Old Jerusalem City Wall

2013–2014 TOWNSEND **PRESS**

SUNDAY SCHOOL
COMMENTARY
BASED ON THE INTERNATIONAL LESSONS SERIES

MW00974803

93
ninety-third edition

KING JAMES
VERSION

NEW
INTERNATIONAL
VERSION

Sunday School Publishing Board
National Baptist Convention, USA, Inc.
Dr. Kelly M. Smith Jr.,
Executive Director

Dr. Julius R. Scruggs, *Convention President;* Dr. Kelly M. Smith Jr., *Executive Director;* Mrs. Kathlyn Pillow, *Associate Director;* Rev. Debra Berry, *Director of Publishing Administration.*
Writers: Dr. Geoffrey V. Guns; Dr. Forrest E. Harris Sr.; Dr. William Franklin Buchanan; *Editor:* Rev. Wellington A. Johnson Sr.; *Copy Editors:* Yalemzewd Worku, Tanae C. McKnight Murdic, Lucinda Anderson; *Layout Designer:* Royetta Davis.

ISBN: 978-1-932972-36-8

CONTENTS

Fall Quarter, 2013—First Things

Winter Quarter, 2013–2014—Jesus and the Just Reign of God

Spring Quarter, 2014—Jesus' Fulfillment of Scripture

Summer Quarter, 2014—The People of God Set Priorities

2010–2016 SCOPE AND SEQUENCE—CYCLE SPREAD

Arrangement of Quarters According to the Church School Year,
September through August

FALL 2010 GOD **The Inescapable God** Exodus; Psalms 8, 19, 46, 47, 63, 66, 90, 91, 139	*WINTER 2010–2011* HOPE **Assuring Hope** Isaiah; Matthew; Mark	*SPRING 2011* WORSHIP **We Worship God** Matthew; Mark; 1 & 2 Timothy; Philippians; Jude; Revelation	*SUMMER 2011* COMMUNITY **God Instructs the People of God** Joshua; Judges; Ruth
FALL 2011 TRADITION **Tradition and Wisdom** Proverbs; Psalms 16, 25, 111, 119; Ecclesiastes; Song of Solomon; Esther	*WINTER 2011–2012* FAITH **God Establishes a Faithful People** Genesis; Exodus; Luke; Galatians	*SPRING 2012* CREATION **God's Creative Word** John	*SUMMER 2012* JUSTICE **God Calls for Justice** Exodus; Leviticus; Deuteronomy; 1 & 2 Samuel; 1 & 2 Kings; 2 Chronicles; Psalm 146; Isaiah; Jeremiah; Ezekiel
FALL 2012 FAITH **A Living Faith** Psalm 46; 1 Corinthians 13:1-13; Hebrews; Acts	*WINTER 2012–2013* GOD: JESUS CHRIST **Jesus Is Lord** Ephesians; Philippians; Colossians	*SPRING 2013* HOPE **Beyond the Present Time** Daniel; Luke; Acts; 1 & 2 Peter; 1 & 2 Thessalonians	*SUMMER 2013* WORSHIP **God's People Worship** Isaiah; Ezra; Nehemiah
FALL 2013 CREATION **First Things** Genesis; Exodus; Psalm 104	*WINTER 2013–2014* JUSTICE **Jesus and the Just Reign of God** Luke; James	*SPRING 2014* TRADITION **Jesus' Fulfillment of Scripture** Zechariah; Malachi; Deuteronomy; Matthew	*SUMMER 2014* COMMUNITY **The People of God Set Priorities** Haggai; 1 & 2 Corinthians
FALL 2014 HOPE **Sustaining Hope** Jeremiah; Habakkuk; Job; Ezekiel; Isaiah 52	*WINTER 2014–2015* WORSHIP **Acts of Worship** Psalm 95:1-7; Daniel; Matthew; Mark; Luke; John; Ephesians; Hebrews; James	*SPRING 2015* GOD: THE HOLY SPIRIT **Work of the Spirit** Mark; John; Acts; 1 Corinthians 12–14; 1 John; 2 John; 3 John	*SUMMER 2015* JUSTICE **God's Prophets Demand Justice** Amos; Micah; Isaiah; Jeremiah; Ezekiel; Zechariah; Malachi
FALL 2015 COMMUNITY **The Community of Believers Comes Alive** Matthew; John; 1 John	*WINTER 2015–2016* TRADITION **Traditions of Israel** Leviticus; Numbers; Deuteronomy	*SPRING 2016* FAITH **The Gift of Faith** Mark; Luke	*SUMMER 2016* CREATION **Toward a New Creation** Genesis; Psalms; Zephaniah; Romans

LIST OF PRINTED TEXTS

The Printed Scriptural Texts used in the *2013-2014 Townsend Press Sunday School Commentary* are arranged here in the order in which they appear in the Bible. Opposite each reference is the page number on which Scriptures appear in this edition of the *Commentary*.

PREFACE

The *Townsend Press Sunday School Commentary*, based on the International Lessons Series, is a production of The Sunday School Publishing Board, National Baptist Convention, USA, Incorporated. These lessons were developed consistent with the curriculum guidelines of the Committee on the Uniform Series, Education Leadership Ministries Commission, National Council of the Churches of Christ in the United States of America. Selected Christian scholars and theologians—who themselves embrace the precepts, doctrines, and positions on biblical interpretation that we have come to believe—are contributors to this publication. By participating in Scripture selection and the development of the matrices for the Guidelines for Lesson Development with the Committee on the Uniform Series, this presentation reflects the historic faith that we share within a rich heritage of worship and witness.

The format of the *Townsend Press Sunday School Commentary* lessons consists of the following: the Unit Title, the general subject with age-level topics, Printed Text from the *King James Version* and the *New International Version* of the Bible, Objectives of the Lesson, Unifying Lesson Principles, Points to Be Emphasized, Topical Outline of the Lesson—with the Biblical Background of the Lesson, Exposition and Application of the Scripture, and Concluding Reflection (designed to focus on the salient points of the lesson), Word Power, and the Home Daily Bible Readings. Each lesson concludes with a prayer.

The *Townsend Press Sunday School Commentary* is designed as an instructional aid for persons involved in the ministry of Christian education. While the autonomy of the individual soul before God is affirmed, we believe that biblical truths find their highest expression within the community of believers whose corporate experiences serve as monitors to preserve the integrity of the Christian faith. As such, the Word of God must not only be understood, but it must also be embodied in the concrete realities of daily life. This serves to allow the Word of God to intersect in a meaningful way with those realities of life.

The presentation of the lessons anticipates the fact that some concepts and Scripture references do not lend themselves to meaningful comprehension by children. Hence, when this occurs, alternative passages of Scripture are used, along with appropriate content emphases, that are designed to assist children in their spiritual growth. There will, however, remain a consistent connection between the children, youth, and adult lessons through the Unifying Principle developed for each session.

We stand firm in our commitment to Christian growth, to the end that lives will be transformed through personal and group interaction with the Word of God. The challenge issued by the apostle Paul continues to find relevance for our faith journey: "Do your best to present yourself to God as one approved by him, a worker who has no need to be ashamed, rightly explaining the word of truth" (2 Timothy 2:15, NRSV). May we all commit ourselves to the affirmation expressed by the psalmist, "Your word is a lamp to my feet and a light for my path" (Psalm 119:105, NIV).

ACKNOWLEDGMENTS

The *Townsend Press Sunday School Commentary* is recognized as the centerpiece of a family of church-school literature designed especially to assist teachers in their presentation of the lessons as well as to broaden the knowledge base of students from the biblical perspective. Our mission has been and will always be to provide religious educational experiences and spiritual resources for our constituency throughout this nation, as well as many foreign countries. To achieve this end, the collaborative efforts of many people provide the needed expertise in the various areas of the production process. Although under the employ of the Sunday School Publishing Board, personnel too numerous to list approach their respective tasks with the dedication and devotion of those who serve God by serving His people. This *Commentary* is presented with gratitude to God for all those who desire a more comprehensive treatment of the selected Scriptures than is provided in the church-school quarterlies, and it is intended to be a complementary resource to the quarterlies.

We acknowledge the Executive Director of The Sunday School Publishing Board in the person of Dr. Kelly M. Smith Jr., who has given a charge to the publishing family to focus on QTC—Quality, Timeliness, and Customer Care—in our interaction with our constituency. Special appreciation is appropriately accorded to Dr. Smith for his continued insightful and inspiring leadership and motivation. Through Dr. Smith's tenure at The Sunday School Publishing Board, the SSPB continues to prosper. It continues as the publisher and printer for the National Baptist Convention, USA, Inc. and its constituent components. There is a greater emphasis on addressing issues germane to the local, national, and international communities, utilizing the latest technologies to promote and distribute our materials—and doing all this based on Christian principles for the advancement of the kingdom of Jesus Christ.

The Sunday School Publishing Board consists of employees with expertise in their assigned areas whose self-understanding is that of "workers together with God" and partners with those who labor in the vineyard of teaching the Word of God in order to make disciples and nurture others toward a mature faith.

Our gratitude is expressed to Dr. William F. Buchanan, expositor for the Fall Quarter, Dr. Forrest E. Harris, expositor for the Winter Quarter, and Dr. Geoffrey V. Guns, expositor for the Spring and Summer Quarters, for their devotion to the development of the respective lessons. These three writers bring diversity and a broad spectrum of ministerial, theological, and educational experience to bear on the exposition and application of the Scripture.

We acknowledge and express our appreciation to Dr. Bruce Alick, pastor of Mt. Zion Baptist Church of Germantown, Pennsylvania, for his theological review of the *2013-2014 Commentary.*

Appreciation is also expressed to Dr. Kelly M. Smith Jr., Executive Director, Mrs. Kathy Pillow, Associate Director, and Rev. Debra Berry, Director of Publishing Administration, for their ongoing leadership. It is a credit to their leadership that the employees have embraced the mission of The Sunday School Publishing Board with a self-perspective that enhances their personal commitment to the cause of Christ as they interact with one another and intersect with the greater community of faith.

The task in which we are all involved would be meaningless and fruitless were it not for the many readers for whom this publication has been so diligently prepared. The faithfulness of our constituency has been enduring for over a century, and we consider ourselves blessed to be their servants in the ministry of the printed Word exalting the living Word, our Lord and Savior Jesus Christ. We pray that God's grace will complement our efforts so that lives will be transformed within and beyond the confines of classroom interaction as the Spirit of God manifests Himself through the intersection of teaching and learning.

Wellington A. Johnson Sr.
Associate Director of Curriculum Publishing

KNOW YOUR WRITERS

Reverend Dr. William F. Buchanan ▼
Fall Quarter

William F. Buchanan was born in Broxton, Georgia—the third of four children born to the late Millinease and John L. Buchanan. He spent his formative years in Georgia, but later the family moved to Florida, where he graduated from high school. In 1976, he received a Bachelor of Science degree from Bethune-Cookman College. He later matriculated at the University of Florida's business school in Gainesville. In 1983, he received a Master of Divinity degree in Pastoral Counseling from the Morehouse School of Religion–Interdenominational Theological Center. Subsequently, he was a Proctor-Booth Fellow at United Theological Seminary, where he earned the Doctor of Ministry degree in 1995.

Dr. Buchanan was ordained into the ministry in 1985, and from 1985 to 1988 served as youth minister at Greenforest Baptist Church in Decatur, Georgia, and as a chaplain intern at Emory University Hospital in Atlanta. He was called to be the senior pastor of First Baptist Church in Huntington, West Virginia, in 1988. In 1994, he was called to the pastorate of the historic Fifteenth Avenue Baptist Church in Nashville, Tennessee.

Since coming to Fifteenth Avenue, Dr. Buchanan has transformed this church into a beacon of light for all persons in the community. The church continues to grow spiritually and numerically, and to serve as a model for twenty-first-century ministry.

Dr. Buchanan has received many awards and honors. He was most recently honored with being named the recipient of the Lily Foundation's Clergy General Grant, which allowed him to take a brief sabbatical to study at Harvard University's School of Divinity. He is a board member of the Nashville Housing Fund, Oasis, Saint Thomas Pastoral Care Advisory Board (chairman), Vanderbilt Divinity School Board of Visitors, and Operation Andrew Group (former board chairman). Dr. Buchanan is an adjunct professor at American Baptist College in Nashville, and a Field Education supervisor at Vanderbilt University's School of Divinity. Additionally, he is in great demand as a preacher, lecturer, and facilitator at churches throughout the nation.

In addition to his busy schedule as a pastor and teacher, Dr. Buchanan is the loving husband of Audrey Cave Buchanan. They are the parents of four children—Kwame, Shani, Dashan, and Aubrey Buchanan—and have six grandchildren.

Reverend Dr. Forrest E. Harris Sr. ▼
Winter Quarter

Forrest Harris was born August 24, 1949, in Memphis, Tennessee, to Wilbur T. and Sallie Mae Harris. Harris's siblings include a twin brother and seven other sisters and brothers.

Harris matriculated at Knoxville College in Knoxville, Tennessee, where he completed a Bachelor's degree in Psychology and Sociology in 1971.

From 1971 to 1979, he was a Federal Compliance Officer with the Energy and Research Development Administration in Oak Ridge, Tennessee. During his tenure as an employee with the federal government, Harris responded to a call to professional Christian ministry. In 1979, he completed a Th.B. (Bachelor of Theology) at American Baptist College in Nashville, Tennessee. He earned a M.Div. (Master of Divinity) and D.Min. (Doctor of Ministry) from Vanderbilt University Divinity School in 1983 and 1989, respectively. At Vanderbilt, Harris was a Benjamin E.

Mays Fellow and a recipient of the Florence Conwell prize for preaching.

Harris was ordained in 1975 at Oak Valley Baptist Church in Oak Ridge, Tennessee. While a seminary student at Vanderbilt, he served as the pastor of this church. During this pastorate, Harris brought together several community organizations and founded the Oak Valley Development Corporation. He also served a three-year term as president of the Oak Ridge Branch of the NAACP. From 1985 to 1987, he taught at Roane State Community College, where he initiated a black studies curriculum and coordinated social outreach programs and special events.

Since 1988, Harris has served on the Vanderbilt Divinity School faculty. He is the Director of the Kelly Miller Smith Institute on Black Church Studies, Assistant Dean for Black Church Studies, and Assistant Professor for the Practice of Ministry. His teaching responsibilities include courses in the theology of ministry in the black church tradition. Under Harris's leadership, the endowment of the Kelly Miller Smith Institute on Black Church Studies has grown to be in excess of one million dollars.

In 1999, Harris was appointed President of American Baptist College in Nashville. During his presidency, the College's endowment has increased by 65 percent.

In addition to his presidential duties, Harris is a husband and father. He is married to Jacqueline Borom Harris, a research nurse at Vanderbilt University Medical Center. They have four children: Kara, Elliot Jr., Morgan, and Alexis.

Reverend Dr. Geoffrey V. Guns ▼
Spring and Summer Quarters

Dr. Geoffrey V. Guns is a native of Newport, Rhode Island. He is the son of a retired Baptist pastor and co-pastor. Dr. Guns received his elementary and secondary education in the Norfolk public school system. He earned his B.S. degree in Business Administration from Norfolk State University in 1972.

In 1981, he earned his Master of Divinity degree from the School of Theology, Virginia Union University, graduating *summa cum laude*. He earned his Doctor of Ministry degree from the School of Religion, Howard University in Washington, D.C., in 1985.

Dr. Guns is the senior pastor of Second Calvary Baptist Church in Norfolk, Virginia, where he has served for over twenty-five years. He is active in his denomination, the National Baptist Convention, USA, Inc. Dr. Guns served as the president of the Virginia Baptist State Convention (VBSC) from 1997 to 2001 and is currently the moderator for the Tidewater Peninsula Baptist Association.

He has written articles for the *Christian Education Informer* of the Division of Christian Education of The Sunday School Publishing Board. Dr. Guns also serves as vice chairman of the Council of Christian Education for the Division of Christian Education of The Sunday School Publishing Board of the NBC. He works with the Home Mission Board of the NBC and serves as the regional representative for the Southeast region.

Dr. Guns is the author of two books: *Church Financial Management* (1997), which is published by Providence House Publishers; and *Spiritual Leadership: A Practical Guide to Developing Spiritual Leaders in the Church* (2000), published by Orman Press, Inc.

He is married to the former Rosetta Harding of Richmond, Virginia. Mrs. Guns is a licensed social worker and works as a school social worker.

First Things

GENERAL INTRODUCTION

This quarter has three units. God's creative work is seen throughout the stories found in the books of Genesis and Exodus. The quarter begins with the creation of the world and of human beings, explores the creation of a nation that began with God's promises to Abraham and Sarah and their heirs, and then studies the stories of the Hebrew people on their journey out of captivity toward freedom.

Unit I, "*First Days*," is a five-lesson unit that explores Israel's earliest stories. The first lesson is a creation hymn that affirms God's creation. The next two lessons focus on God as the Creator of the universe and humanity. The fourth lesson concentrates on God's promise to Noah and the establishment of an everlasting covenant. The fifth lesson explores the scattering of the nations.

Unit II, "*First Nation*," is a four-lesson unit that develops the promise made to Abraham by God. The first two lessons tell of the promise of land and children to Abraham and Sarah. The third lesson sheds light on the blessing promised to family lines from Abraham. The final lesson outlines the blessing that would be passed to Jacob.

Unit III, "*First Freedom*," is a four-lesson unit that explores the power of God to save Israel from oppression. The first and second lessons look at how God prepared and actually delivered Israel from bondage. The last two lessons develop the story of Israel's beginning as a freed nation.

LESSON 1   September 1, 2013

GOD CREATES

FAITH PATHWAY/FAITH JOURNEY TOPIC: **Everything We Need**

DEVOTIONAL READING: **Matthew 6:25-34**
PRINT PASSAGE: **Psalm 104:5-9, 24-30**

BACKGROUND SCRIPTURE: **Psalm 104**
KEY VERSE: **Psalm 104:24**

Psalm 104:5-9, 24-30—KJV

5 Who laid the foundations of the earth, that it should not be removed for ever.

6 Thou coveredst it with the deep as with a garment: the waters stood above the mountains.

7 At thy rebuke they fled; at the voice of thy thunder they hasted away.

8 They go up by the mountains; they go down by the valleys unto the place which thou hast founded for them.

9 Thou hast set a bound that they may not pass over; that they turn not again to cover the earth.

          .....

24 O LORD, how manifold are thy works! in wisdom hast thou made them all: the earth is full of thy riches.

25 So is this great and wide sea, wherein are things creeping innumerable, both small and great beasts.

26 There go the ships: there is that leviathan, whom thou hast made to play therein.

27 These wait all upon thee; that thou mayest give them their meat in due season.

28 That thou givest them they gather: thou openest thine hand, they are filled with good.

29 Thou hidest thy face, they are troubled: thou takest away their breath, they die, and return to their dust.

30 Thou sendest forth thy spirit, they are created: and thou renewest the face of the earth.

Psalm 104:5-9, 24-30—NIV

5 He set the earth on its foundations; it can never be moved.

6 You covered it with the deep as with a garment; the waters stood above the mountains.

7 But at your rebuke the waters fled, at the sound of your thunder they took to flight;

8 they flowed over the mountains, they went down into the valleys, to the place you assigned for them.

9 You set a boundary they cannot cross; never again will they cover the earth.

          .....

24 How many are your works, O LORD! In wisdom you made them all; the earth is full of your creatures.

25 There is the sea, vast and spacious, teeming with creatures beyond number—living things both large and small.

26 There the ships go to and fro, and the leviathan, which you formed to frolic there.

27 These all look to you to give them their food at the proper time.

28 When you give it to them, they gather it up; when you open your hand, they are satisfied with good things.

29 When you hide your face, they are terrified; when you take away their breath, they die and return to the dust.

30 When you send your Spirit, they are created, and you renew the face of the earth.

TOPICAL OUTLINE OF THE LESSON

I. **Introduction**
   A. How Awesome Is Our God!
   B. Biblical Background

II. **Exposition and Application of the Scripture**
   A. The Sovereign Creator (Psalm 104:5-9)
   B. The Greatness of God (Psalm 104:24-26)
   C. The Dependency of Creation (Psalm 104:27-30)

III. **Concluding Reflection**

LESSON OBJECTIVES

Upon the completion of the lesson, the students will be able to do the following:

1. Develop a self-understanding that recognizes their relationship to God and His creation;
2. Experience the awesome wonder of God's creation; and,
3. Name the ways that believers take responsible care of God's gifts in creation.

POINTS TO BE EMPHASIZED

ADULT/YOUTH
Adult Topic: Everything We Need
Youth Topic: Praise the Creator
Adult/Youth Key Verse: Psalm 104:24
Print Passage: Psalm 104:5-9, 24-30

—Psalm 104 most likely drew inspiration from a long tradition of Creation accounts used by Israelites during worship.
—God's reign was demonstrated in control over the powers of chaos, symbolized by the waters of the sea.
—Psalm 104 stated that God ordered water with the pronouncement of His Word (see 104:7); in Genesis 1:1, God separated the waters with His Spirit, breath, or wind.
—God gives blessing and life; without God, there was not only a lack but also a void (see 104:27-30).
—The Psalms have been used in Jewish and Christian worship for thousands of years. For some Christian groups, Psalm 104 is employed in the celebration of Pentecost.

CHILDREN
Children Topic: God Creates It All!
Key Verse: Psalm 104:24
Print Passage: Psalm 104:1-4, 24, 27-29, 31-33

—The psalmist praised and honored God for the greatness and majesty of creation.
—The psalmist extolled the wonder of the heavens, the seas, the clouds, the winds, and fire.
—The psalmist sang of the wisdom with which God created all things.
—The psalmist stressed all of creation's dependence on God for survival.
—The psalmist sang of God's enduring glory and promised to praise God always.
—The psalmist used figurative language to explain the vastness and grandeur of God's creation.

I. INTRODUCTION

A. How Awesome Is Our God!

Psalm 104 testifies to the awesome greatness of Yahweh (God), who created heaven and Earth. How awesome is our God? Rudolph Otto, in his book *The Idea of the Holy,* describes God as the incomparably "wholly other" in creation. There is none like God in heaven above or on Earth below. Hebrew theology speaks of the sophistication and complexity of creation. God has provided, in abundant supply, the necessities of life for all creatures according to each particular need: food, water, territory, and seasons of reproduction.

National Geographic produced a documentary on migratory life on the Serengeti Plains of wildebeests and other big game who migrate from Kenya's Maasai Mara to the southern plains of the Serengeti. "These migratory animals are drawn on a 2000-mile annual trek for fresh grass and water. The trek opens millions of wildebeest and zebras to constant mortal danger: lions lie in wait on granite outcrops, leopards ambush stragglers and calves, and hyenas commute up to forty-five miles to feast on these migrating creatures." As these massive herds migrate in their quest for food and water, they become a part of the vicious cycle of life. As they seek food themselves, many will become food for other beasts. Yet, as food and water dissipate on the Serengeti, these herds will return to the Maasai Mara and next year, when the drought comes again to the Maasai Mara, like a maiden call, they will embark again on the long trek back to the Serengeti Plains.

An interesting insight of this documentary provides a caveat to the wonder of creation. Over two million animals will gather on the Serengeti Plains at one time and no two groups of animals—elephants, wildebeests, zebras, or giraffes—will eat the same foliage. Each animal group will eat only the particular foliage on the plain according to each group's physical attribute. It has been said that animals move by instinct and perhaps this is true—but the Lord had ordered all of life, and even the great mega-herd migrations are according to God's plan for creation.

B. Biblical Background

Although little is known about the author of this particular psalm, it is believed by many Old Testament scholars that it was written around the time of the Babylonian captivity and is a part of a genre of poetic psalms called "Creation Psalms"—i.e., Psalms 29, 93, and 104. Psalm 104 seems to draw inspiration from the Creation narrative of Genesis 1. The psalmist acknowledged that the Lord God of Israel created all things and provided for all creatures that live both on the Earth and in the sea. James L. Mays, Professor Emeritus of the Hebrew Old Testament in *The Interpretation, A Biblical Commentary for Preaching and Teaching,* said, "Heaven and earth exist because the Lord reigns, and all live in God's reign and are dependent on it for life." Mays captured what the psalmist declared: "The earth is the LORD's and the fulness thereof; the world, and they that dwell therein. For he hath founded it upon the seas, and established it upon the floods." Concomitantly, creation is not an accident of nature; it did not come into existence through a process called the "Big Bang Theory," nor did it come into existence by a long evolutionary process whereby the world just evolved (happened) over time; rather, God did it by divine fiat: like a maestro, Yahweh gave meticulous attention to every aspect of creation. Thus, the psalmist celebrated the design of creation, the visible world, as evidence of the greatness and the grandness of Yahweh, Creator God! He also praised God for providing for all creatures that live on the Earth.

II. EXPOSITION AND APPLICATION OF THE SCRIPTURE

A. The Sovereign Creator
(Psalm 104:5-9)

Who laid the foundations of the earth, that it should not be removed for ever. Thou coveredst it with the deep as with a garment: the waters stood above the mountains. At thy rebuke they fled; at the voice of thy thunder they hasted away. They go up by the mountains; they go down by the valleys unto the place which thou hast founded for them. Thou hast set a bound that they may not pass over; that they turn not again to cover the earth.

These verses speak of the sovereignty of Yahweh over all of creation. Everything in nature is under God's authority. Yahweh's meticulous command over every element of nature contradicts the argument that nature is arbitrary or capricious. When the wind blows, it is under Yahweh's direction; when fire rages, it is under Yahweh's command; and when water floods, it is by His permission. God is in nature, yet above nature—and nature operates at His command! As we study this lesson, this is the season of drought, wildfires, hurricanes, and tornados in America. This psalm humbles us, causing us to recognize how finite we are. Even the world (and those "acts of nature" previously mentioned) are accountable to the divine. As you read verses 5-9, notice the assertions of the psalmist—commands and actions taken by Yahweh in the ordering of creation and making it what it is: "Who laid" (verse 5); "Thou coveredst" (verse 6); "At thy rebuke" (verse 5); and "Thou has set" (verse 5).

Finally, there is almost a military image in these verses of God—using the elements of wind, fire (lightning), and water as His companions in the fulfillment of His creative purpose. The Earth and the world were in chaos; water was upon the face of the deep; and darkness was everywhere, when God stepped into chaos and commanded order to come forth out of disorder—and "it was so." These elements of nature are used by God for His creative purposes. Likewise, the world can bear witness to the appalling capacity of these elements to kill and to destroy; yet, God controls them for His good purpose. However, we must be careful concerning the conclusions we reach about horrific acts of nature that destroy lives and properties. Is it God's will for forest fires, floods, hurricanes, and tornados to destroy millions of dollars in property and thousands of lives? This is not the persuasion of the psalmist; rather, it is that God in creation used these elements of wind, water, and fire to order creation.

Likewise, verses 7-9 are inclusive of the ordering of nature by God; and although there is a sense that nature rages at its own will and sometimes appears to be out of control, it is not. God established the Earth on its foundations and commanded the waters—and they obeyed and remain within their boundaries. In May of 2010, Nashville suffered a hundred-year flood: a torrential downpour of rain blanketed Nashville for forty-eight hours, and when it stopped the banks of the Cumberland River were breached and much of Nashville was flooded. It took weeks for the water to recede. However, verse 9 does not allude to this kind of water catastrophe; rather, it is a reference to Earth and its original state when water deluged the Earth. It is construed by some that the language of verse 9—"never again will they cover the earth"—suggests that the psalmist referred to the Noahic flood and promise (see Genesis 9). Although water breached the banks of the Cumberland River, not all of Nashville flooded; and once the water receded, it returned to the boundary of the Cumberland River.

God is in control and is the great river, but God is not a tyrant who rules with an "iron fist" and without benevolence. On the contrary, God is concerned and compassionate and cares about His creation.

B. The Greatness of God (Psalm 104:24-26)

O LORD, how manifold are thy works! in wisdom hast thou made them all: the earth is full of thy riches. So is this great and wide sea, wherein are things creeping innumerable, both small and great beasts. There go the ships: there is that leviathan, whom thou hast made to play therein.

The psalmist spoke rhetorically to God.

How manifold (many) are thy works! The work of creation is obvious and numerous. God created them with all of their complexities and intricacies to operate within the boundaries of a grand scheme. In these verses, the psalmist spoke of the vastness of the sea and its contents: "the fullness of the deep." Perhaps we should find that his description of the sea is indeed interesting, considering the fact that the ancient Hebrew people were not a seagoing people. Although they were neighbors of the Phoenicians, whom ancient history called the greatest maritime people of the ancient world, the Hebrew people were the same. Yet, the psalmist knew about the sea and its content. The sea is indeed a marvel to behold.

In 2008, this writer visited Palestine with a clergy group. Included in that experience was a visit to Caesarea Maritima, located on the shores of the Mediterranean Sea. Caesarea Maritima is an ancient ruin that was built by King Herod and was one of the largest cities in the Roman Empire. The city was named after Herod's patron, Augustus Caesar. As we stood in the ruin of this ancient city, as far as the eye could see was the grand sweep and the beauty of the sea—thousands of miles of water that connected other lands thousands of miles away. At some distant point on the horizon, it appeared that the Earth was flat and everything had just dropped on the face of it. What a beauty to behold—the waters of the Mediterranean Sea. However, with limited transportation and the narrowness of their ancient worldview (compared to what it is today), what did the psalmist see in his mind's eye as he stood where we stood? Whatever he saw, he came to the conclusion that all of life, even that in the sea, was dependent on the reign and reliability of Yahweh.

C. The Dependency of Creation
   ### (Psalm 104:27-30)

These wait all upon thee; that thou mayest give them their meat in due season. That thou givest them they gather: thou openest thine hand, they are filled with good. Thou hidest thy face, they are troubled: thou takest away their breath, they die, and return to their dust. Thou sendest forth thy spirit, they are created: and thou renewest the face of the earth.

Our dependency on Yahweh is irrefutable. It does not matter how high up the social/economic ladder we climb, we can never outdistance our dependency upon God. The psalmist made it seem so simple: "When you open your hand, they are satisfied with good things. When you hide your face they are terrified…" but, it is not quite so simple. Except for one Person, no one has all power—and this is an important point that the psalmist made: that God is so awesome that He provides and takes away from His creatures with little effort. Perhaps humanity is the only part of God's creatures that has yet to realize its absolute dependency upon God for its existence in all things! The ebbs and flow of nature assure us that we are not in control. We all must look to Yahweh to give us even food at the proper time. "When you give it to them, they gather it up; when you open your hand, they are satisfied with good things. When you hide your face, they are terrified; when you take away their breath, they die and return to the dust. When you send your Spirit, they are created, and you renew the face of the earth." The psalmist asserted that God is strong and benevolent!

Finally, the reading of verses 29-30 begs the attention of the reader in the light of some contemporary theological views about God: "God is always at our beck and call"; "We can name it and claim it"; or, "With the right faith we can obligate God." God is always present, but not always available to us. "When you hide your face, they are terrified; when you take away their breath, they die and return to their dust" (verse 29, NIV). God sometimes hides His face from us, suggesting that when He hides His face from us, either we cannot expect favor or God is silent toward us. Both life and death are in the hands of God almighty, who both gives to us and takes from us. God cannot be cajoled or manipulated. Yet, the psalmist said that all creatures are aware of the fact that God gives and God takes away. This is also the discernment that comes to all of us through our creature experiences. "The Lord gives and the Lord takes away; blessed be the name of our God."

III. CONCLUDING REFLECTION

The poem "The Creation," by James Weldon Johnson, describes heaven and Earth in the beginning—with all of its complexity and sophistication—as God created the world out of nothing. Johnson uses great imagination to describe what happened in the beginning: "And God stepped out on space, And He looked around and said, 'I'm lonely—I'll make me a world' As far as the eye of God could see, Darkness covered everything, Blacker than a hundred midnights. Down in a cypress swamp." Just as "The Creation" is full of poetic images of God creating the world, so is Psalm 104 full of the wisdom and wonder of the Creator. There was chaos in heaven and on Earth when Yahweh stepped into space to order the visible world as we see it and experience it. Johnson and the psalmist conclude that

Yahweh did it and is beholden to no one. In contrast, in ancient mythology—to the Greeks, the Egyptians, the Babylonians, the Chinese, etc.—certain acts of nature were ascribed to certain deities (gods), such as fire (*Hephaestus*), the sea (*Poseidon*), wind (*Anemoi*), rain (*Maya*), and drought (*Aphaea*). But Johnson and the psalmist summarily disagreed and reached a different conclusion of the world's origin: Yahweh reigns; He is "Lord of all."

Yahweh has supplied all of our needs "according to his riches in glory." Hence, creation as we have experienced and know it is no accident; Yahweh was intentional when He created heaven and Earth in all of its complexity. The contemporary gospel hit "My God Is Awesome," by Pastor Charles Jenkins and Fellowship Chicago, captures the sentiment of the psalmist: our God is awesome in wisdom, in work, in power, in greatness, and in compassion.

PRAYER

Eternal God, our Father, we are grateful that the kingdoms of this world are a part of the rule and reign of the kingdom of heaven. Yet, You are in need of ambassadors of goodwill to bear Your message in the world. Therefore, oh Lord, cleanse us so that we might be worthy to represent You in the world—as You bring creation to come to its perfect fruition. Also, enable us to get Your message right. In Jesus' name we pray. Amen.

WORD POWER

Breath (*ruach, nephesh*)—life spirit or the act of breathing. This term refers to the essence of life of all living creatures.
Spirit (*ruach, pneuma*)—breath; life spirit. This term refers to divine inspiration.
Wisdom (*chokmah*)—wise or skilled, or the ability to make wise choices.

HOME DAILY BIBLE READINGS
(August 26–September 1, 2013)

God Creates

MONDAY, August 26: "God Knows Our Every Need" (Matthew 6:25-34)
TUESDAY, August 27: "The Greatness of the Creator" (Psalm 104:1-4)
WEDNESDAY, August 28: "Nourishment for All Creatures" (Psalm 104:10-17)
THURSDAY, August 29: "The Cycle of Days and Seasons" (Psalm 104:18-23)
FRIDAY, August 30: "The Exalted God of Creation" (Psalm 97:1-9)
SATURDAY, August 31: "Praise God, the Creator" (Psalm 104:31-35)
SUNDAY, September 1: "God, Our Creator and Sustainer" (Psalm 104:5-9, 24-30)

Sources

Biblos.org
Mays, James Luther. *Interpretation: A Bible Commentary for Teaching and Preaching.* John Knox Press, Louisville, KY, 1994.
Strong, James. *The New Strong Expanded Dictionary of Bible Words.* Thomas Nelson Publishers, Nashville TN, 2001.

LESSON 2   September 8, 2013

GOD'S IMAGE: MALE AND FEMALE

FAITH PATHWAY/FAITH JOURNEY TOPIC: Love and Marriage

DEVOTIONAL READING: **Psalm 8**
PRINT PASSAGE: **Genesis 2:18-25**

BACKGROUND SCRIPTURE: **Genesis 1–2; 5:1-2**
KEY VERSE: **Genesis 2:18**

Genesis 2:18-25—KJV

18 And the LORD God said, It is not good that the man should be alone; I will make him an help meet for him.
19 And out of the ground the LORD God formed every beast of the field, and every fowl of the air; and brought them unto Adam to see what he would call them: and whatsoever Adam called every living creature, that was the name thereof.
20 And Adam gave names to all cattle, and to the fowl of the air, and to every beast of the field; but for Adam there was not found an help meet for him.
21 And the LORD God caused a deep sleep to fall upon Adam, and he slept: and he took one of his ribs, and closed up the flesh instead thereof;
22 And the rib, which the LORD God had taken from man, made he a woman, and brought her unto the man.
23 And Adam said, This is now bone of my bones, and flesh of my flesh: she shall be called Woman, because she was taken out of Man.
24 Therefore shall a man leave his father and his mother, and shall cleave unto his wife: and they shall be one flesh.
25 And they were both naked, the man and his wife, and were not ashamed.

Genesis 2:18-25—NIV

18 The LORD God said, "It is not good for the man to be alone. I will make a helper suitable for him."
19 Now the LORD God had formed out of the ground all the beasts of the field and all the birds of the air. He brought them to the man to see what he would name them; and whatever the man called each living creature, that was its name.
20 So the man gave names to all the livestock, the birds of the air and all the beasts of the field. But for Adam no suitable helper was found.
21 So the LORD God caused the man to fall into a deep sleep; and while he was sleeping, he took one of the man's ribs and closed up the place with flesh.
22 Then the LORD God made a woman from the rib he had taken out of the man, and he brought her to the man.
23 The man said, "This is now bone of my bones and flesh of my flesh; she shall be called 'woman,' for she was taken out of man."
24 For this reason a man will leave his father and mother and be united to his wife, and they will become one flesh.
25 The man and his wife were both naked, and they felt no shame.

BIBLE FACT

The term "Image of God" comes from the Hebrew *elohim* and is translated literally as "image of God." It is the doctrinal belief that human beings are created in God's image and thus have inherent value.

UNIFYING LESSON PRINCIPLE

Finding a suitable companion with whom one can share life can be a struggle—but it can also bring great joy. How does one find a suitable partner? According to Genesis 2, God created Eve as a partner for Adam. The lesson could focus on family ties or friendships in order to make the lesson suitable for children.

TOPICAL OUTLINE OF THE LESSON

I. Introduction
A. We Are Psychological, Spiritual, and Social Beings
B. Biblical Background

II. Exposition and Application of the Scripture
A. A Divine Conclusion (Genesis 2:18)
B. Adam's Incompleteness (Genesis 2:19-21)
C. Yahweh-made (Genesis 2:22-25)

III. Concluding Reflection

LESSON OBJECTIVES

Upon the completion of the lesson, the students will be able to do the following:

1. Explore God's image in connection with the creation as "male and female";
2. Appreciate that God takes an active role in creating loving partnerships; and,
3. Identify spiritual practices that honor strong family and personal bonds with one another.

POINTS TO BE EMPHASIZED

ADULT/YOUTH
Adult Topic: Love and Marriage
Youth Topic: Created for Relationship
Adult Key Verse: Genesis 2:18
Youth Key Verse: Genesis 5:2
Print Passage: Genesis 2:18-25

—The basis in this passage for the affirmation that God loves us is found, in part, in God's desire that humans not be alone but in community.

—The woman was created as a "helper" (Hebrew: *'ezer*) for the man. This word can be understood as "ally," and is used in that sense in the Hebrew Scriptures.

—The passage suggests that, apart from the shame felt after the Fall, God ideally envisioned adults as comfortable with their bodies and with the body of their spouse.

—The order of creation included male and female as a primary relationship.

—Humans are indebted to God, not only for their creation as individual persons but also for the creation of their relationships.

CHILDREN
Children Topic: We Need Family
Key Verse: Genesis 2:18
Print Passage: Genesis 2:7, 15-25

—As part of all that was created, God created man from the dust of the ground and woman from man's rib.

—God provided all that man needed and forbade him to eat from the Tree of the Knowledge of Good and Evil.

—God placed man in the Garden of Eden to care for God's creation and to name every living creature.

—God showed concern for relationships by creating the woman to be a partner with the man.

—The man recognized the relationship that God established between man and woman.

I. INTRODUCTION

A. We Are Psychological, Spiritual, and Social Beings

One of the ironies in Genesis 2 is that after Yahweh had declared that everything was good and very good, He later declared that "It is not good that the man should be alone." Is this an afterthought or a reevaluation of creation? What was it about Adam that made him incomplete? It appears from the complete reading of both Creation narratives (found in Genesis 1 and 2) that Adam had no corresponding helper to enable him to reach his fullest potential. The first Adam, the progenitor of the human race, was created a tripartite being: psychological (mind), spiritual (soul), and sociological (body); hence, there was nothing in all of creation—although it was good and very good—that was compatible with Adam. Adam was the only being who was created in the beginning singular and without an opposite as his equal.

Can you imagine man without woman? Can you imagine an existence without the companionship of another human being? We have heard the colloquial expression that "dog is man's best friend." Well, think how severely handicapped the human race would be if, from the beginning, we only had animal life for companionship. Where would we be as psychological, spiritual, and social beings? What would happen if a child were raised by a colony of apes? The child would take on the characteristics and the language of the ape. Humanity is created in the image and likeness of Yahweh—yet, we are not socialized in heaven, but, rather, on Earth; we need someone of our own likeness to enable us to reach our fullest potential.

B. Biblical Background

Biblical tradition has it that Moses was the author of the first five books of the Bible; however, beyond this church tradition, we cannot be certain of their authorship. Unlike many of the other Old Testament books, these books were not signed. The authorship of these books is of little importance; rather, it is the content of what Yahweh would have us know about His infinite wisdom in the beginning and of the finite nature of our humanity that is important. Except for being too academic, Genesis 2 constitutes the second Creation narrative (chapter 1 is the first); however, they are not in conflict with each other, but complement each other.

The first readers of the text were not critical examiners of it as we are today; they were a "listening community," called to be Yahweh's partnering agents in the world. What is important in the story is not necessarily what we find of interest. Contrarily, we find that in the beginning Yahweh created all things. Walter Brueggemann, Old Testament scholar, says of the book of Genesis: "It is the story of God calling His world into existence to be His faithful world. Therefore, chapter 2 is a part of a larger body of work about creation and the tension between God's will and purpose for creation and the way in which His crown and glory have chosen to answer that call."

Everything that Yahweh created He declared to be good and very good, yet He found Adam incomplete and in need of a partner for companionship. God created Eve out of Adam and gave her to him in order to satisfy the essence of his being.

II. EXPOSITION AND APPLICATION OF THE SCRIPTURE

A. A Divine Conclusion
(Genesis 2:18)

And the Lord God said, It is not good that the man should be alone; I will make him an help meet for him.

Although humans, especially many who are accomplished in their chosen fields of endeavor, often see themselves as sufficient, none of us is truly sufficient. One of the secondary messages of Genesis 2 is that we cannot be made sufficient by external elements of nature. God created the world and all living creatures. He brought them to Adam to see what he would name them. What an awesome responsibility—to name all living creatures: creeping, crawling, walking, and flying. Adam named them all! He must have been an awesome man—intelligent, imaginative, and energetic—to carry out this command without the aid of computer technology or a staff of workers.

Perhaps Adam would be considered a genius in the twenty-first century. But, in spite of Adam's intellect, God declared that it was not good ("best" or "well-being") for man to be alone. God made this declaration after declaring that all things that He had made were *good* and *very good*. The word *good* (1:31 or 2:9) in its original language is not the same

concept of the word *good* in verse 18. In the earlier verses, God declared that creation is excellent—whereas God makes an evaluation of Adam's well-being and concludes that it *was not good*! What conclusion can we reach about this divine proclamation? Adam, in and of himself, was not sufficient without a suitable mate to help him reach sufficiency. God resolved to create someone suitable to help Adam reach sufficiency. The idea of suitability is captured by *Young's Literal Translation Bible*: "I make a helper—as his counter-part." *Barnes' Notes* says, "Adam is formed to be social, to hold conversation, not only with his superior, but also with his equal…. He needs a mate, with whom he may take sweet counsel. And the benevolent Creator resolves to supply this want. One who may not only reciprocate his feelings, but take an intelligent and appropriate part in his active pursuits." No, it is not enough for any of us to achieve notoriety and personal success. We can never outdistance our need for companionship and community. We would be absolutely miserable without one another. *Acting* independent is not the same as *being* independent; by nature, we were created to be co-dependent; thus, we find our completion in one another.

B. Adam's Incompleteness (Genesis 2:19-21)

And out of the ground the LORD God formed every beast of the field, and every fowl of the air; and brought them unto Adam to see what he would call them: and whatsoever Adam called every living creature, that was the name thereof. And Adam gave names to all cattle, and to the fowl of the air, and to every beast of the field; but for Adam there was not found an help meet for him. And the LORD God caused a deep sleep to fall upon Adam, and he slept: and he took one of his ribs, and closed up the flesh instead thereof.

Adam may have been an awesome man, but he was insufficient without Eve. God relied on Adam to name all living creatures, and Adam did so without the aid of computer technology to trace data. Perhaps in today's climate, Adam would be known as a genius. Yet, after creation was complete and all creatures had been named, God recapitulated His ruminations of the insufficiency (see verse 18) of Adam. Adam's insufficiency seems to have been an internal quality that was not part of his personality. He did not have the wherewithal to become all that God had created him to become. This is a startling revelation for many, because as a people we have come to think of the sufficiency of the human personality! We have come to think that our deep insufficiency can be masked or compensated by an abundant supply of the external elements of life, such as recreation, animal companionship, money, possessions, and so forth. But nothing in creation could accommodate Adam's deficiency except someone *like* Adam—but *not* Adam.

God made Eve to complement Adam in ways that nothing else in all of creation could accomplish. The popular adage about dogs' being man's best friend is rubbish. If this were true, how limited and crude we would be! If this were true, what common language could we speak? God in His infinite wisdom made someone with a corresponding DNA for Adam to commune with at the deepest levels of his godlikeness!

C. Yahweh-made (Genesis 2:22-25)

And the rib, which the LORD God had taken from man, made he a woman, and brought her unto the man. And Adam said, This is now bone of my bones, and flesh of my flesh: she shall be called Woman, because she was taken out of Man. Therefore shall a man leave his father and his mother, and shall cleave unto his wife: and they shall be one flesh. And they were both naked, the man and his wife, and were not ashamed.

Because Yahweh determined that it was not a good thing for Adam to be alone (see verse 18), God resolved to make him a helpmate. Eve was made from the rib of Adam and given to him as a helper. When he saw her, Adam affirmed that she was the missing element in his life. She became Adam's soul mate (one flesh), and they were united as husband and wife. They were connected emotionally, spiritually, and socially to each other, and were to depend on each other and reciprocate love for each other. Two can only have this kind of commitment when two are totally committed to the other in nonselfish ways. This is what it means to be one flesh!

Therefore, these verses signify the importance and significance of marriage and why family is essential for the continued sustainability and vitality of community. The genesis of community is family and the genesis of family is two persons who share an irrevocable bond between them. As the family goes, so go the community and nation! Hence, this correlation between the health of the family and the health of a nation is irrefutable. The family is a sacred institution. It is the institution upon which all Judeo-Christian sacred tradition would be founded—the nation of Israel and the church (see Ephesians 5:32-33).

Concomitantly, according to *National Vital Statistics,* 8.3 per 1000 persons will get married, yet 4.5 per 1000 will also get divorces—which means that over 50 percent of all marriages will end in divorce. How many of these divorces are filed on the grounds of "irreconcilable differences"? What does "irreconcilable differences" mean? Basically, "irreconcilable differences" exist when two people are not willing to work together and struggle together, and are unwilling to compromise their individual differences for the sake of the relationship.

Although our society often focuses on the divorce rate, what of the paltry number of people per one thousand who will get married? Only eight people per one thousand will marry—and while life has taught us that marriage is not for everyone, marriage is God's idea. While society over the years has concocted other domestic and social arrangements to supplant marriage, these do not appear to have advanced the health of family life. The family in America is obviously in disarray and the consequences and impact of this on children are devastating. The antecedent for these verses are seen in verses 21-22: God took a rib out of Adam's side and made Eve. When Adam saw Eve, his reaction was to utter that she was bone of his bone and flesh of his flesh. This was the first marriage which was of divine intent and was based in reciprocal love and nurture: "bone of my bones and flesh of my flesh"—the institution of marriage is of God and is God-purposed.

So, if the family is the hub of human life, then can we really expect the church, the community, and the nation to prevail without the survival of the family?

III. CONCLUDING REFLECTION

When we see the words "God's image" as used in this lesson, we need to understand what is being said. Man, meaning male and female, bears the stamp of God in terms of having certain attributes that God has. We are not made in the "physical" image of God, because God is not physical. One of the main areas in which we are made in God's image is that we possess intelligence like God. We were also created as social beings.

There are many points of speculation about the original sin and what it was. Of course we can never be certain, but at its core was selfishness. God told Adam not to eat of the Tree of the Knowledge of Good and Evil, but when Adam and Eve saw what was in it for them, they disobeyed God and ate the forbidden fruit. The essence of selfishness is to look through the narrow lens of "what is in it for me?" and to act, regardless of the consequences. All it takes is a cursory look at human history to see the devastating potential of selfishness—i.e., King David, Samson, Judas, Idi Amin, President Nixon (Watergate), etc. When one only considers himself or herself without regards for the greater good of others and society, that is perhaps the height of sin and is the sin from which all other sins derive. So, perhaps selfishness is the original sin and selfishness has resulted in an assault on the institution of marriage and the family.

However, when Adam saw Eve, he said that she was "bone of [his] bone and flesh of [his] flesh." For this cause a man should leave his mother and father, and the two should become one! Reciprocity seems to no longer be of import in our society. We are a society of "what's in it for me first!" The late Archbishop Oscar Romero said, "Money is good, but selfish persons have made it bad and sinful." Can this not also be said concerning other areas of our lives, such as freedom, politics, and power? Selfishness has contaminated many aspects and resources of life. The institution of marriage is one such resource—marriage is of God and God purposed it. We must fight to preserve it for the good of society!

PRAYER

Lord God, when we look around at the world You made and the people who have been fashioned by Your hands, we cannot help but reflect in awe and amazement. Help us to appreciate Your work in giving us companions to help us achieve sufficiency in You. In Jesus' name we pray. Amen.

WORD POWER

Good—"well-being; suitable."
Rib—from the side.
Suitable—right for a particular purpose; of the right type or quality for a particular purpose or occasion.
Woman—opposite of man; designed to complement man and complete him.

HOME DAILY BIBLE READINGS
(September 2-8, 2013)

God's Image: Male and Female
MONDAY, September 2: "Living Creatures of Every Kind" (Genesis 1:20-25)
TUESDAY, September 3: "Made in the Image of God" (Genesis 1:26-31)
WEDNESDAY, September 4: "Formed from the Dust" (Genesis 2:1-9)
THURSDAY, September 5: "In the Likeness of God" (Genesis 5:1-5)
FRIDAY, September 6: "Made a Little Lower than God" (Psalm 8)
SATURDAY, September 7: "Created in the Likeness of God" (Ephesians 4:17-24)
SUNDAY, September 8: "Created Male and Female" (Genesis 2:18-25)

LESSON 3   **September 15, 2013**

KNOWLEDGE OF GOOD AND EVIL

FAITH PATHWAY/FAITH JOURNEY TOPIC: **Choices and Consequences**

DEVOTIONAL READING: **Deuteronomy 30:11-20**
PRINT PASSAGE: **Genesis 3:8b-17**

BACKGROUND SCRIPTURE: **Genesis 3**
KEY VERSES: **Genesis 3:22-23**

Genesis 3:8b-17—KJV

8 Adam and his wife hid themselves from the presence of the LORD God amongst the trees of the garden.

9 And the LORD God called unto Adam, and said unto him, Where art thou?

10 And he said, I heard thy voice in the garden, and I was afraid, because I was naked; and I hid myself.

11 And he said, Who told thee that thou wast naked? Hast thou eaten of the tree, whereof I commanded thee that thou shouldest not eat?

12 And the man said, The woman whom thou gavest to be with me, she gave me of the tree, and I did eat.

13 And the LORD God said unto the woman, What is this that thou hast done? And the woman said, The serpent beguiled me, and I did eat.

14 And the LORD God said unto the serpent, Because thou hast done this, thou art cursed above all cattle, and above every beast of the field; upon thy belly shalt thou go, and dust shalt thou eat all the days of thy life:

15 And I will put enmity between thee and the woman, and between thy seed and her seed; it shall bruise thy head, and thou shalt bruise his heel.

16 Unto the woman he said, I will greatly multiply thy sorrow and thy conception; in sorrow thou shalt bring forth children; and thy desire shall be to thy husband, and he shall rule over thee.

17 And unto Adam he said, Because thou hast hearkened unto the voice of thy wife, and hast eaten of the tree, of which I commanded thee, saying, Thou shalt not eat of it: cursed is the ground for thy sake; in sorrow shalt thou eat of it all the days of thy life.

Genesis 3:8b-17—NIV

8 They hid from the LORD God among the trees of the garden.

9 But the LORD God called to the man, "Where are you?"

10 He answered, "I heard you in the garden, and I was afraid because I was naked; so I hid."

11 And he said, "Who told you that you were naked? Have you eaten from the tree that I commanded you not to eat from?"

12 The man said, "The woman you put here with me—she gave me some fruit from the tree, and I ate it."

13 Then the LORD God said to the woman, "What is this you have done?" The woman said, "The serpent deceived me, and I ate."

14 So the LORD God said to the serpent, "Because you have done this, Cursed are you above all the livestock and all the wild animals! You will crawl on your belly and you will eat dust all the days of your life.

15 And I will put enmity between you and the woman, and between your offspring and hers; he will crush your head, and you will strike his heel."

16 To the woman he said, "I will greatly increase your pains in childbearing; with pain you will give birth to children. Your desire will be for your husband, and he will rule over you."

17 To Adam he said, "Because you listened to your wife and ate from the tree about which I commanded you, 'You must not eat of it,' Cursed is the ground because of you; through painful toil you will eat of it all the days of your life."

UNIFYING LESSON PRINCIPLE

Everyone at times has given in to lust or greed instead of making a right choice. Why do humans make poor choices? Genesis 3 informs readers that when temptation confronts them, God gives them the freedom to make choices.

TOPICAL OUTLINE OF THE LESSON

I. Introduction
A. The Knowledge of Good and Evil
B. Biblical Background

II. Exposition and Application of the Scripture
A. The Beginning of Autonomy (Genesis 3:8b-11)
B. The Sin of Autonomy (Genesis 3:12-15)
C. The Consequence of Autonomy (Genesis 3:16-17)

III. Concluding Reflection

LESSON OBJECTIVES

Upon the completion of the lesson, the students will be able to do the following:

1. Understand the ways in which sin creates barriers to our having healthy relationships with other people and with God;
2. Confess their wrongs as in-dividual persons, as a church, and as a nation; and,
   Relate experiences in which God has helped them discern right from wrong.

POINTS TO BE EMPHASIZED

ADULT/YOUTH

Adult Topic: Choices and Consequences
Youth Topic: Choices and Consequences
Adult Key Verses: Genesis 3:22-23
Youth Key Verse: Genesis 3:11
Print Passage: Genesis 3:8b-17

—The serpent presented the first occasion for Adam and Eve to choose whether to obey God.
—Genesis 3 is filled with details explaining the origins of snakes' slithering locomotion, weeds, and birth pangs.
—God did not immediately impose the death sentence for disobedience; instead, God pronounced increased pain in childbearing and the difficulties of agriculture.
—It can be debated whether God's words to the man and the woman constitute a divine sentence of judgment or a divine warning of what life from then on would be like in humanity's fallen state.
—God has rules for His creatures that He expects them to keep.
—God's rules are for the good of the creatures.
—God gives His creatures freedom to choose.

CHILDREN

Children Topic: We All Make Choices
Key Verse: Genesis 3:6
Print Passage: Genesis 3:1-13

—Eve said to the serpent that she understood God's instructions.
—Eve was tricked by the serpent's deceptive slant on God's instructions.
—Based on the serpent's words, Eve made a wrong choice by eating the fruit and giving some to Adam.
—Because of guilt, Adam and Eve covered their nakedness and hid in the garden when God approached.
—When God asked the humans what they had done, Adam blamed Eve, and Eve blamed the serpent rather than admitting that they made wrong choices.

I. INTRODUCTION

A. The Knowledge of Good and Evil

The attempt to reconcile evil in a world declared good in the beginning by its Creator has been contemplated by religious men and women (lay theologians) from time immemorial. What was the purpose of the Tree of the Knowledge of Good and Evil? If God was pleased with creation after He had created it, then where does evil come from and what was the need of such a tree? In God's infinite wisdom, what did He have in mind when He created such a tree with such open-ended options for humanity? The fifth-century theologian Augustine of Hippo maintained that "evil exists only as a privation (lack, absence) of that which is good and thus an absence of good such as in *dis*cord, *in*justice, and *loss* of life or of liberty." It stands to reason, then, that if evil is the absence of good, then good must be the absence of all acts and expressions of deprivation and injustice in the world. Yet, these theological questions are not ours alone; rather, they come to us from antiquity and are still unresolved with any absolute certainty.

In this lesson, however, we want to raise a different question: "Can there be knowledge of good and evil without a reality of what constitutes either?" How can we distinguish one from the other in the absence of prior knowledge of what either is? The word *knowledge* (acquaintance, recognition, or understanding) implies some prior experience or awareness of that which is knowable. Can it be that the knowledge of good and evil was etched into the consciousness of humanity in the beginning? Or could it be that the capacity to discern between two opposing forces is what it means to be human, made in the image and likeness of the Creator (free moral agents)?

In the beginning, God gave Adam two commands: to be fruitful and multiply, and not to eat of the Tree of the Knowledge of Good and Evil. It was not until Adam and Eve saw the perceived benefit for them to eat of the Tree of the Knowledge of Good and Evil that they disobeyed God and ate from the tree. Indeed, this knowledge seems to be what distinguishes us from lower primates—the capacity to discern and the ability to make choices of good and evil outcomes. However, our argument about evil must be curtailed and limited for the sake of time and space, but it is worth further communal dialogue beyond the pages of this lesson. Where would we place acts of evil that we characterize as "natural evil" or "acts of God," such as droughts, famine, fires, floods, tornadoes, tsunamis, and so forth? We will explore good and evil from the point of view of humans' responsibility to each other and to God.

B. Biblical Background

The book of Genesis is called the book of beginnings—the beginning of the universe as we know it; but it is also the beginning of the expression of human autonomy (sin).

Adam and Eve violated the divine prohibition that provided limits in their lives. Rather than obey, they chose to rebuff the rule of God. Although many have tried to find out what the forbidden fruit was of which Adam and Eve partook, it is of little consequence, because the cause and effect that brought about condemnation was not the fruit itself—it was their willful disobedience. It is not the hot stove that burns the child; it is the touching of the hot stove that burns. When Adam and Eve saw what the Tree of the Knowledge of Good and Evil could do for them, they chose disobedience over obedience. Dr. Terence E. Fretheim, professor of Old Testament Studies at Luther Northwestern Theological Seminary, says, "Any meaning assigned to the tree must recognize that it has to do with a knowledge that God has." The irony in the text is that they were tempted with the promise that they would be godlike by eating from the tree, when, in fact, they were already godlike—made in God's image and likeness.

It was at this point of discernment that Adam and Eve took and ate from the forbidden tree. To use the colloquial expression, "They saw what was in the deal for them." Is this not the gist of all evil—selfishness (*hubris*): What's in it for me? When we consider historical acts of man's inhumanity to man (the Holocaust, slavery, child abuse, economic exploitation, and greed), the root cause is *hubris* (selfishness and overbearing arrogance). Concomitantly, the gist of good is *unselfishness* (benevolence). Autonomy, in this context, has within it the total disregard for divine rules and expectation for human flourishing. So, in the final analysis, it was after Adam and Eve ate from the Tree of the Knowledge of Good and Evil that their eyes were opened and they realized that they were naked and estranged from God and each other. In this lesson, we cannot ignore the harsh realities that estrangement from one another and from God produces sin and shame in all and for all of us.

II. EXPOSITION AND APPLICATION OF THE SCRIPTURE

A. The Beginning of Autonomy (Genesis 3:8b-11)

Adam and his wife hid themselves from the presence of the LORD God amongst the trees of the garden. And the LORD God called unto Adam, and said unto him, Where art thou? And he said, I heard thy voice in the garden, and I was afraid, because I was naked; and I hid myself. And he said, Who told thee that thou wast naked? Hast thou eaten of the tree, whereof I commanded thee that thou shouldest not eat?

The context for understanding the failure of Adam and Eve in Genesis 3 is seen in verse 25 of chapter 2. The man and his wife were both naked, and they felt no shame. The word *naked* (as a metaphor) connects the psycho-spiritual persona of Adam and Eve before their willful disobedience of the divine command not to eat of the Tree of the Knowledge of Good and Evil. Once they disobeyed, they realized that they were naked and they were ashamed. Because of disobedience, the state of creation transitioned from idyllic to chaotic, characterized by a *lack* of shame and then shame. It is said by some scholars that *naked* was a metaphor for their relationship with each other (chapter 2), and, subsequently, their relationship with God (chapter 3). This transition from one state of existence to the next was marked by their knowledge of good and evil, which was the beginning of human autonomy. Adam and Eve's act of autonomy estranged them from God and consequently from each other, and introduced sin and disgrace into the human family.

So, when Adam and Eve heard God walking in the Garden one evening, they tried to hide themselves from God (as if they could). Upon divine inquiry of their whereabouts, Adam responded that he heard God in the Garden and "was afraid, because I was naked; and I hid myself" (verse 10). According to God's reply, it was Adam and Eve's disobedience that exposed their nakedness. There are many conclusions that can be deduced from their nakedness, but it appears that human nakedness is a psycho-spiritual matter. It is what happens to us psychologically and spiritually when we seek autonomy from God rather than interdependence. Things begin to happen to us that lead us further and further from our Creator and from each other. Adam and Eve became aware of something about themselves that was not previously known to them. How is it that they could be naked and not know it—and then naked and know it? This was the beginning of human autonomy, yet it was not the end of it. Like a snowball rolling down the hill, it has turned into an avalanche, consuming everything in its path. There appears to be no institution—the church, university, government, family, etc.—that is exempt or off-limits to this corrupting spirit of humanity. Every institution known to humankind has suffered at the hand of unbridled human autonomy.

B. The Sin of Autonomy (Genesis 3:12-15)

And the man said, The woman whom thou gavest to be with me, she gave me of the tree, and I did eat. And the Lord God said unto the woman, What is this that thou hast done? And the woman said, The serpent beguiled me, and I did eat. And the Lord God said unto the serpent, Because thou hast done this, thou art cursed above all cattle, and above every beast of the field; upon thy belly shalt thou go, and dust shalt thou eat all the days of thy life: And I will put enmity between thee and the woman, and between thy seed and her seed; it shall bruise thy head, and thou shalt bruise his heel.

God created Adam and Eve as free moral agents capable of choosing between right and wrong, good and bad. Unlike other lower primates in creation, they had the capacity to make choices; however, with those choices came responsibility. After God confronted Adam and Eve about their admission that they were naked, He inquired as to how they knew that they were naked; they then resorted to blaming each other. God created Adam and Eve to be social creatures and to live responsibly together, depending on one another. However, autonomy brought about the sin of estrangement. Hence, Adam and Eve went from shaming to blaming.

What is sin? It depends on whom we ask. There are many definitions of sin, but for the sake of this lesson, *sin* is anything that violates the will of God for human life. God does not desire that we do anything that estranges us from Him or from others within the human family. The quest for human autonomy has morphed into many different sinful and disgraceful expressions in our society—from Bernard Madoff, founder of a billion-dollar securities firm on Wall Street, who defrauded investors out of billions of dollars to see if he could get away with it, to the child abuse scandal at Penn State University and Coach Jerry Sandusky. According to the *Louis Freeh Report*, the leadership at Penn State University was made aware that Coach Sandusky was molesting young boys on campus, but chose to put the well-being of the football program over the sanctity of the lives of young boys who were being sexually exploited by Coach Sandusky. It is interesting that many villains express remorse for their behavior, but only after the fact—when they have been exposed (naked and shamed). It is undeniable that families of villains, victims, and the respective communities suffered irreparable harm and shaming by acts of individual autonomy.

Even as this lesson is being written, the massacre that occurred in Aurora, Colorado, is very much fresh in the psyche of the American people. James Holmes chose autonomy over community; he shot seventy-one persons, killing twelve of them, declaring himself the "joker." We cannot presume to know what is in the minds of these men when they commit their dastardly deeds, but basic to all inhumanity to man is individual autonomy. When persons only think of themselves and what it means to him or her without consideration of the pain and suffering their actions create for others, it is sinful.

C. The Consequence of Autonomy (Genesis 3:16-17)

Unto the woman he said, I will greatly multiply thy sorrow and thy conception; in sorrow thou shalt bring forth children; and thy desire shall be to thy husband, and he shall rule over thee. And unto Adam he said, Because thou hast hearkened unto the voice of thy wife, and hast eaten of the tree, of which I commanded thee, saying, Thou shalt not eat of it: cursed is the ground for thy sake; in sorrow shalt thou eat of it all the days of thy life.

Adam accused Eve of causing him to disobey God. In the same way, Eve accused the serpent of deceiving her. Adam and Eve were not willing to be accountable and accept responsibility for their disobedience. They each blamed someone else—Adam his wife, and Eve the serpent. When they were exposed by God and could not hide, rather than confess their failure, they attempted to escape the consequences of their behavior. The consequence of their quest for autonomy was punishment and banishment from the Garden of Eden (see verses 16-24). It has been said, "The sin belongs to us, but the consequences belong to God." They could not avoid their individual responsibility for their sins. God punished all parties involved—first the woman, then the man, and then the serpent. According to this text, the woman's punishment was pain in childbirth and the dominion of her husband over her. Adam's punishment was to live a life of tilling the soil for food and having difficulty in cultivating it. But beyond Adam and Eve's act of gross disobedience, the real tragedy is that they had everything that they would have needed, but they exchanged it for what Frank E. Gaebelien in his *Exposition's Bible Commentary* calls, "an act of great folly." No matter how we attempt to shift the blame, we cannot shift the blame or the consequences of our actions upon another.

III. CONCLUDING REFLECTION

The tentacles of evil are multiple and varied. We make grave errors in judgment when we attempt to localize expressions of evil in certain groups or in certain stereotypical individuals. In the age of global terrorism and global disaster, our knowledge of both good and evil is obvious and irrefutable. Yet, history has assured us of the reality of evil as both domestic (Oklahoma City bombing) and foreign (car bombings in Israel), corporate (the KKK), individual (Jeffrey Dahmer), and private (pedophiles and spousal abuse) and public (racism), or when a young special needs child was trapped on a third-floor ledge and a passerby (Steve St. Bernard) stood patiently and waited under her to catch her when she fell. Both acts of good and evil are obvious realities in the world. Both Jeffrey Dahmer and Steve St. Bernard were descendents of Adam and Eve—but one was evil and the other is good. St. Bernard said, "I asked God ... I said, 'Let me catch her, please. Don't let me miss.'" When she fell, he said, "We went down. She touched the floor but the impact wasn't on her. It was me and her going down. I guess I absorbed the blow." Is this not what it means to do good—absorbing the blow for another? Is this not what Jesus did for us?

The apostle Paul called Jesus the Second Adam, who reconciled us to God and made us more than conquerors through Him (Jesus) who loves us. Adam and Eve teach us that God has given us enough; therefore, any attempt to get more at any cost will lead to sin. Failure to trust God with our lives is death; however, to trust God with our lives is to live.

PRAYER

Eternal God, Creator of all, we humbly submit our lives to You in obedience to Your call on our lives. We thank You for forgiving us of our sins and providing us with avenues of escape when temptations arise. In Jesus' name we pray. Amen.

WORD POWER

Evil *(aven)*—to exert oneself in vain, or a way of life without God.
Good *(yashar)*—to be straight or to make right.
Knowledge *(yada)*—discerning what is best.

HOME DAILY BIBLE READINGS
(September 9-15, 2013)

Knowledge of Good and Evil

MONDAY, September 9: "Obeying God's Voice" (Exodus 19:3-8)

TUESDAY, September 10: "The Blessing in Obedience" (Deuteronomy 11:26-32)

WEDNESDAY, September 11: "Choosing the Life of Obedience" (Deuteronomy 30:11-20)

THURSDAY, September 12: "Obeying God above All" (Acts 5:27-42)

FRIDAY, September 13: "The Enticement to Disobey" (Genesis 3:1-7)

SATURDAY, September 14: "The Punishment for Disobedience" (Genesis 3:20-24)

SUNDAY, September 15: "The Consequences of Disobedience" (Genesis 3:8b-17)

LESSON 4   September 22, 2013

AN EVERLASTING COVENANT

FAITH PATHWAY/FAITH JOURNEY TOPIC: **Never Again**

DEVOTIONAL READING: **Isaiah 54:9-14**
PRINT PASSAGE: **Genesis 9:8-17**

BACKGROUND SCRIPTURE: **Genesis 6:9–9:28**
KEY VERSE: **Genesis 9:11**

Genesis 9:8-17—KJV

8 And God spake unto Noah, and to his sons with him, saying,

9 And I, behold, I establish my covenant with you, and with your seed after you;

10 And with every living creature that is with you, of the fowl, of the cattle, and of every beast of the earth with you; from all that go out of the ark, to every beast of the earth.

11 And I will establish my covenant with you; neither shall all flesh be cut off any more by the waters of a flood; neither shall there any more be a flood to destroy the earth.

12 And God said, This is the token of the covenant which I make between me and you and every living creature that is with you, for perpetual generations:

13 I do set my bow in the cloud, and it shall be for a token of a covenant between me and the earth.

14 And it shall come to pass, when I bring a cloud over the earth, that the bow shall be seen in the cloud:

15 And I will remember my covenant, which is between me and you and every living creature of all flesh; and the waters shall no more become a flood to destroy all flesh.

16 And the bow shall be in the cloud; and I will look upon it, that I may remember the everlasting covenant between God and every living creature of all flesh that is upon the earth.

17 And God said unto Noah, This is the token of the covenant, which I have established between me and all flesh that is upon the earth.

Genesis 9:8-17—NIV

8 Then God said to Noah and to his sons with him:

9 "I now establish my covenant with you and with your descendants after you

10 and with every living creature that was with you—the birds, the livestock and all the wild animals, all those that came out of the ark with you—every living creature on earth.

11 I establish my covenant with you: Never again will all life be cut off by the waters of a flood; never again will there be a flood to destroy the earth."

12 And God said, "This is the sign of the covenant I am making between me and you and every living creature with you, a covenant for all generations to come:

13 I have set my rainbow in the clouds, and it will be the sign of the covenant between me and the earth.

14 Whenever I bring clouds over the earth and the rainbow appears in the clouds,

15 I will remember my covenant between me and you and all living creatures of every kind. Never again will the waters become a flood to destroy all life.

16 Whenever the rainbow appears in the clouds, I will see it and remember the everlasting covenant between God and all living creatures of every kind on the earth."

17 So God said to Noah, "This is the sign of the covenant I have established between me and all life on the earth."

UNIFYING LESSON PRINCIPLE

A natural disaster can cause great anxiety over the safety and welfare of loved ones. How can loved ones be assured of God's protection in the future? God said that the rainbow would remind Him of the covenant to protect all living creatures.

TOPICAL OUTLINE OF THE LESSON

I. Introduction
  A. God Keeps His Promises
  B. Biblical Background

II. Exposition and Application of the Scripture
  A. God Establishes His Covenant (Genesis 9:8-11)
  B. God Guarantees the Covenant (Genesis 9:12-13)
  C. God Remembers His Covenant (Genesis 9:14-17)

III. Concluding Reflection

LESSON OBJECTIVES

Upon the completion of the lesson, the students will be able to do the following:

1. Explore the covenant that God made with Noah after the Flood;
2. Discover ways in which adults can take delight in signs of God's grace; and,
3. Identify the promises of God on which adults can stake their lives.

POINTS TO BE EMPHASIZED

ADULT/YOUTH

Adult Topic: Never Again
Youth Topic: A Sign of Assurance for the Future
Adult Key Verse: Genesis 9:11
Youth Key Verse: Genesis 9:13
Print Passage: Genesis 9:8-17

—Covenant is a key theological concept first introduced here. God made a covenant with Noah, his offspring, and every living creature that accompanied them off the ark.

—Covenants are accompanied by a symbol or sign—a rainbow in this case—for ratification and reminder.

—The rainbow was a sign and visible seal, just as circumcision was the sign and seal of Abraham (see Genesis 17:11)—and the Sabbath would be the sign and seal of the covenant with Israel at Sinai (see Exodus 31:16-17).

—God initiated the covenant given to Noah and to all creation.

—The rainbow was not a new phenomenon, but, out of this experience, it took on new significance as a reminder of God's covenant.

CHILDREN

Children Topic: A Promise Made
Key Verse: Genesis 9:16
Print Passage: Genesis 7:1, 12-15; 8:13; 9:11-17

—Noah was a righteous man who, along with his family and living creatures, was chosen by God to be saved from death in the Flood.

—After more than a year, the flood waters receded.

—God made a covenant with Noah and symbolized it with a rainbow in the sky.

—God's covenant with Noah was that a flood would never destroy all living things again.

I. INTRODUCTION

A. God Keeps His Promises

Most of us have made promises that we had no intention of keeping, but later someone reminded us that we did not keep the promise. However, the Bible assures us that the God of the universe keeps His promises for a "thousand generations." In this lesson, God's promise is based in His covenant (*diatheke*) with Noah. Although it is understood by some persons that a promise and a covenant are synonymous, they are not. A *covenant* is a legal agreement between two parties who make a promise of commitment to each other and are bound by an oath (guarantor); however, a promise does not have to be reciprocal or relational in nature or sealed by an oath. For instance, a man who makes a promise to himself to never get drunk again or a student who promises herself to be a more disciplined student does not have to seal the promise or guarantee it in any way. There is nothing legal about a promise in and of itself. Likewise, every covenant has a promise in it, but not every promise is a covenant. In the Key Verse (verse 9), we see that God made a two-part covenant with Noah and humanity—humanity would never again be cut off or destroyed by flood water. Thus, the Noahic covenant that all of humanity is bound in is in all reality a covenant of grace.

B. Biblical Background

Perhaps one of the earliest biblical narratives that many African-American children hear is the story of Noah and the fact that "Noah found grace in the eyes of the Lord." For some, this narrative has nursery-rhyme qualities, but the story of Noah is anything but a nursery rhyme. Chapter 9 is part of a larger narrative about the grace of God in the light of human failure. Thus, the genesis of what took place in chapter 9 is chapter 6, in which humanity became vile in the sight of the Lord and God repented that He had made man and woman (see verses 5-6). "The Lord saw how great man's wickedness on the earth had become, and that every inclination of the thoughts of his heart was only evil all the time. The Lord was grieved that he had made man on the earth, and his heart was filled with pain." However, rather than annihilating all of creation, God extended grace to Noah and his family and chose to save Noah, his wife, and his sons and their wives in an ark (see 7:13-14). Sin was so abundant and humanity was so abject that God grieved over creation and decided to destroy all living creatures except two (male and female) of each animal and fowl. The Earth was deluged with water from heaven for forty days, and after the rain ceased, the Earth remained covered with water for 150 days (see Genesis 7:24). After the water receded, God remembered Noah (8:1) and all living creatures and entered into a covenant with him and all of creation.

II. EXPOSITION AND APPLICATION OF THE SCRIPTURE

A. God Establishes His Covenant
(Genesis 9:8-11)

And God spake unto Noah, and to his sons with him, saying, And I, behold, I establish my covenant with you, and with your seed after you; And with every living creature that is with you, of the fowl, of the cattle, and of every beast of the earth with you; from all that go out of the ark, to every beast of the earth. And I will establish my covenant with you; neither shall all flesh be cut off any more by the waters of a flood; neither shall there any more be a flood to destroy the earth.

God extended to Noah and humanity an olive branch when it was time to exit the ark that had kept them from the flood waters. This olive branch is known as a covenant *(diatheke)* and was initiated by God. God was the one who came to humanity in grace to give them another opportunity to do the right thing. In this covenant, the promise is strictly on God and without condition. God declared that He would never again destroy humanity or creation by flood. Before the Flood, God was angry and exacted revenge upon all of creation because of the hearts of humanity—but God seems to have been saying that regardless of the condition of the hearts of men and women, His response to sin would not be human destruction. However, implicit in this covenant is the divine confidence that God had in humanity, in spite of its history or propensity toward disobeying God's will (like Adam, or as seen during the Tower of Babel episode). God imputed a trust to humanity that perhaps has not been earned or deserved heretofore by humanity; however, this is the nature of grace. It has been said that grace is getting what we do not deserve—and in this case, it is true. God remembered Noah in verse 1, and made a covenant with humanity in verse 7. This covenant is established in goodness and love and obligated God not to bring destruction again by flood water.

B. God Guarantees the Covenant
(Genesis 9:12-13)

And God said, This is the token of the covenant which I make between me and you and every living creature that is with you, for perpetual generations: I do set my bow in the cloud, and it shall be for a token of a covenant between me and the earth.

Years ago, as children we were told that there was a pot of gold at the end of a rainbow. In subsequent years, we have come to know that this is an old wives' tale. There is nothing at the end of a rainbow. However, in the reading of this text there is something more precious and eternal behind the rainbow than gold or silver—it is the Word of God. God made an eternal covenant with Noah and every living creature and gave the rainbow as a sign of God's covenant. As a rule, rainbows will appear in the sky after rain has ceased; however, they are sometimes visible to persons or communities who have not experienced rain. Could this speak to the universality of the covenant that it is between God and all living flesh? The rainbow follows the rain and assures all living creatures that never again will rain have the complete catastrophic effect on Earth as it did in the days of Noah. This covenant is not conditional; rather, it is based on the graciousness of God. Concomitantly, this covenant reminds us of the destructive power and consequences of sin. The apostle Paul wrote, "We know that the whole creation has been groaning as in the pains of childbirth right up to the present time" (Romans 8:22). For Paul, this groaning in creation is the result of sin. And since it was the sins of the people (see 6:5-6, 11-12) that caused the Noahic flood, the scope of the promise touches the entire Earth and "all that is in it"—and not just humanity.

Finally, it was God who initiated the covenant, and it was God who guaranteed the covenant. This is evident by the personal pronoun "I" used in verses 12 and 13: "I am" and "I have." God made the covenant ("I am making…," verse 12) and ("I have set my rainbow…," verse 13). This is a unilateral covenant made by God and guaranteed by God. Noah and all living things are merely the recipients of the graciousness of God. Clearly, God took the initiative in establishing this covenant; and, unlike other covenants—Abrahamic, Mosaic, Davidic, etc.—this covenant was neither conditional nor predicated upon the actions of the people. We cannot know the mind of God, but before the Flood, God grieved that He had made humanity because of their wickedness—and after the Flood, God resolved to remember this event and never allow it to happen again. This has to be the highest expression of grace known to humanity, because clearly when we look at human history, the wickedness has been great, and yet we have escaped the vengeance and the wrath of God. In the words of the black deacon, "God has allowed our days to roll on."

C. God Remembers His Covenant (Genesis 9:14-17)

And it shall come to pass, when I bring a cloud over the earth, that the bow shall be seen in the cloud: And I will remember my covenant, which is between me and you and every living creature of all flesh; and the waters shall no more become a flood to destroy all flesh. And the bow shall be in the cloud; and I will look upon it, that I may remember the everlasting covenant between God and every living creature of all flesh that is upon the earth. And God said unto Noah, This is the token of the covenant, which I have established between me and all flesh that is upon the earth.

These verses make it abundantly clear that the rainbow was as much for God as it was for humanity. It was a reminder to God of His promise between Him, Noah, and all living creatures. God made this promise in verse 14; however, if the omniscient attributes we have ascribed to God are true, then the question becomes, "Why is it that God needs to remind Himself of anything?"

In the book of Exodus, after God had set the Israelites free from bondage in Egypt, the people began acting foolishly in the wilderness, and again God repented for having set them free and resolved to destroy them; however, it was Moses who called God to remember the promise God had made with Abraham, Isaac, and Israel. It was at this point that God relented and did not destroy the people (see Exodus 32:11-13). Dr. Terence E. Fretheim says, "The rainbow reminds God and not us. When God sees the rainbow God remembers the covenant. This does not mean that God forgets in between rainbows, because God remembering entails more than mental activity; it involves action with specific reference to prior commitment."

But, perhaps the words of remembrance are as much for humanity as they are for God; it is for the assurance of humankind that God is faithful. Thus, regardless of future deluges, we need not be anxious or fearful about our destruction, because each rainbow is a sign of God's eternal promise to all of creation. Finally, verse 17 demonstrates the interconnectedness between humanity and all of creation. People are indeed a part of an ecological system of all life forms on Earth. As humankind goes, so goes creation. We cannot live our lives with total disregard for the Earth and all that is on it, because the fullness of creation belongs to the Creator.

III. CONCLUDING REFLECTION

When one looks at the arrogance that success and wealth have created in us, it appears that humanity has gravitated toward being more independent. But the reality is that none of us, regardless of our stature and status in life, can ever become an island unto self and independent unto ourselves. This lesson assures us that we are dependent on each other and on our Creator for our existence and continuous well-being.

On May 9, 2010, it rained in Nashville for forty-eight hours and when the rain stopped, the city of Nashville, Tennessee, and many surrounding communities were flooded. Lives and property were lost, and thousands of people were rendered homeless.

In the spring of 2012, more than ten inches of rain fell in Duluth, Minnesota, in a twenty-four-hour period, displacing hundreds of families and costing millions of dollars in property damage and loss. These water disasters do not discriminate between male and female, rich or poor, or among black, white, Hispanic, or any other ethnic groups. Disaster is an equal-opportunity agent and has a way of reducing all of us to our lowest common denominator—being human. We are God's people, living in God's world, and we are dependent on God and one another for our well-being.

PRAYER

Eternal God our Father, Creator of heaven and Earth, we are grateful for all that You do for us, the forgiveness of our sins, and the preservation of our lives. Lord, enable us to be promise keepers, as You are a promise keeper. In Jesus' name we pray. Amen.

WORD POWER
Covenant (*beriyth*)—a legal contract between two parties that is bound by an oath (guarantor). Also, when God establishes a covenant it is expressed in love and loyalty.
Remember (*zakar*)—to mention or to remind oneself.

HOME DAILY BIBLE READINGS
(September 16-22, 2013)

An Everlasting Covenant
MONDAY, September 16: "An Invitation to Covenant with God" (Genesis 6:11-22)
TUESDAY, September 17: "Doing All the Lord Commands" (Genesis 7:1-10)
WEDNESDAY, September 18: "Preserved in the Ark" (Genesis 7:11-24)
THURSDAY, September 19: "Waiting for the Waters to Subside" (Genesis 8:1-12)
FRIDAY, September 20: "A Sacrifice Pleasing to God" (Genesis 8:13-22)
SATURDAY, September 21: "God's Covenant with All Humanity" (Genesis 9:1-7)
SUNDAY, September 22: "Remembering the Everlasting Covenant" (Genesis 9:8-17)

GOD SCATTERS THE NATIONS

FAITH PATHWAY/FAITH JOURNEY TOPIC: **The Proud Brought Low**

DEVOTIONAL READING: **2 Chronicles 34:22-28**
PRINT PASSAGE: **Genesis 11:1-9**

BACKGROUND SCRIPTURE: **Genesis 11:1-9**
KEY VERSE: **Genesis 11:8**

Genesis 11:1-9—KJV

AND THE whole earth was of one language, and of one speech.

2 And it came to pass, as they journeyed from the east, that they found a plain in the land of Shinar; and they dwelt there.

3 And they said one to another, Go to, let us make brick, and burn them thoroughly. And they had brick for stone, and slime had they for mortar.

4 And they said, Go to, let us build us a city and a tower, whose top may reach unto heaven; and let us make us a name, lest we be scattered abroad upon the face of the whole earth.

5 And the LORD came down to see the city and the tower, which the children of men builded.

6 And the LORD said, Behold, the people is one, and they have all one language; and this they begin to do: and now nothing will be restrained from them, which they have imagined to do.

7 Go to, let us go down, and there confound their language, that they may not understand one another's speech.

8 So the LORD scattered them abroad from thence upon the face of all the earth: and they left off to build the city.

9 Therefore is the name of it called Babel; because the LORD did there confound the language of all the earth: and from thence did the LORD scatter them abroad upon the face of all the earth.

Genesis 11:1-9—NIV

NOW THE whole world had one language and a common speech.

2 As men moved eastward, they found a plain in Shinar and settled there.

3 They said to each other, "Come, let's make bricks and bake them thoroughly." They used brick instead of stone, and tar for mortar.

4 Then they said, "Come, let us build ourselves a city, with a tower that reaches to the heavens, so that we may make a name for ourselves and not be scattered over the face of the whole earth."

5 But the LORD came down to see the city and the tower that the men were building.

6 The LORD said, "If as one people speaking the same language they have begun to do this, then nothing they plan to do will be impossible for them.

7 Come, let us go down and confuse their language so they will not understand each other."

8 So the LORD scattered them from there over all the earth, and they stopped building the city.

9 That is why it was called Babel—because there the LORD confused the language of the whole world. From there the LORD scattered them over the face of the whole earth.

TOPICAL OUTLINE OF THE LESSON

I. Introduction
  A. The True Meaning of Pride
  B. Biblical Background

II. Exposition and Application of the Scripture
  A. Man's Plans
    (Genesis 11:1-4)
  B. God "Comes" Down
    (Genesis 11:5-7)
  C. God's Response
    (Genesis 11:8-9)

III. Concluding Reflection

LESSON OBJECTIVES

Upon the completion of the lesson, the students will be able to do the following:

1. Investigate the misguided theology of the plan to build the Tower of Babel;
2. Humbly acknowledge their futile attempts to be like God; and,
3. Identify potential "towers of Babel" that the church attempts to construct today.

POINTS TO BE EMPHASIZED

ADULT/YOUTH

Adult Topic: The Proud Brought Low
Youth Topic: Sounds like Babel
Adult Key Verse: Genesis 11:8
Youth Key Verse: Genesis 11:9
Print Passage: Genesis 11:1-9

—*Babel* means "Gate of God." The Hebrew storyteller, however, linked the name with the Hebrew word *balal*: "to confuse."

—God's use of the plural, "Let *us* go down…" in verse 7 most likely depicts God conferring with the members of the heavenly council, angelic beings who serve as God's royal attendants in various Scripture passages (for example, Job 1:6ff.).

—The people's motive was to "make a name" for themselves (see Genesis 11:4). Their pride and arrogance are subtly ridiculed when God still had to *descend* to reach their heaven-touching tower!

—The sin of the tower builders is sometimes linked to their failure to "fill the earth" (see Genesis 9:1). At least in this instance, being scattered and diverse was preferable in God's plan to being centralized and homogeneous.

—The sin of the tower in this text was selfishly using human skills to build a city and a tower to reach heaven.

—Possessing an ambition to glorify themselves rather than God, the people in this text were trying to make a name for themselves.

CHILDREN

Children Topic: The People Are Scattered
Key Verse: Genesis 11:8
Print Passage: Genesis 11:1-9

—God's desire that humankind "be fruitful and multiply, and fill the earth" (Genesis 1:28) was frustrated by Noah's descendants—who wanted to build a city, stay together, and speak one language.

—God's covenant to be with all people everywhere was endangered by the people's rebellion, pride, and preference to stay in one place.

—The people wanted one language, one city, and a tower that led to the heavens as a safeguard against being scattered across the Earth.

—God knew that the long-term consequences of what the people were doing would be detrimental.

—When God saw what the people were doing, He scattered them over all the Earth, made it impossible for them to understand one another's languages, and terminated the building of the city and the tower.

I. INTRODUCTION
A. The True Meaning of Pride

Pride in our culture has come to be seen as a good thing—but is it? The wisdom writer of the book of Proverbs made two profound statements about pride: it "goes before a fall"; and, "When pride comes, disgrace follows" (see Proverbs 11:2; 16:18). Which is it? Is pride a good thing, or is it a precursor to something bad? The word *pride* is like so many other words in our languages that have evolved over the years to take on new meanings, or a word that people have tried to put a new spin on—but does this work? Can we understand any biblical text apart from the original meaning and understanding of a word?

The etymology of the word *pride* in both the Old and New Testaments is always a negative. In the Old Testament, God is against pride because pride is associated with arrogance. According to some Old Testament writings, pride is "derived from a spirit of error or from Satan." Likewise, according to Old Testament legend, it was *pride* that led to the fall of Lucifer from heaven. In the New Testament, the word *pride* is used infrequently and is never spoken of as a good thing. The apostle Paul listed pride as one of the vices of the pagans (see Romans 1:30). Also, there are three words in the New Testament that have the same roots (*hyperephanos*) as the word *pride: insolent, arrogant,* and *boastful.* Therefore, it does not matter how a word evolves—it does not alter the original intent of the word. The biblical context of pride is that it is a vice against which God is reviled! Thus, it is to this end that some biblical scholars and commentators say that *pride* is the sin behind the fall of the "Tower of Babel" and the scattering of the people. Yet, in the final analysis, it does not really matter what we think about the spirit of pride. God has another view of it: "When pride comes, disgrace follows."

B. Biblical Background

Chapter 11 is a continuation of chapter 10 and what has come to be known as the "Table of Nations." According to biblical lore, all races and nations evolved from the three sons of Noah—Shem, Ham, and Japheth. Chapter 10 consists primarily of the genealogy of the sons of Noah. It is important to note that much of what has come to be said about the racial makeup of these descendants is legendary. In every family, the children tend to take on some of the characteristics and personality of the parents, and there is never a racial identity apart from the racial identity of the parents. Black parents do not give birth to white babies and vice versa. So the inherent question is this: If these are the sons of a set of parents, then how were these three sons (Ham, Shem, and Japheth) the origins of three distinct races of people? Old Testament scholar Walter Brueggemann says, "The basic principle of organization of these clans is not racial, ethnic, linguistic, or territorial, but political. The political reality is that everything points toward the ultimate nation of Israel (Abraham), who descended from the line of Shem. Thus, God (ultimately) used the lineage of Shem to be the hope of a new world and a new order. It would be through Shem's lineage that the nation of Israel would emerge with the hope of one nation and one people."

Nevertheless, it is ironic that humanity and Earth were destroyed because of the sinfulness of humankind—and after the Flood, instead of capitalizing on the opportunity of a new beginning, Noah got drunk, exposed himself, and cursed his grandson, Canaan! Chaos seems to have followed chaos. Thus, the destruction of the Tower of Babel and the scattering of the people seem to be the continuation of humanity's intent to have a vision for themselves and the Earth apart from God's vision. The people of Babel had a common language and sought to build a monument to themselves. This offended God—just as the behavior of the people in Noah's day had offended God. So the things they had in common, rather than being a good thing and a blessing to the community, brought divine judgment that resulted in confusion and subsequent dispersion. Walter Brueggemann said, "All human language has become a language of disobedience." Language is the "word image" of the heart—as Jesus said, "For out of the overflow of the heart the mouth speaks" (Matthew 12:34). So, their common language was used to self-aggrandize rather than to glorify God and honor God's vision for community.

II. EXPOSITION AND APPLICATION OF THE SCRIPTURE

A. Man's Plans
(Genesis 11:1-4)

AND THE whole earth was of one language, and of one speech. And it came to pass, as they journeyed from the east, that they found a plain in the land of Shinar; and they dwelt there. And they said one to another, Go to, let us make brick, and burn them thoroughly. And they had brick for stone, and slime had they for mortar. And they said, Go to, let us build us a city and a tower, whose top may reach unto heaven; and let us make us a name, lest we be scattered abroad upon the face of the whole earth.

The story of the Tower of Babel describes the "whole earth." However, this description is not in reference to the literal Earth and its entire contents but, rather, to certain identifiable people of the Earth. It speaks of the language and the unity of the people in Shinar. Hence, as we read these verses, we must be open to what these verses are *not* saying. The pronouns *we* and *us* suggest that the people had no other people in mind other than themselves. Of course, commentators and scholars differ on whether the expressions "the whole earth" and "all the people of the earth" are to be taken literally or figuratively. The people were in Shinar (Mesopotamia, verse 2) and were settling there, which is hardly the whole Earth.

Also, verses 3 and 4 have no inclusive language: "They said, 'Come, let us build ourselves a city, with a tower that reaches to the heavens, so that we may make a name for ourselves'" (verse 4, NIV). We must bear in mind that these were ordinary people who, like you and me, were without supernatural abilities. They could not see beyond their immediate geographical and social context; rather, they were trying to preserve themselves.

Second, there is no mention of God—only themselves—as they plotted a future without God. However, the very thing that they were attempting to prevent from happening ultimately happened to them. They were attempting to maintain their tribal unity and not be scattered, but God did the very thing to them that they were attempting to avoid. Their decision to make a name for themselves was done without divine consultation. One of the lessons of human history is that humanity is prone to try to make a name for itself without the Lord. The problem in this text is obvious and irrefutable: there was no consultation with God and the people erred in their effort to become self-sufficient and build a future without the Lord. Jesus, in His parable of the "wise and foolish builders," said that two men built a house: one built his house on sand, and the other built his house upon a rock. Yet, only the wise man, who built his house on a rock, was able to withstand the challenges and the crises of life. The quest of the builders of the Tower of Babel for human autonomy fell flat. Therefore, we must learn the lessons of history: humanity cannot find peace and unity and have a sustainable future apart from the Lord.

B. God "Comes" Down (Genesis 11:5-7)

And the Lord came down to see the city and the tower, which the children of men builded. And the Lord said, Behold, the people is one, and they have all one language; and this they begin to do: and now nothing will be restrained from them, which they have imagined to do. Go to, let us go down, and there confound their language, that they may not understand one another's speech.

In these verses, we finally hear the voice of the Lord. The people's quest for autonomy aroused the curiosity of the Lord God in heaven and He came down to see the city. Of course, we know that God did not have to come from heaven to see anything, because one of the attributes we ascribe to God is that God is omniscient—He sees all. The language, again, infers that the effort to build a city was without divine consultation. God came to see the work that the men were building. God's response was decisive and final. It appears that God not only saw the city and the tower, but He also saw the builders' motives. Their hidden motives were not hidden from God—for indeed, God looks not at humanity's outward appearance. God was not pleased with what He saw. God resolved that if the people could accomplish this task, then they would be emboldened to think that nothing was impossible for them. However, "nothing impossible" is an attribute spoken only of God. Was this humanity's attempt to be like God? After all, this was the temptation behind the first satanic temptation of Adam and Eve (see Genesis 3). Whatever their hidden ambitions were, they vexed God and brought about divine judgment against the people of the Earth once again. God saw the need to scatter people over the Earth. We cannot be like God by building things and monuments to ourselves, regardless of how noble our intentions are. God created us in His likeness and image—and in the words of the apostle Paul, we become like God only when we have the mind of Jesus the Christ and allow the Spirit of God to dwell in us. Of course, our likeness must never be confused with our being like God. We are like God only in our human capacity to possess some of the ascribed virtues of God (i.e., love, kindness, joy, peace, etc.; see Galatians 5:22-25).

C. God's Response
(Genesis 11:8-9)

So the LORD scattered them abroad from thence upon the face of all the earth: and they left off to build the city. Therefore is the name of it called Babel; because the LORD did there confound the language of all the earth: and from thence did the LORD scatter them abroad upon the face of all the earth.

It has been said that the actions belong to us, but the consequences belong to God. The people of Shinar decided to build a city and a tower to add permanence to their existence, but obviously what they had in mind for themselves was not what God had in mind. This lesson is clear: God does not find favor in humanity's attempts to find significance in the world apart from Him. So the Lord scattered the people all over the known world (verse 8). God confused their language so that they could not complete the city and left them no choice but to cease and desist. It was the Lord who scattered them, but was this punishment or was it a part of the divine intent for humanity?

In other biblical examples, when God called a person or persons to scatter, it was not punitive. There were three dispensations in which God sent forth His agents as divine ambassadors in the world. The first was God's call to Abram to go to an unknown land… "and all people of the earth will be blessed through you" (see Genesis 12:3). The second was God's call to Moses when He sent Moses to tell Pharaoh to let His people go (see Exodus 3:20). Third, the ultimate call came from Jesus the Christ, who commanded His followers to go into all the world and make disciples (see Matthew 28:19). Jesus commanded His disciples "To be my witnesses in Jerusalem, Judea, Samaria, and the uttermost parts of the world" (see Acts 1:8). God was not *sending* the people of Babel; God was *scattering* the people because their vision of the future did not include God. Nevertheless, we must conclude that God was a God who scattered humankind in order that the first command to have dominion over creation might be fulfilled (see Genesis 1:28). So, in the final analysis, we must ask ourselves about the implications of God's scattering in the world today. How should we apply this text to a Christian lifestyle today? We are God's ambassadors in the world and God commissions and sends us forth as His ambassadors, bearing our gifts of love and justice in the world for the good of all of humanity.

III. CONCLUDING REFLECTION

Can there be a social order in which God is excluded? On the surface, in the reading of this text, the people's quest for unity appears to be a good thing—but God had a problem with their understanding and idea of unity, because not all ideas of unity are equal. When unity is not inclusive of all people, it is not consistent with the will of God for the world. Years ago, when southern politicians talked about a unified South, the Negro was not included in their rhetoric. Likewise, the founding documents of America did not allow and include people of color. "We hold these truths to be self-evident that all men are created equal, that they are endowed by their creator with certain unalienable Rights of life, Liberty, and the pursuit of Happiness." It took the 14th amendment to include people of color.

Walter Brueggemann says, "The unity they were seeking was grounded in fear and they attempted to survive by their own resources. A human unity without the vision of God's will that is inclusive of all people is likely to be ordered in oppressive conformity." God has a plan for all of His people that is grounded in love and justice for all peoples. We must never assume that the talk of unity is a unity that is pleasing to God. There remains a quirk in the human personality that finds comfort in that which is familiar and fears the unknown—i.e., people, places, ideologies, and so forth. Yet, God calls us to a new orientation of community, where people do not live in fear and where God's love and justice are pervasive! So, in spite of the vast resources which God has allowed people of the Earth to amass, any attempt at self-preservation is futile. The Hebrew sage was right in saying, "Trust in the Lord with all your heart and lean not on your own understanding" (Proverbs 3:5, NIV).

PRAYER

Oh Lord, Creator and sustainer of all life, we give thanks today for all that You are doing to put us in the place of Your will for our lives. We confess that we are prone to wander and become preoccupied with our own well-beings, but we plead for Your helping hand to direct and help us to trust You for our future. In Jesus' name we pray. Amen.

WORD POWER

Confused—to disorient or to throw into disorder.
Pride—ascending majesty or arrogance.
Scatter—the process of dispersing; that which happens when a people are forced to leave a homeland or base.

HOME DAILY BIBLE READINGS
(September 23-29, 2013)

God Scatters the Nations
MONDAY, September 23: "Dark Counsel Lacking Knowledge" (Job 38:1-7)
TUESDAY, September 24: "Limited Knowledge and Influence" (Job 38:12-18)
WEDNESDAY, September 25: "The Expanse beyond Human Control" (Job 38:28-38)
THURSDAY, September 26: "Overshadowed by God's Greatness" (Job 40:6-14)
FRIDAY, September 27: "The Wrath of the Lord" (2 Chronicles 34:14-21)
SATURDAY, September 28: "A Humble and Penitent Heart" (2 Chronicles 34:22-28)
SUNDAY, September 29: "Human Achievement without God" (Genesis 11:1-9)

A PROMISE OF LAND

FAITH PATHWAY/FAITH JOURNEY TOPIC: A Lasting Inheritance

DEVOTIONAL READING: Hebrews 11:8-16
PRINT PASSAGE: Genesis 15:7-21
KEY VERSE: Genesis 15:18

BACKGROUND SCRIPTURE: Genesis 12:1-7; 13;
15:7-21; 17:8

Genesis 15:7-21—KJV

7 And he said unto him, I am the LORD that brought thee out of Ur of the Chaldees, to give thee this land to inherit it.

8 And he said, Lord GOD, whereby shall I know that I shall inherit it?

9 And he said unto him, Take me an heifer of three years old, and a she goat of three years old, and a ram of three years old, and a turtledove, and a young pigeon.

10 And he took unto him all these, and divided them in the midst, and laid each piece one against another: but the birds divided he not.

11 And when the fowls came down upon the carcases, Abram drove them away.

12 And when the sun was going down, a deep sleep fell upon Abram; and, lo, an horror of great darkness fell upon him.

13 And he said unto Abram, Know of a surety that thy seed shall be a stranger in a land that is not theirs, and shall serve them; and they shall afflict them four hundred years;

14 And also that nation, whom they shall serve, will I judge: and afterward shall they come out with great substance.

15 And thou shalt go to thy fathers in peace; thou shalt be buried in a good old age.

16 But in the fourth generation they shall come hither again: for the iniquity of the Amorites is not yet full.

17 And it came to pass, that, when the sun went down, and it was dark, behold a smoking furnace, and a burning lamp that passed between those pieces.

18 In the same day the LORD made a covenant with Abram, saying, Unto thy seed have I given this land,

Genesis 15:7-21—NIV

7 He also said to him, "I am the LORD, who brought you out of Ur of the Chaldeans to give you this land to take possession of it."

8 But Abram said, "O Sovereign LORD, how can I know that I will gain possession of it?"

9 So the LORD said to him, "Bring me a heifer, a goat and a ram, each three years old, along with a dove and a young pigeon."

10 Abram brought all these to him, cut them in two and arranged the halves opposite each other; the birds, however, he did not cut in half.

11 Then birds of prey came down on the carcasses, but Abram drove them away.

12 As the sun was setting, Abram fell into a deep sleep, and a thick and dreadful darkness came over him.

13 Then the LORD said to him, "Know for certain that your descendants will be strangers in a country not their own, and they will be enslaved and mistreated four hundred years.

14 But I will punish the nation they serve as slaves, and afterward they will come out with great possessions.

15 You, however, will go to your fathers in peace and be buried at a good old age.

16 In the fourth generation your descendants will come back here, for the sin of the Amorites has not yet reached its full measure."

17 When the sun had set and darkness had fallen, a smoking firepot with a blazing torch appeared and passed between the pieces.

18 On that day the LORD made a covenant with Abram and said, "To your descendants I give this

from the river of Egypt unto the great river, the river Euphrates:

19 The Kenites, and the Kenizzites, and the Kadmonites,

20 And the Hittites, and the Perizzites, and the Rephaims,

21 And the Amorites, and the Canaanites, and the Girgashites, and the Jebusites.

land, from the river of Egypt to the great river, the Euphrates—

19 the land of the Kenites, Kenizzites, Kadmonites,

20 Hittites, Perizzites, Rephaites,

21 Amorites, Canaanites, Girgashites and Jebusites."

TOPICAL OUTLINE OF THE LESSON

I. Introduction
  A. Trust God!
  B. Biblical Background

II. Exposition and Application of the Scripture
  A. I Am the Lord (Genesis 15:7-11)
  B. A Glimpse of the Future (Genesis 15:12-17)
  C. God's Promise Will Be Fulfilled (Genesis 15:18-21)

III. Concluding Reflection

LESSON OBJECTIVES

Upon the completion of the lesson, the students will be able to do the following:

1. Understand the significance of God's covenant with Abraham and Sarah;
2. Measure their level of trust in God to keep promises; and,
3. Describe the inheritance that God promises to give to us.

POINTS TO BE EMPHASIZED
ADULT/YOUTH

Adult Topic: A Lasting Inheritance

Youth Topic: A Promise You Can Trust

Adult/Youth Key Verse: Genesis 15:18

Print Passage: Genesis 15:7-21

—Abram trusted that God's promise would be kept, even if it would not be in his lifetime.

—The story of Abram's family shows how God works with imperfect people to implement the divine plan.

—Since the covenant was made before Abram had a child, there was no evidence in Abram's life beyond God's promise for Abram to believe it to be true.

—The promise of the territorial land was one-third of the blessing offered in Genesis 12. The other two were a name and a commission to bless the nation.

—Abram wanted proof or assurance that the promise would be fulfilled.

—After giving proper identification, God assured Abram that the promise would be fulfilled.

—God confirmed the fulfillment of the promise by giving divine revelation of future events.

—God sealed the covenant, using a Near Eastern covenant ritual that ensured that the covenant would not be broken by God.

CHILDREN
Children Topic: A Promise Given
Key Verse: Genesis 12:7
Print Passage: Genesis 12:1-9
—God instructed Abram (Abraham) to go to a new land and promised to give that land to his offspring.

—God promised to make of Abram (Abraham) a great nation.

—God promised Abram (Abraham) many blessings and a name that would be great.

—Abram (Abraham) took his wife and all his possessions and followed God's instructions to go to the land of Canaan.

—Abram (Abraham) built an altar to God and prayed there in God's name.

I. INTRODUCTION
A. Trust God!

One of the foundational and most important words in the Judeo-Christian tradition is *trust*. The word itself in biblical language is a complex term; it has various possible meanings, depending on context. Trust has to do with fidelity, obedience, confidence, and even proof. There are several biblical references that encourage the believer to trust in the Lord: "Trust in the Lord with all your heart and lean not on your own understanding; in all your ways acknowledge him and he will make your path straight" (Proverbs 3:5-6, NIV). "Those who trust in the Lord will renew their strength" (Isaiah 40:31). In a nutshell, faith and trust are the human reactions to what God is doing in the world. Faith is what we believe about God, and "trust" is what we do with what we say we believe about God.

Thus, trust is an irrefutable quality that endears the believer to the heart of God. In this lesson, Abram was called to follow the voice of God and go to a land that he did not know. Abram believed God and trusted that God would, in fact, do what He had promised. It was Abram's faith in God that enabled him to follow the voice of God with nothing but his internal belief that what he heard was indeed the voice of God, and that God could be trusted to keep His promise. As believers, it takes more than just faith in God; one's faith must be actualized in appropriate action that pleases God. Therefore, we must dare to put our trust in God and live with an assurance that God will keep His promise to us. We must also keep in mind that the promises and works of God, through Abram, were not on an individual level. Rather, they are communal. God blesses us not for personal and private ends, but so that our lives will be a beacon and a blessing to the world.

B. Biblical Background

Last Sunday's lesson ended with the people of the Earth being confused and scattered over the whole Earth—because they tried to make a name for themselves without divine consultation. Their behavior vexed God and God came down from heaven and scattered the people (see chapter 11). After the scattering, the family of Abram was introduced to the reader in verse 27 in the genealogy of his father, Terah. Terah left Ur to journey to Canaan with his family, but they only made it to Haran and it was there that Abram's father, Terah, died and Abram heard the voice of God, calling him to follow the dream of God. Thus, chapters 12–25 chronicle Abram's sojourn as he followed the voice of God. Likewise, these chapters are a continuation of the theme of divine scattering. The former scattering was based in judgment, but the latter was an act of divine love and mercy for humankind. God promised Abram that He would bless him and make of him a great nation through whom all nations of the Earth would be blessed. It is ironic that God scattered the people for trying to make a name for themselves (see 11:4); yet, at another time, He scattered the people as a condition of faith and obedience, in order to make His name great (see 12:2). Terence E. Fretheim says, "The Abram narrative not only describes human faithfulness, but also divine faithfulness to promises made to a specific family."

Abram followed the voice of God. Although his journey was fraught with unpredictable events, famine, and drought, he stayed the course. This call of Abram set in motion a generational pilgrimage that ultimately culminated in a manger in Bethlehem. God gave Abram a lasting inheritance.

II. EXPOSITION AND APPLICATION OF THE SCRIPTURE

A. I Am the Lord
(Genesis 15:7-11)

And he said unto him, I am the Lord that brought thee out of Ur of the Chaldees, to give thee this land to inherit it. And he said, Lord God, whereby shall I know that I shall inherit it? And he said unto him, Take me an heifer of three years old, and a she goat of three years old, and a ram of three years old, and a turtledove, and a young pigeon. And he took unto him all these, and divided them in the midst, and laid each piece one against another: but the birds divided he not. And when the fowls came down upon the carcases, Abram drove them away.

Abram left the land of Ur, and had to detour into Egypt to escape a severe famine in the land in which he lived. While in Egypt, Abram's wife, Sarai, found favor with Pharaoh and Pharaoh bestowed resources of cattle, sheep, donkeys, camels, and men and maidservants on Abram because he thought that Sarai was Abram's sister. Abram left Egypt and settled between Negev and Ai with his family, servants, and his nephew, Lot, whom he brought along with him from Ur. An unfortunate feud broke out between the herdsmen of Abram and those of Lot. Wisdom prevailed, however, and Abram allowed Lot to choose the land for his clan and livestock and Abram took what was left. Lot lifted his eyes and chose the whole plain of Jordan and settled there; however, in time a civil war broke out in the region and Lot and his family were taken captive—victims of being at the wrong place at the wrong time. They were taken captive by the invading kings. When Abram received word that Lot and his family had been taken captive, he gathered his servants and overtook the marauders, rescuing Lot, his family, and his resources. Upon returning from battle, Abram encountered Melchizedek, king of Salem, and priest of the Most High. Abram recognized him as the priest of God Most High and offered him a tenth of all his bounty of war as a tithe. After the conflict and the meeting of Melchizedek, "The word of the LORD came to Abram in a vision" (see Genesis 15:4). Abram asked the Lord what He (the Lord) would give him—since he was "without child." God promised to bless Abram's seed, but as an old man he had no children. As a matter of fact, in verse 3, Abram accused God of not giving him children. However, God assured Abram that his future and posterity were secure and likened his posterity to "the stars of the heaven and the sands of the seashore." Abram again wavered with uncertainty and needed further proof that the land promised to him would be his (verse 7). At this point in the dialogue, God made a covenant with Abram.

Verse 6 says that Abram believed God, and God credited it to him as righteousness. The Lord reminded Abram of who He is and what He had done for him: "I am the LORD, who brought you out of Ur" (see verse 7). Perhaps these words were designed to assure Abram that in spite of the time lag between promise and fulfillment, the promise would come to fruition. In spite of his doubt, Abram reaffirmed his faith in God and brought the necessary animal and bird sacrifices and prepared and placed them on the altar of the Lord.

Doubt might come to all of us who believe, but we must press on through our doubts and fears and know that God is faithful to His promises, even to a thousand generations. There is an old adage in the African-American faith community that asserts that "God may not come when you want Him, but He is always on time." The believer must know something about divine delays: promises delayed are not necessarily promises denied.

B. A Glimpse of the Future (Genesis 15:12-17)

And when the sun was going down, a deep sleep fell upon Abram; and, lo, an horror of great darkness fell upon him. And he said unto Abram, Know of a surety that thy seed shall be a stranger in a land that is not theirs, and shall serve them; and they shall afflict them four hundred years; And also that nation, whom they shall serve, will I judge: and afterward shall they come out with great substance. And thou shalt go to thy fathers in peace; thou shalt be buried in a good old age. But in the fourth generation they shall come hither again: for the iniquity of the Amorites is not yet full. And it came to pass, that, when the sun went down, and it was dark, behold a smoking furnace, and a burning lamp that passed between those pieces.

God not only assured Abram of his posterity—the blessing of his seed—but also informed him that there would be pain and suffering in the future of his descendants. Their pain and suffering was not promised of God, but only forecast by God, which is an important point. There are some religious communities who preach and teach blessing and prosperity and seem to lose sight of the fact that not all of life is filled with good. In fact, Jesus said, "In this world, you will have trouble." God does not call any of us to a pain-free existence. In verse 13, God said to Abram, "Know for certain that your descendants will be strangers in a country and will be enslaved and mistreated." The grandson of Abram was a leader in Egypt and experienced great favor from Pharaoh, but eventually, a "Pharaoh came who did not know Joseph" (see Exodus 1:8). God only foretold their slavery, yet God allowed Abram's descendants to endure their servitude for over four hundred years. This raises the question that if God knew beforehand that slavery was in their future, then why did He not prevent it? We can never be quite certain of why God does what He does, but perhaps God allows things to happen in our lives as a part of the journey to get us to where He would have us to be.

Good Bible readers are familiar with the Exodus story of Moses and the liberation of the children of Israel from Egypt. We know the rest of the story: God interceded and overthrew the hard taskmaster Pharaoh, setting the captives free. Even if God allows it, however, oppression and slavery are never justified. They are the tools of evil men. God set Abram's descendants free from bondage, even though they would not yet be allowed to occupy the Promised Land. Once free, God allowed them to wander in the wilderness for forty years. It took over half a century to occupy the Promised Land, but God and a burning lamp move between the sacrifices. Fire was one of the Old Testament symbols of divine presence (see Exodus 14:20 and 1 Kings 18:38). While Abram slept, God sent fire from heaven to ratify and seal His covenant with Abram.

C. God's Promise Will Be Fulfilled (Genesis 15:18-21)

In the same day the Lᴏʀᴅ made a covenant with Abram, saying, Unto thy seed have I given this land, from the river of Egypt unto the great river, the river Euphrates: The Kenites, and the Kenizzites, and the Kadmonites, And the Hittites, and the Perizzites, and the Rephaims, And the Amorites, and the Canaanites, and the Girgashites, and the Jebusites.

On that day, the Lord made a covenant with Abram and said, "To your descendants I give this land, from the river of Egypt to the great river, the Euphrates—the land of the Kenites, Kenizzites, Kadmonites, Hittites, Perizzites, Rephaites, Amorites, Canaanites, Girgashites and Jebusites" (verses 18-21, NIV).

The Hebrew word for "covenant," *berith*, is translated as "treaty," which is a binding agreement between two parties. However, in this case, the covenant was not between equals; it was God who took the initiative (see verse 18) to establish and to seal the covenant between Himself and Abram. This is what made it everlasting. God is eternal; hence, the promises of God remain until they come to fruition. However, God was more specific in describing the boundary of the land to be occupied by Abram's descendants. The land of the promise was already occupied. Other tribes, and in time the inhabitants, would be driven from the land so that God's promise would be fulfilled. Finally, it is also noteworthy that the promise was made in the present tense: "I give." God made this promise hundreds of years before it would come to fulfillment, but the words "I give" suggest that it happened the moment God said it. God blesses us in the present tense, but the reception of the blessing is sometimes yet to happen in the future.

III. CONCLUDING REFLECTION

God foresaw the oppression of Abram's descendants, but He did not ordain the oppression and in the same breath announced that He would, with a mighty hand, set the captives free. Notwithstanding the forecast of pain and suffering, God assured Abram that his life would come to a good conclusion in old age. The Lord also assured Abram, and us, that His covenant with Abram would be transcendent and would not die with Abram. Rather, it was an everlasting covenant. This text, however, raises a deeper and more profound question that has reverberated over the past decades of liberation theology: Is God on the side of the oppressed? Black and liberation theologians say that God is a God who liberates His people from oppression and works on the side of the oppressed. James Cone—noted theologian of black theology—in his book, *God of the Oppressed,* says, "The Old Testament tells the story of Israel's faith in the faithfulness of God to liberate the lowly and downtrodden from the proud and the mighty." We may not have a definitive understanding of black or liberation theologies, but it is hard to read the books of Genesis and Exodus with objectivity and not see God operating on the side of justice. This was the understanding of our African-American ancestors who found delight in those liberation narratives in the Bible. They believed that the God who defeated Pharaoh, set the Israelites free, and enabled Israel to throw off the shackles of Philistine oppression would also set them free. The African-American legacy of suffering and freedom in America is well documented, and we can draw hope in knowing that God keeps His promises for a thousand generations. Therefore, our belief and awareness that God's covenant of love and justice is an everlasting covenant should continue to inspire patience and hope in all of us.

PRAYER

Eternal God, who keeps promises to a thousand generations, we give You thanks for Your faithfulness toward us. Lord, it is our prayer that we will become more faithful in representing You in the world. Let us love the things You love and rebuke the things You rebuke. In Jesus' name we pray. Amen.

WORD POWER

Covenant (*constitution*)—agreement, pledge.

HOME DAILY BIBLE READINGS
(September 30–October 6, 2013)

A Promise of Land
MONDAY, September 30: "The Faith of Abraham" (Hebrews 11:8-16)
TUESDAY, October 1: "The Call of Abram" (Genesis 12:1-7)
WEDNESDAY, October 2: "Settling in the Land" (Genesis 13:8-18)
THURSDAY, October 3: "The Land and the Covenant" (Genesis 17:1-8)
FRIDAY, October 4: "The Covenant Recounted and Renewed" (Joshua 24:1-13)
SATURDAY, October 5: "The Covenant Remembered" (Psalm 105:1-11)
SUNDAY, October 6: "The Covenant with Abraham" (Genesis 15:7-21)

LESSON 7   October 13, 2013

A PROMISE TO SARAH

FAITH PATHWAY/FAITH JOURNEY TOPIC: A Promise Kept

DEVOTIONAL READING: Isaiah 51:1-6
PRINT PASSAGE: Genesis 17:15-17;
18:9-15; 21:1-7

BACKGROUND SCRIPTURE: Genesis 17:15-17;
18:9-15; 21:1-7
KEY VERSE: Genesis 21:2

Genesis 17:15-17; 18:9-15; 21:1-7—KJV

15 And God said unto Abraham, As for Sarai thy wife, thou shalt not call her name Sarai, but Sarah shall her name be.

16 And I will bless her, and give thee a son also of her: yea, I will bless her, and she shall be a mother of nations; kings of people shall be of her.

17 Then Abraham fell upon his face, and laughed, and said in his heart, Shall a child be born unto him that is an hundred years old? and shall Sarah, that is ninety years old, bear?

.....

9 And they said unto him, Where is Sarah thy wife? And he said, Behold, in the tent.

10 And he said, I will certainly return unto thee according to the time of life; and, lo, Sarah thy wife shall have a son. And Sarah heard it in the tent door, which was behind him.

11 Now Abraham and Sarah were old and well stricken in age; and it ceased to be with Sarah after the manner of women.

12 Therefore Sarah laughed within herself, saying, After I am waxed old shall I have pleasure, my lord being old also?

13 And the LORD said unto Abraham, Wherefore did Sarah laugh, saying, Shall I of a surety bear a child, which am old?

14 Is any thing too hard for the LORD? At the time appointed I will return unto thee, according to the time of life, and Sarah shall have a son.

15 Then Sarah denied, saying, I laughed not; for she was afraid. And he said, Nay; but thou didst laugh.

.....

Genesis 17:15-17; 18:9-15; 21:1-7—NIV

15 God also said to Abraham, "As for Sarai your wife, you are no longer to call her Sarai; her name will be Sarah.

16 I will bless her and will surely give you a son by her. I will bless her so that she will be the mother of nations; kings of peoples will come from her."

17 Abraham fell facedown; he laughed and said to himself, "Will a son be born to a man a hundred years old? Will Sarah bear a child at the age of ninety?"

.....

9 "Where is your wife Sarah?" they asked him. "There, in the tent," he said.

10 Then the LORD said, "I will surely return to you about this time next year, and Sarah your wife will have a son." Now Sarah was listening at the entrance to the tent, which was behind him.

11 Abraham and Sarah were already old and well advanced in years, and Sarah was past the age of childbearing.

12 So Sarah laughed to herself as she thought, "After I am worn out and my master is old, will I now have this pleasure?"

13 Then the LORD said to Abraham, "Why did Sarah laugh and say, 'Will I really have a child, now that I am old?'

14 Is anything too hard for the LORD? I will return to you at the appointed time next year and Sarah will have a son."

15 Sarah was afraid, so she lied and said, "I did not laugh." But he said, "Yes, you did laugh."

.....

UNIFYING LESSON PRINCIPLE

We often rejoice at the birth of a new member in the family or community. What does a birth mean to a family or community? Abraham and Sarah saw their child as evidence of God's faithfulness in keeping the promise to create a nation.

AND THE LORD visited Sarah as he had said, and the LORD did unto Sarah as he had spoken.

2 For Sarah conceived, and bare Abraham a son in his old age, at the set time of which God had spoken to him.

3 And Abraham called the name of his son that was born unto him, whom Sarah bare to him, Isaac.

4 And Abraham circumcised his son Isaac being eight days old, as God had commanded him.

5 And Abraham was an hundred years old, when his son Isaac was born unto him.

6 And Sarah said, God hath made me to laugh, so that all that hear will laugh with me.

7 And she said, Who would have said unto Abraham, that Sarah should have given children suck? for I have born him a son in his old age.

NOW THE LORD was gracious to Sarah as he had said, and the LORD did for Sarah what he had promised.

2 Sarah became pregnant and bore a son to Abraham in his old age, at the very time God had promised him.

3 Abraham gave the name Isaac to the son Sarah bore him.

4 When his son Isaac was eight days old, Abraham circumcised him, as God commanded him.

5 Abraham was a hundred years old when his son Isaac was born to him.

6 Sarah said, "God has brought me laughter, and everyone who hears about this will laugh with me."

7 And she added, "Who would have said to Abraham that Sarah would nurse children? Yet I have borne him a son in his old age."

TOPICAL OUTLINE OF THE LESSON

I. Introduction
A. God's Promise Is Bigger than Our Doubts
B. Biblical Background

II. Exposition and Application of the Scripture
A. God's Promise and Abraham's Response (Genesis 17:15-17)
B. God's Promise and Sarah's Response (Genesis 18:9-15)
C. The Promised Fulfilled (Genesis 21:1-7)

III. Concluding Reflection

LESSON OBJECTIVES

Upon the completion of the lesson, the students will be able to do the following:

1. Understand Abraham and Sarah's joy at the birth of a child in their old age;
2. Weep with those who want children and have none, and laugh with those who rejoice in the birth of a child; and,
3. Identify God's faithfulness to the faith family across generations and give thanks.

POINTS TO BE EMPHASIZED

ADULT/YOUTH

Adult Topic: A Promise Kept

Youth Topic: An Unbelievable Promise

Adult Key Verse: Genesis 21:2

Youth Key Verse: Genesis 17:16

Print Passage: Genesis 17:15-17; 18:9-15; 21:1-7

—In Hebrew, *Isaac* means "He laughs." Among other things, his name expressed the joy his parents experienced at his birth.

—Sarah was told not only that she would give birth to a child but also that she would be the ancestor of kings (see 17:16).

—God changed Sarai's name to Sarah—which means "princess"—in order to validate the promise that she would be the mother of nations and kings.

—God does not look at age when using people to implement His plan.

—Accepting that God can do anything He wants to do—whenever, wherever, and however He wants to do it—can be difficult.

—For Hebrew people, having a child was viewed as a blessing from God, and childlessness was seen as a curse.

—So far-fetched was this promise that, "hoping against hope" (Romans 4:18), Abraham believed that he would become the father of many nations according to God's promise.

CHILDREN
Children Topic: A Promise Kept
Key Verse: Genesis 18:14
Print Passage: Genesis 17:15-17; 18:9-15; 21:1-7

—God promised Abraham that Sarah would have a son who would give rise to new nations.

—Both Sarah and Abraham laughed at the thought that they would have a child in their old age.

—When God heard Sarah laugh, God repeated the promise even though Sarah denied that she had laughed.

—Sarah and Abraham's son, Isaac, was born when Abraham was one hundred years old and Sarah was ninety.

—The birth of Isaac caused Sarah and others to laugh with joy.

I. INTRODUCTION
A. God's Promise Is Bigger than Our Doubts

God made a promise to Sarah in this lesson. Was this promise inferior to God's promise to Abraham? If so, in what way(s)? The birth of their first son meant as much to Sarah as it did to Abraham, because the child represented the faithfulness of God. If this promise were to become real, God had to do it because both husband and wife were old and were beyond child-bearing years. It was God who worked in Sarah to open her womb so that both promises might be fulfilled—the promise could not be fulfilled by any other means, including the use of Hagar as surrogate. Verse 1 of chapter 21 reads, "And the LORD visited Sarah as he had said, and the LORD did unto Sarah as he had spoken." It was through Sarah that God had to work—not Abraham alone—to usher into reality the birth of the child of the promise. It is also interesting that, up to this point, the language in this narrative was exclusively between God and Abraham. Sarah had been like a proverbial spectator—along for the ride—until verse 1 of chapter 21. Heretofore, God spoke to Abraham about Sarah (17:15-16). This time, God spoke directly to Sarah and not Abraham; perhaps just as Abraham informed Sarah of his conversation with God, Sarah informed Abraham of her divine visitation. The promise came to reality, in spite of Sarah and Abraham's doubt. The promise and the implications of the promise for the world were bigger than their doubts and apprehensions.

B. Biblical Background

The promise God made to Abram (in Genesis 12) of becoming a great nation was now critical. Abraham and Sarah were very old and the reality of having a child grew dimmer by the day. God appeared to them in the heat of the day in the persons of three angels appearing in the image of men. Abraham recognized them as messengers of the Lord and showed them hospitality in giving food and water. It would be during their visit that one of the messengers announced the good news that in the next year, Abraham and Sarah would have a son. This would not have been an easy message to digest. The revelation of the coming birth of a son was met with doubt—and so humorous in fact that both laughed (see 17:17; 18:12). They perceived their ages to be an incalculable challenge, but the Lord raised the imponderable question, "Is anything too hard for the Lord? I will return to you at the appointed time next year and Sarah will have a son" (see Genesis 18:13). This was the first time in this long narrative that Sarah moved from behind the veil and became a prominent figure in the narrative about God's plan for humanity. This was evident by the changing of Sarah's name. In Hebrew biblical tradition, one way in which God reaffirmed His covenant with a person was by changing the person's name (Abram to Abraham and Jacob to Israel). God changed her name from Sarai ("my princess") to Sarah ("princess for all the race"). Therefore, whatever we might think biblically and theologically about a plethora of religious and social issues of gender, one must admit that God needs and uses all of us to bring about His purpose and will for humanity. Sarah's life and role in the demonstration of God's faithfulness cannot and must not be underestimated or minimized. Her faith was as radical as Abraham's faith, in that what she heard from the Lord seemed as radical to her as it did to Abraham, and in the end she also was justified by faith.

II. EXPOSITION AND APPLICATION OF THE SCRIPTURE

A. God's Promise and Abraham's Response (Genesis 17:15-17)

And God said unto Abraham, As for Sarai thy wife, thou shalt not call her name Sarai, but Sarah shall her name be. And I will bless her, and give thee a son also of her: yea, I will bless her, and she shall be a mother of nations; kings of people shall be of her. Then Abraham fell upon his face, and laughed, and said in his heart, Shall a child be born unto him that is an hundred years old? and shall Sarah, that is ninety years old, bear?

It was at this point in Abraham and Sarai's sojourn that God changed Sarai's name. Afterward, God reiterated His promise to bless the couple with a son—also stating that Sarai would become the "mother of nations" (verse 16). Abraham's reaction to the good news was disbelief. It seemed most implausible. There is a tendency to look at patron saints of the Old Testament as superheroes, but these passages of Scripture humanized both Abraham and Sarah. When they heard definitively that Sarah was to give birth to a son, her husband laughed in doubt. We cannot be certain of what kind of understanding they had concerning reproduction; however, persons as old as they were could not reasonably expect to have a child for the first time in old age. Their reaction suggests that they had not totally and completely accepted the fact that this was the Lord's doing and not just something that would happen through mere human endeavor. They would soon come to realize that faith in God can do what human activity could not do and take them where human effort had failed. The writer of the book of Hebrews (Hebrews 11:11) wrote that Sarah had no children because she was barren. It also says "that Abram was old and as good as dead" (11:12). Obviously, they had given up the possibility of Sarah's having children, so they conspired and Abraham fathered a son by Sarah's handmaiden, Hagar—but this was not God's plan.

This text is more than just an ancient story. It speaks to us in profound ways in our culture of instant gratification. We tend to be impatient and want what we want now—but God is a faithful God and moves in His own time. Abram and Sarai left Ur almost twenty years prior with an expectation that God would bless them with descendants, even a nation, but as they grew older, they grew impatient. In this context, Abraham and Sarah needed to exercise patience. Patience is the state of endurance under difficult circumstances, which can mean persevering in the face of delay. We must learn from Abraham and Sarah that it pays to wait on the Lord, who is a covenant-keeping God.

B. God's Promise and Sarah's Response (Genesis 18:9-15)

And they said unto him, Where is Sarah thy wife? And he said, Behold, in the tent. And he said, I will certainly return unto thee according to the time of life; and, lo, Sarah thy wife shall have a son. And Sarah heard it in the tent door, which was behind him. Now Abraham and Sarah were old and well stricken in age; and it ceased to be with Sarah after the manner of women. Therefore Sarah laughed within herself, saying, After I am waxed old shall I have pleasure, my lord being old also? And the Lord said unto Abraham, Wherefore did Sarah laugh, saying, Shall I of a surety bear a child, which am old? Is any thing too hard for the Lord? At the time appointed I will return unto thee, according to the time of life, and Sarah shall have a son. Then Sarah denied, saying, I laughed not; for she was afraid. And he said, Nay; but thou didst laugh.

When the time was right, God dispatched three messengers (angels) to visit Abraham's tent, bearing good news to Sarah. She was in her tent and one of the messengers said to Abraham that he would return in about one year and Sarah, his wife, would have given birth to a son. Sarah overheard the conversation. She laughed to herself. What was this laughter about?

I have read views and heard many sermons that have characterized her laughter as doubt or disbelief, but since we cannot be absolutely certain what was in the mind of Sarah at the time, I would like to offer an alternative view of her reaction. Have you ever heard anything that was so remarkable or an unexpected hope coming true that your reaction was surprised laughter—not so much disbelief? Many times, I can attest that in hearing hopeful news, I laughed in amazement and not in disbelief. Years ago, the chairman of deacons called me to inform me that the church had voted me in as their next pastor. My reaction was amazement and laughter at a hoped-for dream which had come to fulfillment. Sarah laughed to herself, thinking that her laughter was private—but the Lord heard her. However, when the messenger asked Abraham why Sarah laughed, she denied it! Fear will make one do some strange things, including lie about the obvious. It is obvious from the reading of the entire narrative about Abraham and Sarah that laughter in and of itself was not the problem, because Abraham also laughed when he heard the news of fathering a child by Sarah his wife—and nothing was made of it. There is no accusatory question as to why Abraham laughed, and it would seem unlikely that God would be critical of Sarah and not of Abraham (see 17:19). I believe that the question is designed to set up the punch line—the rhetorical question, "Is anything too hard for the Lord?" No human construct can ultimately define divine possibilities.

C. The Promised Fulfilled (Genesis 21:1-7)

AND THE Lord visited Sarah as he had said, and the Lord did unto Sarah as he had spoken. For Sarah conceived, and bare Abraham a son in his old age, at the set time of which God had spoken to him. And Abraham called the name of his son that was born unto him, whom Sarah bare to him, Isaac. And Abraham circumcised his son Isaac being eight days old, as God had commanded him. And Abraham was an hundred years old, when his son Isaac was born unto him. And Sarah said, God hath made me to laugh, so that all that hear will laugh with me. And she said, Who would have said unto Abraham, that Sarah should have given children suck? for I have born him a son in his old age.

We have come to the moment of fulfillment. After all of those years of hoping and dreaming, Sarah gave birth to her own son. Up until Genesis 18, the promise of a child had been general. Abraham would be the father of many descendants, but the particulars of when and how were not known. It would happen through their union of husband and wife and not through a servant or Sarah's handmaiden, Hagar. Finally, after years of

doubt and uncertainty, Abraham and Sarah gave affirmation to what the Lord God had promised. The son was named Isaac, which means in the Hebrew language, "he will laugh." I wish we could understand the meaning behind Sarah's words, but she seems to have been suspicious and a bit disbelieving. Sarah and Abraham were not super spiritual beings; they were human like we are, hence they struggled with the same emotional limitations and suspicions that any of us suffer with. She asked her husband who would believe that their child was theirs by birth. Perhaps for them the son would forever remind them that God had a sense of humor in that He favored them at such an unlikely time in their lives. After the son was born, Abraham kept his covenant with the Lord and circumcised Isaac on the eighth day.

III. CONCLUDING REFLECTION

The psalmist declared that "children are the heritage from the Lord; blessed is the man whose quiver is full of them" (see Psalm 127:3). Anyone who has had children knows too well what joy children can be to family life. Yet, we are living in an age in which many husbands and wives have chosen not to have children—and while that is their choice, children are still God's blessing to humanity. Who could imagine how much different our salvation would be without Abraham and Sarah, and without Isaac to perpetuate God's promise for all of humanity? I understand that there are couples who cannot have their own children, yet there are so many others who choose not to have children. Could this mean that they are depriving humanity of a potential blessing that could come only through that child? Abraham and Sarah were only the conduits through which the promises of God were to flow. The phrase "children are a heritage from the Lord" carries more than just the idea of a blessing or gift from God. It seems to have meaning at a deeper and more profound level. A *heritage* is an inheritance that is passed from one generation to another subsequent generation. As God had promised, Sarah gave birth to a son in her old age and it would be from this son that the promise of a great nation (Israel) would be fulfilled. Isaac, the son of Sarah, was the father of Esau and Jacob, and Jacob was the father of Judah, through whose lineage Jesus the Christ would come.

Finally, it is noteworthy that the *voice* of God is not heard in this section, only the *actions* of God are seen. Many people have come to a place in their faith walk where they place a greater priority on the voice of God as opposed to the actions of God. There is tension in salvation history between the time of the spoken word and the spoken word coming to fruition. There was a great space in time between the promise being first spoken to Abraham and Sarah and when the promise was fulfilled. God spoke into the lives of Abraham and Sarah and the Word (promise) of God reverberated down through forty-two generations and culminated in a manger in Bethlehem. In God's own time, He found a way to fulfill His promise to Abraham and Sarah in spite of what appeared to be insurmountable human limitations.

We can be certain that no situation or human limitation can ultimately hinder divine purpose in the world.

PRAYER

God of Abraham and Sarah, we honor You today for Your faithfulness. We are grateful for the insights we have learned from Your Word and we pray that we will be more patient in fulfillment of the things You have called us to be and do. Thank You for being the covenant-keeping God, even of promises to a thousand generations. In Jesus' name we pray. Amen.

WORD POWER

Gracious—indulgent in a pleasantly condescending way; merciful or compassionate.
Heritage—something passing from generation to generation: something that passes from one generation to the next in a social group (e.g., a way of life or traditional culture).

HOME DAILY BIBLE READINGS
(October 7-13, 2013)

A Promise to Sarah

MONDAY, October 7: "A Childless Wife" (Genesis 11:27-32)

TUESDAY, October 8: "A Beautiful Wife" (Genesis 12:10-20)

WEDNESDAY, October 9: "A Threatened Wife" (Genesis 16:1-6)

THURSDAY, October 10: "The Promise of a Covenant" (Genesis 17:18-22)

FRIDAY, October 11: "Dispelling the Competition" (Genesis 21:8-14)

SATURDAY, October 12: "Mourning a Beloved Wife" (Genesis 23:1-6)

SUNDAY, October 13: "Bearing a Child of Promise" (Genesis 17:15-17; 18:9-15; 21:1-7)

LESSON 8   **October 20, 2013**

A BLESSING FOR ISHMAEL AND ISAAC

Faith Pathway/Faith Journey Topic: Sibling Rivalry

Devotional Reading: Hebrews 11:17-22
Print Passage: Genesis 21:13-14, 17-21;
26:2-5, 12-13

Background Scripture: Genesis 15:1-6; 16;
17:1-14, 18, 20-27; 21:9-21; 26:1-25
Key Verses: Genesis 21:12b-13

Genesis 21:13-14, 17-21; 26:2-5, 12-13 —KJV

13 And also of the son of the bondwoman will I make a nation, because he is thy seed.

14 And Abraham rose up early in the morning, and took bread, and a bottle of water, and gave it unto Hagar, putting it on her shoulder, and the child, and sent her away: and she departed, and wandered in the wilderness of Beer-sheba.

. . . . .

17 And God heard the voice of the lad; and the angel of God called Hagar out of heaven, and said unto her, What aileth thee, Hagar? fear not; for God hath heard the voice of the lad where he is.

18 Arise, lift up the lad, and hold him in thine hand; for I will make him a great nation.

19 And God opened her eyes, and she saw a well of water; and she went, and filled the bottle with water, and gave the lad drink.

20 And God was with the lad; and he grew, and dwelt in the wilderness, and became an archer.

21 And he dwelt in the wilderness of Paran: and his mother took him a wife out of the land of Egypt.

. . . . .

2 And the LORD appeared unto him, and said, Go not down into Egypt; dwell in the land which I shall tell thee of:

3 Sojourn in this land, and I will be with thee, and will bless thee; for unto thee, and unto thy seed, I will give all these countries, and I will perform the oath which I sware unto Abraham thy father;

Genesis 21:13-14, 17-21; 26:2-5, 12-13 —NIV

13 "I will make the son of the maidservant into a nation also, because he is your offspring."

14 Early the next morning Abraham took some food and a skin of water and gave them to Hagar. He set them on her shoulders and then sent her off with the boy. She went on her way and wandered in the desert of Beersheba.

. . . . .

17 God heard the boy crying, and the angel of God called to Hagar from heaven and said to her, "What is the matter, Hagar? Do not be afraid; God has heard the boy crying as he lies there.

18 Lift the boy up and take him by the hand, for I will make him into a great nation."

19 Then God opened her eyes and she saw a well of water. So she went and filled the skin with water and gave the boy a drink.

20 God was with the boy as he grew up. He lived in the desert and became an archer.

21 While he was living in the Desert of Paran, his mother got a wife for him from Egypt.

. . . . .

2 The LORD appeared to Isaac and said, "Do not go down to Egypt; live in the land where I tell you to live.

3 Stay in this land for a while, and I will be with you and will bless you. For to you and your descendants I will give all these lands and will confirm the oath I swore to your father Abraham.

4 And I will make thy seed to multiply as the stars of heaven, and will give unto thy seed all these countries; and in thy seed shall all the nations of the earth be blessed;

5 Because that Abraham obeyed my voice, and kept my charge, my commandments, my statutes, and my laws.

.....

12 Then Isaac sowed in that land, and received in the same year an hundredfold: and the LORD blessed him.

13 And the man waxed great, and went forward, and grew until he became very great.

4 I will make your descendants as numerous as the stars in the sky and will give them all these lands, and through your offspring all nations on earth will be blessed,

5 because Abraham obeyed me and kept my requirements, my commands, my decrees and my laws."

.....

12 Isaac planted crops in that land and the same year reaped a hundredfold, because the LORD blessed him.

13 The man became rich, and his wealth continued to grow until he became very wealthy.

TOPICAL OUTLINE OF THE LESSON

I. Introduction
A. The Reality of Sibling Rivalry
B. Biblical Background

II. Exposition and Application of the Scripture
A. Handling Hagar's Issue (Genesis 21:13-14)
B. Divine Intervention (Genesis 21:17-21)
C. Isaac's Future (Genesis 26:2-5, 12-13)

III. Concluding Reflection

LESSON OBJECTIVES

Upon the completion of the lesson, the students will be able to do the following:

1. Explore the theological and political implications of the blessing God gave to Isaac and Ishmael;
2. Confess the jealousies that stand in the way of loving God and neighbor as believers should; and,
3. Pray for world peace, including peace among persons of all faiths.

POINTS TO BE EMPHASIZED
ADULT/YOUTH

Adult Topic: Sibling Rivalry

Youth Topic: You Are Special

Adult Key Verses: Genesis 21:12b-13

Youth Key Verse: Genesis 17:4

Print Passage: Genesis 21:13-14, 17-21; 26:2-5, 12-13

—God promised to bless Abram with numerous heirs and God changed Abram's name to Abraham (see Genesis 17:5).

—After some time had passed, Sarai felt God had not kept His promise—so she encouraged Abram to conceive a child with Hagar, her maidservant.

—Later, Sarah conceived (as God has promised) and gave birth to a son, Isaac, which caused him to be favored over Ishmael.

—Ishmael was rejected but was still blessed by God to become a great nation, because God accepts all people and all people have a role in God's plans.

—Isaac was blessed by God to become a wealthy man and have many offspring.

—Islam, Christianity, and Judaism all recognize Ishmael and Isaac as children of Abraham.

—Sarah demanded that Ishmael, Abraham's son by the slave girl Hagar, be sent away.

CHILDREN

Children Topic: Receiving a Blessing

Key Verse: Genesis 21:18

Print Passage: Genesis 21:9-13; 26:1-5

—Sarah demanded that Ishmael, Abraham's son by the slave girl Hagar, be sent away.

—God promised Abraham that Ishmael would bring forth a great nation.

—God blessed Isaac and promised him and his offspring many lands.

—God's promises to Abraham's two sons were because of Abraham's obedience to God.

I. INTRODUCTION

A. The Reality of Sibling Rivalry

The narrative in this text could have taken place in any era, community, or family. This narrative is about the potential consequences of sibling rivalry—where a parent will choose sides favoring one child over another, to the disadvantage of one of the siblings. Sibling rivalry is no stranger to any of us. If you are not an only child in your family, then perhaps you have firsthand experience with competing against a brother or sister. Abraham, Sarah, and Hagar were a part of what we might call today a blended family—one father and two mothers, with offspring living in the same household. It is not unusual for children of a blended family to suffer unhealthy sibling rivalry as they vie for appropriate attention. Unfortunately, these children often suffer and struggle to find identity in the family unit when one parent does not fully accept the child who is not his or hers. Consequently, the child often suffers.

In today's lesson, we will see both a disturbing family situation and unhealthy parental involvement in resolving the conflict. Therefore, as parents, we must be careful not to instigate the resolution of these conflicts to the disadvantage of one of the siblings. We must always strive for a win-win situation so that children are not further hurt by an adult's inappropriate decisions. Finally, this lesson assures those who might feel victimized and estranged by family dysfunction that there can be divine provisions beyond the family conflict.

B. Biblical Background

It appears that Abraham and Sarah grew impatient as they waited for the child of the promise and decided to intercede and "help" God out. However, their decision complicated family matters and made for an untenable situation. Sarah had a maid servant given to her by Pharaoh when they were in Egypt (see chapter 12). Pharaoh gave Sarah and Abraham parting gifts of treasury and servants when they departed Egypt years earlier. The social arrangement between servant and master was that the servant was a kind of personal valet who cared for the needs of the master. Sarah offered Hagar, her maid servant, to Abraham to be his wife and as it was in antiquity, marriages were consummated by husband and wife engaging in sexual intercourse. A son was born to that relation and they called him Ishmael. Years later, God fulfilled His promise to Abraham and Sarah and Sarah gave birth to a son in her old age. What she and Abraham thought would never happen, happened.

When the child was about three years old, Sarah saw Ishmael taunting her son, Isaac. She became enraged and insisted that her husband expel mother and son (Hagar and Ishmael) from the family compound. Abraham accepted her advice but only after God assured Abraham that mother and son would be all right. So, he expelled them as Sarah had demanded.

One of the troubling parts of this text is that Hagar's voice was not heard in this narrative. The decision to have a son for Abraham was not hers. She was the servant girl of her master and was given to Abraham to be his wife. She and her son found themselves in an unhealthy family arrangement. Too often in our world, children and women are often compromised and exploited by someone else's faulty judgment. Abraham and Sarah brought unnecessary pain and frustration into the life of their family because they did not wait on the Lord.

One of the main points in this text is that we can make a mess of things and cause others to suffer unnecessarily when we get ahead of God. Yet, the good news is that regardless of how fickle and faulty we become, God is faithful and will not allow the innocent to suffer beyond measure at the hands of others. God made promises to Abraham and Sarah, but He also interceded in the plight of Hagar and her son Ishmael and promised him posterity also (see Genesis 21:18).

II. EXPOSITION AND APPLICATION OF THE SCRIPTURE

A. Handling Hagar's Issue
(Genesis 21:13-14)

And also of the son of the bondwoman will I make a nation, because he is thy seed. And Abraham rose up early in the morning, and took bread, and a bottle of water, and gave it unto Hagar, putting it on her shoulder, and the child, and sent her away: and she departed, and wandered in the wilderness of Beer-sheba.

Abraham's family dysfunction came to a head when Ishmael, the surrogate son, began to mock Isaac, the son of the promise—thus disturbing Sarah, the mother of Isaac. The

NRSV translates verse 9 in this way: "Sarah saw the son of Hagar the Egyptian, whom she had borne to Abraham, playing with her son Isaac." We cannot be certain, but perhaps the act of aggression was a little more than child's play. Ishmael was still a child (teenager) himself; nevertheless, Sarah took exception to what she saw and demanded that Abraham expel Hagar and her child from the family compound. There are some scholars who believe that her anger was the result of unresolved conflict between Sarah and Hagar (see Genesis 16:3-9). Sarah allowed Hagar to sleep with her husband to build a family, since she could not have a child. When she realized that Hagar was pregnant, however, she despised her. She also accused Abraham of being responsible for her mental suffering. So about three years later, she was still frustrated and seized the moment to attempt to undo the evidence of the wrong previously committed. Her request initially distressed Abraham, but God appeared to Abraham and assured him that he need not be distressed about the situation; rather, he was to follow the advice of his wife, Sarah.

To quell the feud between the two women, Abraham got food and a flask of water, gave them to Hagar and sent mother and son into the desert of Beersheba. They wandered in the desert until the water and food ran out. The poet was right: "Oh what a tangled web we weave, when first we practice to deceive." Abraham and Sarah became the victims of their own poor decision (the tangled web). Little could Abraham have known that his decision to sleep with Hagar and father a son would have led to this family calamity years later. Abraham's first son and his mother were abandoned in the wilderness and left to make it on their own without the support of Abraham.

B. Divine Intervention
(Genesis 21:17-21)

And God heard the voice of the lad; and the angel of God called Hagar out of heaven, and said unto her, What aileth thee, Hagar? fear not; for God hath heard the voice of the lad where he is. Arise, lift up the lad, and hold him in thine hand; for I will make him a great nation. And God opened her eyes, and she saw a well of water; and she went, and filled the bottle with water, and gave the lad drink. And God was with the lad; and he grew, and dwelt in the wilderness, and became an archer. And he dwelt in the wilderness of Paran: and his mother took him a wife out of the land of Egypt.

This story is the story of many families and blended families all over America that are presently suffering the consequences of the inappropriate and selfish decisions made years prior. Long after the joy and excitement of the moment is over, families are living with the consequences—i.e., a child never fully embraced by the family; a son or a daughter estranged and never having the opportunity to know the rest of their siblings; or a mother and child abandoned by the father to survive as best they can. Many of us are familiar with stories of abuse and abandonment by a father and/or mother, or stepmother and/or stepfather. There are many functioning families in every community, but there are also troubled families in which children are victimized. Little could Abraham have known that his decision to sleep with Hagar and father a son by her would have led to this family calamity years later—yet it did.

Nevertheless, there was good news in the case of Ishmael. God had an alternate plan for Ishmael's life. When his father and stepmother failed him, God lifted him up. When the food and water ran out, Hagar felt hopeless and sat her son under a bush, walked a distance, sat down, and began to cry because she did not want to see her son die. Both mother and son were crying, and the Lord heard the boy's crying and sent an angel to attend to them. The divine messenger assured Hagar that her son would also become a great nation. The implications of this text are far greater than we have time or space to explore. Hagar was Egyptian and her son was not of the will of God, yet he found favor with God and God made a covenant with him (Ishmael) just as God had done with Abraham. The psalmist said, "The eyes of the Lord are on the righteous and his ears are attentive to their cry" (Psalm 34:15).

Verse 20 reads, "God was with [Ishmael] as he grew up." In today's vernacular we would say, "Favor was on him." Ishmael became a great archer and lived his days in the desert of Paran, which is in the current-day Sinai Peninsula between Midian and Egypt. A deeper lesson in this story is that our actions may run counter to God's will for our lives. They bring frustration and deprive us of the peace that God otherwise has for us—but God's faithfulness is greater than our sins. Likewise, we must remember that the actions belong to us, and the consequences belong to God.

C. Isaac's Future
(Genesis 26:2-5, 12-13)

And the LORD appeared unto him, and said, Go not down into Egypt; dwell in the land which I shall tell thee of: Sojourn in this land, and I will be with thee, and will bless thee; for unto thee, and unto thy seed, I will give all these countries, and I will perform the oath which I sware unto Abraham thy father; And I will make thy seed to multiply as the stars of heaven, and will give unto thy seed all these countries; and in thy seed shall all the nations of the earth be blessed; Because that Abraham obeyed my voice, and kept my charge, my commandments, my statutes, and my laws. ... Then Isaac sowed in that land, and received in the same year an hundredfold: and the LORD blessed him. And the man waxed great, and went forward, and grew until he became very great.

Chapter 26 is made up of an odd assortment of material in which Isaac, the son of the promise, served to conclude Abraham's narrative and introduce the reader to Jacob, his son, who would perpetuate the inheritance of Abraham. The life of the son picks up some of the themes that occurred in the father's life. Just as his father Abraham was confronted with a famine in the land and went down to Egypt, so it was with the son (Isaac)—but this time God forbade Isaac to venture to Egypt to escape the famine (verse 2). Just as his father had done in Egypt, Isaac lied about Rebekah, stating that she was his sister and not his wife. But, in spite of Isaac's deception, God blessed him in the land and reiterated the promise that He had made to his father, Abraham.

We hear much talk about generational curses, but what of generational blessings? The latter is much more prevalent in the Bible than is the former. The promises God had made to Abraham were at this point being fulfilled in Isaac. He became great in the land of Gerar and the Philistines were jealous and began scheming against him (see verses 13-14). Note: Verse 14 is not in the printed text for this lesson.

In this hot and arid region, water was a necessary commodity. Each time Isaac and his servant dug a well, it brought about contention—but rather than fight, he dug another well. God gave him success each time and he found water. Finally, the last well he dug was named Rehoboth because he said, "The Lord hath made room for us, and we shall be fruitful in the land" (verse 22).

There is a tendency in the Old Testament to over-spiritualize images, but one has to wonder and find significance in the frequency of the presence of wells and water in this narrative. Water is one of the most powerful and significant images in the Bible; it is a staple of life and is a symbol of divine presence in the life of God's people. Jesus said that He is the water of life (see John 4:14).

Finally, like his father Abraham, Isaac was

a blessed man of wealth and peace, who made peace with the people of the land (verses 17-22). In the end, Isaac, like his father, ultimately relied on the Lord and was bountifully blessed (verse 24).

III. CONCLUDING REFLECTION

As we study the life of Isaac, we see several parallels between his life journey and that of his father, Abraham. Abraham lied about Sarah being his sister when famine forced them to detour into Egypt. Isaac and his wife, Rebekah, also had to detour (this time into Gerar) because of famine—and he lied and said that Rebekah was his sister. There was a family feud that led to Abraham's son Ishmael being exiled by his father. In time, Isaac would have two sons, Esau and Jacob, and a family feud between the two brothers would lead to Jacob, the son of the promise, being exiled by his mother. One of the issues in the story of Abraham and Isaac is the transmission of the promise to the next generation from father to son.

Our lesson does not include the closing verses of chapter 26, which end with peace and not conflict in the land. In the Old Testament, peace in the land was a sign of peace with God. Isaac was at peace in the land, which was a by-product of finding peace with God.

PRAYER

Loving God, who keeps promises to a thousand generations, we give thanks for our awareness that we are because of You. We are who we are not because we have it all together, but rather because Your grace and mercy have been sufficient in our lives. Lord, thank You for preserving our lives. In Jesus' name we pray. Amen.

WORD POWER
Bondwoman—a slave woman; a female slave or servant.
Seed—one's descendants; posterity.

HOME DAILY BIBLE READINGS
(October 14-20, 2013)

A Blessing for Ishmael and Isaac
MONDAY, October 14: "The Promise of Many Descendants" (Genesis 15:1-6)
TUESDAY, October 15: "A Child Born in Affliction" (Genesis 16:7-16)
WEDNESDAY, October 16: "The Symbol of the Covenant" (Genesis 17:9-14)
THURSDAY, October 17: "Abraham's Test of Faith" (Genesis 22:1-8)
FRIDAY, October 18: "Abraham's Obedience Blessed" (Genesis 22:9-18)
SATURDAY, October 19: "The Blessed of the Lord" (Genesis 26:26-31)
SUNDAY, October 20: "Blessing Two Family Branches" (Genesis 21:13-21; 26:2-5, 12-13)

THE BLESSING PASSES TO JACOB

FAITH PATHWAY/FAITH JOURNEY TOPIC: Vision Dreams

DEVOTIONAL READING: **John 4:1-15**
PRINT PASSAGE: **Genesis 28:1a, 10-22**
KEY VERSE: **Genesis 28:15**

BACKGROUND SCRIPTURE: **Genesis 27:19-29;
28:1-4, 10-22; 32:22-30; 35:9-15**

Genesis 28:1a, 10-22—KJV

AND ISAAC called Jacob, and blessed him.

.....

10 And Jacob went out from Beer-sheba, and went toward Haran.

11 And he lighted upon a certain place, and tarried there all night, because the sun was set; and he took of the stones of that place, and put them for his pillows, and lay down in that place to sleep.

12 And he dreamed, and behold a ladder set up on the earth, and the top of it reached to heaven: and behold the angels of God ascending and descending on it.

13 And, behold, the LORD stood above it, and said, I am the LORD God of Abraham thy father, and the God of Isaac: the land whereon thou liest, to thee will I give it, and to thy seed;

14 And thy seed shall be as the dust of the earth, and thou shalt spread abroad to the west, and to the east, and to the north, and to the south: and in thee and in thy seed shall all the families of the earth be blessed.

15 And, behold, I am with thee, and will keep thee in all places whither thou goest, and will bring thee again into this land; for I will not leave thee, until I have done that which I have spoken to thee of.

16 And Jacob awaked out of his sleep, and he said, Surely the LORD is in this place; and I knew it not.

17 And he was afraid, and said, How dreadful is this place! this is none other but the house of God, and this is the gate of heaven.

18 And Jacob rose up early in the morning, and took the stone that he had put for his pillows, and set it up for a pillar, and poured oil upon the top of it.

Genesis 28:1a, 10-22—NIV

SO ISAAC called for Jacob and blessed him.

.....

10 Jacob left Beersheba and set out for Haran.

11 When he reached a certain place, he stopped for the night because the sun had set. Taking one of the stones there, he put it under his head and lay down to sleep.

12 He had a dream in which he saw a stairway resting on the earth, with its top reaching to heaven, and the angels of God were ascending and descending on it.

13 There above it stood the LORD, and he said: "I am the LORD, the God of your father Abraham and the God of Isaac. I will give you and your descendants the land on which you are lying.

14 Your descendants will be like the dust of the earth, and you will spread out to the west and to the east, to the north and to the south. All peoples on earth will be blessed through you and your offspring.

15 I am with you and will watch over you wherever you go, and I will bring you back to this land. I will not leave you until I have done what I have promised you."

16 When Jacob awoke from his sleep, he thought, "Surely the LORD is in this place, and I was not aware of it."

17 He was afraid and said, "How awesome is this place! This is none other than the house of God; this is the gate of heaven."

18 Early the next morning Jacob took the stone he had placed under his head and set it up as a pillar and poured oil on top of it.

UNIFYING LESSON PRINCIPLE

When people feel insecure, they look for a place of security and the assurance of not being alone. Where and with whom can they find sanctuary? God assured Jacob of His presence and promises that through Jacob and his offspring, all the families of the Earth would be blessed.

19 And he called the name of that place Beth-el: but the name of that city was called Luz at the first.
20 And Jacob vowed a vow, saying, If God will be with me, and will keep me in this way that I go, and will give me bread to eat, and raiment to put on,
21 So that I come again to my father's house in peace; then shall the LORD be my God:
22 And this stone, which I have set for a pillar, shall be God's house: and of all that thou shalt give me I will surely give the tenth unto thee.

19 He called that place Bethel, though the city used to be called Luz.
20 Then Jacob made a vow, saying, "If God will be with me and will watch over me on this journey I am taking and will give me food to eat and clothes to wear
21 so that I return safely to my father's house, then the LORD will be my God
22 and this stone that I have set up as a pillar will be God's house, and of all that you give me I will give you a tenth."

TOPICAL OUTLINE OF THE LESSON

I. Introduction
A. Blessed to Be a Blessing
B. Biblical Background

II. Exposition and Application of the Scripture
A. Isaac Gives Jacob a Directive (Genesis 28:1a)
B. Jacob's Dream (Genesis 28:10-15)
C. Jacob's Vow (Genesis 28:16-22)

III. Concluding Reflection

LESSON OBJECTIVES

Upon the completion of the lesson, the students will be able to do the following:

1. Interpret the meaning of Jacob's vision;
2. Recall and cherish the awesomeness of God's presence in their personal experiences; and,
3. Invite God's presence into their everyday activities.

POINTS TO BE EMPHASIZED

ADULT/YOUTH

Adult Topic: Vision Dreams
Youth Topic: Never Alone
Adult/Youth Key Verse: Genesis 28:15
Print Passage: Genesis 28:1a, 10-22

—Why did God refer to Abraham as Jacob's father instead of Isaac? (See verse 13.)
—Within the Bible, dreams were often seen as forms of divine communication in which God was revealed.
—The site marked by a stone pillar became a place where humans could be reminded of God's action at that spot.
—Was Jacob's fear (verse 17) a manifestation of his awe at being in God's presence, of his guilt at deceiving others, or some combination of the two?
—Jacob tricked his father, Isaac, into giving him the covenant blessing instead of Esau.
—Jacob's name translates as "He grasps the heel" (see Genesis 25:26).

—In Jacob's dream, the angels ascending and descending represent an open invitation from the Lord to be Jacob's God.

—God promised to bless the people of the Earth through Jacob, just as God had promised Abraham (see 12:2-3).

—God promised to be with Jacob always and to protect him.

CHILDREN
Children Topic: A Blessing Received
Key Verse: Genesis 28:15a
Print Passage: Genesis 28:1a, 10-22

—Jacob obeyed Isaac's instructions to leave and go to his uncle's house.

—On the way, Jacob dreamed he saw angels and a ladder that extended to heaven.

—In his dream, Jacob was blessed by God.

—When Jacob woke from his dream and realized he had been in God's presence, he named the place Bethel—which means "house of God"—and he set up a stone for a pillar.

—Then Jacob made a vow that, if God would be with him, he would worship God as his God and return to God one-tenth of all that God had given him.

I. INTRODUCTION
A. Blessed to Be a Blessing

There is a tendency to look at some persons in our communities and discount them as incorrigible and/or without redeeming qualities. Most of us know such persons: a drug dealer, an addict, an alcoholic, an ex-felon, a never-married woman with several children, or a person labeled as a derelict by the community and written off. We look at these persons with a scant eye! We hold low estimations of them. But, can we absolutely be certain that these persons are beyond the point of grace? Can we be certain that there is no redeemable quality in them? We cannot be absolutely certain what the end results will be for any of our lives.

Years ago, I knew an upstanding citizen in the community who was married with two children and was a deacon in the church for several years. However, in his late forties something happened to him and he dropped out of the church, divorced, and became a disgrace. He died in shame, without the presence of the friends he had made over the years. What happened? We cannot be certain of when and where any of us might fall or turn our lives around!

This is the story of Jacob, who moved from a low point to a high point as God worked in his life—and in the final analysis, he became the heir of a divine promise. A long journey that began in deception ended in worship! When I was a boy, the elders would say, "When God got His hands on you, there is nothing you could do about it." I cannot be certain of the origin of this wisdom saying, but perhaps it could have been from the reading of the story of Jacob. The blessing God promised Abraham and Isaac ultimately was passed to the son/grandson, Jacob. We cannot live our lives independent of the sacred history of our ancestors; God is still honoring the prayers and promises made to them. We must resolve that there is a force stronger than ourselves that directs what is being played out in our lives; we represent the dreams and visions of our ancestors, being fulfilled in us.

B. Biblical Background

Jacob was not the main character in the drama in this lesson—God is. James Cone called the Old Testament "the drama of God's mighty acts in history that tells the story of the divine acts of grace and judgment as God calls the people of God into an existence of liberation." God used Jacob to fulfill the promises He made to Abraham and his son Isaac—that He would make of them a great nation and that the nations of the Earth would be blessed through them. Jacob was the descendant and beneficiary of those promises. He was one of the twins (Esau was the other) born to Isaac and Rebekah. In antiquity, parents named children according to the expected character of the child. Esau was first in the birth order, and when Jacob was born, he was clutching his brother's heel. His parents named him Jacob ("heel grabber" or "deceiver"). His name was prophetic as he made a life of deception for himself. His lifestyle took him on a circuitous journey that ended in exile in Paddan Aram with his mother's brother, Laban.

Eventually, Jacob's life came full circle and he desired to return home. However, he was also very anxious about going home. He thought that Esau would make good on his promise to kill him. Jacob left home empty, but then returned with two wives, twelve sons, a daughter, and wealth of cattle and servants. As we discover in our Key Verse (verse 15), Jacob's life was in the Lord's hands—and although it appeared that Jacob was making decisions that he thought were for his best interest, he was like a puppet in the hands of a merciful God who kept His promise. Finally, it is noteworthy that in previous lessons, God blessed Abraham and Isaac because of their faithfulness, but there was no such declaration for Jacob. God blessed Jacob in spite of himself; God's faithfulness was greater than the faults and frailties of this one man. This is why the Bible teaches us that "the ways of God are beyond finding out....God's ways are not our ways and God's thoughts are not our thoughts."

Likewise, Jacob's story would be an interesting study in biblical family pathology. Many of the acts and much of the language we discover in Jacob's family are first seen in the lives of his father and grandfather—such as jealousy, competition, anger, and so forth. Just as Sarah gave her handmaiden (Hagar) to Abraham, Jacob's wives gave their handmaidens to Jacob to be his wives. Rachel gave Bilhah, her handmaiden, and she had a son by Jacob; Leah gave Zilpah to him and she had a son (see Genesis 30:3). Many of the family issues that percolated in Jacob's family were first seen in the families of his parents and grandparents. However, in spite of what appears to have been cynical acts within the everyday lives of Jacob and his family, the hand of God was visible and present in the activities of Jacob's family. Thus, we do ourselves a disservice when we do not seek God's presence in our lives, regardless of how mundane the activities and events may be.

II. EXPOSITION AND APPLICATION OF THE SCRIPTURE

A. Isaac Gives Jacob a Directive (Genesis 28:1a)

AND ISAAC called Jacob, and blessed him.

Jacob was about to be exiled to the land of Paddan Aram to live with Rebekah's brother. Jacob feared that Esau would kill him for taking the blessing of his father from him. In order to make Jacob's departure acceptable to his father, his mother Rebekah told Isaac that she feared that her son Jacob would marry a Canaanite woman. Isaac agreed to send him away to get a wife, giving him a directive not to marry a Canaanite woman. Was this a form of racism? It was probably a form of ethnocentrism, not racism! According to the Table of Nations in Genesis 11, after the fall of the Tower of Babel, the descendants of the sons of Noah were scattered throughout the world to repopulate the Earth. The Canaanites were the descendants of Ham's son, Canaan! Abraham, Isaac, and Jacob were the descendants of Shem, the oldest son of Noah. So, the Canaanites were the cousins of Isaac and his family.

Who were the Canaanites? They were members of a Semitic people who inhabited parts of ancient Palestine and were conquered by the Israelites and largely absorbed by them. The question, then, is this: Why did Isaac charge his son Jacob not to marry a Canaanite woman? Isaac followed the stipulation that the Canaanites were a "cursed" people. They were so designated and cut off to prevent Israel and the rest of the world from being corrupted (see Deuteronomy 20:16-18). One of the vile practices of the Canaanites was that of burning their children in honor of their gods (see Leviticus 18:21).

B. Jacob's Dream (Genesis 28:10-15)

And Jacob went out from Beer-sheba, and went toward Haran. And he lighted upon a certain place, and tarried there all night, because the sun was set; and he took of the stones of that place, and put them for his pillows, and lay down in that place to sleep. And he dreamed, and behold a ladder set up on the earth, and the top of it reached to heaven: and behold the angels of God ascending and descending on it. And, behold, the LORD stood above it, and said, I am the LORD God of Abraham thy father, and the God of Isaac: the land whereon thou liest, to thee will I give it, and to thy seed; And thy seed shall be as the dust of the earth, and thou shalt spread abroad to the west, and to the east, and to the north, and to the south: and in thee and in thy seed shall all the families of the earth be blessed. And, behold, I am with thee, and will keep thee in all places whither thou goest, and will bring thee again into this land; for I will not leave thee, until I have done that which I have spoken to thee of.

Isaac granted Jacob's desire to leave. In Jacob's flight to Paddan Aram, he spent the night in the hill country of Luz (see Genesis 28:19). While sleeping, Jacob had a heavenly vision of angels ascending and descending from heaven—and above them stood the Lord, who spoke to Jacob. The Lord reiterated the same promise that He had made to Abraham and Isaac. In spite of the fact that Jacob was a fugitive on the run, the Lord's hand was on his life. God assured Jacob that He was with him wherever his journey took him, and that He would never leave him. We cannot begin to imagine the confidence this must have instilled in Jacob—alone at night, in no man's land; to receive an affirmation from the Lord God must have been a breath of fresh air.

Biblical commentators tell us that God's covenant promise to Abraham and Isaac (Jacob's father and grandfather) was being offered to Jacob as well. Jacob was now establishing his own personal relationship with God. As one Bible scholar stated, "God has no grandchildren." It was of immense importance that Jacob would receive the covenant blessing directly from God. Jacob was promised the land upon which he was lying. His posterity would also be numerous and through him the nations of the Earth would be blessed.

The most important part of this pronouncement from God was the promise of God's presence with Jacob and that wherever Jacob went, God would be with him and bring him back safely to the place of the divine encounter.

C. Jacob's Vow
(Genesis 28:16-22)

And Jacob awaked out of his sleep, and he said, Surely the Lord is in this place; and I knew it not. And he was afraid, and said, How dreadful is this place! this is none other but the house of God, and this is the gate of heaven. And Jacob rose up early in the morning, and took the stone that he had put for his pillows, and set it up for a pillar, and poured oil upon the top of it. And he called the name of that place Beth-el: but the name of that city was called Luz at the first. And Jacob vowed a vow, saying, If God will be with me, and will keep me in this way that I go, and will give me bread to eat, and raiment to put on, So that I come again to my father's house in peace; then shall the Lord be my God: And this stone, which I have set for a pillar, shall be God's house: and of all that thou shalt give me I will surely give the tenth unto thee.

When Jacob awoke, he declared that the Lord was in the place where he sojourned. He called the place Bethel, or "house of God." Up to this point in Jacob's life there was nothing said to indicate that he knew the God of his fathers. His life before this had been blighted by selfish behavior, but this vision was an "aha moment" that transformed Jacob's life. He

acknowledged the Lord which, for him, was the beginning of a new life. In recognition of this new life, Jacob took steps to memorialize the experience and the place. He took the stone he had used for a "pillow" and set it up as a "pillar." He also poured oil upon it as a symbolic anointing.

Following this memorializing service, Jacob then made a vow to God. When we read the details of this vow, it would appear that Jacob was bargaining with God. He was saying that if God did something for him, then he would let the Lord be his God and he would "give the tenth unto thee." Scholars have raised the question as to whether Jacob was trying to bargain with God. Some scholars take the view that Jacob was not really trying to bargain with God, but was pledging his future to God. He may not have "said it right." It is usually accepted that Jacob was saying in reality that since God blessed him, he would follow God. The bottom line is this: whether Jacob was bargaining or pledging, God blessed him.

III. CONCLUDING REFLECTION

One of the unspoken realities in the story of Jacob is the role that lies and deception had in Jacob's becoming the person whom God would ultimately have him to become. He deceived his brother, Esau (see Genesis 25:29), his father, Isaac (see Genesis 27:19), and his father-in-law, Laban (see Genesis 31:20). His life makes one wonder what would have happened had he and his mother not deceived his father, Isaac, and Isaac had given the blessing to Esau instead. It appears that by hook or by crook Jacob would become the son of the promise and receive the promise of God. How can we reconcile this discrepancy between a good God who rewarded Abraham and Isaac for their faithfulness, but who also affirmed a trickster with all of his trickery to become the heir to a divine promise? Joan D. Chittister, in her book, *Scarred by Struggle, Transformed by Hope,* says this of Jacob's story: "It is an archetype for our own struggles." Jacob's story helps us to understand our own struggle (that of humanity) and that God works with all of us and through all of us in spite of our limitations and frailties to accomplish His work in the world. This narrative ebbs and flows throughout several chapters, but in the end God brought Jacob's life to a place of posterity and blessedness. Thus, the long view of Jacob's life and who he became is really not about Jacob, but about the faithfulness of God. We must persevere in spite of our particular struggles, because we never know which prayers and promises of our ancestors are being fulfilled in us. God is an awesome God, yet our frailties and limitations are little more than opportunities for God to be God. This is our hope, because we want our lives to come to fruitful and blessed conclusions!

PRAYER

God of our ancestors who would dare allow us to wrestle with You, we are grateful that all our struggles are not intended to end in death, but rather to lead us to a place of a new beginning. We surrender ourselves to You. Make us and mold us after Your will. In Jesus' name we pray. Amen.

WORD POWER

Charged—to have imposed a duty, responsibility, or obligation on someone.
Dreadful—awe-inspiring: inspiring awe.
Vow—a solemn promise, pledge, or personal commitment.

HOME DAILY BIBLE READINGS
(October 21-27, 2013)

The Blessing Passes to Jacob
MONDAY, October 21: "One Greater than Jacob" (John 4:1-15)
TUESDAY, October 22: "The Plot to Gain a Blessing" (Genesis 27:1-10)
WEDNESDAY, October 23: "Planning the Deception" (Genesis 27:11-17)
THURSDAY, October 24: "A Blessing Gained through Deceit" (Genesis 27:18-29)
FRIDAY, October 25: "Jacob Received God's Blessing" (Genesis 32:22-30)
SATURDAY, October 26: "Jacob's Name Changed to Israel" (Genesis 35:9-15)
SUNDAY, October 27: "God's Assurance for Jacob" (Genesis 28:1a, 10-22)

PREPARATION FOR DELIVERANCE

FAITH PATHWAY/FAITH JOURNEY TOPIC: **Get Ready!**

DEVOTIONAL READING: **Exodus 4:10-16**
PRINT PASSAGE: **Exodus 3:7-17**

BACKGROUND SCRIPTURE: **Exodus 1–4**
KEY VERSES: **Exodus 3:16-17**

Exodus 3:7-17—KJV

7 And the LORD said, I have surely seen the affliction of my people which are in Egypt, and have heard their cry by reason of their taskmasters; for I know their sorrows;

8 And I am come down to deliver them out of the hand of the Egyptians, and to bring them up out of that land unto a good land and a large, unto a land flowing with milk and honey; unto the place of the Canaanites, and the Hittites, and the Amorites, and the Perizzites, and the Hivites, and the Jebusites.

9 Now therefore, behold, the cry of the children of Israel is come unto me: and I have also seen the oppression wherewith the Egyptians oppress them.

10 Come now therefore, and I will send thee unto Pharaoh, that thou mayest bring forth my people the children of Israel out of Egypt.

11 And Moses said unto God, Who am I, that I should go unto Pharaoh, and that I should bring forth the children of Israel out of Egypt?

12 And he said, Certainly I will be with thee; and this shall be a token unto thee, that I have sent thee: When thou hast brought forth the people out of Egypt, ye shall serve God upon this mountain.

13 And Moses said unto God, Behold, when I come unto the children of Israel, and shall say unto them, The God of your fathers hath sent me unto you; and they shall say to me, What is his name? what shall I say unto them?

14 And God said unto Moses, I AM THAT I AM: and he said, Thus shalt thou say unto the children of Israel, I AM hath sent me unto you.

15 And God said moreover unto Moses, Thus shalt thou say unto the children of Israel, The LORD God of

Exodus 3:7-17—NIV

7 The LORD said, "I have indeed seen the misery of my people in Egypt. I have heard them crying out because of their slave drivers, and I am concerned about their suffering.

8 So I have come down to rescue them from the hand of the Egyptians and to bring them up out of that land into a good and spacious land, a land flowing with milk and honey—the home of the Canaanites, Hittites, Amorites, Perizzites, Hivites and Jebusites.

9 And now the cry of the Israelites has reached me, and I have seen the way the Egyptians are oppressing them.

10 So now, go. I am sending you to Pharaoh to bring my people the Israelites out of Egypt."

11 But Moses said to God, "Who am I, that I should go to Pharaoh and bring the Israelites out of Egypt?"

12 And God said, "I will be with you. And this will be the sign to you that it is I who have sent you: When you have brought the people out of Egypt, you will worship God on this mountain."

13 Moses said to God, "Suppose I go to the Israelites and say to them, 'The God of your fathers has sent me to you,' and they ask me, 'What is his name?' Then what shall I tell them?"

14 God said to Moses, "I AM WHO I AM. This is what you are to say to the Israelites: 'I AM has sent me to you.'"

15 God also said to Moses, "Say to the Israelites, 'The LORD, the God of your fathers—the God of Abraham,

your fathers, the God of Abraham, the God of Isaac, and the God of Jacob, hath sent me unto you: this is my name for ever, and this is my memorial unto all generations.

16 Go, and gather the elders of Israel together, and say unto them, The LORD God of your fathers, the God of Abraham, of Isaac, and of Jacob, appeared unto me, saying, I have surely visited you, and seen that which is done to you in Egypt:

17 And I have said, I will bring you up out of the affliction of Egypt unto the land of the Canaanites, and the Hittites, and the Amorites, and the Perizzites, and the Hivites, and the Jebusites, unto a land flowing with milk and honey.

the God of Isaac and the God of Jacob—has sent me to you.' This is my name forever, the name by which I am to be remembered from generation to generation.

16 Go, assemble the elders of Israel and say to them, 'The LORD, the God of your fathers—the God of Abraham, Isaac and Jacob—appeared to me and said: I have watched over you and have seen what has been done to you in Egypt.

17 And I have promised to bring you up out of your misery in Egypt into the land of the Canaanites, Hittites, Amorites, Perizzites, Hivites and Jebusites—a land flowing with milk and honey.'"

TOPICAL OUTLINE OF THE LESSON

I. Introduction
A. Facing the Unknown
B. Biblical Background

II. Exposition and Application of the Scripture
A. God Sees the Situation! (Exodus 3:7-10)
B. God Sends Help! (Exodus 3:11-13)
C. God Will Deliver! (Exodus 3:14-17)

III. Concluding Reflection

LESSON OBJECTIVES

Upon the completion of the lesson, the students will be able to do the following:

1. Explore the significance of God's assignment to Moses;
2. Explore the value of allowing the heart to say yes to God; and,
3. Name the ways in which adults resist God's call on their lives and the ways in which they can open themselves to obey.

POINTS TO BE EMPHASIZED

ADULT/YOUTH

Adult Topic: Get Ready!
Youth Topic: You Can Do It
Adult Key Verses: Exodus 3:16-17
Youth Key Verse: Exodus 3:11
Print Passage: Exodus 3:7-17

—The rescue of the ancient Israelites from slavery in Egypt foreshadowed the rescue from the slavery of sin in the Christian Scriptures.

—God often accomplished His work through human intermediaries—and chose some unlikely people at that.

—The conversation between God and Moses occurred in Midian. The people of Midian were also descendants of Abraham.

—Moses' name in Hebrew means "to draw out."

—An angel of the Lord appeared to Moses in flames of fire from within a bush.

—God called and commissioned Moses to lead the Israelites out of slavery in Egypt.

—Moses made excuses when God called him.

—God promised Moses that God's presence, power, and direction would enable him to fulfill the call.

CHILDREN
Children Topic: A Special Job

Key Verse: Exodus 3:12
Print Passage: Exodus 3:1-12

—God's angel appeared to Moses in a burning bush that was not consumed.

—God told Moses that he was standing on holy ground.

—God told Moses that He was the God of Moses' ancestors.

—Moses was afraid to look at God.

—God intended to deliver the people from the oppression of the Egyptians.

—God promised to be with Moses as he led the Israelites out of Egypt.

I. INTRODUCTION

A. Facing the Unknown

In our lesson today, the children of Israel were on the precipice of a different future that was unlike anything they had experienced before. They were set to leave a situation, albeit oppressive, that was all they had known for generations. As the descendants of Abraham, Isaac, and Jacob, they had been trapped in Egypt for over 420 years and had adapted to their lives in Egypt, although they were greatly oppressed. For the Israelites, along with freedom came a different set of options; they must leave the confines of Egypt and go to a strange and foreign land with more questions than answers.

There is a profound scene in the movie *Shawshank Redemption* when "Red" (Morgan Freeman) is paroled from prison after decades of incarceration. He said, "All I do anymore is think of ways to break my parole so maybe they'd send me back; terrible thing to live in fear. Brooks Hatlen knew it; he knew it all too well. All I want is to be back where things make sense, where I won't have to be afraid all the time." Conversely, there is another character, Andy, who dreams big and made plans for the day when freedom would be his. He dreamed of going far away and living by the Pacific Ocean, the place which the Mexicans said "has no memory." I cannot claim that Andy was following the voice of God, but he had a voice inside of him that was calling him to dream and imagine a life beyond the walls that confined him. We, too, must have a dream or vision that God has something more for us than our current realities. There is an old adage that is appropriate for this lesson: "God does not call us to a place where His love cannot keep us."

B. Biblical Background

The Jacob narrative drew to a conclusion with his sons' selling the younger brother, Joseph, to a caravan of Ishmaelites, who sold him as a slave in Egypt (see Genesis 37).

Young Joseph succeeded in Egypt over time and became a government official during a time when a severe famine plagued his native land, Canaan. Jacob, his father, heard that there was corn or grain in Egypt and sent his sons to Egypt to buy grain. The sons had to appear before Joseph to make the purchase, but not without fanfare. Joseph recognized his brothers, although they did not recognize him, and he set as a condition of the sale that they must return home and bring their youngest brother, Benjamin, with them to Egypt. Upon their return home, with the condition of the sale, Jacob grudgingly allowed Benjamin to return with them. Joseph ultimately revealed himself as their brother and sent for his father, Jacob. Jacob and his entire clan relocated to Egypt and spent the rest of their days there. They all prospered in Egypt. In time, the family members of the original group that relocated to Egypt all died and the book of Exodus opened with the words that "there came a Pharaoh who knew not Joseph." Pharaoh needed cheap labor to build his empire, so he enslaved the descendants of Jacob and Joseph. They languished in Egypt for 420 years, most of the time as slaves. They were the victims of injustice and oppression until the Lord raised up an emancipator named Moses, who was of the tribe of Levi, one of the sons of Jacob.

The book of Exodus is primarily a narrative of liberation and has become the core of Jewish identity in history. However, the main character in this drama was Yahweh, the God of Abraham, Isaac, and Jacob. God worked through Moses to fulfill His promise to Abraham in Genesis 12. Moses was a miracle child who was rescued from a genocidal maniac, Pharaoh—who issued an edict that all Jewish infant boys were to be put to death (see Exodus 1). Moses' birth and rescue coincided with this edict. However, through a series of circumstances, Moses was raised in the house of Pharaoh as the prince of Egypt until he ran afoul of Egyptian law and was forced into exile in Midian. It was in Midian that Moses was arrested by the voice of God with a command to return to Egypt as God's agent of social transformation and liberation. Yahweh revealed Himself as the God of compassion, who had seen the misery and heard the cry of His people. God commissioned Moses to return to Egypt as the emancipator and lead His people to freedom and into the Land of Promise.

II. EXPOSITION AND APPLICATION OF THE SCRIPTURE

A. God Sees the Situation!
(Exodus 3:7-10)

And the Lord said, I have surely seen the affliction of my people which are in Egypt, and have heard their cry by reason of their taskmasters; for I know their sorrows; And I am come down to deliver them out of the hand of the Egyptians, and to bring them up out of that land unto a good land and a large, unto a land flowing with milk and honey; unto the place of the Canaanites, and the Hittites, and the Amorites, and the Perizzites, and the Hivites, and the Jebusites. Now therefore, behold, the cry of the children of Israel is come unto me: and I have also seen the oppression wherewith the Egyptians oppress them. Come now therefore, and I will send thee unto Pharaoh, that thou mayest bring forth my people the children of Israel out of Egypt.

The God, who called Abraham to leave the land of Ur and who was with Isaac and Jacob in their sojourn, broke His silence after 420 years. Yahweh saw the misery and heard the cries of His people in Egypt. God chose to break His silence on the backside of a remote mountain in Horeb, where Moses was tending the flock of his father-in-law. An angel of the Lord appeared out of a burning bush that was not being consumed. The bush attracted Moses' attention and when he went over to inspect the bush, God spoke, calling Moses' name twice. When Moses answered "Here I am," God instructed him not to get any closer because the ground he was standing on was holy ground (verse 5).

According to *Strong's Exhaustive Concordance of the Bible*, this is the first use of the word *holy* in the Hebrew Bible. It is used as an adjective to describe the ground around the bush. The word *holy* means "sacred" or "set apart." God "set apart" the ground around the burning bush. He allowed Moses to stand on it, but without his sandals. His sandals were a symbol of his defilement and unworthiness to stand in the presence of God. Herding a flock in the desert would have been a dirty, dusty business. Moses' feet were just as dirty as the sandals; therefore, it was obedience that God demanded. Thus, the issue was not really about the sandals, but, rather, about Moses' obedience to the voice speaking to him. God's call to obedience is God's way of affirming one's commitment and devotion to Him. God announced that He had come down to rescue His people. The word *rescue* is also translated "snatches." God had come to take His people—who were being oppressed—out of the hand of Pharaoh. However, it was only after Moses' obedience that the drama moved forward. Moses received his commission to return to Egypt as a divine agent of transformation and liberation from God: "Now, go. I am sending

you" (verse 10, NIV). We must never minimize the simplicity of any demand that comes from God, because God's covenant relationship with His people is based in obedience.

B. God Sends Help! (Exodus 3:11-13)

And Moses said unto God, Who am I, that I should go unto Pharaoh, and that I should bring forth the children of Israel out of Egypt? And he said, Certainly I will be with thee; and this shall be a token unto thee, that I have sent thee: When thou hast brought forth the people out of Egypt, ye shall serve God upon this mountain. And Moses said unto God, Behold, when I come unto the children of Israel, and shall say unto them, The God of your fathers hath sent me unto you; and they shall say to me, What is his name? what shall I say unto them?

In the previous section of this lesson, Yahweh commissioned Moses to return to Egypt as the great emancipator to bring God's people, the Israelites (the descendants of Jacob), out of Egypt. However, Moses' reaction to his new assignment was trepidation. He knew the power and might of the Egyptian empire. He knew Pharaoh to be a mighty foe with enormous military might and resources at his disposal. So Moses raised the pragmatic question that perhaps all of us would raise: "Who am I that I should go to Pharaoh?" and make such a demand of such a world power? Pharaoh represented the impenetrable force that appears to constitute most oppressive regimes. The assignment not only appeared to be a daunting task, but impossible as well. But, in verse 12, Yahweh gave Moses the assurance that He would be with him, and offered him a sign. However, it is noteworthy that the sign would be manifested after the deliverance and not before.

Moses must walk by faith and not by sight.

He must trust the journey to God, because the sign would take place after the people left Egypt, which suggests that his assurance would be in retrospect. Moses then talked with God and asked a follow-up question that clearly suggests that Moses was not fully convinced at this point: "Suppose I go with your message and my people ask me what your name is? What shall I tell them?" In other words, Moses was saying to God, "Let us assume" or "For the sake of argument, assume" that I go—who do I tell that the people sent me? I am often asked by younger people trying to discern the voice of God, "How can I be sure that it is the voice of God speaking to me?" There is no cookie-cutter answer of knowing! But, in this particular paradigm, Moses listened with an ear of faith, engaged the voice in follow-up questions, and was patient.

C. God Will Deliver!
(Exodus 3:14-17)

And God said unto Moses, I AM THAT I AM: and he said, Thus shalt thou say unto the children of Israel, I AM hath sent me unto you. And God said moreover unto Moses, Thus shalt thou say unto the children of Israel, The LORD God of your fathers, the God of Abraham, the God of Isaac, and the God of Jacob, hath sent me unto you: this is my name for ever, and this is my memorial unto all generations. Go, and gather the elders of Israel together, and say unto them, The LORD God of your fathers, the God of Abraham, of Isaac, and of Jacob, appeared unto me, saying, I have surely visited you, and seen that which is done to you in Egypt: And I have said, I will bring you up out of the affliction of Egypt unto the land of the Canaanites, and the Hittites, and the Amorites, and the Perizzites, and the Hivites, and the Jebusites, unto a land flowing with milk and honey.

At this point, God reiterated His promise to Moses that He would be with him. All that God is went with Moses as he returned to Egypt as God's ambassador of liberation. It is the hope of all of us that God will be with us in our endeavors of goodwill.

God's assurance to Moses was based on who God is. God said, "I AM THAT I AM." The literal meaning of this phrase is "I am that I will be." God's name is indicative of who God is in all of His infinite capacity. God has no limits—neither can God be limited by human predicaments or circumstances. God becomes who He needs to be in order to accomplish His purpose and vision for the world. God would ultimately demonstrate His limitless capacity to effectuate change in Egypt (see Exodus 4–10). God gave a message of deliverance to Moses; he was to tell the elders of Israel, the older men in the Hebrew community, the message of God and who God is. Long before the establishment of formal religious ceremonies and ritual, religious tradition was passed through oral communication. It would, therefore, be the role of the elders to persuade the Hebrew people to follow Moses.

The message of liberation was connected to the covenant that God made with their ancestors. There was a dual reference to the God of their history and the promises made eons ago; now God was ready to act again in their lives to honor those promises. Therefore, we do ourselves a grave disservice when we attempt to understand our current realities apart from our history and the lives of our ancestors. God reiterated the promises made to Abraham, Isaac, and Jacob to give them a great land, "flowing with milk and honey." Also, the mentioning of the occupants of the land was consistent with God's limitless authority and power. These groups pale in might to that of Pharaoh; and surely if God could defeat Pharaoh, then God could overcome the Canaanites, Hittites, Amorites, Perizzites, Hivites, and Jebusites.

III. CONCLUDING REFLECTION

The issue of obedience was not just Moses' issue to deal with—it is ours also. God demands obedience of His people. Obedience is essential to God's covenant with us. Thus, after Moses pulled off his sandals, God identified Himself and gave the reasons for His visitation. God said this: I have seen and heard the misery and cries of My people and had come down to see about them. This text is normative for doing liberation theology—God is concerned with the plight of the oppressed. Therefore, the main character is God, who hears and sees and comes down from His place in glory to attend to the needs of the people. Through

His commission to Moses, God reaffirmed His faithfulness to the promises made to Abraham, Isaac, and Jacob.

God often appears in the mundane areas of our lives in fulfillment of an old-age promise. Deuteronomy 7:9 declares that "The LORD your God is God; he is the faithful God, keeping His covenant of love to a thousand generations of those who love Him and keep His commands" (NIV). We must never underestimate the faithfulness of God and the spiritual legacy of our ancestors who made covenants with God.

PRAYER

"God of our weary years, God of our silent tears, thou who hast brought us thus far on the way....": We are grateful for all that You have done and are doing in our lives to lead us to a place of peace, where we can better serve You. In Jesus' name we pray. Amen.

WORD POWER
Obedience—"to hear correctly"; dutiful or submissive compliance.
Rescue—is the same verb in (2:19) that means "snatches."

HOME DAILY BIBLE READINGS
(October 28–November 3, 2013)

Preparation for Deliverance
MONDAY, October 28: "Oppression under a New King" (Exodus 1:7-14)
TUESDAY, October 29: "The King's Evil Plan" (Exodus 1:15-22)
WEDNESDAY, October 30: "The Sparing of the Infant Moses" (Exodus 2:1-10)
THURSDAY, October 31: "Moses Flees from Pharaoh" (Exodus 2:15-25)
FRIDAY, November 1: "The People Worship God" (Exodus 4:27-31)
SATURDAY, November 2: "Moses' Encounter with God" (Exodus 3:1-6)
SUNDAY, November 3: "Moses' Commission from God" (Exodus 3:7-17)

BEGINNING OF PASSOVER

FAITH PATHWAY/FAITH JOURNEY TOPIC: Remember and Celebrate

DEVOTIONAL READING: John 1:29-37
PRINT PASSAGE: Exodus 12:1-14

BACKGROUND SCRIPTURE: Exodus 6:2-30; 12
KEY VERSE: Exodus 12:14

Exodus 12:1-14—KJV

AND THE LORD spake unto Moses and Aaron in the land of Egypt, saying,

2 This month shall be unto you the beginning of months: it shall be the first month of the year to you.

3 Speak ye unto all the congregation of Israel, saying, In the tenth day of this month they shall take to them every man a lamb, according to the house of their fathers, a lamb for an house:

4 And if the household be too little for the lamb, let him and his neighbour next unto his house take it according to the number of the souls; every man according to his eating shall make your count for the lamb.

5 Your lamb shall be without blemish, a male of the first year: ye shall take it out from the sheep, or from the goats:

6 And ye shall keep it up until the fourteenth day of the same month: and the whole assembly of the congregation of Israel shall kill it in the evening.

7 And they shall take of the blood, and strike it on the two side posts and on the upper door post of the houses, wherein they shall eat it.

8 And they shall eat the flesh in that night, roast with fire, and unleavened bread; and with bitter herbs they shall eat it.

9 Eat not of it raw, nor sodden at all with water, but roast with fire; his head with his legs, and with the purtenance thereof.

10 And ye shall let nothing of it remain until the morning; and that which remaineth of it until the morning ye shall burn with fire.

11 And thus shall ye eat it; with your loins girded, your shoes on your feet, and your staff in your hand; and ye shall eat it in haste: it is the Lord's passover.

12 For I will pass through the land of Egypt this night, and will smite all the firstborn in the land of

Exodus 12:1-14—NIV

THE LORD said to Moses and Aaron in Egypt,

2 "This month is to be for you the first month, the first month of your year.

3 Tell the whole community of Israel that on the tenth day of this month each man is to take a lamb for his family, one for each household.

4 If any household is too small for a whole lamb, they must share one with their nearest neighbor, having taken into account the number of people there are. You are to determine the amount of lamb needed in accordance with what each person will eat.

5 The animals you choose must be year-old males without defect, and you may take them from the sheep or the goats.

6 Take care of them until the fourteenth day of the month, when all the people of the community of Israel must slaughter them at twilight.

7 Then they are to take some of the blood and put it on the sides and tops of the doorframes of the houses where they eat the lambs.

8 That same night they are to eat the meat roasted over the fire, along with bitter herbs, and bread made without yeast.

9 Do not eat the meat raw or cooked in water, but roast it over the fire—head, legs and inner parts.

10 Do not leave any of it till morning; if some is left till morning, you must burn it.

11 This is how you are to eat it: with your cloak tucked into your belt, your sandals on your feet and your staff in your hand. Eat it in haste; it is the LORD's Passover.

12 On that same night I will pass through Egypt

Egypt, both man and beast; and against all the gods of Egypt I will execute judgment: I am the LORD. 13 And the blood shall be to you for a token upon the houses where ye are: and when I see the blood, I will pass over you, and the plague shall not be upon you to destroy you, when I smite the land of Egypt. 14 And this day shall be unto you for a memorial; and ye shall keep it a feast to the LORD throughout your generations; ye shall keep it a feast by an ordinance for ever.

and strike down every firstborn—both men and animals—and I will bring judgment on all the gods of Egypt. I am the LORD. 13 The blood will be a sign for you on the houses where you are; and when I see the blood, I will pass over you. No destructive plague will touch you when I strike Egypt. 14 This is a day you are to commemorate; for the generations to come you shall celebrate it as a festival to the LORD—a lasting ordinance."

TOPICAL OUTLINE OF THE LESSON

I. Introduction
A. What Is True Freedom?
B. Biblical Background

II. Exposition and Application of the Scripture
A. Preparing for Deliverance (Exodus 12:1-6)
B. The Feast of Passover (Exodus 12:7-11)
C. God Will Act! (Exodus 12:12-14)

III. Concluding Reflection

LESSON OBJECTIVES

Upon the completion of the lesson, the students will be able to do the following:

1. Understand the historical events that lie behind the Jewish celebration of Passover;
2. Empathize with those who are in need of deliverance; and,
3. Identify ways in which the church can participate in freeing those who need deliverance.

POINTS TO BE EMPHASIZED

ADULT/YOUTH
Adult Topic: Remember and Celebrate
Youth Topic: A New Beginning
Adult/Youth Key Verse: Exodus 12:14
Print Passage: Exodus 12:1-14

—The Passover celebration was instituted as a communal reminder of God's mighty deeds and as a tool for faith formation.
—The Passover was both a familial celebration and a community celebration.
—The command to put blood on the doorposts was a test of faith and obedience.
—The elements of the Passover imply a "ready to go" state, such as unleavened bread and the complete consumption of the meal.

—God promised to redeem the Israelites from slavery and to give them a new home in the Promised Land.

—In Jewish tradition, Passover marks the beginning of a new year.

—After the Passover, Pharaoh released the Israelites from captivity.

—Passover served to remind future generations of Israelites that they were freed from slavery and should always be kind to the oppressed.

CHILDREN
Children Topic: A Day of Remembrance
Key Verse: Exodus 12:14a

Print Passage: Exodus 12:1-14

—God gave Moses and Aaron instructions concerning the Passover.

—The people were to slay a young lamb and place its blood on the two doorposts and lintel of their houses.

—The people were to roast the lamb and eat all of it the same night.

—God's plan was to pass through Egypt—sparing only those houses marked by the blood.

—The Passover was to be celebrated by the Israelites throughout all generations.

I. INTRODUCTION
A. What Is True Freedom?

There is so much talk about freedom (liberty) in the political world that the word itself has become trite and without the substance it demands. Freedom is a state of being that is without mental or physical restraint.

Dr. Martin Luther King Jr. raised the implicit question of freedom in his statement about justice: "Justice (freedom) denied somewhere is justice (freedom) denied everywhere." Once freedom is denied to one person or group, invariably it also denies others an aspect of freedom indirectly. None can be free until all are free, because the reality is that freedom is a yearning that is in all of us! One cannot have liberty without freedom, nor freedom without liberty—the words are synonymous!

This lesson is a lesson about true liberation that avails the people of God with liberty and justice from oppression. God sees oppression and hears the cries of the oppressed and comes down to not only see about them, but also to set them free from a system of oppression (as it was with the Hebrew people in Egypt). According to "Liberation Theologies," God is on the side of those who are oppressed and denied the flourishing of their humanity. Thus, for many, the African-American story of slavery and freedom rivals this ancient story. God set the captive free from a system that denied and restricted the flourishing of the humanity of people of color in America. Freedom is God-given and the reality of it is that it yearns in all of us!

B. Biblical Background

When Moses arrived in Egypt, he delivered the Lord's message to Pharaoh: "Let my people go." The Lord said to Moses, "Pharaoh will refuse to listen to you, so that my wonders may be multiplied in Egypt" (Exodus 11:9). True to God's words, Pharaoh resisted and God showed His power through a series of plagues in Egypt that would compel Pharaoh to set God's people free (see Exodus 4–11). Thus, it was through these series of divine plagues—even the death of Pharaoh's son—that Pharaoh would finally succumb and set the people free. In the final night before their departure from Egypt, God commanded the Israelites to mark this event of liberation with a ritual to be celebrated for all generations. This ritual was to commemorate their freedom and became known as the Passover. The meal which commemorated the Passover consisted of roasted sheep or goat and bitter herbs. The blood of the animal sacrifice was to be placed on the doorpost of the doorway of each Jewish home as a marker of covering.

The stubbornness of Pharaoh and his resistance to the command of Yahweh caused Yahweh to dispatch a death angel to kill all firstborn boys "of man and beast" in the homes not marked by the blood on the doorposts. It is interesting that the narrative of Moses began with an edict of death against Hebrew infant boys and the power of God afflicted the Egyptians with the death of their firstborn sons as a force of liberation (see Exodus 11).

II. EXPOSITION AND APPLICATION OF THE SCRIPTURE

A. Preparing for Deliverance
(Exodus 12:1-6)

AND THE LORD spake unto Moses and Aaron in the land of Egypt, saying, This month shall be unto you the beginning of months: it shall be the first month of the year to you. Speak ye unto all the congregation of Israel, saying, In the tenth day of this month they shall take to them every man a lamb, according to the house of their fathers, a lamb for an house: And if the household be too little for the lamb, let him and his neighbour next unto his house take it according to the number of the souls; every man according to his eating shall make your count for the lamb. Your lamb shall be without blemish, a male of the first year: ye shall take it out from the sheep, or from the goats: And ye shall keep it up until the fourteenth day of the same month: and the whole assembly of the congregation of Israel shall kill it in the evening.

God spoke to Moses and Aaron with a message for the Israelite community. God would liberate the Hebrew community; therefore, the community would have a role in their own deliverance. We are living in an age when it appears that individual piety and faith seem to take precedence and priority over the collective faith of the community. While God does call us individually, the call is never exclusionary and without consequences that impact the entire community. God does not just deliver individuals—God delivers communities. In verse 3, Moses and Aaron were instructed to speak to "all the congregation" with the instruction that each man on the tenth day of the month take a male lamb of a year old without blemish, sequester it for fourteen days, and then slaughter it in the evening and offer a sacrifice unto the Lord. If a household was too small to consume a lamb or a goat, then families were to share so that the entire animal was consumed. The people were to eat roasted lamb, bread, and bitter herbs. However, if by chance some meat was not consumed that night it was to be burned the next morning.

This event became the landmark event around which Israel would become a compassionate community, which in time, by law, would make provisions for orphans, widows, aliens, and strangers. This event carried profound social implications for Israel and the nation they were to become. God commanded the people to make provisions for persons who were at risk of being left out or who might be deprived of participation in the liberation event. It was vital that all Hebrew people in Egypt be fully able to participate in this ritual of departure.

It is in this Exodus experience that we get the first glimpse of a divine call to community. The chosen family of Jacob from the beginning had been troubled by one conflict after another, but finally after four centuries of slavery, God called them to community around a common meal and a common table, and a common deliverance. They would have these images in common and it would be around these images—the Passover, Unleavened Bread, and the Exodus experience of liberation—that God would establish a covenant and call His people to community.

B. The Feast of Passover
(Exodus 12:7-11)

And they shall take of the blood, and strike it on the two side posts and on the upper door post of the houses, wherein they shall eat it. And they shall eat the flesh in that night, roast with fire, and unleavened bread; and with bitter herbs they shall eat it. Eat not of it raw, nor sodden at all with water, but roast with fire; his head with his legs, and with the purtenance thereof. And ye shall let nothing of it remain until the morning; and that which remaineth of it until the morning ye shall burn with fire. And thus shall ye eat it; with your loins girded, your shoes on your feet, and your staff in your hand; and ye shall eat it in haste: it is the Lord's passover.

The people were to slaughter a lamb or a goat and the blood from the slaughtered animals was to be posted on the doorpost of each house as a sign to the death angel that passed through Egypt to "pass over" the house. But the blood sign was not merely a "marker," as one would use paint or a magic marker to identify each house; the blood on the doorpost was a sign of life. The lives of all firstborn boys and male animals that belonged to the household with the blood on the doorpost were spared.

In the Bible, blood, at a practical level, represented life; its presence in the body distinguishes the living from the dead—it is vital to all life. This is why when a person is sick and loses an inordinate amount of blood, a blood transfusion is essential to sustain life. The Lord said in Leviticus 17:11, "The life of a creature is in the blood... it is the blood that makes atonement for one's life" (NIV). In history, this sign of blood has become an integral part of Israel's covenant and ritual practice for generations. Even to this day, Jews all over the world still celebrate this sacred ritual of Passover and Unleavened Bread, and each time Jews observe these rituals, they are reminded of what God did for their ancestors thousands of years earlier.

Finally, Dr. Terence E. Fretheim, professor of Old Testament classes at Luther Northwestern Theological Seminary, says, "The blood of creation is shed so that Israel's blood might be spared." The blood in this Exodus narrative is a "type" that points to something else beyond itself and a more significant event or thing in the future. The blood image of the Passover in the Old Testament is such a type that points beyond itself to the blood of Jesus that would become the marker in the believer's life. According to the book of Hebrews (chapter 9), Jesus became a better sacrifice. Christ did not enter by means of the blood of goats and calves, "but he entered the Most Holy Place once for all by his own blood" (verse 12). Therefore, inasmuch as in the Moses narrative those who were in a house marked by blood were protected from divine wrath, we believers also are the beneficiaries of the presence of the shed blood of Jesus in our lives. A line from an old hymn goes, "O the blood done signed my name." Indeed, this is what happened in Jesus.

C. God Will Act!
(Exodus 12:12-14)

For I will pass through the land of Egypt this night, and will smite all the firstborn in the land of Egypt, both man and beast; and against all the gods of Egypt I will execute judgment: I am the Lord. And the blood shall be to you for a token upon the houses where ye are: and when I see the blood, I will pass over you, and the plague shall not be upon you to destroy you, when I smite the land of Egypt. And this day shall be unto you for a memorial; and ye shall keep it a feast to the Lord throughout your generations; ye shall keep it a feast by an ordinance for ever.

Finally, the text reaches the essence of the narrative—God acting to compel Pharaoh to set God's people free. In the night of the Passover observance, God would dispatch a death angel to pass through Egypt, striking down every firstborn male of both men and animals. In our day and time, we would view such genocide of children and the killing of animals as horrific and unthinkable, but it is really not the act itself that begs our attention—it is the cosmic struggle between the God of Abraham, Isaac, and Jacob and worldly power (Pharaoh) that challenged the authority of God. This reality of life and death is part of what the sovereignty of God means. Thus, God used a series of plagues to demonstrate His power over Egypt; and each time Pharaoh resisted, God ratcheted up the ante until Pharaoh relented and obeyed God. In God's final act, God used His authority

over life and death as a demonstration of His authority.

When Moses performed the first miracle before Pharaoh (see chapter 4), Pharaoh had his magicians who could perform a similar miracle by sleight of hand. But, death was something that neither he nor his magicians could replicate by sleight of hand. At the end of this night, there would be no doubt in Pharaoh's mind of who is Lord of all. So, the Lord had the power and authority to bring judgment on the gods of Egypt, because "I am the Lord" (verse 12). Israel was instructed to remember and reenact this "Passover event" each year at the same time for generations to come.

There is plenty of history that we remember in our communities, but we do not reenact it, which carries the notion of repeating the events of the past. It is not enough to remember; the people of God developed a practice or reenactment around those moments of grace in which God set His people free (liberated us).

God commanded Israel to reenact this event of liberation each year; they must not forget what the Lord did for them and their ancestors in Egypt (verse 14). The weight of the commemoration is that it is an ordinance to be celebrated as "a feast to the Lord."

Thus, the Passover is the centerpiece of both Jewish and Christian faith traditions. The Lord's Supper and the Passover are inseparable events in salvation history. In the Passover, a lamb is sacrificed—but on Calvary, Jesus became our sacrificial lamb, slain to deliver us from sin that entangles us. Thus, each time the Christian church celebrates the Lord's Supper, she is also celebrating the acts of God in salvation history; and inasmuch as God asked the Jews to commemorate the Exodus event, believers are also asked to commemorate the night Jesus spent with His disciples before going to the Cross. In spite of the horrific acts of this narrative, in the end it (this narrative) is about both death and new life in the hands of God.

III. CONCLUDING REFLECTION

As we read these instructions given to the Israelites, it is difficult to ignore the particularity of the instructions that the people were to follow; they were to prepare the meat a certain way, bake the bread a certain way, and dress in a certain way as they ate the Passover. God even gave specific instructions for the disposal of any leftover meat. These detailed instructions were important for two reasons: they allowed the people to participate in their deliverance from Egypt, and they also allowed the people to follow the instructions as an act of obedience. God is a God who demands obedience of His people. Thus, we must never underestimate the seeming simplicity of God's commands, because it is not about simplicity or complexity—rather, it is about obedience.

Finally, whereas the Israelites were to commemorate the Passover for generations to come, Jesus would add new meaning to the Passover. Jesus established a covenant with the community of believers and said to His disciples, "He took bread, and gave thanks, and brake it, and gave unto them, saying, This is my body which is given for you: this do in remembrance of me." Centuries later it would be around these same images, meal and table, that God's Son would establish this covenant with all believers. As we mark the spot of our liberation, we must commemorate them in such a way that generations to come will know what the Lord has done for us.

PRAYER

Oh Lord, our Lord, how great You are. We honor You this day, for indeed, You are a God of freedom who created us for freedom. Oh Lord, give us clean hearts so that we might serve others as we serve You in Spirit and in truth, for those whom You have set free are free indeed. In Jesus' name we pray. Amen.

WORD POWER

Commemorate *(memorial)*—means to "rehearse" or "recount."
Ordinance—"something prescribed" or "enactment."

HOME DAILY BIBLE READINGS
(November 4-10, 2013)

Beginning of Passover
MONDAY, November 4: "The Lamb of God" (John 1:29-37)
TUESDAY, November 5: "The Troubles Multiply" (Exodus 5:19-23)
WEDNESDAY, November 6: "Broken Spirits and Closed Ears" (Exodus 6:2-9)
THURSDAY, November 7: "The Final Plague" (Exodus 11)
FRIDAY, November 8: "The First Passover" (Exodus 12:21-28)
SATURDAY, November 9: "The Lord Delivered Israel" (Exodus 12:43-51)
SUNDAY, November 10: "The Promise to Pass Over" (Exodus 12:1-14)

BEGINNING OF FREEDOM

FAITH PATHWAY/FAITH JOURNEY TOPIC: From Despair to Deliverance

DEVOTIONAL READING: **Galatians 5:13-21**
PRINT PASSAGE: **Exodus 14:21-30**

BACKGROUND SCRIPTURE: **Exodus 13:17-22; 14**
KEY VERSE: **Exodus 14:30**

Exodus 14:21-30—KJV

21 And Moses stretched out his hand over the sea; and the LORD caused the sea to go back by a strong east wind all that night, and made the sea dry land, and the waters were divided.

22 And the children of Israel went into the midst of the sea upon the dry ground: and the waters were a wall unto them on their right hand, and on their left.

23 And the Egyptians pursued, and went in after them to the midst of the sea, even all Pharaoh's horses, his chariots, and his horsemen.

24 And it came to pass, that in the morning watch the LORD looked unto the host of the Egyptians through the pillar of fire and of the cloud, and troubled the host of the Egyptians,

25 And took off their chariot wheels, that they drave them heavily: so that the Egyptians said, Let us flee from the face of Israel; for the LORD fighteth for them against the Egyptians.

26 And the LORD said unto Moses, Stretch out thine hand over the sea, that the waters may come again upon the Egyptians, upon their chariots, and upon their horsemen.

27 And Moses stretched forth his hand over the sea, and the sea returned to his strength when the morning appeared; and the Egyptians fled against it; and the LORD overthrew the Egyptians in the midst of the sea.

28 And the waters returned, and covered the chariots, and the horsemen, and all the host of Pharaoh that came into the sea after them; there remained not so much as one of them.

29 But the children of Israel walked upon dry land in

Exodus 14:21-30—NIV

21 Then Moses stretched out his hand over the sea, and all that night the LORD drove the sea back with a strong east wind and turned it into dry land. The waters were divided,

22 and the Israelites went through the sea on dry ground, with a wall of water on their right and on their left.

23 The Egyptians pursued them, and all Pharaoh's horses and chariots and horsemen followed them into the sea.

24 During the last watch of the night the LORD looked down from the pillar of fire and cloud at the Egyptian army and threw it into confusion.

25 He made the wheels of their chariots come off so that they had difficulty driving. And the Egyptians said, "Let's get away from the Israelites! The LORD is fighting for them against Egypt."

26 Then the LORD said to Moses, "Stretch out your hand over the sea so that the waters may flow back over the Egyptians and their chariots and horsemen."

27 Moses stretched out his hand over the sea, and at daybreak the sea went back to its place. The Egyptians were fleeing toward it, and the LORD swept them into the sea.

28 The water flowed back and covered the chariots and horsemen—the entire army of Pharaoh that had followed the Israelites into the sea. Not one of them survived.

29 But the Israelites went through the sea on dry

the midst of the sea; and the waters were a wall unto them on their right hand, and on their left.

30 Thus the LORD saved Israel that day out of the hand of the Egyptians; and Israel saw the Egyptians dead upon the sea shore.

ground, with a wall of water on their right and on their left.

30 That day the LORD saved Israel from the hands of the Egyptians, and Israel saw the Egyptians lying dead on the shore.

TOPICAL OUTLINE OF THE LESSON

I. Introduction
    A. Help Will Come!
    B. Biblical Background

II. Exposition and Application of the Scripture
    A. A Way Out of No Way!
        (Exodus 14:21-25)
    B. The Enemy Destroyed!
        (Exodus 14:26-28)
    C. God Did It!
        (Exodus 14:29-30)

III. Concluding Reflection

LESSON OBJECTIVES

Upon the completion of the lesson, the students will be able to do the following:

1. Connect the deliverance of Israel from Egypt to the rest of Israel's history;
2. Experience gratitude for God's deliverance in their lives; and,
3. Identify the importance of the Exodus to the Christian faith.

POINTS TO BE EMPHASIZED
ADULT/YOUTH
Adult Topic: From Despair to Deliverance
Youth Topic: We're Free!
Adult/Youth Key Verse: Exodus 14:30
Print Passage: Exodus 14:21-30

—God often works through human intermediaries.
—The central drama of Exodus 14 was the triumph of the power of God over the power of Pharaoh, Egypt, and Egypt's supposed gods.
—God's will for liberation and freedom was revealed when the sea opened up and a dry path appeared.
—The crossing of the Red Sea provided an enduring point of reference to the power of God (see Psalm 106:9; Acts 7:36; and so forth).
—God guided the Israelites by a pillar of cloud by day and a pillar of fire by night as reassurance of His presence.
—After the Israelites left Egypt, God directed them to travel a longer route on the way to the Red Sea.
—Pharaoh's heart was hardened by God so he pursued the Israelites across the Red Sea.
—God performed a miracle by using Moses to part the Red Sea so that the Israelites could cross over to safety.
—God destroyed Pharaoh and his army in the Red Sea.

CHILDREN
Children Topic: The Great Escape
Key Verse: Exodus 14:29
Print Passage: Exodus 14:8-9, 21-30

—When he heard that the Israelites were leaving Egypt, Pharaoh decided to pursue them.
—When Moses stretched out his hand, the Red Sea parted and the Israelites went through it on dry land.
—God saw the Egyptians pursuing the Israelites and threw the Egyptians into a panic.
—The Egyptians followed the Israelites and the waters came together, drowning the Egyptians.
—The Lord saved Israel.

I. INTRODUCTION

A. Help Will Come!

The Bible says, "What is impossible with men is possible with God." Therefore, the task of believers is not to question how, but to trust that if it is God's will, then it will happen. The ways of God are beyond finding out! When John F. Kennedy Jr. ran for president in 1960, he chose as his running mate a senator from Texas—Lyndon B. Johnson—to appeal to the southern voter. President Kennedy was assassinated in November of 1963 and Lyndon B. Johnson became president. In 1964, the pressing issues confronting America were the struggle of the Negro for equal and voting rights. Although there had been some progress made on the political front, the "Southern Dixiecrats" in Congress had been successful in blocking such legislation. Although he had never voted on Civil Rights legislature, President Lyndon B. Johnson used his political clout to push the Civil Rights Bill through Congress. The Civil Rights Movement, in full swing, had struggled for years to gain political traction, but in spite of the objections and resistance from his southern colleagues, President Johnson signed into law the Civil Rights Bill in July of 1964.

We cannot be certain which corner of the universe our help will come from, but we can be certain that if God is in it, then it will come. God works in the hearts of men and women everywhere to bring about His purpose and will in the world. This is the lesson of the book of Exodus. God worked through persons to bring His people to freedom. Just as Moses was divinely engaged in the process of liberation so that the Israelites could escape to freedom, the political leadership in Washington, DC in 1964 had to exercise its will and judgment to bring the Civil Rights Bill into law for the American Negro. We must conclude that God is still offering opportunities for new possibilities to bring a fuller and more flourishing life to all of God's people. Even when it seems impossible, we must trust that God will make a way out of no way for those whose backs are against the wall in every generation!

B. Biblical Background

The history of the Israelites has been covered over the last ten lessons. Their lives as a people began with the call of Abraham by God to become a great nation. He was the progenitor of a son, Isaac, who was the father of two sons, Esau and Jacob. However, it was Jacob who would become heir of the promise first given to his grandfather, Abraham. Jacob had twelve sons, one of whom was precocious (Joseph) and incurred the wrath of his older brothers, who abducted him and sold him into slavery in Egypt. The Lord's hand was on Joseph, however, and he prospered while in Egypt and became a political leader in the government of Pharaoh. Over time, Joseph brought his father, Jacob, and his brothers and their families to Egypt to live because of the famine. They all prospered in Egypt, but eventually both Pharaoh and Joseph died and there came to the throne of Egypt a pharaoh "who knew not Joseph" (Exodus 1:8).

The Jewish descendants of Jacob were placed into bondage for several centuries, until God saw their misery and heard their cry. God raised up a liberator named Moses in Midian, who was in exile from Pharaoh. Moses returned to Egypt with God's message to Pharaoh to let His people go; however, it took a series of miracles to persuade Pharaoh to set the people free. Finally, after the death angel struck his son, Pharaoh set the Israelites free. The people of Israel left Egypt bound for the Promised Land (Canaan) that God had promised Abraham, Isaac, and Jacob. However, after Pharaoh had set them free, he had a change of heart and sent his soldiers to overtake them and bring them back. He realized the impact that their freedom would have on the economy in Egypt—no more free labor. Therefore, lesson 11 picks up on the narrative as the children of Israel there would be in an impossible dilemma: caught between the desert, a charging army, and the Red Sea. The children of Israel complained against Moses and even insinuated that they asked him to leave them alone in Egypt. So, the main character in this narrative is Yahweh (God), who calls a people into existence and works in and through their lives over several generations to bring to fulfillment that which God had promised.

II. EXPOSITION AND APPLICATION OF THE SCRIPTURE

A. A Way Out of No Way!
(Exodus 14:21-25)

And Moses stretched out his hand over the sea; and the LORD caused the sea to go back by a strong east wind all that night, and made the sea dry land, and the waters were divided. And the children of Israel went into the midst of the sea upon the dry ground: and the waters were a wall unto them on their right hand, and on their left. And the Egyptians pursued, and went in after them to the midst of the sea, even all Pharaoh's horses, his chariots, and his horsemen. And it came to pass, that in the morning watch the LORD looked unto the host of the Egyptians through the pillar of fire and of the cloud, and troubled the host of the Egyptians, And took off their chariot wheels, that they drave them heavily: so that the Egyptians said, Let us flee from the face of Israel; for the LORD fighteth for them against the Egyptians.

The Israelites were granted the freedom to leave Egypt by Pharaoh, but as often happens, when it is realized that the freedom of the oppressed required the yielding of control and power over another, often remorse sets in (see verse 8). It was Frederick Douglass who said, "Power concedes nothing without a demand. It never did and it never will." After the demands placed upon Pharaoh by Yahweh, Pharaoh relented and set the Israelites free, but changed his mind when he realized the cost to the empire with the loss of free labor. Pharaoh pursued the Israelites to return them to Egypt in order to maintain the status quo (as his slaves). The Israelites' response to being pursued by the Egyptian army was fear and trepidation. In fear, they turned on Moses and began taunting him (verse 11) and demanded to know why he brought them out of Egypt to die in the desert. "Didn't we say to you in Egypt, 'Leave us alone; let us serve the Egyptians'? It would have been better for us to serve the Egyptians than to die in the desert!" (verse 12). Their dialogue with Moses highlights the mindset of those who are summarily oppressed; often they prefer the certainty of slavery over the uncertainty and challenges of freedom.

Slavery for them had become a state of mind and they desired the certainty of slavery against the uncertainty of a future with freedom—but God had other ideas. Their freedom was a justice issue and God is a God of justice; so it was not just their freedom that was at stake, but also God's faithfulness. We established in lesson 1 that Yahweh is Lord over all of creation (Psalm 8); therefore, in chapter 12 (verses 19-21), Yahweh used light and darkness, fire, clouds, and wind to confuse the Egyptian army and delay their aggression to enable the people to escape through the Red Sea. Yahweh used two agents to deliver the people—humans and nature. When the wheels came off of the chariots, the Egyptians understood that God was fighting against them.

Therefore, we must never underestimate the power of God to bring under His authority both human and natural agencies to effectuate God's purpose and plan in the world. Divine power is unlimited in us and in nature as God

sees fit. Was this not the testimony of Jesus in His conversation with Nicodemus: "The wind blows wherever it pleases…so it is with the Spirit" (John 3:8)? We can never be certain where and when the hand of God will appear in the work of human freedom.

B. The Enemy Destroyed!
(Exodus 14:26-28)

And the Lord said unto Moses, Stretch out thine hand over the sea, that the waters may come again upon the Egyptians, upon their chariots, and upon their horsemen. And Moses stretched forth his hand over the sea, and the sea returned to his strength when the morning appeared; and the Egyptians fled against it; and the Lord overthrew the Egyptians in the midst of the sea. And the waters returned, and covered the chariots, and the horsemen, and all the host of Pharaoh that came into the sea after them; there remained not so much as one of them.

After Israel had crossed over the sea and had arrived safely on the other side, God instructed Moses to again stretch out his hand so that the sea might return to normal. The sea returned to its normal state and the Egyptians were drowned in the same passage that yielded freedom and life to the Israelites. In this narrative, we witness the grace and the wrath or judgment of God in the same event. Israel was no more a people of faith at this time than the Egyptians. They grumbled and murmured against Moses and desired to return to slavery; nonetheless, they found grace in the sight of God. On the other hand, the Egyptians were no better or worse. They were trying to recover what they had lost (slave labor) and they suffered the wrath and the judgment of God in the process. However, the issue was not the merit of either group; rather, it is God's faithfulness and strength that was on display in the sea and in Moses in order to fulfill God's promise to Abraham, Isaac, and Jacob and set the captives free! It was God who allowed the sea to roll back as a path of liberation—and it was God who allowed the sea to return to its bed as a tool of destruction. Verse 27 reads, "The Lord overthrew the Egyptians in the midst of the sea"; so it was not just the actions of Moses, but the Lord who swept them into the sea.

Concomitantly, Moses' experience with the people and the power of God would serve him well later on, when his leadership would be questioned and tested time and time again. The people would become stiff-necked and rebel against Moses; therefore, the promise God made "to be with Moses" (Exodus 3:12) would be needed for Moses as much with the people in their rebellion as it was with the stubbornness of Pharaoh. Finally, this Exodus passage was the signal moment in the history of the Hebrew people—all subsequent experiences in Israel's history point back to their deliverance. Both poet and prophet in future generations would use this moment as the basis of encouragement and hope in God. Perhaps the crossing of the Red Sea was a rite of passage by which the people would become a nation. This narrative later became the paradigm for other oppressed people in history such as the Negro. James Cone, in his book, *God of the Oppressed*, says, "Liberation is not only a relationship with God but an encounter grounded in the historical struggle to be free."

C. God Did It!
(Exodus 14:29-30)

But the children of Israel walked upon dry land in the midst of the sea; and the waters were a wall unto them on their right hand, and on their left. Thus the Lord saved Israel that day out of the hand of the Egyptians; and Israel saw the Egyptians dead upon the sea shore.

One of the miracles that is not often discussed in this text is that the people crossed through the Red Sea on dry ground. The Red Sea had sat in its bed for centuries prior to this event. The wind of God did not just divide the water—it also evaporated the water from the sea bed and dried it out so the people and their carts could cross on dry ground. To evaporate the water from a sea bed instantaneously required a miracle.

In 2010, a flood inundated Davidson County/Nashville, Tennessee. It took over a week for the waters to completely recede into the rivers and tributaries, and it took another several weeks for parks and golf courses to open to the public, because the areas that were flooded were too muddy and soggy on which to walk or ride. It took weeks for the ground where the water stood to become dry—but God dried the ground of the Red Sea in a moment. There is no doubt that their liberation was the Lord's doing! However, what was available to the Israelites was not available to the enemy. When the enemy tried to cross through the same passage, wheels got stuck and came off chariots, and the Lord allowed the water to return, so that the Egyptians who entered the passage perished as the churning water returned to its bed. God allowed the Israelites to see the destruction of evil—and what they saw strengthened their faith both in the Lord and in Moses for the road ahead. That which Israel could not do for itself was accomplished by God! They did not deserve and were not able to contribute to their liberation, but because of the faithfulness of God to His promise to Abraham, Isaac, and Jacob, they were set free.

Therefore, we, too, must take courage in this narrative because the sages are correct: "There is no secret what God can do, for what He's done for others, He'll do for you."

III. CONCLUDING REFLECTION

The Israelites at the Red Sea ultimately had to exercise faith in God for their liberation; and we, too, must exercise a similar faith that God will hold back the watery walls from collapsing in on us as well. Thus, the Exodus experience was not just a significant moment in the history of the Hebrew people; it also bears eternal truth for all of us.

Finally, what happened in the Exodus liberation narrative points to the New Testament and what Jesus the Christ ultimately meant to the world. Moses was the human agent through whom God worked to accomplish His will in Egypt. Therefore, Moses was a type of Christ in the Old Testament who liberated God's people from the clutches of injustice. Jesus the Christ in the New Testament became the human agent through whom God worked and continues to work to set the captives free (see Luke 4:18-20). Thus, we have been set free to live lives of love and justice in the world. In doing so, just as God got the glory in Israel's liberation, God will get the glory through our liberation, and our lives will become examples of love and justice in the world.

PRAYER

Lord God, who set the captives free, we are grateful for all that You have done and are doing to set us free from the shackles that hinder and constrain us from becoming all that You have ordained us to be. Lord, as we are set free, let us also be Your agents of love and justice in the world. Let our lives in Christ glorify You. In Jesus' name we pray. Amen.

WORD POWER

Deliverance—rescue from something: rescue from captivity, hardship, or domination by evil. Freedom—release from captivity or slavery: release or rescue from being physically bound, or from being confined, enslaved, captured, or imprisoned.

HOME DAILY BIBLE READINGS
(November 11-17, 2013)

Beginning of Freedom
MONDAY, November 11: "Called to Live in Freedom" (Galatians 5:13-21)
TUESDAY, November 12: "Setting Apart the Firstborn" (Exodus 13:11-16)
WEDNESDAY, November 13: "Guided by Pillars of Cloud and Fire" (Exodus 13:17-22)
THURSDAY, November 14: "Pharaoh's Change of Heart" (Exodus 14:5-9)
FRIDAY, November 15: "The Lord Will Fight for You" (Exodus 14:10-14)
SATURDAY, November 16: "Guarded from the Approaching Enemy" (Exodus 14:15-20)
SUNDAY, November 17: "The Lord Saved Israel That Day" (Exodus 14:21-30)

BEGINNING OF THE TABERNACLE

Faith Pathway/Faith Journey Topic: Traveling Light

Devotional Reading: Hebrews 9:11-15
Print Passage: Exodus 40:16-30, 34, 38

Background Scripture: Exodus 35–40
Key Verse: Exodus 40:38

Exodus 40:16-30, 34, 38—KJV

16 Thus did Moses: according to all that the Lord commanded him, so did he.

17 And it came to pass in the first month in the second year, on the first day of the month that the tabernacle was reared up.

18 And Moses reared up the tabernacle, and fastened his sockets, and set up the boards thereof, and put in the bars thereof, and reared up his pillars.

19 And he spread abroad the tent over the tabernacle, and put the covering of the tent above upon it; as the Lord commanded Moses.

20 And he took and put the testimony into the ark, and set the staves on the ark, and put the mercy seat above upon the ark:

21 And he brought the ark into the tabernacle, and set up the vail of the covering, and covered the ark of the testimony; as the Lord commanded Moses.

22 And he put the table in the tent of the congregation, upon the side of the tabernacle northward, without the vail.

23 And he set the bread in order upon it before the Lord; as the Lord had commanded Moses.

24 And he put the candlestick in the tent of the congregation, over against the table, on the side of the tabernacle southward.

25 And he lighted the lamps before the Lord; as the Lord commanded Moses.

26 And he put the golden altar in the tent of the congregation before the vail:

27 And he burnt sweet incense thereon; as the Lord commanded Moses.

28 And he set up the hanging at the door of the tabernacle.

Exodus 40:16-30, 34, 38—NIV

16 Moses did everything just as the Lord commanded him.

17 So the tabernacle was set up on the first day of the first month in the second year.

18 When Moses set up the tabernacle, he put the bases in place, erected the frames, inserted the crossbars and set up the posts.

19 Then he spread the tent over the tabernacle and put the covering over the tent, as the Lord commanded him.

20 He took the Testimony and placed it in the ark, attached the poles to the ark and put the atonement cover over it.

21 Then he brought the ark into the tabernacle and hung the shielding curtain and shielded the ark of the Testimony, as the Lord commanded him.

22 Moses placed the table in the Tent of Meeting on the north side of the tabernacle outside the curtain

23 and set out the bread on it before the Lord, as the Lord commanded him.

24 He placed the lampstand in the Tent of Meeting opposite the table on the south side of the tabernacle

25 and set up the lamps before the Lord, as the Lord commanded him.

26 Moses placed the gold altar in the Tent of Meeting in front of the curtain

27 and burned fragrant incense on it, as the Lord commanded him.

28 Then he put up the curtain at the entrance to the tabernacle.

UNIFYING LESSON PRINCIPLE

In the midst of a difficult transition, people look for security and guidance. Where can they find the security and direction they seek? While the Israelites were on their way to the Promised Land, God instructed the people to create the tabernacle—a place where they could always find God's presence and guidance.

29 And he put the altar of burnt offering by the door of the tabernacle of the tent of the congregation, and offered upon it the burnt offering and the meat offering; as the LORD commanded Moses.

30 And he set the laver between the tent of the congregation and the altar, and put water there, to wash withal.

.....

34 Then a cloud covered the tent of the congregation, and the glory of the LORD filled the tabernacle.

.....

38 For the cloud of the LORD was upon the tabernacle by day, and fire was on it by night, in the sight of all the house of Israel, throughout all their journeys.

29 He set the altar of burnt offering near the entrance to the tabernacle, the Tent of Meeting, and offered on it burnt offerings and grain offerings, as the LORD commanded him.

30 He placed the basin between the Tent of Meeting and the altar and put water in it for washing.

.....

34 Then the cloud covered the Tent of Meeting, and the glory of the LORD filled the tabernacle.

.....

38 So the cloud of the LORD was over the tabernacle by day, and fire was in the cloud by night, in the sight of all the house of Israel during all their travels.

TOPICAL OUTLINE OF THE LESSON

I. Introduction
   A. On the Move with God!
   B. Biblical Background

II. Exposition and Application of the Scripture
   A. Following Instructions
     —Part 1
     (Exodus 40:16-23)
   B. Following Instructions
     —Part 2
     (Exodus 40:24-30)
   C. God's Presence Shows Up!
     (Exodus 40:34, 38)

III. Concluding Reflection

LESSON OBJECTIVES

Upon the completion of the lesson, the students will be able to do the following:

1. Explore the significance of God's instructions to Moses regarding the tabernacle;
2. Explore how people respond emotionally to the furnishings of worship spaces; and,
3. Compare and contrast the tabernacle and its furnishings with modern places of worship.

POINTS TO BE EMPHASIZED

ADULT/YOUTH
Adult Topic: Traveling Light
Youth Topic: I'm Here!
Adult Key Verse: Exodus 40:38
Youth Key Verse: Exodus 40:34
Print Passage: Exodus 40:16-30, 34, 38
—The (movable) tabernacle was a precursor of the (permanent) Temple.

—The "filling" of the tabernacle with the glory of the Lord (see Exodus 40:34) was followed several centuries later by the departure of that glory from the Temple (see Ezekiel 10).

—While Moses was obedient to the task and finished the work to which God had called him, he had to wait with hope and anticipation for it to be completed by the indwelling of God's presence.

—The Israelites liberally donated the materials and furniture needed for the construction of the tabernacle, which was constructed in accordance with God's commands.

—The tabernacle was constructed a year after the institution of the Passover.

—The tabernacle represented the presence of God and housed the ark of the covenant. For their faithfulness, God blessed the people by filling the tabernacle with His glory.

—The tabernacle was God's home on Earth until a Temple was built in Jerusalem many years later.

CHILDREN

Children Topic: Great Job!
Key Verse: Exodus 40:34
Print Passage: Exodus 40:16-30, 34, 38

—The tabernacle was a sacred tent that functioned as a portable sanctuary, signifying God's presence with the Israelites wherever they went.

—Moses followed God's explicit instructions for setting up the tabernacle and its furnishings.

—At the completion of the tabernacle, God's glory filled it.

—The cloud and the fire accompanied the tabernacle as the Israelites journeyed toward the Promised Land.

I. INTRODUCTION

A. On the Move with God!

Israel's narrative was coming to a close in the book of Exodus, but not before God gave them a blueprint for a traveling sanctuary that would serve two purposes: as a place of worship, and a place that symbolized the presence of God. Although God had promised Moses that He would be with them, the people had nothing permanent or tangible that represented God's presence. The Israelites were secure in the wilderness and out of Egyptian bondage, but they were anything but secure in their new freedom. This must have been a bittersweet experience for them—free to go and do what they pleased for the first time in their lives, but not knowing where they were going. They had to trust their leader, Moses.

The tabernacle that they would construct would be a visible expression of the willingness and the capacity of God to be present with the people in the world. The tabernacle provided the assurance the people needed in spite of their fears and uncertainty that the Lord was with them. But this is the assurance that all people need and search for—that in spite of life's fears and uncertainties the Lord of creation is ever present with us.

B. Biblical Background

The book of Exodus comes to a close with the building of the tabernacle, or the Tent of Meeting. The details of this sacred space are significant. They reflect the mind of God.

The specificity of fabrics, colors, textures, oils, garments for the priests, anointing, liturgy, and so forth (see chapters 35–40) highlight the divine details of the first house of the Lord and the accompanying rituals. The children of Israel left the Red Sea and were wandering in the wilderness. They were rebellious and stiff-necked against God and Moses. They built a golden calf to worship and when life got tough, they grumbled that they had been better off in Egypt. Their behavior was so offensive to God that God repented of what He had done for them and resolved to destroy them. However, Moses interceded on their behalf and reminded God that it would not be good for Him to destroy the people in the wilderness. "Why should the Egyptians say, 'It was with evil intent that he brought them out, to kill them in the mountains and to wipe them off the face of the earth'? Turn from your fierce anger; relent and do not bring disaster on your people" (Exodus 32:12). God relented and spared the people; therefore, obedience is of upmost significance to God. It demonstrates the willingness to follow the voice and dictates of God.

The antecedent of chapter 40 is the close of chapter 39: "So all the work on the tabernacle, the Tent of Meeting, was completed. The Israelites did everything just as the LORD commanded Moses" (Exodus 39:32, NIV). "The Israelites had done all the work just as the LORD had commanded Moses; Moses inspected the work and saw that they had done it just as the LORD had commanded" (39:42-43). The people's obedience in this matter was of paramount importance as they constructed the "Tent of Meeting," because they were stubborn and had proven that they were incapable of sustained obedience to God. Perhaps it would have been easy for the people to take shortcuts on this project, because some of the details seem to have been miniscule—but with God, the smallest of details is precious and connotes one's willingness not only to pay attention, but also to follow divine instructions. The apostle Paul said, "God uses the foolish things of this world to confound the wise" (1 Corinthians 1:27).

After the people had built the tabernacle, they brought the finished product to Moses. Chapter 40 begins with an adverb of time, *then*—"Then the LORD said to Moses: 'Set up the tabernacle'" (NIV). After this, he was to anoint the tabernacle with oil. "Moses did everything just as the LORD commanded him" (verse 16).

II. EXPOSITION AND APPLICATION OF THE SCRIPTURE

A. Following Instructions—Part 1
(Exodus 40:16-23)

Thus did Moses: according to all that the LORD commanded him, so did he. And it came to pass in the first month in the second year, on the first day of the month that the tabernacle was reared up. And Moses reared up the tabernacle, and fastened his sockets, and set up the boards thereof, and put in the bars thereof, and reared up his pillars. And he spread abroad the tent over the tabernacle, and put the covering of the tent above upon it; as the LORD com-manded Moses. And he took and put the testimony into the ark, and set the staves on the ark, and put the mercy seat above upon the ark: And he brought the ark into the tabernacle, and set up the vail of the covering, and covered the ark of the testimony; as the LORD commanded Moses. And he put the table in the tent of the congregation, upon the side of the tabernacle northward, without the vail. And he set the bread in order upon it before the LORD; as the LORD had commanded Moses.

The time came to set up the tabernacle; it was on the first day of the first month in the second year of their departure from Egypt. The word tabernacle (*shakhan*) means "to inhabit or to reside" and was the symbol of God's presence among His people. The laity (artisans) built it, but Moses was to assemble it according to the blueprint of assembly that God had given him. Thus, these verses give us the step-by-step details of both the assembly and the placing of the artifacts and furniture within the tabernacle. Everything had a particular place in the tabernacle, according to its function and the significance of its service to the Lord.

Moses hung the curtains (veil) that separated the Holy of Holies from the Holy Place, and the ark of the covenant sat in the Holy of Holies. The ark of the covenant was a sacred box that contained the testimony of God (the Law), Aaron's rod, and a remnant of the manna that the people ate while in the wilderness. On top of the ark were two winged creatures and the object resting upon the ark called the "mercy seat." The ark was the embodiment of the very presence of God and access to it was restricted; it was only to be approached once a year on the Day of Atonement by the high priest as he offered burnt offerings on behalf of the sins of the people. Finally, the Aaronic priesthood had not yet been consecrated, so it is noteworthy that Moses was the priestly leader of the people at this point in their history. He was the only consecrated leader and provided spiritual guidance in the absence of the priestly order. However, once the Aaronic priesthood was consecrated, *they* would serve the Lord in the tabernacle and offer sacrifices to the Lord on behalf of the people (see verses 13-15). This section is of little news other than the fact that Moses followed the instructions of the Lord and it pleased the Lord. Terence E. Fretheim

says, "Obedience is an external demonstration of loyalty to Yahweh." Thus, there is no substitute for obedience in the kingdom of God—and although much credence is given today to praise and "naming it and claiming it," obedience was the most sacred thing in the Old Testament and the most sacred act we can render to the Lord.

B. Following Instructions—Part 2 (Exodus 40:24-30)

And he put the candlestick in the tent of the congregation, over against the table, on the side of the tabernacle southward. And he lighted the lamps before the Lord; as the Lord commanded Moses. And he put the golden altar in the tent of the congregation before the vail: And he burnt sweet incense thereon; as the Lord commanded Moses. And he set up the hanging at the door of the tabernacle. And he put the altar of burnt offering by the door of the tabernacle of the tent of the congregation, and offered upon it the burnt offering and the meat offering; as the Lord commanded Moses. And he set the laver between the tent of the congregation and the altar, and put water there, to wash withal.

The Holy Place was the foyer of the Holy of Holies and was a kind of anteroom for the preparation of worship for the high priest before he entered the Holy of Holies. In the Holy Place sat the table of showbread, the golden lamp stand, and the altar of incense. The golden lamp stand had seven oil lamps that provided the only light in the tabernacle and was representative of the fact that where God dwells, there is light. The table of showbread and the altar of incense were also symbolic; however, the richer symbolism of these artifacts will be given later in the book of Leviticus. The significance of their arrangements was such because it was the Lord's house. God worked through Moses to make holy the tabernacle (verses 9-11, 13). "Take the anointing oil and anoint the tabernacle and everything in it; consecrate it and all its furnishings, and it will be holy. Then anoint the altar of burnt offering and all its utensils; consecrate the altar, and it will be most holy. Anoint the basin and its stand and consecrate them. Then dress Aaron in the sacred garments, anoint him, and consecrate him so he may serve me as priest. Bring his sons and dress them in tunics. Anoint them just as you anointed their father, so they may serve me as priests. Their anointing will be to a priesthood that will continue for all generations to come." The text then says, "Moses did everything just as the LORD commanded him." (See Exodus 40:9-16.)

Then the basin of water was put in place for Moses, Aaron, and his sons to wash their hands and feet before they entered into the presence of the Lord. The importance of obedience to God cannot be overemphasized. There are eighteen references to Moses' doing as God commanded (35–40), which suggests that one's holiness is a function of obedience. If the prophet was right—that "obedience is better than sacrifice" (1 Samuel 15:22)—then it does not matter what one's worship/sacrifice is if he/she has not done as the Lord commanded. It is interesting that it is the small things that often trip us up in our spiritual sojourn. This is why Jesus said, "Whosoever can be trusted with very little can also be trusted with much, and whosoever is dishonest with very little will also be dishonest with much." We must be obedient in doing the smallest of things that God commands us to do; otherwise, our worship is in vain. As Moses did everything the Lord had commanded, so must we.

C. God's Presence Shows Up!
(Exodus 40:34, 38)

Then a cloud covered the tent of the congregation, and the glory of the Lord filled the tabernacle. ... For the cloud of the LORD was upon the tabernacle by day, and fire was on it by night, in the sight of all the house of Israel, throughout all their journeys.

Again, chapter 40 closes with an adverb of time: *then.* "Then the cloud covered the Tent of Meeting and the glory of the LORD filled the tabernacle" (verse 34). The antecedent to these last two verses was Moses' obedience, so after Moses did all that the Lord had commanded, then God responded with His presence, and the glory of God filled the tabernacle. God is willing to be present with His people, but only in God's holiness. This passage makes it clear that God's holiness cannot be compromised by His people. It is not enough to be chosen or to have the favor of God on our lives; we have a responsibility to live up to the divine expectations for our lives.

Finally, the "b" part of verse 38 tells us that the tabernacle was a mobile structure that traveled with the people of Israel as they journeyed to the Land of Promise. As they traveled from place to place, God's presence went with them. This was their reassurance and this is our assurance—that God's people are not sent out alone into a world that is hostile and filled with challenges; God is with us. The faithfulness of God is evident in the tabernacle as God resided among His people. Therefore, the God of the Hebrew people is also our God, and He will not lead us to a place where He will not go and cannot keep us. The hymnologist says appropriately, "In shady, green pastures, so rich and so sweet, God leads His dear children along; where the water's cool flow bathes the weary one's feet, God leads His dear children along. Some through the waters, some through the flood, some through the fire, but all through the blood; some through great sorrow, but God gives a song, in the night season and all the day long." Indeed, God is with us as we journey through life!

III. CONCLUDING REFLECTION

God's presence was in the tabernacle, and He resided among the people. The tabernacle was the visible image of God's presence among the people. The tabernacle was what the church is supposed to be today—the place of God's dwelling and presence in the world; but unfortunately, for too many, the church has become a symbol of human activity and culture. I had a conversation recently with an associate who said that he knows many persons, like himself, who are refugees from the church-persons—"who have been hurt or offended by the culture of the church and are in rebellion against her." Perhaps, the church has come to identify with culture and human activity rather than with the presence of God in our communities.

Finally, one of the themes expressed so vividly in the last chapters (see 39–40) of the book of Exodus is "finish." The workers finished the construction of the tabernacle (see 39:32). Then they brought it to Moses and he assembled it, putting everything in place until it was finished (40:33). The word *finish* in the Hebrew language carries the idea of a task being accomplished. The people and Moses finished their assignment according to divine instruction, but God's will and plan for the people was accomplished only in their obedience.

PRAYER

Eternal God, our Father, we are grateful that You are omnipresent in the world and there is no place we can go from Your presence. Let our lives bring glory and honor to Your name. In Jesus' name we pray. Amen.

WORD POWER

Rituals—performance of formal acts: the observance of actions or procedures in a set, ordered, and ceremonial way.

Symbol—something that represents something else: something that stands for or represents something else, especially an object representing an abstraction.

Tabernacle—a tent for carrying the ark of the covenant: in the Bible, a portable tent used as a sanctuary for the ark of the covenant by the Israelites during the Exodus.

HOME DAILY BIBLE READINGS
(November 18-24, 2013)

Beginning of the Tabernacle

MONDAY, November 18: "Offering Our Possessions" (Exodus 35:4-9)
TUESDAY, November 19: "Offering Our Skills" (Exodus 35:10-19)
WEDNESDAY, November 20: "Stirred Hearts and Willing Spirits" (Exodus 35:20-29)
THURSDAY, November 21: "Skills for Every Kind of Work" (Exodus 35:30-35)
FRIDAY, November 22: "An Overabundance of Offerings" (Exodus 36:2-7)
SATURDAY, November 23: "Blessing the Faithful Workers" (Exodus 39:32-43)
SUNDAY, November 24: "God Affirms the Completed Work" (Exodus 40:16-30, 34, 38)

Jesus and the Just Reign of God

GENERAL INTRODUCTION

This quarter has three units centering on the overall theme of "justice." God's power is proclaimed through the person of Jesus Christ, resulting in Christians' being empowered to live under God's rule.

Unit I, *God Sends Jesus,* is a five-lesson study. The gospel of Luke is the biblical context for these lessons. Lesson 1 presents readers with the prophecy regarding the birth of Jesus. Lesson 2 recounts Mary's response to the angel's announcement concerning her future. In lesson 3, Zachariah prophesied concerning his son, John, who would be the forerunner of the Lord. Lesson 4 recalls the Christmas story of Jesus' birth. In lesson 5, Jesus is presented as the Messiah and a light to the Gentiles.

Unit II, *Jesus Ushers in the Reign of God,* has four lessons. These lessons continue the study from the book of Luke. The first lesson encourages us to honor the Sabbath. The second lesson challenges us to live as God's people. The third lesson instructs us concerning Jesus' teachings about relationships. The fourth lesson looks at Jesus' teachings concerning compassion for the poor.

Unit III, *Live Justly in the Reign of God,* is a four-lesson study on the book of James. The first lesson provides a challenge for us to hear and do the Word. The second lesson is an admonishment for us to treat everyone equally and not show preference for those who "have" at the expense of those who "have not." In the third lesson, James encouraged believers to show their faith by their works. The final lesson contains a challenge for believers to control their speech.

LESSON 1   December 1, 2013 (First Sunday in Advent)

JESUS' BIRTH FORETOLD

FAITH PATHWAY/FAITH JOURNEY TOPIC: Surprised and Expectant

DEVOTIONAL READING: Psalm 89:1-7
PRINT PASSAGE: Luke 1:26-40

BACKGROUND SCRIPTURE: Luke 1:26-45
KEY VERSE: Luke 1:31

Luke 1:26-40—KJV

26 And in the sixth month the angel Gabriel was sent from God unto a city of Galilee, named Nazareth,

27 To a virgin espoused to a man whose name was Joseph, of the house of David; and the virgin's name was Mary.

28 And the angel came in unto her, and said, Hail, thou that art highly favoured, the Lord is with thee: blessed art thou among women.

29 And when she saw him, she was troubled at his saying, and cast in her mind what manner of salutation this should be.

30 And the angel said unto her, Fear not, Mary: for thou hast found favour with God.

31 And, behold, thou shalt conceive in thy womb, and bring forth a son, and shalt call his name JESUS.

32 He shall be great, and shall be called the Son of the Highest: and the Lord God shall give unto him the throne of his father David:

33 And he shall reign over the house of Jacob for ever; and of his kingdom there shall be no end.

34 Then said Mary unto the angel, How shall this be, seeing I know not a man?

35 And the angel answered and said unto her, The Holy Ghost shall come upon thee, and the power of the Highest shall overshadow thee: therefore also that holy thing which shall be born of thee shall be called the Son of God.

36 And, behold, thy cousin Elisabeth, she hath also conceived a son in her old age: and this is the sixth month with her, who was called barren.

37 For with God nothing shall be impossible.

38 And Mary said, Behold the handmaid of the Lord; be it unto me according to thy word. And the angel departed from her.

39 And Mary arose in those days, and went into the hill country with haste, into a city of Judah;

Luke 1:26-40—NIV

26 In the sixth month, God sent the angel Gabriel to Nazareth, a town in Galilee,

27 to a virgin pledged to be married to a man named Joseph, a descendant of David. The virgin's name was Mary.

28 The angel went to her and said, "Greetings, you who are highly favored! The Lord is with you."

29 Mary was greatly troubled at his words and wondered what kind of greeting this might be.

30 But the angel said to her, "Do not be afraid, Mary, you have found favor with God.

31 You will be with child and give birth to a son, and you are to give him the name Jesus.

32 He will be great and will be called the Son of the Most High. The Lord God will give him the throne of his father David,

33 and he will reign over the house of Jacob forever; his kingdom will never end."

34 "How will this be," Mary asked the angel, "since I am a virgin?"

35 The angel answered, "The Holy Spirit will come upon you, and the power of the Most High will overshadow you. So the holy one to be born will be called the Son of God.

36 Even Elizabeth your relative is going to have a child in her old age, and she who was said to be barren is in her sixth month.

37 For nothing is impossible with God."

38 "I am the Lord's servant," Mary answered. "May it be to me as you have said." Then the angel left her.

39 At that time Mary got ready and hurried to a town in the hill country of Judea,

UNIFYING LESSON PRINCIPLE

People are always amazed and often perplexed when unexpected things happen in their lives. How can Christians handle these unanticipated events that occur? Mary responded at first with surprise and then with dedication to the angel's announcement about the birth of her baby.

40 And entered into the house of Zacharias, and saluted Elisabeth.

40 where she entered Zechariah's home and greeted Elizabeth.

TOPICAL OUTLINE OF THE LESSON

I. Introduction
A. Behind the Scenes of Jesus' Birth
B. Biblical Background

II. Exposition and Application of the Scripture
A. An Expectant People (Luke 1:26-28)
B. Mary's Surprise (Luke 1:29-38)
C. Mary's Good News and Elizabeth's Joy (Luke 1:39-40)

III. Concluding Reflection

LESSON OBJECTIVES

Upon the completion of the lesson, the students will be able to do the following:

1. Review the foretelling of Jesus' birth;
2. Reflect on the unexpected and perplexing events of their lives; and,
3. Dedicate themselves to the purposes of God.

POINTS TO BE EMPHASIZED

ADULT/YOUTH
Adult Topic: Surprised and Expectant
Youth Topic: Coming Near You
Adult/Youth Key Verse: Luke 1:31
Print Passage: Luke 1:26-40

— The angel Gabriel was sent to a culturally and economically insignificant city called Nazareth.
— The word *favor* was mentioned twice, and it affirmed God's selection of Mary as the vehicle (channel) through whom the Messiah would be born.
— Mary questioned the angel's prophecy and pointed out the obstacles involving the fulfillment of the prophecy—as did Abraham and Sarah. (See Genesis 17:17-18; 18:9-15.)
— Mary accepted God's purpose for her life and declared her faith in the angel's words.
— After journeying to Judea, Mary found Elizabeth, and Elizabeth's baby recognized the presence of the Lord and leapt for joy.

CHILDREN
Children Topic: A Special Gift
Key Verses: Luke 1:30-31, 32a
Print Passage: Luke 1:26-38

—God chose to use a young, poor female, who lived in an insignificant town, for one of the most important acts of obedience.
—God's favor upon Mary led to great pain and it carried no guarantee of earthly fame or success; but it included the world's only hope for salvation.
—God sent Jesus, His own Son, to fulfill God's promise to King David—to establish a kingdom that will never end.
—God's Son was named Jesus, and He came to save people and lead them to eternal life.
—Jesus was both human and divine.

I. INTRODUCTION

A. Behind the Scenes of Jesus' Birth

Beginning with this lesson, the students will engage in a series of five lessons that respond to the question of why God sent Jesus into the world. To understand the biblical narratives of Jesus' birth, one must understand the ancient worldview of prophecy that underlines Jesus' universal meaning as Savior of the world. To understand how Jesus became accepted as Lord and Christ for first-century followers and for Christians worldwide, the whole of Jesus' life must be held together—beginning with His birth at Bethlehem and ending in a cruel execution on a Roman cross. It is also important to understand that the ordinary occurrences of human life were used as channels for the incarnation of God in the world.

The gospel of Luke offers another perspective of Jesus' birth that is different from Matthew's account. Luke and Matthew were the only gospel writers who provided a biblical birth narrative. What did Luke believe to be the most significant thing for his readers to understand about Jesus' birth? This is the question that this lesson seeks to answer.

Luke was not concerned with practical matters of Jesus' birth, but with the sacred, transcendent purpose and meaning it held for human existence. Thus, biblical myths help us link life to matters of ultimate concern and how life connects to or fits in the scheme of God's world. Luke's birth narrative, properly understood, conveys the idea that we exist in God through ordinary circumstances of family, work, community living, and the common struggles of human life. In Luke's ancient world, such meaning was revealed through angelic appearances and announcements, a free-moving star that guided the shepherds, and dreams—all of which were a part of God's active presence in the events surrounding Jesus' birth. When the meaning of Jesus' birth is understood from Luke's worldview and filtered through contemporary struggles for spiritual meaning and purposeful existence, we can better attend to the stirrings of God within ourselves and open our familiar relationships for the activity and purpose of God.

B. Biblical Background

There are two birth narratives in the New Testament gospels—one written by Matthew and the other by Luke. The community to whom Luke wrote was influenced by Greek culture. Matthew's story was to link Jewish heritage and prophecy, which sought to confirm God's power and presence in the origin and roots of Judaism, beginning with Abraham. Luke's gospel was written from a universal perspective of the Greek world, which included material that expands the hope of Judaism to the universal Gentile world (see Acts 1:8). Matthew began his genealogy of Jesus with Abraham, the father of the Jewish nation. Luke, in contrast, traced the genealogy of Jesus all the way back to Adam. If Gentiles were to be incorporated into the divine promise, as was Luke's concern, then Adam, the father of all—not Abraham—was the common point of origin.

Jesus was born when Herod was king of Judea (see Matthew 2:1; Luke 1:5). Luke went on to say that the birth occurred when Quirinius was governor of Syria (see Luke 2:2).

The characters in Luke's birth narrative were as follows: Mary, a virgin teenager who accepted God's will for the miracle conception of Jesus; Joseph, who was engaged to marry Mary and, after a dream, trusted God for what the unexpected pregnancy of Mary meant for his life; and Elizabeth and Zechariah (Elizabeth was a cousin of Mary), the parents of John. They were all deeply vested in the messianic tradition and lived with the hope of a deliverer bringing God's salvation into the world.

II. EXPOSITION AND APPLICATION OF THE SCRIPTURE

A. An Expectant People
(Luke 1:26-28)

And in the sixth month the angel Gabriel was sent from God unto a city of Galilee, named Nazareth, To a virgin espoused to a man whose name was Joseph, of the house of David; and the virgin's name was Mary. And the angel came in unto her, and said, Hail, thou that art highly favoured, the Lord is with thee: blessed art thou among women.

Mary, Joseph, Elizabeth, and Zechariah were expectant Jews living daily with the hope of the coming of God's kingdom. Luke's birth narrative was written from the perspective of the Jewish experience waiting for God to bring *Shalom* (*Shelama*, the Aramaic equivalent of "peace") to their land. When Jesus was born, the word *shalom* gained fresh vigor for every Jew under Roman dominance who saw Jesus' birth as fulfillment of the enduring covenant and promise of God to Abraham. Mary and Joseph, Elizabeth and Zechariah lived as other Jews—with the hope and promise of *Shalom*.

Luke was very much aware of the first-century climate of oppression in which Jesus was born, and how devastating it was to the Jewish community. New Testament scholar Obery M. Hendricks, in his book, *The Politics of Jesus: Rediscovering the True Revolutionary Nature of Jesus' Teachings and How They Have Been Corrupted,* points out that around the time Jesus was born, the ancient historian Josephus documented that the Roman military crucified some two thousand people in the Galilean city of Sepphoris as punishment for rebelling against Roman rule. It was in this kind of environment of continuous threats of violence—enduring defeat, genocide, and colonized oppression at the hand of past oppressors, along with the prejudice and dominance of the Roman Empire—that we find the expectant promise of Shalom in the hope of Zechariah and Elizabeth, Mary and Joseph. Generation after generation, the expectation of freedom through the coming of the Messiah was the faith that undergirded the prayers and worship of every Jew. Obedience to the covenant and through the ritual of offering the appropriate sacrifice to God kept hope alive in the Jewish community. Annual pilgrimages were taken by Jewish families to the Temple in Jerusalem in order to offer sacrifices to God. Worship renewed the people who were constantly under the threat of the Roman Empire. They took refuge in the covenant of God as their only hope for a new future. They were an expectant people whose hope refused to be buried in Roman oppression.

The theological power of the story of Jesus' birth broke upon the scene in Judea in the first century and then moved on to supplant the Roman Empire in the fourth century—opening up for us all a way to enter the reality of God.

B. Mary's Surprise
(Luke 1:29-38)

And when she saw him, she was troubled at his saying, and cast in her mind what manner of salutation this should be. And the angel said unto her, Fear not, Mary: for thou hast found favour with God. And, behold, thou shalt conceive in thy womb, and bring forth a son, and shalt call his name JESUS. He shall be great, and shall be called the Son of the Highest: and the Lord God shall give unto him the throne of his father David: And he shall reign over the house of Jacob for ever; and of his kingdom there shall be no end. Then said Mary unto the angel, How shall this be, seeing I know not a man? And the angel answered and said unto her, The Holy Ghost shall come upon thee, and the power of the Highest shall overshadow thee: therefore also that holy thing which shall be born of thee shall be called the Son of God. And, behold, thy cousin Elisabeth, she hath also conceived a son in her old age: and this is the sixth month with her, who was called barren. For with God nothing shall be impossible. And Mary said, Behold the handmaid of the Lord; be it unto me according to thy word. And the angel departed from her.

Many Christians are angered or feel deceived when others suggest that Jesus was not born of a virgin and that a star did not travel through the sky and come to rest over a particular place in Bethlehem. Luke's intent was not to report the scientific or biological facts about how Jesus was born, but to report the reason why Jesus was born. The strength of the Christian faith provides people with a context that makes sense of life; it directs attention to the eternal and the universal meaning of Jesus' life. Luke's account of the Virgin Birth cannot be demonstrated by rational proofs. Rather, what is worthy of our faith is Luke's intuitive theological insights about its meaning and how its reality became embodied in the faith, rituals, and worship of Mary and Joseph, Elizabeth and Zechariah—and in our faith, rituals, and worship today.

Mary was surprised at the announcement that she had been favored by God to be the mother of "the Son of the Most High." Jesus was conceived before Mary was married to Joseph. The early pregnancy perhaps touched off vicious rumors in the surrounding neighborhoods about Jesus' paternity. Mary's response to the angel's announcement—"But how can this happen? I am a virgin" (verse 34)—is at the center of this controversy. Concerning the birth account of Jesus, neither Luke nor Matthew focused on the biological virginity of Mary, except for declaring that Jesus' miraculous birth fulfilled prophecy from the Scripture of Israel (see Isaiah 7:14).

Luke's story invokes within our faith a theological sense of the sacredness of Jesus' birth, enabling us to grasp the deeper truths of God's presence and action in the world. This was indeed Mary's surprise—that her own agency and body had been chosen as the vessel for birthing the One whose kingdom would last forever (see Luke 1:33). As Christians, we embrace the belief that a loving God is active in the affairs of the world. The fact that Jesus was born into the world as the Son of God validates our faith. We believe that the Jesus of history, who was born of Mary, became the Christ of faith. We believe that Jesus is the bringer of peace; we believe He is Savior of the world.

The early church needed celebrations to remind Christians who they were. The Advent season, the Lord's Supper, and baptism became the avenues through which to remember the birth, death, and resurrection of Jesus. For Luke, the birth narrative was the perfect symbol for a celebration of God's reign through Jesus' coming into the world. Luke proclaimed this message with poetic beauty in his birth narrative. When Luke's birth story is put into its broader historic and religious context of sacred transmission and symbol, it becomes a theological narration of truth telling and a witness to the joyful fulfillment of life.

Throughout the Christian story and in the history of human existence, the surprises of God turn up in unsuspecting people and places. No one would have suspected that the providential arrangements of God would have included a peasant teenage girl as the mother of Jesus.

C. Mary's Good News and Elizabeth's Joy (Luke 1:39-40)

And Mary arose in those days, and went into the hill country with haste, into a city of Judah; And entered into the house of Zacharias, and saluted Elisabeth.

When Mary visited her cousin Elizabeth in the hill country of Judea, Elizabeth was filled with the Holy Spirit. Elizabeth was also pregnant at that time with the one who would become known as John the Baptist, whom Scripture describes as the forerunner and preparer of the way for the Messiah (see John 1:6-10, 15). Luke portrayed Mary and Joseph (the parents of Jesus) and Elizabeth and Zechariah (the parents of John) after the pattern of Abraham and Sarah from the book of Genesis. Both sets of parents were called righteous (see Genesis 11:30; Luke 1:6-7). In both stories, the angelic annunciation came to a disbelieving father (see Genesis 18:11;

Luke 1:11-13). Both fathers were assured that nothing was impossible with God (see Genesis 18:14; Luke 1:37).

Why did Luke write the birth narrative of Jesus in the light of the Genesis stories? Luke was convinced of the theological connection of the founding fathers and mothers of Israel to Jesus, who was to inaugurate the New Israel into the world.

In the light of this same purpose, Luke's story of the birth of Jesus also parallels that of Isaac's wife, Rebekah, who was expecting twins. Genesis 25:19-23 informs us that these unborn children struggled in Rebekah's womb, and she went to inquire of the Lord about them. The word of the Lord that Rebekah heard in the Genesis story was that the destiny of these two boys had been set by divine providence while they were still in the womb. It was revealed that the older one, who would be named Esau, would serve the younger one, who would be named Jacob (see Genesis 25:19-23).

After Mary learned that her pregnancy was a part of divine providence, she went to visit her cousin, Elizabeth, who was also pregnant. When she arrived, the babe in Elizabeth's womb leapt to acknowledge the lordship of Jesus, who was still in Mary's womb. The destiny of these two lives, like Jacob and Esau, was revealed while they were still in the womb. That destiny was that the older would serve the younger.

Elizabeth's words of joy at the news of Mary's pregnancy explain the content of the living hope which she and many Jews nurtured for centuries. "God has blessed you above all women, and your child is blessed. Why am I so honored, that the mother of my Lord should visit me?" (verse 43).

III. CONCLUDING REFLECTION

God's response to a despairing people whose identity and future were under siege by Roman oppression was the birth of a child. A young teenager just beginning to make choices about her life in the context of Jewish culture under the colonized rule of the Roman Empire willingly became the vessel, through providential arrangements, that would make real the promise of God's kingdom. Mary was surprised and confused, but the overwhelming expectancy of a new kingdom gave rise to humble submission to the will of God.

This kind of expectant hope has long lived in the faith tradition and sojourn of black people in America. God has answered the pleas regarding the oppression of black people with liberation and salvation through the birth of a child. It is akin to what the black religious mystic Howard Thurman describes in his book, *The Growing Edge*: "Old worlds are dying and new worlds are being born." Thurman further says that God's most dramatic answer to death, destruction, and human despair is the birth of a child. In the midst of human suffering, oppression, blood, sweat, and tears, the Christ experience has prevailed through black people's unrelenting faith in the One who was born of Mary and died under Pontius Pilate.

In our contemporary day of evil and injustice, we would do well to look to the divine—"the growing edge"—with an expectant faith in God's eternal purpose and enduring reign of peace through Jesus, who has become God's Christ and our Lord.

PRAYER

Our Father, for those who have lost hope in the future, we pray that Jesus' life will renew them spiritually and make them expectant of life's new possibilities with God. In Jesus' name we pray. Amen.

WORD POWER

Jesus Christ—considered by Christians to be the promised deliverer.
Messiah—in Judaism, the awaited redeemer of the Jews, to be sent by God to free them.
Virgin Birth—the doctrine that Jesus was miraculously begotten by God and born of the Virgin Mary without the agency of a human father. (Read more: http://www.answers.com/topic/virgin-birth#ixzz2IizJC9yo.)

HOME DAILY BIBLE READINGS
(November 25–December 1, 2013)

Jesus' Birth Foretold
MONDAY, November 25: "A Covenant with David" (Psalm 89:1-7)
TUESDAY, November 26: "God's Faithfulness and Steadfast Love" (Psalm 89:19-24)
WEDNESDAY, November 27: "The Highest of Earthly Kings" (Psalm 89:26-34)
THURSDAY, November 28: "A Promise for a Distant Future" (2 Samuel 7:18-29)
FRIDAY, November 29: "A Child Named Immanuel" (Isaiah 7:10-15)
SATURDAY, November 30: "Elizabeth's Blessing" (Luke 1:41-45)
SUNDAY, December 1: "The Announcement to Mary" (Luke 1:26-40)

LESSON 2   December 8, 2013

MARY'S SONG OF PRAISE

Faith Pathway/Faith Journey Topic: Jubilant!

Devotional Reading: Psalm 111
Print Passage: Luke 1:46-56

Background Scripture: Luke 1:46-56
Key Verse: Luke 1:47

Luke 1:46-56—KJV

46 And Mary said, My soul doth magnify the Lord,

47 And my spirit hath rejoiced in God my Saviour.

48 For he hath regarded the low estate of his handmaiden: for, behold, from henceforth all generations shall call me blessed.

49 For he that is mighty hath done to me great things; and holy is his name.

50 And his mercy is on them that fear him from generation to generation.

51 He hath shewed strength with his arm; he hath scattered the proud in the imagination of their hearts.

52 He hath put down the mighty from their seats, and exalted them of low degree.

53 He hath filled the hungry with good things; and the rich he hath sent empty away.

54 He hath holpen his servant Israel, in remembrance of his mercy;

55 As he spake to our fathers, to Abraham, and to his seed for ever.

56 And Mary abode with her about three months, and returned to her own house.

Luke 1:46-56—NIV

46 And Mary said: "My soul glorifies the Lord

47 and my spirit rejoices in God my Savior,

48 for he has been mindful of the humble state of his servant. From now on all generations will call me blessed,

49 for the Mighty One has done great things for me—holy is his name.

50 His mercy extends to those who fear him, from generation to generation.

51 He has performed mighty deeds with his arm; he has scattered those who are proud in their inmost thoughts.

52 He has brought down rulers from their thrones but has lifted up the humble.

53 He has filled the hungry with good things but has sent the rich away empty.

54 He has helped his servant Israel, remembering to be merciful

55 to Abraham and his descendants forever, even as he said to our fathers."

56 Mary stayed with Elizabeth for about three months and then returned home.

BIBLE FACT

Mary's Song of Praise is called "The Magnificat." The Latin name comes from the phrase that begins the hymn. Mary praised God for how He had treated her and how He had/has treated the righteous throughout the ages.

UNIFYING LESSON PRINCIPLE

People usually respond with great joy when good things happen to them. What is the origin of such joyful responses? Mary responded from the depths of her soul by praising her God of justice for receiving such a wonderful gift.

TOPICAL OUTLINE OF THE LESSON

I. Introduction
A. Mary Magnifies God for His Salvation
B. Biblical Background

II. Exposition and Application of the Scripture
A. Mary's Image of God (Luke 1:46-50)
B. God's Dream Is Mary's Praise (Luke 1:51-53)
C. The Universal Elements in Mary's Praise (Luke 1:54-56)

III. Concluding Reflection

LESSON OBJECTIVES

Upon the completion of the lesson, the students will be able to do the following:

1. Explore themes of justice in Mary's song of praise;
2. Appreciate the deepest meanings of praise in response to God; and,
3. Develop new ways of praising God.

POINTS TO BE EMPHASIZED

ADULT/YOUTH

Adult Topic: Jubilant!
Youth Topic: Joy
Adult Key Verse: Luke 1:47
Youth Key Verses: Luke 1:46-47
Print Passage: Luke 1:46-56

—"The Magnificat" was based largely on Hannah's prayer (see 1 Samuel 2:1-10).
—The poor, who have nothing to lose, seem best able to receive God's grace.
—The self-defined "low estate" of Mary paralleled the servant theme of Jesus and the servant songs of Isaiah.
—Mary verified the angel's prophecy in her song to God.
—Mary expressed her praise to God in her song called "The Magnificat." Notice the similarities between her song, Zechariah's song (Benedictus; see Luke 1:68-79), and the prayer of Simeon (Nunc Dimittis; see Luke 2:29-32).
—Mary's song of praise foreshadowed the major themes of Luke's gospel (ministry to the poor, feeding the hungry, and so forth).

CHILDREN

Children Topic: A Mother Rejoices
Key Verses: Luke 1:46-47, 49
Print Passage: Luke 1:39-50, 54-56

—Mary hastened to visit her elderly cousin Elizabeth because the angel said that God had already wrought a miraculous conception in Elizabeth's womb.
—God's Spirit revealed to Elizabeth that Mary had conceived the Messiah—for Elizabeth greeted Mary as "the mother of my Lord."

—Elizabeth's joyous greeting to Mary strengthened her young cousin's belief that nothing is impossible with God.

—Mary glorified God in song for what He was going to do through her for the world.

—Mary humbly and joyfully recognized and accepted the favored gifts that God had given to her.

—Mary was a young woman, yet she understood that the Messiah's birth fulfilled God's promise.

I. INTRODUCTION

A. Mary Magnifies God for His Salvation

The lesson study today highlights Mary's song. Mary's song, called "The Magnificat," in many ways parallels Hannah's prayer of praise in 1 Samuel 2:1-10.

Mary's song, like Hannah's, highlights the praise of God for bringing down the rich and powerful and exalting the poor and downtrodden (see 1 Samuel 2:7-8; Luke 1:52-55). From the historical perspective of black churches in America, Mary's song of praise has similar features of the spiritual songs of black folk who endured the hardship of slavery. Both Mary's song of praise and the known "Negro Spirituals" are examples of music developed out of the belief that the nature and character of God are devoted to justice. This is why black Christians in particular find Mary's song about the justice and mercy of God inspiring. Against disillusionment, despair, and the vicissitudes of American history, the religious traditions of black people hold to a faith that believes that at the center of God's creation is the principle of love in the service of justice.

The black Christian tradition parallels the Jewish tradition—in the belief that God is a God of justice. We shall learn through the study of Mary's song how important it is to worship God with songs of praise and lives that reflect God's justice. Students should pay particular attention to how Mary committed herself willingly as an instrument of God's mercy and justice in the world. The theological emphasis of Mary's song is that Christians should strive to better know the will of God in their personal lives and conduct, but they should also do justice in the world.

B. Biblical Background

In our previous lesson study, students saw how first-century Jews were under the constant strain of Roman injustice, subjugation, and oppression. The emperor Augustus extolled himself as the savior and lord of *Pax romana,* a season of peace in the Roman Empire. The village in which Mary and Joseph lived was under the constant strain of structural poverty and political subjugation. Roman oppression touched virtually every facet of life among the Jews.

After many years of the debilitating effects of impoverishment and Roman oppression, the psychological and emotional health of Jewish villagers clung to the messianic hope of a deliverer. Luke highlighted this feature of hope in Mary's song as she responded to being chosen to be the mother of Jesus. The announcement to Mary that she was chosen to be the mother of Jesus was for her the realization that the prophet's sign of Emmanuel, as the triumph over oppression and injustice, was no longer a dream deferred—because through Jesus, God's deliverance had come. Mary praised God for Jesus as the bringer of a new age of liberation and justice.

As the students will see in the study of this lesson, praise and justice are inseparable elements in Mary's song.

II. EXPOSITION AND APPLICATION OF THE SCRIPTURE

A. Mary's Image of God
(Luke 1:46-50)

And Mary said, My soul doth magnify the Lord, And my spirit hath rejoiced in God my Saviour. For he hath regarded the low estate of his handmaiden: for, behold, from henceforth all generations shall call me blessed. For he that is mighty hath done to me great things; and holy is his name. And his mercy is on them that fear him from generation to generation.

Mary's song of praise begins with a poetic lyric that describes her relationship with God. The religious identity, cultural heritage, and political context of Mary's life were radically impacted by the news of the angel Gabriel. Mary's personal anxiety shifted to that of praising God as she accepted her chosen role to be the mother of Jesus. Mary's image of herself and the image of God brought about spiritual fulfillment that she had not known before receiving the news of God's favoring her life as a channel for the miraculous activity of divine providence.

Mary's praise of God as Savior is the primary theme of her song. Verse 47 is theologically clear: God is our Savior. The image Mary had of God as Savior is theologically consistent with the voices of Moses, the prophets, and Jesus' own understanding of the imminent reign of God. Mary knew the tradition of conflict between God's covenant people and the empires that oppressed Israel. The historical backdrop of Mary's song was the conflict between the lordship of God and the lordship of the emperor—the kingship of Herod or the kingship of Jesus. The lens through which Mary understood this history is through the God-human relationship and the image of God as Savior, who is "the mighty and holy one" (verse 49). These images of God come out of the Hebrew tradition of seeing God as a deliverer, a righteous lawgiver, and a King above all earthly kings and kingdoms. Mary's reference of God as "the Mighty One" models God as a transcendent power that subverts the existing social order of injustice and replaces it with a new order of divine mercy and justice. Mary's acknowledgment of God as Savior expressed the desperate need of the lowly, the poor, the oppressed, and the hungry.

Mary's view of God changed and impacted the view she had of herself and the context of her community's struggle for alternatives to Roman rule. Mary's faith was shaped by the hope that the radical reversal of injustice would occur and the new social order of God's kingdom was soon to come. The kingdom of God, in Mary's understanding, would be the basis of radical opposition to the existing social order. It was a different vision of individual and social existence for humankind, wherein Mary saw the justice of God at work. Mary saw herself as participating in something larger than even her personal joy of having been chosen as a vessel of God. Mary's joyous humility of being chosen of God became praise for the work of divine justice. "For the Mighty One is holy, and he has done great things for me" (Luke 1:49).

How an individual views God directly relates to how he or she understands God's presence and action in the world. Mary's praise of God reflects an image of God that involves her participation in divine purposes. God is not distant in Mary's understanding of herself and the world she inhabits. God is intimately involved in the day-to-day struggles against the inauthentic realities of Empire oppression. Mary's image of God as a Savior represents the view of first-century Jews who had been recipients throughout their history of God's constant mercies and repeated deliverances. In her phrase, "How my spirit rejoices in God my savior" (Luke 1:47), Mary indicated an awareness that God's salvation was personal and purposive, communal and collective. Mary saw her own salvation bound up and interrelated with the movement of God to bring salvation to all the people. Mary also recognized that her social status was not a barrier in God's choice of her. Although a poor peasant teenager, Mary was God's choice as an instrument for divine action.

B. God's Dream Is Mary's Praise (Luke 1:51-53)

He hath shewed strength with his arm; he hath scattered the proud in the imagination of their hearts. He hath put down the mighty from their seats, and exalted them of low degree. He hath filled the hungry with good things; and the rich he hath sent empty away.

Mary's song is reflective of Jewish history and hope for "the Son of God," the Anointed One. Such titles as "Messiah" were given to earthly personalities whose lives reflected the hope of deliverance. This began with the coronation of King David and it ended in the destruction of Jerusalem at the time of the Babylonian exile (586 BC). After this time, when no human occupant was sitting on the Jewish throne, the Jewish people began to dream of the ideal king who would someday restore the throne of David and who would inaugurate anew the kingdom of God.

The Jews were indentured subjects of the Roman Empire, and their cultural and religious activities were confined within the restrictions of Roman governance. In addition, the pervasive political power of Rome also defined who they were in terms of social status, rendering them to be a part of a permanent underclass. But in Mary's village community, the dream of God for them was alive in their faith. In every way, Roman society attempted to turn the Jewish dream of the "anointed one" into a nightmare of brokenness and social abandonment. The covenant promise of the dawning of the kingdom of God was their last defense against the seemingly permanent control of Rome over their lives and future. The Jews believed that God's kingdom would ultimately supersede every form of injustice and oppression suffered by the people. Thus, Mary praised God as the "helper" of Israel who remembered to be merciful to the heritage of Abraham (see Luke 1:54-55). Mary's complete identification of the child in her womb as the one to usher in the reign of God inspired her praise. The dream of God would find fulfillment in Jesus.

With the coming of the kingdom of God, the needs of the people often were an affront to the Roman system and were deemed holy. This is perhaps what Mary meant by uttering the phrase "He [God] has filled the hungry with good things and sent the rich away with empty hands" (Luke 1:53). Radical reversals will take place in the kingdom of God. "Princes are brought down from their throne and the humble are exalted in their place" (Luke 1:52). Indeed, Mary may have seen this reversal as a revolution of love—where the people and their needs were seen as holy.

The ethical mandate of the reign of God is based on the Hebrew biblical concepts of *hesed* (love, strength, and steadfastness) and *justice* (*mishpat* in Hebrew). Justice involves equity, fairness, and the right ordering of relationships. The *King James Version* of the Holy Bible translates *hesed* as "lovingkindness" and *justice* as "righteousness." Mary saw God's mysterious use of her body to birth Jesus as a demonstration of God's *hesed* (steadfast love) and *mishpat* (justice). In other words, God's love is toward justice and is the reason for divine intervention in the plight of the poor. Thus, Mary's praise song is reflective of "[God] shows mercy from generation to generation to all who fear him" (Luke 1:50). The dream of God in the world is the right ordering of relationships. Mary's praise song matches this divine dream.

C. The Universal Elements in Mary's Praise (Luke 1:54-56)

He hath holpen his servant Israel, in remembrance of his mercy; As he spake to our fathers, to Abraham, and to his seed for ever. And Mary abode with her about three months, and returned to her own house.

Mary's whole life was bound up in the reality of Jesus' birth. Through her womb, Mary was the bearer of a "God-presence" into the world. While Mary understood what this meant for her personal life, she was unaware of its full implication for the world around her and even beyond her time. We see this in how Mary lifted up the theme of an everlasting kingdom and its enduring impact on the lives of all people. Mary's song focuses on the particularity of God's response to the plight of the Jews. However, the universal implication of this divine response is beyond the particularity of the Jewish hope for salvation. God, as the Savior of the world, is a theological feature that Luke did not want his audience to miss in Mary's song of praise.

What we learn from reflecting on Mary's song of praise is that a person's worship of God must align with an appropriate image of God. When our image of God is inconsistent with the character of God's work and presence in the world, our praise of God is likely to be off-key and out of sync with God's purpose in the world. The image Mary had of God is consistent with the history and tradition of the Jews. Mary had to interpret the meaning of Jesus for the time in which she lived. Mary's song about the salvation and justice of God reflected what it meant not only for her own life, but also the changes it would bring and the inevitable demands it would make upon the Roman world.

God came among us in Jesus, offering new life, love, healing, and justice. Mary's song of praise lifted faith to the realm of the Spirit as a celebration of God as the Savior of *all* people. This is a salvation where we are transformed by the God we meet in Jesus. Through the salvation Jesus offers, God forgives sin and reconciles our lives to God. This should be not only Mary's praise but also the jubilant praise of every person who trusts and knows the power of this transformation and salvation.

III. CONCLUDING REFLECTION

Mary's song of praise is an affirmation of God's salvation that black churches can fully embrace. The jubilant praise of a people struggling against and overcoming the vicissitudes and injustices in the world is what the worship of God is all about. A common phrase often heard in the worship experience of black churches is, "If the Lord had not been on our side, where would we be?" In 1865, when the Emancipation Proclamation declared freedom in the United States for all slaves, jubilation overwhelmed the souls of the slaves—for salvation had finally come. On that day salvation came in two forms: liberation of the inner self from the psychological bondage of slavery; and transformation of the outward social conditions of slavery that condemned the self. To acknowledge God as our Savior means that we receive who God is into our lives along with what God does, and God's love and justice as the guide for life.

God brought Jesus into the world for the purpose of redeeming the world in justice and love. As Mary trusted God's purpose and gave herself fully to its power in her life, Christians must trust God's salvation in every situation of life. To trust God as Savior means not looking to some other power for salvation. The injustices of the world are mounting in disease, crime, murder, war, and poverty. Neither technology nor social progress, neither education nor legislative reforms, will in and of themselves deliver us from social ruin. Knowledge of God, doing God's will, living inside the reality of God's purpose, and openness to the transformation of both the head and heart are the only ways to salvation.

PRAYER

Thank You, God, for sending Jesus into the world. Our hearts rejoice and praise looms large for the justice, liberation, healing, and salvation we know through Jesus. In Jesus' name we pray. Amen.

WORD POWER

Magnificat—the title commonly given to the Latin text and vernacular translation of the Canticle (or Song) of Mary. It is the opening word of the Vulgate (Latin translation) text of Luke 1:46-55: "Magnificat anima mea, Dominum," etc. (My soul doth magnify the Lord, etc.). (From www.newadvent.org.)

HOME DAILY BIBLE READINGS
(December 2-8, 2013)

Mary's Song of Praise
MONDAY, December 2: "My Heart Exults in the Lord" (1 Samuel 2:1-10)
TUESDAY, December 3: "O Magnify the Lord with Me" (Psalm 34:1-8)
WEDNESDAY, December 4: "Give Thanks to the Lord" (Psalm 100)
THURSDAY, December 5: "Bless the Compassionate Lord" (Psalm 103:13-22)
FRIDAY, December 6: "Praise the Gracious and Merciful Lord" (Psalm 111)
SATURDAY, December 7: "The Lord Reigns for All Generations" (Psalm 146)
SUNDAY, December 8: "God Has Done Great Things" (Luke 1:46-56)

LESSON 3   December 15, 2013

ZECHARIAH PROPHESIES ABOUT HIS SON JOHN

FAITH PATHWAY/FAITH JOURNEY TOPIC: Opening the Way

DEVOTIONAL READING: **Luke 1:59-66**   BACKGROUND SCRIPTURE: **Luke 1:57-80**
PRINT PASSAGE: **Luke 1:57-58, 67-79**   KEY VERSES: **Luke 1:76-77**

Luke 1:57-58, 67-79—KJV

57 Now Elisabeth's full time came that she should be delivered; and she brought forth a son.
58 And her neighbours and her cousins heard how the Lord had shewed great mercy upon her; and they rejoiced with her.

....

67 And his father Zacharias was filled with the Holy Ghost, and prophesied, saying,
68 Blessed be the Lord God of Israel; for he hath visited and redeemed his people,
69 And hath raised up an horn of salvation for us in the house of his servant David;
70 As he spake by the mouth of his holy prophets, which have been since the world began:
71 That we should be saved from our enemies, and from the hand of all that hate us;
72 To perform the mercy promised to our fathers, and to remember his holy covenant;
73 The oath which he sware to our father Abraham,
74 That he would grant unto us, that we being delivered out of the hand of our enemies might serve him without fear,
75 In holiness and righteousness before him, all the days of our life.
76 And thou, child, shalt be called the prophet of the Highest: for thou shalt go before the face of the Lord to prepare his ways;
77 To give knowledge of salvation unto his people by the remission of their sins,

Luke 1:57-58, 67-79—NIV

57 When it was time for Elizabeth to have her baby, she gave birth to a son.
58 Her neighbors and relatives heard that the Lord had shown her great mercy, and they shared her joy.

....

67 His father Zechariah was filled with the Holy Spirit and prophesied:
68 "Praise be to the Lord, the God of Israel, because he has come and has redeemed his people.
69 He has raised up a horn of salvation for us in the house of his servant David
70 (as he said through his holy prophets of long ago),
71 salvation from our enemies and from the hand of all who hate us—
72 to show mercy to our fathers and to remember his holy covenant,
73 the oath he swore to our father Abraham:
74 to rescue us from the hand of our enemies, and to enable us to serve him without fear
75 in holiness and righteousness before him all our days.
76 And you, my child, will be called a prophet of the Most High; for you will go on before the Lord to prepare the way for him,
77 to give his people the knowledge of salvation through the forgiveness of their sins,

78 Through the tender mercy of our God; whereby the dayspring from on high hath visited us,
79 To give light to them that sit in darkness and in the shadow of death, to guide our feet into the way of peace.

78 because of the tender mercy of our God, by which the rising sun will come to us from heaven
79 to shine on those living in darkness and in the shadow of death, to guide our feet into the path of peace."

TOPICAL OUTLINE OF THE LESSON

I. Introduction
  A. The Praise and Rejoicing of Common People
  B. Biblical Background

II. Exposition and Application of the Scripture
  A. The Special Birth of John (Luke 1:57-58)
  B. The Preparer of the Way (Luke 1:67-77)
  C. Through the Children, God Opens the Way to Peace (Luke 1:78-79)

III. Concluding Reflection

LESSON OBJECTIVES

Upon the completion of the lesson, the students will be able to do the following:

1. Review the story of Zechariah's prophecy concerning his son, John the Baptist;

2. Gain an appreciation for prophecy and reflect on expectations that they have for the next generation; and,

3. Address the justice modeled in Zechariah's prophecy.

POINTS TO BE EMPHASIZED

ADULT/YOUTH

Adult Topic: Opening the Way
Youth Topic: Great Expectations
Adult Key Verses: Luke 1:76-77
Youth Key Verses: Luke 1:67-68
Print Passage: Luke 1:57-58, 67-79

—Scholars suggest that Zechariah's song (also called the Benedictus) was an adaptation of two Jewish Christian hymns (see verses 68-75, 76-79).

—The name *John* means "the grace of the Lord."

—The birth of John the Baptist was a cause for celebration by Elizabeth, her family, and her neighbors.

—Zechariah and Elizabeth upheld Jewish traditions, such as naming and circumcising John on the eighth day. However, Zechariah broke with tradition when he named the child according to the directions of the angel.

—Zechariah's song of praise included praise to God for keeping God's promise of redemption to his ancestors.

—His song of praise was filled with the Holy Spirit, and it prophesied the ministry of John as paramount to preparing for the coming of the Lord.

CHILDREN

Children Topic: A New Dad Celebrates
Key Verse: Luke 1:76

Print Passage: Luke 1:67-79

—Zechariah praised God with the first words he spoke, after having been unable to speak for several months because he doubted the angel's words.

—In a song often called "The Benedictus," Zechariah foretold of the coming of a Savior who would redeem God's people.

—Zechariah's song of prophecy further predicted that his son John would prepare the way for the Messiah by giving the people the knowledge of salvation.

—Zechariah praised God for keeping promises to show mercy on the faithful by delivering them from their enemies and guiding them in paths of peace.

I. INTRODUCTION

A. The Praise and Rejoicing of Common People

The motif of praise and rejoicing are prominent features of Luke's story regarding the birth of Jesus. In the previous lesson study, Mary's praise song was highlighted. Today's lesson features the prophecy of Zechariah, the father of John, who later became known as the preparer of the way for the Messiah. Elizabeth (the wife of Zechariah) and Mary and Joseph (the earthly parents of Jesus) were common people. They lived within the hopes and aspirations of a spirituality and covenant tradition that kept hope for deliverance from oppression vibrantly alive in their faith.

This lesson study challenges Christians to take the birth of every child seriously as the potential for a new beginning in the world. The faith and spiritual resolve of Zechariah's prophecy in today's lesson should inspire us toward honoring the life of every newborn child as having great potential for fulfilling godly purposes. When Elizabeth and Zechariah received the wonderful news that they would be the parents of a child who would prepare the way for the Messiah, they rejoiced and praised God as recipients of divine grace.

B. Biblical Background

Following the meeting of Mary in the home of Elizabeth (see Luke 1:39-43), Luke's birth narrative turned to Zechariah, husband of Elizabeth. As a local priest, Zechariah received the news that he and his wife would become parents in their old age. Zechariah received the angelic news in disbelief (see Luke 1:18) and as a result, he became mute after the encounter with the angel. Luke's theological interpretation of the event highlights the divine activity surrounding the birth of Jesus and the foreshadowing of John's birth as it related to his future role in preparing the way for the Messiah. Luke's account of the birth of John and the insight of Elizabeth and Zechariah was to illumine for the reader the understanding of the person and work of Jesus. John's birth was miraculous, but it was not of the same magnitude as the birth of Jesus. The parents of John were old. They were beyond childbearing age. Conception would therefore require an act of God.

Luke, who was a physician, was sensitive to the biological realities of conception in old age and was aware of this phenomena occurring throughout Jewish history (see Genesis 18:14). Luke was not concerned about reporting the science behind the birth of John or how Mary conceived Jesus. Rather, Luke's birth narrative parallels accounts in the book of Genesis to reveal the meaning of the births of John and Jesus. In the theology of the gospel of Luke, Zechariah and Elizabeth emerged with their son, John, out of Hebrew history to play their roles in the drama of salvation that was being described in the story of Jesus' birth.

II. EXPOSITION AND APPLICATION OF THE SCRIPTURE

A. The Special Birth of John
(Luke 1:57-58)

Now Elisabeth's full time came that she should be delivered; and she brought forth a son. And her neighbours and her cousins heard how the Lord had shewed great mercy upon her; and they rejoiced with her.

The names of Zechariah and Elizabeth bring to mind a familiar reference in the Hebrew tradition. The name of Elizabeth's husband—Zechariah—enabled Luke to journey back in the Hebrew Temple tradition to find a theological connection with divine activity in the nation of Israel (see Zechariah 1:4-14). Zechariah was a local village priest with the most sacred duties associated with the ancient Temple priest. Zechariah had been chosen by divine lot to offer the incense in that portion of the Temple known as the Holy of Holies. While he went about this duty, his prayers were interrupted by the message of the angel Gabriel (see Luke 1:10-11). Zechariah was petrified. His disbelief caused the angel to render him mute until the baby was born (see Luke 1:20). Zechariah responded to the angelic message with a song that pointed to a fulfillment yet to come "when he raises up a mighty savior for us" (Luke 1:69).

According to Luke's story, Zechariah's encounter with Gabriel occurred at the time he was offering prayers and incense in the Holy of Holies. *Prayer* can be defined as "practicing the presence of God or living with a divine consciousness and human awareness of God's constant presence, purpose, and power." Revelatory moments of truth seemingly occur, cultivated and made ready by prayers in solidarity with God's purpose. Zechariah's prophecy proceeded out of the living tradition kept vibrant by the prayers, the hope, and the heritage of ancient Judaism.

The naming of John was for Luke an important inclusion for unfolding the theological meaning behind his birth narrative. The patriarchal tradition of the Hebrew community gave naming authority of children to the male. Zechariah was speechless when Elizabeth's child was born. The local villagers were confused when Elizabeth named the child John and not after the genealogy of Zechariah. In his mute condition, however, Zechariah wrote on a tablet and confirmed Elizabeth's choice of the name *John* (see Luke 1:61-63). Names sent messages. Names embodied proclamations. The naming of John brought fear and amazement throughout the village communities. The people knew that a special child had been born to Elizabeth and Zechariah. God's power was at work in the birth of John to play a special role in the salvation of the people.

B. The Preparer of the Way
(Luke 1:67-77)

And his father Zacharias was filled with the Holy Ghost, and prophesied, saying, Blessed be the Lord God of Israel; for he hath visited and redeemed his people, And hath raised up an horn of salvation for us in the house of his servant David; As he spake by the mouth of his holy prophets, which have been since the world began: That we should be saved from our enemies, and from the hand of all that hate us; To perform the mercy promised to our fathers, and to remember his holy covenant; The oath which he sware to our father Abraham, That he would grant unto us, that we being delivered out of the hand of our enemies might serve him without fear, In holiness and righteousness before him, all the days of our life. And thou, child, shalt be called the prophet of the Highest: for thou shalt go before the face of the Lord to prepare his ways; To give knowledge of salvation unto his people by the remission of their sins.

Zechariah began his prophecy with a blessing or *Benedictus*. The blessing is the acknowledgment that God was at work anew on behalf of the people. John would play a central role as preparer of the way of Jesus in the coming reign of God. The kingdom of God was the principal theme of Zechariah's prophecy. It was the pivotal covenant hope alive in the priestly order of Zechariah and of Judaism. Luke understood the births of John and Jesus as part of God's fulfillment of the promises to David (see 2 Samuel 7:8-16) and to Abraham (see 12:1-3; 26:3).

The world in which Zechariah lived made no distinction between politics and religion. Jews not only worshipped God but also believed that God's reign would be the only power on Earth and in heaven. That belief was wound into Zechariah's prophecy and sense of the Jews as a people and nation ultimately to be ruled by God. From the book of Exodus through the prophetic book of Malachi, there are literary claims that God helps His chosen people conquer their enemies when they keep God's covenant, and lets them fall victim to oppression when they stray from righteousness. This conviction accounts for Zechariah's discipline and loyalty to his priestly duties and why his prophecy speaks of God dealing mercifully with Israel and remembered the holy covenant, the oath sworn to Abraham (see Luke 1:72). Jesus was the "horn of salvation" (Luke 1:69) and John was the preparer of the way (see Luke 1:76) for its fulfillment. Through the personage of John and Jesus, Zechariah affirmed his long-held conviction that the visitation of the Lord would fulfill the promises of the covenant to Abraham.

According to the gospel of Luke, Zechariah's son, John—who later became known as the Baptist—would come "with the spirit and power of Elijah" (Luke 1:17). John the Baptist came to be identified with the messenger of the Lord "who will prepare the way" (Luke 1:76), and "as one crying in the wilderness" (Mark 1:3). As a messenger of the Lord, Luke saw John the Baptist in the light of the messenger from Malachi (see 3:1) and from Isaiah (see 40:3).

John's special role as preparer of the way for the Lord gave Zechariah spontaneous joy. He praised God for divine mercy and for remembering the plight of the people. Every aspect of life would be radically affected by the salvation to come. The covenant people would be rescued from oppression by God's hand. They would be free again to worship God unhindered.

C. Through the Children, God Opens the Way to Peace
(Luke 1:78-79)

Through the tender mercy of our God; whereby the dayspring from on high hath visited us, To give light to them

that sit in darkness and in the shadow of death, to guide our feet into the way of peace.

Zechariah's prophecy affirms the belief that enemies to the dream of God will ultimately be defeated. Luke's story of Zechariah's prophecy reweaves the sacred moments of the Jews' past struggles to become the people of God. John's role in the salvation of God opens the way for the divine presence to appear in human form. Zechariah's encounter with the angel Gabriel left him convinced that this divine presence was to be fully incarnate in the life of Jesus of Nazareth. The life of God in Jesus would open up the way for access to God and usher in the dawning of the kingdom of God. As a local Temple priest, Zechariah lived with the hope (without having much to account for its actual reality). A passion for Jewish solidarity with the dream and will of God inspired Zechariah to keep pace with the disciplines of righteousness of his daily Temple duties. Rare were the moments of sacred encounter for Zechariah. Not every moment of worship in the Temple resulted in divine revelation. Zechariah, like the village community he served, waited through long intervals of divine silence upon the Lord to renew their strength for a new beginning. Zechariah's loyalty to the Abrahamic covenant created an environment in which God spoke to him through an angelic encounter.

It was the hope of every Jewish household that a male child born in it would grow up to be special in God's covenant promise of salvation. The birth of John fulfilled the hopes and aspirations of his parents. It reaffirmed for them that God's purposes are never confined to any distinct class of people. Among the oppressed God raises a deliverer to open up the way for His reign. The people of Israel had long expected that God's deliverance would eventually dawn, but through whom and in what form was left within the unfolding mystery of God. The Roman Empire was not too old when Jesus and John were born. Rome's policy of violently protecting its power was ruthless. John would open up the way to a new reign of peace and justice.

Zechariah's prophecy reveals the true purpose of God's salvation. The true end of God's salvation of the people is not only for deliverance from political domination, but also the creation of conditions in which God's people can worship and serve God without fear and live in righteousness. Deliverance makes worship—unhindered peace—possible.

John opened up the way for the dawning of the light of God. The light is the light of God's salvation and forgiveness of the people's sins. The darkness of oppression must give way to the light of God's merciful compassion to guide the people into the ways of peace (see Luke 1:79). God's salvation comes "to guide our feet into the way of peace" (Luke 1:79). The promise of salvation and redemption are inseparably linked with peace—for each is necessary for the realization of the other. Zechariah's prophecy affirms that God's purposes are being fulfilled by His delivering His people from unjust oppression to justice. Their lives are being blessed with the ways of peace so that they may worship God without the barriers of fear.

III. CONCLUDING REFLECTION

Luke's story of the births of Jesus and John theologically informs us that God is at work to remove all barriers that prevent His salvation from transforming life. In the case of Zechariah and Elizabeth, the parents of John, Luke told us that salvation comes through channels of divine grace into the lives of ordinary people and circumstances of life. God visited an elderly priest and his barren wife with news of a new beginning through the birth of their child. The awareness that God is at work in the life of a child makes a difference in the life of a family and community. Every birth in an ancient Jewish household held out the hope that the child being born might be a sign of God's future salvation. When parents have the special consciousness of God's purpose and of the possibility that God can use their child's life to achieve something great in the world, it makes a difference in how those parents raise, nurture, and teach their child.

Zechariah's prophecy about John's special role in God's salvation should inspire us with the kind of faith that looks for godly signs of hope in the world around us. The Roman situation that confronted the village community of Zechariah was indeed formidable. God's favor and blessing came in the midst of the people's oppression. God's salvation came through the unsuspecting lives of ordinary people. God's salvation came to deliver and free Zechariah's community to be the true people of God. John prepared the way for Jesus, who would open up access to God and the dawning of the reign of God.

PRAYER

God, we thank You for the blessed lives of John and Jesus. Help us to see the divinity that was in Jesus and John in every child's life as a gift of possibility for a new beginning. In Jesus' name we pray. Amen.

WORD POWER

Prophecy—(1) an inspired utterance of a prophet, viewed as a revelation of divine will; (2) a prediction of the future, made under divine inspiration; (3) such an inspired message or prediction transmitted orally or in writing. (www.thefreedictionary.com/prophecy)
Salvation—Christianity: (1) deliverance from the power or penalty of sin; redemption; (2) the agent or means that brings about such deliverance. (www.thefreedictionary.com/salvation)

HOME DAILY BIBLE READINGS
(December 9-15, 2013)

Zechariah Prophesies about His Son John

MONDAY, December 9: "What Will This Child Become?" (Luke 1:59-66)
TUESDAY, December 10: "John's Call to Repentance" (Luke 3:1-6)
WEDNESDAY, December 11: "What, Then, Should We Do?" (Luke 3:7-14)
THURSDAY, December 12: "One More Powerful than John" (Luke 3:15-20)
FRIDAY, December 13: "The Baptizer of Jesus" (Matthew 3:13-17)
SATURDAY, December 14: "A Prophet and More" (Luke 7:18-27)
SUNDAY, December 15: "A Prophet of the Most High" (Luke 1:57-58, 67-79)

LESSON 4 — December 22, 2013 (Christmas Sunday)

JESUS IS BORN

FAITH PATHWAY/FAITH JOURNEY TOPIC: A Bundle of Joy

DEVOTIONAL READING: Galatians 4:1-7
PRINT PASSAGE: Luke 2:1-17

BACKGROUND SCRIPTURE: Luke 2:1-20
KEY VERSE: Luke 2:7

Luke 2:1-17—KJV

AND IT came to pass in those days, that there went out a decree from Caesar Augustus, that all the world should be taxed.

2 (And this taxing was first made when Cyrenius was governor of Syria.)

3 And all went to be taxed, every one into his own city.

4 And Joseph also went up from Galilee, out of the city of Nazareth, into Judaea, unto the city of David, which is called Bethlehem; (because he was of the house and lineage of David:)

5 To be taxed with Mary his espoused wife, being great with child.

6 And so it was, that, while they were there, the days were accomplished that she should be delivered.

7 And she brought forth her firstborn son, and wrapped him in swaddling clothes, and laid him in a manger; because there was no room for them in the inn.

8 And there were in the same country shepherds abiding in the field, keeping watch over their flock by night.

9 And, lo, the angel of the Lord came upon them, and the glory of the Lord shone round about them: and they were sore afraid.

10 And the angel said unto them, Fear not: for, behold, I bring you good tidings of great joy, which shall be to all people.

11 For unto you is born this day in the city of David a Saviour, which is Christ the Lord.

12 And this shall be a sign unto you; Ye shall find the babe wrapped in swaddling clothes, lying in a manger.

13 And suddenly there was with the angel a multitude of the heavenly host praising God, and saying,

Luke 2:1-17—NIV

IN THOSE days Caesar Augustus issued a decree that a census should be taken of the entire Roman world.

2 (This was the first census that took place while Quirinius was governor of Syria.)

3 And everyone went to his own town to register.

4 So Joseph also went up from the town of Nazareth in Galilee to Judea, to Bethlehem the town of David, because he belonged to the house and line of David.

5 He went there to register with Mary, who was pledged to be married to him and was expecting a child.

6 While they were there, the time came for the baby to be born,

7 and she gave birth to her firstborn, a son. She wrapped him in cloths and placed him in a manger, because there was no room for them in the inn.

8 And there were shepherds living out in the fields nearby, keeping watch over their flocks at night.

9 An angel of the Lord appeared to them, and the glory of the Lord shone around them, and they were terrified.

10 But the angel said to them, "Do not be afraid. I bring you good news of great joy that will be for all the people.

11 Today in the town of David a Savior has been born to you; he is Christ the Lord.

12 This will be a sign to you: You will find a baby wrapped in cloths and lying in a manger."

13 Suddenly a great company of the heavenly host appeared with the angel, praising God and saying,

14 Glory to God in the highest, and on earth peace, good will toward men.

15 And it came to pass, as the angels were gone away from them into heaven, the shepherds said one to another, Let us now go even unto Bethlehem, and see this thing which is come to pass, which the Lord hath made known unto us.

16 And they came with haste, and found Mary, and Joseph, and the babe lying in a manger.

17 And when they had seen it, they made known abroad the saying which was told them concerning this child.

14 "Glory to God in the highest, and on earth peace to men on whom his favor rests."

15 When the angels had left them and gone into heaven, the shepherds said to one another, "Let's go to Bethlehem and see this thing that has happened, which the Lord has told us about."

16 So they hurried off and found Mary and Joseph, and the baby, who was lying in the manger.

17 When they had seen him, they spread the word concerning what had been told them about this child.

TOPICAL OUTLINE OF THE LESSON

I. Introduction
A. Bringing the Messiah into the World
B. Biblical Background

II. Exposition and Application of the Scripture
A. A Child Born under Oppression (Luke 2:1-6)
B. Great News of Great Joy (Luke 2:7-14)
C. Joy in Abundance (Luke 2:15-17)

III. Concluding Reflection

LESSON OBJECTIVES

Upon the completion of the lesson, the students will be able to do the following:

1. Review the story of Joseph and Mary's journey to Bethlehem and Jesus' birth;
2. Reflect on the meaning of the term *Messiah* in contemporary times; and,
3. Identify the saving work of Jesus in the world today.

POINTS TO BE EMPHASIZED

ADULT/YOUTH
Adult Topic: **A Bundle of Joy**
Youth Topic: **A Child Is Born!**
Adult Key Verse: **Luke 2:7**
Youth Key Verses: **Luke 2:10-11**
Print Passage: **Luke 2:1-17**

—"All the world" referred to the Roman Empire, of which Quirinius was a military governor in Syria.
—The distance from Nazareth to Bethlehem of sixty-three miles and an elevation change of one thousand feet indicate a strenuous trip for a pregnant woman.
—Early Christian tradition speculated that Jesus was born in a cave.
—The shepherds, representing people at the margins of society, served as witnesses and heralds to the birth of Jesus.

—Luke set the birth of Jesus within the historical context of the Roman census requirement.

—Joseph's journey to Bethlehem fulfilled the prophecy that the Messiah would be born of the lineage and house of David.

—Jesus was born to humble beginnings.

—The angelic appearance to the shepherds suggested that salvation would be a gift for all people.

—The heavenly host recognized the magnificent work that God did in redemption and gave praise to God.

CHILDREN

Children Topic: Rejoice! Good News!

Key Verse: Luke 2:7

Print Passage: Luke 2:1-17

—The Roman emperor's decree was made to facilitate the taxation of all people, but the decree was activated to coincide with God's perfect timing to bring His Son into the world in the town of Bethlehem.

—As Mary and Joseph obeyed God's will, God did not give them comfort and convenience, but rather He provided for their needs as His Son was born in the humblest environment.

—God revealed the news of the birth of His Son to the least expected—lowly shepherds in the field.

—The fear of the shepherds turned to joy as they hastened to visit the long-awaited Messiah.

—After the shepherds visited Mary, Joseph, and the newborn baby, they told the Good News they had heard and seen as they glorified and praised God.

I. INTRODUCTION

A. Bringing the Messiah into the World

Christmas is a time to put all human strivings into a larger context. The liturgical calendar of Christian churches recognizes Christmas as part of the Advent season of new beginnings. Although pagan rituals have distorted the symbolic meaning of Jesus' birth—and there has been much controversy about the time, place, and literal interpretation surrounding the conception of Jesus—still, God's most dramatic act and affirmation of life is the birth of a child. In the case of Mary and Joseph, the most miraculous birth recorded in the history of the world is the birth of Jesus, whom Luke declared is the Savior of the world. Luke was not concerned with the literal details of how Jesus' birth happened; rather, he was concerned with what it meant theologically as a timeless revelation and constant reality for humankind.

In the study of this lesson, students should not miss the salient point that Luke made in his story of Jesus' birth. What is important to note is that through common people and ordinary circumstances, the presence, purpose, and salvation of the holy God came through one born of Mary. Luke was convinced that such a God-presence and divine purpose was beyond the capacity of human beings to create. When the shepherds told their experience of encountering an angelic host with the news of a Savior being born, Mary treasured the news in her heart; the God-presence and divinity in Jesus brought joy to the world.

B. Biblical Background

Luke began his account of Jesus' birth by citing an edict issued by Emperor Augustus—that all the people must return to their home villages in order to register in a census for taxation purposes (see Luke 2:1). Luke's reference to the Roman emperor (Caesar Augustus) and the governor of Syria (Quirinius) is a significant background for understanding the circumstances surrounding Jesus' birth. What was Luke's theological reason for linking Jesus' birth to the census and rulers of the Empire?

For Luke, the theological significance of Jesus' birth was that Jesus was the Savior of both the Jewish and Gentile worlds. Jesus was born under the reign of Caesar Augustus, whose promise of peace was a false peace. True peace for the oppressed came with the birth of the Promised Messiah. Students should take away from the study of this lesson Luke's theological understanding of Jesus as a universal Savior and bringer of peace to all people. In Jesus, we meet a divine presence—offering life, love, and peace. How does the understanding of Jesus as the bringer of peace impact our world today? What are the barriers to true peace in our world? The theological challenge of Luke's story for us today is how to expose the purveyors and vendors of false peace in the world.

II. EXPOSITION AND APPLICATION OF THE SCRIPTURE

A. A Child Born under Oppression
(Luke 2:1-6)

AND IT came to pass in those days, that there went out a decree from Caesar Augustus, that all the world should be taxed. (And this taxing was first made when Cyrenius was governor of Syria.) And all went to be taxed, every one into his own city. And Joseph also went up from Galilee, out of the city of Nazareth, into Judaea, unto the city of David, which is called Bethlehem; (because he was of the house and lineage of David:) To be taxed with Mary his espoused wife, being great with child. And so it was, that, while they were there, the days were accomplished that she should be delivered.

Among the greatest theological problems regarding Jesus is how both His birth and life have been depoliticized by the Christian church. Unfortunately, Jesus' birth has been domesticated to fit a contemporary western worldview of private religious piety and personal salvation that encourages an individualistic worldview. Contrary to this view, Luke disclosed that the revelation of God was in a person born under oppression to bring peace and salvation to the oppressed. For Luke, the heart, character, and passion of God are revealed in the birth of Jesus as liberator-prophet, who is God's anointed for the salvation of the world.

Under the strain of travel, Joseph made his way to Bethlehem with a pregnant Mary. The distance from Nazareth to Bethlehem of sixty-three miles and an elevation change of one thousand feet made the trip a strenuous one for a pregnant woman.

Having to make their way to Joseph's hometown for taxation is but one example of the suffering endured by Jewish communities. The census conjured up fears that oppression would deepen with new taxation. Luke was insistent that Jesus' story be seen as God's identification with the poor and oppressed. Jesus was not born to wealthy parents. The "bands of cloth" in which Jesus was wrapped and "the feeding trough" in which the Baby was laid were signs of humility and poverty.

Against the backdrop of power and opulence of Roman rulers and poverty of the oppressed, the holy God—in and through the birth of Jesus—radically enters the world.

Jesus' birth in Bethlehem became the battleground where all the hopes and fears across years of exile and oppression met to win supremacy. Theologically, Luke's story opens up this battle of "hopes and fears" to cosmic significance. God entered human history and took on human form through the vulnerable life of that Baby, who ultimately would be victorious over a world of fear, oppression, and injustice. The world of the Roman Empire was dying and the new world of hope—God's reign of love, justice, and human flourishing—was being born.

B. Great News of Great Joy
(Luke 2:7-14)

And she brought forth her firstborn son, and wrapped him in swaddling clothes, and laid him in a manger; because there was no room for them in the inn. And there were in the same country shepherds abiding in the field, keeping watch over their flock by night. And, lo, the angel of the Lord came upon them, and the glory of the Lord shone round about them: and they were sore afraid. And the angel said unto them, Fear not: for, behold, I bring you good tidings of great joy, which shall be to all people. For unto you is born this day in the city of David a Saviour, which is Christ the Lord. And this shall be a sign unto you; Ye shall find the babe wrapped in swaddling clothes, lying in a manger. And suddenly there was with the angel a multitude of the heavenly host praising God, and saying, Glory to God in the highest, and on earth peace, good will toward men.

Luke's gospel was heard with special inspiration by working-class folks, the oppressed, and the impoverished. In highlighting God's choice of poor peasants for the parents of Jesus, Luke sent the message that no one is excluded from God's purpose, regardless of social or economic status. The birth of Jesus fulfilled the divine promise of salvation for everyone. Luke was the only gospel writer who included the experience of ordinary field shepherds. The shepherd's routine work of "keeping watch over their flock by night" was interrupted by the angelic news of Jesus' birth. The ancient economy of agriculture and of harnessing the energy and resources of cattle and sheep was a vital means of survival for Jewish peasants. Most likely the shepherds struggled to eke out a bare existence for their families. According to biblical historians, often farmers and sheepherders were subjected to the brutality of Roman soldiers who entered their villages and simply took bread or wine or animals and sexually assaulted the village women. The shepherds like Mary and Joseph lived with the burden of an uncertain future. The reversal of their plight meant that something new must have occurred in the arrangement of the world they knew. They lived with the mundane circumstances of changelessness in the way things appear. They accepted their lot of being a permanent underclass.

Yet, the hope and faith of these field shepherds' expectations were alive with the divine possibilities. Their hearts and spirits (like that of many Jewish households) were active and attentive for signs pointing to something new. The light that Luke recorded as shining round the shepherds on the night of Jesus' birth can be understood as a miraculous culmination of "hopes and fears" in which God—through that angelic encounter—announced to the field shepherds that something new in the world had happened. The news of Jesus' birth meant that the life of the shepherds would be impacted by radical reversals, and the reign of God was at hand (see Mark 1:14-15). With this announcement by the angels, the shepherds were amazed and they became participants in the cosmic significance of Jesus' birth; Christ the Lord was born—a Savior in the tradition and royal line of David. The greatness of the news was the greatness of its message. Divine presence was in Jesus, born to Mary.

C. Joy in Abundance
(Luke 2:15-17)

And it came to pass, as the angels were gone away from them into heaven, the shepherds said one to another, Let us now go even unto Bethlehem, and see this thing which is come to pass, which the Lord hath made known unto us. And they came with haste, and found Mary, and Joseph, and the babe lying in a manger. And when they had seen it, they made known abroad the saying which was told them concerning this child.

On a typical night of watching over their sheep, the shepherds' field task was disrupted with a visit to the manger scene. They rushed to Bethlehem of Judea, the City of David, to the scene of the birth with the accompaniment of a heavenly host of angels—praising God and singing, "Glory to God in the highest, and on earth peace, good will toward men" (Luke 2:14). Just as the angel had announced to them, they found Mary's baby in flesh, lying in the manger. What is most miraculous about the shepherds' story is that against the backdrop of their ancient world of oppression and marginalization they were allowed to receive news of a new beginning. After receiving the angelic news, the shepherds not only rushed to the scene of Jesus' birth to confirm what had been told to them, but they also dared to live in the creative tension between what the news meant and the reality of what was. The establishment

of a peaceful reign of love, justice, and community on Earth were possibilities and promises of hope that the shepherds had not experienced before. But because "divine presence" was with them, the announcement of the birth of Jesus brought an abundance of joy.

The Advent season celebrates God's sending Jesus into the world. Advent is a season of hope, expectation, longing, and anticipation of the newness of God. Against the heaps of human despair in our world, sickness, poverty, and grief, what accounts for the Christian joy about Jesus? To avoid an honest confrontation with the hope of Jesus' advent, we could simply (as many do) opt for cheap Christmas optimism, joining the consumerism and commercial markets that glibly assume that things will get better. But the shepherds rejoiced over the birth of Jesus, even though they were in a dark world of Roman oppression that dashed their dreams and distorted their future. The joy that became the basis of their witness was capable of sustaining life through any crisis. This joy gave the shepherds defiant courage against the realities of the Roman rulers. They rushed to Bethlehem to confirm what they had heard from the angels. From that moment on their faith was enlarged and they were given the spiritual capacity to live in and before the presence of God.

III. CONCLUDING REFLECTION

The shepherds, representing people on the margins of society, served as witnesses and heralds to the birth of Jesus. They became messengers of God's great news for all people. They represented the hopes and fears of common people who were vulnerable to the fatalistic conclusion that nothing was ever going to change. The announcement of God's active presence in the world through Jesus gave the shepherds great joy. Such joy is the basis of Christianity today, confirming that God's salvation is active and available to everyone in every place or circumstance. As a result of Jesus' birth, the world of women and men radically changed in the first century and has, up to the present era, made a difference in the destiny of the world.

Jesus' birth holds a deeper meaning than a literal view of what happened in His miraculous conception. Without Jesus' birth, we would be left without an adequate response to life's tough questions, continuing dilemmas, and enduring toil. Tough questions about life in a divine future remain with us. Are the reversals of life through divine possibilities and promise a reality we can trust? What makes life count? Against the backdrop of poverty and oppression that discounts the significance of one's humanity, we ask this: Is there salvation? In a world of war and extreme violence, we ask this: Is peace a realistic hope for the human family? Is it possible to find a place that confirms an ultimate worth for all persons, regardless of their station or status in life? If we fully grasp the message of Luke's birth story of Jesus, then the answer to these questions is a joyful yes! History confirms that the birth of Jesus has given the human family hope and joy through a salvation impossible without the active love and grace of God.

PRAYER

O God, our hearts rejoice that Jesus is Your gift to all people. We are grateful for the salvation and joy of Jesus. Enable us to share this gift with people and in places where this joy and salvation are not known. In Jesus' name we pray. Amen.

WORD POWER

Decree—an authoritative order having the force of law. (www.thefreedictionary.com/decree)

Espoused—to be engaged to marry (in marriage). (www.BibleStudyTools.com)

Lineage—lineal descent from an ancestor; ancestry or extraction; the line of descendants of a particular ancestor; family; race. (www.dictionary.reference.com/browse/lineage)

HOME DAILY BIBLE READINGS
(December 16-22, 2013)

Jesus Is Born

MONDAY, December 16: "A Child Dedicated to the Lord" (1 Samuel 1:21-28)

TUESDAY, December 17: "Blessing the Children of Israel" (Numbers 6:22-27)

WEDNESDAY, December 18: "Hope for the Coming One" (Isaiah 9:1-5)

THURSDAY, December 19: "A Ruler from Bethlehem and Judah" (Micah 5:1-5)

FRIDAY, December 20: "God's Blessings on David's Descendants" (Psalm 18:46-50)

SATURDAY, December 21: "The Fullness of Time" (Galatians 4:1-7)

SUNDAY, December 22: "The Birth of Jesus in Bethlehem" (Luke 2:1-17)

JESUS IS PRESENTED IN THE TEMPLE

FAITH PATHWAY/FAITH JOURNEY TOPIC: **Dreams Come True**

DEVOTIONAL READING: **Isaiah 49:8-13**   BACKGROUND SCRIPTURE: **Luke 2:21-40**
PRINT PASSAGE: **Luke 2:25-38**   KEY VERSES: **Luke 2:30-31**

Luke 2:25-38—KJV

25 And, behold, there was a man in Jerusalem, whose name was Simeon; and the same man was just and devout, waiting for the consolation of Israel: and the Holy Ghost was upon him.

26 And it was revealed unto him by the Holy Ghost, that he should not see death, before he had seen the Lord's Christ.

27 And he came by the Spirit into the temple: and when the parents brought in the child Jesus, to do for him after the custom of the law,

28 Then took he him up in his arms, and blessed God, and said,

29 Lord, now lettest thou thy servant depart in peace, according to thy word:

30 For mine eyes have seen thy salvation,

31 Which thou hast prepared before the face of all people;

32 A light to lighten the Gentiles, and the glory of thy people Israel.

33 And Joseph and his mother marvelled at those things which were spoken of him.

34 And Simeon blessed them, and said unto Mary his mother, Behold, this child is set for the fall and rising again of many in Israel; and for a sign which shall be spoken against;

35 (Yea, a sword shall pierce through thy own soul also,) that the thoughts of many hearts may be revealed.

36 And there was one Anna, a prophetess, the daughter of Phanuel, of the tribe of Aser: she was of a great age, and had lived with an husband seven years from her virginity;

Luke 2:25-38—NIV

25 Now there was a man in Jerusalem called Simeon, who was righteous and devout. He was waiting for the consolation of Israel, and the Holy Spirit was upon him.

26 It had been revealed to him by the Holy Spirit that he would not die before he had seen the Lord's Christ.

27 Moved by the Spirit, he went into the temple courts. When the parents brought in the child Jesus to do for him what the custom of the Law required,

28 Simeon took him in his arms and praised God, saying:

29 "Sovereign Lord, as you have promised, you now dismiss your servant in peace.

30 For my eyes have seen your salvation,

31 which you have prepared in the sight of all people,

32 a light for revelation to the Gentiles and for glory to your people Israel."

33 The child's father and mother marveled at what was said about him.

34 Then Simeon blessed them and said to Mary, his mother: "This child is destined to cause the falling and rising of many in Israel, and to be a sign that will be spoken against,

35 so that the thoughts of many hearts will be revealed. And a sword will pierce your own soul too."

36 There was also a prophetess, Anna, the daughter of Phanuel, of the tribe of Asher. She was very old; she had lived with her husband seven years after her marriage,

37 and then was a widow until she was eighty-four.

37 And she was a widow of about fourscore and four years, which departed not from the temple, but served God with fastings and prayers night and day.

38 And she coming in that instant gave thanks likewise unto the Lord, and spake of him to all them that looked for redemption in Jerusalem.

She never left the temple but worshiped night and day, fasting and praying.

38 Coming up to them at that very moment, she gave thanks to God and spoke about the child to all who were looking forward to the redemption of Jerusalem.

TOPICAL OUTLINE OF THE LESSON

I. Introduction
A. God's Dream for Us
B. Biblical Background

II. Exposition and Application of the Scripture
A. Mary and Joseph Meet Simeon (Luke 2:25-35)
B. Mary and Joseph Meet Anna (Luke 2:36-38)

III. Concluding Reflection

LESSON OBJECTIVES

Upon the completion of the lesson, the students will be able to do the following:

1. Explore Jesus' being presented in the Temple;
2. Express their feelings about the phrase in Luke 2:34, "This child is destined for the falling and rising of many"; and,
3. Decide how they might be holy.

POINTS TO BE EMPHASIZED
ADULT/YOUTH
Adult Topic: Dreams Come True
Youth Topic: The Moment We've Been Waiting For
Adult Key Verses: Luke 2:30-31
Youth Key Verse: Luke 2:22
Print Passage: Luke 2:25-38

—The Greek word translated "consolation" is *paraklesis*. This is a form of the word used in the Septuagint translation of Isaiah 40:1—"Comfort, O comfort my people, says your God."

—*Simeon* means "God has heard." *Anna* means "grace." The pairing of Anna and Simeon mirrored Elizabeth and Zechariah, who demonstrated that men and women stand side by side before God.

—Joseph and Mary obeyed the law of Moses by eighth-day circumcision and fortieth-day redemption and purification.

—Jesus was named and circumcised within the traditional framework of Jewish law.

—The Holy Spirit played a very active role in the gospel of Luke and its sequel, the book of Acts. The Spirit was present not only in the birth narrative but also in moments of Jesus' life. In this passage, the Holy Spirit led Simeon to witness Jesus' rite of purification as verification of God's promise to the aged believer to send the Messiah.

—Simeon's prayer, the Nunc Dimittis, hinted that Jesus' ministry would include the non-Jewish world and, therefore, fit within Luke's theme of universal salvation. Simeon's blessings on

Mary and Joseph also pointed to Jesus' rejection and death.

CHILDREN
Children Topic: Simeon Gives Thanks
Key Verse: Luke 2:22b
Print Passage: Luke 2:25-38
—God revealed to Simeon that he would not die before he had seen the Messiah, Israel's spiritual deliverer.
—The Holy Spirit led Simeon into the Temple just before Mary and Joseph presented Jesus in fulfillment of the Law.
—Simeon took the baby Jesus in his arms, and he praised and thanked God for allowing him to see Israel's salvation before he died.
—Simeon's words of prophecy amazed Mary and Joseph, because Simeon affirmed that Jesus was a gift from God, recognized Jesus as the long-awaited Messiah, and proclaimed Jesus as the Light to the entire world.
—Simeon prophesied that, because of Jesus, many would rise and fall and that Mary would be greatly grieved because of the widespread rejection of her Son.
—Anna, a devout prophetess, proclaimed God's truth about the Christ child to all who were looking for the redemption of Jerusalem.

I. INTRODUCTION
A. God's Dream for Us
The infamous play by poet and playwright Lorraine Hansberry, *A Raisin in the Sun*, begins with a few lines from the poem "A Dream Deferred," by the poet Langston Hughes:

> *What happens to a dream deferred?*
> *Does it dry up*
> *like a raisin in the sun?*

Today's Bible lesson focuses on the lives of Simeon and Anna, who for many years lived with "a dream deferred." Both of them had grown old in a tradition alive with the dream of God. After many years of delay and deferment, the dream that Israel would inherit freedom in a land given them by God remained active in their memories and alive in their faith. Anna and Simeon knew the history of God's constant deliverances and repeated mercies on behalf of the dream for Israel. They were daily dwellers at the Temple, awaiting signs of hope of the fulfillment of this dream. Through many decades of Roman political hostility, poverty, and suppression, the ritualistic life of Temple worship sustained the dream of God in the hearts of Anna and Simeon. God's dream had not become "like a raisin dried by the sun" for them. Hope was alive. For Anna and Simeon, God's dream remained alive in them through the nurturing atmosphere of daily worship. It was in the Temple atmosphere of worship that they came into intimate contact with the revelation about Jesus—as He was presented for consecration by Mary and Joseph.

The study of this lesson will give us spiritual insight into how to sustain faith in God's dreams when in life they appear to be deferred by the brokenness of social and political circumstances. As students study this lesson, they should ask this question: "What dreams are worthy of our highest engagement in life?" Is God's dream the basis for your own dreaming about the world and divine possibilities for life? Do our individual dreams align with God's dream of justice, love, and human flourishing for all? What spiritual disciplines keep God's dream of freedom alive and active in us?

B. Biblical Background

Luke composed his gospel between AD 59–62. This would be close to sixty years after Jesus' birth. The world of Luke was a world where records were not written down, and biographical information was based on memory and oral tradition. Memories and stories were passed on from generation to generation, based on their enduring sacred meaning and value to preserve the hope, faith, and spirituality of the people. Therefore, the story of Anna and Simeon appear in Luke's gospel as anchoring stories that accentuate the divine presence and holy purpose in the birth and life of Jesus.

Luke included the story of a priest named Simeon who saw God's salvation in the baby Jesus. As Mary and Joseph passed by him on the way to the Temple altar for consecration, Simeon praised God (see Luke 2:30). Luke also included the witness of Anna, an old prophetess, who was identified as the daughter of Phanuel (similar to the Hebrew word *Peniel* in Genesis 32:30), who spoke of this child as one to whom all were looking for salvation (see Luke 2:36).

Many ancient Jews like Anna and Simeon believed that if they lived in accord with God's covenant and commandments, then God would intervene in human affairs, drive their oppressors from the land, and institute a reign of justice. Anna and Simeon lived daily with a consciousness of God's dream through worship and the rituals and traditions of the Torah.

II. EXPOSITION AND APPLICATION OF THE SCRIPTURE

A. Mary and Joseph Meet Simeon
(Luke 2:25-35)

And, behold, there was a man in Jerusalem, whose name was Simeon; and the same man was just and devout, waiting for the consolation of Israel: and the Holy Ghost was upon him. And it was revealed unto him by the Holy Ghost, that he should not see death, before he had seen the Lord's Christ. And he came by the Spirit into the temple: and when the parents brought in the child Jesus, to do for him after the custom of the law, Then took he him up in his arms, and blessed God, and said, Lord, now lettest thou thy servant depart in peace, according to thy word: For mine eyes have seen thy salvation, Which thou hast prepared before the face of all people; A light to lighten the Gentiles, and the glory of thy people Israel. And Joseph and his mother marvelled at those things which were spoken of him. And Simeon blessed them, and said unto Mary his mother, Behold, this child is set for the fall and rising again of many in Israel; and for a sign which shall be spoken against; (Yea, a sword shall pierce through thy own soul also,) that the thoughts of many hearts may be revealed.

When Mary and Joseph came to present Jesus for dedication and consecration they were obligated to meet all of the requirements for dedicating their child to the Lord. The dedication of the child to God was a declaration of the child's heritage and character. Both Jesus' name (*Yeshua* in Aramaic) and circumcision underscored the significance of His birth.

Mary and Joseph were seeking their own

vindication as they shared in the circumcision and dedication of Jesus. Both the naming of Jesus and His circumcision pointed to His role as Savior and were acts and signs of fulfillment for Mary and Joseph.

At the Temple, while fulfilling their obligations under the Law, they came into contact with a man by the name of Simeon. The name *Simeon* means "God has heard." The text describes Simeon as a just and devout man waiting for the consolation of Israel. The text tells us that the Holy Spirit came upon Simeon. Simeon was blessed in a special way by God. He was told that he would not see death until he had seen "the Lord's Christ" (verse 26). This was a special favor placed upon Simeon's life. He would live to see the Messiah, who was/is considered "The consolation of Israel" (verse 25).

On this special occasion, the Spirit brought him into the Temple. At that same time Mary and Joseph were there to dedicate their Son Jesus to the Lord. This was indeed what could be called "divine orchestration." God so designed it that Mary and Joseph would meet Simeon, an old, saintly man who was expecting the "consolation of Israel."

Upon seeing Mary and Joseph with their child Jesus, Simeon then took the child in his arms and blessed God. Simeon's pronouncement (song) is referred to as the *Nunc Dimittis*, because they are the first words in Latin of the song that Simeon sang. The first line of Simeon's song in Latin is as follows: "Nunc dimittis servum tuum." In English, it means "Lord, now you are dismissing your servant in peace" (verse 29). Simeon then referred to Jesus, God's salvation, and a light to lighten the Gentiles and the glory of God's people Israel.

When Joseph and Mary heard these words coming from Simeon, they marveled (or were amazed). Simeon, after blessing Joseph, Mary, and Jesus, said something specifically to Mary. He told her the following: "Behold, this child is set for the fall and rising again of many in Israel; and for a sign which shall be spoken against"; ("Yea, a sword shall pierce through thy own soul also"), that the thoughts of many hearts may be revealed (Luke 2:34-35).

B. Mary and Joseph Meet Anna (Luke 2:36-38)

And there was one Anna, a prophetess, the daughter of Phanuel, of the tribe of Aser: she was of a great age, and had lived with an husband seven years from her virginity; And she was a widow of about fourscore and four years, which departed not from the temple, but served God with fastings and prayers night and day. And she coming in that instant gave thanks likewise unto the Lord, and spake of him to all them that looked for redemption in Jerusalem.

While still at the Temple, Mary and Joseph were blessed to meet an aged prophetess by the name of Anna. Anna was also well advanced in age. Both Simeon and Anna, led by the Spirit, were among the first to bear witness to Jesus. The name *Anna* means "grace." Anna was called a prophetess, indicating her close relationship with God. In fact, the text tells us that she stayed at the Temple continually, serving God with fasting and prayers night and day.

Prophets and prophetesses did not necessarily predict the future, but had a main role of speaking the truth for God. In this instance, Anna joined Simeon in thanking God for the privilege of seeing the Messiah, and also spoke to those in attendance who were looking for the redemption in Jerusalem.

The combination of Simeon's and Anna's names suggests that "God had heard" the people's cry for justice and divine "grace" for the salvation for all people. Both Anna and Simeon met Jesus in the Temple. They were Temple dwellers. By being Temple worshippers, Anna and Simeon stayed close to the spiritual ethos of Jewish religious tradition. The hope and consolation of Israel had not calcified in their faith, even though for centuries the dream of freedom had been deferred. Anna and Simeon held on to the prerogatives of their faith heritage and religious tradition. Their faith reached back to the promised fulfillment of the Abrahamic covenant. Although Anna and Simeon were well advanced in age, they remained faithful to this hope—even through the sometimes violent domination of Roman rulers.

No doubt Luke placed the experience of Anna and Simeon in his birth narrative to make the point that God's salvation can be seen and received by those who become one with the dream of God. Temple worship, over many years, prepared the eyes and spirits of Simeon and Anna to see in the baby Jesus the dream of God being fulfilled.

The birth of a child, the fulfillment of God's covenant promise, the consolation of Israel, and the dawning of the reign of justice set the occasion for Anna and Simeon to prophesy about a divine dream that for them had come true. The sage prophecies of Anna and Simeon gave way to a deeper mystery that Mary and Joseph humbly accepted as the special destiny of Jesus. A salvation for Jews and Gentiles has come through the birth of Jesus. Simeon blessed Jesus and Anna praised God for the peace and salvation of the people. In Simeon's blessing of the child, he foretold that the salvation Jesus brought also came with judgment and rejection. "This child is destined for the falling and the rising of many in Israel" (Luke 2:34). The one who brought salvation would also bring judgment and rejection by many.

God's dream of justice was alive and active in the faith of Anna and Simeon, who dwelt in the Temple and waited for the "consolation of Israel." After many decades of injustice and deferment, their dream came true. Jesus' birth and life were the embodiment of their dream of the reign of God. Just as the parents of Jesus were obedient to the process of fulfilling the covenant requirements of Jewish tradition regarding the circumcision of Jesus and purification of Mary, Anna and Simeon were rewarded for their faithful devotion and received God's blessing. The Temple was the site of the ritual performance that kept the memory and mystery of God's dream active and alive in the hearts of Anna and Simeon. Unfortunately, rituals, rites of passage, and religious disciplines have less weight in the spirituality of churchgoers today. We know that the Jewish rituals of circumcision and purification were external requirements that are not required of Christians today. Yet, these ancient observances serve to remind us that life without rituals of meaning inevitably become void of internal devotion and spiritual union with the purpose of God. Divine dreams remain alive in the hearts of people through worship and the exercise of spiritual disciplines of prayer and sacrifice. Neglecting to practice meaningful rituals in the life of the church could lead to disregard for the divine dream of justice and sincerity in one's love of God and neighbor.

III. CONCLUDING REFLECTION

It is important that the spirituality and culture of African Americans are maintained with rituals and observances that keep the dream of God alive in the hearts of succeeding generations. The increasing criminal activity of black life and decline of morality in black youth may be linked not only to structural and systemic injustice, but also to the loss of rituals that tie generations together in worthy dreams. The testimony and wisdom of the older people should be passed down to the young. Special days and events that remind the community of black people's struggle for freedom and justice should be observed with a view of God's grace and salvation. In parts of the South, the 1865 emancipation of slaves is celebrated. Other events like the annual celebration of the life of Martin Luther King Jr. should not be allowed to become empty rituals on the holiday calendar. The dedication of children at church altars should be a part of family rituals in order to affirm God's special destiny at work in the life of every child. We must find rituals that cultivate the spirit of justice in the formation of children's spirituality. There are "Freedom Schools" sponsored by the Children's Defense Fund, which serve to help young people recognize the sacredness of life and the presence of God in everyday events. Through rituals of meaning, the language of love in the service of justice becomes powerfully alive in a community. People become one with divine dreams of love and justice.

PRAYER

O God, many have lost hope in the divine dream of justice and love in the world. Help us keep the dream of God alive and active in us and in the lives of our children. In Jesus' name we pray. Amen.

WORD POWER

Circumcision—the Hebrew (*milah*), like the Greek (*peritome*) and the Latin (*circumcisio*), signifies a cutting and, specifically, the removal of the prepuce, or foreskin, from the penis.
Consolation of Israel—a name for the Messiah in common use among the Jews, probably suggested by Isaiah 12:1; 49:13.
Prophetess—noun: (1) a woman who speaks for God or a deity, or by divine inspiration; (2) a woman who foretells future events; (3) a woman who is a spokesperson of some doctrine, cause, or movement; (4) the wife or female companion of a prophet.

HOME DAILY BIBLE READINGS
(December 23-29, 2013)

Jesus Is Presented in the Temple
MONDAY, December 23: "Parents Committed to the Law" (Luke 2:21-24)
TUESDAY, December 24: "Circumcising on the Eighth Day" (Leviticus 12:1-5)
WEDNESDAY, December 25: "Offering a Sacrifice to the Lord" (Leviticus 12:6-8)
THURSDAY, December 26: "Consolation for Israel" (Isaiah 40:1-5)
FRIDAY, December 27: "The Lord's Comfort and Compassion" (Isaiah 49:8-13)
SATURDAY, December 28: "A Light to the Nations" (Isaiah 42:1-7)
SUNDAY, December 29: "Jesus' Presentation in the Temple" (Luke 2:25-38)

LESSON 6   January 5, 2014

HONORING THE SABBATH

FAITH PATHWAY/FAITH JOURNEY TOPIC: Living with Justice and Mercy

DEVOTIONAL READING: **John 5:2-17**
PRINT PASSAGE: **Luke 6:1-11**

BACKGROUND SCRIPTURE: **Luke 6:1-47**
KEY VERSE: **Luke 6:9**

Luke 6:1-11—KJV

AND IT came to pass on the second sabbath after the first, that he went through the corn fields; and his disciples plucked the ears of corn, and did eat, rubbing them in their hands.

2 And certain of the Pharisees said unto them, Why do ye that which is not lawful to do on the sabbath days?

3 And Jesus answering them said, Have ye not read so much as this, what David did, when himself was an hungred, and they which were with him;

4 How he went into the house of God, and did take and eat the shewbread, and gave also to them that were with him; which it is not lawful to eat but for the priests alone?

5 And he said unto them, That the Son of man is Lord also of the sabbath.

6 And it came to pass also on another sabbath, that he entered into the synagogue and taught: and there was a man whose right hand was withered.

7 And the scribes and Pharisees watched him, whether he would heal on the sabbath day; that they might find an accusation against him.

8 But he knew their thoughts, and said to the man which had the withered hand, Rise up, and stand forth in the midst. And he arose and stood forth.

9 Then said Jesus unto them, I will ask you one thing; Is it lawful on the sabbath days to do good, or to do evil? to save life, or to destroy it?

10 And looking round about upon them all, he said unto the man, Stretch forth thy hand. And he did so: and his hand was restored whole as the other.

11 And they were filled with madness; and communed one with another what they might do to Jesus.

Luke 6:1-11—NIV

ONE SABBATH Jesus was going through the grainfields, and his disciples began to pick some heads of grain, rub them in their hands and eat the kernels.

2 Some of the Pharisees asked, "Why are you doing what is unlawful on the Sabbath?"

3 Jesus answered them, "Have you never read what David did when he and his companions were hungry?

4 He entered the house of God, and taking the consecrated bread, he ate what is lawful only for priests to eat. And he also gave some to his companions."

5 Then Jesus said to them, "The Son of Man is Lord of the Sabbath."

6 On another Sabbath he went into the synagogue and was teaching, and a man was there whose right hand was shriveled.

7 The Pharisees and the teachers of the law were looking for a reason to accuse Jesus, so they watched him closely to see if he would heal on the Sabbath.

8 But Jesus knew what they were thinking and said to the man with the shriveled hand, "Get up and stand in front of everyone." So he got up and stood there.

9 Then Jesus said to them, "I ask you, which is lawful on the Sabbath: to do good or to do evil, to save life or to destroy it?"

10 He looked around at them all, and then said to the man, "Stretch out your hand." He did so, and his hand was completely restored.

11 But they were furious and began to discuss with one another what they might do to Jesus.

TOPICAL OUTLINE OF THE LESSON

I. Introduction
A. Jesus' Understanding of Justice and Mercy
B. Biblical Background

II. Exposition and Application of the Scripture
A. Jesus, Lord of the Sabbath (Luke 6:1-5)
B. Doing Justice by Healing Others (Luke 6:6-7)
C. To Do Good or Evil (Luke 6:8-11)

III. Concluding Reflection

LESSON OBJECTIVES

Upon the completion of the lesson, the students will be able to do the following:

1. Review Sabbath laws and their conflicts with human need;
2. Appreciate the priority of human needs being met; and,
3. Live in such a way that they honor the Sabbath from the perspective of Jesus.

POINTS TO BE EMPHASIZED

ADULT/YOUTH
Adult Topic: Living with Justice and Mercy
Youth Topic: Just Do Good!
Adult/Youth Key Verse: Luke 6:9
Print Passage: Luke 6:1-11

—The rules and regulations of Sabbath keeping reflect a long history of practice of the Jewish faith community.
—The Pharisees interpreted Exodus 20:8-11 as prohibiting plucking grain on the Sabbath.
—Jesus challenged the traditional understanding of the Sabbath by highlighting the biblical call for justice and love.
—Jesus refused to be constricted by the pharisaic way.
—Jesus proclaimed His lordship over the Sabbath in numerous instances—two of which are recorded in this passage: rubbing and eating the grain, and healing on the Sabbath.

CHILDREN
Children Topic: Doing Good
Key Verse: Luke 6:9
Print Passage: Luke 6:1-11

—The disciples took the "heads of grains" (verse 1) to eat for themselves on the Sabbath and Jesus defended their actions.
—Jesus recalled the time when David broke the tradition by entering the Temple, eating the bread, and giving some to his companions on the Sabbath.
—Jesus healed a man with a withered hand on the Sabbath.
—Jesus challenged the scribes and Pharisees about whether it is right to do good on the Sabbath.

I. INTRODUCTION

A. Jesus' Understanding of Justice and Mercy

The formation of Jesus' understanding of justice and mercy began in the context of His looking outside of the rules and regulations of the synagogue for understanding of who He was and what the traditions of the Torah meant for His life and future.

In the study of this lesson, students might explore how institutions, religious or political, present formidable barriers to the flourishing of justice and mercy for all persons. As you reflect on the lesson, ask how welfare reform in the United States might be carried out in ways that embrace Jesus' love ethic of justice and mercy. Who are the outsiders in our contemporary society? Are the rules that governed the life of the poor fair and on par with the advantages of the wealthy in America? In what ways are the beliefs, practices, or traditions of the church complicit with injustices that prevent showing mercy and justice to outsiders? How can Christians be part of the world's healing and transformation and not block it? Living with mercy and justice will require gleaning honest theological responses to these questions.

B. Biblical Background

The Greek meaning of the word for "mercy," *eleos*, means "compassion or pity; a readiness to help those in trouble" (see Matthew 9:13). Mercy is a spiritual quality that shows kindness or goodwill toward the miserable and afflicted, joined with a desire to relieve or liberate them (see *Strong's Concordance*). The Hebraic understanding of justice (*mishpat* in Hebrew) is the establishment of right relationships among all things in God's creation. Not only does biblical understanding of *mishpat* (justice) call for what is fair, but also it upholds the idea that people and their needs should be treated as sacred and holy solely because they are children of God's creation. Our conventional conception of justice is centered on a legal framework which passes over or misdiagnoses Jesus' understanding of justice. For Jesus, anything that is a barrier or prevents people and their legitimate human needs from fulfillment or diminishes their position as children of God is an injustice. Recognizing the importance of people and their needs is the basis for understanding Jesus' conception of doing good or harm toward others. Jesus was often offended by the rules and regulations of Sabbath laws and traditions that were in conflict with compassionate acts of justice. Any practice that isolated people and made them outsiders to the mercy and justice of God was offensive to Jesus.

Jesus' conception of justice and mercy also included the notion of God's loving-kindness (*hesed* in Hebrew). Jesus understood loving-kindness to be the enduring ethical basis and fundamental principle of the kingdom of God. It was in divine love (*hesed*) that Jesus reconciled His own self-identity in the mercy and justice of God and came to believe that no institutional barrier or practice, political or religious, should prevent its extension to all persons.

II. EXPOSITION AND APPLICATION OF THE SCRIPTURE

A. Jesus, Lord of the Sabbath
(Luke 6:1-5)

AND IT came to pass on the second sabbath after the first, that he went through the corn fields; and his disciples plucked the ears of corn, and did eat, rubbing them in their hands. And certain of the Pharisees said unto them, Why do ye that which is not lawful to do on the sabbath days? And Jesus answering them said, Have ye not read so much as this, what David did, when himself was an hungred, and they which were with him; How he went into the house of God, and did take and eat the shewbread, and gave also to them that were with him; which it is not lawful to eat but for the priests alone? And he said unto them, That the Son of man is Lord also of the sabbath.

In the gospel of Luke, the first Sabbath controversy Jesus encountered was the plucking of corn on the Sabbath day. The disciples of Jesus were charged with a Sabbath violation when they satisfied their hunger by plucking corn while going through a grain field. Luke used this incident to make the theological case that Jesus as the "Son of Man" is also "Lord of the Sabbath." The Pharisees interpreted Exodus 20:8-11 as prohibiting the plucking of grain on the Sabbath because it was seen as a form of work, which was forbidden on the Sabbath day. They accused Jesus' disciples of violating the Sabbath law by plucking corn on the holy day. The Torah's rule of no work on the Sabbath is linked with Israel's system of purity before God. Purity laws sought to assure holiness and to avoid impurity, which in the mind of ancient Judaism separates one from God. Purity observances were meant to regulate action and behavior, so as to maintain unhindered access and connection to God. Although Jesus was a devoted Jew observing many of the traditions of Judaism (see Mark 1:44; 14:12-16), He did violate many of the laws of Judaism when He saw that the legalistic practice of those laws was in conflict with the treatment of persons and their needs as holy and sacred. Jesus challenged the traditional understanding of the Sabbath by highlighting the biblical call for justice and love.

Jesus' response to the Pharisees' accusation illustrates how the ethic of mercy was absent from the practice of the Sabbath law. For Jesus, the priority of human hunger superseded the Sabbath law. Although the disciples violated the Sabbath law by gathering grain for food, Jesus saw their activity as meeting a vital human need. The Pharisees' question to Jesus as to why the disciples were plucking corn on the Sabbath focused on an important theological point—which Luke was concerned that his readers understand. What was at the core of the Pharisees' disposition was a concern for *orthodoxy* (right belief), while the larger significance of discerning divine presence in responding to human need required *orthopraxis,* meaning "right action or practice." Jesus challenged the Pharisees on the grounds of their own tradition as He compared what His disciples did to what David did when, due to hunger, he ate the bread prescribed only for the priest. The event Jesus recalled is recorded in 1 Samuel 21:1-6, when David overturned the rule of Leviticus by entering the Temple and eating bread set aside for the priest (see Leviticus 24:5-9). Jesus juxtaposed the action of David (with his own authority as a king) to His authority as the "Son of Man" to allow His disciples to pluck corn to satisfy their hunger on the Sabbath day. Jesus' love ethic of mercy and compassion for meeting the needs of others took precedence over and superseded the Sabbath law. Jesus annulled or passed over the Sabbath law prohibition of work when that work was needed to meet a real human need. Jesus passed over what was false, destructive, and oppressive in the Law while preserving what was true, good, and liberating for fulfilling human needs.

Luke's juxtaposition of Jesus with David in this synagogue conflict is consistent with Luke's theological perspective of Jesus as "Son of Man" and "son of David" (Luke 1:27). Later, Jesus justified His actions by making the claim to be one greater than David (see Luke 20:41-44). The theological point that Luke made is that Jesus, the son of David, is the Son of Man and, thus, is also Lord of the Sabbath.

B. Doing Justice by Healing Others (Luke 6:6-7)

And it came to pass also on another sabbath, that he entered into the synagogue and taught: and there was a man whose right hand was withered. And the scribes and Pharisees watched him, whether he would heal on the sabbath day; that they might find an accusation against him.

The kingdom of God and its love ethic of mercy and justice were the driving forces behind Jesus' teaching and healing ministry. Through the lens of God's kingdom, Jesus discerned the difference between legalistic obedience to Sabbath laws and the communal call of God's love and compassion to be applied in every life situation. Jesus lived with the possibility of re-creation of the world through the channel of God's love, mercy, and justice—as it found collective embodiment and expression in every life. It was this elemental theological interpretation in Jesus' teaching that stood out in contrast to the teaching of the Pharisees and

Scribes. Luke highlighted this basic premise of Jesus' teaching in the second Sabbath controversy in Luke 6. On this occasion, Jesus' commitment to save life was put in opposition to one's obligation to keep the Sabbath law. Driven by the vision of God's love ethic, Jesus went into the synagogue to teach. Luke told the readers at the outset that the day was the Sabbath and added that Jesus went into the synagogue for the purpose of teaching (see Luke 4:15, 31; 5:3, 17).

Present among the synagogue worshippers was a man with a withered, shriveled, or crippled hand. For a period of time, Luke did not tell how long the condition of the man's hand had prevented him from having an industrious and productive life. The man left with this physical disability was placed at a social and economic disadvantage. Mercy for the man's condition overtook Jesus' compassion—thus, He healed on the Sabbath day. In the tension of the moment, competing priorities forced Jesus to decide whether to be a healer or a keeper of the Law. The scribes and Pharisees were aware of a rabbinic tradition that permitted healing on the Sabbath when faced with a life-threatening condition. Since the man's condition was chronic and not life-threatening, they watched to see what Jesus would do. Jesus made no distinction between the man's condition being chronic or whether it was an immediate life-threatening situation. Jesus' priority was to liberate him from a condition that rendered his life inadequate and useless. Love and compassion took precedence. Jesus healed the man. Jesus saw strict obedience to the Sabbath laws as having the potential for idolatry. The Sabbath laws had the tendency to push over-adherence to extremes in the face of threats and insecurities. This is a critical issue in our own time—as people attempt to make sense of religion in the public areas of life. What should contemporary Christians do when faced with good things conflicting with established and time-honored traditions?

C. To Do Good or Evil
(Luke 6:8-11)

But he knew their thoughts, and said to the man which had the withered hand, Rise up, and stand forth in the midst. And he arose and stood forth. Then said Jesus unto them, I will ask you one thing; Is it lawful on the sabbath days to do good, or to do evil? to save life, or to destroy it? And looking round about upon them all, he said unto the man, Stretch forth thy hand. And he did so: and his hand was restored whole as the other. And they were filled with madness; and communed one with another what they might do to Jesus.

Jesus posed the following question to the Pharisees who had been watching Him to see whether He would violate the Sabbath law: when is the right time to do good or to resist evil? For Jesus, saving life always took precedence over rules that were barriers to saving life. In Jesus' thinking, healing the man with the crippled hand should take place—whether it was on the Sabbath or not. The Pharisees, however, trapped in fundamentalist beliefs and ideological practices, could not discern the significance of healing over against strict adherence to the Sabbath law. Jesus lived with a vision arising out of the love ethic of the kingdom of God that made the treating of human needs sacred and holy. The Pharisees, who did not have this vision, placed Sabbath observances above the meeting of human needs. The conflict heightened when Jesus answered His own question to the Pharisees by healing the man on the Sabbath day. Any barrier allowed

to stand in the way of doing good is evil. By implication, the Pharisees were doing harm or evil when they resisted the action of Jesus to heal the man.

Cultural and religious beliefs being promulgated today are unsettling, because in many instances the love ethic of Jesus is easily superseded by competing loyalties that separate mercy from justice. In situations of life and death, healing and disease, fundamentalist beliefs and right doctrine sometimes take precedence over the practice of justice and mercy. For example, the belief in individual rights and freedom do not correspond to the needs for welfare and health care reform. Traditional and conventional forms of religious beliefs, when combined with capitalist priorities, put the lives of the poor at risk. Opposition to the Affordable Health Care Act in the halls of government is illustrative of the point that laws devoid of a love ethic create injustice for the poor, who cannot afford the care which others have as an advantage. The chasm between love and law is also seen in debates related to abortion. Seemingly, the debate has lost sight of the ethic of mercy and justice when a woman conceives as a victim of rape or when conception occurs in circumstances of extreme poverty. In such cases, resources should be provided to support and enhance the child's life chances. The danger becomes acute when rigid stands take the form of violence against those who believe and behave differently. Ultimately, it should be remembered by Christians that the violation of purity and Sabbath laws were a major factor in causing Jesus' crucifixion.

III. CONCLUDING REFLECTION

The two Sabbath controversies in this lesson point to the theological clarity that Christians need in order to live with a commitment to mercy and justice. Such clarity is needed as Christians apply the love ethic of Jesus to the competing values and practices of religious institutions. Micah 6:8 explains that what God requires is not ceremonial observance but justice, kindness, and humility. Jesus had the courage to think and act with clarity about whether to heal the crippled man or to obey the Sabbath law. Jesus resolved the Sabbath controversy with an unapologetic commitment to God's kingdom love ethic of mercy and justice.

The identification of contemporary Christians with Jesus' love ethic will create conflict between a society that objectifies life rather than seeing the communal and relational qualities of God's love committed to healing and restoring life. The stress falls on loving whom and what God loves more than supporting the institutions and traditions that perpetuate beliefs and religious practices that may at times be in conflict with this ethic.

PRAYER

God, help us to live and act receptively in every situation of life. Teach us how to live with mercy and justice as we confront resistance to Your divine presence and healing in the world. In Jesus' name we pray. Amen.

WORD POWER

Lord of the Sabbath—Jesus proclaimed that He is the one who exercised authority, even over the rules and regulations that govern the Sabbath day. (From: www.gotquestions.org/Lord-of-the-Sabbath.html.)

Son of Man—the term "Son of Man" refers to Jesus, who was both a man and God. It means many things, but Jesus used it to identify with us and the prophets. This does not mean that He was declining to be Messiah or the only begotten Son of God. (From: wiki.answers.com › ... › Christianity › The Bible.)

HOME DAILY BIBLE READINGS
(December 30, 2013–January 5, 2014)

Honoring the Sabbath
MONDAY, December 30: "God Is Still Working" (John 5:2-17)
TUESDAY, December 31: "A Day of Thanksgiving" (Psalm 92:1-8)
WEDNESDAY, January 1: "A Day of Rest" (Exodus 16:22-30)
THURSDAY, January 2: "A Day of Remembrance" (Deuteronomy 5:11-15)
FRIDAY, January 3: "A Holy Convocation" (Leviticus 23:1-8)
SATURDAY, January 4: "A Holy Day" (Jeremiah 17:19-27)
SUNDAY, January 5: "Lord of the Sabbath" (Luke 6:1-11)

LESSON 7   January 12, 2014

HOW TO LIVE AS GOD'S PEOPLE

FAITH PATHWAY/FAITH JOURNEY TOPIC: Living Justly with Others

DEVOTIONAL READING: **Matthew 18:21-35**
PRINT PASSAGE: **Luke 6:17-31**

BACKGROUND SCRIPTURE: **Luke 6:17-36**
KEY VERSE: **Luke 6:27**

Luke 6:17-31—KJV

17 And he came down with them, and stood in the plain, and the company of his disciples, and a great multitude of people out of all Judaea and Jerusalem, and from the sea coast of Tyre and Sidon, which came to hear him, and to be healed of their diseases;

18 And they that were vexed with unclean spirits: and they were healed.

19 And the whole multitude sought to touch him: for there went virtue out of him, and healed them all.

20 And he lifted up his eyes on his disciples, and said, Blessed be ye poor: for yours is the kingdom of God.

21 Blessed are ye that hunger now: for ye shall be filled. Blessed are ye that weep now: for ye shall laugh.

22 Blessed are ye, when men shall hate you, and when they shall separate you from their company, and shall reproach you, and cast out your name as evil, for the Son of man's sake.

23 Rejoice ye in that day, and leap for joy: for, behold, your reward is great in heaven: for in the like manner did their fathers unto the prophets.

24 But woe unto you that are rich! for ye have received your consolation.

25 Woe unto you that are full! for ye shall hunger. Woe unto you that laugh now! for ye shall mourn and weep.

26 Woe unto you, when all men shall speak well of you! for so did their fathers to the false prophets.

27 But I say unto you which hear, Love your enemies, do good to them which hate you,

28 Bless them that curse you, and pray for them which despitefully use you.

29 And unto him that smiteth thee on the one cheek

Luke 6:17-31—NIV

17 He went down with them and stood on a level place. A large crowd of his disciples was there and a great number of people from all over Judea, from Jerusalem, and from the coast of Tyre and Sidon,

18 who had come to hear him and to be healed of their diseases. Those troubled by evil spirits were cured,

19 and the people all tried to touch him, because power was coming from him and healing them all.

20 Looking at his disciples, he said: "Blessed are you who are poor, for yours is the kingdom of God.

21 Blessed are you who hunger now, for you will be satisfied. Blessed are you who weep now, for you will laugh.

22 Blessed are you when men hate you, when they exclude you and insult you and reject your name as evil, because of the Son of Man.

23 Rejoice in that day and leap for joy, because great is your reward in heaven. For that is how their fathers treated the prophets.

24 But woe to you who are rich, for you have already received your comfort.

25 Woe to you who are well fed now, for you will go hungry. Woe to you who laugh now, for you will mourn and weep.

26 Woe to you when all men speak well of you, for that is how their fathers treated the false prophets.

27 But I tell you who hear me: Love your enemies, do good to those who hate you,

28 bless those who curse you, pray for those who mistreat you.

29 If someone strikes you on one cheek, turn to him

offer also the other; and him that taketh away thy cloke forbid not to take thy coat also.

30 Give to every man that asketh of thee; and of him that taketh away thy goods ask them not again.

31 And as ye would that men should do to you, do ye also to them likewise.

the other also. If someone takes your cloak, do not stop him from taking your tunic.

30 Give to everyone who asks you, and if anyone takes what belongs to you, do not demand it back.

31 Do to others as you would have them do to you."

TOPICAL OUTLINE OF THE LESSON

I. Introduction
   A. Good News for the Poor
   B. Biblical Background

II. Exposition and Application of the Scripture
   A. Blessings of Divine Justice (Luke 6:17-23)
   B. The Reversals of Divine Justice (Luke 6:24-26)
   C. "Strength to Love" (Luke 6:27-31)

III. Concluding Reflection

LESSON OBJECTIVES

Upon the completion of the lesson, the students will be able to do the following:

1. Interpret the meanings of love and justice as principles of the kingdom of God;

2. Deal with the difficult feelings associated with their loving people who show total disdain for them; and,

3. Understand the importance of spiritual disciplines that encourage and express love for the enemy.

POINTS TO BE EMPHASIZED
ADULT/YOUTH

Adult Topic: **Living Justly with Others**
Youth Topic: **Loving Your Haters!**
Adult Key Verse: **Luke 6:27**
Youth Key Verses: **Luke 6:27-28**
Print Passage: **Luke 6:17-31**

—The idea of nonviolent resistance found in verses 27-31 was important to the philosophies and teachings of Mahatma Gandhi and Martin Luther King Jr. (See Matthew 5–7 for further examples.)

—The order of the Beatitudes is different in the books of Matthew and Luke, perhaps indicating that the authors drew from different sources.

—Jesus' command to love one's enemies superseded Jewish law, which authorized retaliation or revenge.

—Instead of repaying evil for evil, Jesus emphasized four activities His disciples were to carry out: love, do good, bless, and pray for their adversaries. (See verses 27-28.)

—Jesus' disciples, then and now, must love not only those who love them in return but also those who do not.

—Jesus established that the authority for judging is with God and not with men, and that Christians should be more concerned with giving and forgiving.

CHILDREN

Children Topic: Loving People
Key Verses: Luke 6:35a, 36
Print Passage: Luke 6:17-19, 27-36
—Jesus preached and many people were healed of diseases and unclean spirits.

—Jesus taught His disciples to love their enemies.

—Jesus taught His followers to treat others as they would like to be treated.

—Jesus promised that the reward would be great for doing good to others.

I. INTRODUCTION

A. Good News for the Poor

The lesson for today focuses on the content of Jesus' preaching and teachings to the poor. Luke and the other gospel writers told us that the poor heard Jesus gladly, while others were offended by His teachings. The foremost reason why the poor greeted Jesus' teachings with enthusiasm and the rich with rejection was the announcement of God's new age of justice and liberation. Different from the other gospel writers, Luke presented Jesus' teachings in the social context of human misery and suffering. The setting for Jesus' instruction to the crowd of disciples was the political plight and disenfranchisement of Jews who lived on the margins of Roman society.

This lesson also highlights what it meant to live in a hostile culture of abusive power, dominating political hierarchies, and oppressive systems of inhumanity. The followers of Jesus found that embracing Jesus' love ethic was the most challenging yet effective strategy for liberation. Love was the revolutionary weapon of the kingdom of God, and learning how to trust and be active agents of its power in the world took the form of ethical choices and decisions. It called for a "love ethic" that radically reversed the power of those in control and a faith identity that the religious status quo was unprepared to accept. Jesus warned His disciples that identification with God's kingdom would create conflict, disturb religious traditions, and put one's life at odds with the "Power that be."

An important concept we should take away from the study of this lesson is that of living with the reality of God's new age. The theological challenge that invites our response is how to live justly with the Good News of God's new age. How do we apply the kingdom principles of love and justice to the human condition and struggle for peace and justice in a violent world? How should love of one's enemies be applied to faith and action? The study of this lesson will help students see that at the core of Jesus' teachings is the theme of spiritual and social liberation, which involves the revolutionary actions of Jesus, who taught His disciples about the rewards and blessings of divine justice.

B. Biblical Background

Biblical scholars interpret Luke 6:17-36 as God's "scandalous" good news for the poor. The Greek word *skandalon*, from which we get the English word *scandal*, means "stumbling blocks" or "that which offends." What made the preaching and teachings of Jesus a "stumbling block" or an "offense" is key to understanding Luke's account of Jesus' "Sermon on the Plain"—known by Christians as the Beatitudes (see Luke 6:20-23). The beatitudes announced God's blessings upon the poor. This aspect of Jesus' teachings was heavily influenced by the eighth-century prophets who prophesied God's deliverance of Israel from the misery of exile and oppression. Jesus' teachings were shaped by the ancient prophets' vision of reversing the hardship, exile, and oppression of ancient Israel. Isaiah 40 proclaims "comfort," good tidings to Zion, and total restoration of the weak. Jesus often referenced Isaiah's proclamation (see Isaiah 61) over the course of His life, which developed in Him the unyielding conviction that God will not falter in establishing a new age of divine governance (the reign of God) on Earth (see Isaiah 42:3). Luke picked up this prophetic vision in his account of Jesus' instructions to the disciples, who listened attentively to the implications and impact that the reign of God would have upon the social condition of the people.

Unlike Matthew, whose writings focused on Jesus' teachings concerning the Judaic laws, the theological lens of Luke reveals features of Jesus' teachings as they relate to the social conditions of the poor. Also different from Matthew's treatment of the Beatitudes, Luke combined "blessings" with lists of "woes" or judgments that come with God's new age. Luke described four blessings and four woes. The woes were in reverse order from the Beatitudes given in the book of Matthew. Matthew listed nine beatitudes and no woes. The scandal of "blessings" and "woes" feature Luke's account of Jesus' teaching. Thus, Luke provided a condensed version of the Beatitudes that fit the concept of God's new age of Good News to the oppressed. In total, this Good News proclaimed that God was at work in history to reverse systems that distorted what God intended to be human reality.

II. EXPOSITION AND APPLICATION OF THE SCRIPTURE

A. Blessings of Divine Justice

(Luke 6:17-23)

And he came down with them, and stood in the plain, and the company of his disciples, and a great multitude of people out of all Judaea and Jerusalem, and from the sea coast of Tyre and Sidon, which came to hear him, and to be healed of their diseases; And they that were vexed with unclean spirits: and they were healed. And the whole multitude sought to touch him: for there went virtue out of him, and healed them all. And he lifted up his eyes on his disciples, and said, Blessed be ye poor: for yours is the kingdom of God. Blessed are ye that hunger now: for ye shall be filled. Blessed are ye that weep now: for ye shall laugh. Blessed are ye, when men shall hate you, and when they shall separate you from their company, and shall reproach you, and cast out your name as evil, for the Son of man's sake. Rejoice ye in that day, and leap for joy: for, behold, your reward is great in heaven: for in the like manner did their fathers unto the prophets.

Luke's "Sermon on the Plain" is often compared to the longer version in Matthew's account of the "Sermon on the Mount" (see Matthew 5–7). In this setting, Matthew's list of Jesus' teachings focused on the "poor in Spirit," while Luke focused on the physical conditions of the "poor." Poverty of spirit that diminishes the human spirit and physical poverty that decimates the body were inseparable concerns of God's liberating love and justice. Considering Jesus' vision of human oneness in God's kingdom, both perspectives are applicable for participating in God's new age of justice and love. Luke used the term *blessed* (*markarios* in the Greek) to highlight God's love for the poor and divine justice to liberate them. In Luke's version of the Beatitudes, Jesus said that the kingdom of God belongs to the poor. Everyone (down to the least in society) has new possibilities as sharers in God's new age. Luke often referenced Jesus' statements about the kingdom and His commitment to its fulfillment. Luke 4:18, 43 illustrates Jesus' prophetic commitment to proclaim the kingdom's Good News to all cities and villages in the region of Galilee. Jesus lived with a singular mission—the fulfillment of the kingdom of God. By Jesus' complete identification with the poor, He made it plain through His teaching and action that poverty, hunger, and injustice robbed people of all dignity and that the kingdom of God would fill them bodily with the blessings of God.

Jesus alerted the disciples to the impact that the blessings of divine justice would have upon their existence and that of the poor, those whom they would later teach and serve, and for whom they would do works of liberation. Jesus' teachings appealed to His disciples and the growing crowd of followers because they were anxious for an alternative reality. For Jesus, the only viable alternative was God's new age of divine justice and love that involved the radical reversal of positions of power and political circumstances. When God's new age dawned, its blessings would take away mourning and replace it with the laughter of people participating in God's new age.

B. The Reversals of Divine Justice (Luke 6:24-26)

But woe unto you that are rich! for ye have received your consolation. Woe unto you that are full! for ye shall hunger. Woe unto you that laugh now! for ye shall mourn and weep. Woe unto you, when all men shall speak well of you! for so did their fathers to the false prophets.

The causes and consequences of poverty are inseparable and produce social alienation and social grief for the poor. Jesus said to people trapped in the social grief of human misery, "Blessed are ye that weep now: for ye shall laugh" (Luke 6:21). The laughter which Jesus promised to those beset by social grief was tied to the new transformation in God's new age. The divine blessings of justice cause radical transformation of conditions of oppression. The rewards of God's new age reverse social grief to laughter. God's blessings in the kingdom change and reverse everything. The hungry are fed; those who weep become joyful as they look back at their journey from oppression to liberation (see Isaiah 61:2; Matthew 5:4; Luke 6:25). Laughter and joy among the oppressed are elements of praise in the kingdom of God (see Psalm 126). The blessing is the joyful noise made unto the Lord by those delivered to a new existence.

African-American Christians can relate to the way God works to reverse conditions of injustice to justice, and social grief to social liberation. The history of black people's struggle for human liberation in America reveals God's unrelenting will and love for justice. We have seen how God's new age of love and justice reverse conditions of brutal slavery, inhumane practices of racial segregation, dehumanizing forms of discrimination, and economic exploitation to the rewards of freedom. Today, at every level of human progress there is African-American leadership. From the president of the United States to leaders in education, health, economics, and public media, there is an African-American presence.

The divine blessings of justice reverse realities of human misery. As witnesses and recipients of kingdom blessings, we have the responsibility of discipleship that honors justice and love in our moral choices and decisions. Luke's gospel account of Jesus' teaching reminds us of the inseparable tie between joys and costs of discipleship in the kingdom of God. Fulfillment of God's kingdom promises do not come without sacrifice and persecutions. The joys of transformation and the reversal of human injustice outweigh their costs and sacrifices. Christians must ask themselves what the evils in our churches and communities are that we should commit ourselves to destroy. When the church becomes complicit with systems of oppression, it forfeits the blessings of divine justice.

Jesus gave the disciples a social strategy for sustaining faith to overcome oppression. Responses of hate, abuse, and social alienation at the hands of those who resisted God's future could be expected. Jesus relayed to the disciples the long tradition of persecution of the prophets, opposition by the religious status quo, and rejection of justice. These responses, Jesus taught, can only be successfully confronted by the moral imperatives of God's kingdom. Jesus told the disciples to be "exceeding glad" that they were on the right side of God's redemptive purpose in history. Their reward would be great in the kingdom of God. The Civil Rights Movement of the 1960s taught us that justice does not come without persecution. Black churches were bombed, individuals were beaten and killed, and protesters were put in jail. But the rewards of the struggle for justice are the blessings of justice and freedom for future generations.

Luke saw in Jesus' teaching both "blessings" and "woes" or judgments. The message of divine blessings for the poor was followed by a list of judgments against those who hold power and wealth to the disadvantage of others. Luke made use of the ancient word *woe* to drive home the consequences of injustice. Just as the divine blessing of justice is an occasion for joy among the poor, Jesus saw the coming of God's new age as a time of judgment among the wealthy. "Woe to you who are rich, for you have received your consolation." Jesus' teaching does not condemn people for the honest achievement of wealth; the judgment is against the unethical use of systems for gain at the expense of others. "Woe to you who are well fed now, for you will go hungry" (Luke 6:25). Wealth often leads to arrogance and the disparagement of others. People who embrace values different from the values of divine justice tend to elevate possessions above the value of people (see Luke 14:15-24). Compassionate concern for neighbor and vindication for the poor are not the values and priorities of a society driven solely by profit motives. Because the kingdom of God is invested in justice, those who cooperate with systems that abandon the poor and put them at a disadvantage invite God's judgment. Justice requires more than charity—it requires non-participation in systems of exploitation for one's personal gain.

C. "Strength to Love"
(Luke 6:27-31)

But I say unto you which hear, Love your enemies, do good

to them which hate you, Bless them that curse you, and pray for them which despitefully use you. And unto him that smiteth thee on the one cheek offer also the other; and him that taketh away thy cloke forbid not to take thy coat also. Give to every man that asketh of thee; and of him that taketh away thy goods ask them not again. And as ye would that men should do to you, do ye also to them likewise.

The principle of divine love is a thread that runs throughout Luke's theological account of Jesus' teachings. The moral force behind Jesus' teaching was the Greek word *agape,* translated "love," which means "to have unconditional goodwill toward all persons." When Jesus bid His disciples to love their enemies, He spoke of *agape*-type love, understanding, and creative, redemptive goodwill for all persons. The application of agape-type love in all situations of human reality is a difficult matter requiring a range of moral reasoning and choices. For Jesus, God's unconditional love must be applicable—even toward an enemy—in order to avoid the violence that proceeds from the ruins of complete moral failure. Who, in the best of circumstances—not to speak of the worst situations of hate and oppression—does not find loving his/her enemy difficult to do? Among the teachings of Jesus, the admonition to "love your enemies" was the most challenging moral directive given to His disciples. It is easy to love those who love you—but to love those who oppress you, who stand in the way of justice and block social flourishing, is another matter. When Jesus said "love your enemy," He was not unmindful of its moral demands. Jesus understood that living on the basis of the power of love transforms one's enemies and is the best strategy for moral victory over oppression. When Jesus spoke of love, He meant the manifestation of God's love working to harmonize human relationships to create freedom and justice for all persons. God is "love in action," overcoming political, economic, and social conflict and reconciling us to His purpose in the world. Jesus realized that returning hate for hate multiplies hate, adding deeper darkness and moral and social oppression.

Living justly with others requires love and forgiveness. Those who persecute and seek to do harm to us are not themselves the evil they do. Those who perpetuate evil systems of injustice are not the evil those systems produce but are persons whose reality has been distorted by evil. Our natural response to those who do us harm is to strike back through some form of violence and/or revenge. But Jesus saw that to reciprocate hate for hate leaves people in moral ruin. So Jesus taught a love ethic of nonviolence to win over one's enemy to a higher moral ground. Jesus realized that achieving this high moral place requires a genuine expression of love that grows out of a consistent and total surrender to God. Breaking the cycle of hate can only occur by having love that is willing to forgive those who perpetuate evil against us.

In admonishing the disciples to "love your enemies," Jesus recognized that the evil and unjust deeds of a person to harm and injure us do not express all that the person is. To see another's true essence and reality with clarity requires love and forgiveness. Love allows us to see that the possible good or the worst we see in our enemies are also possibilities that dwell in us. There is some good in the worst of us and some evil in the best of us. Jesus taught the disciples to look beneath the hate of their enemies and see God's image and love deeply etched into their being. This was the basis of Jesus' nonviolent love ethic—as He admonished His disciples to win over their opponents by blessing and doing good to those who persecuted and despitefully abused them.

III. CONCLUDING REFLECTION

Our society's failure to love and live justly is having global moral consequences. Our world cannot overcome social alienation and injustice without love. The world must live in the kind of community it creates. A world of human competition, individualism, and materialism devoid of love will isolate individuals in camps of social division, hate, and insecurity. We see this kind of society manifesting itself politically across the landscape of America. The lesson study today calls us back to the teachings of Jesus that mandate that our moral choices and treatment of others be guided by divine justice and love in order to overcome injustice and oppression. Jesus' teachings remind us that our humanity is interwoven with the destiny of the poor and the least members of our society. We need others in order to fulfill ourselves. The happier and healthier the community, the happier and healthier are our own lives. The liberating love of God operating in our hearts provides us the moral clarity to work for justice and love for the brother or sister further down. By surrendering ourselves to the love ethic of God's kingdom, we will find the strength to love even our enemies and those who resist the will of God for us. Love is the antidote for hatred, division, and human misery in our world. Jesus calls us to be disciples of this love ethic as the basis for Christian service to others.

PRAYER

God, in a world of hate and malice, injustice and ill will, give us the strength to love even our enemies so that we might be instruments of justice—channeling Your liberating love to everyone we meet. In Jesus' name we pray. Amen.

WORD POWER
Blessed—having God's favor.
Unclean spirits—wicked spirits; demons.
Woe—deep distress or misery, as from grief; wretchedness. (www.answers.com)

HOME DAILY BIBLE READINGS
(January 6-12, 2014)

How to Live as God's People
MONDAY, January 6: "Judged by the Righteous God" (Psalm 7:7-17)
TUESDAY, January 7: "The Righteous and Upright" (Proverbs 11:3-11)
WEDNESDAY, January 8: "Enslaved to God" (Romans 6:16-23)
THURSDAY, January 9: "Living as God's Servants" (1 Peter 2:11-17)
FRIDAY, January 10: "Forgiveness and Mercy" (Matthew 18:21-35)
SATURDAY, January 11: "Blessings and Woes" (Luke 6:20-26)
SUNDAY, January 12: "Do Not Judge" (Luke 6:27-42)

JESUS TEACHES ABOUT RELATIONSHIPS

FAITH PATHWAY/FAITH JOURNEY TOPIC: **Welcoming All People**

DEVOTIONAL READING: **Psalm 147:1-11**
PRINT PASSAGE: **Luke 14:7-18a, 22-24**

BACKGROUND SCRIPTURE: **Luke 14:7-24**
KEY VERSE: **Luke 14:11**

Luke 14:7-18a, 22-24—KJV

7 And he put forth a parable to those which were bidden, when he marked how they chose out the chief rooms; saying unto them,

8 When thou art bidden of any man to a wedding, sit not down in the highest room; lest a more honourable man than thou be bidden of him;

9 And he that bade thee and him come and say to thee, Give this man place; and thou begin with shame to take the lowest room.

10 But when thou art bidden, go and sit down in the lowest room; that when he that bade thee cometh, he may say unto thee, Friend, go up higher: then shalt thou have worship in the presence of them that sit at meat with thee.

11 For whosoever exalteth himself shall be abased; and he that humbleth himself shall be exalted.

12 Then said he also to him that bade him, When thou makest a dinner or a supper, call not thy friends, nor thy brethren, neither thy kinsmen, nor thy rich neighbours; lest they also bid thee again, and a recompence be made thee.

13 But when thou makest a feast, call the poor, the maimed, the lame, the blind:

14 And thou shalt be blessed; for they cannot recompense thee: for thou shalt be recompensed at the resurrection of the just.

15 And when one of them that sat at meat with him heard these things, he said unto him, Blessed is he that shall eat bread in the kingdom of God.

16 Then said he unto him, A certain man made a great supper, and bade many:

Luke 14:7-18a, 22-24—NIV

7 When he noticed how the guests picked the places of honor at the table, he told them this parable:

8 "When someone invites you to a wedding feast, do not take the place of honor, for a person more distinguished than you may have been invited.

9 If so, the host who invited both of you will come and say to you, 'Give this man your seat.' Then, humiliated, you will have to take the least important place.

10 But when you are invited, take the lowest place, so that when your host comes, he will say to you, 'Friend, move up to a better place.' Then you will be honored in the presence of all your fellow guests.

11 For everyone who exalts himself will be humbled, and he who humbles himself will be exalted."

12 Then Jesus said to his host, "When you give a luncheon or dinner, do not invite your friends, your brothers or relatives, or your rich neighbors; if you do, they may invite you back and so you will be repaid.

13 But when you give a banquet, invite the poor, the crippled, the lame, the blind,

14 and you will be blessed. Although they cannot repay you, you will be repaid at the resurrection of the righteous."

15 When one of those at the table with him heard this, he said to Jesus, "Blessed is the man who will eat at the feast in the kingdom of God."

16 Jesus replied: "A certain man was preparing a great banquet and invited many guests.

17 At the time of the banquet he sent his servant to

17 And sent his servant at supper time to say to them that were bidden, Come; for all things are now ready.
18 And they all with one consent began to make excuse.

.....

22 And the servant said, Lord, it is done as thou hast commanded, and yet there is room.
23 And the lord said unto the servant, Go out into the highways and hedges, and compel them to come in, that my house may be filled.
24 For I say unto you, That none of those men which were bidden shall taste of my supper.

tell those who had been invited, 'Come, for everything is now ready.'
18 But they all alike began to make excuses."

.....

22 "'Sir,' the servant said, 'what you ordered has been done, but there is still room.'
23 Then the master told his servant, 'Go out to the roads and country lanes and make them come in, so that my house will be full.
24 I tell you, not one of those men who were invited will get a taste of my banquet.'"

TOPICAL OUTLINE OF THE LESSON

I. Introduction
  A. Hospitality for All
  B. Biblical Background

II. Exposition and Application of the Scripture
  A. Humility and Fellowship (Luke 14:7-11)
  B. Host at the Table (Luke 14:12-14)
  C. The Parable of the Great Banquet (Luke 14:15-18a, 22-24)

III. Concluding Reflection

LESSON OBJECTIVES

Upon the completion of the lesson, the students will be able to do the following:

1. Explore Jesus' teachings about humility and exaltation;
2. Evaluate their attitudes and behavior toward those who are disenfranchised; and,
3. Invite persons who do not normally participate in the local church to do so.

POINTS TO BE EMPHASIZED
ADULT/YOUTH

Adult Topic: Welcoming All People
Youth Topic: How Low Can You Go?
Adult/Youth Key Verse: Luke 14:11
Print Passage: Luke 14:7-18a, 22-24

—Jesus maintained that the meaning of hospitality was found in inviting someone who cannot repay you—someone who is unfamiliar to you.
—Dinner conversations were common teaching settings in the Greek and Jewish worlds.
—Jesus often used parables to help others understand His point of emphasis concerning the kingdom of God.
—Jesus was using His circumstances of being at a dinner to teach about the humility and hospitality that both the host and the guests should show one another.

—Self-exaltation contradicts the spirit of humility that Jesus sought to teach His disciples.

—When completing a list of invitees, a host of an event should include those who cannot repay the favor or invitation. The less fortunate should be remembered and included.

CHILDREN

Children Topic: Respecting Others

Key Verses: Luke 14:13-14a

Print Passage: Luke 14:15-24

—Jesus taught the Pharisees to be humble and hospitable.

—Jesus challenged the Pharisees to do for others without looking for anything in return.

—Jesus challenged the Pharisees to interact with everyone, not just people like them.

—Some people make excuses when they are given an invitation to come to Christ—but the invitation goes out to all people.

I. INTRODUCTION

A. Hospitality for All

In today's lesson, Luke 14:7-24 includes parables that highlight Jesus' values of fairness, humility, and hospitality. These parables illustrate how attitudes of superiority based on social status are barriers not only to good human relations, but also to the creation of civility and enfranchising the lives of the poor and marginal in society.

From a historical perspective, this lesson teaches how hospitality is a social imperative for justice and building community, based on the values of the kingdom of God. The value of social hospitality requires humility, spirituality, and solidarity that recognize the inherent value of all persons.

Living without social barriers requires humility that gives persons a right estimate of themselves. Jesus taught His disciples lessons in kingdom etiquette that focused on humility and respect for the boundaries of others. Jesus' ethic of hospitality saw the spiritual and social value of persons as the criteria for social relations and inclusion in community.

B. Biblical Background

The parables in Luke 14 convey in narrative form the teaching of Jesus' sermon in the synagogue, recorded in Luke 4:18. Luke documented what is considered to have been Jesus' inaugural sermon in the synagogue—in which Jesus announced His prophetic mission of hospitality and preaching to the poor, the brokenhearted, prisoners, and the blind and bruised of society. The original Greek word for "hospitality" in the Bible is *philo* (love) *xenia* (stranger). The fear of strangers blocks hospitality. Other social phobias such as the fear of difference and fear of social isolation played a significant role in ancient Jewish communities where groups were formed around social biases and prejudices to protect group status and security. Jesus overcame those social fears by embodying a spiritual openness to all persons. Jesus embodied a spirituality of equality and mutuality that was inclusive of all aspects of social relationships and common life of people. For Jesus, no one is a stranger to God's inclusive love. All are welcome to the table of hospitality, love, and justice (see John 3:16).

Jesus taught His disciples lessons in kingdom etiquette which recognize the human dignity and worth of others. Since all persons are created in the image of God, Jesus taught that all persons should be treated and seen as God sees them. In other words, we should see all persons as created in the image of God and in the light of God's unconditional love, even for one's enemies (see Luke 6:29-31).

Jesus saw the possibility of fulfilling God's communal love in the most basic relationships in the common lives of people. The meal table, social gatherings, banquets, weddings, and public ceremonial occasions were opportunities for demonstrating spiritual hospitality and etiquette of the kingdom of God. For example, Jesus' hospitality at the wedding in Cana of Galilee responded to a crisis of wine shortage to avoid embarrassment to the host's family (see John 2:1-11).

Samaritans, lepers, and poor widows were beneficiaries of Jesus' hospitality—as He invited them to relationships within the kingdom of God. The meal setting was often used as an occasion by Jesus for demonstrating humility and hospitality, healing and teaching (see John 14:1-14). At these gatherings, Jesus taught how social dispositions ought to serve the higher values of God's kingdom.

Jesus despised how the elaborate banquets of the wealthy imposed social rules and hierarchal status. Jesus taught His disciples not to seek the preferred high places of honor. In Jesus' estimation, honor was not gained by seizing prominence—it was earned by being alert to the needs and longings of others for truth, justice, and compassion. Because truth, justice, and compassion were standard bearers of the kingdom of God, Jesus used them as ethical measures for all social relations.

II. EXPOSITION AND APPLICATION OF THE SCRIPTURE

A. Humility and Fellowship
(Luke 14:7-11)

And he put forth a parable to those which were bidden, when he marked how they chose out the chief rooms; saying unto them, When thou art bidden of any man to a wedding, sit not down in the highest room; lest a more honourable man than thou be bidden of him; And he that bade thee and him come and say to thee, Give this man place; and thou begin with shame to take the lowest room. But when thou art bidden, go and sit down in the lowest room; that when he that bade thee cometh, he may say unto thee, Friend, go up higher: then shalt thou have worship in the presence of them that sit at meat with thee. For whosoever exalteth himself shall be abased; and he that humbleth himself shall be exalted.

The meal setting introduced in Luke 14:1 was brought to the forefront in this section of Luke's gospel. How to host the spirits of others during occasions where food and fellowship bring people together was the focus of Jesus' parable and teaching regarding kingdom etiquette and social graces. Jesus' life is the highest model of hospitality. Jesus knew how to host the spirits of others in all settings of common life. The stranger, the diseased, and the socially outcast were candidates for inclusion in God's kingdom. In Luke 14:7-11, a contrast between the banquet of the Pharisees and the eschatological banquet of God's kingdom can be seen. As described in Jesus' parables, the eschatological banquet invited all to the table of the Lord. God is the host of the spirit of strangers and outcasts. For Jesus, God's eschatological table foreshadows the inclusiveness of the kingdom. The social etiquette of humility and hospitality is the social grace to be practiced at occasions of meal and fellowship.

The important thing to recognize during occasions of food and fellowship is that in greeting and recognizing persons, we are acting as hosts of the spirits of others. Jesus warned the disciple that banquet occasions should not be settings to establish one's social rank and assumed prominence. He taught them not to behave like buffoons who set themselves up for embarrassment. Jesus taught them to exercise to others humility as a social grace. Jesus warned against seeking high places of honor, because they were traps for self-deception and social arrogance.

The Pharisees and lawyers were seen by Jesus as seekers of honor. The word *honor* points to a kind of "glory" that goes beyond the person on which it is bestowed to the glory that belongs to God. Seeking honor for public recognition excludes glory to God. The Pharisees and lawyers used social gatherings to exert their assumed prominence in contrast to the social ranking of others. Jesus saw public recognition and honor as something one should not seek, but one that is earned as a result of treating others with compassion and justice. "All who exalt themselves will be humbled, and those who humble themselves will be exalted" (Luke 7:11).

B. Host at the Table
(Luke 14:12-14)

Then said he also to him that bade him, When thou makest a dinner or a supper, call not thy friends, nor thy brethren, neither thy kinsmen, nor thy rich neighbours; lest they also bid thee again, and a recompence be made thee. But when thou makest a feast, call the poor, the maimed, the lame, the blind: And thou shalt be blessed; for they cannot recompense thee: for thou shalt be recompensed at the resurrection of the just.

Jesus was often at meals with others. The meals, for Jesus, were not only occasions for food and fellowship, but were also times for building genuine community with others. Jesus saw the meal as an occasion for sacredness, affirming the goodness of life and an opportunity to affirm the dignity and spirit of others. Jesus warned against using these occasions for one's own private advantage. As hosts of others, humility and hospitality were essential for honoring and recognizing the worth and dignity of others. In ancient Jewish society, banquets and social gatherings were exclusive and elaborate occasions for establishing social status. The guest lists only included those who were seen as a benefit for one's social ambition. Jesus despised such gatherings, since they only served to exclude those whom God had accepted—the lame and the blind were barred from community fellowship. Exclusion of others based solely on social merit and benefits to oneself violated a cardinal principle of God's kingdom. Meals and experiences of community round the table appeared in many places in Jesus' ministry. Jesus maintained that the meaning of hospitality was found in one's inviting someone into his or her house who could not repay him or her, or someone who was unfamiliar with another. Jesus' inclusion of the crippled, the lame, and the blind challenged the purity code of Leviticus 21:17-23. Jesus taught His disciples to live without social barriers so that they could be free to create human community. Jesus stood against discriminatory hospitality practices. For Jesus, meals were times of celebration and an inclusive fellowship that foreshadowed the inclusiveness of God's kingdom. Banquets and common meals were seen by Jesus as opportunities to be in solidarity with the broken of society.

C. The Parable of the Great Banquet
(Luke 14:15-18a, 22-24)

And when one of them that sat at meat with him heard these things, he said unto him, Blessed is he that shall eat bread in the kingdom of God. Then said he unto him, A certain man made a great supper, and bade many: And sent his servant at supper time to say to them that were bidden, Come; for all things are now ready. And they all with one consent began to make excuse. ...And the servant said, Lord, it is done as thou hast commanded, and yet there is room. And the lord said unto the servant, Go out into the highways and hedges, and compel them to come in, that my house may be filled. For I say unto you, That none of those men which were bidden shall taste of my supper.

The teaching of Jesus against discriminatory hospitality practices are reintroduced in the parable of the great banquet. The guest list of the host was reversed to include unfavorable people, strangers, and outsiders—because the priorities of the invited elite got in the way of their attendance at the banquet. The host and invited guests had a relationship that warranted recognition in the form of a banquet celebration. Those who made up the guest list were seen by others as truly blessed to have been on the VIP list. The host was a wealthy person who employed methods of social stratification to determine his guest list. The invited guests were those who could reciprocate the host with honor and benefits of possessions. The host had the resources to put on an elaborate banquet for his social peers. Every arrangement was made for a great banquet. However, the banquet was radically disrupted when the invited guests politely offered excuses that prevented them from attending. Their excuses revealed their true priorities. They declined the invitation of the host because their priorities shifted. The excuses given were absurd and illustrated lack of respect for the host. Protection and securing possessions got in the way of building communal fellowship and community. Family obligations were offered as excuses that kept the invited guests from attending the banquet. In total, all the excuses offered by the invited guests come to an evaluation of the importance of the benefits for attending the banquet. The excuses were pretenses for covering a "what is in it for me?" disposition, which was the reason for their decisions. For example, the just-married couple's pretense could have meant, in the midst of their own celebration, that they needed to spend time alone with each other, or possibly that as a result of the wedding they were paying bills and could not afford the elaborate expense of attending the banquet. In the case of the property owner, his excuse for not attending was solely based on a need to protect and secure his land. The excuses offered were mere pretenses. The banquet of the host was snubbed.

The parable that Jesus inserted into His teaching to the disciples contrasted the social banquet of the elite with the true blessing of being a guest at the Lord's Table in the eschatological banquet. The Lord's eschatological or kingdom banquet will not be empty of guests. The seats at all tables will be filled with those whom society has abandoned.

Having been rejected by his social peers, the host sought new guests with an open invitation for "Whosoever will let him or her come." The host was driven by a new goal. The diversity of guests was inclusive of outsiders and strangers.

III. CONCLUDING REFLECTION

Jesus' teaching regarding humility and hospitality challenges us to evaluate our social priorities and goals. Exposure of our true priorities might reveal that they are aligned with God's kingdom and works of mercy and compassion. The excuses we offer for nonparticipation in social ministries that honor God's kingdom reveal the activities and commitments we hold in greater esteem. The Lord's banquet table has been set for all to come without barriers of sin, social ostracism, social status, or rank. All are welcome to the table of the Lord. The kingdom banquet of communal love and justice invites "the huddled masses, the tired, and the poor" to a future where all exclusionary and discriminatory social practices are eliminated. A ministry to the homeless and disenfranchised in our society is a gift to those whom Jesus invites to His own table of love and sacrifice, forgiveness and compassion.

PRAYER

Lord, teach us the ways of spiritual and social hospitality. Infuse Your love into our spirits so that we might truly be hosts of those abandoned and abused by the cruelties of life. In Jesus' name we pray. Amen.

WORD POWER

Parable—(1) moral or religious story: a simple short story intended to illustrate a moral or religious lesson; (2) a story ascribed to Jesus Christ: a parable that appears in the Bible, as told by Jesus Christ.

HOME DAILY BIBLE READINGS
(January 13-19, 2014)

Jesus Teaches about Relationships
MONDAY, January 13: "The Danger of Self-exaltation" (Isaiah 14:12-20)
TUESDAY, January 14: "Humble Yourself before the Lord" (James 4:7-12)
WEDNESDAY, January 15: "God Gives Grace to the Humble" (1 Peter 5:1-7)
THURSDAY, January 16: "God Gathers the Outcasts" (Psalm 147:1-11)
FRIDAY, January 17: "God Lifts the Poor and Needy" (Psalm 113)
SATURDAY, January 18: "God Shows No Partiality" (Romans 2:1-11)
SUNDAY, January 19: "Honor and Disgrace" (Luke 14:7-18a, 22-24)

JESUS TEACHES COMPASSION FOR THE POOR

FAITH PATHWAY/FAITH JOURNEY TOPIC: Compassion and Generosity at the Gate

DEVOTIONAL READING: Luke 19:1-10
PRINT PASSAGE: Luke 16:19-31

BACKGROUND SCRIPTURE: Luke 16
KEY VERSE: Luke 16:10

Luke 16:19-31—KJV

19 There was a certain rich man, which was clothed in purple and fine linen, and fared sumptuously every day:

20 And there was a certain beggar named Lazarus, which was laid at his gate, full of sores,

21 And desiring to be fed with the crumbs which fell from the rich man's table: moreover the dogs came and licked his sores.

22 And it came to pass, that the beggar died, and was carried by the angels into Abraham's bosom: the rich man also died, and was buried;

23 And in hell he lift up his eyes, being in torments, and seeth Abraham afar off, and Lazarus in his bosom.

24 And he cried and said, Father Abraham, have mercy on me, and send Lazarus, that he may dip the tip of his finger in water, and cool my tongue; for I am tormented in this flame.

25 But Abraham said, Son, remember that thou in thy lifetime receivedst thy good things, and likewise Lazarus evil things: but now he is comforted, and thou art tormented.

26 And beside all this, between us and you there is a great gulf fixed: so that they which would pass from hence to you cannot; neither can they pass to us, that would come from thence.

27 Then he said, I pray thee therefore, father, that thou wouldest send him to my father's house:

28 For I have five brethren; that he may testify unto

Luke 16:19-31—NIV

19 "There was a rich man who was dressed in purple and fine linen and lived in luxury every day.

20 At his gate was laid a beggar named Lazarus, covered with sores

21 and longing to eat what fell from the rich man's table. Even the dogs came and licked his sores.

22 The time came when the beggar died and the angels carried him to Abraham's side. The rich man also died and was buried.

23 In hell, where he was in torment, he looked up and saw Abraham far away, with Lazarus by his side.

24 So he called to him, 'Father Abraham, have pity on me and send Lazarus to dip the tip of his finger in water and cool my tongue, because I am in agony in this fire.'

25 But Abraham replied, 'Son, remember that in your lifetime you received your good things, while Lazarus received bad things, but now he is comforted here and you are in agony.

26 And besides all this, between us and you a great chasm has been fixed, so that those who want to go from here to you cannot, nor can anyone cross over from there to us.'

27 He answered, 'Then I beg you, father, send Lazarus to my father's house,

28 for I have five brothers. Let him warn them, so that they will not also come to this place of torment.'

them, lest they also come into this place of torment. 29 Abraham saith unto him, They have Moses and the prophets; let them hear them. 30 And he said, Nay, father Abraham: but if one went unto them from the dead, they will repent. 31 And he said unto him, If they hear not Moses and the prophets, neither will they be persuaded, though one rose from the dead.

29 Abraham replied, 'They have Moses and the Prophets; let them listen to them.' 30 'No, father Abraham,' he said, 'but if someone from the dead goes to them, they will repent.' 31 He said to him, 'If they do not listen to Moses and the Prophets, they will not be convinced even if someone rises from the dead.'"

TOPICAL OUTLINE OF THE LESSON

I. Introduction
A. Compassion for the Poor
B. Biblical Background

II. Exposition and Application of the Scripture
A. Moral Disregard for the Poor (Luke 16:19-21)
B. The Lack of Compassion and Its Consequences (Luke 16:22-28)
C. The Lament and Sorrow of the Rich Man (Luke 16:29-31)

III. Concluding Reflection

LESSON OBJECTIVES

Upon the completion of the lesson, the students will be able to do the following:

1. Review the story of the rich man and Lazarus;
2. Discuss their feelings about having compassion toward the poor; and,
3. Involve their congregation in developing a project that addresses their selfishness and has a positive effect on their congregation's attitudes and actions toward the poor.

POINTS TO BE EMPHASIZED

ADULT/YOUTH
Adult Topic: Compassion and Generosity at the Gate
Youth Topic: Lend a Helping Hand
Adult Key Verse: Luke 16:10
Youth Key Verse: Luke 16:13
Print Passage: Luke 16:19-31
—The rich man, though unnamed, is traditionally called "Dives," which is Latin for "rich man."
—The person named here is not the same Lazarus as in John 11–12.
—This is the only parable of Jesus in which one character is given a name.
—"Lazarus" is a form of the name *Eliezer* (Eleazar), which means "God will help." In the book of Genesis, it is the name of Abraham's servant, who thus becomes a paradigm of the faithful servant in Jewish piety.
—Jesus contrasted the relationships between one who is physically rich and one who is rich in humility in order to

show that human wealth and affluence are not determinants used by God concerning salvation.

—Eternal life may involve a reversal of human fortunes.

—The message of salvation is a call to the living to repent.

CHILDREN
Children Topic: First Things First
Key Verse: Luke 16:13

Print Passage: Luke 16:19-31
—Jesus told a story to teach the Pharisees about caring for others.

—Jesus told the Pharisees that people could not serve two masters: God and wealth.

—The Pharisees cared more for material possessions than for people's well-beings.

—Jesus taught about the importance of treating the rich and the poor the same.

—God knows people's hearts.

I. INTRODUCTION
A. Compassion for the Poor

In this section of his gospel, Luke gave a prophetic critique of wealth and material greed. The two main characters in the parable—the rich man and Lazarus—illustrate the parable's principal ethical teaching. What the rich man in the parable prized during his life is a moral offense to the ethics of God's kingdom. Lazarus's condition of poverty called for compassion from the rich man and the society in which he lived—which they clearly lacked. The study of this parable raises important social and moral questions for Christians and society as a whole.

Students should study this lesson from the perspective of poverty being a structural problem requiring individual Christian advocacy and moral compassion for the poor. The teachings of Jesus call Christians to live compassionately toward the poor and to work actively for social and economic justice on their behalf. The parable illustrates the moral insensitivity of the rich man, who had no compassion to attend to the needs of Lazarus.

This lesson is also instructive regarding the Christian obligation to join love with justice in responding to the poor. Not only Christians but all members of society have a moral obligation to the poor and vulnerable. We learn from Jesus' teaching that this justice is reciprocal. What we do or do not do for the weak and vulnerable results in judgment. Society is judged by its treatment of the poor. The parable of the rich man and Lazarus challenges contemporary Christians as consumers, citizens, workers, and owners to "love one's neighbor."

B. Biblical Background

By the inclusion of the parable of the rich man and Lazarus in his gospel record, Luke offered Jesus' prophetic critique of empire wealth and its impact upon the poor. For Jesus, no dimension of human life lies beyond God's care and concern. In opposition to the worldly reality of materialism, Jesus taught that every individual possessed an inalienable dignity of being created in the image of God (see Genesis 1:27) and thus were not subjects of Rome but citizens of the kingdom of God.

Jesus' parable teaches the love and justice mandate of the coming reign of God. God is a "God of justice" (Isaiah 30:18), who loves justice (see Isaiah 61:8). God demanded justice from the whole community (see Deuteronomy 16:20) and executed justice for the needy (see Psalm 140:12). Central to Jesus' understanding of justice was how the poor and the stranger (non-Israelites) were treated.

In the case of the rich man, Jesus' critique and judgment of materialism and greed plays out in what occurred at the end of his life. The rich man's neglect and treatment of Lazarus's poverty became the basis for eternal judgment. The judgment of the rich man is one that tells Christians to have regard for human dignity— in ourselves and in others—and the showing of justice through service and compassion.

II. EXPOSITION AND APPLICATION OF THE SCRIPTURE

A. Moral Disregard for the Poor (Luke 16:19-21)

There was a certain rich man, which was clothed in purple and fine linen, and fared sumptuously every day: And there was a certain beggar named Lazarus, which was laid at his gate, full of sores, And desiring to be fed with the crumbs which fell from the rich man's table: moreover the dogs came and licked his sores.

Luke presented the parable of the rich man and Lazarus in a cluster of parables that Jesus spoke to audiences that resonated with His message of the kingdom of God. A principal feature of these parables is the reordering of relationships in love and justice. The rich man in the parable illustrates the fate of those whose lifestyles reject the ethical demands of the kingdom of God. The rich man was a person who was insensitive to the poverty-stricken Lazarus. The wealth of the rich man and the poverty of Lazarus represented extreme disparities that reflected the economic systems of society. The society in which they lived is a tableau of economic disparities. The rich man was oblivious to the concerns of a just society marked by love and compassion. His daily routine was undisturbed by the poverty beyond the gate of his lavish home. He dressed in fine linen and feasted sumptuously every day. Minimal justice and compassion asked the rich man to at least recognize the condition of Lazarus by stopping to render aid and help. But the rich man showed no moral consciousness toward the poor condition of Lazarus. The rich man was undisturbed by the kind of poverty that deeply disturbs God. The rich man lived with an economic surplus while Lazarus lived in rags. Poverty may have caused ill health for Lazarus, with sores breaking out on his body. The dogs licked his sores while the rich man did nothing to help.

The name *Lazarus* meant "God helps." The inhumanity of the rich man was his refusal to help one whom God would help. Lazarus was a crippled beggar whose body was covered with running sores, yet he received help from no one. In the urban density of the city, Lazarus sat daily at the gate to the rich man's house. The surplus of the rich man, whether bread or medicine, did not go to aid Lazarus. Lazarus would have gladly received the thrown-away food or other used items for his sores. At feasts hosted by the rich, crumbs would have been under the table (see Mark 7:28). The rich man saw how the ravages of starvation decimated the body of Lazarus.

The sin of the rich man is both spiritual and social. His deep contempt for the poor while living in luxury and a self-absorbed lifestyle is a violation of what it means to honor the sacredness and dignity of human life. Lazarus was diseased in his body; the rich man was diseased in his soul. Wealth functioned to separate and insulate the rich man from the poverty surrounding him. The rich man's disregard for Lazarus paralleled his disregard for God (see Luke 16:13).

B. The Lack of Compassion and Its Consequences (Luke 16:22-28)

And it came to pass, that the beggar died, and was carried by the angels into Abraham's bosom: the rich man also died, and was buried; And in hell he lift up his eyes, being in torments, and seeth Abraham afar off, and Lazarus in his bosom. And he cried and said, Father Abraham, have mercy on me, and send Lazarus, that he may dip the tip of his finger in water, and cool my tongue; for I am tormented in this flame. But Abraham said, Son, remember that thou in thy lifetime receivedst thy good things, and likewise Lazarus evil things: but now he is comforted, and thou art tormented. And beside all this, between us and you there is a great gulf fixed: so that they which would pass from hence to you cannot; neither can they pass to us, that would come from thence. Then he said, I pray thee therefore, father, that thou wouldest send him to my father's house: For I have five brethren; that he may testify unto them, lest they also come into this place of torment.

After both the rich man and Lazarus died, their realities were reversed. The rich became poor and the poor man became rich. The ultimate end for Lazarus was in the bosom of Abraham—the place of highest bliss in Jewish eschatology. Lazarus was the honored guest at the eschatological banquet, feasting while the rich man was in torment. The rich man ended up in "Hades," the place where the dead await the final judgment. Their realities were reversed, which was in clear sight of the rich man. The disciples and others who may have heard the parable were perhaps surprised by the turn of events. It was believed that blessings in life and earthly blessings were a sign of God's favor, while suffering, poverty, and hardship were signs of God's displeasure. The hearers of the parable may have been puzzled. "How could a beggar go to heaven?" they might have thought. The parable does not refer to any righteous disposition of Lazarus that would merit him a place of bliss in the bosom of Abraham. This emphasis is not on the personal righteousness of Lazarus but rather on God's claim of His humanity as sacred.

The rich man pleaded to Abraham for relief from his miserable state. "Father Abraham" was admonished to send Lazarus to dip his finger in water to cool the rich man's tongue. Because he knew Lazarus by name, it can be assumed that the rich man had known of the suffering of the beggar at his gate. Lazarus was requested to render service to the rich man, which the rich man did not offer Lazarus as he suffered daily at the rich man's gate. Lazarus finally found voice in the bosom of Abraham. He had no voice on Earth amidst poverty and suffering. The rich man pleaded for compassion. He pleaded to Abraham, "Send Lazarus to relieve my torment." Abraham's response was one of judgment. Abraham connected the lives and rewards of the rich man and Lazarus. He called for the rich man to remember the disregarded opportunities to show compassion toward Lazarus (see Luke 16:25). It is a "dangerous memory" for the rich man, in the sense that he must hold himself accountable for his failures to be compassionate—but in his own miserable state, he needed the service and compassion of Lazarus. Now that the positions were reversed, the rich man had the clarity he wished he had when presented with opportunities to do justice and love mercy. The rich man had unhindered access to Lazarus during the time of their earthly lives; however, all he displayed were apathy and indifference. Now that the positions were reversed, a chasm existed that prevented Lazarus from responding to the rich man's torment with compassion.

The rich man realized what this judgment meant eternally for him and then pleaded for his brothers to be told of the consequences of leading a non-compassionate lifestyle that neglected the poor—so that they might repent.

C. The Lament and Sorrow of the Rich Man (Luke 16:29-31)

Abraham saith unto him, They have Moses and the prophets; let them hear them. And he said, Nay, father Abraham: but if one went unto them from the dead, they will repent. And he said unto him, If they hear not Moses and the prophets, neither will they be persuaded, though one rose from the dead.

In judgment, the rich man lamented in sorrow. In the torment of "Hades" he had clarity about his wrong moral choices. The consequences of judgment brought finality to what he might have done differently. The great chasm between the rich man in "Hades" and Lazarus in the bosom of Abraham is fixed. The rich man's repentance took the form of a request for warning his brothers to reverse their ways of life and regard for the poor. His last hope was that his brothers would not follow

him to the horrible place of torment which was his permanent abode. Abraham's response to the rich man's request concludes the parable. The rich man's request carried an urgent appeal to convince his family to repent. The record of Moses and prophets, however, had not influenced the rich man's morality, while he had opportunity to repent during his life. The rich man's neglect of Lazarus corresponded to his neglect of the laws of Moses and the prophets' call for justice and mercy toward the poor and strangers. The rich man's brothers had the same opportunity that he had been given to repent. Abraham's response to his request is indicative of a non-repentant generation that resisted the ethical demands of God's kingdom. If the brothers would not hear Moses and the prophets, then they would not be convinced even if one should rise from the dead. The language of Abraham's reply anticipates how people will respond to the transforming reality of Jesus' resurrection (see Luke 18:33). Repentance is an act of the human will—and even in the face of God's demonstration of power in Jesus' resurrection, some still will refuse to repent. The tragic conclusion of the parable is that a non-repentant generation rejected God's mercy.

The sin of the rich man was rooted in a hardhearted contempt for the poor. His moral disposition toward the poor resisted a change of heart to take a new moral path. The rich man's moral failure is a fundamental challenge to all Christians to work to humanize life by responding to the social wounds of poverty. The teaching of Jesus' parable goes beyond a charitable flinging of a coin to a beggar on the street corner. Ameliorations such as food and medicine are necessary, but there is need for love and social justice and a change in the conditions that place victims of poverty in a public light.

III. CONCLUDING REFLECTION

The pattern of poverty and wealth presents challenges to Christians today. Luke's gospel has been described as a "social gospel" for the liberation of the poor. The first public proclamation of Jesus included a commitment to preach Good News to the poor and liberate them to the alternatives of the kingdom of God (see Luke 4:18; cf. Isaiah 61:2). The parable of Jesus warns the prosperous not to be blind to the great poverty that exists beside great wealth. Jesus took the side of Lazarus and warned of the dangers of wealth. A constant biblical refrain is that the poor must be cared for and protected and that when they are exploited, God hears their cries (see Proverbs 22:22-23). The teaching of Jesus calls for openness to God's reign of love and justice for the transformation of life for all persons.

PRAYER

O God, Your mercies have touched our lives in compassionate ways, giving us transformation and hope. As receivers of mercy, make us instruments of Your love and justice for the poor in the world. Turn our love toward those for whom Your divine love is dedicated. In Jesus' name we pray. Amen.

WORD POWER

Abraham's Bosom—refers to the place of comfort in sheol (Greek: hades) where the Jews said the righteous dead awaited Judgment Day.

Hell—(1) the abode of condemned souls and devils in some religions; the place of eternal punishment for the wicked after death, presided over by Satan; (2) a state of separation from God; exclusion from God's presence; (3) the abode of the dead, identified with the Hebrew *Sheol* and the Greek *Hades*; the underworld.

Sumptuously—splendid: magnificent or grand in appearance; extravagant: entailing great expense.

HOME DAILY BIBLE READINGS
(January 20-26, 2014)

Jesus Teaches Compassion for the Poor

MONDAY, January 20: "An Open Hand to the Poor" (Deuteronomy 15:7-11)

TUESDAY, January 21: "The Cry of the Poor and Afflicted" (Job 34:17-30)

WEDNESDAY, January 22: "False Concern for the Poor" (John 12:1-8)

THURSDAY, January 23: "I Will Give to the Poor" (Luke 19:1-10)

FRIDAY, January 24: "Shrewdness and the Future" (Luke 16:1-9)

SATURDAY, January 25: "Master of the Heart" (Luke 16:10-18)

SUNDAY, January 26: "Comfort and Agony" (Luke 16:19-31)

HEAR AND DO THE WORD

FAITH PATHWAY/FAITH JOURNEY TOPIC: Committed to Action

DEVOTIONAL READING: 1 John 3:14-20
PRINT PASSAGE: James 1:19-27

BACKGROUND SCRIPTURE: James 1:19-27
KEY VERSE: James 1:22

James 1:19-27—KJV

19 Wherefore, my beloved brethren, let every man be swift to hear, slow to speak, slow to wrath:

20 For the wrath of man worketh not the righteousness of God.

21 Wherefore lay apart all filthiness and superfluity of naughtiness, and receive with meekness the engrafted word, which is able to save your souls.

22 But be ye doers of the word, and not hearers only, deceiving your own selves.

23 For if any be a hearer of the word, and not a doer, he is like unto a man beholding his natural face in a glass:

24 For he beholdeth himself, and goeth his way, and straightway forgetteth what manner of man he was.

25 But whoso looketh into the perfect law of liberty, and continueth therein, he being not a forgetful hearer, but a doer of the work, this man shall be blessed in his deed.

26 If any man among you seem to be religious, and bridleth not his tongue, but deceiveth his own heart, this man's religion is vain.

27 Pure religion and undefiled before God and the Father is this, To visit the fatherless and widows in their affliction, and to keep himself unspotted from the world.

James 1:19-27—NIV

19 My dear brothers, take note of this: Everyone should be quick to listen, slow to speak and slow to become angry,

20 for man's anger does not bring about the righteous life that God desires.

21 Therefore, get rid of all moral filth and the evil that is so prevalent and humbly accept the word planted in you, which can save you.

22 Do not merely listen to the word, and so deceive yourselves. Do what it says.

23 Anyone who listens to the word but does not do what it says is like a man who looks at his face in a mirror

24 and, after looking at himself, goes away and immediately forgets what he looks like.

25 But the man who looks intently into the perfect law that gives freedom, and continues to do this, not forgetting what he has heard, but doing it—he will be blessed in what he does.

26 If anyone considers himself religious and yet does not keep a tight rein on his tongue, he deceives himself and his religion is worthless.

27 Religion that God our Father accepts as pure and faultless is this: to look after orphans and widows in their distress and to keep oneself from being polluted by the world.

TOPICAL OUTLINE OF THE LESSON

I. Introduction
A. Good Religion
B. Biblical Background

II. Exposition and Application of the Scripture
A. Put It Down (James 1:19-21)
B. Pick It Up (James 1:22-24)
C. Pass It On (James 1:25-27)

III. Concluding Reflection

LESSON OBJECTIVES

Upon the completion of the lesson, the students will be able to do the following:

1. Review the relationship that is expressed in the Scripture between hearing and doing the Word;
2. Express their feelings about hearing and doing God's Word; and,
3. Develop practical strategies for taking actions that adhere to the Word.

POINTS TO BE EMPHASIZED

ADULT/YOUTH
Adult Topic: Committed to Action
Youth Topic: Just Do It!
Adult/Youth Key Verse: James 1:22
Print Passage: James 1:19-27

—James labeled as deceptive and worthless belief that is merely mental or verbal assent and that fails to translate into tempered speech and right action.
—James's "doers of the word" admonition of verse 22 is a primary theme, resurfacing in 2:2-4, 12, 14, 17, 24, and 26.
—James described faithful living as both rejecting some things and internalizing and embracing others.
—Authentic faith moves beyond hearing and knowing the Word of God to doing the will of God, and demonstrating the love of God through acts of charity and justice among the poor and powerless.
—James contrasted human anger with the righteousness of God. He cautioned disciples to exemplify God's Word in their lives.
—"Religion that is pure" is expressed by doing ministry and living in a manner that pleases God.

CHILDREN
Children Topic: Obeying Rules
Key Verse: James 1:22
Print Passage: James 1:19-27

—Anger does not lead to righteousness.
—The Word of God is an appeal to action—so hearing God's Word must lead to putting God's Word into action.
—The Word of God is like a mirror that reflects who one is.
—Those people who do or obey God's Word will be blessed.
—Caring for those who are in need puts God's Word into practice.
—One's speech demonstrates one's character as a Christian.

I. INTRODUCTION

A. Good Religion

The epistle of James is the most practical treatment of the meaning of religion found in the early literature of the first-century church. The Latin word for "religion," *religare*—which means "to tie, to bind"—highlights the emphasis that James placed upon the ethical practice of Christian faith. James understood religion as being something more than having a simple belief system that affirmed the existence of God. Religion is living under the guidance of "wisdom from above" that holds together the meaning of life with the reality of God. Religion that is false or unauthentic bases one's morality in wisdom from below, which leads to envy, oppression, and unbridled judgment against others. The letter of James includes clear moral exhortation that focuses on the practical wisdom which Christians must embrace if their lives are to be "living demonstrations" of faith in God. The necessity of acting out one's faith convictions is a prominent ethical feature in the letter of James, which demands *orthodoxy* (right belief) that coheres with and matches *orthopraxis* (right action).

James understood religious faith in terms of allegiance to God that translated into relevant action. In other words, wisdom that God gives from above lives itself out in the common life of daily relationships. Those who are wise adhere to God's wisdom that shuns moral behaviors based in envy, individualism, and immorality. Thus, the letter of James draws from the traditional wisdom of the Hebrew prophets and the life of Jesus—which honors the practical outcomes of love and justice and recognizes regard for one's neighbor as the pure essence of religion.

The study of this lesson will challenge the church to give close scrutiny to how its faith matches up with action, and how having an understanding of God correlates with the church's mission and ministry.

B. Biblical Background

The letter of James is a moral discourse for theological and ethical guidance to the early church. Written in the style of brief diatribe—a characteristic of the Wisdom Literature—the content of the letter offers moral exhortations for living effectively in a pagan world (see James 2:14-19). James imparted moral imperatives to the Christian community, similar to those found in Hebrew Wisdom Literature. James viewed the Law positively and understood its purpose as producing right actions that benefitted others and kept believers morally pure. James sought to persuade the early church to live up to their profession of faith to which they had committed themselves—namely, the faith "in our glorious Lord Jesus Christ" (see James 2:1).

The letter of James covers a range of moral rhetoric aimed at sustaining Christian discipline and perseverance against extreme challenges to the faith of the church. Scholars label these instructions as "wisdom from above" that respond to the misleading moral calculations of "wisdom from below." The wisdom from below is the wisdom of the world, which is based in desire and envy and leads to every form of competition, violence, and eventually murder and war (see James 3:13–4:3). In contrast, the "wisdom from above" is given by God through the "implanted word" (Jesus Christ). Human wisdom or "wisdom from below" lacks the imperatives as moral literature with wisdom characteristics. James was more concerned with morality, moral attitudes, and behavior than with gaining worldly honor and success.

The theological ethics of James considers true religion to include the visiting of the sick, orphans, and widows, and hearing the cry of the oppressed.

For James, "the faith of Jesus" means living before God in a manner shaped by the words of Jesus; and, by Jesus' declaration, that loving one's neighbor as oneself is the "moral law" of a profession of faith in Jesus Christ. The letter of James is a clear rejection of immorality in "the world" as measured by God.

The study of this lesson will enable the students to grasp a strong basis for applying Christian "social ethics" in daily living and determine what Christian morality means as measured by God's gift of love through Jesus Christ.

II. EXPOSITION AND APPLICATION OF THE SCRIPTURE

A. Put It Down
(James 1:19-21)

Wherefore, my beloved brethren, let every man be swift to hear, slow to speak, slow to wrath: For the wrath of man worketh not the righteousness of God. Wherefore lay apart all filthiness and superfluity of naughtiness, and receive with meekness the engrafted word, which is able to save your souls.

The strong admonition to "be swift to hear, slow to speak, (and) slow to wrath" may be a reference to readers' accusations against God, or it may simply be a general statement about hearing and speaking. It is written as a proverb and has all of the power and wisdom of the ancient sayings. There is a strong correlation between listening and outbursts of anger. The correlation is, however, notably negative. The more the outburst in anger, the less we actually listen to what is being said and are capable of giving a righteous word to help someone through a tough and trying situation. When a Christian gives place to wrath, it makes him or her incapable of acting justly or righteously—as the person becomes blinded by his or her selfish rage. To add weight to the folly of wrath and to act in such a way hinders and possibly prevents the vindication of God's righteousness in the world. In verse 21, we are charged to "lay apart all filthiness." Since the Word is a seed, it must have good soil in order to thrive. We cannot be used by God to bring others to Him if we are entangled in sin and shame, disgracing our names and causing others to look down on us rather than up to us. In order to truly be equipped to handle the challenges of the world and be positioned to help someone in need, we must have the "engrafted word." Note the fact that this is something you must accept with meekness. This means that you must willingly accept what God allows and learn from the process.

B. Pick It Up
(James 1:22-24)

But be ye doers of the word, and not hearers only, deceiving your own selves. For if any be a hearer of the word, and not a doer, he is like unto a man beholding his natural face in a glass: For he beholdeth himself, and goeth his way, and straightway forgetteth what manner of man he was.

Christianity is a religion of action. As important as it is to listen, one must not stop there. *Doing* must follow *listening*. To be a hearer only is a form of deception, a trap into which the enemy loves for Christians to fall. We cannot sit idle, allowing the Word to not take root and grow; once it is planted and takes root, it will produce. It is not enough to remember what we hear and to be able to repeat it—we must take our faith in the Word to the next level. A proverb is introduced; this one challenges our intellects with a common phrase about looking into the mirror and forgetting what we just saw. As looking glasses show us spots and blemishes to be cleaned up, so the Word of God does the same for us. The problem comes when we look at our faces, do nothing about the dirt on them, and then later try to remember what was wrong. The same is true with sin. When God exposes our sin to us, we should make every effort to repent and seek to change. We cannot wait until later to get it right. This self-serving attitude belittles the grace of God and puffs up humans, causing them only to fall harder at a later time. The tenses of the verbs in verse 24 are interesting; note "beholdeth," "goeth," and "forgetteth."

James said that the impression was momentary. If something was not done in that moment to engage and sustain the momentum of any change, then all would be lost. While this is a form of action, it is a form of unfocused action. This is not the way that Christians are to behave. We must move with active intentionality, just as God has moved and continues to move in our lives.

C. Pass It On
(James 1:25-27)

But whoso looketh into the perfect law of liberty, and continueth therein, he being not a forgetful hearer, but a doer of the work, this man shall be blessed in his deed. If any man among you seem to be religious, and bridleth not his tongue, but deceiveth his own heart, this man's religion is vain. Pure religion and undefiled before God and the Father is this, To visit the fatherless and widows in their affliction, and to keep himself unspotted from the world.

The mirror analogy or proverb applies to the issue of a believer's behavior or doing. The mirror, which reveals the imperfection of the outer man, is now contrasted with the "perfect law"—the law of freedom—which reflects the inner person. This is the first reference to *law* in this epistle. James used the term to denote the ethical side of Christianity—the *diache*, or "teaching." Here, James called the law *perfect*. Compare this with Psalm 19:7. For James, the Law was made perfect because of Christ. The "law of liberty" probably means that it applies to those who were free—not from the law, but from sin and self through the Word of truth. Remember, Jesus did not come to destroy the Law, but to fulfill the Law. The man who looks into the Law and makes a habit of doing so (*paramenias*) will become a "doer of the word" and will find true happiness—for he "shall be blessed in his deed." Following this prescription leads to walking in liberty. This process sheds light on the evolution of the Law—as that it moves from being a burden upon the people, mainly due to human misuse of the Law, to a perfect Law as Christ concisely and precisely penetrates the heart of humanity. It is from this piercing that man becomes free to dwell in love with God, even in this sinful, sick world. This is the freedom we enjoy in Christ Jesus: not the freedom to do whatever we want, but to speak, walk, and act in love.

III. CONCLUDING REFLECTION

As people of faith, we seek to change the way we live in order to match what we say we believe. This is never easy, but it is our charge and task. Christians understand human life within the context of community and relationship rather than in isolated individualism. We understand the power and need of community. This was a powerful testimony of the early church. How can we get this back? People of faith live with consistent commitment to a God-defined reality and allow the Word of God to show them not only who they are, but also who they can become. This revelation stretches and strengthens as we grow to live more like Christ. Because of our love for God, we realize that human freedom comes from allegiance to wisdom from above. This connection gives us power to make wise choices that benefit all of humanity. We can display acts of charity and champion the cause of justice for the voiceless and powerless.

PRAYER

O God, when our faith is tested, give us wisdom and patience until Your purpose is realized through us. Grant us courage in our hours of trial. Teach us how to be hearers and doers of Your Word. In Jesus' name we pray. Amen.

WORD POWER

Wisdom—the quality or state of being wise; knowledge of what is true or right coupled with just judgment to act; sagacity, discernment, or insight. (www.dictionary.reference.com/browse/wisdom)

HOME DAILY BIBLE READINGS
(January 27–February 2, 2014)

Hear and Do the Word
MONDAY, January 27: "A People Who Will Not Listen" (Jeremiah 7:21-28)
TUESDAY, January 28: "A Lamp to Lighten My Darkness" (2 Samuel 22:26-31)
WEDNESDAY, January 29: "The Voice of the Living God" (Deuteronomy 5:22-27)
THURSDAY, January 30: "Neither Add nor Take Away Anything" (Deuteronomy 4:1-10)
FRIDAY, January 31: "Denying God by Actions" (Titus 1:10-16)
SATURDAY, February 1: "Love in Truth and Action" (1 John 3:14-20)
SUNDAY, February 2: "Hearers and Doers of the Word" (James 1:19-27)

TREAT EVERYONE EQUALLY

FAITH PATHWAY/FAITH JOURNEY TOPIC: **Playing Favorites**

DEVOTIONAL READING: **Romans 13:8-14**
PRINT PASSAGE: **James 2:1-13**

BACKGROUND SCRIPTURE: **James 2:1-13**
KEY VERSE: **James 2:5**

James 2:1-13—KJV

MY BRETHREN, have not the faith of our Lord Jesus Christ, the Lord of glory, with respect of persons.
2 For if there come unto your assembly a man with a gold ring, in goodly apparel, and there come in also a poor man in vile raiment;
3 And ye have respect to him that weareth the gay clothing, and say unto him, Sit thou here in a good place; and say to the poor, Stand thou there, or sit here under my footstool:
4 Are ye not then partial in yourselves, and are become judges of evil thoughts?
5 Hearken, my beloved brethren, Hath not God chosen the poor of this world rich in faith, and heirs of the kingdom which he hath promised to them that love him?
6 But ye have despised the poor. Do not rich men oppress you, and draw you before the judgment seats?
7 Do not they blaspheme that worthy name by the which ye are called?
8 If ye fulfil the royal law according to the scripture, Thou shalt love thy neighbour as thyself, ye do well:
9 But if ye have respect to persons, ye commit sin, and are convinced of the law as transgressors.
10 For whosoever shall keep the whole law, and yet offend in one point, he is guilty of all.
11 For he that said, Do not commit adultery, said also, Do not kill. Now if thou commit no adultery, yet if thou kill, thou art become a transgressor of the law.
12 So speak ye, and so do, as they that shall be judged by the law of liberty.
13 For he shall have judgment without mercy, that hath shewed no mercy; and mercy rejoiceth against judgment.

James 2:1-13—NIV

MY BROTHERS, as believers in our glorious Lord Jesus Christ, don't show favoritism.
2 Suppose a man comes into your meeting wearing a gold ring and fine clothes, and a poor man in shabby clothes also comes in.
3 If you show special attention to the man wearing fine clothes and say, "Here's a good seat for you," but say to the poor man, "You stand there" or "Sit on the floor by my feet,"
4 have you not discriminated among yourselves and become judges with evil thoughts?
5 Listen, my dear brothers: Has not God chosen those who are poor in the eyes of the world to be rich in faith and to inherit the kingdom he promised those who love him?
6 But you have insulted the poor. Is it not the rich who are exploiting you? Are they not the ones who are dragging you into court?
7 Are they not the ones who are slandering the noble name of him to whom you belong?
8 If you really keep the royal law found in Scripture, "Love your neighbor as yourself," you are doing right.
9 But if you show favoritism, you sin and are convicted by the law as lawbreakers.
10 For whoever keeps the whole law and yet stumbles at just one point is guilty of breaking all of it.
11 For he who said, "Do not commit adultery," also said, "Do not murder." If you do not commit adultery but do commit murder, you have become a lawbreaker.
12 Speak and act as those who are going to be judged by the law that gives freedom,
13 because judgment without mercy will be shown to anyone who has not been merciful. Mercy triumphs over judgment!

People show partiality toward others for a variety of reasons. How can we avoid favoritism? James reminded his followers of the importance of justice practiced through taking care of the poor and loving our neighbors as ourselves.

TOPICAL OUTLINE OF THE LESSON

I. Introduction
A. A Religion without Prejudice
B. Biblical Background

II. Exposition and Application of the Scripture
A. The Sin of Partiality (James 2:1-7)
B. Practice What Your Religion Preaches (James 2:8-11)
C. The Working of Mercy (James 2:12-13)

III. Concluding Reflection

LESSON OBJECTIVES

Upon the completion of the lesson, the students will be able to do the following:

1. Review James' writings concerning partiality and ways to avoid it;
2. Explore the full meaning of the phrase, "Love your neighbor as yourself"; and,
3. Investigate ways that they discriminate against certain groups and come up with ways to express love to those groups.

POINTS TO BE EMPHASIZED

ADULT/YOUTH
Adult Topic: Playing Favorites
Youth Topic: Hey! Do Not Play Favorites!
Adult Key Verse: James 2:5
Youth Key Verse: James 2:1
Print Passage: James 2:1-13

—James addressed an apparently common situation concerning discrimination and partiality; Paul reported two similar incidents (see 1 Corinthians 11:17-34; Galatians 2:11-14).
—James recognized that Jewish law was extremely difficult if not impossible to keep, and believed that a Christian must work that much harder not to break it in any way. To break the Law in any way was to break it in all ways.
—James concluded that the principle of mercy is more important than the Law.
—James forbade disciples from being partial to the wealthy and affluent. All are to be made welcome to worship the Lord.
—Loving your neighbor includes loving people who are different from you.
—Disciples are to keep the entire Law rather than just parts of it; disobeying one part of the Law is essentially the same as disobeying the entire Law.
—Those who judge others according to the Law must remember that they will likewise be judged by the Law.
—God is a merciful God, but God will judge those who refuse to show mercy to others.

CHILDREN
Children Topic: Do Not Play Favorites
Key Verse: James 2:8
Print Passage: James 2:1-13

—Believers demonstrate a lack of faith when they show favoritism.

—God has chosen the poor of the world to be rich in faith.

—The rich of the world may take advantage of the poor of the world.

—The royal law—"love your neighbor"—should cancel out the practice of favoritism.

—Believers must not show favoritism.

I. INTRODUCTION

A. A Religion without Prejudice

The letter of James deals with the enduring problem of partiality and bias in public and religious life. The letter of James seeks to ensure that the religious practices of the church do not mimic worldly prejudice against the poor and oppressed at the hands of rich and powerful persons. When worldly ambitions of power and wealth take over the religion of the church, it is a "religion" which James declared was an offense to God. The problems of race, gender, and social discrimination are a continuing dilemma for Christians today.

In the first century, when James sat down to write a letter to the first Christians, he had no concept of the religious pluralism that would characterize American life today. But the teaching of the letter of James parallels the concern for the practice of religion without favoritism, bias, and discrimination, which today is a huge social problem.

As we study this section of the letter of James, we should note how easily cultural biases and prejudices hide in religious beliefs and how such beliefs are complicit with racism, sexism, and discrimination against those who are different from the majority.

The letter of James challenges every Christian to examine the basis of discrimination in religious practices, social relations, and moral decisions. We must realize that no religious faith, whether Christian or otherwise, is exempt from cultural practices incoherent with the law of God's love. James reaffirmed that the love of God and neighbor was the bottom line of authentic religion, which roots out all forms of fear, bias, prejudice, and discrimination against minority groups based on class, race, gender, and sex.

B. Biblical Background

James 2:1-13 addresses a common human problem concerning discrimination and partiality. James declared that all forms of favoritism based on wealth, social hierarchies, and rank stand against the love ethic of Jesus. In addressing the problem of religious discrimination, James upheld teachings from both Hebrew Scripture and from the teaching of Jesus (see Matthew 5:3; Luke 6:20). The Torah forbade discriminating between the rich and the poor based on appearance and insisted that leaders judge cases impartially (see Leviticus 19:15). James understood that the purpose of the Law was to ensure love, equality, and impartiality to all, regardless of social status. James 2:1-13 can be divided into verses 1-7—which present a vivid example of how a religious community acts in opposition to its professed ideal; and verses 8-13—which show how such behavior is inconsistent with the claim to live by the law of love taught by Jesus. This section of the letter addresses favoritism as incompatible with the faith of the inclusive love ethic of Jesus (see James 2:1). James made the point that discrimination and exploitation of the poor was not only a serious offense, but also a situation against which people of faith must take action. According to James, people of faith discover that the law of love is specific rather than vague or abstract, and it finds expression in seemingly simple things, such as the way people are treated in public spaces. James insisted that people of faith recognize that the law of love extends not just to those they find attractive or valuable, but far beyond to those they find unlovely, undesirable, or even threatening as well. James insisted that compassion defines the morality of people of faith. Compassion and mercy were seen by James as the test of bearing the name of Jesus, and as the only hope for participating in the coming reign of God.

II. EXPOSITION AND APPLICATION OF THE SCRIPTURE

A. The Sin of Partiality
(James 2:1-7)

MY BRETHREN, have not the faith of our Lord Jesus Christ, the Lord of glory, with respect of persons. For if there come unto your assembly a man with a gold ring, in goodly apparel, and there come in also a poor man in vile raiment; And ye have respect to him that weareth the gay clothing, and say unto him, Sit thou here in a good place; and say to the poor, Stand thou there, or sit here under my footstool: Are ye not then partial in yourselves, and are become judges of evil thoughts? Hearken, my beloved brethren, Hath not God chosen the poor of this world rich in faith, and heirs of the kingdom which he hath promised to them that love him? But ye have despised the poor. Do not rich men oppress you, and draw you before the judgment seats? Do not they blaspheme that worthy name by the which ye are called?

James insisted that the practice of religion must be without partiality. Classism and caste had no place in the spirit of religion that represents the teachings of Jesus. The faith of Jesus is not compatible with deference and discrimination between persons because of their social or financial status. James saw such biased judgments as leading to evil. Evil practices manifest themselves in social dispositions that favor one group over another. The faith which represents the religion of Jesus disavows distinctions based upon birth, race, property, or gender (see Galatians 3:28). Samaritans, lepers, women, and the socially outcast were the focus of Jesus' love and ministry (see Luke 4:18). Jesus lived without social barriers and with a conviction that all have access to God. The letter of James was written to help people of faith make the distinction between Jesus' example and worldly practices of deference and discrimination. James denounced partiality at the expense of the poor or rich. The word *partiality* means "to estimate people superficially rather than on the basis of their fundamental humanity." James stood against the logic of partiality because it denied what God affirms: the full humanity of every person.

The letter of James pushes against such social attitudes—being that they are the opposite of the love of Jesus. There are many tragic examples of partiality based on gender, race, and sex—denying access to education and resources to people of color.

James declared that the practice of good religion ought to provide an alternative consciousness to the practice of partiality based on social status. Many persons have been turned away by the church because of a difference in skin color. James reminded us that God has chosen the poor of this world to be heirs of the kingdom of God. Since the poor are claimed by God, James declared that when the poor are despised, the name by which they are called is despised. The words of James reveal the contrast between good in the form of freedom and justice, and evil in the form of oppression and partiality. The words of James are unequivocal: "If you show partiality, you commit sin."

James's words declare that the evil fueled by partiality and racism will not prevail against the coming reign of God. The letter of James asked the Christian church what it had done and what it was called to do for the realization of God's justice in social life. James declared that justice and mercy must be characteristic of those who profess to serve the Lord (see Isaiah 3:13-15; 10:1-2; Luke 20:46-47).

The Christian fellowship who read the letter of James was admonished to practice "disciplines of the spirit" such as prayer and alms, along with giving and works of mercy among the poor.

B. Practice What Your Religion Preaches (James 2:8-11)

If ye fulfil the royal law according to the scripture, Thou shalt love thy neighbour as thyself, ye do well: But if ye have respect to persons, ye commit sin, and are convinced of the law as transgressors. For whosoever shall keep the whole law, and yet offend in one point, he is guilty of all. For he that said, Do not commit adultery, said also, Do not kill. Now if thou commit no adultery, yet if thou kill, thou art become a transgressor of the law.

Practicing what your religion preaches is the mandate that the letter of James outlines for the first-century church—as he said, "If you really fulfill the royal law according to the Scripture, 'You shall love your neighbor as yourself,' you do well" (James 2:8).

The letter of James punctuates the law of love as God's judgment, which establishes common ground upon which the rich and the poor stand together. For James, charitable gestures toward the poor while harboring attitudes of prejudice and inattention to systems that cause their suffering violate the law of love. Heartlessness toward the needy is excused so long as one has faith. A people whose faith is without deeds of justice are part of the problem of religious racism. If Christians want to be part of the solution (rather than part of the problem) when it comes to racism, then it seems that we need to reflect on how to change practices for Sunday mornings as a first step to changing the larger society. James declared that good religion must be consistent with good religious practice. The law of love is the basis of good religion; James insisted that it must manifest deeds commensurate with faith that honors God's wisdom in Jesus. In other words, love informs faith and the moral decisions that follow. The law of love is inclusive of all. Partiality and bias against the poor are inconsistent with the law of love. Christians cannot practice love toward the privileged if at the same time they are discriminating against the poor. James declared that the Christian life should be under the control of a single dominant motive: "Love thy neighbor as thyself." Since love cannot be divided, it can show partiality toward one group of persons at the disparagement of another. James punctuated the fact that if one violates the intention of the law of love, then he/she is guilty of violating the principle which underlies all the commandments of God (see James 1:9-11).

C. The Working of Mercy (James 2:12-13)

So speak ye, and so do, as they that shall be judged by the law of liberty. For he shall have judgment without mercy, that hath shewed no mercy; and mercy rejoiceth against judgment.

More frequently than not, the internal workings of the church itself are affected by partiality and favoritism. The status and honor of a few in chosen positions of authority outweigh the inclusion of those deemed unworthy in status and social influence. The principle of inclusive love in the letter of James challenges the unspoken "qualifications" of persons ranked as superior who are chosen to lead the church over persons seen as inferior. For example, women have suffered from the sexist bias of male dominance in the church, denying them the free exercise of their gifts and spiritual calling. Churches have been known to impose unspoken codes of dress and behavior before acceptance is granted to those who are different. A person's place of employment along with his/her network of friends weigh as important factors for acceptance into the church's fellowship circles. The letter of James is clear. When we violate a person's worth at the level of favoritism, or consider them inferior—or practice bias or slander, adultery or murder, or hate or violence—the basic principle of love is violated. It is immaterial what the particular offense against the person might be—the law of love demands forgiveness and just treatment of all persons.

James attacked the notion that a confession of faith guaranteed salvation, regardless of the conduct of the believer. "Creeds without deeds" is what James called dead faith. Worship of God that does not translate into works of mercy and justice offends God (see Amos 5:21-24). Dead faith has plagued the church, from James's time to contemporary times—when charity replaces justice and individualism takes precedence over communal relationships. There is only one answer to James's question of "Can faith save us?" If faith is manifested in deeds of justice and love, compassion and reconciliation, then it can.

III. CONCLUDING REFLECTION

The letter of James offers much wisdom for the church. It is the kind of spiritual wisdom that invites spiritual formation around the law of God's love. Love is the bottom line against all forms of discrimination: partiality, xenophobia, racism, and gender bias. The church cannot afford to have such dispositions in it and still seek to proclaim the Gospel to a world that needs liberation from these very same sins. Of what significance is membership in a church if one does not honestly seek to live in accordance with the principles of Jesus upon which it was founded? What is the profit in pious words such as "God loves everybody" and "go in peace" if they are dissociated from works of mercy and justice? James declared that such piety without love in action was good for nothing. A useful and effective future for the Christian church depends upon its practicing what its religion preaches.

PRAYER

O God, many of Your children have suffered injury and deep wounds from experiences of prejudice and bias, even in the church. Forgive us of the sins of partiality that have caused people to suffer due to race, sex, or gender bias. Heal us with the law of Your divine love so that we may become a demonstration of Your love in action. In Jesus' name we pray. Amen.

WORD POWER

Favoritism—(1) unfairly favoring a person or group: the practice of giving special treatment or unfair advantages to a person or group; (2) status as a preferred person: the state of being a favorite person or group.

Judgment—the process of forming an opinion or evaluation by discerning and comparing.

Mercy—compassion or forbearance shown especially to an offender or to one subject to one's power.

(www.dictionary.reference.com)

HOME DAILY BIBLE READINGS
(February 3-9, 2014)

Treat Everyone Equally

MONDAY, February 3: "Judging Rightly and Impartially" (Deuteronomy 1:9-18)

TUESDAY, February 4: "Judging on the Lord's Behalf" (2 Chronicles 19:1-7)

WEDNESDAY, February 5: "Giving Justice to the Weak" (Psalm 82)

THURSDAY, February 6: "Showing Partiality Is Not Good" (Proverbs 28:18-22)

FRIDAY, February 7: "God Shows No Partiality" (Acts 10:34-43)

SATURDAY, February 8: "Put On the Lord Jesus Christ" (Romans 13:8-14)

SUNDAY, February 9: "Faith and Favoritism" (James 2:1-13)

SHOW YOUR FAITH BY YOUR WORKS

Faith Pathway/Faith Journey Topic: Live What You Believe

DEVOTIONAL READING: **Luke 7:1-10**   BACKGROUND SCRIPTURE: **James 2:14-26**
PRINT PASSAGE: **James 2:14-26**   KEY VERSE: **James 2:26**

James 2:14-26—KJV

14 What doth it profit, my brethren, though a man say he hath faith, and have not works? can faith save him?
15 If a brother or sister be naked, and destitute of daily food,
16 And one of you say unto them, Depart in peace, be ye warmed and filled; notwithstanding ye give them not those things which are needful to the body; what doth it profit?
17 Even so faith, if it hath not works, is dead, being alone.
18 Yea, a man may say, Thou hast faith, and I have works: shew me thy faith without thy works, and I will shew thee my faith by my works.
19 Thou believest that there is one God; thou doest well: the devils also believe, and tremble.
20 But wilt thou know, O vain man, that faith without works is dead?
21 Was not Abraham our father justified by works, when he had offered Isaac his son upon the altar?
22 Seest thou how faith wrought with his works, and by works was faith made perfect?
23 And the scripture was fulfilled which saith, Abraham believed God, and it was imputed unto him for righteousness: and he was called the Friend of God.
24 Ye see then how that by works a man is justified, and not by faith only.
25 Likewise also was not Rahab the harlot justified by works, when she had received the messengers, and had sent them out another way?
26 For as the body without the spirit is dead, so faith without works is dead also.

James 2:14-26—NIV

14 What good is it, my brothers, if a man claims to have faith but has no deeds? Can such faith save him?
15 Suppose a brother or sister is without clothes and daily food.
16 If one of you says to him, "Go, I wish you well; keep warm and well fed," but does nothing about his physical needs, what good is it?
17 In the same way, faith by itself, if it is not accompanied by action, is dead.
18 But someone will say, "You have faith; I have deeds." Show me your faith without deeds, and I will show you my faith by what I do.
19 You believe that there is one God. Good! Even the demons believe that—and shudder.
20 You foolish man, do you want evidence that faith without deeds is useless?
21 Was not our ancestor Abraham considered righteous for what he did when he offered his son Isaac on the altar?
22 You see that his faith and his actions were working together, and his faith was made complete by what he did.
23 And the scripture was fulfilled that says, "Abraham believed God, and it was credited to him as righteousness," and he was called God's friend.
24 You see that a person is justified by what he does and not by faith alone.
25 In the same way, was not even Rahab the prostitute considered righteous for what she did when she gave lodging to the spies and sent them off in a different direction?
26 As the body without the spirit is dead, so faith without deeds is dead.

UNIFYING LESSON PRINCIPLE

People often make great declarations of faith but show no evidence of it in their actions. What gives evidence of faith? James stated that faith, which by itself is dead, becomes active when carried out through works of justice.

TOPICAL OUTLINE
OF THE LESSON

I. Introduction
A. Faith and Works
B. Biblical Background

II. Exposition and Application of the Scripture
A. Worthless Faith
(James 2:14-18)
B. Corruptible Faith
(James 2:19-24)
C. The Working of Faith
(James 2:25-26)

III. Concluding Reflection

LESSON OBJECTIVES

Upon the completion of the lesson, the students will be able to do the following:

1. Review James's relationship of faith to works;
2. Express the meaning of declaring faith by doing works; and,
3. Consider a faith statement and identify its expression in works.

POINTS TO BE EMPHASIZED

ADULT/YOUTH

Adult Topic: Live What You Believe
Youth Topic: It's Show Time!
Adult Key Verse: James 2:26
Youth Key Verse: James 2:18
Print Passage: James 2:14-26

—To introduce the discussion of faith and works, James portrayed a Christian who chose not to provide for the needs of another Christian.

—James explained that the works of Abraham completed his faith—and he pointed to actions of Abraham in response to God's call to sacrifice Isaac as a burnt offering (see Genesis 22:1-19).

—To emphasize the nature of the relationship between faith and works, James used the analogy of body and spirit.

—Paul and James both appealed to the same example of Abraham (see Genesis 15) to support their seemingly conflicting statements about the relationship between faith, grace, and works.

—Faith requires action.

—Faith as an action supports and verifies one's words.

CHILDREN

Children Topic: Faith and Works Walk Together
Key Verse: James 2:18b
Print Passage: James 2:14-26

—Words without action do not help the person in need.

—A person demonstrates his or her faith by what he or she does.

—God tested Abraham so that others could see Abraham's faith.

—Good deeds show that faith is growing and active.

—The story of Rahab showed that God accepts anyone who comes to Him by faith.

—What one believes determines how one behaves.

I. INTRODUCTION

A. Faith and Works

The theme of faith and works is a prominent theological feature detailed in the letter of James. James based his theological view of "faith and works" in the God-human relationship and the law of divine love. Throughout the letter, James showed impatience with faith without commensurate works of mercy and justice. James understood the centrality of faith as necessary for the flourishing of God's love in the first-century world. Faith, love, and works are inseparable from what James understood as good religion. James saw any religious logic that separated faith from responding effectively to human needs as deeply flawed and morally inconsistent.

James was aware that faith did not change the demonic character that also believed in the reality of God and "shuddered." The demonic was not a friend to good people and worked against God's coming reign of love, justice, and acceptance of all persons in divine righteousness. Thus, James stood against that which the demonic perpetuated: fear, bias, prejudice, and elitist favoritism—all of which have no transforming effect upon the world. Unless faith manifests deeds in opposition to these attitudes, it is dead. Barren faith was a moral problem for James. When such faith defines the church, "the living faith of the dead becomes the dead faith of the living." Most people who attend Protestant and Catholic churches proudly profess faith in God. The expression of religious faith in America, however, has many Christians split between belief systems and religious activity. What kind of activity reflects good religion? Today, religion is driven by issue positions rather than love and justice. One wonders how James would respond to "pro-life" anti-abortion advocates and the use of religion to bolster angry opposition rather than right actions (orthopraxis) to save children from poor health care and poverty once they are born. A majority of churchgoing Americans proudly make the claim that America is a Christian democracy, while at the same time voting to limit the life chances of Native Americans and minority groups. Many people around the world are questioning the claim that America is a Christian nation. American democracy is broken by wide disparities between the rich and the poor, along with criminal incarceration of a disproportionate number of African Americans and Latino groups.

One of the great tragedies of contemporary religious traditions is the gulf between practice and profession—between doing and saying. A profession of Christian faith followed by practices that express the very antithesis of the principles of Christianity is a moral problem upon which the letter of James focuses. James reminded us that the religion of Jesus matched love with commensurate action.

B. Biblical Background

The misunderstanding of the relationship between Paul and James has arisen in reference to the use of the word *works* (see Romans 3:38; James 2:18). This word *Works* had the same meaning for both Paul and James, but differed in usage. In the book of James, *works* was directed to the question of whether a profession of faith was valid if there were no deeds to substantiate it (works commensurate with actions). In the book of Romans, Paul was concerned with the theological issue of how one comes into a right relationship with God. Does one—as he, when a Pharisee—establish acceptance from God by living flawlessly or keeping the law, or does faith alone justify one's life before God? In this regard, Paul used the term *works* as earning righteousness rather than receiving it as a gift of God's grace. Justification by faith only brings God's forgiveness and righteousness. All one has to do is in full self-surrender respond to the love of God freely offered in Jesus Christ. In this self-surrender, a life separate from God is united to God in love and righteousness. It is not earned or merited; the fullness of God's life in a human being's life is a gift of God.

In Paul's usage of the word *faith* is not the mere belief in God nor is it the profession of a set of doctrinal beliefs about God. Faith is an event of grace, fully and freely offered through the life, ministry, death, and resurrection of Jesus Christ. It is a relationship of trust and gratitude for God's liberating action in Jesus. Paul and James were in agreement that evidence of authentic faith was manifested in deeds of love that honor justice (see Romans 12:1; 1 Corinthians 13). It is the realization of and openness to the love of God which motivates works of mercy and love. Both James and Paul saw eye to eye that "faith without works is dead." James's moral disapproval was with those who claimed that faith in the existence of God was all that was necessary in order to make one a Christian. It was this concern that James had for those who may become church members but who were not Christians. Many modern-day pastors complain about this continuing dilemma of having "pew members" who are not justice seekers and disciples of the kingdom of God. Anyone who has faith in God—who is in right relationship with God—will demonstrate the reality of that faith and relationship by right behavior, moral deeds, and social actions which are consistent with that faith.

II. EXPOSITION AND APPLICATION OF THE SCRIPTURE

A. Worthless Faith
(James 2:14-18)

What doth it profit, my brethren, though a man say he hath faith, and have not works? can faith save him? If a brother or sister be naked, and destitute of daily food, And one of you say unto them, Depart in peace, be ye warmed and filled; notwithstanding ye give them not those things which are needful to the body; what doth it profit? Even so faith, if it hath not works, is dead, being alone. Yea, a man may say, Thou hast faith, and I have works: shew me thy faith without thy works, and I will shew thee my faith by my works.

On one occasion, Jesus was asked by a Jewish lawyer, "Master, what shall I do to inherit eternal life?" Jesus replied, "Thou shall love the Lord thy God with all your heart, and with all your soul, and with all your strength, and with all your mind; and love your neighbor as yourself" (Luke 10:29). The lawyer then inquired, "Who is my neighbor?" Jesus told a parable of the good Samaritan that gave clarity to an ethic of love—to which the lawyer was able to answer in sum that one's neighbor is anyone to whom one shows love, whether a Samaritan or Jew, male or female. James defined "worthless faith" as the absence of the "love ethic" of Jesus. Worthless faith results in unprofitable religious practices, empty rituals, and worship void of spiritual power and substance. In first-century society, communities were defined by tribalism, clan, family, race, or nation. These social barriers set up blockades, limiting neighborly acceptance and compassion to strangers. Into this environment Jesus introduced a love ethic which the letter of James framed as the foundation of authentic faith. The faith of Jesus went beyond race, religion, and nationality. James understood this faith as a call to demonstrate love in action toward the least among the community. James was an alert theologian/moral thinker whose idea of religion went against Roman aristocratic thought and Jewish patriarchy—to include Gentiles, slaves, and the poor as the focus of God's liberating love and salvation. James's understanding of faith required true spiritual altruism and humanness. Faith profits a person nothing when it is void of love. In the eyes of God, it is worthless.

For much of America's religious history, faith has been trapped in a narrow group-centered attitude based on race, gender, and culture. Injustice and social injury that happens to persons outside these groups did not activate the kind of faith (love in action) which was the concern of James. When faith is guided by narrow provincialism, it is worthless.

The letter of James seeks to address the kind of profitless faith that isolates Christians from seeking justice and true works of love and mercy. The living out of this faith is not only a matter of authentic and meaningful living for Christians but is also a matter of life and death for others. In his book *Strength to Love*, Martin Luther King Jr. included a story of several members of an African-American basketball team who were severely injured in an automobile accident while traveling on a highway in the South in the 1960s. "An ambulance was immediately called, but on arriving at the place of the accident, the driver, who was white, said without apology that it was not his policy to "service Negroes," and drove away. It so happened that another driver stopped and drove the injured players to the nearest hospital, but the attending physician had the same belligerent racist attitude of the white driver and refused to attend to their wounds. When the boys finally arrived at a "colored" hospital fifty miles from the scene of the accident, all of the injured had died. Imagine if the religious profession of the white driver and physician were the Christian faith. Their faith was trapped in American racism that prevented them from doing works of mercy and compassion. It is this kind of faith that James called *worthless*.

B. Corruptible Faith
(James 2:19-24)

Thou believest that there is one God; thou doest well: the devils also believe, and tremble. But wilt thou know, O vain man, that faith without works is dead? Was not Abraham our father justified by works, when he had offered Isaac his son upon the altar? Seest thou how faith wrought with his works, and by works was faith made perfect? And the scripture was fulfilled which saith, Abraham believed

God, and it was imputed unto him for righteousness: and he was called the Friend of God. Ye see then how that by works a man is justified, and not by faith only.

In James 2:19-24, James offered a mirror to reflect the kind of religious practice that corrupts faith. In the estimation of James, bad religion occurred when a system of belief about God became a substitute for righteous works that honor or glorify God. Such religion corrupts faith. Thus, for James, belief in God was not enough. The demons also believed in God and "shuddered," James said. A division between belief in God and activity that honors God not only corrupts faith but also opens the door for the demonic distortion of life. When religion is distorted, demonic forces fuel prejudice—wherein life becomes a platform for hate and violence. For example, the Jewish Holocaust was fueled by religious distortion of a "superior" race. Racial segregation fueled "religious" racism, which spun violent responses by Southern Christians. The ideological battle between Muslims and Christians fuels contemporary terrorism. These are examples of bad "religion" that corrupts faith. Organized religion struggles to express faith beyond a narrow group-centered prejudice. James took corruptible faith and religious prejudice head-on, as he made the point that God cannot be divided into camps of private beliefs. Faith is dynamic. Faith is driven by ultimate concerns that lead to an authentic relationship with God.

The faith of Abraham, the religious patriarch of Judaism, illustrates the point that James made about authentic faith. Nothing merits God's righteousness—only grace. Abraham's attitude of trust was based on the faith that God provides which works alone cannot produce. Abraham's faith in God was the vanguard for all who seek a relationship with God. Laws, codes of moral conduct, or a strict performance of religious rituals do not merit God's righteousness. In Abraham's case, the attempt to offer Isaac, his son, upon an altar was stopped because it was an acceptable sacrifice for being established in God's righteousness. Simply, Abraham believed God and God blessed him with divine righteousness. Abraham's faith in God brought him into right relationship with God. Christians today would do well to examine the internal life of the church in order to expose practices that corrupt faith. Are there practices in worship that fuel disunity within the body and beyond the church? Are the church's beliefs consistent with Jesus' love ethic? What activities in the church show a commitment to works of mercy and justice? Faith that joins with God's love and justice is a vital witness needed in the world today. Authentic faith begins at the altars and worship experiences of churches. Christian practice born of authentic faith plays a vital role in transforming life. Think how the world would be without the faith of people who followed Jesus' love ethic in principle and practice. Slavery was defeated by faith in a God of freedom. Racial segregation was defeated by faith in a God of justice. The stronghold of discrimination against black people, Jews, racial minorities, and women has been defeated by those who sacrifice their lives for a better world. Authentic faith—when utilized for transforming the world in God's righteousness—operates without barriers and it serves the needs of humanity without consideration of race, tribe, or ethnicity.

C. The Working of Faith
(James 2:25-26)

Likewise also was not Rahab the harlot justified by works, when she had received the messengers, and had sent them out another way? For as the body without the spirit is dead, so faith without works is dead also.

James mentioned the story of Rahab, a Gentile harlot, as an example of works that authenticate faith. Rahab provided refuge and safety for those sent by Joshua to spy out the land of Canaan. The movement of God in the lives of the Israelites impressed upon Rahab the need to trust her family's future with God. She harbored the Hebrew spies because of her faith in God's purpose. James celebrated Rahab's faith because it represented an unforced act of mercy and compassion. Rahab was more concerned about the mission of the Hebrew people than the safety of her own family. She endorsed the mission of God's liberation with faith. Rahab displayed what Martin Luther King Jr. once described as "dangerous altruism." She took a risk. Rather than ask what would happen to her and her family, Rahab was more concerned for the movement of God. Many decades ago the university professor Albert Schweitzer launched a mission to Africa. It was a great risk to his career and life. However, he did not ask, "What will happen to my prestige and security as a university professor and to my status if I work with the people of Africa?" Rather, he asked, "What will happen to these millions of people who have been wounded by the forces of injustice if I do not go to them?" Authentic faith reclaims works of mercy. Many persons consider themselves good Christians because of personal habits of self-discipline, while at the same time not being involved in works of mercy.

Jesus took risks to illustrate that love has no barriers. Speaking with a Samaritan woman and healing a crippled man on the Sabbath day were risks Jesus took, because fear was not allowed to trump mercy and compassion. Reclaiming mercy goes far beyond sympathy. Works of mercy require a faith in God's own compassion in the world. Faith in God's compassion broadens our capacity to sympathize. Such faith in divine compassion transforms pity into works of mercy. Often the church's zeal is to do something for people, rather than to do something with people. In the church's missionary zeal, millions of dollars have gone to Africa from the hands of church people who would not welcome an African to live next door to them or establish a lasting relationship with such a person. James declared that Christian faith cannot be one-sided; it must be concerned for the whole person. How the church today might share in reclaiming mercy "as the doing of the word and not hearing only" is a challenge to what it means to be Christian. When works of mercy are reclaimed beyond narrow provincialism and rigid belief claims, the church stands with a great opportunity to represent God's mission in the world and live out its beliefs.

III. CONCLUDING REFLECTION

Living what one believes is the challenge of every Christian. Belief in God should unite us with the things that God loves. Christians are challenged not to allow division to occur between faith and works or between beliefs and compassion. Living what we believe does not mean we are to segregate ourselves from others who are different from us or who are guided by different religious claims or convictions. Living what we believe means holding consistently to an understanding of God's love and justice that transcends barriers of race, class, and gender. Loving justice and doing mercy is not to be isolated in group identity but goes beyond group interests to others. Living what Christians believe will bring transformation to neighborhoods and communities—only if persons avoid the temptation of separating love from justice and faith from works. There is a push to save humanity on different levels of human need across the world. Each Christian must find his or her place of service in God's movement of love and liberation. It would be tragic if, because of habits and attitudes that fuel prejudice and bias, many who call themselves Christians miss this opportunity.

PRAYER

O God, only through Your strength can we be given power to live what we believe. Grant us the strength and courage to do works of mercy toward all people, no matter their status in life. Help us make real in the world what is real in our hearts. In Jesus' name we pray. Amen.

WORD POWER

Faith—(1) belief and trust in and loyalty to God; (2) belief in the traditional doctrines of a religion; (3) firm belief in something for which there is no proof; (4) complete trust; (5) something that is believed, especially with strong conviction; especially: a system of religious beliefs.

Justified/justification—a process that conforms us to Christ's likeness (moral likeness). Justification is a legal declaration of a sinner becoming righteous.

Righteousness—personal holiness, obedience to God, and the maintaining of an upright character.

HOME DAILY BIBLE READINGS
(February 10-16, 2014)

Show Your Faith by Your Works

MONDAY, February 10: "The Work of Faith with Power" (2 Thessalonians 1:3-12)

TUESDAY, February 11: "Faith Distracted by Loving Money" (1 Timothy 6:6-12)

WEDNESDAY, February 12: "Completing What's Lacking in Faith" (1 Thessalonians 3:4-13)

THURSDAY, February 13: "An Example of Great Faith" (Luke 7:1-10)

FRIDAY, February 14: "A Faith that Saves" (Luke 7:36-50)

SATURDAY, February 15: "Living Your Life in Christ" (Colossians 2:1-7)

SUNDAY, February 16: "Faith Demonstrated through Works" (James 2:14-26)

CONTROL YOUR SPEECH

FAITH PATHWAY/FAITH JOURNEY TOPIC: Unfork Your Tongue

DEVOTIONAL READING: **Proverbs 18:2-13**
PRINT PASSAGE: **James 3:1-12**

BACKGROUND SCRIPTURE: **James 3:1-12**
KEY VERSE: **James 3:10**

James 3:1-12—KJV

MY BRETHREN, be not many masters, knowing that we shall receive the greater condemnation.

2 For in many things we offend all. If any man offend not in word, the same is a perfect man, and able also to bridle the whole body.

3 Behold, we put bits in the horses' mouths, that they may obey us; and we turn about their whole body.

4 Behold also the ships, which though they be so great, and are driven of fierce winds, yet are they turned about with a very small helm, whithersoever the governor listeth.

5 Even so the tongue is a little member, and boasteth great things. Behold, how great a matter a little fire kindleth!

6 And the tongue is a fire, a world of iniquity: so is the tongue among our members, that it defileth the whole body, and setteth on fire the course of nature; and it is set on fire of hell.

7 For every kind of beasts, and of birds, and of serpents, and of things in the sea, is tamed, and hath been tamed of mankind:

8 But the tongue can no man tame; it is an unruly evil, full of deadly poison.

9 Therewith bless we God, even the Father; and therewith curse we men, which are made after the similitude of God.

10 Out of the same mouth proceedeth blessing and cursing. My brethren, these things ought not so to be.

11 Doth a fountain send forth at the same place sweet water and bitter?

12 Can the fig tree, my brethren, bear olive berries? either a vine, figs? so can no fountain both yield salt water and fresh.

James 3:1-12—NIV

NOT MANY of you should presume to be teachers, my brothers, because you know that we who teach will be judged more strictly.

2 We all stumble in many ways. If anyone is never at fault in what he says, he is a perfect man, able to keep his whole body in check.

3 When we put bits into the mouths of horses to make them obey us, we can turn the whole animal.

4 Or take ships as an example. Although they are so large and are driven by strong winds, they are steered by a very small rudder wherever the pilot wants to go.

5 Likewise the tongue is a small part of the body, but it makes great boasts. Consider what a great forest is set on fire by a small spark.

6 The tongue also is a fire, a world of evil among the parts of the body. It corrupts the whole person, sets the whole course of his life on fire, and is itself set on fire by hell.

7 All kinds of animals, birds, reptiles and creatures of the sea are being tamed and have been tamed by man,

8 but no man can tame the tongue. It is a restless evil, full of deadly poison.

9 With the tongue we praise our Lord and Father, and with it we curse men, who have been made in God's likeness.

10 Out of the same mouth come praise and cursing. My brothers, this should not be.

11 Can both fresh water and salt water flow from the same spring?

12 My brothers, can a fig tree bear olives, or a grape-vine bear figs? Neither can a salt spring produce fresh water.

TOPICAL OUTLINE OF THE LESSON

I. Introduction
   A. Speech that Heals or Harms
   B. Biblical Background

II. Exposition and Application of the Scripture
   A. Teachers, Watch What You Say
   (James 3:1)
   B. The Power of the Tongue
   (James 3:2-8)
   C. A Wise Use of Words
   (James 3:9-12)

III. Concluding Reflection

LESSON OBJECTIVES

Upon the completion of the lesson, the students will be able to do the following:

1. Review James's teachings concerning the use and/or misuse of the tongue;
2. Express how it feels to be criticized and praised; and,
3. Find ways to contrast praise and criticism.

POINTS TO BE EMPHASIZED

ADULT/YOUTH

Adult Topic: Unfork Your Tongue
Youth Topic: Words Do Hurt
Adult/Youth Key Verse: James 3:10
Print Passage: James 3:1-12

—As James began to teach about how humans use language, he warned his readers that teachers carry extra responsibility.

—James, by comparing the tongue to a horse's bit and a ship's rudder, taught that the tongue could control a wide swath of life.

—James also taught that the tongue is very hard, if not impossible, to control—by comparing it to a raging fire, an untamable creature, restless evil, and poison.

—The images at the end of this passage indicated that what is said by the tongue shows the nature of the speaker and insisted that believers should not be split. This might make some think of Jesus' warning to the religious leaders about the need to be careful in speech (see Matthew 12:33-37).

—The book of Proverbs indicated that wise speech and controlling the tongue demonstrate wisdom.

—Although disciples should seek to be perfect, they must remember that all are prone to mistakes.

—Believers must seek to control their behavior by making an effort to keep in check those parts (organs) that can cause the most harm to themselves and others.

—The tongue must be controlled by believers, and it should be used to praise God and to build up others.

—God considers it unacceptable to curse others with the same tongue used to praise God.

CHILDREN

Children Topic: Watch Your Tongue!
Key Verse: James 3:10
Print Passage: James 3:1-12
—James showed how teachers have both a great influence on and a responsibility to their students.
—The tongue is responsible for many mistakes and imperfections.

—James commanded the followers of Jesus to be swift to hear and slow to speak.

—Words can be as devastating and destructive as fire.

—Both blessing and cursing can come from the same mouth.

I. INTRODUCTION

A. Speech that Heals or Harms

In this section of the letter of James, the focus is on the connection between wisdom and speech within a community where meaning and purpose were formed. James described the power of language as a gift to create goodwill or a tool of peril that destroys human community. Since James viewed human beings as "first fruits of God's creatures" (James 1:18), he warned his readers regarding the dangers and perilous use of the tongue. As a tool for forming speech or language, the tongue can either create a universe of good or cause distortion and darkness. James saw the use of language or speech as an awesome responsibility, because it gave/gives humans the freedom to either bless life according to "the word of truth" or condemn life.

The lesson today affords students an opportunity to examine the ways in which words (or speech) communicate hatred or love. James warned that harmful speech against others brings God's judgment. What we allow to come through our mouths matters. Thus, this lesson raises a red flag of a moral caution for us to think before we must speak judgmentally about others. James's moral caution went beyond speaking angry words or incidental petty issues of negative speech about a person whom one does not like. It targeted the use of harmful speech to create a distorted world of falsehood that could cause someone's downfall and the misdirection of an entire community. James's connecting speech and moral wisdom is a challenge for every Christian who seeks to cultivate and nurture genuine community among and with others.

B. Biblical Background

In last's week lesson, we saw that faith and deeds were complementary and that authentic faith always expresses itself in action or activity commensurate with the meaning of faith in Jesus Christ. In this section of James's letter, the major issue of moral speech surfaces as a moral and theological challenge to the Christian community. James used the genre of Wisdom Literature to illustrate the need for discipline or control in the way one speaks to others as an ethical and practical matter for building community. Three themes emerge in this section of the book of James: the power of the tongue and its destructive character (see

James 3:5-6); the human inability to control speech (see James 3:9-10); and the double-mindedness of wicked speech (see James 3:11-12). James saw it as one's moral obligation to guard against having a pretense of religion without concern for control of one's tongue.

James pulled together a solid moral argument for the proper and improper use of the tongue or speech. Improper use of speech is aimed at the distortion of truth. In contrast to slanderous speech and distorted use of language, James showed the readers how moral speech in the faith community functions and the practical outcomes one can expect (see James 5:12-20). When James said that his readers should be "quick to listen, slow to speak and slow to become angry" (James 1:19), he was repeating the wisdom that accompanies the speech of those who seek the kingdom of God. For James, then, human speech should be a productive agent of righteousness and placed in the context of God's Word. As God spoke creation into existence, human beings can speak goodwill into existence.

II. EXPOSITION AND APPLICATION OF THE SCRIPTURE

A. Teachers, Watch What You Say
(James 3:1)

MY BRETHREN, be not many masters, knowing that we shall receive the greater condemnation.

Since teachers will be held to greater accountability for teaching and guiding the community of faith, they need to ensure that they emulate speech characterized by "wisdom from above." James began chapter 3 by warning his readers that teachers or leaders carry extra responsibility for guarding against the use of harmful speech. In the ancient community of James, teaching was a prestigious position in the community. People were eager for the reputable designation of being recognized as a sage of the community. The rabbis of the Jewish community were highly respected for their wisdom. Many were eager to teach various philosophies and schools of thought. But teaching or moral leadership carried a dimension of responsibility that James highlighted for those so inclined to fulfill those roles. James issued a stark warning for those who were called to teach "the law of liberty." Teachers will be judged more strictly for what they say and the speech they employ under the cover of service to the Lord (see Romans 14:10, 11; 1 Corinthians 3:10-15). Those who teach will face an even stricter judgment because they have influenced the faith and life of others by their teaching. It seems that the judgment James was speaking about was not primarily concerned with doctrinal matters (although it is vital that those who teach are faithful to God's Word)—but his concern was regarding the attitude and moral disposition behind the speech of the teacher. Intellectual pride, absolutism, and arrogance about what one believes leads to speech that harms the listener. James warned teachers to resist the temptation to use speech or what they taught to damage others.

James warned leaders and teachers of their responsibility to guard against harmful speech—because of his keen awareness of their heavy challenge as public and moral leaders. Preachers and Christian teachers deal with the most challenging aspect of life: human personality. Any mishandling or misdirecting or moral miscalculating could mean life or death, spiritual flourishing or condemnation for persons entrusted to their care. Thus, James warned leaders and teachers to watch what they said because it could either create goodwill or bring the judgment of God. We will be judged for our speech.

B. The Power of the Tongue
(James 3:2-8)

For in many things we offend all. If any man offend not in word, the same is a perfect man, and able also to bridle the whole body. Behold, we put bits in the horses' mouths, that they may obey us; and we turn about their whole body. Behold also the ships, which though they be so great, and are driven of fierce winds, yet are they turned about with a very small helm, whithersoever the governor listeth. Even so the tongue is a little member, and boasteth great things. Behold, how great a matter a little fire kindleth! And the tongue is a fire, a world of iniquity: so is the tongue among our members, that it defileth the whole body, and setteth on fire the course of nature; and it is set on fire of hell. For every kind of beasts, and of birds, and of serpents, and of things in the sea, is tamed, and hath been tamed of mankind: But the tongue can no man tame; it is an unruly evil, full of deadly poison.

In the normal functions of the human body, the tongue is not seen as the central part for control of the whole person. James's characterization of the tongue as "a restless evil, full of deadly poison" alerts the reader to the potential that the tongue has for good or evil. Biblical scholar Timothy Johnson notes that James's treatment of the tongue heightens the capacity of speech to a cosmic force set to evil. The tongues within our bodies in effect represent or constitute the "world" that for James was related to God. The tongue is a little member of the body—but depending upon how it is used, it can cause a "world of iniquity"

(James 3:6). James, by comparing the tongue to a horse's bit and a ship's rudder, taught that the tongue could control a wide swath of life. James also taught that the tongue is very hard, if not impossible, to control by comparing it to a raging fire, an untamable creature, restless evil, and poison. While James offered no direct word of hope with respect to the tongue in this passage, the letter does presume that the believer can exercise control over what is said (see James 2:12; 4:11).

The images at the end of this passage indicate that what is said by the tongue shows the nature of the speaker and insisted that believers should not be split between what one says and who one is. This might make some think of Jesus' warning to the religious leaders about the need to be careful in speech (see Matthew 12:33-37). In other words, wise speech and controlling the tongue demonstrate wisdom. James's discussion of the tongue as an instrument of speech for good or evil is fundamentally a religious call to Christian virtue. The tongue should be used to cultivate human virtue and goodwill. The ridicule and shame that an uncontrolled tongue can bring is the antithesis of good religion. The use of the tongue as an instrument of human speech must be representative of God, who spoke creation into existence for good.

A person with an uncontrollable tongue is what the older people in the church community called a person with "a bad mouth." This phrase was not only associated with those who used curse words often, but also with those whose speech was consistently "bad mouthing" others. They were persons who seemingly had nothing good to say about anyone or the circumstances of life. They were labeled as having negative personalities. The use of their tongues was that of what James metaphorically called "a fire from hell" that sets aflame the cycle of evil. Wicked use of the tongue spreads evil to everything that nurtures life and takes away from the importance of speech. What one says is a sign of personality. The human personality is heavily influenced by one's context, culture, and environment, but one does not have to let it determine one's character. James insisted that the use of one's tongue ought not to compromise religious convictions that tie life to God. Our words ought to be inspired by relationships that honor Christ.

C. A Wise Use of Words
(James 3:9-12)

Therewith bless we God, even the Father; and therewith curse we men, which are made after the similitude of God. Out of the same mouth proceedeth blessing and cursing. My brethren, these things ought not so to be. Doth a fountain send forth at the same place sweet water and bitter? Can the fig tree, my brethren, bear olive berries? either a vine, figs? so can no fountain both yield salt water and fresh.

Because of the use of the tongue to produce evil speech, James emphasized the proper use of words for spiritual empowerment. James pointed out that the tongue could be used to bless God and at the same time curse a human being who was created in the image of God. This is what James called "double-tongued." For James, a "double-tongued" person was not merely a person who said one thing and did another. When the same tongue is used to both bless God and curse, it renders what was said to bless God worthless. The allegiance by which one claims to live is betrayed in a fundamental way. There is not only moral failure here, but also sin. Words matter as a moral agent

of good or evil. All cooperation between human beings depends upon the success of verbal communication. Verbal understanding involves an exchange of words. No plans can be made or implemented without words. Even in international negotiations, peace cannot be achieved without a clever use of words. People of faith work to control what they say and how they say it—because they know that their words can be powerful influences for good. People of faith find ways to say things that strengthen other people.

In the previous verses of the book of James, he showed how words can both hurt and heal. Christians therefore strive to speak words of blessing and constructive criticism. People of faith should examine the ways that the culture at-large thinks about the power or powerlessness of what people say. For example, social and electronic media, sound bytes, and film productions can be used to communicate messages of good or ill will. Recently a film was produced to disparage the Muslim religion, and it caused a violent reaction across the Islamic world. Character is revealed by one's speech.

James was not far from wrong when he placed great emphasis upon the clever use of the tongue or human speech. History has shown how words can inflame a mob to a dastardly lynching or inspire a nation to heroic action. Words can start quarrels or inspire reconciliation, destroy friendships, break up homes, instigate wars, or create an environment for peace. The wise use of words can bring transformation and healing. Courageous words can be the catalyst for justice and inspire understanding for social change. The speeches of Martin Luther King Jr. inspired hope for racial justice and reconciliation at a time when the nation was marked by hateful speech and violence.

III. CONCLUDING REFLECTION

When we realize that words have a world-creating capacity, then we begin to appreciate James's wisdom concerning the clever use of words. Words have power for creating good. Words can also create peril. How we use the gift of language and speech depends upon our moral character and commitment to human flourishing. Ultimately, what we *say* ought to be synchronized with what we *do* as Christians. And what we say and do ought to both represent and dignify our relationship with Jesus Christ. James's writing has led us to reflect on human speech as a potent instrument for the continuation of God's kingdom. Our language should not misrepresent Christ but honor the purpose of Christ in the world. Thus, we have an obligation to pay attention to the words and language we use. We must always be aware that God works through our human speech to reach others. Just one word in the direction of love can work wonders upon someone whose life feels loveless. A word of justice can start a movement to establish God's beloved community. A word of forgiveness can reverse ill will.

PRAYER

Heavenly Father, help us to be cognizant of what we say, how we say it, and why we say it. Help us to guard our tongues and allow them to be reflective of Your grace and goodness. In Jesus' name we pray. Amen.

WORD POWER

Bless—to wish somebody or something well: to declare approval and support for somebody or something.

Curse—the expression of a wish that misfortune, evil, doom, etc., befall a person, group, etc.

(www.dictionary.reference.com)

HOME DAILY BIBLE READINGS
(February 17-23, 2014)

Control Your Speech

MONDAY, February 17: "Lying and Flattering Lips" (Psalm 12)

TUESDAY, February 18: "Words that Intimidate" (1 Samuel 17:1-11)

WEDNESDAY, February 19: "Words that Lead to Repentance" (2 Chronicles 15:1-12)

THURSDAY, February 20: "Words that Lead to Mourning" (Nehemiah 1)

FRIDAY, February 21: "Words that Lead to Worship" (Genesis 24:42-52)

SATURDAY, February 22: "Words Guided by Wisdom" (Proverbs 18:2-13)

SUNDAY, February 23: "Taming the Tongue" (James 3:1-12)

Jesus' Fulfillment of Scripture

GENERAL INTRODUCTION

The purpose of the spring quarter is to explore connections between Jesus and the Hebrew Scriptures. Each of the three units approaches this relationship from a different perspective.

Unit I, *Jesus and the Davidic Covenant,* explores a variety of texts that make connections between the reign of David and the lordship of Christ. Lesson 1 studies the narrative of God's promise of a Davidic line that would sit on the throne forever. Lesson 2 looks at Matthew's gospel as an interpretation of how God fulfilled this promise in the birth of Christ. In lesson 3, Peter's message on the Day of Pentecost gave witness to Christ as God's promised Messiah. In lesson 4, the scene takes place in the heavenly court of John's vision and Christ is seated; the Lamb of Judah is on the eternal throne.

Unit II, *What the Prophets Foretold,* looks at the Christian Scriptures' use of Hebrew Scriptures in recording the events that led to Jesus' crucifixion. The unit opens with the story of Jesus' triumphal entry into Jerusalem, followed by a lesson of Jesus' cleansing of the Temple in conjunction with passages from the books of Isaiah and Jeremiah. The next lesson moves to the scene after Jesus' trial in which the soldiers mocked Him and beat Him. On Easter Sunday, the lesson celebrates the Resurrection and explores the significance of the "third day" as a Hebrew Scripture reference to deliverance. The final lesson of Unit II looks at the Emmaus Road story and the ways in which Jesus' life, death, and resurrection would fulfill Hebrew Scripture promises.

Unit III, *Jesus' Use of Scripture,* has four lessons from the Gospels that demonstrate how Jesus incorporated the Hebrew Scriptures into His own life and teaching. Lesson 10 looks at Jesus' use of Scripture in confronting temptation. Lesson 11 helps the participants to understand Jesus' mission through His interpretation of the Law and the Prophets, and it offers Jesus' life as a pattern for Christian discipleship. Lesson 12 deals with Jesus' respect for tradition and also His warnings about its misuse. Lesson 13 is a study of the Great Commandment in its Hebrew Scripture context, as well as its continued importance for Christian lives today.

LESSON 1   March 2, 2014

AN ETERNAL KINGDOM

FAITH PATHWAY/FAITH JOURNEY TOPIC: A Change of Plans

DEVOTIONAL READING: Psalm 98
PRINT PASSAGE: 2 Samuel 7:4-16

BACKGROUND SCRIPTURE: 2 Samuel 7:1-17
KEY VERSE: 2 Samuel 7:16

2 Samuel 7:4-16—KJV

4 And it came to pass that night, that the word of the LORD came unto Nathan, saying,

5 Go and tell my servant David, Thus saith the LORD, Shalt thou build me an house for me to dwell in?

6 Whereas I have not dwelt in any house since the time that I brought up the children of Israel out of Egypt, even to this day, but have walked in a tent and in a tabernacle.

7 In all the places wherein I have walked with all the children of Israel spake I a word with any of the tribes of Israel, whom I commanded to feed my people Israel, saying, Why build ye not me an house of cedar?

8 Now therefore so shalt thou say unto my servant David, Thus saith the LORD of hosts, I took thee from the sheepcote, from following the sheep, to be ruler over my people, over Israel:

9 And I was with thee whithersoever thou wentest, and have cut off all thine enemies out of thy sight, and have made thee a great name, like unto the name of the great men that are in the earth.

10 Moreover I will appoint a place for my people Israel, and will plant them, that they may dwell in a place of their own, and move no more; neither shall the children of wickedness afflict them any more, as beforetime,

11 And as since the time that I commanded judges to be over my people Israel, and have caused thee to rest from all thine enemies. Also the LORD telleth thee that he will make thee an house.

12 And when thy days be fulfilled, and thou shalt sleep with thy fathers, I will set up thy seed after thee, which

2 Samuel 7:4-16—NIV

4 That night the word of the LORD came to Nathan, saying:

5 "Go and tell my servant David, 'This is what the LORD says: Are you the one to build me a house to dwell in?

6 I have not dwelt in a house from the day I brought the Israelites up out of Egypt to this day. I have been moving from place to place with a tent as my dwelling.

7 Wherever I have moved with all the Israelites, did I ever say to any of their rulers whom I commanded to shepherd my people Israel, "Why have you not built me a house of cedar?"'

8 Now then, tell my servant David, 'This is what the LORD Almighty says: I took you from the pasture and from following the flock to be ruler over my people Israel.

9 I have been with you wherever you have gone, and I have cut off all your enemies from before you. Now I will make your name great, like the names of the greatest men of the earth.

10 And I will provide a place for my people Israel and will plant them so that they can have a home of their own and no longer be disturbed. Wicked people will not oppress them anymore, as they did at the beginning

11 and have done ever since the time I appointed leaders over my people Israel. I will also give you rest from all your enemies. The LORD declares to you that the LORD himself will establish a house for you:

12 When your days are over and you rest with your fathers, I will raise up your offspring to succeed you,

UNIFYING LESSON PRINCIPLE

People value permanence and seek to build things that will outlast themselves. How do people seek to build a legacy? When David wanted to build a house for God, God promised to build a house for David—a dynasty, a tradition of royalty.

shall proceed out of thy bowels, and I will establish his kingdom.

13 He shall build an house for my name, and I will stablish the throne of his kingdom for ever.

14 I will be his father, and he shall be my son. If he commit iniquity, I will chasten him with the rod of men, and with the stripes of the children of men:

15 But my mercy shall not depart away from him, as I took it from Saul, whom I put away before thee.

16 And thine house and thy kingdom shall be established for ever before thee: thy throne shall be established for ever.

who will come from your own body, and I will establish his kingdom.

13 He is the one who will build a house for my Name, and I will establish the throne of his kingdom forever.

14 I will be his father, and he will be my son. When he does wrong, I will punish him with the rod of men, with floggings inflicted by men.

15 But my love will never be taken away from him, as I took it away from Saul, whom I removed from before you.

16 Your house and your kingdom will endure forever before me; your throne will be established forever.'"

TOPICAL OUTLINE OF THE LESSON

I. Introduction
A. A Denial and a Promise
B. Biblical Background

II. Exposition and Application of the Scripture
A. God Changes David's Plans (2 Samuel 7:4-7)
B. God Reminds David of His Past (2 Samuel 7:8-11a)
C. God Makes a Covenant with David (2 Samuel 7:11b-16)

III. Concluding Reflection

LESSON OBJECTIVES

Upon the completion of the lesson, the students will be able to do the following:

1. Understand the connection between the house David wanted to build for God and the house God promised to build for David;

2. Name the feelings associated with discovering that God sometimes has designs for persons' lives that are different from what they had planned; and,

3. Prayerfully discern God's promises for their future.

POINTS TO BE EMPHASIZED

ADULT/YOUTH
Adult Topic: A Change of Plans
Youth Topic: Let's Get It Started
Adult/Youth Key Verse: 2 Samuel 7:16
Print Passage: 2 Samuel 7:4-16

—Many of the prophecies about the Messiah draw on this promise made to David.

—In 1 Chronicles 22:8, God told David that he would not

be allowed to build the Temple because he was a man of war.

—Why did God's promise continue through David's line, despite frequent occurrences of sin in some of those rulers?

—God promised to sustain and make great the name of David as a continuation of the Abrahamic covenant.

—God instructed David not to build a temple for God—because he was a warrior (see 1 Chronicles 28:3).

—God fulfilled the promise through David's ancestry—beginning with David's son, Solomon.

CHILDREN
Children Topic: Keeping Promises
Key Verse: 2 Samuel 7:13
Print Passage: 2 Samuel 7:4-16

—David was not pleased that he lived in a palace and the ark resided in a tent.

—Nathan encouraged David to build a permanent house for the ark.

—God challenged David's desire to build a house for the Lord.

—God protected David from his enemies.

—God honored David by promising to establish his throne and family forever.

—God's mercy and love would be with David's family forever.

I. INTRODUCTION
A. A Denial and a Promise

Much of today's preaching and teaching is based on the premise that if one believes sincerely and deeply enough, then he/she will be able to secure his/her greatest desire from God. Yet, the truth is that many of us can tell stories that mirror the heartbreak and disappointment we felt when God said *no* to what we wanted and believed we deserved. There is nothing more disappointing than to have great plans for the future, only to face the disheartening prospect of being denied. Every person alive has experienced the agony of unfulfilled dreams, dashed hopes, and shipwrecked desires. Consider for a moment the broken dreams and the times we thought that something was God's will for our lives, only to find that it was not to be so.

Sometimes our dreams do not necessarily match up with God's will and purpose for our ministries. Many people have a deep sensitivity for what King David felt when God denied him the privilege to build a Temple for the ark of the covenant. Building a temple was the one great desire of David—but it was not to be. Like David, we value permanence and seek to build things that will outlast ourselves. How do people seek to build a legacy? When David wanted to build a house for God, God promised to build a house for David—a dynasty, or tradition of royalty.

B. Biblical Background

Historically, David was and remains the most important king in Israel's history. The reign of David was significant for several reasons. First, shortly after the death of Saul and his sons, David became king over the tribe of Judah, establishing his headquarters in Hebron (see 2 Samuel 2:1-4). Second, within a few months of his coronation, civil war broke out between the house of David and the house of Saul (see 2 Samuel 3:1). David proved to be the stronger leader and after enduring intrigue and conspiracy, he was crowned king over all Israel at Hebron (see 2 Samuel 5:1-5). Third, David captured Jerusalem, which was strategically located in the central mountains between the southern tribes and the northern tribes (see 2 Samuel 5:6-12). Fourth, David defeated and subdued all of Israel's historic enemies, giving Israel an unprecedented period of peace and prosperity (see 2 Samuel 8; compare 5:25). Fifth, David brought the ark of the covenant into Jerusalem and placed it in the tent that he had made (see 2 Samuel 6:12-17).

Things could not have been better in David's life. He was living in his palace and had peace on all sides (see 2 Samuel 7:1). He felt that the one thing he could do at that point in his life would be to build a Temple for the name of the Lord and provide a place for the ark of the covenant. David shared his vision with the prophet Nathan, who told David to do whatever the Lord had put into his heart and spirit to do (see 2 Samuel 7:3). Later that night, God told Nathan to go back and pose this question to David: "Are you the one who should build Me a house to dwell in?" (verse 5). The implication of the question was that David was not the one, but his son Solomon would build a house for the Lord God of Israel. Solomon would later say in 1 Kings 8:18 that God blessed David because he had it in his heart to build Him a house. Sometimes our greatest blessings come from God—not because we have lived spotless and unblemished lives, but because we had it in our hearts to do the right thing.

II. EXPOSITION AND APPLICATION OF THE SCRIPTURE

A. God Changes David's Plans
(2 Samuel 7:4-7)

And it came to pass that night, that the word of the LORD came unto Nathan, saying, Go and tell my servant David, Thus saith the LORD, Shalt thou build me an house for me to dwell in? Whereas I have not dwelt in any house since the time that I brought up the children of Israel out of Egypt, even to this day, but have walked in a tent and in a tabernacle. In all the places wherein I have walked with all the children of Israel spake I a word with any of the tribes of Israel, whom I commanded to feed my people Israel, saying, Why build ye not me an house of cedar?

Nathan the prophet was mentioned for the first time in the Old Testament in verse 2 (Background Scripture) when David shared his concern that the ark did not have a permanent dwelling place (see 2 Samuel 12 and 1 Kings 1 for the other appearances of Nathan). Nathan encouraged David to do whatever the Lord had placed in his heart to do, because God was with him (verse 3).

In verse 4, the statement that the "word of the LORD came to Nathan" is typical of how all of the prophets received their instructions from God. We are not told how this came about; we are only told that it did. During the course of the night, the plans of David were reversed by God. The reasons would be stated later. Why did God speak to Nathan and not David? This was primarily because David had a great deal of respect for the prophet of God and he would be much more open to receiving the Word of the Lord than Saul had been before him (see 1 Samuel 15:1-23). God told Nathan to return and raise this question with David: "Are you the one to build me a house to dwell in?" The question was laced with divine irony. Who is God that He should be limited to a fixed structure? There is no building that can contain Him!

In verse 6, God reminded Nathan that since the Exodus and the construction of the original tabernacle, He had not dwelt in nor needed a permanent manmade structure (see Exodus 25:1-8). The purpose of the tabernacle was not to house God, but to serve as the visible symbol of His presence among His people (see Exodus 33:14; 40:35-38; Deuteronomy 23:14).

The Lord stated in verse 7 that He had never asked the Israelites to build Him a house. None of Israel's rulers were instructed to build a permanent dwelling place for the ark. Here we see the sovereignty of God, which is one of His principal attributes. God is free to be whoever He wishes to be and His freedom does not tie nor restrict Him to the houses we build for worship. What David came to realize (and all Christians would do well to learn) is this: our plans and desires do not always correspond to God's plans (see Isaiah 55:8-11).

B. God Reminds David of His Past
(2 Samuel 7:8-11a)

Now therefore so shalt thou say unto my servant David, Thus saith the LORD of hosts, I took thee from the sheepcote, from following the sheep, to be ruler over my people, over Israel: And I was with thee whithersoever thou wentest, and have cut off all thine enemies out of thy sight, and have made thee a great name, like unto the name of the great men that are in the earth. Moreover I will appoint a place for my people Israel, and will plant them, that they may dwell in a place of their own, and move no more; neither shall the children of wickedness afflict them any more, as beforetime, And as since the time that I commanded judges to be over my people Israel, and have caused thee to rest from all thine enemies.

This section of the lesson contains statements that reflect both the past and what appear to be future blessings in the life of David and Israel. In verse 8, God gave Nathan a second oracle to share with David, which focused on his past and how God had blessed his life. David was referred to as the servant of the Lord, a title of affection and one that denotes an intimate relationship with the Lord (see Joshua 1:2, 7, 13). There is no greater title that one can receive from God than to be called His servant. God had been very gracious to David and the evidence of His gracious favor was about to be spelled out to Nathan. Four statements were made that reflected God's gracious favor in David's life. First, God took David from tending the sheep and made him the ruler over His chosen people. David had held one of the lowest occupations in all of Israel and from that lowly perch God raised him up to be the king (see 1 Samuel 9:16; 10:1; 16:11-12).

Second, God had personally been with him wherever he went (see verse 9). David had been a man of war from the time that he defeated Goliath. His life was marred by conflict and combat. And in all of those campaigns, he had never been wounded or hurt (see 2 Samuel 5:10; 8:6, 14; 22:30; compare Psalm 91:7). David was evidence that God can keep His own in the midst of life's most turbulent and dangerous moments.

Third, God was going to make David's name great, like all of the great men of that day.

The words of that promise were also echoed in the promise made to Abraham (see Genesis 12:2; 1 Samuel 2:8; 1 Chronicles 17:8; Luke 1:52).

Fourth, God promised to provide safety and security. This would be a place of rest, peace, and prosperity. This life of security would be characterized by the absence of any of Israel's historic enemies. The period would be unlike anything or time that Israel had ever known (verse 11).

C. God Makes a Covenant with David (2 Samuel 7:11b-16)

Also the LORD telleth thee that he will make thee an house. And when thy days be fulfilled, and thou shalt sleep with thy fathers, I will set up thy seed after thee, which shall proceed out of thy bowels, and I will establish his kingdom. He shall build an house for my name, and I will stablish the throne of his kingdom for ever. I will be his father, and he shall be my son. If he commit iniquity, I will chasten him with the rod of men, and with the stripes of the children of men: But my mercy shall not depart away from him, as I took it from Saul, whom I put away before thee. And thine house and thy kingdom shall be established for ever before thee: thy throne shall be established for ever.

This passage has been historically understood as a messianic passage that points to the establishment of the kingdom of God through Jesus of Nazareth. After the time of David, all of the prophets interpreted the covenant between God and David in messianic overtones. They all made references to the promise made by God to David (see Isaiah 11:1, 10; Jeremiah 23:5; 33:15, 17, 22; Ezekiel 37:24; Hosea 3:5; Amos 9:11; Micah 5:2-5; Zechariah 12:8). David was the ideal king. He had been chosen by God over his other brothers to lead God's people. He was not the oldest, tallest, or what some would consider the brightest—but he was God's choice.

The break between verses 11 and 12 is an artificial one. The theme of the oracle changed from what God had done in David's past to what He was going to do in David's future. God declared that He was going to establish a house for David, which is a strange twist of irony. David wanted to build a house for the Lord, but it was David who would be on the receiving end.

In verse 12, God made three promises to David. First, when he slept with his fathers (a reference to his death), God was going to raise up his offspring to succeed him as king. Second, the successor to David would not be a stepchild nor a servant, but one who would come from his own body. Third, God was going to establish David's kingdom.

God was going to allow the offspring of David to build the Temple for the name of the Lord. His throne and kingdom would be established forever. Everything about the relationship between God and David's heir would be different. God would be his father and he would be considered as a son. Unlike Saul, who had the kingdom stripped from him because of his disobedience, this son would receive chastisement from God through human agents (verse 14). Regardless of what happened, the relationship between God and this son would never change. Saul's disobedience effectively ended his relationship as the chosen one.

The heart of the promise or covenant was its perpetuity. Not only would the house of David last forever—a reference to a continuous line of descendants—but his kingdom would last.

III. CONCLUDING REFLECTION

David was the ideal king. He had been chosen by God, over his other brothers—who were older, perhaps taller, and maybe more mature—to lead His people. He was God's choice. The lesson provides several valuable insights into the nature and ways of God. First, there are times in our lives when our personal interests and desires are in conflict with the plan of God. When God says no to our desires, it may be that He has something better or greater in store. This means that it is important that we learn to discern the plan of God and then be open to obediently follow His plan for our lives. Second, it is useful to spend time reflecting on the great things that God has done in our lives. Remembering the challenging times in life empowers us for the times when God redirects our efforts in the direction that suits His plan. What is the appropriate response to the blessings of God? It is always praise, worship, and hearts overflowing with gratitude.

PRAYER

Lord, teach us how to live in full acknowledgment of Your will for our lives. Grant that we will never turn away from the grand design that You have for our lives. In Jesus' name we pray. Amen.

WORD POWER

Servant (Hebrew: *ebed*)—is a very important word in the Old and New Testaments, especially when used in connection with individuals whom God called "servants." Servants were persons who performed tasks or assignments for a superior. Within the context of the Old Testament the designation of someone as the "servant of the Lord" was a title of great honor, which showed the person's humility and spiritual relationship to God.

HOME DAILY BIBLE READINGS
(February 24–March 2, 2014)

An Eternal Kingdom
MONDAY, February 24: "The Lord Is King" (Psalm 93)
TUESDAY, February 25: "You Are My Son" (Psalm 2)
WEDNESDAY, February 26: "An Eternal Throne" (Psalm 45:1-9)
THURSDAY, February 27: "God's Heritage" (Psalm 94:8-15)
FRIDAY, February 28: "God's Steadfast Love and Faithfulness" (Psalm 98)
SATURDAY, March 1: "The Messiah Will Reign Forever" (Revelation 11:15-19)
SUNDAY, March 2: "A Throne Established Forever" (2 Samuel 7:4-16)

SON OF DAVID

FAITH PATHWAY/FAITH JOURNEY TOPIC: Family Connections

DEVOTIONAL READING: **Mark 10:46-52**
PRINT PASSAGE: **Psalm 89:35-37; Isaiah 9:6-7;**
Matthew 1:18-21
KEY VERSES: **Matthew 1:21-22**

BACKGROUND SCRIPTURE: **Psalm 89:3-14, 30-37;**
Isaiah 9:1-7; Matthew 1:18–2:6; Mark 12:35-37;
Luke 1:26-33

Psalm 89:35-37; Isaiah 9:6-7; Matthew 1:18-21—KJV

35 Once have I sworn by my holiness that I will not lie unto David.

36 His seed shall endure for ever, and his throne as the sun before me.

37 It shall be established for ever as the moon, and as a faithful witness in heaven. Selah.

.....

6 For unto us a child is born, unto us a son is given: and the government shall be upon his shoulder: and his name shall be called Wonderful, Counsellor, The mighty God, The everlasting Father, The Prince of Peace.

7 Of the increase of his government and peace there shall be no end, upon the throne of David, and upon his kingdom, to order it, and to establish it with judgment and with justice from henceforth even for ever. The zeal of the LORD of hosts will perform this.

.....

18 Now the birth of Jesus Christ was on this wise: When as his mother Mary was espoused to Joseph, before they came together, she was found with child of the Holy Ghost.

19 Then Joseph her husband, being a just man, and not willing to make her a publick example, was minded to put her away privily.

20 But while he thought on these things, behold, the angel of the Lord appeared unto him in a dream, saying, Joseph, thou son of David, fear not to take unto

Psalm 89:35-37; Isaiah 9:6-7; Matthew 1:18-21—NIV

35 "Once for all, I have sworn by my holiness—and I will not lie to David—

36 that his line will continue forever and his throne endure before me like the sun;

37 it will be established forever like the moon, the faithful witness in the sky."

.....

6 For to us a child is born, to us a son is given, and the government will be on his shoulders. And he will be called Wonderful Counselor, Mighty God, Everlasting Father, Prince of Peace.

7 Of the increase of his government and peace there will be no end. He will reign on David's throne and over his kingdom, establishing and upholding it with justice and righteousness from that time on and forever. The zeal of the LORD Almighty will accomplish this.

.....

18 This is how the birth of Jesus Christ came about: His mother Mary was pledged to be married to Joseph, but before they came together, she was found to be with child through the Holy Spirit.

19 Because Joseph her husband was a righteous man and did not want to expose her to public disgrace, he had in mind to divorce her quietly.

20 But after he had considered this, an angel of the Lord appeared to him in a dream and said, "Joseph son of David, do not be afraid to take Mary home as

thee Mary thy wife: for that which is conceived in her is of the Holy Ghost.

21 And she shall bring forth a son, and thou shalt call his name JESUS: for he shall save his people from their sins.

your wife, because what is conceived in her is from the Holy Spirit.

21 She will give birth to a son, and you are to give him the name Jesus, because he will save his people from their sins."

TOPICAL OUTLINE OF THE LESSON

I. Introduction
A. Family Roots
B. Biblical Background

II. Exposition and Application of the Scripture
A. The Promise and Permanence of the Covenant (Psalm 89:35-37)
B. The Prophecy Concerning the Coming King (Isaiah 9:6-7)
C. The Announcement of the Birth of the Messiah (Matthew 1:18-21)

III. Concluding Reflection

LESSON OBJECTIVES

Upon the completion of the lesson, the students will be able to do the following:

1. Understand the genealogical connection between David and Jesus;
2. Experience the significance of Christians' familial kinship with Jesus; and,
3. Create a "spiritual" family tree of those who have nurtured their faith from their birth to their present age.

POINTS TO BE EMPHASIZED

ADULT/YOUTH

Adult Topic: Family Connections
Youth Topic: To Be Continued…
Adult Key Verses: Matthew 1:21-22
Youth Key Verse: Matthew 2:6
Print Passage: Psalm 89:35-37; Isaiah 9:6-7; Matthew 1:18-21

—The book of Isaiah passage came to be seen as an assurance of divine mercy mediated through a descendant of David.

—Psalm 89 rearticulates God's eternal promise that would be fulfilled through David's line, to a people who had broken God's covenant.

—Psalm 89 reiterates Nathan's vision concerning the Davidic dynasty (see 2 Samuel 7).

—In the book of Matthew passage, Joseph is addressed as a "son of David," indicating his connection with the kingly line.

—The name *Jesus* means, "God will save." The English form of the name goes back to the Latin transliteration of the Greek. The original Hebrew form was *yeshua* (Joshua), and was associated with God's deliverance of His people from their enemies.

—God promised that David's royal lineage would sit on the throne of Israel forever.

—Joseph accepted the angel's instructions to marry Mary, despite cultural traditions and implications.

—The Virgin Birth is important to the Christian faith—because Jesus does not embody the sinful nature passed on to humanity by Adam.

—God's promise was fulfilled ultimately through the birth of Jesus.

CHILDREN
Children Topic: Family Ties

Key Verse: Psalm 89:4

Print Passage: Psalm 89:1-4, 26-29; Matthew 1:17-18

—The psalmist sang praises to God for His mercy.

—The psalmist restated a covenant made by God with David.

—David was highly favored by God—so David's family would continue forever.

—The promise of God for Jesus' birth was brought to fulfillment.

—According to Matthew, there were twenty-eight generations between David and Jesus.

I. INTRODUCTION

A. Family Roots

In 1977, the ABC television network broadcast the Emmy Award-winning miniseries *Roots: The Saga of an American Family.* The series was based on a novel written by Alex Haley (1921-1992) depicting the life and story of a young boy named Kunte Kinte, born in Gambia, West Africa. It was 1750, and Kinte was fifteen years old when he was captured one day and sold to white slave traders. The book and the miniseries were billed as true accounts of the ancestry of Alex Haley. Several years after the release of the book and the successful miniseries, however, Alex Haley was sued by a man named Harold Courlander in a federal district court, claiming that Haley's book was not an original work. In his lawsuit, Courlander claimed that Haley had taken excerpts from his own book, *The African,* which was published in 1967. From the very beginning, there were researchers who doubted the validity of Haley's claims that he had successfully traced his family tree back to Gambia. The civil trial which lasted for nearly five weeks was eventually settled out of court, with Haley paying an undisclosed financial settlement. He regrettably admitted later that there were some portions of *The African* which may have been included in his book.

Alex Haley's masterpiece points to the desire that many people have to know where their families originated, especially African Americans. In the previous lesson, we learned how God had made a promise to King David that his family would continue and that his throne would be established forever. People have expectations and hopes regarding their descendants. What assurances do people have that their line of descendants will continue? As God promised David and as Isaiah prophesied, Matthew reported that the birth of Jesus fulfilled the traditional expectation that a descendant of David would be coming as the Savior.

B. Biblical Background

The lesson today comes from three separate passages: two are from the Old Testament and one is from the New Testament. The passages from the Old Testament, Psalm 89:35-37 and Isaiah 9:6-7, both have messianic overtones and have been used to point back to God's intention to bring forth a Savior, who would come through the lineage of Abraham and David (see Genesis 12:1-3; 2 Samuel 7:12-16). The passage from the book of Isaiah came to be interpreted as an assurance of divine mercy mediated through a descendant of David. Isaiah's prophecy was delivered to Israel, the northern kingdom. After the death of Solomon, the northern tribes rejected the Davidic legacy (see 1 Kings 12:16). King Ahaz, who ruled the southern kingdom of Judea, was facing a major political and military crisis which had been precipitated by the Assyrian invasion and conquest of the northern tribes (see 2 Kings 16:1-17:18). God reassured Ahaz that the Davidic line would continue in the birth of a son, who turned out to be Hezekiah.

Psalm 89 is a royal psalm that celebrates God's faithfulness to David and the promise that He would establish his throne forever. It was probably written during the time of the Babylonian Exile or shortly afterward as a means of affirming God's presence with His people. Psalm 89 reiterated God's eternal promise that nothing would prevent the Davidic dynasty from lasting forever. God had sworn by His name that it would endure, just as the heavenly bodies had stood in their places since creation.

In the passage from the book of Matthew, Joseph was addressed as a "son of David," indicating his connection to the Davidic dynasty. Mary's firstborn Son would be called Jesus, and He, too, would be a descendant of the seed of David and would be the ultimate fulfillment of the promise of God. The name *Jesus* comes from a Hebrew root *Jeshua* (Joshua) and it, too, is a name that is associated with divine deliverance. Each of these passages speaks to the promise of God to David and its fulfillment.

II. EXPOSITION AND APPLICATION OF THE SCRIPTURE

A. The Promise and Permanence of the Covenant (Psalm 89:35-37)

Once have I sworn by my holiness that I will not lie unto David. His seed shall endure for ever, and his throne as the sun before me. It shall be established for ever as the moon, and as a faithful witness in heaven. Selah.

The words in this section continue the reinforcement of the promise made to David through the prophet Nathan (see 2 Samuel 7:11b-16). In these verses, the promise is even more emphatic, proclaiming the permanence of the covenant between God and David. The word *covenant* is invoked in verse 34 (in the Background Scripture) as an unalterable proclamation from the lips of God.

According to verse 35, God swore by His holiness, a reference to the very sacredness and character of God. God is holy and His holiness cannot be changed. For God to fail to honor His promise would be both a contradiction and violation of His very nature (see Psalms 104:4; 132:11; Amos 4:2; 8:7; Hebrews 6:13; Titus 1:2; 2 Peter 3:9). God will never lie to us and we can be sure that His promises are sure and steadfast. One of the great promises of God is His abiding and continuing presence in every situation and phase of our lives (see Joshua 1:5; 2 Corinthians 4:7-18).

In verses 36 and 37, God called upon the sun and moon to become His personal witnesses to the validity of His promise. These two bodies have stood in the sky since the dawn of creation and have never wavered in what they were created to do and be. There is no better witness to the permanence of God's Word than the sun and moon (see Psalm 72:5, 17; Isaiah 59:21; Jeremiah 33:20).

B. The Prophecy Concerning the Coming King (Isaiah 9:6-7)

For unto us a child is born, unto us a son is given: and the government shall be upon his shoulder: and his name shall be called Wonderful, Counsellor, The mighty God, The everlasting Father, The Prince of Peace. Of the increase of his government and peace there shall be no end, upon the throne of David, and upon his kingdom, to order it, and to establish it with judgment and with justice from henceforth even for ever. The zeal of the LORD of hosts will perform this.

There came a period in the history of Israel when it looked like the promise of an everlasting throne and lineage of David would be snuffed out by the powerful armies of Assyria and later Babylon. The northern kingdom had already been decimated by idolatry, sin, and the continuing invasions and conquest by the Assyrians. The leaders in the south were at their wits end over how to respond to the situation. God raised up a prophet who preached of deliverance in the near term and of a greater future deliverance of which he had no knowledge. Isaiah 9:6-7 must be read in historical context to appreciate the importance of the prophecy. During the time of Isaiah's ministry, there was widespread despair, discouragement, and dejection throughout the land of Judah. Many of the common people saw no hope for a brighter and better future. Life was fragile and tenuous. One never knew what would happen from day to day.

One of the unique aspects of the message of Isaiah was his messianic pronouncements. Isaiah preached that God was going to send a Messiah, one anointed with the Spirit of God, who would reverse the situation of His people. These messianic announcements are in Isaiah 7:14; 9:1-7; 11:1; and the Servant passages that appear in Isaiah chapters 40–55.

Isaiah declared that a son had been born and a child had been given. Was this the announcement of the birth of Hezekiah who would reign in the place of his father? Yes— and much more! God was raising up a leader for then and one for the future. God gave the people a leader who would execute His will in the person of Hezekiah. Yet, there was one to come whom John said was not even worthy to stoop down and tie up his shoelaces (see John 1:27).

In these verses, we have a galaxy of names that surround us with joy. Who is this child? In what child can the government of the universe rest? His name is called Wonderful. That which He does surpasses all that we can think and expect. Jesus Christ did mighty and wonderful things. He is a Counselor whose wisdom exceeds even that of Solomon's. He leads us in the paths of righteousness. None need go astray when they follow Him. He is the mighty God. He is the everlasting Father who is the same yesterday, today, and forever. He lives in eternity, but His greatest works are in time. He is the Prince of Peace who keeps us in perfect peace when our minds are stayed upon Him. Through the prophetic preaching of Isaiah that a son would be born, God reaffirmed the original promise to David that a descendant would sit upon the throne of Judah forever. And even if they sinned, they would be punished—but their reckless behavior would not nullify the promise made by God to David.

C. The Announcement of the Birth of the Messiah (Matthew 1:18-21)

Now the birth of Jesus Christ was on this wise: When as his mother Mary was espoused to Joseph, before they came together, she was found with child of the Holy Ghost. Then Joseph her husband, being a just man, and not willing to make her a publick example, was minded to put her away privily. But while he thought on these things, behold, the angel of the Lord appeared unto him in a dream, saying, Joseph, thou son of David, fear not to take unto thee Mary thy wife: for that which is conceived in her is of the Holy Ghost. And she shall bring forth a son, and thou shalt call his name JESUS: for he shall save his people from their sins.

The final passage in today's lesson comes from the birth narrative of the gospel of Matthew. In the verses, we have a clear statement as to why Jesus was born and the circumstances surrounding His birth (see Genesis 3:15; Galatians 4:4-5; Hebrews 7:26; 10:5; compare Luke 1:25). Jesus was born in fulfillment of the promise made first to Abraham and then to King David that there would always be an heir on the throne. Joseph was of the house and lineage of David. The account begins with the engagement of two young people who lived in Nazareth. Mary, the birth mother of Jesus, was impregnated by the Holy Spirit at a critical point in their engagement. In that day, an engagement was tantamount to being married. It was a very important time in the life of the young couple, both of whom had made the decision to give themselves to each other.

According to verse 19, Joseph planned on putting Mary away privately. When Joseph found out that Mary was pregnant, it was his intention to quietly and discreetly give her a writ of divorcement which would in effect nullify the marital agreement (see Leviticus 19:20; Deuteronomy 22:21-23). In verse 20, we see the reversal of Joseph's decision to divorce Mary. While Joseph slept, the angel of the Lord spoke to him in a dream and encouraged him not to be afraid, but to go ahead and take Mary as his wife because what had been conceived in her womb was through the Holy Spirit.

In verse 21, we see the statement regarding why Jesus came into the world. Jesus came into the world for a specific purpose and mission: to save His people (Jews) and all people. Matthew made it clear that Jesus came in fulfillment of the Jewish expectation of a coming Messiah. In the Jewish extra-biblical writings (non-canonical writings that do not appear in the Bible), Jewish rabbis wrote extensively about the Messiah. One belief held that during the age of the Messiah, sin would be vanquished and people would live free of its power and dominance.

According to ancient Hebrew prophecy, the age of Messiah would be characterized by unusual peace, prosperity, and progress. In the writings of Micah, this period is characterized as a time of great peace and prosperity and one where Jerusalem would become the center of the Earth and all nations would come to this place to worship (see Micah 4:1-4).

III. CONCLUDING REFLECTION

Christians believe in the Virgin Birth. The

central affirmation of the New Testament is that Jesus Christ is the only answer for human sinfulness. The Scriptures affirm that Jesus was not just a prophet, preacher, and faith healer; rather, He was, is, and always will be God, who became a living human being in the person of Jesus of Nazareth. He is the only way to God. The affirmation of the witness of Scripture does not make one a religious extremist, or a narrow-minded person who is locked into an ancient world belief that is no longer relevant for our age of freedom and tolerance. We know that the only answer to the problems of this world is not more legislation, bank bailouts, job bills, sealed borders, drug rehabilitation programs, or more and better schools. No, the answer is Jesus! Jesus saves! Christians take comfort in the eternal nature of God's promises. Although we see through a glass darkly and know only in part, one day all things will be fully revealed.

PRAYER

Lord God Almighty, teach us how to trust You in the narrow places of life. When our hopes and dreams have been shattered by the unseen and unpredictable, bless us to wait before You for grace and mercy. In Jesus' name we pray. Amen.

WORD POWER

Holiness (Hebrew: *Qodesh* [ko' desh])—The words *holiness* and *holy* are words that are rich in spiritual depth and theological importance. The words literally mean "apartness, separateness, or sacredness." In the lesson, they denote something of the uniqueness and exclusive character of God (see Exodus 15:11; Psalms 30:4; 108:7; Amos 4:2).

HOME DAILY BIBLE READINGS
(March 3–9, 2014)

Son of David
MONDAY, March 3: "A Son Named Emmanuel" (Matthew 1:22-25)
TUESDAY, March 4: "The King of the Jews" (Matthew 2:1-6)
WEDNESDAY, March 5: "Is This the Son of David?" (Matthew 12:15-23)
THURSDAY, March 6: "Hosanna to the Son of David" (Matthew 21:12-17)
FRIDAY, March 7: "Whose Son Is the Messiah?" (Matthew 22:41-45)
SATURDAY, March 8: "Following the Son of David" (Mark 10:46-52)
SUNDAY, March 9: "The Son of David" (Psalm 89:35-37; Isaiah 9:6-7; Matthew 1:18-21)

LESSON 3   March 16, 2014

PETER'S REPORT

FAITH PATHWAY/FAITH JOURNEY TOPIC: Looking Forward and Looking Back

DEVOTIONAL READING: Psalm 16:7-11
PRINT PASSAGE: Psalm 110:1-4; Acts 2:22-24, 29-32

BACKGROUND SCRIPTURE: Psalm 110; Acts 2:22-36
KEY VERSE: Acts 2:31

Psalm 110:1-4; Acts 2:22-24, 29-32—KJV

THE LORD said unto my Lord, Sit thou at my right hand, until I make thine enemies thy footstool.

2 The LORD shall send the rod of thy strength out of Zion: rule thou in the midst of thine enemies.

3 Thy people shall be willing in the day of thy power, in the beauties of holiness from the womb of the morning: thou hast the dew of thy youth.

4 The LORD hath sworn, and will not repent, Thou art a priest for ever after the order of Melchizedek.

.....

22 Ye men of Israel, hear these words; Jesus of Nazareth, a man approved of God among you by miracles and wonders and signs, which God did by him in the midst of you, as ye yourselves also know:

23 Him, being delivered by the determinate counsel and foreknowledge of God, ye have taken, and by wicked hands have crucified and slain:

24 Whom God hath raised up, having loosed the pains of death: because it was not possible that he should be holden of it.

.....

29 Men and brethren, let me freely speak unto you of the patriarch David, that he is both dead and buried, and his sepulchre is with us unto this day.

30 Therefore being a prophet, and knowing that God had sworn with an oath to him, that of the fruit of his loins, according to the flesh, he would raise up Christ to sit on his throne;

31 He seeing this before spake of the resurrection of Christ, that his soul was not left in hell, neither his flesh did see corruption.

Psalm 110:1-4; Acts 2:22-24, 29-32—NIV

THE LORD says to my Lord: "Sit at my right hand until I make your enemies a footstool for your feet."

2 The LORD will extend your mighty scepter from Zion; you will rule in the midst of your enemies.

3 Your troops will be willing on your day of battle. Arrayed in holy majesty, from the womb of the dawn you will receive the dew of your youth.

4 The LORD has sworn and will not change his mind: "You are a priest forever, in the order of Melchizedek."

.....

22 "Men of Israel, listen to this: Jesus of Nazareth was a man accredited by God to you by miracles, wonders and signs, which God did among you through him, as you yourselves know.

23 This man was handed over to you by God's set purpose and foreknowledge; and you, with the help of wicked men, put him to death by nailing him to the cross.

24 But God raised him from the dead, freeing him from the agony of death, because it was impossible for death to keep its hold on him."

.....

29 "Brothers, I can tell you confidently that the patriarch David died and was buried, and his tomb is here to this day.

30 But he was a prophet and knew that God had promised him on oath that he would place one of his descendants on his throne.

31 Seeing what was ahead, he spoke of the resurrection of the Christ, that he was not abandoned to the grave, nor did his body see decay.

32 This Jesus hath God raised up, whereof we all are witnesses.

32 God has raised this Jesus to life, and we are all witnesses of the fact."

TOPICAL OUTLINE OF THE LESSON

I. Introduction
- A. The Past Prepares Us for the Future
- B. Biblical Background

II. Exposition and Application of the Scripture
- A. The Picture of the Messiah as King and Priest (Psalm 110:1-4)
- B. Peter's Witness of the Messiah (Acts 2:22-24)
- C. David's Witness of the Messiah (Acts 2:29-32)

III. Concluding Reflection

LESSON OBJECTIVES

Upon the completion of the lesson, the students will be able to do the following:

1. Study Peter's insights of David's connection to Jesus, with a view to expanding their understanding of Jesus' relationship to God;
2. Give their testimonies of the saving power of Jesus; and,
3. Develop a method for sharing their faith in Christ with others.

POINTS TO BE EMPHASIZED

ADULT/YOUTH

Adult Topic: Looking Forward and Looking Back
Youth Topic: Jesus Is Lord
Adult Key Verse: Acts 2:31
Youth Key Verse: Acts 2:36
Print Passage: Psalm 110:1-4; Acts 2:22-24, 29-32

—The book of Acts passage is a portion of Peter's sermon on the day of Pentecost.

—Peter connected David to messianic hopes fulfilled in Jesus.

—Peter taught that everything that happened to Jesus was foreknown by God.

—Psalm 110 has clear references to the Messiah.

—Melchizedek is the first named priest-king in Scripture. He honored God and counseled Abraham.

—Ultimate victory was promised by God and fulfilled through Jesus Christ.

CHILDREN

Children Topic: A King Forever
Key Verse: Acts 2:32
Print Passage: Acts 2:22-25, 29-36

—Peter reminded the Israelites that God raised Jesus, whom they crucified.

—Peter reminded his hearers that David knew God would fulfill His promises through one of David's descendants.

—God resurrected the Messiah.

—Jesus was placed at the right hand of God.

—Jesus gave the gift of the Holy Spirit to His followers.

—Peter declared with certainty that God made Jesus both Lord and Messiah.

I. INTRODUCTION
A. The Past Prepares Us for the Future

There is much that can be gained from the stories of the past. We can learn a great deal about how they dealt with disappointment, failure, and the keys to their successes. During our annual church celebrations, we remember the past, but we also look forward to where we believe the Lord Jesus Christ is calling us and taking us as a congregation. God is always calling us to live in the future. The past is the footprints of where we have come from and reminds us of the road on which we have traveled. It is important for the people of God to reflect over the past, but also to look with expectancy toward the future.

People need to understand what they have received as a legacy in order for them to perceive any value in it. How can people correlate tradition and legacy? In the lesson today, Peter's sermon, preached on the Day of Pentecost, is an interpretation of the coming of Jesus into the world. He came in fulfillment of the prophecies of a Messiah-King who would descend from the lineage of David. In the previous lesson, we learned that the birth of Jesus Christ occurred in fulfillment of the prophecy of Isaiah (see Isaiah 7:14; 9:1-7).

B. Biblical Background

There are three passages that comprise the lesson today. The first is found in the Old Testament book of Psalms and the remaining two passages come out of the Acts of the Apostles. The first verse in Psalm 110 is one of the most frequently quoted verses in the New Testament (see Matthew 26:64; Mark 14:62; Luke 22:69; Acts 2:34-34; 7:35-56; Romans 8:34; Ephesians 1:20; Colossians 3:1; Hebrews 1:3, 13; 8:1; 10:12; 1 Peter 3:22). There is some disagreement among biblical scholars as to the exact context out of which this psalm emerged. Some believe that it may have been written at a time prior to the Babylonian Exile and that it served primarily as an enthronement psalm used during the coronation of the king. Others see it as a battle psalm, without any identifiable historical context. Then finally, others see it coming out of the post-exilic period and believe that it functioned as a psalm of remembrance and affirmation regarding the covenant between God and David. David was the author, as seen on the superscription (title); therefore, it has historically been used as a messianic psalm remembering the covenant between God and David.

The other two passages are parts of the first Christian sermon preached by Peter on the

Day of Pentecost (see Acts 2:14-39). Pentecost was an annual Jewish festival celebrated fifty days after Passover. Pentecost was one of the three major Jewish festivals and it annually drew very large crowds of people to Jerusalem (see Acts 2:5-11). In his sermon, Peter connected David to the messianic expectations of the people. Peter maintained that David spoke about Jesus and His resurrection in Psalms 16 and 110. In the life and ministry of Jesus, there was a clear expectation that the Messiah-King had come forth with great pomp and majesty (see Matthew 11:2-6).

II. EXPOSITION AND APPLICATION OF THE SCRIPTURE

A. The Picture of the Messiah as King and Priest (Psalm 110:1-4)

THE LORD said unto my Lord, Sit thou at my right hand, until I make thine enemies thy footstool. The LORD shall send the rod of thy strength out of Zion: rule thou in the midst of thine enemies. Thy people shall be willing in the day of thy power, in the beauties of holiness from the womb of the morning: thou hast the dew of thy youth. The LORD hath sworn, and will not repent, Thou art a priest for ever after the order of Melchizedek.

The title of the psalm declares that it is the work of King David. This particular psalm is considered to be one of the enthronement psalms—but like many of the psalms the context cannot be definitely known. Three questions can be asked which helps us better understand a particular psalm. First, what did the psalm mean in its original context? Second, what did the psalm mean to the people who helped shape it and included it in the book of Psalms? Third, what did the psalm mean to the first Christians who saw these words in light of the life of Jesus Christ?

In verse 1, the very first question raised is one surrounding the identity of the speaker and whom he was addressing. We can assume that the speaker was either David or some other royal personage who was addressing someone else of royal stature. The speaker offered a word of encouragement that his enemies would be defeated. In the meantime, he was invited to sit at the right hand of the Lord. The right hand represents support, strength, and a place of honor.

Verses 2-3 exclaim that the king would be successful and that his army would reign supreme—beginning with Zion or Jerusalem. The scepter was the symbol of authority and denoted the rule of the king. The willingness of the troops likely referred to the soldiers who were willing to sacrifice themselves in the heat of battle. Biblical scholars are not quite sure of the real meaning of the second part of verse 3.

Verse 4 was a clear reference to David and the promise made regarding the establishment of his throne forever. The covenant stood and God would never renege on His promise. Here in this verse, we see the combination of the functions of priest and king. The declaration is that of an eternal priesthood after the order of Melchizedek that looked back to the time of Abraham, where Melchizedek is discussed (see Genesis 14:18; Hebrews 5:6, 10; 6:20; 7:17).

Psalm 110 has been historically interpreted in light of the ministry of Jesus of Nazareth. The early Christians saw in these words a clear prophetic reference to Jesus by David, and this was reflected in the sermon of Peter on the Day of Pentecost. The early Christians never had doubts that these words were a clear reference to the messiah-ship of Jesus Christ.

B. Peter's Witness of the Messiah (Acts 2:22-24)

Ye men of Israel, hear these words; Jesus of Nazareth, a man approved of God among you by miracles and wonders and signs, which God did by him in the midst of you, as ye yourselves also know: Him, being delivered by the determinate counsel and foreknowledge of God, ye have taken, and by wicked hands have crucified and slain: Whom God hath raised up, having loosed the pains of death: because it was not possible that he should be holden of it.

This section of the lesson comes from the first recorded Christian sermon preached by one of the apostles. Peter's message began in Acts 2:14 as he connected the events of Pentecost to the fulfillment of the prophecy of Joel (see 2:28-32). The coming of the Messiah was not an unknown or an unforeseen event in history. Peter reminded the Jews that Jesus of Nazareth was and is the Messiah, and the evidence of this claim is well-documented. There were occasions when the Pharisees accused Jesus of being an instrument of the devil (see Matthew 12:23; Mark 3:22; Luke 11:15). They attributed His miraculous power to the devil. Peter's message declared that God validated the work and ministry of Jesus in three ways: through miracles, wonders, and signs (refer to the "Word Power" section for specific definitions). Peter pointed out that Jesus was the instrument through whom God worked. These miracles were not unknown to them, for many of the people who heard Peter had no doubt either been a personal witness to them or may have even been a recipient of the mercy of God. The words "you yourselves know" comprise an emphatic phrase that points out that the people were also witnesses of the very life and ministry of Jesus of Nazareth.

Verse 23 is a change in the tone and content of the message. First, Howard Marshall remarked that in verse 23, we have "the paradox of divine predestination and human freewill in its strongest form."[1] Although the Jews thought that they were carrying out their own plans to get rid of Jesus, they were in fact fulfilling God's eternal purpose. Several thoughts are expressed about the salvific work of God in this verse. First, this very same man whom God used to work miracles was handed over to the men of Israel by God. Second, this was not their doing but was part of the set purpose and foreknowledge of God. It was all within the redemptive plan of God to save the world from sin and death (see Genesis 3:15; Isaiah 53). Third, Peter accused the Jews of participating in the death of the Messiah when they joined with the wicked Roman establishment to have Jesus arrested and crucified. Fourth, Jesus was nailed to the cross, a clear reference to the pain and agony He endured.

In verse 24, the phrase "but God" points out that the wickedness of humankind was no match for the power of God. Peter announced what is at the very heart and center of apostolic preaching and witness: God raised Jesus from the dead (see Acts 2:32; 3:15, 26; 4:10; 5:30; 10:40; 13:30, 33-34; 17:31; 1 Corinthians 15:1-4, 19-20). The Resurrection was the greatest miracle of God—as He freed Jesus from death. Peter declared that it was impossible for death to hold Him. Why? He is the Creator, who is both the giver and sustainer of life. How could death possibly overpower Him?

C. David's Witness of the Messiah (Acts 2:29-32)

Men and brethren, let me freely speak unto you of the

patriarch David, that he is both dead and buried, and his sepulchre is with us unto this day. Therefore being a prophet, and knowing that God had sworn with an oath to him, that of the fruit of his loins, according to the flesh, he would raise up Christ to sit on his throne; He seeing this before spake of the resurrection of Christ, that his soul was not left in hell, neither his flesh did see corruption. This Jesus hath God raised up, whereof we all are witnesses.

Verses 29-32 have to be read in light of Peter's quote of Psalm 16:8-11 (see Acts 2:25-28 in the Background Scripture). Peter changed the tone of his address and referred to his audience as his brothers. He spoke with confidence, calling David a patriarch (chief father or leader of a tribe; compare Acts 7:8-9). This is the only reference to David as a patriarch in the Bible. The term is specifically used for Abraham, Isaac, and Jacob (see Exodus 3:6, 15-16; 32:13; Jeremiah 33:26). Peter stated that when David spoke the words of the psalm, he could not possibly have been speaking of himself. David died and was buried, and his tomb was visibly present with them.

Verse 30 contains the only reference to David as a prophet. Peter declared that David was a prophet who foresaw the coming of the Messiah. The coming forth of the Messiah-King would be the fulfillment of the promise made to David that there would always be one of his descendants sitting on his throne (see 2 Samuel 7:12-14). The reference to Jesus as the fulfillment of this promise is not interpreted as a literal civic ruler, but as King who comes to establish the rule and reign of God in the world.

As a prophet, David foresaw the resurrection of Jesus Christ. There are no specifics regarding what David saw—such as the time

of year, the occasion of the Resurrection, or any of the details noted in the Gospels. Rather, when Jesus was crucified and buried, He was not abandoned to the grave. His physical body did not decay; rather, God raised Him to new life. This was not mere speculation; the apostles were all witnesses of the fact of the resurrection of Jesus Christ. We must note that Jesus did not become Messiah by virtue of His resurrection; rather, He was already God and His coming was the final revelation of God's plan and purpose to save the world from sin (see John 1:14; 2 Corinthians 5:19-20; 8:9).

III. CONCLUDING REFLECTION

There are several important truths for believers to take away from this lesson. First, we see the importance of being able to make connections between the prophecies of the Old Testament and their fulfillment in the New Testament. The Old Testament is the bedrock of our faith and is the foundation for understanding God's final revelation in Jesus Christ (see Hebrews 1:1-2).

Second, we learn that believers must always declare their faith in God without reservation or apprehensions. We are, first and foremost, witnesses of His resurrection (see Acts 1:8; 2:32; 3:15; 5:32). The central and most important tenet of the Christian faith is that Jesus Christ lives. He was crucified and buried, but God has raised Him from the dead (see Acts 13:30; Romans 6:4; 8:11; 10:9; Ephesians 1:20; 1 Thessalonians 1:10). Peter never tried to explain how the resurrection of Jesus occurred, nor did he seek to offer a defense of his faith. He merely proclaimed what God had done through Jesus Christ, and he allowed the

Holy Spirit to do the rest. Like the first apostles and early Christians, we, too, are called to be witnesses of His resurrection. When we witness for Christ, we must do so with boldness and without apology.

PRAYER

Heavenly Father, we thank You for the gift of eternal life through our Lord Jesus Christ. We thank You that You have loved us with an everlasting love. In Jesus' name we pray. Amen.

WORD POWER

Miracles (Greek: *dunamis* [doo'nam-is])—literally, strength, power, or ability, and is the most commonly used expression of the power of God. Within the Gospels, the ministry of Jesus is characterized by the performance of mighty deeds of power. He healed the sick, gave sight to the blind, and even overcame the forces of nature.

Signs (Greek: *semeion* [say-mi'-on])—This word is often used with the word *wonders* (Greek: *teras*) and denotes an unusual occurrence that transcends the normal course of events. It is a great cosmic miracle or event that has no other explanation other than being of God. Its roots are deeply embedded in the Old Testament and are particularly seen in connection with the deliverance of the children of Israel from slavery in Egypt. In the gospel of John, *signs* are viewed as the evidence of the divinity of Jesus, and it is the commonly used word for "miracles."

HOME DAILY BIBLE READINGS
(March 10–16, 2014)

Peter's Report

MONDAY, March 10: "Protect Me, O God" (Psalm 16:1-6)

TUESDAY, March 11: "Show Me the Path of Life" (Psalm 16:7-11)

WEDNESDAY, March 12: "Freed from the Fear of Death" (Hebrews 2:14-18)

THURSDAY, March 13: "The Power of the Resurrection" (Philippians 3:7-11)

FRIDAY, March 14: "The Heavenly Call of God" (Philippians 3:12-16)

SATURDAY, March 15: "Made Both Lord and Messiah" (Acts 2:33-36)

SUNDAY, March 16: "Placed on David's Throne" (Psalm 110:1-4; Acts 2:22-24, 29-32)

End Note

[1] I. Howard Marshall, *Acts (Tyndale New Testament Commentaries)* (Grand Rapids: Wm. B. Eerdmans Publishing Co., 1980), 75.

LESSON 4   March 23, 2014

WORTHY IS THE LAMB

FAITH PATHWAY/FAITH JOURNEY TOPIC: **Victory Celebration**

DEVOTIONAL READING: **Matthew 9:35–10:1**
PRINT PASSAGE: **Revelation 5:6-13**
KEY VERSE: **Revelation 5:12**

BACKGROUND SCRIPTURE: **Revelation 3:7; 5:5-13; 6:12–7:17; 22:16**

Revelation 5:6-13—KJV

6 And I beheld, and, lo, in the midst of the throne and of the four beasts, and in the midst of the elders, stood a Lamb as it had been slain, having seven horns and seven eyes, which are the seven Spirits of God sent forth into all the earth.

7 And he came and took the book out of the right hand of him that sat upon the throne.

8 And when he had taken the book, the four beasts and four and twenty elders fell down before the Lamb, having every one of them harps, and golden vials full of odours, which are the prayers of saints.

9 And they sung a new song, saying, Thou art worthy to take the book, and to open the seals thereof: for thou wast slain, and hast redeemed us to God by thy blood out of every kindred, and tongue, and people, and nation;

10 And hast made us unto our God kings and priests: and we shall reign on the earth.

11 And I beheld, and I heard the voice of many angels round about the throne and the beasts and the elders: and the number of them was ten thousand times ten thousand, and thousands of thousands;

12 Saying with a loud voice, Worthy is the Lamb that was slain to receive power, and riches, and wisdom, and strength, and honour, and glory, and blessing.

13 And every creature which is in heaven, and on the earth, and under the earth, and such as are in the sea, and all that are in them, heard I saying, Blessing, and honour, and glory, and power, be unto him that sitteth upon the throne, and unto the Lamb for ever and ever.

Revelation 5:6-13—NIV

6 Then I saw a Lamb, looking as if it had been slain, standing in the center of the throne, encircled by the four living creatures and the elders. He had seven horns and seven eyes, which are the seven spirits of God sent out into all the earth.

7 He came and took the scroll from the right hand of him who sat on the throne.

8 And when he had taken it, the four living creatures and the twenty-four elders fell down before the Lamb. Each one had a harp and they were holding golden bowls full of incense, which are the prayers of the saints.

9 And they sang a new song: "You are worthy to take the scroll and to open its seals, because you were slain, and with your blood you purchased men for God from every tribe and language and people and nation.

10 You have made them to be a kingdom and priests to serve our God, and they will reign on the earth."

11 Then I looked and heard the voice of many angels, numbering thousands upon thousands, and ten thousand times ten thousand. They encircled the throne and the living creatures and the elders.

12 In a loud voice they sang: "Worthy is the Lamb, who was slain, to receive power and wealth and wisdom and strength and honor and glory and praise!"

13 Then I heard every creature in heaven and on earth and under the earth and on the sea, and all that is in them, singing: "To him who sits on the throne and to the Lamb be praise and honor and glory and power, for ever and ever!"

UNIFYING LESSON PRINCIPLE

When long-hoped-for dreams come about, people express their joy in celebration. In what ways do people celebrate? The result of the fulfillment of the salvific tradition is the extravagant praise and worship of God by the multitude of the redeemed.

TOPICAL OUTLINE OF THE LESSON

I. Introduction
  A. Worship Now—Worship Then!
  B. Biblical Background

II. Exposition and Application of the Scripture
  A. Christ the Lamb Revealed (Revelation 5:6-7)
  B. The Twenty-four Elders and Four Living Creatures Worship the Lamb (Revelation 5:8-10)
  C. The Myriads of Angels Worship the Lamb (Revelation 5:11-13)

III. Concluding Reflection

LESSON OBJECTIVES

Upon the completion of the lesson, the students will be able to do the following:

1. Understand Jesus' final triumph as the Lamb;
2. Worship in the spirit of Revelation, at the feet of the only One worthy to receive blessing and honor and glory; and,
3. Identify hymns and songs of praise that are influenced by the praise passages in the book of Revelation.

POINTS TO BE EMPHASIZED
ADULT/YOUTH
Adult Topic: Victory Celebration
Youth Topic: Celebrate!
Adult/Youth Key Verse: Revelation 5:12
Print Passage: Revelation 5:6-13

—The figure of the lamb represented the Christ who acted as a redeeming sacrifice. The passage implies that to triumph involves one's giving him- or herself on behalf of others.
—The horn was employed in the Hebrew Scriptures as a symbol of power (verse 6). The "seven horns" suggest power that is full and complete. The "seven eyes" (verse 6) symbolize omniscience. The "harp" was a common biblical instrument of praise (verse 8).
—The salvation purchased is for people of "every tribe and language and people and nation" (verse 9, NIV).
—The Lamb was praised and adored by all the created order.
—People are praising God from every nation and culture, which demonstrates a message that reaches diverse groups.

CHILDREN
Children Topic: Giving Praise, Honor, and Thanksgiving
Key Verse: Revelation 7:12
Print Passage: Revelation 7:9-17

—John saw a vast number of persons from various backgrounds and countries standing before God's throne.
—Praises were given to God by all who were around the throne.
—Those in heaven will praise and worship God forever.
—John used vivid imagery to explain who was around the throne and the ways in which they worshipped.
—God will provide peace, victory, and comfort to those who have gone through great trials.
—In describing Jesus as the Lamb, John was connecting Jesus to the promises made to David.

I. INTRODUCTION

A. Worship Now—Worship Then!

One day, the Lord Jesus Christ will appear and claim His glorious bride, the church (see Revelation 21:1-4). Unlike various denominational gatherings, this will be a gathering of all of the saints of God from every generation and nation. Our feeble minds cannot begin to grasp the magnitude of such a gathering. Our earthly experiences, no matter how powerful, are only minute glimpses of heaven's glory.

In this lesson, we look into the future and see the events of the celebration of the triumph of the Lamb of God. Believers live in hope of that blessed day when the saints of God will gather before the Great White Throne and celebrate the victory of the Lamb. When Jesus Christ died on the cross and was raised to new life, He completed the plan of the Father to save the world from sin. The result of the fulfillment of the salvific tradition is the extravagant praise and worship of God by the multitude of the redeemed. Worship is more than a weekly obligation; rather, it is a celebration of our new life in Christ. Let the celebration begin!

B. Biblical Background

The book of Revelation was written by John, a first-century Christian. The book of Revelation was written to seven churches in Asia Minor that were all experiencing some form of religious persecution.

Chapter 5 continues the vision of heaven and the scene of the throne that John saw. The twenty-four elders and the four living creatures which were in chapter 4 are found in this chapter as well, and added to this group are myriads of angels. The action of the vision shifted to the Lamb, who stood around the throne. John saw a book (more properly called a scroll) sealed with seven seals. God, who sat upon the throne, held the book in His right hand. The seven-sealed book was one of the dominant themes of the chapter. It is referred to in eight of the fourteen verses in the chapter. A strong angel asked who was worthy to open the book. No person was found worthy, prompting John to weep bitterly.

After the Lamb took the scroll, the heavenly chorus of angels, the twenty-four elders, and the four living creatures all broke out in jubilant praise of the Lamb. Jesus Christ is the Lamb who is worthy to open the seven-sealed book. He is the subject of the chapter and the object of the heavenly praise. All who formed the heavenly court bowed before His presence.

II. EXPOSITION AND APPLICATION OF THE SCRIPTURE

A. Christ the Lamb Revealed (Revelation 5:6-7)

And I beheld, and, lo, in the midst of the throne and of the four beasts, and in the midst of the elders, stood a Lamb as it had been slain, having seven horns and seven eyes, which are the seven Spirits of God sent forth into all the earth. And he came and took the book out of the right hand of him that sat upon the throne.

John continued to look and he saw something else that changed the attitude of his heart completely: "And I saw between the throne (with the four living creatures) and the elders a Lamb standing, as if slain, having seven horns and seven eyes, which are the seven Spirits of God, sent out into all the earth" (verse 6). Instead of a lion, John saw a Lamb, as if it had been slain. John was so consumed by what he initially saw that he missed the Lamb altogether. Here the Old Testament references are numerous, but clearly they point back to the initial sacrifice of the lamb without a blemish in Exodus 12:1ff (see also Exodus 29; Numbers 28-29; Isaiah 53:7). Jesus was the Lamb of God who took away the sins of the world (see John 1:29, 35-36; Acts 8:32; Hebrews 9:13-14; 1 Peter 1:19). He died one time for all time.

The seven horns represent the complete, perfect, omnipotent power of God. Here again we are faced with an allusion to an Old Testament event that depicts the use of the number 7. Seven would be the number that would display God's awesome power. The seven eyes represent God's omniscience. There is nothing that God does not know. The end will come according to the perfect knowledge and will of God—and no power in the universe will be able to stay His hand of justice.

The Lamb took the scroll out of the hand of the One who sat upon the throne (see verses 1-3). Jesus Christ is heir of all things and He is the very one before whom all nations will stand for judgment (see Matthew 25:31-46; 2 Corinthians 5:10). When Jesus Christ takes the scroll or book out of the hand of God, the events leading up to the end of the world will commence.

B. The Twenty-four Elders and Four Living Creatures Worship the Lamb (Revelation 5:8-10)

And when he had taken the book, the four beasts and four and twenty elders fell down before the Lamb, having every one of them harps, and golden vials full of odours, which are the prayers of saints. And they sung a new song, saying, Thou art worthy to take the book, and to open the seals thereof: for thou wast slain, and hast redeemed us to God by thy blood out of every kindred, and tongue, and people, and nation; And hast made us unto our God kings and priests: and we shall reign on the earth.

The beginning of the end will be preceded by a period of tremendous worship of the Lamb, which will be the acknowledgment of His role as Savior. The four living creatures and the twenty-four elders will fall down before the Lamb. Each of the four living creatures and the twenty-four elders will have in one hand a harp, which is the instrument of praise and worship. They will also hold golden bowls full of the incense which are the prayers of the saints.

John MacArthur made this comment about verse 8: "These wide-mouthed bowls were used in the tabernacle and the temple, where they were connected with the altar. They symbolized the priestly work of intercession for the people. The Scriptures elsewhere associates the burning of incense with the prayers of the saints in Psalm 141:2; Luke 1:9-10; and Revelation 8:3-4. The incense in these bowls represents the prayers of believers through the ages that God's prophesied and promised redemption of the earth might come. Taken together, the harps and the bowls indicate that all that the prophets ever prophesied and all that God's children ever prayed for is finally to be fulfilled."

In John's vision, heaven was suddenly filled with the sounds of a new song. "New," in this instance, refers to the idea of newness in terms of the quality of the music. It is a song that has never been sung. What will be the reasons for the rejoicing? John recorded three in this verse: First, the sealed book is about to be opened and the revelation of God's plan for the ages will be unfolded. Second, the Lamb was slain for the sin of the whole world; through His sacrificial death we received redemption and salvation from our sins (see Ephesians 1:7; 1 Peter 1:18-19). Third, the redeemed would be men, women, boys, and girls from every tribe, tongue, people, and nation on the face of the Earth. The use of four nouns to depict the inclusiveness of people is significant. "Four" is the number for the sum total of all creation. "Four" is the number of the elements—earth, air, fire, and water; for the regions of the Earth—north, south, east, and west; for the division of the day—morning, noon, evening, and midnight; for the seasons of the year—winter, spring, summer, and fall.[1] There will be people from every nation in heaven—every social, economic, educational, and political persuasion. Not only are we redeemed, but also the Lamb makes us a kingdom of priests to our God—and together with the Lamb, we will reign upon the Earth.

C. The Myriads of Angels Worship the Lamb (Revelation 5:11-13)

And I beheld, and I heard the voice of many angels round about the throne and the beasts and the elders: and the number of them was ten thousand times ten thousand, and thousands of thousands; Saying with a loud voice, Worthy is the Lamb that was slain to receive power, and riches, and wisdom, and strength, and honour, and glory, and blessing. And every creature which is in heaven, and on the earth, and under the earth, and such as are in the sea, and all that are in them, heard I saying, Blessing, and honour, and glory, and power, be unto him that sitteth upon the throne, and unto the Lamb for ever and ever.

In verse 11, the word *the* introduced another sight that filled John's view: thousands and tens of thousands of angels worshipping and praising the Lamb. Throughout heaven the voice of many angels is heard in celebrative praise of the Lamb. The number of angels was beyond John's ability to count them. These combined voices included the angels around the throne, the living creatures, and the twenty-four elders joined by a host made up of tens of thousands worshipping and singing praises to the Lamb with a loud (Greek: *megas*) voice.

In verse 12, the heavenly hosts sing a sevenfold acclamation of praise to the Lamb. The first four celebrate the attributes of Christ—power, wealth, wisdom, and strength. And the final three extol the praise that is due Him—honor, glory, and praise.[2] Every living creature in heaven and on Earth will bow before the Lamb and acknowledge His lordship (see 2 Corinthians 5:10; Philippians 2:5-11; Revelations 20:11-15). The only ones who will not be in this heavenly throng are the demonic angels who rebelled against God's sovereign authority and were thrown out of heaven. The tens of thousands (not literal, but figurative) will join together and sing a great chorus of praise to the Lamb. The scene concludes with the four living creatures and the twenty-four elders falling down and worshipping Him who lives forever and ever. They said "Amen," meaning, "So let it be as it was stated."

III. CONCLUDING REFLECTION

Grant Osborne says that there are three great theological themes evident in the fifth chapter of the book of Revelation: Christology (the doctrine of Jesus Christ), soteriology (the doctrine of salvation), and eschatology (the doctrine of the last things). Many Christians have lost sight of the biblical image of Jesus Christ. We see Him in this age as less than who He is—King of Kings and Lord of Lords. Some may see Him as Savior, but certainly not the One to whom absolute loyalty and devotion are to be given. Jesus is at the same time both our conquering hero who saves us from the ravages of sin and its destructive power, and our Savior who died in our place and ushered humankind into a perfect relationship with the Father.

PRAYER

Heavenly Father, who is the source of infinite love and mercy, grant that Your servants may know the joy of worship and the peace that surpasses all understanding. May we learn to live in hope of that blessed day when the saints gather before Your throne. In Jesus' name we pray. Amen.

WORD POWER

Scroll (Greek: *biblion*)—literally, a small book. Robert Mounce observed of the scroll that it was "Filled to overflowing and sealed with seven seals to insure the secrecy of its decrees; it contains the full account of what God in his sovereign will has determined as the destiny of the world."[3]

HOME DAILY BIBLE READINGS
(March 17–23, 2014)

Worthy Is the Lamb

MONDAY, March 17: "Sheep without a Shepherd" (Matthew 9:35–10:1)
TUESDAY, March 18: "The One at God's Right Hand" (Psalm 80:8-19)
WEDNESDAY, March 19: "The Lord Cares for the Flock" (Zechariah 10:1-5)
THURSDAY, March 20: "The Wrath of the Lamb" (Revelation 6:12-17)
FRIDAY, March 21: "Salvation Belongs to Our God" (Revelation 7:9-12)
SATURDAY, March 22: "The Lamb Will Be Their Shepherd" (Revelation 7:13-17)
SUNDAY, March 23: "Worthy Is the Lamb" (Revelation 5:5-13)

End Notes

[1] E. W. Bullinger, *Number in Scripture: Its Supernatural Design and Spiritual Significance* (Grand Rapids: Kregel Publications, 1967), 123.

[2] Grant R. Osborne, *Revelation: Baker Exegetical Commentary on the New Testament* (Grand Rapids: Baker Academic, 2002), 262.

[3] Ibid., 129.

TRIUMPHANT AND VICTORIOUS

FAITH PATHWAY/FAITH JOURNEY TOPIC: **Joy and Celebration**

DEVOTIONAL READING: **Psalm 47**
PRINT PASSAGE: **Zechariah 9:9; Matthew 21:1-11**
KEY VERSE: **Matthew 21:9**

BACKGROUND SCRIPTURE: **Zechariah 9:9-10; Matthew 21:1-11**

Zechariah 9:9; Matthew 21:1-11—KJV

9 Rejoice greatly, O daughter of Zion; shout, O daughter of Jerusalem: behold, thy King cometh unto thee: he is just, and having salvation; lowly, and riding upon an ass, and upon a colt the foal of an ass.

.....

AND WHEN they drew nigh unto Jerusalem, and were come to Bethphage, unto the mount of Olives, then sent Jesus two disciples,

2 Saying unto them, Go into the village over against you, and straightway ye shall find an ass tied, and a colt with her: loose them, and bring them unto me.

3 And if any man say ought unto you, ye shall say, The Lord hath need of them; and straightway he will send them.

4 All this was done, that it might be fulfilled which was spoken by the prophet, saying,

5 Tell ye the daughter of Sion, Behold, thy King cometh unto thee, meek, and sitting upon an ass, and a colt the foal of an ass.

6 And the disciples went, and did as Jesus commanded them,

7 And brought the ass, and the colt, and put on them their clothes, and they set him thereon.

8 And a very great multitude spread their garments in the way; others cut down branches from the trees, and strawed them in the way.

9 And the multitudes that went before, and that followed, cried, saying, Hosanna to the Son of David: Blessed is he that cometh in the name of the Lord; Hosanna in the highest.

Zechariah 9:9; Matthew 21:1-11—NIV

9 Rejoice greatly, O Daughter of Zion! Shout, Daughter of Jerusalem! See, your king comes to you, righteous and having salvation, gentle and riding on a donkey, on a colt, the foal of a donkey.

.....

AS THEY approached Jerusalem and came to Bethphage on the Mount of Olives, Jesus sent two disciples,

2 saying to them, "Go to the village ahead of you, and at once you will find a donkey tied there, with her colt by her. Untie them and bring them to me.

3 If anyone says anything to you, tell him that the Lord needs them, and he will send them right away."

4 This took place to fulfill what was spoken through the prophet:

5 "Say to the Daughter of Zion, 'See, your king comes to you, gentle and riding on a donkey, on a colt, the foal of a donkey.'"

6 The disciples went and did as Jesus had instructed them.

7 They brought the donkey and the colt, placed their cloaks on them, and Jesus sat on them.

8 A very large crowd spread their cloaks on the road, while others cut branches from the trees and spread them on the road.

9 The crowds that went ahead of him and those that followed shouted, "Hosanna to the Son of David!" "Blessed is he who comes in the name of the Lord!" "Hosanna in the highest!"

10 And when he was come into Jerusalem, all the city was moved, saying, Who is this?	10 When Jesus entered Jerusalem, the whole city was stirred and asked, "Who is this?"
11 And the multitude said, This is Jesus the prophet of Nazareth of Galilee.	11 The crowds answered, "This is Jesus, the prophet from Nazareth in Galilee."

TOPICAL OUTLINE OF THE LESSON

I. Introduction
A. Fit for a King
B. Biblical Background

II. Exposition and Application of the Scripture
A. The Prophecy: The Triumphal Entry of the King (Zechariah 9:9)
B. The Instructions Given to the Disciples (Matthew 21:1-3)
C. The Fulfillment of the Prophecy (Matthew 21:4-5)
D. The Presentation of the King-Messiah (Matthew 21:6-11)

III. Concluding Reflection

LESSON OBJECTIVES

Upon the completion of the lesson, the students will be able to do the following:

1. Investigate what motivated the people to praise and honor Jesus on the day He rode into Jerusalem;
2. Step into the place and time of the Gospel story and feel the joy of the people who were celebrating Jesus' entry into Jerusalem; and,
3. Evaluate their expectations of who Christ is for them in light of who Christ claims to be in the Gospel story.

POINTS TO BE EMPHASIZED

ADULT/YOUTH

Adult Topic: Joy and Celebration

Youth Topic: Praise Him!

Adult/Youth Key Verse: Matthew 21:9

Print Passage: Zechariah 9:9; Matthew 21:1-11

—The Gospel writer Matthew took great care to document the fulfillment of prophecy.

—The importance of Jesus' triumphal entry is evident in that all four of the Gospel writers documented it.

—Jesus' riding a donkey might represent humility rather than military power.

—The crowd's conclusions about Jesus were partly correct, but partly mistaken.

—All four gospels relate that on this trip to Jerusalem, either Jesus or His disciples proclaimed His true identity as the Messiah.

—The triumphal entry was recounted in all four gospels, but only Matthew and John connected this event to the prophecy in Zechariah 9:9.

—The donkey was a lowly beast of burden that symbolized humility and peace, contrasted with the warhorse of Zechariah 9:10.

—The cheering crowd used three messianic phrases to refer to Jesus: (a) Son of David; (b) the one who comes in the name of the Lord (see Psalm 118:26); (c) the prophet (see Deuteronomy 18:15).

CHILDREN
Children Topic: Welcome a Hero!

Key Verses: Matthew 21:10-11
Print Passage: Zechariah 9:9; Matthew 21:1-11
—Zechariah foretold the coming of a Messiah.
—Jesus' disciples helped in preparing for His entry.
—Jesus entered Jerusalem on a donkey.
—Jesus' disciples placed their clothing on the donkey and on the road as signs of welcome and respect.
—The people were jubilant and chanted "Hosanna" and called Jesus "Blessed" when He rode into Jerusalem.

I. INTRODUCTION
A. Fit for a King

In the Fall of 2008, this writer led a short-term mission team to Port Harcourt, Nigeria. One of the highlights of the trip was a private meeting with the tribal king of the region where our team was working. Prior to going to the home of the king, we were given strict instructions regarding how we were to stand, bow, and greet the king upon his entry into the room. The women had to wear scarves or some form of headdress. It was the first time that I had personally been in the presence of a king. There are many nations that have kings and queens today and they all have their unique protocols regarding how to greet and show respect for the king and queen.

What is the most fitting way to celebrate the arrival of an honored person? The crowds who welcomed Jesus into Jerusalem spread their cloaks on the road as a special gesture to recognize Him as Messiah. The events that are taught in the lesson today are traditionally referred to as Palm Sunday, which marks the start of the holiest week in the Christian faith. Christians around the world will join with each other to celebrate the start of Holy Week, which will culminate with the Easter celebration next Sunday. The name PALM Sunday comes from a description of the event in the gospel of John (see 12:13), where we are told that the people greeted the arrival of Jesus by laying palm branches in front of His borrowed donkey as He rode down the side of the Mount of Olives.

B. Biblical Background

The lesson today comes from two related passages. The first comes from the Old Testament book of Zechariah, which covers events that took place during the Restoration, the period when the Jews returned from exile in Babylon (see also the books of Ezra, Nehemiah, Haggai, and Malachi). The second passage comes out of the gospel of Matthew and describes the events that began the final week of Jesus' earthly ministry. The events described in the lesson have come to be known as His triumphal entry into Jerusalem. Jesus sat upon the back of a donkey and He rode into Jerusalem in full view of the people and the religious leaders. The people hailed Him as a king by spreading their garments before His donkey. The coming of Jesus riding on a donkey fulfills several of the messianic prophecies of the Old Testament (see 2 Samuel 7:12-14; Isaiah 7:14; 9:7; Zechariah 9:9). Did the people in that day miss the full impact of Jesus' coming? Their concept of the coming of the king was centered on an earthly kingdom, and no doubt mixed with images of the coming of Solomon, who would succeed David as king of Israel (see 1 Kings 1:32-40; compare also 2 Samuel 15:30, where David returned to Jerusalem over the Mount of Olives). During this event, neither Jesus nor His disciples proclaimed Him to be the Messiah.

II. EXPOSITION AND APPLICATION OF THE SCRIPTURE

A. The Prophecy: The Triumphal Entry of the King (Zechariah 9:9)

Rejoice greatly, O daughter of Zion; shout, O daughter of Jerusalem: behold, thy King cometh unto thee: he is just, and having salvation; lowly, and riding upon an ass, and upon a colt the foal of an ass.

The destruction of Jerusalem by the Babylonians in 598-597 BC crushed and demoralized the spirit of the people of God (see 2 Kings 24:1-25:30; compare with Psalm 137; Ezra 3:1-13). When the Jews began to return to Jerusalem, God raised up several prophets to speak words of encouragement to them. One of the prophets was Zechariah (see Ezra 5:1). He called upon the people of God to "rejoice greatly" (verse 9). Shout for joy! These two parallel statements express the imperative command to get excited about what God was about to do in their midst. The people had walked in darkness, but now a new day of light was coming. Zechariah proclaimed that God was sending them a king, who was righteous and would bring salvation. He would not come riding upon a great stallion, like the military leaders who conquered Israel. Rather, He would come in humility, riding upon a donkey. The early Christian church saw these words fulfilled in the life and ministry of Jesus Christ. Jesus came to bring hope, reconciliation, and salvation.

B. The Instructions Given to the Disciples (Matthew 21:1-3)

AND WHEN they drew nigh unto Jerusalem, and were come to Bethphage, unto the mount of Olives, then sent Jesus two disciples, Saying unto them, Go into the village over against you, and straightway ye shall find an ass tied, and a colt with her: loose them, and bring them unto me. And if any man say ought unto you, ye shall say, The Lord hath need of them; and straightway he will send them.

The final stages of the journey to Jerusalem which passed through Jericho (see Matthew 20:29) came to a conclusion with the arrival of Jesus and the disciples to the small village of Bethphage. Jesus came to Jerusalem to claim His rightful place as the King who would sit upon the throne of David, establishing His kingdom forever (see 2 Samuel 7:12-14). In each of the Synoptic Gospels (Matthew, Mark, and Luke), the journey from Jericho concluded at Bethphage. The name *Bethphage* means "house of unripened figs" and refers to a type of fig tree that rarely ever produces ripened figs.

Bethphage was located between Jerusalem and Bethany and was situated on the eastern slopes of the Mount of Olives, which was one of three primary mountain ranges surrounding Jerusalem. The others are Mount Zion and Mount Scopus. The arrival of Jesus on the Mount of Olives fulfilled the prophecy of Zechariah 14:4, which spoke of the feet of the Messiah standing upon the Mount of Olives.

Jesus called two of His disciples and gave them instructions to go into the village, which was Bethphage, where they would find a donkey that was tied up. The two disciples did not raise any questions with Jesus regarding why, where, what, or when. Obediently and without hesitation they carried out the task. They were to bring the donkey, along with her colt, to Jesus. If they were stopped and asked why they were doing this, their response was simply "the Lord needs them." Jesus can request the animals because He is the creator of the Earth—and all that is within it belong to Him (see Psalm 24:1).

C. The Fulfillment of the Prophecy (Matthew 21:4-5)

All this was done, that it might be fulfilled which was spoken by the prophet, saying, Tell ye the daughter of Sion, Behold, thy King cometh unto thee, meek, and sitting upon an ass, and a colt the foal of an ass.

Matthew made it clear that all of the events that occurred with the coming of Jesus into Jerusalem were in fulfillment of the Scriptures (see 1 Corinthians 15:1-4). This is critical because Jesus did not come as a pretender or usurper to the throne of David. He was and is the rightful heir, whose coming was foretold by the prophets.

The "Daughter of Zion" refers to the inhabitants of Jerusalem (see Psalm 9:5; Isaiah

12:6; 40:9; 62:11; Zephaniah 3:14). Jesus went into Jerusalem, not riding a stallion or in a chariot of iron, but sitting on the colt of a donkey. This speaks to the humility and grace with which He came (see 2 Corinthians 8:9). As King, Jesus did not need the pomp and circumstance of a parade, nor did He need to be surrounded by soldiers wearing armor. His kingdom is not of this world.

D. The Presentation of the King-Messiah (Matthew 21:6-11)

And the disciples went, and did as Jesus commanded them, And brought the ass, and the colt, and put on them their clothes, and they set him thereon. And a very great multitude spread their garments in the way; others cut down branches from the trees, and strawed them in the way. And the multitudes that went before, and that followed, cried, saying, Hosanna to the Son of David: Blessed is he that cometh in the name of the Lord; Hosanna in the highest. And when he was come into Jerusalem, all the city was moved, saying, Who is this? And the multitude said, This is Jesus the prophet of Nazareth of Galilee.

The disciples responded by doing exactly what Jesus had instructed them to do. In this act of simple obedience, they followed the example of the Lord Himself, who reminded them on various occasions that He always obeyed the Father (see John 4:34; 5:30; 6:38; 8:29; 14:31; 15:10; compare Colossians 1:9-10).

In the remaining verses, we have three different responses and reactions to the Lord. First, in verse 7, there is the reaction of the disciples who showed absolute respect to Jesus. In their willingness to take their own garments and place them on the back of the colt, they showed their love and respect for Jesus.

Second, we see the reaction of a very large crowd as Jesus rode down the side of the mountain going to Jerusalem. They took their own garments and created a pathway of respect for their King. Some cut down branches and put them along the route of travel. Only John mentioned that the crowd took palm branches and spread them along the road (see John 12:13). The crowd shouted "Hosanna!" which means "Save Us!" They were thinking that Jesus would save them from their political enemies and reestablish the glory days of the past. The reference to David is a reference to King David, who had been king during the glory days of Israel. Between King David and Jesus more than 950 years had passed, and people were still looking for a Davidic King/Messiah. Who was the crowd of people around Jesus? Mark 10:46 reminds us that it was the same crowd that had been with Him in Jericho. They had just witnessed the healing of Bartimaeus and the conversion of Zacchaeus.

Third, there was the response of the dwellers or visitors to Jerusalem who had come for the celebration of Passover. It is obvious that not everyone in Jerusalem knew who Jesus was, nor were they familiar with His teachings or mighty works of power. There were people who had gathered from across the Roman Empire for the Passover (see Acts 2:9-11). It would not be surprising that some would ask who the man riding on the donkey could be and who was accompanied by such an enthusiastic and massive crowd. Jesus was called the prophet from Nazareth, a label which specifically identified Him with His ministry in Galilee.

III. CONCLUDING REFLECTION

Laurence W. Veinott of New Life Presbyterian Church (Canton, New York) made the following observation about the dramatic experience of Jesus riding triumphantly into Jerusalem on a donkey: When you read about Jesus' entry into Jerusalem and how it fulfilled the prophecy in the book of Zechariah, and how it fit in exactly with Jesus' teaching and His mission—and you see how Jesus planned it all with the Father's approval and Jesus telling His disciples to go and that they would find a donkey and her colt, and how, in fact, they were there (indicating God the Father's approval)—this ought to fill you with wonder and awe and you should know that here, Jesus was claiming to be the Messiah.

Throughout today's lesson, there is one overarching theme—that Jesus Christ came into the world in fulfillment of the prophecies of the Old Testament. He came for one specific purpose—which was to save the world from sin (see Matthew 21:21; John 3:16-17; 2 Corinthians 5:17-20). Jesus saved us and He continues to save the world from its ideological beliefs and political agendas that often limit the quality of life of billions of people on the Earth. Jesus came to set up a different type of rule and kingdom. The kingdom was not about David; he was merely a representative of its founder. The kingdom was and is about the rule and reign of God in the lives of people. What then is our challenge? It is just this: that the political ideology of the church is driven by the Word of God. Political ideologies, such as existed in the day of Jesus, cannot overtake who we are as Christians. Jesus refused to be lured into the false ideas of that large crowd that greeted Him and who wanted to make a different kind of king out of Him. The church must seek to establish a political agenda that is based upon our belief that God is King of the world and that His Word calls upon us to promote justice, righteousness, equity, and peace. The prophet wrote in Micah 6:8 (NASB), "He has told you, O man, what is good; And what does the LORD require of you, But to do justice, to love kindness, And to walk humbly with your God?"

PRAYER

Lord God, grant that Your servants will love and honor You—not with lip service, but with lives that are replete with good works. May we follow the examples of those who have gone before us and learn from them how to love, honor, worship, and reverence You. In Jesus' name we pray. Amen.

WORD POWER

Rejoice (Hebrew: *gily* [gheel])—The root meaning is "to circle around." From this word comes the idea of encircling in joy or rejoicing. Within the Old Testament, the word is used to express a wide range of joy or rejoicing. The majority of the time the word expresses the excitement or enthusiasm that results from what God has done in the lives of His people. Righteous (Hebrew: *tsaddiyq* [tsad-deek])—The Hebrew literally means "just or righteous in conduct." The righteous person is someone who executes the will of God. Salvation (Hebrew: *yasha* [yaw-shah])—The word *salvation* has its origin in Arabic and literally means "make wide" or "make sufficient." Within the Old Testament, the word is used to denote God's deliverance of His people out of danger or life-threatening situations. Unlike the New Testament meaning—which is primarily spiritual, moral, and ethical in the Old Testament—God is the one who literally saves.

HOME DAILY BIBLE READINGS
(March 24–30, 2014)

Triumphant and Victorious

MONDAY, March 24: "The Lord Enthroned as King" (Psalm 29)

TUESDAY, March 25: "The Lord Protects" (Zechariah 9:10-15a)

WEDNESDAY, March 26: "The Lord Gives Victory" (Psalm 20)

THURSDAY, March 27: "Loud Songs of Joy" (Psalm 47)

FRIDAY, March 28: "Your Salvation Comes!" (Isaiah 62:8-12)

SATURDAY, March 29: "Coming in the Lord's Name" (Psalm 118:21-29)

SUNDAY, March 30: "The Triumphal Entry" (Zechariah 9:9; Matthew 21:1-11)

LESSON 6   **April 6, 2014**

JESUS CLEANSES THE TEMPLE

FAITH PATHWAY/FAITH JOURNEY TOPIC: **Preserving Places of Heritage**

DEVOTIONAL READING: **Psalm 27:1-5**
PRINT PASSAGE: **Isaiah 56:6-7;**
Jeremiah 7:9-11; Mark 11:15-19

BACKGROUND SCRIPTURE: **Isaiah 56:6-8;**
Jeremiah 7:8-15; Mark 11:15-19
KEY VERSE: **Jeremiah 7:11**

Isaiah 56:6-7; Jeremiah 7:9-11; Mark 11:15-19—KJV

6 Also the sons of the stranger, that join themselves to the LORD, to serve him, and to love the name of the LORD, to be his servants, every one that keepeth the sabbath from polluting it, and taketh hold of my covenant;

7 Even them will I bring to my holy mountain, and make them joyful in my house of prayer: their burnt offerings and their sacrifices shall be accepted upon mine altar; for mine house shall be called an house of prayer for all people.

.....

9 Will ye steal, murder, and commit adultery, and swear falsely, and burn incense unto Baal, and walk after other gods whom ye know not;

10 And come and stand before me in this house, which is called by my name, and say, We are delivered to do all these abominations?

11 Is this house, which is called by my name, become a den of robbers in your eyes? Behold, even I have seen it, saith the LORD.

......

15 And they come to Jerusalem: and Jesus went into the temple, and began to cast out them that sold and bought in the temple, and overthrew the tables of the moneychangers, and the seats of them that sold doves;

16 And would not suffer that any man should carry any vessel through the temple.

17 And he taught, saying unto them, Is it not written, My house shall be called of all nations the house of prayer? but ye have made it a den of thieves.

Isaiah 56:6-7; Jeremiah 7:9-11; Mark 11:15-19—NIV

6 "And foreigners who bind themselves to the LORD to serve him, to love the name of the LORD, and to worship him, all who keep the Sabbath without desecrating it and who hold fast to my covenant—

7 these I will bring to my holy mountain and give them joy in my house of prayer. Their burnt offerings and sacrifices will be accepted on my altar; for my house will be called a house of prayer for all nations."

.....

9 "'Will you steal and murder, commit adultery and perjury, burn incense to Baal and follow other gods you have not known,

10 and then come and stand before me in this house, which bears my Name, and say, "We are safe"—safe to do all these detestable things?

11 Has this house, which bears my Name, become a den of robbers to you? But I have been watching! declares the LORD.'"

.....

15 On reaching Jerusalem, Jesus entered the temple area and began driving out those who were buying and selling there. He overturned the tables of the money changers and the benches of those selling doves,

16 and would not allow anyone to carry merchandise through the temple courts.

17 And as he taught them, he said, "Is it not written: 'My house will be called a house of prayer for all nations'? But you have made it 'a den of robbers.'"

18 And the scribes and chief priests heard it, and sought how they might destroy him: for they feared him, because all the people was astonished at his doctrine.

19 And when even was come, he went out of the city.

18 The chief priests and the teachers of the law heard this and began looking for a way to kill him, for they feared him, because the whole crowd was amazed at his teaching.

19 When evening came, they went out of the city.

TOPICAL OUTLINE OF THE LESSON

I. Introduction
A. Tradition versus Progress
B. Biblical Background

II. Exposition and Application of the Scripture
A. Blessings Promised to Non-Israelites in the Covenant Community (Isaiah 56:6-7)
B. Exposure of False Worship in the Temple (Jeremiah 7:9-11)
C. Expulsion of the Money Changers from the Temple (Mark 11:15-19)

III. Concluding Reflection

LESSON OBJECTIVES

Upon the completion of the lesson, the students will be able to do the following:

1. Understand the breadth of possibilities for Jesus' reaction in the Temple;
2. Subject their hearts to a thorough cleansing of all that falls short of God's will for their lives; and,
3. Evaluate the "traditions" of their congregation to see if the church is failing in some ways to be a house of prayer for all peoples.

POINTS TO BE EMPHASIZED

ADULT/YOUTH
Adult Topic: Preserving Places of Heritage
Youth Topic: The Praying Place
Adult Key Verse: Jeremiah 7:11
Youth Key Verse: Mark 11:17
Print Passage: Isaiah 56:6-7; Jeremiah 7:9-11; Mark 11:15-19

—Jesus connected the misuse of the Temple in His time to the abuse of the Temple during the time of Jeremiah. In both cases, the Temple was destroyed within decades of the prophetic denunciation of abuse.

—Jeremiah 7:9-11 is part of Jeremiah's Temple sermon (see 7:1–8:3), accusing Judah of breaking the Ten Commandments, and then using the Temple as a safe haven just as robbers use their den as a hideout.

—All four gospels included this account of Jesus' cleansing the

Temple (see Matthew 21:12-16; Mark 11:15-18; Luke 19:45-47; John 2:13-16).

—Only Mark and Luke link the Jewish leaders' intent to kill Jesus to a reaction against Jesus' cleansing of the Temple.

CHILDREN
Children Topic: Clean House!
Key Verse: Mark 11:15
Print Passage: Jeremiah 7:9-15; Mark 11:15-19

—When Jesus entered the Temple and saw dishonest people selling worship items, He became angry.
—Jesus reacted by overthrowing tables and chairs and stopping those who brought items to the Temple to be sold.
—Jesus quoted from Jeremiah 7:9-15, in which the Lord vows to destroy those who defame His house of worship.
—The scribes and chief priests responded by looking for ways to destroy Jesus, despite their fear of the crowd who followed Him.

I. INTRODUCTION

A. Tradition versus Progress

Often in congregations the things that we do and the dates that we observe take on a sacrosanct character, becoming more important than why the congregation meets each week for worship. When an activity becomes rote, the original helpful intents and purposes may be lost and replaced by new, harmful intents and purposes. How can a good activity be prevented from evolving into an unintended harmful result? During the days of His ministry in Galilee, Jesus often came into conflict with the scribes and Pharisees over the importance they attached to the traditions of their elders (see Mark 2:18-27). Jesus' angry action in the Temple called attention to the ways in which the priests and worshippers had lost sight of the tradition of God's dwelling place being a house of prayer for all people.

B. Biblical Background

Jesus had nothing good to say about the traditions of the Jewish elders. He was criticized on several occasions because He did not encourage His disciples to honor their traditions. The traditions of the elders were interpretations of the Old Testament laws that were handed down from one generation to the next. In last week's lesson, Jesus entered Jerusalem with great fanfare as He was greeted by large crowds of adoring followers. The religious leaders, instead of seeing Jesus as the Messiah, resisted Him.

When He entered the Temple, Jesus connected the abuse that He saw to the abuse of the Temple during the time of Jeremiah. In both cases, the Temple was destroyed within decades of the prophetic denunciation of abuse. In 597-587 BC, the Babylonians swept through Israel and completely destroyed the Temple, taking all of the precious vessels and ornaments back to Babylon. In AD 70, the Romans destroyed the Temple and it was never rebuilt.

As reported in the Synoptic Gospels, Jesus' cleansing of the Temple occurred after Palm Sunday. However, in the gospel of John, Jesus cleansed the Temple at the beginning of His ministry (see John 2:13-16). The Temple in Jesus' day was a huge commercial enterprise for the religious leaders, who cared little for the religious life of the masses. It was Jesus' act of righteous indignation that led to the plot to kill Him.

II. EXPOSITION AND APPLICATION OF THE SCRIPTURE

A. Blessings Promised to Non-Israelites in the Covenant Community (Isaiah 56:6-7)

Also the sons of the stranger, that join themselves to the LORD, to serve him, and to love the name of the LORD, to be his servants, every one that keepeth the sabbath from polluting it, and taketh hold of my covenant; Even them will I bring to my holy mountain, and make them joyful in my house of prayer: their burnt offerings and their sacrifices shall be accepted upon mine altar; for mine house shall be called an house of prayer for all people.

The edict of Cyrus (538 BC) released the Jews from captivity in Babylon (see 2 Chronicles 36:22-23). This passage, which is taken from the writings of the prophet Isaiah, was spoken and written during the post-exilic period. That period was some time after the return from Babylon—as the Jews sought to rebuild their lives and reclaim the past glory of their relationship with God. The people of Israel came to be known as Jews (separate ones) after the Exile, as they sought to purify themselves from the pagan and idolatrous ways of the nations around them. One of the results of their return from Babylon was their insistence that only Jews would be able to participate in their religious observances and enter the Temple. All others were to be excluded from the covenant community.

God spoke through the prophet Isaiah to remind Israel that just as had been done with the eunuchs mentioned in verses 1-5, no one was to be excluded from the covenant community. Foreigners were non-Jewish residents of Israel. They were without citizenship and civil rights. However, God said that even these non-citizens who did four things were welcome into the covenant community. Those four things were as follows: they were to bind themselves to the Lord to serve and love Him, worship Him, keep the Sabbath, and hold fast to the covenant (see Exodus 19:1-7; Jeremiah 50:5; Mark 12:30-34; compare Ephesians 2:11-18).

God is inclusive and does not eliminate anyone from the covenant of grace. Jesus Christ came into the world to die for all people, not just a select few (see John 3:16). The church must never see itself or set itself up as an exclusive religious community that marginalizes some and gives enormous honor to others.

In verse 7, the foreigners would be brought to the holy mountain (Zion) and they, too, would experience and know the joy of the Lord. Their gifts of love would not be rejected nor belittled, but God would receive their offerings as well. Instead of the Temple being the exclusive worship center of the Jews, it would become and remain a house of prayer for all nations.

B. Exposure of False Worship in the Temple (Jeremiah 7:9-11)

Will ye steal, murder, and commit adultery, and swear

falsely, and burn incense unto Baal, and walk after other gods whom ye know not; And come and stand before me in this house, which is called by my name, and say, We are delivered to do all these abominations? Is this house, which is called by my name, become a den of robbers in your eyes? Behold, even I have seen it, saith the Lord.

Jeremiah lived and preached during the latter days of the southern kingdom. His ministry was concentrated in and around Jerusalem. At that time, Judah was full of social and economic injustice. Jeremiah preached that Judah should amend their ways and practice justice and righteousness. The legal system was rigged to support those who were the wealthiest. And what was more tragic was the shallowness and hypocrisy that was practiced in the Temple religious observances.

In verse 9, the people of Judah were accused of breaking the covenant by failing to obey the Law (see Deuteronomy 6:4-9, 16-19; compare Exodus 22:25; Leviticus 19:15; Psalm 10:4-11; Isaiah 10:2; Romans 1:29). Specifically, the crimes listed were all violations of one of the Ten Commandments (see Exodus 20:1-17). They were accused of stealing (quite possibly from the poor), committing murder, adultery, and the most heinous of all of the crimes— idolatry. They were following gods that they had not known and creating a climate of spiritual darkness in the land (see Psalm 50:16-21; Isaiah 59:1-8; Jeremiah 9:2-9; Ezekiel 18:10; Hosea 4:1-3).

According to verse 10, they practiced all of the things listed in verse 9 and then would come to the Temple and act as though nothing was wrong. They would come and stand before the Lord, maybe with hands lifted up in praise and bowing as though they were honestly seeking God. Is it possible that we can become so absorbed in the acts of religion, practicing the rituals of baptism and the Lord's Supper, reading our creeds, and reciting our covenants that we leave all of this locked behind the doors of the church on Monday morning?

The phrase "We are safe" (verse 10) probably refers to the continuing presence of the Babylonian army in and around Jerusalem. The belief that Jerusalem would never be overrun by an enemy went back to the time of Solomon's dedication of the Temple (see 2 Chronicles 7:12-18). The fallacy of the peoples' position regarding the unconquerable status of Jerusalem was that God's promise of protection was conditional. They must walk upright and keep the Commandments (see 2 Chronicles 7:19-22). The last phrase is steeped in irony. By claiming to be safe, God declared this in the form of a question to them: "Do you honestly feel that you can do all of these things and find safety in this house?"

The final phrase makes three strong statements about God's indignation over what was going on in the Temple. First, He reminded them that the Temple bore His name. It was not their house of worship, but it was His house (see Exodus 25:8; 1 Chronicles 29:1). Second, He said that they had converted the Temple from a house of worship to a den of thieves and robbers. Third, they failed to realize that God was watching. They were not going to get away with their crimes and sin forever (see Psalm 34:15; compare Romans 6:23).

C. Expulsion of the Money Changers from the Temple
(Mark 11:15-19)

And they come to Jerusalem: and Jesus went into the temple, and began to cast out them that sold and bought in the temple, and overthrew the tables of the

moneychangers, and the seats of them that sold doves; And would not suffer that any man should carry any vessel through the temple. And he taught, saying unto them, Is it not written, My house shall be called of all nations the house of prayer? but ye have made it a den of thieves. And the scribes and chief priests heard it, and sought how they might destroy him: for they feared him, because all the people was astonished at his doctrine. And when even was come, he went out of the city.

Each of the Synoptic Gospels (Matthew, Mark, and Luke) placed the cleansing of the Temple at the end of the ministry of Jesus. This event occurred shortly after Jesus entered Jerusalem on that first Palm Sunday. John placed it at the beginning of His ministry (see John 2:14-22). There has been much debate as to whether we should reject John's account because it does not coincide with the synoptic tradition. However, there in John's gospel, Jesus spent a few months in the region of Judea before heading north to Galilee. And it is possible that He could have cleansed the Temple twice.

Verse 15 states that upon reaching Jerusalem, Jesus entered the Temple area. The Temple was not an enclosed building—like a church building—but it consisted of a large, open area where men and women gathered, worshipped, and offered sacrifices. The area that is referred to as an outer court was quite possibly the Court of the Gentiles. The moneychangers and the people selling sacrifices were located in this area. All sacrifices had to meet certain standards (see Exodus 12:5; 29:1; Leviticus 1:3, 10; 3:1, 6; 4:3; 14:10; 22:19; 23:18). Many people coming to Jerusalem to observe Passover would simply buy an approved sacrifice rather than endure the rigors of having their sacrifice inspected and quite possibly rejected. The law permitted people to sacrifice doves if they were unable to buy or own an animal that could be sacrificed (see Leviticus 1:14; 5:7; 12:6; Luke 2:24). According to the Law of Moses, every male had to appear three times a year at the tabernacle/Temple in order to present their annual Temple tax (see Exodus 30:13, 15). Payments had to be made with the sanctuary shekel (see Leviticus 5:15). Roman currency bore the image of the emperor, thus making it a violation of the law to own or possess it—because it bore a graven image (see Exodus 20:4). Further, the currency used to pay the Temple tax was minted in Tyre and was of a specific quality and weight. Pilgrims traveling from outside of Israel would have to exchange their local currency for the Temple shekel. As with all currency exchanges, there was a fee. The moneychangers may have charged excessive fees, thereby reaping huge profits. Jesus went in and began to overturn their tables and benches. As people were coming in to sell their merchandise, Jesus would stop them (verse 17). He quoted from the books of Isaiah and Jeremiah that the house of the Lord was a house of prayer, but that it had been turned into a den of robbers. The word *you* was emphatic and referred specifically to the religious leaders. Not only had they perverted the sacred space, but they had also turned it into a commercial place for selfish gain.

Verse 18 points out that it was this act of aggression against the Temple business that aroused the anger of the religious leaders—prompting them to plot to have Jesus killed. At that very moment they began to look for ways to kill Him. They would not openly attempt to do this, because Jesus was adored and respected by many of the people who were present in Jerusalem for Passover. The religious leaders literally feared Jesus. We are not told why they feared Him. It may have been due to the presence of such a large crowd of followers. The primary reason for these large crowds probably had to do with the amazement of the crowd as Jesus taught about respecting the Temple (see Mark 1:27; 2:12; 6:51; 9:15; 10:32).

III. CONCLUDING REFLECTION

In this lesson, several key issues are identified that often plague congregations today. First, how does a congregation reconcile what it believes with what it practices? The current economic recession has put enormous pressure upon the financial positions of every congregation in America, to say nothing of congregations in developing and poorer nations. Leaders may teach tithing and freewill giving, but at the same time may find it difficult to give in order to support denominational mission causes or meaningful causes within their own communities—such as homelessness, hunger, violence, or family disintegration. Second, congregations may knowingly allow persons whose personal lives are a sham to remain in key leadership positions because they are major givers or they come from very prominent families in the church. On Sundays, this kind of man or woman is an upstanding member—but on Monday, he or she may live an immoral or indecent life. Third, the lesson raises the question of whether or not it is ever proper to sell goods and services in the church. The issue causes a great deal of division on either side of the question. My answer to the question of commercializing the church is the same one that Jesus gave when questioned about divorce: "From the beginning it was not so" (Matthew 19:8).

PRAYER

Heavenly Father, may this lesson today arouse within us the desire to walk upright before You. Forgive us of our sins. In Jesus' name we pray. Amen.

WORD POWER

Sabbath (Hebrew: *Shabbath* [shab-bawth])—*Sabbath* means "rest" and refers to the cessation of work. The Sabbath is first mentioned in the Old Testament in Genesis 2:2-3. God instituted the Sabbath as a day of rest when He had finished all of the work of creating the heavens and the Earth.

HOME DAILY BIBLE READINGS
(March 31–April 6, 2014)

Jesus Cleanses the Temple
MONDAY, March 31: "The Holy Temple" (Habakkuk 2:18-20)
TUESDAY, April 1: "The House of the Lord" (Psalm 27:1-5)
WEDNESDAY, April 2: "I Cried for Help" (Psalm 18:1-6)
THURSDAY, April 3: "My Prayer Came to You" (Jonah 2:1-9)
FRIDAY, April 4: "Something Greater than the Temple" (Matthew 12:1-8)
SATURDAY, April 5: "A Holy Temple in the Lord" (Ephesians 2:11-22)
SUNDAY, April 6: "A House of Prayer" (Isaiah 56:6-7; Jeremiah 7:9-11; Mark 11:15-19)

LESSON 7   **April 13, 2014**

A MESSIANIC PRIEST-KING

FAITH PATHWAY/FAITH JOURNEY TOPIC: **A Perceived Threat**

DEVOTIONAL READING: **Hebrews 7:11-19**
PRINT PASSAGE: **Jeremiah 23:5-6;**
Zechariah 6:9-15; John 19:1-5

BACKGROUND SCRIPTURE: **Jeremiah 23:5-6;**
Zechariah 6:9-15; John 19:1-5; Hebrews 7:13
KEY VERSE: **John 19:3**

Jeremiah 23:5-6; Zechariah 6:9-15; John 19:1-5—KJV

5 Behold, the days come, saith the LORD, that I will raise unto David a righteous Branch, and a King shall reign and prosper, and shall execute judgment and justice in the earth.

6 In his days Judah shall be saved, and Israel shall dwell safely: and this is his name whereby he shall be called, THE LORD OUR RIGHTEOUSNESS.

.....

9 And the word of the LORD came unto me, saying,

10 Take of them of the captivity, even of Heldai, of Tobijah, and of Jedaiah, which are come from Babylon, and come thou the same day, and go into the house of Josiah the son of Zephaniah;

11 Then take silver and gold, and make crowns, and set them upon the head of Joshua the son of Josedech, the high priest;

12 And speak unto him, saying, Thus speaketh the LORD of hosts, saying, Behold the man whose name is The BRANCH; and he shall grow up out of his place, and he shall build the temple of the LORD:

13 Even he shall build the temple of the LORD; and he shall bear the glory, and shall sit and rule upon his throne; and he shall be a priest upon his throne: and the counsel of peace shall be between them both.

14 And the crowns shall be to Helem, and to Tobijah, and to Jedaiah, and to Hen the son of Zephaniah, for a memorial in the temple of the LORD.

15 And they that are far off shall come and build in the temple of the LORD, and ye shall know that the LORD of hosts hath sent me unto you. And this shall

Jeremiah 23:5-6; Zechariah 6:9-15; John 19:1-5—NIV

5 "The days are coming," declares the LORD, "when I will raise up to David a righteous Branch, a King who will reign wisely and do what is just and right in the land.

6 In his days Judah will be saved and Israel will live in safety. This is the name by which he will be called: THE LORD OUR RIGHTEOUSNESS."

.....

9 The word of the LORD came to me:

10 "Take silver and gold from the exiles Heldai, Tobijah and Jedaiah, who have arrived from Babylon. Go the same day to the house of Josiah son of Zephaniah.

11 Take the silver and gold and make a crown, and set it on the head of the high priest, Joshua son of Jehozadak.

12 Tell him this is what the LORD Almighty says: 'Here is the man whose name is the Branch, and he will branch out from his place and build the temple of the LORD.

13 It is he who will build the temple of the LORD, and he will be clothed with majesty and will sit and rule on his throne. And he will be a priest on his throne. And there will be harmony between the two.'

14 The crown will be given to Heldai, Tobijah, Jedaiah and Hen son of Zephaniah as a memorial in the temple of the LORD.

15 Those who are far away will come and help to build

UNIFYING LESSON PRINCIPLE

People tend to lash out at perceived threats to established power. How do people form a perception of threat? The perception of Jesus as a King who would exercise political rule and power caused Him to be seen as a threat to the existing Roman and Jewish powers.

come to pass, if ye will diligently obey the voice of the LORD your God.

.....

THEN PILATE therefore took Jesus, and scourged him.

2 And the soldiers platted a crown of thorns, and put it on his head, and they put on him a purple robe,

3 And said, Hail, King of the Jews! and they smote him with their hands.

4 Pilate therefore went forth again, and saith unto them, Behold, I bring him forth to you, that ye may know that I find no fault in him.

5 Then came Jesus forth, wearing the crown of thorns, and the purple robe. And Pilate saith unto them, Behold the man!

the temple of the LORD, and you will know that the LORD Almighty has sent me to you. This will happen if you diligently obey the LORD your God."

.....

THEN PILATE took Jesus and had him flogged.

2 The soldiers twisted together a crown of thorns and put it on his head. They clothed him in a purple robe

3 and went up to him again and again, saying, "Hail, king of the Jews!" And they struck him in the face.

4 Once more Pilate came out and said to the Jews, "Look, I am bringing him out to you to let you know that I find no basis for a charge against him."

5 When Jesus came out wearing the crown of thorns and the purple robe, Pilate said to them, "Here is the man!"

TOPICAL OUTLINE OF THE LESSON

I. **Introduction**
   A. Perception versus Reality
   B. Biblical Background

II. **Exposition and Application of the Scripture**
   A. The Messianic King Predicted (Jeremiah 23:5-6)
   B. The Restored Israel under Messiah King-Priest (Zechariah 6:9-15)
   C. Behold the Man (John 19:1-5)

III. **Concluding Reflection**

LESSON OBJECTIVES

Upon the completion of the lesson, the students will be able to do the following:

1. Study the connection between the prophecy in the Hebrew Scriptures and the brutal death that Jesus suffered;
2. Identify with Christ in His suffering; and,
3. Reach out to those who are suffering in ways that will relieve their pain.

POINTS TO BE EMPHASIZED

ADULT/YOUTH
Adult Topic: **A Perceived Threat**
Youth Topic: **Vote Up or Down**
Adult Key Verse: **John 19:3**
Youth Key Verses: **John 19:2-3**
Print Passage: **Jeremiah 23:5-6; Zechariah 6:9-15; John 19:1-5**

—Pilate knew that Jesus was innocent, but he feared the consequences of doing what he knew was right.

—The statement in Jeremiah 23:5, "The days are surely coming," was a messianic formula used by the prophets in the Bible and is recognized by Jewish and Christian scholars as introducing something about the promised and expected Messiah.

—In Zechariah 6:9-15, the crowning of Joshua, though an actual event, was made by the prophet into a sign-oracle that communicated a message through vividly dramatizing God's truth—much as did Isaiah walking around Jerusalem naked (see 20:2-4), Jeremiah wearing a yoke (see 27:2-7), and Ezekiel carrying his bag through a hole in the Jerusalem wall (see 12:1-12).

—Although scourging was a usual accompaniment of crucifixion, Pilate used it in John 19 in the hopes that the Jewish leaders would accept this punishment of Jesus as sufficient and would stop demanding that an innocent person be crucified.

—Although Pilate's words to introduce Jesus were meant to convince the Jewish leaders that this persecuted and punished human could not possibly be their king, "Here is the man!" (verse 5) was taken by the Jews as Pilate's confirming messianic announcement, coming from their prophet Zechariah—and thus the Jewish leaders were further infuriated.

CHILDREN

Children Topic: Here's the Man!

Key Verses: John 19:2-3

Print Passage: Jeremiah 23:5-6; Zechariah 6:9-14; John 19:1-5

—Jeremiah prophesied of a time when Judah and Israel would be saved by God's Righteous One.

—In the book of Zechariah, the Lord declared that He would commission the Branch to build the Temple of the Lord and ordered a crown to be made for the Chosen One.

—Following His trial before Pilate, Jesus was whipped and mocked.

—The soldiers fashioned a crown and robe for Jesus and mockingly called Him "King."

—Pilate declared that Jesus was innocent and handed Him over to the chief priests and police.

I. INTRODUCTION

A. Perception versus Reality

Young African-American males are often viewed as a threat to society. Within inner-city communities they are viewed as rebellious, driven by the lure of easy money, and attached to gangs and the violence that it spawns. They are more likely to be stopped, searched, and arrested for the most minor offenses. The racist stereotypes that have existed for decades in America continue to be driven by a society that perceives anyone who is different as a threat, whether in dress or practices.

People tend to lash out at perceived threats to established power. How do people form a perception of threat? The answers are probably as numerous as the number of people in the world. The religious and political leaders of Jesus' day perceived Him as a threat to the religious and social life of the nation. The perception that Jesus was a King who would exercise political rule and power caused Him to be seen as a threat to the existing Roman and Jewish powers.

B. Biblical Background

The early Christians believed and preached that the birth, death, and resurrection of Jesus of Nazareth were all events that had been foretold by the prophets of old. Within the Hebrew Scriptures the positions of prophet, priest, and king were all fulfilled in Jesus of Nazareth (see Mark 6:14-15; 8:28; Hebrews 5:5-6; Revelation 17:14; 19:16).

Throughout the Old Testament, particularly in the preaching of the prophets, there was the expectation that the Lord God of Israel would raise up a Messiah-King. He would rule in righteousness and practice justice according to the Law of Moses (see Deuteronomy 18:10; Isaiah 9:6-7). According to Jeremiah, he would be called "the Lord our Righteousness." Zechariah was one of the prophets who preached and inspired the exiles who were returning from captivity in Babylon (c.a. 520 BCE). In a series of symbolic acts, he announced that God was going to ensure the rebuilding of the Temple and the raising up of a new high priest who would lead the people of God in worship of Him. This new high priest would also be a king who would rule in righteousness. It would not be one from the earthly lineage of David, but the Messiah-Savior, who would come and take away the sins of the world. The passage from the gospel of John includes scenes from the trial of Jesus. They depict the passion of Christ as a time of intense suffering and humiliation caused by Pilate and the Jews. Although Pilate knew that Jesus was innocent of the charges leveled against Him, he would not drop them, because he feared the backlash by the Jewish religious leaders.

II. EXPOSITION AND APPLICATION OF THE SCRIPTURE

A. The Messianic King Predicted (Jeremiah 23:5-6)

Behold, the days come, saith the LORD, that I will raise unto David a righteous Branch, and a King shall reign and prosper, and shall execute judgment and justice in the earth. In his days Judah shall be saved, and Israel shall dwell safely: and this is his name whereby he shall be called, THE LORD OUR RIGHTEOUSNESS.

The leaders of Judah had been rightly accused of destroying the flock of God (see Jeremiah 23:1-4). Judah was headed to exile in Babylon because her religious leaders had turned away from God and their covenant relationship. Judah's political leaders had polluted the land with wickedness and tolerated injustice. The past had been a time of spiritual darkness in the land, but there was a new day coming when God was going to do a new thing in Judah (see Isaiah 43:17-19). During the time of Jeremiah, the land of Judah was economically, spiritually, morally, and socially in a shambles. Yet, all was not lost, because God was going to raise up a new king in Judah, one who would come from the lineage of David. David is remembered as the ideal king of Israel, one to whom all of the kings after him were compared.

According to verse 6, three things would characterize the reign of the Davidic Messiah. Judah would be saved, which more than likely is a reference to being delivered from their captivity in Babylon. The second promise centered on Israel, which is a reference to the northern kingdom. Under the Davidic heir, Israel would be restored and the land would live in safety. Third, the Davidic ruler would be called "the Lord our Righteousness," which is a term that symbolizes the Messiah-King.

Why did God need to raise up new leaders? The answer was clearly visible to Jeremiah. The current leaders had failed to care for the people of God. The poor were mistreated and abused. The widows were neglected and the strangers within their borders were not welcomed. Those who lead the people of God are required to ensure that justice and righteousness are the standards by which the society lives (see Micah 6:6-8). When the leaders fail, the people suffer.

B. The Restored Israel under Messiah King-Priest (Zechariah 6:9-15)

And the word of the LORD came unto me, saying, Take of them of the captivity, even of Heldai, of Tobijah, and of Jedaiah, which are come from Babylon, and come thou the same day, and go into the house of Josiah the son of Zephaniah; Then take silver and gold, and make crowns, and set them upon the head of Joshua the son of Josedech, the high priest; And speak unto him, saying, Thus speaketh the LORD of hosts, saying, Behold the man whose name is The BRANCH; and he shall grow up out of his place, and he shall build the temple of the LORD: Even he shall build the temple of the LORD; and he shall bear the glory, and shall sit and rule upon his throne; and he shall be a priest upon his throne: and the counsel of peace shall be between them both. And the crowns shall be to Helem, and to Tobijah, and to Jedaiah, and to Hen the son of Zephaniah, for a memorial in the temple of the LORD. And they that are far off shall come and build in the temple of the LORD, and ye shall know that the LORD of hosts hath sent me unto you. And this shall come to pass, if ye will diligently obey the voice of the LORD your God.

In verse 9, Zechariah began using typical prophetic form by announcing that the "Word of the Lord" had come to him. He had received the Word through visions, which is the same form in which he previously had received his prophecies from God (see Zechariah 1:8, 18, 20; 2:1; 3:1; 4:2; 5:1; 6:1). Some interpreters see this prophecy as pertaining to just the future. However, we must remember that the prophets also spoke to the times in which they lived. God would never raise up a prophet to speak to just the future without having something definitive to say to the current situation of His people.

The prophecy has to be understood on two levels. There is the level on which God was speaking specifically to the people of that day regarding the rebuilding of the Temple in Jerusalem. The Jews had come back from Babylon and were attempting to rebuild their lives (see Zechariah 4:8-9). God raised up prophets and priests to give leadership and encouragement to the exiles. The prophet spoke not only to his time, but to the fulfillment of promises which were off into the future. In this instance, the "far off" focus envisioned a time when God, the future Messiah-King, would come and rule over a kingdom that was not made by hands. He would wear not only the crown symbolizing kingship, but He would also wear the garments of the high priest and hold the office of the priest. He would build a Temple that would be an everlasting Temple, eternal in the heavens.

According to verse 10, God commanded Zechariah to take silver and gold from specific exiles who had recently returned from Babylon. Their names are as follows: Haldea, Tobijah, and Jedaiah; they would all be found in the house of a man named Josiah, who was the son of Zephaniah. This was not the prophet Zephaniah. Zechariah was to make a crown and set it on the head of Joshua, who was the high priest. This was a highly unusual act because there had never been a time when the priest was anointed and crowned king. The office of the priest and king were always separate. At the time of this action, Zerubbabel was governor and he would have been the most likely person to wear the crown (see Haggai 2:2; compare Haggai 1:1, 12, 14; Ezra 2:2; 3:2, 8; 4:2-3; 5:2; Nehemiah 7:7; 12:1). Zechariah was told to let Joshua know that what was being done was not strange nor out of place. God was combining the offices of priest and king for His purposes. The reason the crown was given to the three men mentioned earlier (verse 14) is not stated, other than as a perpetual memorial. The people who were "afar off" were not identified. This usually meant strangers or foreigners who in this instance would come and help rebuild Jerusalem and the Temple.

Within the Christian tradition, these verses have been a source of great and messianic hope and expectation. Christians see prophecy concerning the Messiah—Jesus Christ, who fulfills the Law and the Prophets—in these verses. Through the coming of Jesus Christ, God built and continues to build an everlasting kingdom.

C. Behold the Man
(John 19:1-5)

THEN PILATE therefore took Jesus, and scourged him. And the soldiers platted a crown of thorns, and put it on his head, and they put on him a purple robe, And said, Hail, King of the Jews! and they smote him with their hands. Pilate therefore went forth again, and saith unto them, Behold, I bring him forth to you, that ye may know that I find no fault in him. Then came Jesus forth, wearing the crown of thorns, and the purple robe. And Pilate saith unto them, Behold the man!

Pilate was the Roman governor, whose responsibility it was to collect taxes and maintain order in the province. Passover was always a tense time, because the Jews had a reputation for sparking uprisings or discontent during the annual celebration. Jesus had been arrested, tried before the Sanhedrin, and delivered to Pilate for punishment. Pilate found no fault with Jesus and knew that there was nothing that He had done to warrant execution. Each year during the Passover, the Romans would release a political prisoner to placate the Jews. He offered the Jews a choice between Jesus and Barabbas, and they chose Barabbas (see John 18:40). The truth of the release of Barabbas is attested to in the other three canonical gospels (see Matthew 27:15-26; Mark 15:6-15; Luke 23:18-25).

In an effort to relieve himself of any responsibility for the torture and mistreatment of Jesus, Pilate had Jesus beaten by his soldiers. This was a very cruel and inhumane form of punishment that alone could have killed Jesus. The victim was tied to a pole with his back facing away from the pole and stripped of his upper garments. He was then whipped with an instrument made of three leather cords. The Jewish law allowed for up to forty lashes (see Deuteronomy 25:3). We do not know how many lashes that Jesus received.

In verse 2, the soldiers continued to mock Jesus by twisting together a crown made of thorns and pressing it upon His head. Thorns in that region can be up to an inch in length and are very sharp. They further humiliated Him by dressing Him in a purple robe, hitting Him in the face, and referring to Him in derogatory terms, such as "Hail, King of the Jews!" Hitting a Jew in the face is the worst form of public humiliation and disgrace.

Pilate brought Jesus out into the courtyard and presented Him to the Jews. This was his final attempt to release Jesus, because he found no fault in Him. He presented Jesus to the Jews and declared, "Here is the man!" This was in fulfillment of Zechariah 6:12. Dressed in a royal robe and crown of thorns upon His head, Jesus was led away to be crucified.

III. CONCLUDING REFLECTION

Jesus Christ suffered humiliation, enormous pain, and the agony of death for us. All of this was done, not because He had committed a crime or had violated the Law of Moses, but because it was in fulfillment of the Hebrew Scriptures and the promise of God that a Messiah-King would come and bring in the long-awaited day of righteousness and peace.

PRAYER

Lord God, give us the determination and courage to stand against the injustices we see in our world. May we cease to be silent partners in the struggle for social and economic justice—but may our voices be heard and our presence felt in our communities. In Jesus' name we pray. Amen.

WORD POWER

Branch (Hebrew: *tsemakh*)—This word is used as a term to describe the legitimate Davidic heir. The word came to be used with messianic overtones of the One who would come and occupy the throne of David. A Phoenician inscription dating from the third century contained the phrase *semah sedek*, "the righteous shoot," which meant that the individual was the legitimate heir to the throne.[1]

HOME DAILY BIBLE READINGS
(April 7–13, 2014)

A Messianic Priest-King

MONDAY, April 7: "An Established Throne Forever" (1 Chronicles 17:7-14)
TUESDAY, April 8: "Light Has Dawned" (Matthew 4:12-17)
WEDNESDAY, April 9: "Seated on the Throne of Glory" (Matthew 19:23-30)
THURSDAY, April 10: "The Kingdom of God's Beloved Son" (Colossians 1:9-14)
FRIDAY, April 11: "A Better Hope" (Hebrews 7:11-19)
SATURDAY, April 12: "King of Kings, Lord of Lords" (Revelation 19:11-16)
SUNDAY, April 13: "Here Is the Man!" (Jeremiah 23:5-6; Zechariah 6:9-14; John 19:1-5)

End Note

[1]R. Larid Harris, Gleason L. Archer Jr., and Bruce K. Waltke, *Theological Word Book of the Old Testament*, Vol. 2 (Chicago: Moody Bible Institute, 1980), 769.

LESSON 8 — April 20, 2014 (Easter)

THE THIRD DAY

FAITH PATHWAY/FAITH JOURNEY TOPIC: Deliverance!

DEVOTIONAL READING: 1 Corinthians 15:12-20
PRINT PASSAGE: Hosea 6:1-3; Luke 24:1-12
KEY VERSES: Luke 24:6-7

BACKGROUND SCRIPTURE: Hosea 6:1-3;
Luke 24:1-12

Hosea 6:1-3; Luke 24:1-12—KJV

COME, AND let us return unto the LORD: for he hath torn, and he will heal us; he hath smitten, and he will bind us up.

2 After two days will he revive us: in the third day he will raise us up, and we shall live in his sight.

3 Then shall we know, if we follow on to know the LORD: his going forth is prepared as the morning; and he shall come unto us as the rain, as the latter and former rain unto the earth.

.....

NOW UPON the first day of the week, very early in the morning, they came unto the sepulchre, bringing the spices which they had prepared, and certain others with them.

2 And they found the stone rolled away from the sepulchre.

3 And they entered in, and found not the body of the Lord Jesus.

4 And it came to pass, as they were much perplexed thereabout, behold, two men stood by them in shining garments:

5 And as they were afraid, and bowed down their faces to the earth, they said unto them, Why seek ye the living among the dead?

6 He is not here, but is risen: remember how he spake unto you when he was yet in Galilee,

7 Saying, The Son of man must be delivered into the hands of sinful men, and be crucified, and the third day rise again.

8 And they remembered his words,

Hosea 6:1-3; Luke 24:1-12—NIV

"COME, LET us return to the LORD. He has torn us to pieces but he will heal us; he has injured us but he will bind up our wounds.

2 After two days he will revive us; on the third day he will restore us, that we may live in his presence.

3 Let us acknowledge the LORD; Let us press on to acknowledge him. As surely as the sun rises, he will appear; he will come to us like the winter rains, like the spring rains that water the earth."

.....

ON THE first day of the week, very early in the morning, the women took the spices they had prepared and went to the tomb.

2 They found the stone rolled away from the tomb,

3 but when they entered, they did not find the body of the Lord Jesus.

4 While they were wondering about this, suddenly two men in clothes that gleamed like lightning stood beside them.

5 In their fright the women bowed down with their faces to the ground, but the men said to them, "Why do you look for the living among the dead?

6 He is not here; he has risen! Remember how he told you, while he was still with you in Galilee:

7 'The Son of Man must be delivered into the hands of sinful men, be crucified and on the third day be raised again.'"

8 Then they remembered his words.

Sometimes people do not recognize the accomplishment of long-held goals because they are achieved in a different fashion from what was expected. What sustains the motivation of people to keep going when victory looks improbable? Jesus' forecast of His resurrection on the third day alluded to the Hebrew Scripture theme (tradition) of deliverance in defiance of the horror of the Crucifixion.

9 And returned from the sepulchre, and told all these things unto the eleven, and to all the rest.
10 It was Mary Magdalene, and Joanna, and Mary the mother of James, and other women that were with them, which told these things unto the apostles.
11 And their words seemed to them as idle tales, and they believed them not.
12 Then arose Peter, and ran unto the sepulchre; and stooping down, he beheld the linen clothes laid by themselves, and departed, wondering in himself at that which was come to pass.

9 When they came back from the tomb, they told all these things to the Eleven and to all the others.
10 It was Mary Magdalene, Joanna, Mary the mother of James, and the others with them who told this to the apostles.
11 But they did not believe the women, because their words seemed to them like nonsense.
12 Peter, however, got up and ran to the tomb. Bending over, he saw the strips of linen lying by themselves, and he went away, wondering to himself what had happened.

TOPICAL OUTLINE OF THE LESSON

I. Introduction
  A. Faith and Hope versus Skepticism and Doubt
  B. Biblical Background

II. Exposition and Application of the Scripture
  A. Israel's Plea for Deliverance (Hosea 6:1-3)
  B. A Startling Discovery (Luke 24:1-8)
  C. The First Witnesses of the Resurrection (Luke 24:9-12)

III. Concluding Reflection

LESSON OBJECTIVES

Upon the completion of the lesson, the students will be able to do the following:

1. Explore the biblical use of "third day" in order to better understand Jesus' reference to resurrection and deliverance;
2. Experience Resurrection power in their lives; and,
3. Pray for the deliverance of oppressed people and to consider what more can be done to bring God's justice to Earth here and now.

POINTS TO BE EMPHASIZED
ADULT/YOUTH
Adult Topic: Deliverance!
Youth Topic: Rise Up!
Adult/Youth Key Verses: Luke 24:6-7
Print Passage: Hosea 6:1-3; Luke 24:1-12
—All four gospels attest to the importance of the death, burial, and resurrection of Jesus.
—"Son of man" was Jesus' most often used self-designation.
—The crucifixion of Christ demonstrated God's love and holiness.
—The standard time allowed for the Israelites to assemble at the central sanctuary for a pilgrim festival in which they received rejuvenated life was three days (see Exodus 3:18; 5:3; 8:27;

Joshua 9:16-17; 2 Samuel 20:4; Ezra 10:8-9). Thus, the phrase "third day" came to signify a return to life by God's power, and is so used in the Christian Scriptures for the resurrection of Jesus (see Matthew 16:21; 17:23; Mark 9:31; Luke 9:22; 18:31-33; 24:7; 1 Corinthians 15:4).

—The Septuagint version of Hosea 6:2 shares the same Greek wording for "on the third day" as Luke 24:7 and 1 Corinthians 15:4.

—Early Christian preaching (see Acts 3:15; 4:10; 5:30; 10:40-42; 13:30-31) affirmed the message given by the angels (see Luke 24:6-7) regarding Jesus' resurrection.

CHILDREN
Children Topic: He's Alive!
Key Verse: Luke 24:5
Print Passage: Hosea 6:1-3; Luke 24:1-12

—Following the Crucifixion, women went to the tomb to complete the burial preparation.

—Messengers met the women and told them that Jesus was alive.

—The messengers reminded the women of Jesus' promise to rise on the third day—in accord with the prophecy in the book of Hosea.

—The women went to tell the Eleven and others, but they were met with unbelief.

—Peter ran to the tomb to see for himself—and, yet, he wondered what had happened.

I. INTRODUCTION
A. Faith and Hope versus Skepticism and Doubt

Skepticism and doubt are two of the biggest threats and challenges to our faith in God. Each of us, from time to time, has wrestled with the question of the historical reliability of the biblical record. We wonder if the Bible is true. Are the stories that are told about the great heroes of faith accurate and reliable? Can I trust the Bible to provide the answers to my most pressing and agonizing questions? One of the most urgent questions of life is this: "What happens to us after we die?" Indeed, this is life's most imperative issue and one of our most central concerns of the Resurrection. The Christian Gospel removes the veil of secrecy and allows us to see behind the curtain of eternity to the everlasting throne of God. The Christian Gospel proclaims that on the first Easter Sunday morning God raised Jesus Christ from the dead to new life. The One crucified on Friday was raised and enthroned as both Lord and King (see Acts 2:24, 32). With Jesus' resurrection, those who had been captive to death and the grave had been freed by the power of God (see Ephesians 4:7-9). The Resurrection was a historic event seen and experienced by several hundred persons. The Resurrection is the basis of eternal hope for all who believe.

B. Biblical Background

There are two biblical passages that form this week's lesson: Hosea 6:1-3 and Luke 24:1-12. Hosea 6:1-3 has been interpreted as the passage in the Old Testament that foretells the resurrection of Jesus in three days. In Hosea 6:2, there is the mention of "the third day."

Biblical scholars have mixed views about this interpretation—because to simply see it as a prediction of the resurrection of Jesus in three days denies the historical connection to the context in which Hosea preached and made this pronouncement. The historical context of the book of Hosea saw its events take place during the time of Jeroboam II, who ruled the north (see Hosea 1:1-2). Hosea preached in the northern kingdom of Israel sometime between 750–734 BC. As a contemporary of Amos, he saw firsthand the callousness and disobedience that characterized life in Israel at the time. He called for the nation to return to God and said that God would have mercy and forgive their sins. During his ministry, God used the prophet to foretell of an event that was off into the future, even though he did not know the full impact of his message.

The second passage comes from the Resurrection narrative of the gospel of Luke. The women who went to the tomb of Jesus to anoint His body were greeted by two men who were dressed in clothes that glowed brightly as lightning. They were told not to fear because the Lord Jesus Christ had risen on the third day just as He told them He would.

II. EXPOSITION AND APPLICATION OF THE SCRIPTURE

A. Israel's Plea for Deliverance (Hosea 6:1-3)

COME, AND let us return unto the LORD: for he hath torn, and he will heal us; he hath smitten, and he will bind us up. After two days will he revive us: in the third day he will raise us up, and we shall live in his sight. Then shall we know, if we follow on to know the LORD: his going forth is prepared as the morning; and he shall come unto us as the rain, as the latter and former rain unto the earth.

Hosea preached at a time when the people of God had closed their ears to the message of the prophets. The rebellion and the practice of idolatry had produced a society reeking with injustice and corruption. They sought help from the Assyrians in their attempts to stave off conquest at the hands of their enemies (see Hosea 5:13). However, God's fierce wrath would come upon them like a lion pursuing its prey—there would be no escape (see Hosea 5:14).

Hosea 6:1 introduces a call by either the priests or the people to return to the Lord. The Hebrew word for "return," *shuwb*, has in it the idea of going back to the beginning. The people were summoned to go back to their covenant relationship with the Lord, not the idols they had created which could neither help nor save them. The prophet declared that God is just as merciful as He is vengeful. He not only executes the fierceness of His wrath, but He also delights in mercy and compassion (see Micah 6:19-20). He will bind up the wounds of those whom He has injured (see Deuteronomy 32:39; Job 5:18).

In verse 2, the reference to *two days and the third day* are not to be taken literally, but are references to time. The prophet had in view the complete and total restoration of the relationship between God and Israel. Restoration would allow them to live in His presence. At the other end of the hermeneutical spiral is the faith of the New Testament church, which saw in these words a clear reference to the death and resurrection of Jesus of Nazareth. The earliest Christians found in these words a clear messianic prophecy concerning the resurrection of Jesus of Nazareth (see Luke 24:21; Acts 10:40; 1 Corinthians 15:4). Just as God reversed the lot of the people in Hosea 6:2, so, too, did He reverse the sinful acts of men who killed the Lord of glory. The fact that God raised Jesus from the dead is the central tenet of the Christian faith.

Verse 3 looks back to Hosea 5:16, where God said that He would go away from them until they admitted their sin and guilt. The NIV translates the Hebrew word *yada* as "acknowledge"; however, it is best understood as "know," which increases the intensity of the passage. They could acknowledge God's presence just as someone waves his or her hand to acknowledge one's presence. They could wink at God and continue to live in sin and rebellion. Here, the call was to know God in the most intimate of ways. The call was to strive diligently to know God by renewing their covenant relationship.

B. A Startling Discovery
(Luke 24:1-8)

NOW UPON the first day of the week, very early in the morning, they came unto the sepulchre, bringing the spices which they had prepared, and certain others with them. And they found the stone rolled away from the sepulchre. And they entered in, and found not the body of the Lord Jesus. And it came to pass, as they were much perplexed thereabout, behold, two men stood by them in shining garments: And as they were afraid, and bowed down their faces to the earth, they said unto them, Why seek ye the living among the dead? He is not here, but is risen: remember how he spake unto you when he was yet in Galilee, Saying, The Son of man must be delivered into the hands of sinful men, and be crucified, and the third day rise again. And they remembered his words.

The trauma of Jesus' crucifixion on Friday was behind them and the women were free to go to the grave site and formally anoint the body of Jesus for burial. We are not immediately told who these women were—that comes later in verse 10. They were prohibited from visiting the tomb on the Sabbath because of Jewish legal restrictions (see Exodus 20:8-11; Deuteronomy 5:12-15). However, Joseph of Arimathea had hastily buried Jesus' body in his personal tomb and rolled a huge stone in front to seal the grave (see Matthew 27:59-60; Mark 15:46). The first day of the week is Sunday, which became the day of worship for the early Christian church (see 1 Corinthians 16:1-2). It was early in the morning—probably about 6:00 a.m., which would be considered very early in the morning—of the first day. When the women arrived, they found the stone rolled away. This was a large, round stone and would have required considerable strength to move, even for men. Graves in ancient Israel were sealed with a large, round stone that resembled a wheel, which was then placed on a track which made it easy to move back and forth in front of the tomb's entrance.

Verse 3 is the first report of the empty tomb. The women expected to find the motionless body of Jesus; instead, they found an empty tomb. Surely, there were some words exchanged. As they stood there wondering what had happened, two men in shining garments appeared. These men, or angels, appeared out of nowhere, creating a scene of disbelief and absolute fear. Out of reverence, the women bowed with their faces to the ground. This does not infer that they thought of the strange men as gods; rather, it was customary for people to bow as an act of respect. The two men spoke in tones that were a mild rebuke, yet at the same time they reassured the women that no one had stolen the body of Jesus. What followed was just as astonishing as the appearance of the two men. The statement of the men looked back to the preaching and teaching ministry of Jesus and called upon the women to remember His words about His rejection, suffering, death, and resurrection (see John 2:2; compare with John 12:16; 14:6; and Luke 9:22). At that very moment things started to crystallize in their minds and spirits as they remembered the words of Jesus.

C. The First Witnesses of the Resurrection (Luke 24:9-12)

And returned from the sepulchre, and told all these things unto the eleven, and to all the rest. It was Mary Magdalene, and Joanna, and Mary the mother of James, and other women that were with them, which told these things unto the apostles. And their words seemed to them as idle tales, and they believed them not. Then arose Peter, and ran unto the sepulchre; and stooping down, he beheld the linen clothes laid by themselves, and departed, wondering in himself at that which was come to pass.

All of the Gospels report that women were the first witnesses of the resurrection of Jesus Christ. Each of the Gospel writers reported the account of the empty tomb and the presence of angels or men in stunning and glistening clothes. Verse 9 records the women leaving the sepulcher, going back to the eleven disciples, and telling them and the other disciples with them what had just happened. The "Eleven" refers to the disciples of Jesus, minus Judas. We are not told who the others were, but more than likely they were among the followers of Jesus who had come from Galilee.

Verse 10 identifies the women who went to the tomb. All of the gospels report that Mary Magdalene was among them (see Matthew 28:1; Mark 16:1; Luke 8:2; John 20:1, 18). Joanna was one of the early financial supporters of the ministry of Jesus (see Luke 8:3). Women were among the most committed financial supporters of Jesus' ministry (see Matthew 27:55). There has been some question regarding the exact identity of Mary the mother of James. Some interpreters have thought that maybe she was the wife of Zebedee, but that seems unlikely, given the fact that John was not mentioned with James by Luke. Others have thought that she may have been the Mary the mother of Jesus, since one of the brothers of Jesus was named James. The most likely option is that she was the mother of James, son of Alphaeus (see Matthew 10:3; Mark 15:40). Again, we do not know who the others were who accompanied them.

They went and found the apostles who were in hiding, probably within the confines of Jerusalem. Exactly where they were has never been known. When the women shared their story with the apostles, they were met with sarcasm and total disbelief. Their witness was dismissed as nonsense. Peter, however, must have thought about what he heard and took time to remember the things that Jesus had said to them on three separate occasions about what would happen to Him and how, on the third day, He would be raised from the dead (see Mark 8:31; 9:31; 10:33-34). Peter got up and ran to the tomb. Upon arriving, he bent over and looked in and saw the grave clothes in which Jesus had been wrapped. He did not know what to make of this development and there is no record of him saying anything.

III. CONCLUDING REFLECTION

Today, known as Easter Sunday, is the

day that we celebrate the resurrection of Jesus Christ from the dead. Christians believe and affirm that the resurrection of Jesus of Nazareth is the single-most important event in all of history. There is nothing that compares to the resurrection of Jesus of Nazareth. By virtue of His resurrection, God made Him both Lord and Christ. When we say that Jesus Christ is Lord, we mean that He is the one to whom we owe our total loyalty, love, and devotion. When we say that He is Christ, we mean that He is the Anointed One of God who came to save us from sin, death, hell, and the grave. The Resurrection is the simple and timeless truth of our faith that Jesus Christ lives. One of the tenets that Easter affirms is that our darkest moments are not to be viewed through the lenses of pessimism. Rather, we understand and know that God is able to take our most woeful moments and our most despicable circumstances and turn them into the sunshine of a new day. Resurrection is the ultimate message of hope (see 1 Corinthians 15:19-21).

PRAYER

Heavenly Father, for the joy that was set before Your Son, Jesus, He endured the Cross and despised the shame. Grant that we may live in such ways that our lives will be reflections of the new life that we have through His death and resurrection. In Jesus' name we pray. Amen.

WORD POWER

First day of the week—How did Sunday come to be regarded as the Christian day of worship? It has already been noted that many Jewish Christians continued practicing Jewish religious customs and traditions well into the first Christian century. Jewish Christians continued to attend the synagogues until they were eventually forced out.[1]

HOME DAILY BIBLE READINGS
(April 14–20, 2014)

The Third Day
MONDAY, April 14: "Death and Despair" (Job 30:20-31)
TUESDAY, April 15: "Ransomed from the Power of Death" (Psalm 49:5-15)
WEDNESDAY, April 16: "Received by God with Honor" (Psalm 73:16-28)
THURSDAY, April 17: "You Shall Live!" (Ezekiel 37:1-14)
FRIDAY, April 18: "God of the Living" (Mark 12:18-27)
SATURDAY, April 19: "Christ Has Been Raised" (1 Corinthians 15:12-20)
SUNDAY, April 20: "Raised on the Third Day" (Hosea 6:1-3; Luke 24:1-12)

End Note

---

[1] *The New International Dictionary of the Christian Church*, Rev. ed., "Sunday," H. L. Ellison.

FROM SUFFERING TO GLORY

FAITH PATHWAY/FAITH JOURNEY TOPIC: Greater Understanding

DEVOTIONAL READING: John 1:10-18
PRINT PASSAGE: Isaiah 53:5-8;
Luke 24:25-27, 44-47

BACKGROUND SCRIPTURE: Isaiah 52:13–53:12;
Luke 24:25-27, 44-50
KEY VERSE: Luke 24:27

Isaiah 53:5-8; Luke 24:25-27, 44-47—KJV

5 But he was wounded for our transgressions, he was bruised for our iniquities: the chastisement of our peace was upon him; and with his stripes we are healed.

6 All we like sheep have gone astray; we have turned every one to his own way; and the LORD hath laid on him the iniquity of us all.

7 He was oppressed, and he was afflicted, yet he opened not his mouth: he is brought as a lamb to the slaughter, and as a sheep before her shearers is dumb, so he openeth not his mouth.

8 He was taken from prison and from judgment: and who shall declare his generation? for he was cut off out of the land of the living: for the transgression of my people was he stricken.

.....

25 Then he said unto them, O fools, and slow of heart to believe all that the prophets have spoken:

26 Ought not Christ to have suffered these things, and to enter into his glory?

27 And beginning at Moses and all the prophets, he expounded unto them in all the scriptures the things concerning himself.

.....

44 And he said unto them, These are the words which I spake unto you, while I was yet with you, that all things must be fulfilled, which were written in the law of Moses, and in the prophets, and in the psalms, concerning me.

45 Then opened he their understanding, that they might understand the scriptures,

Isaiah 53:5-8; Luke 24:25-27, 44-47—NIV

5 But he was pierced for our transgressions, he was crushed for our iniquities; the punishment that brought us peace was upon him, and by his wounds we are healed.

6 We all, like sheep, have gone astray, each of us has turned to his own way; and the LORD has laid on him the iniquity of us all.

7 He was oppressed and afflicted, yet he did not open his mouth; he was led like a lamb to the slaughter, and as a sheep before her shearers is silent, so he did not open his mouth.

8 By oppression and judgment he was taken away. And who can speak of his descendants? For he was cut off from the land of the living; for the transgression of my people he was stricken.

.....

25 He said to them, "How foolish you are, and how slow of heart to believe all that the prophets have spoken!

26 Did not the Christ have to suffer these things and then enter his glory?"

27 And beginning with Moses and all the Prophets, he explained to them what was said in all the Scriptures concerning himself.

.....

44 He said to them, "This is what I told you while I was still with you: Everything must be fulfilled that is written about me in the Law of Moses, the Prophets and the Psalms."

UNIFYING LESSON PRINCIPLE

Confusion, disappointment, and sorrow in life often result from not understanding fully what has happened. How can the true meaning be discovered and understood? After Jesus explained His life, death, and resurrection within the context of Hebrew Scriptures, the two travelers on the road to Emmaus understood better what had happened.

46 And said unto them, Thus it is written, and thus it behoved Christ to suffer, and to rise from the dead the third day:

47 And that repentance and remission of sins should be preached in his name among all nations, beginning at Jerusalem.

45 Then he opened their minds so they could understand the Scriptures.

46 He told them, "This is what is written: The Christ will suffer and rise from the dead on the third day,

47 and repentance and forgiveness of sins will be preached in his name to all nations, beginning at Jerusalem."

TOPICAL OUTLINE OF THE LESSON

I. Introduction
A. Tragedy Can Be Confusing
B. Biblical Background

II. Exposition and Application of the Scripture
A. The Passion of the Suffering Servant (Isaiah 53:5-6)
B. The Passivity of the Suffering Servant (Isaiah 53:7-8)
C. The Exposition of the Scriptures Concerning the Suffering Servant (Luke 24:25-27)
D. The Explanation of Jesus Concerning the Suffering Servant (Luke 24:44-47)

III. Concluding Reflection

LESSON OBJECTIVES

Upon the completion of the lesson, the students will be able to do the following:

1. Deepen their understanding of God's salvation story, from Genesis to Revelation;
2. Meditate on the presence of the risen Christ; and,
3. Recognize and give thanks to those who explain the Scriptures in ways that bring Christ closer.

POINTS TO BE EMPHASIZED

ADULT/YOUTH

Adult Topic: Greater Understanding
Youth Topic: No Pain, No Gain
Adult Key Verse: Luke 24:27
Youth Key Verses: Luke 24:46-47
Print Passage: Isaiah 53:5-8; Luke 24:25-27, 44-47

—The Gospel writers were careful to depict Jesus' death and resurrection as fulfilled prophecy.
—Jesus' discussion on the road to Emmaus was unique to Luke's rendition in the Gospel accounts.
—Isaiah 53:5-8 presented the messianic Suffering Servant, highlighting the submissiveness of the sacrificial Lamb.
—The account of the resurrection of Christ in Luke 24 stressed the importance of the empty tomb—and the bodily appearances of the risen Jesus Christ further confirmed it.

—Luke saw so much importance in the fact that Jesus was resurrected on the third day that he included this fact in his Resurrection account three times (see Luke 24:7, 21, 46).

—The two on the road to Emmaus (see Luke 24:27, 31) and the disciples in Jerusalem (see Luke 24:45) received divine help to understand the prophecies in the Hebrew Scriptures about the Messiah's rising from the dead.

CHILDREN
Children Topic: From Sorrow to Joy
Key Verse: Luke 24:36

Print Passage: Isaiah 53:11-12; Luke 24:44-50

—Through His death and resurrection, Jesus fulfilled the words of the Law, the Prophets, and the psalms about Him.

—Jesus authorized the disciples to tell others about Him.

—Jesus told the disciples to wait on the Holy Spirit, who had been promised by God.

—Jesus explained that the Holy Spirit would fill the disciples with power.

—Jesus blessed the people before leaving Earth.

I. INTRODUCTION
A. Tragedy Can Be Confusing

On September 11, 2012, a group of heavily armed men overran the U.S. Consulate in Benghazi, Libya. The three-man security detail, comprised of all Americans, was killed, along with Ambassador Christopher Stevens. The American government was initially confused regarding what happened, and had no idea who had perpetrated this heinous act of aggression and murder. A few days after the attack, the White House issued a statement that blamed the attack on Muslim extremism and overreaction to a hideous video that had been released earlier, which depicted the Prophet Muhammad in a very negative manner. Political rivals of President Obama began to seize upon the confusing statements, declaring that the White House was hiding the details of what really happened that night. As it turned out, the attack was not a random, unorganized effort, but was orchestrated by members of al-Qaeda. This tragic event highlights how the world has grown increasingly more violent. Further, it points to how unfortunate events that happen in life can create massive confusion, blame, sorrow, and disappointment. No one knows what fully happened and the investigations never yielded the full story.

The account of what happened at the U.S. Embassy in Libya is a stark reminder that tragic events have happened throughout the history of the human race. No doubt the disciples of Jesus were baffled and bewildered by the events that culminated in His arrest, trial, and public crucifixion. But, three days later, when they saw Him alive, they were moved with exuberant joy and expectation. The resurrected Jesus appeared to several people on that first Easter Sunday. On the road to Emmaus, He met two travelers who were still struggling with the events surrounding the death of Jesus. After Jesus explained the necessity of His life, death, and resurrection within the context of the Hebrew Scriptures, they understood better what had happened.

B. Biblical Background

The lesson today comes from two important passages of Scripture. The first is found in Isaiah 53:5-8, which is one of the most significant prophecies in the Bible concerning the plan of God to bring redemption and salvation to the whole world. The second passage (Luke 24:25-27, 44-47) contains two of the post-Resurrection appearances of Jesus Christ. One passage is the prophecy concerning the Suffering Servant, and the second passage is the explanation and exposition by Jesus concerning the necessity of the servant of the Lord to suffer at the hands of evil people.

The passage from the book of Isaiah is part of a large corpus of prophetic writings on the servant of the Lord, who came to bring the people of God back into covenant relationship with Him (see Isaiah 42:1-9; 49:1-13; 50:4-11; 52:13–53:12). In Isaiah 53, the Servant of the Lord is seen as one who comes without distinguishing characteristics. Yet, He was rejected, despised, and ultimately crucified for the sins of the world.

In the passages from the book of Luke, we see two post-Resurrection appearances. The first took place on the road to Emmaus, as two of the followers of Jesus were met by the risen Lord Himself. The second occurrence was Jesus' appearance to His disciples in Jerusalem. In each of the appearances, Jesus reminded His hearers that He had to suffer, die, and be raised again on the third day. In both appearances, Jesus helped the disciples and the two men on the road to Emmaus to understand all of the prophecies in the Hebrew Scriptures concerning Him and the resurrection of the Messiah from the dead.

II. EXPOSITION AND APPLICATION OF THE SCRIPTURE

A. The Passion of the Suffering Servant (Isaiah 53:5-6)

But he was wounded for our transgressions, he was bruised for our iniquities: the chastisement of our peace was upon him; and with his stripes we are healed. All we like sheep have gone astray; we have turned every one to his own way; and the LORD hath laid on him the iniquity of us all.

There is no messianic prophecy in the Old Testament that rises to the height and zenith of these words of Isaiah. They are the pinnacle of messianic prophecy.

Isaiah made it perfectly clear that the Servant of the Lord did not suffer for Himself. In verses 5-6 there is a graphic description of the reasons why and for whom He suffered. He was pierced for our transgressions; He was crushed for our iniquities. The prophet did not identify who the "our" referred to, but it is obvious that he included himself in the group. The Hebrew word for *pierced* has in it the idea of being fatally wounded. These were wounds so severe that there was no way to possibly recover from them. The Suffering Servant was wounded for us, and the Lord laid upon Him the iniquities of humankind, referring to their depravity and guilt before God.

Verse 6 states that we are all like the sheep that Isaiah described as having gone astray. Within the Scriptures, Israel was viewed as the flock of God that sometimes wandered from the fold (see Isaiah 56:11; Jeremiah 13:20; 23:1; 49:20; Ezekiel 34:1-10; Zechariah 10:2).

The prophet did not exclude himself from those who brought the wrath of God upon the Suffering Servant. The Servant of the Lord was humanity's substitute.

B. The Passivity of the Suffering Servant (Isaiah 53:7-8)

He was oppressed, and he was afflicted, yet he opened not his mouth: he is brought as a lamb to the slaughter, and as a sheep before her shearers is dumb, so he openeth not his mouth. He was taken from prison and from judgment: and who shall declare his generation? for he was cut off out of the land of the living: for the transgression of my people was he stricken.

In verse 7, Isaiah made a comparison between the Suffering Servant who suffered death and the sacrificial death that an innocent lamb faces when it is about to be sacrificed: The lamb has no idea what is about to happen. As the lamb is sheared of its wool, it cannot even begin to anticipate the horror of being sacrificed on an altar. Likewise, the Suffering Servant was pressured by the pains of physical and emotional affliction. The word *oppressed* has in it the idea of being driven by tormentors. When Jesus Christ was arrested, tried, and tortured, He, too, was traumatized—but He was moved neither to tears nor to cries of agony by the suffering He endured (see Matthew 26:63; 27:12). There were no cries that His tormentors offered Him as reasons for their hatred. He was led as an innocent lamb to the slaughter (see Psalm 44:22; compare with Romans 8:34-39).

Verse 8 hints at the Servant's being oppressed, denied due process, and deprived of His legal rights. The question regarding the descendants of the Servant is not a reference to His personal descendants. Rather, it is intended to raise a question about the attitude of the people who witnessed this grave miscarriage of justice. What did they think about what happened, or did they have an opinion at all? Jesus was cut off—that is, He literally died for the transgressions and sins of the people.

C. The Exposition of the Scriptures Concerning the Suffering Servant (Luke 24:25-27)

Then he said unto them, O fools, and slow of heart to believe all that the prophets have spoken: Ought not Christ to have suffered these things, and to enter into his glory? And beginning at Moses and all the prophets, he expounded unto them in all the scriptures the things concerning himself.

Verse 25 is a continuation of the conversation that the risen Christ had with two men who were traveling from Jerusalem going to Emmaus. As they walked they revealed their lack of understanding regarding the mission of the Messiah. As they walked, Jesus seized the moment and began to reveal to them the Scriptures concerning the Messiah. Jesus was not just another traveler on the road, but the very One in whom they had cast their hope for eternal life. Luke used language that expressed in a very strong and stern manner Jesus' rebuke of the two men. "How foolish" and "slow of heart" (verse 25) denotes Jesus' deep disappointment that these men did not have an understanding regarding the events that took place in Jerusalem (see Luke 24:5-7; compare also Matthew 16:11 and Mark 7:18 for instances of the failure to understand). The men had failed not only to comprehend the mission and message of Jesus, but also—as they revealed an even more startling reality—in that they did not believe all that the prophets had spoken concerning the Christ (see Deuteronomy 18:15; Psalms 2:7; 16:8-11; 110:1; Isaiah 53).

As Jesus continued to teach the men, He reminded them of the absolute necessity of the Christ suffering these things. This was a reference to His previous arrest, trial, torture, and crucifixion. There were no options given to Jesus; this was the only way that He could enter His glory (see Luke 22:41-43). Glory (Greek: *doxa*) denotes the majesty and splendor that belongs to the King of Kings. Throughout the gospel of Luke, Jesus moved on to His final glory—which began with the singing of the angels at His birth and culminated with His ascension.

According to verse 27, Jesus began at the beginning—the writings of Moses—and went through all of the prophets, explaining the Scriptures. The word *explained* means "to open up" or "unfold." Jesus opened to the two men everything that had ever been written and spoken concerning Him.

D. The Explanation of Jesus Concerning the Suffering Servant (Luke 24:44-47)

And he said unto them, These are the words which I spake unto you, while I was yet with you, that all things must be fulfilled, which were written in the law of Moses, and in the prophets, and in the psalms, concerning me. Then opened he their understanding, that they might understand the scriptures, And said unto them, Thus it is written, and thus it behoved Christ to suffer, and to rise from the dead the third day: And that repentance and remission of sins should be preached in his name among all nations, beginning at Jerusalem.

Verse 44 took place in a different location from that of the previous scene in Emmaus. Jesus appeared in Jerusalem at an undisclosed location. Not only were the two men whom He met on the road to Emmaus present, but the Eleven and several other disciples of the Lord were also present (see verse 33). After calming their fears and doubts, Jesus reminded the gathering that all of the things that had come to pass during the previous week had already been told to them while they were together in Galilee. Everything concerning Jesus, His death, burial, and resurrection had to be fulfilled beginning with the Law, the Prophets, and the psalms. Here we have a reference to what was considered to be the sum total of all the Scriptures.

With the previous encounter, Jesus opened the Scriptures; at this appearance, He opened the minds of the disciples (see verse 45). The eyes of their understanding were enlightened and they were able to see with spiritual understanding the things that pertained to the revelation of God's plan for human redemption as it unfolded in the life and ministry of Jesus. The very spiritual nature of the Scriptures and their meaning cannot be grasped apart from the work of the Holy Spirit. The natural person cannot comprehend the deep things of God (see 1 Corinthians 2:6-16; Ephesians 1:18).

Verses 46-47 contain three very important parts of the teachings of Scripture concerning the Christ: First, Christ must suffer (see Psalms 22; 31; 69; 118; Isaiah 53); second, Christ must rise from the dead on the third day (see Psalms 16:10; 110:1); third, repentance and forgiveness must be preached in His name. Repentance means turning from the past and the old ways of life and embracing the new man or new woman (see 2 Corinthians 5:17; Ephesians 4:22-24). Forgiveness is the gracious act of wiping clean the slate of our lives, thus freeing us from the power and stench of sin. The disciples were sent to preach the Resurrection and its aftermath—first in Jerusalem then to the ends of the Earth. The charge and mandate still stands to this very day. The church is charged to go into the entire world and preach the Gospel to every human being. Mission begins at our local churches and spreads to the ends of the Earth.

III. CONCLUDING REFLECTION

The justice and righteousness of God demand that all sin be punished. According to 2 Corinthians 5:10, we must all appear before the judgment seat of Christ in order to give an account of the deeds done in the body (whether they be good or bad)—for sin does have a heavenly remedy, which is the reason for the coming of the Suffering Servant. Sin has been dealt a decisive defeat once and for all time. Romans 5:8 reads, "God commends His own love toward us, in that while we were yet sinners, Christ died for us." Verse 10 reads, "For if while we were enemies we were reconciled to God through the death of His Son, much more, having been reconciled, we shall be saved by His life.

PRAYER

Lord God, grant that Your servants may live lives that are well-pleasing in Your sight. Grant that we will have the will to obey and never transgress Your Word. In Jesus' name we pray. Amen.

WORD POWER

Transgressions (Hebrew: *pasha* [peh-shah])—The word *Pesha* appears forty-eight times in the Old Testament. It has been translated as "trespass, sin, or rebellion." In the context of the OT, the word denotes those who reject the authority of God and seek to live in the world without Him. The word also has in it the idea of the breaking of the covenant between God and Israel. Humanity's willingness to violate the terms of the covenant and live in opposition to God is what is at the heart of the sacrifice of Jesus Christ. He healed the rebellion brought on by man's sin.

HOME DAILY BIBLE READINGS
(April 21–27, 2014)

From Suffering to Glory

MONDAY, April 21: "Seeking the Answer to Suffering" (Job 23:1-7)
TUESDAY, April 22: "The Completion of God's Plans" (Job 23:8-14)
WEDNESDAY, April 23: "A Man of Suffering" (Isaiah 52:13–53:4)
THURSDAY, April 24: "Undergoing Great Suffering" (Matthew 16:21-28)
FRIDAY, April 25: "Servant of All" (Mark 9:30-37)
SATURDAY, April 26: "We Have Seen His Glory" (John 1:10-18)
SUNDAY, April 27: "The Messiah's Necessary Suffering" (Luke 24:25-27, 44-47; Isaiah 53:5-8)

JESUS RESISTS TEMPTATION

FAITH PATHWAY/FAITH JOURNEY TOPIC: **Just Say No!**

DEVOTIONAL READING: Psalm 91:1-12
PRINT PASSAGE: Deuteronomy 6:13-16;
Matthew 4:4-11

BACKGROUND SCRIPTURE: Deuteronomy 6:13-16;
8:3; Psalm 91:11-12; Matthew 4:1-11
KEY VERSE: Matthew 4:4

Deuteronomy 6:13-16; Matthew 4:4-11 —KJV

13 Thou shalt fear the LORD thy God, and serve him, and shalt swear by his name.

14 Ye shall not go after other gods, of the gods of the people which are round about you;

15 (For the LORD thy God is a jealous God among you) lest the anger of the LORD thy God be kindled against thee, and destroy thee from off the face of the earth.

16 Ye shall not tempt the LORD your God, as ye tempted him in Massah.

.....

4 But he answered and said, It is written, Man shall not live by bread alone, but by every word that proceedeth out of the mouth of God.

5 Then the devil taketh him up into the holy city, and setteth him on a pinnacle of the temple,

6 And saith unto him, If thou be the Son of God, cast thyself down: for it is written, He shall give his angels charge concerning thee: and in their hands they shall bear thee up, lest at any time thou dash thy foot against a stone.

7 Jesus said unto him, It is written again, Thou shalt not tempt the Lord thy God.

8 Again, the devil taketh him up into an exceeding high mountain, and sheweth him all the kingdoms of the world, and the glory of them;

9 And saith unto him, All these things will I give thee, if thou wilt fall down and worship me.

Deuteronomy 6:13-16; Matthew 4:4-11 —NIV

13 Fear the LORD your God, serve him only and take your oaths in his name.

14 Do not follow other gods, the gods of the peoples around you;

15 for the LORD your God, who is among you, is a jealous God and his anger will burn against you, and he will destroy you from the face of the land.

16 Do not test the LORD your God as you did at Massah.

.....

4 Jesus answered, "It is written: 'Man does not live on bread alone, but on every word that comes from the mouth of God.'"

5 Then the devil took him to the holy city and had him stand on the highest point of the temple.

6 "If you are the Son of God," he said, "throw yourself down. For it is written: 'He will command his angels concerning you, and they will lift you up in their hands, so that you will not strike your foot against a stone.'"

7 Jesus answered him, "It is also written: 'Do not put the Lord your God to the test.'"

8 Again, the devil took him to a very high mountain and showed him all the kingdoms of the world and their splendor.

9 "All this I will give you," he said, "if you will bow down and worship me."

UNIFYING LESSON PRINCIPLE

In a world that offers persons countless ways to satisfy their lusts and appetites, discipline is required in order to maintain high ethical and moral standards. What helps people stick to their principles when other options tempt them? Jesus' thorough knowledge of Scripture gave Him strength to withstand difficult temptations.

10 Then saith Jesus unto him, Get thee hence, Satan: for it is written, Thou shalt worship the Lord thy God, and him only shalt thou serve.
11 Then the devil leaveth him, and, behold, angels came and ministered unto him.

10 Jesus said to him, "Away from me, Satan! For it is written: 'Worship the Lord your God, and serve him only.'"
11 Then the devil left him, and angels came and attended him.

TOPICAL OUTLINE OF THE LESSON

I. Introduction
A. Count the Cost
B. Biblical Background

II. Exposition and Application of the Scripture
A. The Exhortation to Serve Only the Lord God (Deuteronomy 6:13-16)
B. The First Temptation (Matthew 4:4)
C. The Second Temptation (Matthew 4:5-7)
D. The Third Temptation (Matthew 4:8-11)

III. Concluding Reflection

LESSON OBJECTIVES

Upon the completion of the lesson, the students will be able to do the following:

1. Gain new insight from studying the story of Jesus' temptation in the wilderness;

2. Appreciate the importance of regular prayer and the Scripture reading in shaping their attitudes and actions; and,
3. Make a commitment to memorize key verses of the Scriptures.

POINTS TO BE EMPHASIZED

ADULT/YOUTH
Adult Topic: Just Say No!
Youth Topic: Just Say No!
Adult Key Verse: Matthew 4:4
Youth Key Verse: Matthew 4:10
Print Passage: Deuteronomy 6:13-16; Matthew 4:4-11

—Jesus' wilderness experience—with its temptations—followed closely after His baptism by John (see Matthew 3:13-17).
—The passage from the book of Deuteronomy was the source for two of Jesus' Scripture quotations in the wilderness. The other was from Deuteronomy 8.
—The name *Satan* (verse 10) means "adversary."
—Following the major event of His baptism, Jesus was led by the Spirit into the wilderness—where Jesus faced significant temptations.
—The temptations included physical needs, opportunities for status, and the priority of whom or what Jesus would worship.
—Jesus addressed each of Satan's temptations with words from the Hebrew Scriptures.

CHILDREN

Children Topic: Making the Right Choice

Key Verse: Matthew 4:10

Print Passage: Matthew 4:1-11

—This passage presented three central temptations in the human experience: to satisfy personal hunger, pride, and power.

—Jesus was tempted after forty days of fasting and He was famished.

—Jesus demonstrated how knowing the Word of God would assist one in resisting temptation.

—Although tempted three times, Jesus persisted in following the will of God.

—Temptation comes to people in various ways and when they are most vulnerable.

—After the Temptation, God sent angels to minister to Jesus.

I. INTRODUCTION
A. Count the Cost

Greed is a powerful lure. The apostle Paul cautioned Timothy about the love of money and its fatal attractions (see 1 Timothy 6:6-10). The lust for things—money, power, prominence, and sex—has led many men and women down the path of self-destruction. Interestingly, the lure of money has often led men and women to undertake very dangerous, even life-threatening challenges without counting the cost.

One of the lessons of temptations is its appearance of being good, while the outcome of giving in is disastrous.[1] Today's lesson helps believers to see the value of sticking to their principles when other options are trying to lead them into temptation. Jesus' thorough knowledge of Scripture gave Him strength to withstand difficult temptations.

B. Biblical Background

Today's lesson comes from two passages. The first comes from the book of Deuteronomy, which literally means "second law." The Deuteronomic Law was a series of sermons God gave to Moses for the people of Israel. These messages were all delivered just prior to their going into the Promised Land and shortly before the death of Moses. Israel was repeatedly reminded of the grace and goodness of God, which was seen in the fulfillment of the promises to the patriarchs—Abraham, Isaac, and Jacob (see Deuteronomy 6:10-11). Moses exhorted them not to forget the Lord their God, which would be easy for them to do, since all of the people who entered the land of Canaan had no real recollection of the trials of the wilderness, nor what it was like to live in slavery (see Deuteronomy 6:12; 8:1-19).

The second part of the lesson comes out of the gospel of Matthew and is the record of Jesus' encounter with Satan in the wilderness. Jesus' wilderness experience, with its temptations, followed closely after His baptism by John the Baptist (see Matthew 3:13-17). All three Synoptic Gospels present some aspect of the wilderness experience of Jesus.

Luke's account reversed the order of the last two temptations (see Luke 4:1-13). Further, Luke did not mention that Jesus was attended to by angels. Mark included an account of the Temptation, but because it was not central to his narrative, he provided very few details regarding the Temptation (see Mark 1:13). He did mention that there were "wild beasts" present in the wilderness. Throughout the assault on His Personhood and purpose, Jesus stood firm and resolute.

II. EXPOSITION AND APPLICATION OF THE SCRIPTURE

A. The Exhortation to Serve Only the Lord God (Deuteronomy 6:13-16)

Thou shalt fear the Lord thy God, and serve him, and shalt swear by his name. Ye shall not go after other gods, of the gods of the people which are round about you; (For the Lord thy God is a jealous God among you) lest the anger of the Lord thy God be kindled against thee, and destroy thee from off the face of the earth. Ye shall not tempt the Lord your God, as ye tempted him in Massah.

Verse 13 follows the command or exhortation in verse 12 not to forget the Lord, who had brought Israel out of slavery in Egypt. In verse 13, Moses exhorted the people to do three things: First, they were to fear the Lord, which literally meant to have a deep and abiding reverence for God; second, they were to serve Him only, which has reference to their worship and can also refer to working for the Lord. Rather than look back at the gods that their parents served in Egypt, they were to worship and adore the God who brought them out of bondage; third, they were to take their oaths in His name, which means that they were not to swear by any name other than the name of the Lord their God.

Verse 14 is an imperative command and looks back to the first two commandments that had reference to not having any other gods before the Lord their God. It was the central command of the covenant and of the *Shema* (Hebrew for "hear"; see verse 4). Israel would be entering a new land, one filled with idolatry and paganism. Unlike the nations around them that created idol gods with their hands, Israel's God lived among the people and His presence was seen and experienced in the tabernacle. God would not share His glory with any other gods and His anger would be kindled against Israel when they became unfaithful.

Moses reminded the people in verse 15 that God was not only a transcendent deity, but He was also the God who lived in their midst. He was also a jealous God who would not leave one of them standing or alive if they followed after other gods. Just as He would not permit their parents and grandparents to enter the land of Canaan, He would do no less to them (see Deuteronomy 28:14ff.). One of the problems of the generation of Israelites who died in the wilderness was their propensity to test the Lord.

B. The First Temptation (Matthew 4:4)

But he answered and said, It is written, Man shall not live by bread alone, but by every word that proceedeth out of the mouth of God.

The first temptation is recorded as part of the Background Scripture in verse 3. In that first temptation, Satan focused on the point where he believed Jesus appeared to be the most vulnerable—he attacked Jesus' need for food. The enemy comes when he thinks that we are at our weakest points—when life becomes a struggle and we could easily give in. He appears as an angel of light with conflicting and confusing messages (see 2 Corinthians 11:14). The devil approached Jesus and wanted Him to do something that would meet an immediate need, but would lead to absolute disobedience to the Father.

Matthew 4:3 (Background Scripture, KJV) says that when the tempter came to Jesus, he said, "If thou be the Son of God, command that these stones be made bread." Jesus responded by quoting Deuteronomy 8:3, which looked back into the life of Israel's sojourn in the wilderness when God fed them with manna from heaven: "And he humbled thee, and suffered thee to hunger, and fed thee with manna, which thou knewest not, neither did thy fathers know; that he might make thee know that man doth not live by bread only, but by every word that proceedeth out of the mouth of the Lord doth man live." Jesus wanted it to be clear that humans need food, but that food is not all we need. God will provide the food.

It is clear from the words of Jesus that He never lost sight of His primary purpose. He did not lose sight of His place in God's plan. Jesus responded by saying that it was written that humans do not live by food alone. Yes, we need food, water, shelter, air, and the other essentials of life—but that is not all there is to life (see Luke 12:15; compare Matthew 6:19-34). Our heavenly Father knows that His children have needs and it is His good pleasure to meet those needs.

C. The Second Temptation (Matthew 4:5-7)

Then the devil taketh him up into the holy city, and setteth him on a pinnacle of the temple, And saith unto him, If thou be the Son of God, cast thyself down: for it is written, He shall give his angels charge concerning thee: and in their hands they shall bear thee up, lest at any time thou dash thy foot against a stone. Jesus said unto him, It is written again, Thou shalt not tempt the Lord thy God.

The second temptation attacked Jesus' confidence in the Father. Matthew 4:5-7 reads, "Then the devil taketh him up into the holy city, and setteth him on a pinnacle of the temple, And saith unto him, If thou be the Son of God, cast thyself down: for it is written, He shall give his angels charge concerning thee: and in their hands they shall bear thee up, lest at any time thou dash thy foot against a stone."

Again, Satan dared Jesus to trust God with a foolhardy request—to jump down and let God catch Him. He was saying (in essence), "Go ahead, Jesus; put Your money where Your mouth is. If You are all that spiritual, let me see You jump off of this building and summon the God of creation to send a bunch of angels to hold You up. That will really get the crowd going."

Here, Satan revealed his knowledge and his ability to use the Scriptures to confuse and confound many believers. Watch out when you are tempted to fall into a situation that is clearly outside of God's will and plan for your life. Sometimes the devil will tempt us to try God to the point of excess—that is, he wants to push us to a point of being absolutely irreverent with God. There are some things that God will not do in our lives, no matter how much we name it, claim it, speak it, and stand on it. It is not going to happen. We have to know when we are in God's will and when we have just stepped outside of it. Sometimes we can put ourselves in jeopardy, thinking that God will deliver us when we have simply set ourselves up for a major, catastrophic spiritual meltdown.

Again, Jesus responded with the Word of God. Verse 7 reads, "Jesus said unto him, It is written again, Thou shalt not tempt the Lord thy God." This quote is found in Deuteronomy 6:16, "Ye shall not tempt the Lord your God, as ye tempted him in Massah." This text looks back into Israel's history to a time when they tried God's patience unnecessarily. They complained about not having water.

D. The Third Temptation
(Matthew 4:8-11)

Again, the devil taketh him up into an exceeding high mountain, and sheweth him all the kingdoms of the world, and the glory of them; And saith unto him, All these things will I give thee, if thou wilt fall down and worship me. Then saith Jesus unto him, Get thee hence, Satan: for it is written, Thou shalt worship the Lord thy God, and him only shalt thou serve. Then the devil leaveth him, and, behold, angels came and ministered unto him.

The third temptation attacked Jesus at the point of His worship. One of Satan's tactics is to lure people into idolatry and false worship. The devil never gives up. He will try and try until we either defeat him or we succumb to his pressure and tactics. Matthew 4:8-10 reads, "Again, the devil taketh him up into an exceeding high mountain, and sheweth him all the kingdoms of the world, and the glory of them; And saith unto him, All these things will I give thee, if thou wilt fall down and worship me."

Frederick Bruner says that this is the temptation to make our *work* our *God*. Jesus is the anointed Messiah of God, sent into the world to redeem and release men and women from the power of sin and death. Satan would have had Jesus think that he controlled the world—that he was running the universe and was, therefore, in a position to help Jesus succeed in His mission.

Notice what Jesus said, as seen in verse 10: "Then saith Jesus unto him, Get thee hence, Satan: for it is written, Thou shalt worship the Lord thy God, and him only shalt thou serve." Jesus clearly showed the only proper object of all worship—the Lord!

III. CONCLUDING REFLECTION

Temptation is a force and evil so powerful that it was the first spiritual battle that Jesus fought and won. The temptations of Jesus were the first real tests of His resolve and commitment to the Father's anointing and purpose for sending Him into the world. We can learn how to recognize and resist temptation from this narrative that describes the experience of Jesus in the wilderness. The battle against temptation is the first major spiritual conflict that we face after conversion, and it is one that we will all face again and again. The enemy never tires or grows weary in his efforts to lure us into destruction through succumbing to temptations.

The inability to resist and ward off temptation is one of the most powerful retardants to our spiritual growth. Satan uses temptation to hinder our growth in grace. He does it with such cunning skill that by the time we realize what has happened, the tragic consequences of sin have already started to take hold. Adam and Eve plunged the whole world into sin before they realized the gravity of their mistake. Samson was too naïve, and assumed that he could tamper with God's commandments without any consequences. David reveled in the beauty of Bathsheba while the devil tricked him into committing the most heinous sin of his life. Judas was duped into thinking that having thirty pieces of silver was worth selling out His Lord and Master. Temptation is a powerful weapon in the hand of Satan. Jesus taught that the key to victory over sin and temptation is the knowledge of the Word of God and our absolute commitment to obedience (see Psalms 1; 119:1-24).

PRAYER

Heavenly Father, grant that we will love You with hearts of obedience, as we commit ourselves to Your purpose. Give us the determination and will to face and defeat every temptation that the devil presents to us. In Jesus' name we pray. Amen.

WORD POWER

Jealous (Hebrew: *qana'* [kan–naw])—This is a critically important theological term because it expresses the strongest emotions that God felt for Israel. The word *jealous* can be used in a negative manner to express hostile and disruptive human characteristics.[2] However, the particular Hebrew word that is used in Deuteronomy 6:15 is used only in connection with God. *Qana*, in this context, is a term of deep, indescribable endearment and love. God loved Israel with an everlasting love and would not share His relationship with any other god.

HOME DAILY BIBLE READINGS
(April 28–May 4, 2014)

Jesus Resists Temptation
MONDAY, April 28: "Testing What Is in Your Heart" (Deuteronomy 8:1-11)
TUESDAY, April 29: "Keep Watching and Praying" (Matthew 26:36-41)
WEDNESDAY, April 30: "Take Care against Being Tempted" (Galatians 6:1-5)
THURSDAY, May 1: "Do Not Lead Us into Temptation" (Matthew 6:9-13)
FRIDAY, May 2: "Kept from Trial and Testing" (Revelation 3:8-13)
SATURDAY, May 3: "Guarded in All Your Ways" (Psalm 91:1-12)
SUNDAY, May 4: "Serve Only God" (Deuteronomy 6:13-16; Matthew 4:4-11)

End Notes

[1]Adapted from Greg Brian Larson and Phyllis Ten Elshof, *1001 Illustrations that Connect* (Grand Rapids: Zondervan, 2008), 454.

[2]R. Laird Harris, Gleason L. Archer Jr., and Bruce K. Waltke, *Theological Wordbook of the Old Testament* (Chicago: Moody Press, 1980), 802.

JESUS' MISSION ON EARTH

FAITH PATHWAY/FAITH JOURNEY TOPIC: A Fulfilling Vocation

DEVOTIONAL READING: **John 10:1-10**
PRINT PASSAGE: **Luke 4:14-21**
KEY VERSE: **Luke 4:21**

BACKGROUND SCRIPTURE: **Leviticus 25:8-55;**
Isaiah 61:1-2; Luke 4:14-21

Luke 4:14-21—KJV

14 And Jesus returned in the power of the Spirit into Galilee: and there went out a fame of him through all the region round about.

15 And he taught in their synagogues, being glorified of all.

16 And he came to Nazareth, where he had been brought up: and, as his custom was, he went into the synagogue on the sabbath day, and stood up for to read.

17 And there was delivered unto him the book of the prophet Esaias. And when he had opened the book, he found the place where it was written,

18 The Spirit of the Lord is upon me, because he hath anointed me to preach the gospel to the poor; he hath sent me to heal the brokenhearted, to preach deliverance to the captives, and recovering of sight to the blind, to set at liberty them that are bruised,

19 To preach the acceptable year of the Lord.

20 And he closed the book, and he gave it again to the minister, and sat down. And the eyes of all them that were in the synagogue were fastened on him.

21 And he began to say unto them, This day is this scripture fulfilled in your ears.

Luke 4:14-21—NIV

14 Jesus returned to Galilee in the power of the Spirit, and news about him spread through the whole countryside.

15 He taught in their synagogues, and everyone praised him.

16 He went to Nazareth, where he had been brought up, and on the Sabbath day he went into the synagogue, as was his custom. And he stood up to read.

17 The scroll of the prophet Isaiah was handed to him. Unrolling it, he found the place where it is written:

18 "The Spirit of the Lord is on me, because he has anointed me to preach good news to the poor. He has sent me to proclaim freedom for the prisoners and recovery of sight for the blind, to release the oppressed,

19 to proclaim the year of the Lord's favor."

20 Then he rolled up the scroll, gave it back to the attendant and sat down. The eyes of everyone in the synagogue were fastened on him,

21 and he began by saying to them, "Today this scripture is fulfilled in your hearing."

BIBLE FACT

Jesus' "Mission Statement" is contained in Luke 4:14-21. The word *Mission* means "to send." Jesus was sent by God the Father to bring liberation to all who are bound in sin.

UNIFYING LESSON PRINCIPLE

Many people wrestle with the circumstances of finding or choosing a job. What considerations should drive their decision-making process when it comes to vocation? Jesus' identity and mission was informed by the prophetic tradition of the Hebrew Scriptures.

TOPICAL OUTLINE OF THE LESSON

I. **Introduction**
   A. Who Am I and What Am I to Do?
   B. Biblical Background

II. **Exposition and application of the Scripture**
   A. The Ministry of Jesus Begins in Galilee (Luke 4:14-15)
   B. Jesus Preaches in Nazareth (Luke 4:16-17)
   C. Jesus Announces His Role as Messiah (Luke 4:18-21)

III. **Concluding Reflection**

LESSON OBJECTIVES

Upon the completion of the lesson, the students will be able to do the following:

1. Learn how to make deeper connections between God's Word to us in the Hebrew Scriptures and the texts of the Christian Scriptures;
2. Experience anew God's call in their lives; and,
3. Identify opportunities for discipleship and act on them.

POINTS TO BE EMPHASIZED

ADULT/YOUTH

Adult Topic: A Fulfilling Vocation

Youth Topic: What Will You Do?

Adult Key Verse: Luke 4:21

Youth Key Verse: Luke 4:18

Print Passage: Luke 4:14-21

—Nazareth was the town in which Jesus "had been brought up," but He had since moved to Capernaum (see Matthew 4:13).

—The "year of the Lord's favor" (Luke 4:19) was a reference to the Jubilee year mentioned in Leviticus 25:8-55.

—The background text from the book of Isaiah is the passage Jesus read in the synagogue.

—"To proclaim the year of the Lord's favor" (4:19) echoed the Year of Jubilee, described in the book of Leviticus as rooted in the Law given by God to Moses.

—The Year of Jubilee offered mercy and hope—as it called for release from oppression and offered opportunities for fresh starts.

CHILDREN

Children Topic: Life Goals

Key Verse: Luke 4:18

Print Passage: Luke 4:14-21

—Jesus returned to His hometown in order to reveal the nature of His ministry.

—Jesus set His ministry in the context of Isaiah's hope for the redemption of Israel.

—Jesus claimed the power of God as He initiated His ministry.

—Jesus' ministry was one of word and of deed that was directed toward healing and helping those who could not help themselves.

I. INTRODUCTION
A. Who Am I and What Am I to Do?

My life has been an interesting journey. I have gone from being a prodigal to becoming a preacher of the Gospel. At the age of twelve, I knew that God had a call to preach upon my life—but it was not something I wanted to pursue as a lifelong vocation. In 1967, I graduated from Booker T. Washington High School in Norfolk, Virginia. On the day of my graduation, I had no idea what I planned to do with the rest of my life. I had taken the SAT, but I could not brag about how well I had performed on the test. During the summer of 1967 I worked in a restaurant at Virginia Beach, earning the minimum wage (which was about $1.25 an hour). As the weeks passed by, my father insisted that I enroll in a local college. After a little parental coercion, in September of 1967 I enrolled in Norfolk State University. Prior to starting school in the fall of 1967, I had no idea what to select as a major. At one point I considered majoring in history, but I soon dismissed that idea because I did not want to pursue a teaching career in history. I finally settled on business administration with a minor in marketing. At the time, all male students enrolled as full-time students were required to enlist in ROTC. After nearly five years in college, I graduated in 1972 and was commissioned as a second lieutenant in the United States Army. After six years in the army, I finally reached a point when I knew that there was only one course for my life: I was to acknowledge my call to ministry. I resigned my commission and enrolled in seminary. In 1978, I took on a new assignment and I have been trying to live out that assignment every day.

There are many people whose stories are similar to mine. They wrestle with very important questions such as choosing a mate, deciding on what college to enroll in and/or where to purchase a home, or simply choosing a lifelong vocation. What are the considerations that should drive the decision-making process when it comes to a vocation? Jesus' identity and mission were informed by the prophetic tradition of the Hebrew Scriptures.

B. Biblical Background

Each of the Synoptic Gospels records a visit by Jesus to His hometown of Nazareth (see Matthew 13:54-58; Mark 6:1-6). Some scholars believe that the passage in the book of Luke may have occurred early in the Galilean ministry of Jesus, because neither Matthew nor Mark mentioned the attempts of the people to kill Jesus. It may be possible that Jesus embarked on multiple visits to Nazareth and the writers of the Gospels summarized them in one event. Shortly after His forty days of fasting in the Judean wilderness, Jesus moved to Galilee, settling in the city of Capernaum. It was in the northern region of Galilee that He began His ministry. Luke did not report many of the early details of His work, just that Jesus became very popular as news about Him spread throughout the countryside.

Luke did not say at what point Jesus decided to go home to Nazareth, nor did he report that Jesus was accompanied by anyone. When the time came for the reading of the Scriptures, Jesus stood and read from Isaiah 61:1-2.

These words from Isaiah are messianic in their interpretation. Scholars believe that the book of Isaiah was written in three stages: chapters 1–39 (the Assyrian Period), chapters 40–55 (the Babylonian Period), and chapters 56–66 (the Persian Period). The Persian Period was a time of great optimism and hope that at long last Israel would be restored to its former glory. The words read by Jesus referred to Israel's belief and hope in the coming of the Messiah (Hebrew designation), or the Christ (Greek designation). According to Hebrew tradition, the Messiah would break the yoke of Roman bondage, restore prosperity, heal the hurting, and usher in a new age of freedom and peace in Israel. The lion and the lamb would lie down together; men would beat their swords into plowshares and their spears into pruning hooks (see Isaiah 2:4; Micah 4:1-4). By reading the words of Isaiah, Jesus announced the arrival of the Year of Jubilee and in Him these promises would be fulfilled.

II. EXPOSITION AND APPLICATION OF THE SCRIPTURE

A. The Ministry of Jesus Begins in Galilee (Luke 4:14-15)

And Jesus returned in the power of the Spirit into Galilee: and there went out a fame of him through all the region round about. And he taught in their synagogues, being glorified of all.

At some point Jesus left Nazareth and joined the work of John the Baptist in the Jordan River Valley. Each of the Synoptic Gospels reports that the ministry of Jesus began during the latter days of the ministry of John the Baptist (see Matthew 3:13; 4:12-17; Mark 1:14; Luke 3:2-9). The Gospels are silent as to what prompted Jesus to begin His work and missionary activities. Luke stated that Jesus was about thirty years old when He began to preach (see Luke 3:23). He spent some portion of His early ministry in and around the area near Jericho and the Dead Sea in a place known today as Bethany beyond the Jordan (see John 1:28). The area where John was baptizing is in the southern region of modern-day Jordan and is not far from the modern city of Jericho, which is approximately a thirty-minute ride from the modern city of Amman, Jordan.

In verse 14, Jesus returned to Galilee, which was the commercial and economic hub of Israel (see Matthew 4:12). It was also the most likely place for Jesus to begin His ministry, since He was from Nazareth. At that time, Nazareth was a very small village nestled in the hill country of Galilee, an area that forms the northern boundary of the Jezreel Valley. Jesus spent just about the entire time of His ministry in and around Galilee (see Mark 1:9, 14, 16, 28, 39; 3:7; 6:21; 7:31; 9:30). From the very beginning there is a distinct difference drawn between the ministry of Jesus and that of other teachers. Jesus was filled with the power of the Holy Spirit, which made His teaching authoritative (see Mark 1:22).

Verse 15 is a summary statement that

describes what Jesus was doing (see Matthew 4:23-25; Mark 1:14-16): He was teaching in their synagogues. Synagogues were local meeting places, serving as both houses of worship and civic gathering places. We are not told what He was teaching. It is assumed that He was teaching from the Old Testament, just as He had done in Nazareth; He was announcing the arrival of the messianic age.

B. Jesus Preaches in Nazareth (Luke 4:16-17)

And he came to Nazareth, where he had been brought up: and, as his custom was, he went into the synagogue on the sabbath day, and stood up for to read. And there was delivered unto him the book of the prophet Esaias. And when he had opened the book, he found the place where it was written.

Nazareth was the hometown of Jesus. "Christian tradition holds that the announcement of the birth of Christ was made to Mary in Nazareth."[1] During the sixth month of Elizabeth's pregnancy with John, the angel Gabriel was sent by God to a city in Galilee named Nazareth (see Luke 1:26). The angel of the Lord announced to Mary that God had highly favored her and that she would be pregnant with a child who would be called the Son of the Most High.

Jesus was reared and spent the early years of His life in Nazareth. When Joseph and Mary returned from Egypt, they settled in Nazareth (see Matthew 2:19-23). In the synagogue of Nazareth, Jesus made His first public preaching and teaching appearance, announcing the beginning of His messianic ministry (see Luke 4:14-21). The book of Luke is the only one of the Synoptic Gospels to record this event in the life of Jesus. In Nazareth, Jesus came to realize that a prophet is not without honor except among those who are His own people (see Mark 6:4). Nazareth was the place where He experienced His first bout with rejection and doubt over His ministry and mission in the world.

According to verse 16, Jesus went to Nazareth, timing His visit to coincide with the Sabbath. He went to the local synagogue, which was customary for Jewish males to do. There is no conclusive archaeological or biblical evidence given as to the exact date or period that synagogues first appeared in history. Further, there is very little known about the early administrative functioning of synagogues.[2] Biblical scholars generally accept the belief that synagogues may have first appeared during the time of the Babylonian Exile in 587 BC. One of the earliest known synagogues was found in Egypt and is believed to have been established during the third century BC. Adin Steinsaltz has noted that there were synagogues in Jerusalem before the time of the Roman destruction of Jerusalem.[3] He notes further that there were synagogues that catered to people of the same profession or social group.[4] Several roles of the local synagogues have been noted by scholars: houses of public prayer, places for instruction in the Torah, community meeting places, and schools for children.

Synagogues were in wide use during the time of Jesus' ministry. In the Gospels, Jesus often attended the religious meetings held in the synagogues, taught in them, healed the sick, and generally participated in the life of the local synagogue—particularly on the Sabbath (see Matthew 4:23; Mark 6:2; Luke 4:16-21). He received some of His harshest criticisms from members of the local synagogues (see Mark 6:1-4; Luke 4:28-29).

C. Jesus Announces His Role as Messiah (Luke 4:18-21)

The Spirit of the Lord is upon me, because he hath anointed me to preach the gospel to the poor; he hath sent me to heal the brokenhearted, to preach deliverance to the captives, and recovering of sight to the blind, to set at liberty them that are bruised, To preach the acceptable year of the Lord. And he closed the book, and he gave it again to the minister, and sat down. And the eyes of all them that were in the synagogue were fastened on him. And he began to say unto them, This day is this scripture fulfilled in your ears.

Verses 18-21 are among the most significant words of Jesus in the New Testament. They set the tone for His ministry and they have provided direction for the work of the Christian church for nearly two thousand years. Jesus took the scroll of the prophet Isaiah and read 61:1-2. He probably gave a short exposition of the passage and how it related to Him. Jesus proclaimed that the Spirit of the Lord was upon Him for a specific purpose. Luke noted that Jesus identified several tasks that would be associated with His ministry: preaching the Gospel to the poor, proclaiming freedom to those in prison, helping the blind to recover their sight, and releasing those who were oppressed (see Isaiah 42:7; 49:8-9; 56:6; 63:4).

One question that comes to mind is this: Why would these words from Isaiah be significant to the people of Galilee during the time of Jesus? The first reason was because the nation of Israel at the time was a vassal state of Rome. The people lived in bondage, although the Romans granted them a lot of freedom to move and conduct daily life according to their own dictates. Second, there was a real class distinction within Jewish society. The very wealthy classes controlled much of the wealth and the land, which explains the large number of people that Jesus fed. Third, it was the time of the arrival of the kingdom of God (see Mark 1:16-17). The new age had arrived and Jesus was the primary proclaimer of that age.

In verse 19, Jesus announced that the "year of the Lord's favor" had come. Jesus was anointed with the Holy Spirit from birth to do the work of ministry. The Holy Spirit is the Agent of power in the ministry and work of the church. These words from Isaiah were messianic. They referred to Israel's belief and hope in the coming of the Messiah. According to tradition, the Messiah would break the yoke of bondage, restore prosperity, heal the hurting, and usher in a new age of freedom and peace in Israel. The lion and the lamb would lie down together and men would beat their swords into plowshares and their spears into pruning hooks. The Messiah would come as God's conquering hero. The Messiah was a liberator and deliverer of those who were in bondage.

Jesus did come as the Messiah. He did come to set men and women free from bondage. His coming did usher in a new age of peace and prosperity. This is the message that we must take to the ends of the Earth. God is able to set us free.

III. CONCLUDING REFLECTION

The call to Christian ministry begins with first understanding the mission of God, which is visibly seen and demonstrated in the life and ministry of Jesus of Nazareth. Christian ministry and missions are an extension of the work of Jesus (see Matthew 25:31-46; 28:18-20). Believers must come to grips with the reality in the twenty-first century that Jesus did not call us to become church members; rather, we are called to be disciples. Our call is a call to follow Jesus and continue the work of redemption. We do this through preaching, teaching, ministry, missions, and worship. Often when we talk about being called to ministry, we see it through the eyes of pulpit ministry. There are many venues by which we can exercise the call to ministry—and local church pastoral ministry is only one of those venues. God has called us to go into all the world, but many believers only get as far as the local church—and for many this is only occasionally.

PRAYER

Heavenly Father, we thank You for the example of Your Son, Jesus of Nazareth, who shows us what it means to commit ourselves to serving You. Grant that we may never grow weary in doing well. In Jesus' name we pray. Amen.

WORD POWER

Anointed (Greek: *chrio* [khree'-o])—The Greek root of "anoint" gives us the English word *christos*. Thus, Christ is not a formal name, but a title that designated Jesus as the one anointed by the Father for a specific purpose. In the Old Testament, the act of anointing was used to dedicate people, places, or objects to the service of the Lord. The word *Messiah* is the English translation of a Hebrew word (*mashia*), which means "the Lord's anointed or anointed one."

HOME DAILY BIBLE READINGS
(May 5–11, 2014)

Jesus' Mission on Earth
MONDAY, May 5: "I Came from the Father" (John 16:25-33)
TUESDAY, May 6: "I Came to Do God's Will" (John 6:35-40)
WEDNESDAY, May 7: "I Came to Bring Light" (John 12:44-50)
THURSDAY, May 8: "I Came to Testify to Truth" (John 18:33-38)
FRIDAY, May 9: "I Came to Draw All People" (John 12:27-32)
SATURDAY, May 10: "I Came to Give Abundant Life" (John 10:1-10)
SUNDAY, May 11: "The Lord's Spirit Is upon Me" (Luke 4:14-21)

End Notes

---

[1]Charles R. Page II & Carl A. Volz, *The Land and the Book: An Introduction to the World of the Bible* (Nashville: Abingdon Press, 1993), 162.

[2]Howard F. Vos, *Nelson's New Illustrated Bible Manners and Customs: How the People of the Bible Really Lived* (Nashville: Thomas Nelson Publishers, 1999), 412.

[3]Adin Steinsaltz, *The Essential Talmud* (Philadelphia, PA: Basic Books, 1976), 103-104.

[4]Ibid.

LESSON 12   **May 18, 2014**

JESUS' TEACHING ON THE LAW

FAITH PATHWAY/FAITH JOURNEY TOPIC: Get It Right

DEVOTIONAL READING: Matthew 5:14-20
PRINT PASSAGE: Matthew 15:1-11, 15-20
KEY VERSES: Matthew 15:8-9

BACKGROUND SCRIPTURE: Exodus 20; Isaiah 29:13-14a; Matthew 5:17-48; 15:1-19; Romans 3:31

Matthew 15:1-11, 15-20—KJV

THEN CAME to Jesus scribes and Pharisees, which were of Jerusalem, saying,

2 Why do thy disciples transgress the tradition of the elders? for they wash not their hands when they eat bread.

3 But he answered and said unto them, Why do ye also transgress the commandment of God by your tradition?

4 For God commanded, saying, Honour thy father and mother: and, He that curseth father or mother, let him die the death.

5 But ye say, Whosoever shall say to his father or his mother, It is a gift, by whatsoever thou mightest be profited by me;

6 And honour not his father or his mother, he shall be free. Thus have ye made the commandment of God of none effect by your tradition.

7 Ye hypocrites, well did Esaias prophesy of you, saying,

8 This people draweth nigh unto me with their mouth, and honoureth me with their lips; but their heart is far from me.

9 But in vain they do worship me, teaching for doctrines the commandments of men.

10 And he called the multitude, and said unto them, Hear, and understand:

11 Not that which goeth into the mouth defileth a man; but that which cometh out of the mouth, this defileth a man.

.....

15 Then answered Peter and said unto him, Declare unto us this parable.

Matthew 15:1-11, 15-20—NIV

THEN SOME Pharisees and teachers of the law came to Jesus from Jerusalem and asked,

2 "Why do your disciples break the tradition of the elders? They don't wash their hands before they eat!"

3 Jesus replied, "And why do you break the command of God for the sake of your tradition?

4 For God said, 'Honor your father and mother' and 'Anyone who curses his father or mother must be put to death.'

5 But you say that if a man says to his father or mother, 'Whatever help you might otherwise have received from me is a gift devoted to God,'

6 he is not to 'honor his father' with it. Thus you nullify the word of God for the sake of your tradition.

7 You hypocrites! Isaiah was right when he prophesied about you:

8 'These people honor me with their lips, but their hearts are far from me.

9 They worship me in vain; their teachings are but rules taught by men.'"

10 Jesus called the crowd to him and said, "Listen and understand.

11 What goes into a man's mouth does not make him 'unclean,' but what comes out of his mouth, that is what makes him 'unclean.'"

.....

16 And Jesus said, Are ye also yet without understanding?

17 Do not ye yet understand, that whatsoever entereth in at the mouth goeth into the belly, and is cast out into the draught?

18 But those things which proceed out of the mouth come forth from the heart; and they defile the man.

19 For out of the heart proceed evil thoughts, murders, adulteries, fornications, thefts, false witness, blasphemies:

20 These are the things which defile a man: but to eat with unwashen hands defileth not a man.

15 Peter said, "Explain the parable to us."

16 "Are you still so dull?" Jesus asked them.

17 "Don't you see that whatever enters the mouth goes into the stomach and then out of the body?

18 But the things that come out of the mouth come from the heart, and these make a man 'unclean.'

19 For out of the heart come evil thoughts, murder, adultery, sexual immorality, theft, false testimony, slander.

20 These are what make a man 'unclean'; but eating with unwashed hands does not make him 'unclean.'"

TOPICAL OUTLINE OF THE LESSON

I. Introduction
A. Traditionalism versus Biblicism
B. Biblical Background

II. Exposition and Application of the Scripture
A. The Religious Leaders and a Meaningless Quarrel (Matthew 15:1-6)
B. Jesus' Denunciation of the Pharisees and Teachers (Matthew 15:7-11)
C. Peter's Question (Matthew 15:15-20)

III. Concluding Reflection

LESSON OBJECTIVES

Upon the completion of the lesson, the students will be able to do the following:

1. Understand the sacred traditions of the church in light of Scripture;
2. Recount stories of traditions that touch their hearts most deeply; and,
3. Assess aspects of tradition that might be creating a barrier to a fresh experience of the Spirit in their churches.

POINTS TO BE EMPHASIZED
ADULT/YOUTH

Adult Topic: Get It Right
Youth Topic: Do the Right Thing
Adult Key Verses: Matthew 15:8-9
Youth Key Verse: Matthew 15:3
Print Passage: Matthew 15:1-11, 15-20
—Jesus criticized the Pharisees for paying attention to the minutiae of the Law and for their failure to observe the

weightier matters of the Law: justice, mercy, and faith (see Matthew 23:23).

—When Jesus said that eating something cannot defile a person (see Matthew 15:10), He declared, as Mark pointed out, that there is no "unclean" food. (See Mark 7:19.)

—Although the Pharisees viewed the Law as God's gift, their vast array of literal applications made it difficult to obey one law without breaking another.

—Jesus made it clear that He had come not to abolish the Law but rather to fulfill the intent with which God had given it.

—Jesus responded to the Pharisees and scribes' question by citing other passages of the Law and of tradition from Scripture that emphasized justice and mercy.

CHILDREN

Children Topic: Traditions Connect Us
Key Verse: Matthew 15:18
Print Passage: Matthew 15:1-18

—Jesus confronted the Pharisees and scribes about beliefs in the spiritual value of certain traditions.

—Jesus demonstrated that knowing the Word of God is essential to interpreting the correctness of traditions.

—Jesus explained how religious traditions might be oppositional to God's Word.

—Jesus taught that people could honor God with their lips while also having unclean hearts.

—Jesus taught that one's words reflect the condition of his or her heart and can indicate a corrupt spirit.

—Human traditions are often taught as if they emanated from God's Word.

I. INTRODUCTION

A. Traditionalism versus Biblicism

What is traditionalism? Joe Ellis writes in his book, *The Church on Purpose,* that traditionalism is "the elevation of expedient forms or practices to a sacrosanct position and insists upon their perpetuation."[1] What does he mean by that statement? It basically means that congregational leaders or members can begin a simple practice such as wearing a particular color of clothes for communion and declare them to be God's will. Many practices observed by congregations have no biblical foundation. They are things that we have simply been doing and they have taken on a life all of their own.

Traditions should not be totally discarded as useless and irrelevant in the twenty-first century. Traditions are powerful guides for determining actions and behavior. A central issue revolves around determining how Christians can avoid using traditions to set up the word of the Law against the spirit of the Law. While Jesus was a firm believer in tradition, He warned against a misuse of tradition that "makes void the Word of God" (Matthew 15:6).

B. Biblical Background

The Pharisees and teachers of the law (scribes), particularly those from Jerusalem, had very little (if any) concern about the positive impact that the ministry of Jesus had in Galilee. Rather than be supportive of the work, they were more concerned about the failure of His disciples to adhere to the traditions of the elders, especially their failure to follow the ritual of washing their hands prior to eating.

In today's lesson, there are three separate episodes: First, there is the confrontation with the religious leaders over the washing of hands (see Matthew 15:1-6); second, there is Jesus' answer to their criticism and His quoting of the Prophet Isaiah (see verses 7-11). Third, we see Jesus' answer to a question raised by Peter regarding the meaning of the parable of eating (see verses 15-20).

The center of the controversy with Jesus over the hand washing revolved around whose vision of morality and obedience would prevail in Israel.[2] The issue of the hand washing was not about hygiene but about ritual purity and the need for all to strictly adhere to the tradition of the elders. The Pharisees were appalled that Jesus would not instruct His disciples to follow the tradition of the elders. Jesus responded to the criticism of the religious leaders by quoting a passage from the book of Isaiah and declaring that they (the Pharisees and scribes) had taken their own rituals and rules and set them up above the Word of God. Jesus reminded them that God was not interested in whether a man or woman washed his/her hands before eating. It was not what went into a person but, rather, what came out of a person that had moral relevance.

II. EXPOSITION AND APPLICATION OF THE SCRIPTURE

A. The Religious Leaders and a Meaningless Quarrel (Matthew 15:1-6)

THEN CAME to Jesus scribes and Pharisees, which were of Jerusalem, saying, Why do thy disciples transgress the tradition of the elders? for they wash not their hands when they eat bread. But he answered and said unto them, Why do ye also transgress the commandment of God by your tradition? For God commanded, saying, Honour thy father and mother: and, He that curseth father or mother, let him die the death. But ye say, Whosoever shall say to his father or his mother, It is a gift, by whatsoever thou mightest be profited by me; And honour not his father or his mother, he shall be free. Thus have ye made the commandment of God of none effect by your tradition.

Verse 1 is a continuation of the healing and preaching activity of Jesus in Gennesaret (see Matthew 14:34-36). Jesus was in the midst of healing and teaching when a delegation of religious leaders from Jerusalem approached Him. We are not told how many were in the entourage. What is clear is that this was an international act of investigation. Jerusalem is about seventy-five miles south of Galilee, and for these men to have traveled that distance signified that the reputation of Jesus had ballooned and that they were very concerned about His work in Galilee. Jesus was often accompanied by large crowds of people and His ministry reached thousands of people. The Pharisees and teachers of the law questioned the work of Jesus by challenging Him about the failure of His disciples to wash their hands before eating. The question addressed to Jesus was intended to imply that as a teacher, He permitted His disciples to do what was unlawful—which was to fail to keep the tradition of the elders. The tradition of the elders refers to a body of teachings that was based upon interpretations of the Law of Moses. These traditions (Greek: *paradosis*) were oral teachings or interpretations that had been handed down through several generations. Some Jews claimed that they were actually delivered by Moses. During the time of Jesus, the traditions of the elders were as highly regarded as the written law. The Pharisees were extremely adamant about following the oral traditions and the law.

The Pharisees regarded the practice of eating with unclean hands as a matter of grave concern. In verse 3, Jesus' response was a direct rebuke of their religiosity and their willingness to break the Fifth Commandment (see Exodus 20:12) for the sake of their traditions. The Pharisees, who devoted their lives to keeping the Law of Moses, were in many cases the biggest offenders when it came to certain aspects of the Law. The Law clearly taught that anyone who failed to honor his or her parents would be put to death. *Honor* not only meant respect, but it also had other connotations. Here, the reference was to providing financial support for parents in their old age (see Exodus 20:17; Leviticus 19:3; 20:9; Deuteronomy 21:18; 27:16; Proverbs 20:20; compare Ephesians 6:1-2).

In verse 5, Jesus referred to the practice of "Corban," which was a method used in setting aside property or money for God. From Jesus' point of view, the command from the Law of Moses to honor parents far exceeded the tradition of dedicating money or property to the Temple when one's parents were suffering. The Pharisees insisted through their tradition that a parent had no right to the property—if the son had previously dedicated it to the work of the Lord. Further, the son could claim to be in violation of the Law because He took what belonged to God and gave it to his parent, even though he never intended to follow through. It was this reckless interpretation of the law that provoked Jesus to accuse the Pharisees and teachers of the Law of having taken their own rituals and rules and set them up above the Word of God.

B. Jesus' Denunciation of the Pharisees and Teachers (Matthew 15:7-11)

Ye hypocrites, well did Esaias prophesy of you, saying, This people draweth nigh unto me with their mouth, and honoureth me with their lips; but their heart is far from me. But in vain they do worship me, teaching for doctrines the commandments of men. And he called the multitude, and said unto them, Hear, and understand: Not that which goeth into the mouth defileth a man; but that which cometh out of the mouth, this defileth a man.

Jesus denounced the Pharisees and teachers of the Law, calling them hypocrites. What did He mean by this epitaph? Jesus was saying that the Pharisees and teachers of the Law were more concerned about religious practice that was invented by men than they were about the actual keeping of the Law. When Jesus referenced Isaiah, He was recalling a time when the prophet spoke to the people of His day about their own insincerity when it came to doing the will of God (see Isaiah 29:13; Ezekiel 33:31). Jesus quoted the prophet Isaiah more than any other (compare Matthew 3:3; 8:17; 12:17; 13:14; 22:18; 23:23).

In verse 9, the reference to "honoring with the lips" spoke to the practice of saying one thing and doing something else altogether. It is quite easy to profess faith and obedience in the midst of a gathered congregation of believers, but quite a challenge when one is put in a different context. One can worship and serve in a local congregation and be moved only by the obligation to serve on a particular day. Jesus said that their hearts were not in obeying the Lord.

In verses 10-11, Jesus called the crowd and publicly and openly challenged the teachings and traditions of the Pharisees and teachers of the Law. He called upon the people to listen, which meant to give complete attention to His words. Not only were they to listen, but also, He wanted them to "understand," which meant taking what they had heard and coming to some decision about its truthfulness. In an outright refutation of the most religious people in the nation, Jesus declared them and their traditions to be outright wrong. It was not what went into people that defiled them—it was what came out of their mouths that made them unclean (see Matthew 12:34; Acts 10:14-15).

C. Peter's Question
(Matthew 15:15-20)

Then answered Peter and said unto him, Declare unto us this parable. And Jesus said, Are ye also yet without understanding? Do not ye yet understand, that whatsoever entereth in at the mouth goeth into the belly, and is cast out into the draught? But those things which proceed out of the mouth come forth from the heart; and they defile the man. For out of the heart proceed evil thoughts, murders, adulteries, fornications, thefts, false witness, blasphemies: These are the things which defile a man: but to eat with unwashen hands defileth not a man.

In his typical fashion, Peter spoke for the group when he asked Jesus to explain the parabolic illustration that He had just shared with them (verse 11). The nature of the question was interesting to Jesus. They were the very last people that He would expect to miss the point of the teaching. Why was it necessary for Him to explain to them a teaching that they should have fully grasped the moment they heard it? The disciples had been with Jesus for quite some time. During this time they had heard His teachings, witnessed the miracles, and seen His impact upon the lives of thousands of people. Yet, they had not perceived nor understood the magnitude of His ministry. The level of comprehension displayed by the disciples was also symptomatic of the kind of spiritual infancy in existence in many churches today. When longtime members should be teaching others, they are still being taught and learning the elementary doctrines of the faith (see 1 Corinthians 3:1-10; Hebrews 5:11–6:3).

In a loving and gentle fashion, Jesus explained the meaning of the parable to them. Whether or not people washed their hands prior to eating had no bearing on what was in their hearts, which was a real gauge of their spirituality. What went into the stomach came out of the body through natural processes (see 1 Corinthians 6:13). What a man or woman really felt and thought were the products of the human heart. The heart is the seat and center of all human emotions; hence, it is the genesis of our actions and words. Jesus was saying that one's eating food with unwashed hands had no bearing on his or her attitude.

III. CONCLUDING REFLECTION

One of the central problems of human tradition or church traditions is that they lack biblical foundations. Often, congregations assume that because we engage in these practices, they must be rooted in the Scriptures.[3] Human traditions can and have often severely limited a congregation's growth potential. The church in Sardis (Revelation 3:1-6) is a prime example; it was a congregation with a certain reputation and name that indicated that it was alive, but in reality it was dead. Traditional churches can die spiritually and never realize it. Congregations can drift into apathy, into lethargy, and into a culture that slams the door on new ways of looking at the church's ministry. One of the mistakes that congregational leaders must avoid making is tending toward a disregard of sacred traditions that are anchored in Scripture—such as the Lord's Supper, baptism, and prayer.

PRAYER

Lord, may we never be guilty of worshipping You with our lips only, but failing to honor You with pure and undefiled hands. Grant that we may find forgiveness for our acts of hypocrisy. Give us the courage to live authentically as Your Son did. In Jesus' name we pray. Amen.

WORD POWER

Hypocrite (Greek: *hupoktrites* [hoop-ok-ree-tace])—someone who plays a part or wears a mask.

Pharisees (Greek: *Pharisaios* [far-is-as'yos])—The Pharisees were the largest and most influential religious party in Israel. They are said to have numbered more than six thousand. The Pharisees had their origin during the time of the Maccabean Revolt (ca. 168–165 BC). They were primarily concerned with protecting Israel from the growing presence of Hellenism. The name *Pharisee* comes from a Hebrew word, *parash*, and means to "separate."[4]

HOME DAILY BIBLE READINGS
(May 12–18, 2014)

Jesus' Teaching on the Law

MONDAY, May 12: "Commandments Learned by Rote" (Isaiah 29:13-19)
TUESDAY, May 13: "Testing and Fear" (Exodus 20:12-21)
WEDNESDAY, May 14: "We Uphold the Law" (Romans 3:21-31)
THURSDAY, May 15: "Fulfilling the Law" (Matthew 5:14-20)
FRIDAY, May 16: "But I Say to You" (Matthew 5:27-37)
SATURDAY, May 17: "Be Perfect" (Matthew 5:38-48)
SUNDAY, May 18: "What Proceeds from the Heart" (Matthew 15:1-18)

End Notes

[1]Joe S. Ellis, *The Church on Purpose* (Cincinnati, Ohio: Standard Publishing Co., 1984), 96.
[2]David Garland, *Mark: The NIV Application Commentary* (Grand Rapids: Zondervan, 1996), 271.
[3]Aubrey Malphurs, *A New Kind of Church: Understanding Models of Ministry for the 21st Century* (Grand Rapids: Baker Books, 2007), 63.
[4]Joachim Jeremias, *Jerusalem in the Time of Jesus* (Philadelphia: Fortress Press, 1962), 247.

LESSON 13   May 25, 2014

THE GREATEST COMMANDMENT

FAITH PATHWAY/FAITH JOURNEY TOPIC: **First Things First**

DEVOTIONAL READING: **Psalm 15**
PRINT PASSAGE: **Leviticus 19:18;**
Deuteronomy 6:4-9; Mark 12:28-34

BACKGROUND SCRIPTURE: **Leviticus 19:18;**
Deuteronomy 4:35; 6:1-9; Mark 12:28-34
KEY VERSES: **Mark 12:30-31**

Leviticus 19:18; Deuteronomy 6:4-9; Mark 12:28-34—KJV

18 Thou shalt not avenge, nor bear any grudge against the children of thy people, but thou shalt love thy neighbour as thyself: I am the LORD.

.....

4 Hear, O Israel: The LORD our God is one LORD:
5 And thou shalt love the LORD thy God with all thine heart, and with all thy soul, and with all thy might.
6 And these words, which I command thee this day, shall be in thine heart:
7 And thou shalt teach them diligently unto thy children, and shalt talk of them when thou sittest in thine house, and when thou walkest by the way, and when thou liest down, and when thou risest up.
8 And thou shalt bind them for a sign upon thine hand, and they shall be as frontlets between thine eyes.
9 And thou shalt write them upon the posts of thy house, and on thy gates.

.....

28 And one of the scribes came, and having heard them reasoning together, and perceiving that he had answered them well, asked him, Which is the first commandment of all?
29 And Jesus answered him, The first of all the commandments is, Hear, O Israel; The Lord our God is one Lord:
30 And thou shalt love the Lord thy God with all thy heart, and with all thy soul, and with all thy mind, and with all thy strength: this is the first commandment.
31 And the second is like, namely this, Thou shalt love thy neighbour as thyself. There is none other commandment greater than these.
32 And the scribe said unto him, Well, Master, thou

Leviticus 19:18; Deuteronomy 6:4-9; Mark 12:28-34—NIV

18 "'Do not seek revenge or bear a grudge against one of your people, but love your neighbor as yourself. I am the LORD.'"

.....

4 Hear, O Israel: The LORD our God, the LORD is one.
5 Love the LORD your God with all your heart and with all your soul and with all your strength.
6 These commandments that I give you today are to be upon your hearts.
7 Impress them on your children. Talk about them when you sit at home and when you walk along the road, when you lie down and when you get up.
8 Tie them as symbols on your hands and bind them on your foreheads.
9 Write them on the doorframes of your houses and on your gates.

.....

28 One of the teachers of the law came and heard them debating. Noticing that Jesus had given them a good answer, he asked him, "Of all the commandments, which is the most important?"
29 "The most important one," answered Jesus, "is this: 'Hear, O Israel, the Lord our God, the Lord is one.
30 Love the Lord your God with all your heart and with all your soul and with all your mind and with all your strength.'
31 The second is this: 'Love your neighbor as yourself.' There is no commandment greater than these."
32 "Well said, teacher," the man replied. "You are

hast said the truth: for there is one God; and there is none other but he:

33 And to love him with all the heart, and with all the understanding, and with all the soul, and with all the strength, and to love his neighbour as himself, is more than all whole burnt offerings and sacrifices.

34 And when Jesus saw that he answered discreetly, he said unto him, Thou art not far from the kingdom of God. And no man after that durst ask him any question.

right in saying that God is one and there is no other but him.

33 To love him with all your heart, with all your understanding and with all your strength, and to love your neighbor as yourself is more important than all burnt offerings and sacrifices."

34 When Jesus saw that he had answered wisely, he said to him, "You are not far from the kingdom of God." And from then on no one dared ask him any more questions.

TOPICAL OUTLINE OF THE LESSON

I. Introduction
  A. Misplaced Priority
  B. Biblical Background

II. Exposition and Application of the Scripture
  A. Love Your Neighbor (Leviticus 19:18)
  B. Love the Lord Your God (Deuteronomy 6:4-9)
  C. The Great Commandment (Mark 12:28-34)

III. Concluding Reflection

LESSON OBJECTIVES

Upon the completion of the lesson, the students will be able to do the following:

1. Appreciate better why the Great Commandment is considered a summary of all the Law and the Prophets;
2. Confess what has been done and left undone with regards to loving their neighbors; and,
3. Identify ways that Christians can be the hands, feet, eyes, and ears of Jesus in this world.

POINTS TO BE EMPHASIZED

ADULT/YOUTH

Adult Topic: First Things First

Youth Topic: Top Priority!

Adult Key Verses: Mark 12:30-31

Youth Key Verse: Mark 12:33

Print Passage: Leviticus 19:18; Deuteronomy 6:4-9; Mark 12:28-34

—The events recorded in Mark 12:28-34 occurred during Jesus' "final week," a time during which He was repeatedly questioned by several hostile groups.

—In the book of Mark, the scribe who asked Jesus about the great commandment appears to be an honest inquisitor. In

Matthew's account (22:34-40), the scribe was selected by the Pharisees to test Jesus.

—Leviticus 19:18 is one of many verses in that chapter that tell of how to treat one's neighbor.

—The passage from the book of Deuteronomy is sometimes called the Shema.

—The Greek word for "love" in Mark 12:30, 31, and 33—as well as the Septuagint version of Leviticus 19:18 and Deuteronomy 6:5—is *agape*, which speaks of one's demonstrating active, intelligent goodwill toward another without regard to a response.

—Love of God and love of neighbor are foundational in the Hebrew Scriptures and in Jewish tradition.

CHILDREN
Children Topic: The Most Important Rule
Key Verses: Mark 12:30, 31
Print Passage: Leviticus 19:18; Deuteronomy 6:4-9; Mark 12:28-34

—A scribe asked Jesus what the most important commandment is.

—Jesus answered the scribe by reciting Deuteronomy 6:4-9.

—Jesus included "with all your mind" because it connoted that loving God is a conscious decision.

—Jesus connected the second greatest commandment (found in Leviticus 19:18)—to love one's neighbor as oneself—to the greatest commandment.

—Once Jesus affirmed the scribe's response to His teaching, the crowd was silenced.

I. INTRODUCTION
A. Misplaced Priority

Each summer, some child is accidently locked in an automobile and subsequently dies from heat exhaustion and dehydration. One extremely hot summer day in San Antonio, a ten-month-old baby girl was accidently locked inside a parked car by her aunt. When she realized what she had done, the woman panicked and ran repeatedly around the car trying to find a door that would open. A passerby came up and tried to help her open the car by using a clothes hanger to unlock the door. His efforts were futile and within a matter of a few minutes the child began to lose consciousness, foam at the mouth, and start turning purple.

As the situation grew increasingly more desperate, up drove a man in a wrecker. Sensing the gravity of the situation and that time was of the essence, he grabbed a hammer and broke out one of the windows of the car, enabling the little girl to be rescued. As the situation started to calm down, the aunt became incensed at the man because he broke the window in her car. Puzzled by the behavior, the man could not understand why the woman would value the window more than the life of the child.[1]

It appears as though the woman's priorities were directed more at her car than saving the life of a little girl. In some ways, the woman in this story is a reflection of how many people live their lives. They place enormous value on the things that matter the least in life. This same attitude is often on display in many contemporary congregations. Within many local congregations there is the continuing saga of wasted time and resources on things that matter very little within the scope of the kingdom of God. When Jesus quoted Deuteronomy 6:4-5, He reminded the disputants that tradition had already determined which commandment was greatest. There was no need to debate or discuss the primacy of the commandments.

B. Biblical Background

Today's lesson comes from three passages of Scripture that teach the importance of giving absolute priority to the things that matter most. The first two passages come from the Old Testament books of Leviticus and Deuteronomy, both of which are books of the Law of Moses. The book of Leviticus appears third in the canon of the Old Testament Law. Its primary concern is with ritual holiness and the practice of the Hebrew religion (see Leviticus 1-6; 16:1-34). The book contains passages that were often quoted by Jesus, such as the command to love one's neighbor (found in Leviticus 19:18).

The second passage is from the book of Deuteronomy, which means "second law." It is the fifth and final book of the Law and perhaps one of the most important among the books of law in the Old Testament. The passage comprising the lesson is often referred to as the Shema, which gets its name from the Hebrew word *shama,* which means "hear" or "give attention." The Shema is the primary affirmation of Hebrew and Jewish faith and it is recited daily in the homes and synagogues of Jewish people to this very day. Its purpose is to affirm the oneness and sovereignty of God (see Deuteronomy 6:4-9; 11:13-21; Numbers 15:37-41).

The third passage comes from the gospel of Mark and describes an encounter that Jesus had with Jewish religious leaders in the final week of His earthly ministry. During that week, a man came to Jesus and wanted to know what the most important commandment was.

II. EXPOSITION AND APPLICATION OF THE SCRIPTURE

A. Love Your Neighbor
(Leviticus 19:18)

Thou shalt not avenge, nor bear any grudge against the children of thy people, but thou shalt love thy neighbour as thyself: I am the LORD.

Leviticus 19 contains a list of various laws and commands that God gave Moses to teach Israel. These laws began with the command to be holy because the Lord was holy (see verse 1; compare Leviticus 11:44 and 1 Peter 1:13-16). There are two types of laws in the Old Testament: casuistic law and apodictic. *Casuistic* means "case by case"—these are laws

that apply to specific types of situations. An example is found in Deuteronomy 25:1-3. The second kind of law, *apodictic,* is a direct command that Israel could not violate under any circumstances. These laws usually begin with the words "Thou shalt not" or "Do not." The command in verse 18 is an apodictic law.

The command in verse 18 involves three distinct parts. First, they were not to seek revenge. The command was quite clear and did not leave room for exceptions. The key to understanding this command is found in its Old Testament theological underpinnings.

Vengeance was always reserved as a divine prerogative; therefore, because it belonged to God, humans were never given the right or authority to exercise vengeance without God's permission. God does not give us the right to justify exacting revenge upon others because they have done us wrong.

Second, they were not to even bear a grudge against any of their own people. The Hebrew word for "grudge" is *natar,* which literally means "to keep" or "maintain." Vengeance, or the need to take revenge, is always a byproduct of someone's harboring a grudge against others. The third command in the verse stands in stark contrast to the first two; they were to love their neighbors as they loved themselves. The declaration, "I am the Lord" gives weight to the command and validates its origin and importance.

B. Love the Lord Your God (Deuteronomy 6:4-9)

Hear, O Israel: The Lord our God is one Lord: And thou shalt love the Lord thy God with all thine heart, and with all thy soul, and with all thy might. And these words, which I command thee this day, shall be in thine heart: And thou shalt teach them diligently unto thy children, and shalt talk of them when thou sittest in thine house, and when thou walkest by the way, and when thou liest down, and when thou risest up. And thou shalt bind them for a sign upon thine hand, and they shall be as frontlets between thine eyes. And thou shalt write them upon the posts of thy house, and on thy gates.

The passage begins with the Hebrew word *Shama* [shaw-maw], the Hebrew imperative command "to hear." In this context, hearing is not passive; rather, it is an urgent matter that calls upon the believer to hear and listen intently with the determination to obey God.

Verse 4 makes a strong theological statement regarding the faith of Israel and reinforces its monotheistic belief in the oneness of God. "Lord," YAHWEH, is the proper name for Israel's God. Israel was reminded that the Lord is not just any God—rather, He was *their* God, the One who had been active in their existence and history from the days of the patriarchs (see Deuteronomy 5:6; 6:3; compare with Numbers 10:29). *God* (Hebrew: *Elohim* [El-o-heem]) is the word used in the Old Testament to denote the true God of Israel.

Verse 5 introduces a second command to love the Lord in three ways: with all of their hearts, all of their souls, and all of their might. *Heart* (Hebrew: *lebab*) denotes the seat of human thinking and reflection. *Soul* (Hebrew: *nephesh*; refer to the "Word Power" section) is the very essence of human personality. *Might* (Hebrew: *me'-od*) does not imply nor mean strength; rather, it is a noun that means "exceedingly or abundantly." God is to be lavished with our love.

Israel was commanded to take these commands and impress them upon their hearts, and to sow the seed of faith in the lives of their children (see Genesis 18:19; Exodus 12:26-27; Psalm 78:5-6; Proverbs 22:6; Ephesians 6:4). Israel was commanded to teach their children diligently (Hebrew: *shanan* [shaw-nan]). The word *Shanan* literally means "to sharpen" and also has in it the idea of piercing through and through. The implication is that children were not to be left alone to discover truth on their own. Rather, they were to be pierced through and through with the Word of God, sharpened against the attacks of idolatry and disobedience. The seriousness with which parents were to teach their children is intensified by the number of places and times that teaching was to take place—in the home, walking along the road, when they lie down, and even as they rose. The point is that every opportunity for one to teach his/her child was to be taken and cherished.

Verses 8-9 conclude the passage and express in figurative language the fact that the Word or the Law was to be an integral part of their lives. Writing on the hands and foreheads was symbolic, although in later years some people came to regard it literally. Within Hebrew religious culture, people would write a small portion of Scripture on a paper and put it in a box on the doorpost in what is called a *mezuzah* (a small box).

C. The Great Commandment
(Mark 12:28-34)

And one of the scribes came, and having heard them reasoning together, and perceiving that he had answered them well, asked him, Which is the first commandment of all? And Jesus answered him, The first of all the commandments is, Hear, O Israel; The Lord our God is one Lord: And thou shalt love the Lord thy God with all thy heart, and with all thy soul, and with all thy mind, and with all thy strength: this is the first commandment. And the second is like, namely this, Thou shalt love thy neighbour as thyself. There is none other commandment greater than these. And the scribe said unto him, Well, Master, thou hast said the truth: for there is one God; and there is none other but he: And to love him with all the heart, and with all the understanding, and with all the soul, and with all the strength, and to love his neighbour as himself, is more than all whole burnt offerings and sacrifices. And when Jesus saw that he answered discreetly, he said unto him, Thou art not far from the kingdom of God. And no man after that durst ask him any question.

Jesus had just finished answering questions by His critics when He was approached once more (see Mark 11:27-33; 12:13, 18).

Instead of the Pharisees and Herodians, Jesus was approached by a teacher (Greek: *grammateus* [gram-mat-yooce]) who was obviously impressed by the answer that Jesus had given to the Pharisees and Herodians. The teacher asked Jesus a legitimate question—and from its tone, it appeared to have no pretense or evil intention. "Which is the most important commandment?" Walter Wessel and Mark Strauss pointed out that later, rabbis counted 613 individual commandments and statutes of the Law, of which 365 were negative and 248 were positive.[2] Jewish rabbis often engaged in debates about which were the weightier of the statutes.

Jesus did not hesitate, quoting two passages from the Old Testament—Leviticus 19:18 and Deuteronomy 6:4-5 (see the discussion in the previous section regarding these two passages). There is one difference between the passages in Deuteronomy 6:5 and the words of Jesus. In His response, Jesus added the word *mind*, which is further reinforcement that one's love for God is to be complete. Jesus took the command a step further and pointed out that not only are we to love God, but that love should lead to love of others, especially our neighbors. The neighbor is to be loved equally as much as one loves oneself. Unlike the Jews of His day who restricted their interpretation of neighbors to fellow Jews, Jesus saw the neighbor as anyone needing help, even if they were not of the same ethnicity (see Luke 10:25-37).

In verse 32, the man gave Jesus a surprising word of commendation. The teacher was impressed with Jesus' answer and remarked that loving God and neighbor was more important and more impressive than all of the burnt offerings and sacrifices. When Jesus heard the man's response, He remarked that he was not far from the kingdom. What did Jesus mean by this statement? It probably was intended to push the teacher to abandon his old ways of legalism and become a disciple.

III. CONCLUDING REFLECTION

What happens to the spiritual life of a believer when he or she is more in love with his position, ministry, pastor, or church than he or she is with God? First, it is a sign that the individual has little understanding about what it means to be a disciple of the Lord Jesus Christ. Second, it is easy to be disappointed by human failures, congregational conflict, and setbacks in the progress or lack of progress in a ministry. Christians recognize that loving God and loving one's neighbor are hallmarks of the kingdom of God.

PRAYER

Heavenly Father, giver and sustainer of all life, grant that we will love You with all of our hearts, minds, souls, and strength. May we never be moved to retaliate against others because of the wrongs we suffer. In Jesus' name we pray. Amen.

WORD POWER

Soul (Hebrew: *nephesh* [neh'-fesh])—There are two distinct biblical understandings of the word *soul*. In the New Testament, *psyche* is the word used and it denotes the principle or essence of life. Within the Scriptures, the word *soul* appears 458 times in both the Old and New Testaments. In its original context, Genesis 2:7, the word *nephesh* denotes the totality of human life. When God created Adam, he was not given a soul; rather, he became a living soul through the in-breathing of the breath of God.

HOME DAILY BIBLE READINGS
(May 19–25, 2014)

The Greatest Commandment

MONDAY, May 19: "Love and Commandment Keeping" (Deuteronomy 7:7-16)
TUESDAY, May 20: "Serving God with Heart and Soul" (Deuteronomy 10:12-21)
WEDNESDAY, May 21: "Keeping God's Commandments Always" (Deuteronomy 11:1-7)
THURSDAY, May 22: "Relating to Your Neighbor" (Leviticus 19:11-17)
FRIDAY, May 23: "Sin against a Neighbor or God" (1 Kings 8:31-36)
SATURDAY, May 24: "They Shall Not Be Moved" (Psalm 15)
SUNDAY, May 25: "Loving God and Neighbor" (Leviticus 19:18; Deuteronomy 6:4-9; Mark 12:28-34)

End Notes

---

[1]Brian Larson and Leadership Journal, *750 Engaging Illustrations for Preachers, Teachers, and Writers* (Grand Rapids: Baker Books, 1993), 424.

[2]Walter W. Wessel and Mark L. Strauss, *Mark: The Expositors Bible Commentary, Revised Edition* (Grand Rapids: Zondervan, 2010), 906.

The People of God Set Priorities

GENERAL INTRODUCTION

This quarter has three units. The first unit is from the book of Haggai in the Hebrew Scriptures and involves a call to community through the rebuilding of the Temple. The second and third units are from the letters of 1 and 2 Corinthians in the Christian Scriptures and reflect a call to community through the believers.

Unit I, *Hope and Confidence Come from God*, has four lessons. Each lesson attempts to convey a message of the importance of community in attaining the goal of rebuilding the Temple. The lessons develop key aspects to living in a community as obedience and trust in God, living in a right relationship with God, and maintaining hope in God.

Unit II, *Living as a Community of Believers*, looks at the church of Corinth in order to learn how to build and maintain community among believers. The unit has five lessons. It lifts up the importance of unity, glorifying God, building up colleagues in ministry, dealing with situations that threaten community, and seeking the good of others.

Unit III, *Bearing One Another's Burdens*, has five lessons. The unit outlines from the book of 2 Corinthians list ways to sustain community among believers. The lessons place specific emphasis on prayer, forgiveness, love, cooperation, and sharing.

OBEY THE LORD

Faith Pathway/Faith Journey Topic: Do What Is Required

Devotional Reading: Luke 19:41-48
Print Passage: Haggai 1:1-11

Background Scripture: Haggai 1:1-11
Key Verses: Haggai 1:3-4

Haggai 1:1-11—KJV

IN THE second year of Darius the king, in the sixth month, in the first day of the month, came the word of the LORD by Haggai the prophet unto Zerubbabel the son of Shealtiel, governor of Judah, and to Joshua the son of Josedech, the high priest, saying,

2 Thus speaketh the LORD of hosts, saying, This people say, The time is not come, the time that the LORD's house should be built.

3 Then came the word of the LORD by Haggai the prophet, saying,

4 Is it time for you, O ye, to dwell in your cieled houses, and this house lie waste?

5 Now therefore thus saith the LORD of hosts; Consider your ways.

6 Ye have sown much, and bring in little; ye eat, but ye have not enough; ye drink, but ye are not filled with drink; ye clothe you, but there is none warm; and he that earneth wages earneth wages to put it into a bag with holes.

7 Thus saith the LORD of hosts; Consider your ways.

8 Go up to the mountain, and bring wood, and build the house; and I will take pleasure in it, and I will be glorified, saith the LORD.

9 Ye looked for much, and, lo, it came to little; and when ye brought it home, I did blow upon it. Why? saith the LORD of hosts. Because of mine house that is waste, and ye run every man unto his own house.

10 Therefore the heaven over you is stayed from dew, and the earth is stayed from her fruit.

11 And I called for a drought upon the land, and upon the mountains, and upon the corn, and upon the new wine, and upon the oil, and upon that which the ground bringeth forth, and upon men, and upon cattle, and upon all the labour of the hands.

Haggai 1:1-11—NIV

IN THE second year of King Darius, on the first day of the sixth month, the word of the LORD came through the prophet Haggai to Zerubbabel son of Shealtiel, governor of Judah, and to Joshua son of Jehozadak, the high priest:

2 This is what the LORD Almighty says: "These people say, 'The time has not yet come for the LORD's house to be built.'"

3 Then the word of the LORD came through the prophet Haggai:

4 "Is it a time for you yourselves to be living in your paneled houses, while this house remains a ruin?"

5 Now this is what the LORD Almighty says: "Give careful thought to your ways.

6 You have planted much, but have harvested little. You eat, but never have enough. You drink, but never have your fill. You put on clothes, but are not warm. You earn wages, only to put them in a purse with holes in it."

7 This is what the LORD Almighty says: "Give careful thought to your ways.

8 Go up into the mountains and bring down timber and build the house, so that I may take pleasure in it and be honored," says the LORD.

9 "You expected much, but see, it turned out to be little. What you brought home, I blew away. Why?" declares the LORD Almighty. "Because of my house, which remains a ruin, while each of you is busy with his own house.

10 Therefore, because of you the heavens have withheld their dew and the earth its crops.

11 I called for a drought on the fields and the mountains, on the grain, the new wine, the oil and whatever the ground produces, on men and cattle, and on the labor of your hands."

TOPICAL OUTLINE OF THE LESSON

I. Introduction
A. What Is of Priority?
B. Biblical Background

II. Exposition and Application of the Scripture
A. The Recipients of the Prophecy (Haggai 1:1)
B. The Accusation of Procrastination (Haggai 1:2-7)
C. The Explanation of the People's Impoverishment (Haggai 1:8-11)

III. Concluding Reflection

LESSON OBJECTIVES

Upon completion of the lesson, the students will be able to do the following:

1. Reveal why God commanded Haggai to encourage the Israelite community to rebuild the Temple;

2. Understand the connection between the neglect of God's house and the poor results of the Israelite community's selfish efforts; and,

3. Explore ways to attend to God's business before personal wants and needs, and then link those with specific actions that adults can take.

POINTS TO BE EMPHASIZED

ADULT/YOUTH

Adult Topic: Do What Is Required
Youth Topic: From Start to Almost Finish
Adult Key Verses: Haggai 1:3-4
Youth Key Verse: Haggai 1:8
Print Passage: Haggai 1:1-11

—Zerubbabel was a direct Davidic descendant and the last to be governor in the postexilic period.
—Haggai spoke directly to the governor, the high priest, and the people.
—The Jews began to use excuses to postpone the rebuilding and Haggai was called to remind them of their goal.
—The Jews were preoccupied with building their own houses and God was not pleased with them.
—God's judgment of them left them suffering in the poverty of a drought.
—They were not aware of the consequences of disobeying God.

CHILDREN

Children Topic: We Will Do It Together!
Key Verse: Haggai 1:14
Print Passage: Haggai 1:1-4, 8-14

—Through Haggai, God made Zerubbabel and Joshua aware of the remnants' lack of interest in rebuilding the Temple.
—The remnant living in Judah experienced natural disasters, physical hardships, and spiritual restlessness.
—God's house was in ruins while the people lived in luxury.
—God gave specific instructions for gathering the supplies needed to rebuild the Temple.
—God promised to withhold blessings from the people because their selfishness dishonored and displeased Him.
—After the remnant and their leaders agreed to obey God, their spirits were stirred to complete the work assigned to them.

I. INTRODUCTION
A. What Is of Priority?

The First Church of Raymondville was growing by leaps and bounds. The new young pastor had come into a congregation that had reached a plateau, but within a few months, he had ignited a fresh burst of energy and excitement. Young families were filling the pews; young adults were excited because now they had a peer who was their pastor. Many of the seniors in the congregation reminisced about what First Church was like in their childhood. The weekly offerings had swelled and nearly doubled, and everything was going extremely well. New ministries were being started and the congregation was about to send two people on their first short-term mission trip to Kenya. Everyone in town was buzzing about the new pastor and his visionary leadership. However, there was one glaring problem: the church facility was very old and very outdated. The building had been built in 1946, and very few improvements had been made to the church building since it was constructed. Pastor Jones knew that if the congregation was going to continue to grow, they would need a new facility. After much reflection, study, and prayer, Pastor Jones developed a long-range plan that included building a new church facility—which also included relocating the church to a prime piece of real estate that would further fuel the church's long-term growth prospects. When he presented his plan to the senior leaders of the congregation, however, the plan was voted down. Many of the most influential leaders felt that there was no need to invest millions of dollars in a building when things were just fine. Pastor Jones tried to convince the leaders, but to no avail. The leaders simply did not see the project as a priority for the congregation. After several more months of intense pressure and hostility from many of the senior leaders, he resigned and moved to another city.

The story of Pastor Jones and First Church is not new. Sometimes, personal needs and desires prevent Christians from giving priority to the things that are most important in their lives. How can Christians identify and give priority to what is important? God spoke through Haggai, saying that the people's first priority should be rebuilding God's house and not their own houses. Today's lesson will teach us the importance of following leaders who are led by God. We will learn why it is important to give attention to the house of God.

B. Biblical Background

The prophetic writings of Haggai are listed among the twelve Minor Prophets. The only reason that these books are called "minor" is because of the length of each book. Each of the Minor Prophets was given a major responsibility when it came to delivering their respective messages. One of the most important prophets of the Old Testament era was a man named Haggai. The prophetic ministry of Haggai took place during the period of Hebrew history that is referred to as the Restoration. This period detailed the events that took place when the Jews returned from captivity in Babylon in 539/538 BC.

In 538 BC, King Cyrus of Persia released all the captive peoples whom the Babylonians had taken into captivity (see 2 Kings 24-25; 2 Chronicles 36:22). The release of the people of Judea from captivity began a new era in Israel's history known as the "postexilic period." The actual number of people who returned to Judea was 42,360, along with another 7,337 male and female servants (see Ezra 2:64-65). Within two years of returning to Jerusalem, they began the arduous process of rebuilding the Temple that had been destroyed by the army of King Nebuchadnezzar. It was not long before opposition to the work arose and the entire project was stopped and lay dormant for nearly sixteen years (see Ezra 3:8–5:1). According to Ezra 4:4, the people of the land (those living in Judea at the time) discouraged the people of God and they stopped work on the rebuilding project.

During this lull between the start of construction and the actual completion, the people showed very little interest in finishing the work. The Temple lay dormant for years until 520 BC, when God used two prophets, Haggai and Zechariah, to inspire and encourage the people to rise up and continue with the reconstruction project. The preaching ministry of Haggai lasted for about three and one half months (see Haggai 1:1; 2:1, 20). And although it was a brief period, he was instrumental in helping to spur the people to rebuild the Temple—which stood for nearly six hundred years until it was destroyed by the Romans in AD 70.

This is the only place in the Old Testament where we find anyone with the name *Haggai*. It comes from a Hebrew word that means "feast" or "festival." There is virtually no information available about the personal life of Haggai. We have no information about his family, or whether he was married, or had children; nor do we have any idea of his age at the time of his preaching ministry. Scholars have never uncovered any information that helps to answer any questions about the personal life of one of the most important prophets in the postexilic period. Although shrouded in mystery, Haggai remains one of the most relevant prophets in the Scriptures.

II. EXPOSITION AND APPLICATION OF THE SCRIPTURE

A. The Recipients of the Prophecy (Haggai 1:1)

IN THE second year of Darius the king, in the sixth month, in the first day of the month, came the word of the Lord by Haggai the prophet unto Zerubbabel the son of Shealtiel, governor of Judah, and to Joshua the son of Josedech, the high priest, saying.

Haggai began his preaching ministry in 520 BC, during the second year of Darius Hystapses's rule over the Persian Empire. Darius came to the throne in 522 BC and ruled until 486 BC. The sixth month would have been Elul, and would have coincided with the months of August–September. According to Numbers 10:10, the people were to gather for a celebration of the New Moon, which was the first day of each month (see also Numbers 28:11; Psalm 83:3; Isaiah 1:13-14; Hosea 2:11). Haggai was a contemporary of the prophet Zechariah, who began his preaching in the eighth month of the second year of Darius (see Zechariah 1:1 and also chapters 1–8). Both prophets are mentioned together in the book of Ezra and are given credit for helping to inspire the leaders and people to complete the rebuilding of the Temple in Jerusalem (see Ezra 5:1; 6:14).

The word that God sent to the people came first to the prophet Haggai and was directed to Zerubbabel, the son of Shealtiel, the appointed governor of Judah. His name meant "seed of Babylon," indicating that he had been born in Babylon and was among the first group of returnees from the captivity (see Ezra 2:2; 3:2-3). He was among the group that laid the foundation for the rebuilding of the second Temple in 536 BC (see Ezra 3:8-13). The other key leader was a man named Joshua, who was the high priest (see Ezra 2:2; the name may appear as Jeshua). He was from the priestly line of Zadok. His father, Jehozadak, was the high priest at the time of the deportation to Babylon (see 1 Chronicles 6:15).

Haggai is simply referred to as the prophet, which indicated that he was very well known in the area. The designation of him as the prophet also pointed to the high regard and respect he had among the people.

B. The Accusation of Procrastination (Haggai 1:2-7)

Thus speaketh the Lord of hosts, saying, This people say, The time is not come, the time that the Lord's house should be built. Then came the word of the Lord by Haggai the prophet, saying, Is it time for you, O ye, to dwell in your cieled houses, and this house lie waste? Now therefore thus saith the Lord of hosts; Consider your ways. Ye have sown much, and bring in little; ye eat, but ye have not enough; ye drink, but ye are not filled with drink; ye clothe you, but there is none warm; and he that earneth wages earneth wages to put it into a bag with holes. Thus saith the Lord of hosts; Consider your ways.

The word that was sent to the people was a very specific word. The phrase "Lord of hosts" refers to the armies of God and is a name that is frequently found in the Old Testament (see Exodus 12:41; 1 Samuel 1:11; 4:4; 15:2; 17:45; 1 Kings 18:15). Haggai spoke the word of the Lord to this people who declared that now was not "the time for the house of the Lord to be rebuilt" (Haggai 1:2). A spirit of procrastination and indifference had gripped the hearts of the people. Instead of working to complete the rebuilding of the Temple, they found excuses for their failures.

In this verse, the people of Judah are referred to as "This people." They were not referred to as the Lord's people nor as "My people"—just "this people." The use of this reference can mean that the people had been rejected by God (see Isaiah 6:9-10; Hosea 1:9). If this were not the time, then when would it be appropriate for the people to undertake the most important construction project in their history? No explanation was given for why the people felt the time had not come to rebuild the Temple. Haggai's purpose was twofold: first, he wanted to encourage the leaders to rise up and lead the effort to rebuild the Temple; second, he wanted to remind the people that they would never be blessed if they put God second in their lives.

The second part of Haggai's first oracle was directed to the people of Judah. The same word that had come to the leaders was directed to the people. The people were more concerned about their personal needs than the rebuilding of the Temple (see Philippians 2:21; compare to 2 Samuel 7:2). Haggai raised a question:

"Is it time for you to live in your well-built and finely decorated homes while the Lord's house sits in ruins?" (see verse 4). There is a direct comparison between the houses of the people—which have been given priority—and "this house," the Lord's house, which lay in ruins. It is difficult for someone living in the twenty-first century to imagine what Haggai was describing. The Temple built by King Solomon was not a small place—it was spacious, large, and visible from all directions as one headed up toward Jerusalem. When the Babylonians destroyed the Temple, burning it to the ground, what were left were piles of rubble, huge stones, and burned-out timber.

In verse 5, there is the call to "Consider your ways." The reason why the Lord's house was in ruins was because the people had not given serious consideration to its care. In this instance, the word *consider* reinforces the imperative command to put this matter in its proper place. The command is very clear: "Do not neglect to give the Lord's house the importance it deserves." The word *ways* is from the Hebrew word *Derek*, and it can refer to moral behavior, or, when used figuratively, it refers to "the course of life." Haggai wanted the people to look at their lives and realize that everything that had gone wrong was due to one single cause—their neglect of the house of the Lord.

Verse 6 identifies the heart of Judah's problem: they were not able to get ahead or make progress (see Joshua 1:9-10; compare it with Deuteronomy 28:1-14, especially verse 38). Although they were blessed with all of the necessities of life—food, shelter, clothing, and water—something was still missing. J. Alec Motyer, in his work, *The Minor Prophets: An Exegetical and Expository Commentary*, said, "What the prophet exposes here is not

hardship but non-fulfillment. They had seed to sow, food to eat, wine to drink, clothes to wear, gainful employment—but no true satisfaction. Their problem was not a lack of goods but of good."[1] The people were not suffering destitution. They had more than enough to meet their needs and the needs of the Lord's house. Their dilemma was expressed in the series of dramatic statements in verse 6. They had planted a lot of seeds, but the harvest was skimpy. There was never enough food to be full and satisfied—just enough to keep from starving. Ironically, they could not even get drunk, because there was not enough wine to satisfy that desire. Their clothes were never sufficient for the weather conditions. In the final analysis, the people were like so many today, who have earned money only to see it go out to pay creditors and other bills. Their pockets had holes. Just as fast as it came in, it dripped out. In verse 7, they were again called upon to consider their ways and give attention to the thing that was most important—the rebuilding of the Lord's house.

C. The Explanation of the People's Impoverishment (Haggai 1:8-11)

Go up to the mountain, and bring wood, and build the house; and I will take pleasure in it, and I will be glorified, saith the Lord. Ye looked for much, and, lo, it came to little; and when ye brought it home, I did blow upon it. Why? saith the Lord of hosts. Because of mine house that is waste, and ye run every man unto his own house. Therefore the heaven over you is stayed from dew, and the earth is stayed from her fruit. And I called for a drought upon the land, and upon the mountains, and upon the corn, and upon the new wine, and upon the oil, and upon that which the ground bringeth forth, and upon men, and upon cattle, and upon all the labour of the hands.

Given the dire economic situation of the people of Judah, it could hardly be expected that they would be in a position to actually rebuild the house of the Lord (see 2 Corinthians 8:1-5 for an example of people who were poor financially, but were generous in their support of the kingdom's work). Verse 8 begins with a series of three imperative commands: "Go up to the mountains," "bring wood," and "rebuild the temple." The reason for the commands are expressed in the words, "that I may be pleased with it and be glorified." It had been many years since real worship had taken place on Mount Zion. The rebuilding of the Temple would bring renewal and revival of the Temple sacrifices and the great festival celebrations that characterized Judah's worship. The nations surrounding Judah would know that there was a God in Israel. The Lord understood the plight and condition of the people and what they were facing. His concern centered in the attitude of their not even trying to rebuild the Temple.

The mountains more than likely refer to the mountains of Lebanon. It is highly unlikely that there would have been sufficient lumber in the mountains surrounding Jerusalem for such an undertaking. However, there was plenty of limestone available, given its abundance in that region. Their expectations were very high, but what was produced was very disappointing. No sooner had they brought the produce of their labors home that they saw it blown away. There is the image of grain that is laid on a mat or blanket to be winnowed, only to see it blown away by a strong wind. There was a simple reason for why things were going terribly wrong in the lives of the people of Judah. All they needed to do was to look at Mount Zion, which had stood idle for sixteen years. No work on the Temple had been done since the laying of the foundation. The Lord's house lay in total desolation, while the people sought refuge in their own homes. The absence of the Temple was not just the absence of a physical structure—it was the absence of the very symbol of God's presence in their midst as well (see 1 Kings 8:12-19; 1 Chronicles 29:1; 2 Chronicles 7:1-3).

It was because of the attitude of indifference of the people of Judah—and their failure to respond to the gracious opportunity to rebuild the Temple—that they were experiencing such hardship. Is it reasonable to expect that men and women would want to live in God's world and not give Him His due? Yet, it is often the case that men and women, some being born-again believers, will give only token allegiance to the house of the Lord.

Rain in that part of the world is vital and the lack of any measurable rain can easily lead to drought, crop failure, and major economic collapse. Haggai again spoke for God and declared that God had called for the land to suffer a drought. He literally summoned the sun to bring its brightness to bear and the clouds to shut themselves up in the Mediterranean Sea and not come ashore. The drought affected the mountain, grain, the new wine, the oil, and everything that the ground produced. Not only did the drought extend to the land, but even the labor of their hands. Nothing would work, nothing would change, and nothing would be different until the people took seriously the Word of God to rebuild the Temple on Mount Zion.

III. CONCLUDING REFLECTION

What should be the primary priority of the people of God? The passage makes several key points that believers in every age should and must consider. The first priority of the people of God is to love the Lord with the total heart, mind, and spirit (see Mark 12:28). Loving God means loving the people and the things that God loves. How does one love God in an age driven by self-centeredness, consumerism, and the quest for personal satisfaction? Believers love God by giving themselves unselfishly to the work of ministry and missions. Second, we are challenged to nurture our relationship to God, even in the midst of difficult circumstances. Economic hardship can place an enormous burden on tapped-out finances. Yet, we are reminded that God is the giver of every good and perfect gift. Believers are encouraged to prioritize their support for the work of the kingdom. Consider this week how you allocate your time and resources for kingdom work.

PRAYER

Heavenly Father, may we learn how to prioritize the things that matter most in Your kingdom. May the Holy Spirit give us the will and determination to apply the lessons we have learned today. In Jesus' name we pray. Amen.

WORD POWER

Consider (Hebrew: *sumw* [soom])—literally means "to place, to put something somewhere." In this passage, the word is written in the imperative mood, which means that the people were to give the matters presented to them urgent attention.

Paneled (Hebrew: *sapun*)—refers to a type of material used in construction of either the roof of a house or its interior. Haggai may have been referring to the use of cedar and other high-quality materials that were used to build private homes. The message shows the stark contrast between the efforts that were made to build and beautify personal residences versus rebuilding the Temple.

HOME DAILY BIBLE READINGS
(May 26—June 1, 2014)

Obey the Lord

MONDAY, May 26: "A House of Prayer" (Luke 19:41-48)

TUESDAY, May 27: "The Fall of Jerusalem" (Jeremiah 52:1-9)

WEDNESDAY, May 28: "The Temple Destroyed" (Jeremiah 52:10-14)

THURSDAY, May 29: "Given into Enemy Hands" (2 Chronicles 36:15-21)

FRIDAY, May 30: "Carried Away into Captivity" (2 Kings 24:8-17)

SATURDAY, May 31: "Rebuild God's House" (Ezra 1:1-8)

SUNDAY, June 1: "God's House Lies in Ruins" (Haggai 1:1-11)

End Note

[1]J. Alec Motyer, *Haggai: The Minor Prophets*, Thomas Edward McComiskey, ed. (Grand Rapids: Baker Book House, 1998), 976-977.

UNIT I: Hope and Confidence Come from God
CHILDREN'S UNIT: Building a Community of Believers
SUMMER QUARTER

LESSON 2   June 8, 2014

TRUST GOD'S PROMISES

FAITH PATHWAY/FAITH JOURNEY TOPIC: Build for the Future

DEVOTIONAL READING: Psalm 27:7-14
PRINT PASSAGE: Haggai 1:12; 2:1-9

BACKGROUND SCRIPTURE: Haggai 1:12–2:9
KEY VERSE: Haggai 2:9

Haggai 1:12; 2:1-9—KJV

12 Then Zerubbabel the son of Shealtiel, and Joshua the son of Josedech, the high priest, with all the remnant of the people, obeyed the voice of the LORD their God, and the words of Haggai the prophet, as the LORD their God had sent him, and the people did fear before the LORD.

.....

IN THE seventh month, in the one and twentieth day of the month, came the word of the LORD by the prophet Haggai, saying,

2 Speak now to Zerubbabel the son of Shealtiel, governor of Judah, and to Joshua the son of Josedech, the high priest, and to the residue of the people, saying,

3 Who is left among you that saw this house in her first glory? and how do ye see it now? is it not in your eyes in comparison of it as nothing?

4 Yet now be strong, O Zerubbabel, saith the LORD; and be strong, O Joshua, son of Josedech, the high priest; and be strong, all ye people of the land, saith the LORD, and work: for I am with you, saith the LORD of hosts:

5 According to the word that I covenanted with you when ye came out of Egypt, so my spirit remaineth among you: fear ye not.

6 For thus saith the LORD of hosts; Yet once, it is a little while, and I will shake the heavens, and the earth, and the sea, and the dry land;

7 And I will shake all nations, and the desire of all nations shall come: and I will fill this house with glory, saith the LORD of hosts.

8 The silver is mine, and the gold is mine, saith the LORD of hosts.

9 The glory of this latter house shall be greater than of

Haggai 1:12; 2:1-9—NIV

12 Then Zerubbabel son of Shealtiel, Joshua son of Jehozadak, the high priest, and the whole remnant of the people obeyed the voice of the LORD their God and the message of the prophet Haggai, because the LORD their God had sent him. And the people feared the LORD.

.....

ON THE twenty-first day of the seventh month, the word of the LORD came through the prophet Haggai:

2 "Speak to Zerubbabel son of Shealtiel, governor of Judah, to Joshua son of Jehozadak, the high priest, and to the remnant of the people. Ask them,

3 'Who of you is left who saw this house in its former glory? How does it look to you now? Does it not seem to you like nothing?

4 But now be strong, O Zerubbabel,' declares the LORD. 'Be strong, O Joshua son of Jehozadak, the high priest. Be strong, all you people of the land,' declares the LORD, 'and work. For I am with you,' declares the LORD Almighty.

5 'This is what I covenanted with you when you came out of Egypt. And my Spirit remains among you. Do not fear.'

6 This is what the LORD Almighty says: 'In a little while I will once more shake the heavens and the earth, the sea and the dry land.

7 I will shake all nations, and the desired of all nations will come, and I will fill this house with glory,' says the LORD Almighty.

8 'The silver is mine and the gold is mine,' declares the LORD Almighty.

9 'The glory of this present house will be greater than the glory of the former house,' says the LORD

the former, saith the LORD of hosts: and in this place will I give peace, saith the LORD of hosts.

Almighty. 'And in this place I will grant peace,' declares the LORD Almighty."

TOPICAL OUTLINE OF THE LESSON

I. Introduction
   A. The Challenge of Building
   B. Biblical Background

II. Exposition and Application of the Scripture
   A. They Obeyed the Lord (Haggai 1:12)
   B. The Second Message of the Prophet (Haggai 2:1-2)
   C. Who Remembers the First Temple? (Haggai 2:3-5)
   D. The Best Is Yet to Come (Haggai 2:6-9)

III. Concluding Reflection

LESSON OBJECTIVES

Upon completion of the lesson, the students will be able to do the following:

1. Review what God promised the Israelites when they obeyed God's command to rebuild the Temple;
2. Believe that God pledges assistance and prosperity to His response to obedience; and,
3. Identify ways that God asks for the class's obedience and to demonstrate that obedience.

POINTS TO BE EMPHASIZED

ADULT/YOUTH

Adult Topic: Build for the Future
Youth Topic: Promise Made; Promise Kept
Adult Key Verse: Haggai 2:9
Youth Key Verse: Haggai 1:13
Print Passage: Haggai 1:12; 2:1-9

—The former exiles did not have the resources to rebuild the Temple to the grandeur of Solomon's building.
—Haggai offered a broader perspective on why the second Temple eventually would be greater than the first.
—God's people, called the remnant, responded to Haggai's message.
—Zerubbabel and Joshua were chosen as the new leaders to continue rebuilding the Temple.
—God promised to be with the remnant and bless them with joy as they rebuilt the Temple.
—God promised that the future glory of the Temple would be greater than the former glory.

CHILDREN

Children Topic: Working Together
Key Verse: Haggai 2:4b
Print Passage: Ezra 6:13-15; Haggai 2:1-9

—Haggai, as God's messenger, encouraged Zerubbabel, Joshua, and the remnant of the people to obey God's command to rebuild the Temple.
—God told Haggai to remind the people of God's past interventions on their behalf.
—Through Haggai, God urged the people to be obedient in building the Temple, which was central to their worship.
—God told Haggai to assure the people that the Temple and their lives would be greatly enriched if the Temple was rebuilt.

I. INTRODUCTION
A. The Challenge of Building

Church construction and renovation projects are extremely difficult undertakings. There are several reasons why church construction projects are so challenging. First, the majority of church leaders may have never been involved in a multimillion-dollar church construction project and may lack the management skills that are vital to the success of the project. Second, construction projects can take years to finish and the longer they drag on, the less enthusiasm members may have for completing the project. Third, church construction projects come with enormous costs, many of which may not be anticipated by church building committees. Fourth, the internal politics of a congregation can doom a simple project before it has a chance to get off the ground. Whether some or all of these forces were in play during the time of the rebuilding of the Temple is not known. What is known is that the people of Judah began to rebuild but soon became discouraged by the people of the land (see Ezra 4:4).

B. Biblical Background

According to the *Quest Study Bible*, eighteen years before Haggai's prophecy, the Persian king Cyrus allowed thousands of Jews to return from Babylon to Judah (538 BC). Even though the Jews had started rebuilding the Temple sixteen years earlier, the opposition of their neighbors had demoralized them and caused them to abandon the plans for rebuilding. The book of Haggai includes messages that were directed specifically to Zerubbabel, who was the governor of Judah at that time, and to Joshua, the high priest. The fact that they were the civil and religious leaders placed them in the position of representing the people who had returned from the exile. What was the main thrust of Haggai's message? Haggai wanted the people to recognize that they had deprived themselves of God's blessings by failing to complete the rebuilding process on the Temple.

II. EXPOSITION AND APPLICATION OF THE SCRIPTURE

A. They Obeyed the Lord
(Haggai 1:12)

Then Zerubbabel the son of Shealtiel, and Joshua the son of Josedech, the high priest, with all the remnant of the people, obeyed the voice of the LORD their God, and the words of Haggai the prophet, as the LORD their God had sent him, and the people did fear before the LORD.

The preaching of Haggai had a clear and immediate impact on the leaders and the people. Within a matter of weeks, the attitudes of the leaders and the people changed. Two results were clearly visible: first, the obedience of the leaders and people; and second, their reverence for God. Central to being blessed by the Lord God is the necessity to hear God with the intention of obeying what we have heard. The word *Then* introduces the outcome of Haggai's preaching to Zerubbabel,

Joshua, and the people, who are referred to in this section as "the remnant of the people." The word *remnant* (Hebrew: *she'eriyth* [sheh–ay–reeth]) can mean one of three things: the rest, descendants, or residue. In this instance, it refers to the people who had come out of Babylon, including Zerubbabel and Joshua. We must remember that not all of the people of Jerusalem were deported to Babylon in 587 BC (see 2 Kings 24:14). It is possible that there were two classes of people living in Jerusalem during the Restoration: the descendants of the people who remained and were not carried to Babylon, and the returnees.

In the earlier verses the people are called "this people," which indicated that they were not in relationship with God. A change of heart produced a change in their status with the Lord God; they were then referred to as "the remnant." Note that the three major segments of the Judean community responded to the preaching of the prophet: civil leaders, religious leaders, and the people.

The second part of the verse points out why their status changed—they obeyed the voice of the Lord their God and the words of Haggai the prophet. Many of the prophets did not have the benefit of seeing their preaching so readily accepted and followed. Haggai's preaching made an immediate impact. Many men and women of God have labored untiringly for years with no visible results from their work. The people obeyed. The word *Obeyed* (Hebrew: *shama* [shaw–mah]) means "to hear—specifically to hear with the intention of acting upon what has been heard or received."

B. The Second Message of the Prophet (Haggai 2:1-2)

IN THE seventh month, in the one and twentieth day of the month, came the word of the LORD by the prophet Haggai, saying, Speak now to Zerubbabel the son of Shealtiel, governor of Judah, and to Joshua the son of Josedech, the high priest, and to the residue of the people, saying.

Verse 1 of the above passage of Scripture provides a definitive time at which the word of the Lord came through the prophet Haggai. The writer was very specific in providing the details of when and to whom the prophet delivered the word of the Lord. We are told that the word of the Lord came through the prophet Haggai on the twenty-first day of the seventh month. This would work out to be October 17, 520 BC. Bible scholars suggest that Haggai's messages were given specific dates in order to provide them with an official aura.

Haggai was told by the Lord to "speak now to Zerubbabel the son of Shealtiel, governor of Judah, to Joshua the son of Jehozadak (NIV), Josedech (KJV), the high priest, and to the residue of the people. In essence, no one was to be left out from hearing the word of the Lord.

The reason for this direct word from the Lord is that several weeks had passed since the people began to go up and work on the Temple. We are not told anything about the progress of the work or anything about the identity of the primary workers. But it appears from the context that things were not going as well as they had perhaps intended. Haggai was commanded to speak a word that was needed just for that moment. God will always send the right word in due season.

C. Who Remembers the First Temple? (Haggai 2:3-5)

Who is left among you that saw this house in her first glory? and how do ye see it now? is it not in your eyes in comparison of it as nothing? Yet now be strong, O

Zerubbabel, saith the Lord; and be strong, O Joshua, son of Josedech, the high priest; and be strong, all ye people of the land, saith the Lord, and work: for I am with you, saith the Lord of hosts: According to the word that I covenanted with you when ye came out of Egypt, so my spirit remaineth among you: fear ye not.

The contents of the passage seem to suggest that a spirit of depression or despondency had set in when the people saw what was coming up from the ground. Verse 3 contains three rhetorical questions. The first question asks who remembered what the first Temple looked like. It had been nearly seventy years since the first Temple had been destroyed, and those who did remember were probably in their late seventies or eighties and above.[1] There is no way of knowing how many people were present who had lived through the horror of seeing the Temple destroyed, along with the precious artifacts that symbolized Israel's faith in God being stolen while they helplessly watched (see 2 Kings 24:13).

The second question asked how they viewed the current Temple, which was under construction. Evidently, the current Temple was nothing like the first. While there were those who focused on the past glory of the Temple, there were others who failed to remember that the Temple was not for the glory of man but for the Lord (see 1 Chronicles 29:1). The third question drew a comparison between the first Temple and the second one, which was under construction. Obviously there could be no comparisons between the first Temple and the one under construction. David had assembled the best craftsmen and set aside a vast personal fortune to pay for the finest materials (see 1 Chronicles 28:9-19; 29:2-5).

In verses 4-5, there is a reinforcement of the earlier promise of God's presence with them (see Haggai 1:13). The message of the Lord through Haggai was for the leaders and the people to take courage. God has often sent messengers to encourage His people to be strong in the face of difficult circumstances (see Joshua 1:6; Zechariah 8:9; Ephesians 6:10). The message exhorted the people to be strong and work, because the Lord was with them. His very presence was a genuine guarantee that they would succeed. God's presence makes us stronger and often is the source of our favor with people (see Genesis 39:2, 4, 21, 23; 2 Samuel 5:10; 1 Chronicles 28:20).

The second part of the message recalls the period of the Exodus when the Lord brought the children of Israel out of slavery with a high and mighty hand. The promise mentioned in verse 5a is found in Exodus 19:4-6, where God promised to keep Israel as a special possession and bless them if they would obey His voice (see also Exodus 29:45-46; 33:12, 14; 34:8-10). The prophet assured the leaders and the people that God had never deserted them nor left them. His Spirit was abiding in their midst and therefore there was no need to fear.

D. The Best Is Yet to Come (Haggai 2:6-9)

For thus saith the Lord of hosts; Yet once, it is a little while, and I will shake the heavens, and the earth, and the sea, and the dry land; And I will shake all nations, and the desire of all nations shall come: and I will fill this house with glory, saith the Lord of hosts. The silver is mine, and the gold is mine, saith the Lord of hosts. The glory of this latter house shall be greater than of the former, saith the Lord of hosts: and in this place will I give peace, saith the Lord of hosts.

The word *For* looks forward to something

cataclysmic that the Lord is about to do. It also reinforces the reason why Zerubbabel, Joshua, and the remnant of the people were not to be afraid. What was about to happen was specified as an event that was similar to things in the past. "Once more in a little while" a cataclysmic event was about to unfold, because the emphasis in the verses was on what the Lord was about to do: "shake the heavens, and the earth" "and the sea and the dry land" (verse 6). What does the use of these two phrases mean? Old Testament scholars refer to them as "merisms," which was a literary device used in either prophecy or biblical poetry to mention "extremes of some category in order to portray it as a totality."[2] The declaration that God was going to shake the heavens and the Earth, along with the sea and dry land, means that nothing and no place would be spared or overlooked. Shaking is not understood as a destructive force; rather, it is language expressing God's coming in the fullness of His glory and divinity to do something cosmic and worldwide.[3] The coming of Jesus Christ into the world is an example of God's shaking the heavens and the Earth. His presence in the world changed the course of human history.

In verse 7, the nations would also feel the thunderous power of God. The term "nations" refers to the surrounding nations and those in far-off places. Unlike the preaching of Amos—where the nations were judged—here they became participants in the large plan of God's restoration of His people. They would all participate in the rebuilding of the Temple by sharing their wealth (Hebrew: hemdat). This prophecy was fulfilled in the decree of Darius I that the treasury of Persia would provide the financial resources to assist in the rebuilding of the Temple in Jerusalem (see Ezra 6:8-12).

Verse 8 states that all of the silver and gold is God's. God owns the cattle upon a thousand hills and because He is the Creator of the heavens and Earth, He is also the owner of the silver and gold. Hans Walter Wolff observed, "For since Yahweh is the owner of everything that is of value, he has the power to change present conditions completely."[4]

The word *glory* is used twice in the passage (verses 7, 9) to denote the presence, provision, and protection of God. The house of the Lord was glorious or impressive not because of how it looked, but because it was the dwelling place of the Lord's Spirit. It was His presence that made the place glorious.

Verse 9 states that the latter glory will be greater than the former glory. Is this present or future glory? Is this physical or spiritual glory? Present ruins and desolation were not an indication of what the Lord could do or was about to do. God is the One who makes all things new and who does new things that are able to transform even the deserts into streams of rivers (see Isaiah 43:18-21; compare also 2 Corinthians 5:17). The message ends with the promise of peace (Hebrew: *shalom*). The word *Shalom* has in it the idea of completeness, welfare, health, prosperity, and tranquility. The presence of "shalom" not only guaranteed peace in the land, but it also produces prosperity and the environment where the people of God could experience increase.

III. CONCLUDING REFLECTION

One of the emotions addressed by Haggai was the fear that the leaders and people may have had about failing in their efforts to rebuild the Temple. Their fear may have sprung from the perspective that their work would be small and puny in comparison to the Temple built by Solomon. Fear can destroy motivation and determination. God raised up a man to speak to the situation and to the hearts and minds of His people. They must not grow weary in doing the work. Although the second Temple did not match the earlier Temple, it was God who would nonetheless be glorified.

PRAYER

Heavenly Father, may we never lose hope when we find ourselves facing delays and disappointments with the assignments You give us. Grant that our hearts will remain fixed on You. In Jesus' name we pray. Amen.

WORD POWER

Courage (Hebrew: *chazaq* [khaw–zak])—*Chazaq* literally means "to become hardened, make strong, be firm, resolute, or grow rigid."

Glory (Hebrew: *kabod*)—literally means "weighty" or "heaviness," from which we get the connotation of honor or glory. In this instance, *kabod* is figurative language indicating that which is noteworthy or impressive.[5]

HOME DAILY BIBLE READINGS
(June 2-8, 2014)

Trust God's Promises

MONDAY, June 2: "My Spirit Seeks You" (Isaiah 26:1-13)

TUESDAY, June 3: "The Blessings of Obedience" (Leviticus 26:3-13)

WEDNESDAY, June 4: "The Consequences of Disobedience" (Leviticus 26:14-26)

THURSDAY, June 5: "The Fear of the Lord" (Deuteronomy 6:17-25)

FRIDAY, June 6: "I Am with You" (Isaiah 41:1-10)

SATURDAY, June 7: "Take Courage!" (Psalm 27:7-14)

SUNDAY, June 8: "Obeying the Voice of God" (Haggai 1:12–2:9)

End Notes

[1] J. Alec Motyer, *The Minor Prophets: An Exegetical and Expository Commentary, Vol. 3 Haggai* (Grand Rapids: Baker Book House, 1998), 987.

[2] William W. Klein, Craig L. Blomberg, and Robert L. Hubbard Jr., *Introduction to Biblical Interpretation: Revised and Updated* (Nashville: Thomas Nelson, Inc., 2004), 302.

[3] Motyer, 990.

[4] Hans Walter Wolff, *Haggai* (Minneapolis: Augsburg Publishing House, 1988), 82.

[5] *Theological Wordbook of the Old Testament*, 426.

LESSON 3

June 15, 2014

LIVE PURE LIVES

FAITH PATHWAY/FAITH JOURNEY TOPIC: Live Honorable Lives

DEVOTIONAL READING: **1 Peter 1:13-21**
PRINT PASSAGE: **Haggai 2:10-19**

BACKGROUND SCRIPTURE: **Haggai 2:10-19**
KEY VERSE: **Haggai 2:19**

Haggai 2:10-19—KJV

10 In the four and twentieth day of the ninth month, in the second year of Darius, came the word of the LORD by Haggai the prophet, saying,

11 Thus saith the LORD of hosts; Ask now the priests concerning the law, saying,

12 If one bear holy flesh in the skirt of his garment, and with his skirt do touch bread, or pottage, or wine, or oil, or any meat, shall it be holy? And the priests answered and said, No.

13 Then said Haggai, If one that is unclean by a dead body touch any of these, shall it be unclean? And the priests answered and said, It shall be unclean.

14 Then answered Haggai, and said, So is this people, and so is this nation before me, saith the LORD; and so is every work of their hands; and that which they offer there is unclean.

15 And now, I pray you, consider from this day and upward, from before a stone was laid upon a stone in the temple of the LORD:

16 Since those days were, when one came to an heap of twenty measures, there were but ten: when one came to the pressfat for to draw out fifty vessels out of the press, there were but twenty.

17 I smote you with blasting and with mildew and with hail in all the labours of your hands; yet ye turned not to me, saith the LORD.

18 Consider now from this day and upward, from the four and twentieth day of the ninth month, even from the day that the foundation of the LORD's temple was laid, consider it.

19 Is the seed yet in the barn? yea, as yet the vine, and the fig tree, and the pomegranate, and the olive tree, hath not brought forth: from this day will I bless you.

Haggai 2:10-19—NIV

10 On the twenty-fourth day of the ninth month, in the second year of Darius, the word of the LORD came to the prophet Haggai:

11 "This is what the LORD Almighty says: 'Ask the priests what the law says:

12 If a person carries consecrated meat in the fold of his garment, and that fold touches some bread or stew, some wine, oil or other food, does it become consecrated?'" The priests answered, "No."

13 Then Haggai said, "If a person defiled by contact with a dead body touches one of these things, does it become defiled?" "Yes," the priests replied, "it becomes defiled."

14 Then Haggai said, "'So it is with this people and this nation in my sight,' declares the LORD. 'Whatever they do and whatever they offer there is defiled.

15 Now give careful thought to this from this day on—consider how things were before one stone was laid on another in the LORD's temple.

16 When anyone came to a heap of twenty measures, there were only ten. When anyone went to a wine vat to draw fifty measures, there were only twenty.

17 I struck all the work of your hands with blight, mildew and hail, yet you did not turn to me,' declares the LORD.

18 'From this day on, from this twenty-fourth day of the ninth month, give careful thought to the day when the foundation of the LORD's temple was laid. Give careful thought:

19 Is there yet any seed left in the barn? Until now, the vine and the fig tree, the pomegranate and the olive tree have not borne fruit. From this day on I will bless you.'"

UNIFYING LESSON PRINCIPLE

Almost everyone wants to belong to something that will make a difference in the world. What or who could help Christians feel that sense of belonging? God rewards and blesses the community of believers that lives in righteousness and fear of God.

TOPICAL OUTLINE OF THE LESSON

I. Introduction
   A. God's Measure of Holiness
   B. Biblical Background

II. Exposition and Application of the Scripture
   A. Come Clean!
      (Haggai 2:10-14)
   B. Remember the Cause of the Past Problems
      (Haggai 2:15-17)
   C. The Lord Promised to Bless His People
      (Haggai 2:18-19)

III. Concluding Reflection

LESSON OBJECTIVES

Upon completion of the lesson, the students will be able to do the following:

1. Review Haggai's message of encouragement to the Israelite community to resume work when the Temple rebuilding effort lagged;
2. Realize that failing to follow through on promises made to God leads to unholiness and catastrophic results for the community; and,
3. Discuss the class's conduct within God's purpose for their community and commit to help one another in doing God's work.

POINTS TO BE EMPHASIZED

ADULT/YOUTH
Adult Topic: Live Honorable Lives
Youth Topic: Wholly Holy
Adult/Youth Key Verse: Haggai 2:19
Print Passage: Haggai 2:10-19

—Haggai compared the people's selfish building of their homes and the neglect of God's house with ritual uncleanness.

—By speaking of uncleanness to the people, Haggai encouraged them to continue rebuilding the Temple.

—In speaking of the uncleanness of death, Haggai indicated the great importance and urgency of completing the rebuilding of the Temple.

—Haggai indicated that the ability to do good works (rebuilding the Temple) was possible only with God in the lives of the people.

—He explained that the people's right actions and attitudes (holy living) would bring God's blessings.

—He also told them that God was not pleased with their attitude toward the work that God had commanded them to do.

CHILDREN
Children Topic: Do the Right Thing!
Key Verse: 2 Corinthians 6:16b
Print Passage: 2 Corinthians 6:14-18; 7:1

—Believers are strengthened by associating with others who have similar values, standards, and morals.

—Persons in the body of Christ are called to be holy as God is holy.

—A believer's body is the temple of God, because God dwells within.

—God dwells among the body of believers.

I. INTRODUCTION

A. God's Measure of Holiness

Holiness is an elusive term for many believers—not because they have never heard the word, but because in many congregations the word is rarely used. I remember growing up in a "traditional" Baptist church and hearing my father preach about "living right," "living above the world," and "living holy." At the time, like most young people, I did not pay attention to the calls to live holy. In fact, I did everything to make sure that my life was a reflection of just the opposite of holiness. However, when I responded to my call to preach the Gospel, I immediately enrolled in seminary. During my senior year of seminary, I enrolled in an elective course on spiritual formation and the spiritual life. The Roman Catholic nun who taught the course helped reshape my thinking and belief regarding what it means to be holy and what it takes to reach the pinnacle of spiritual maturity.

In today's lesson, the Judeans were called to consider how they measured up to God's standards of righteousness and holiness. It was not a single individual who was considered unholy, but the whole community which was contaminated by sin. God wants us to make a difference in the world—but we cannot make a difference if our lives are shrouded in the stench of sin. The people of Haggai's day came to see that God rewards and blesses the community of believers that lives in righteousness and fear of God.

B. Biblical Background

Today's lesson summarizes Haggai's third message to the Judeans regarding the rebuilding of the Temple in Jerusalem. Haggai compared the people's selfish building of their own homes and the neglect of God's house with ritual uncleanness. When he spoke of uncleanness, his intent was to encourage them to continue building the Temple. Every word and message of Haggai was focused on one primary goal—motivating the leaders and the people to rebuild the house of the Lord. Although they had attempted to rebuild the Temple sixteen years earlier, their efforts would never amount to much because they had taken God out of the equation altogether. The people of God are only capable of doing great and mighty works when God is at the center of their efforts.

II. EXPOSITION AND APPLICATION OF THE SCRIPTURE

A. Come Clean!
(Haggai 2:10-14)

In the four and twentieth day of the ninth month, in the second year of Darius, came the word of the LORD by Haggai the prophet, saying, Thus saith the LORD of hosts; Ask now the priests concerning the law, saying, If one bear holy flesh in the skirt of his garment, and with his skirt do touch bread, or pottage, or wine, or oil, or any meat, shall it be holy? And the priests answered and said, No.

Then said Haggai, If one that is unclean by a dead body touch any of these, shall it be unclean? And the priests answered and said, It shall be unclean. Then answered Haggai, and said, So is this people, and so is this nation before me, saith the LORD; and so is every work of their hands; and that which they offer there is unclean.

The central theme of this section of the book of Haggai is ritual purity or holiness. Haggai drove home the truth that it was easy for the people of God to contaminate everything that they touched, rendering them unclean because of their disobedience and neglect of the house of God.

This was the third message of Haggai, which was preached on December 18, 520 BC. Haggai preached this message two months after the first message was delivered. At this point, the people had begun to work on rebuilding the Temple, which they ceased to do in 536 BC (see Ezra 4:24). The foundation of the Temple was laid and work had begun. The previous two messages were preached during the time of festival celebrations, because there would be a large gathering in the area of the Temple. This message was not preached during the time of the new moon or any other festival.

The middle of December was usually the time of year when crops had been planted and farmers were awaiting the rains to water the Earth, causing the crops to grow. Haggai mentioned Darius simply by name, not calling him the king. There is no apparent reason for this change from the previous mentions of Darius. In this message, Haggai declared that the Word of the Lord came to him. This was different from the first two messages, where the Word came by him or to him (see 1:3; 2:1). We are not told how the Word of the Lord came to Haggai; it may have been in a dream or through a revelatory event (see Jeremiah 18:1-12; Ezekiel 1:1; 2:1). Nonetheless, Haggai received the Word of God and he promptly obeyed.

In verse 11, Haggai stated that the Lord wanted him to raise two questions with the priests regarding ritual or ceremonial purity. The questions would be built around hypothetical situations concerning ritual purity. Within the ancient Hebrew religious system, the priest led in all aspects of the religious life of the tabernacle and later the Temple. It was the Lord God who established the priesthood and prescribed who would be priests and how they would serve (see Exodus 28:1-4). The priests were all from the tribe of Levi and descendants of Aaron and his sons. The priests were charged with the responsibility of instructing the people in the Word of God and deciding all questions related to ritual or ceremonial purity.

In Mark 1:40-44, Jesus healed a man of leprosy, after which He instructed him to go and show himself to the priest. According to the Law of Moses, only the priest could announce that someone had been healed of leprosy (see Leviticus 14:1-9; compare also Leviticus 10:10-11; Deuteronomy 17:8-12; Zechariah 7:2-3; Malachi 2:7). Haggai was instructed to ask the priests for a ruling or an opinion on the question of holiness and whether or not it could be transferred from one thing to another. This clearly points out that there was a distinct difference between the role that priests played and the role of a prophet. It is important to note that neither stepped outside of their calling.

Verse 12 requires a little understanding of the example that was being used. According to Levitical practices, the priests and Levites were permitted to take a portion of the meat used in the daily or annual sacrifices for personal use. It was their portion. If someone brought a lamb for sacrifice and not all of it was used, then the priests were given a portion for their families to eat (see Leviticus 6:6-17, especially verse 17). The meat was holy because it was used in one of the daily sacrifices. During this period, men wore long, free-flowing robes. It was possible to take an item and wrap it in the excess garment and create what amounted to a bag—hence the "fold." The scenario suggested this: if the priest entered the home or someplace where food items were kept and the robe came into contact with one of those items, then would that render the items touched *holy*? The answer was no!

The law permitted the priest to carry the sacred meat in the fold of his garment. This in turn meant that the garment became holy because of its contact with the meat that had been made holy by virtue of its use in the sacrifices. However, the garment that the meat was wrapped in did not have the power to transmit holiness to anything that it came into contact with (see Leviticus 6:24-30).

The second situation in verse 13 involved a man touching a corpse, which automatically rendered him unclean (see Numbers 19:11; Leviticus 21). If he in turn touched something that was holy and clean, then he rendered it unclean through direct contact (see Leviticus 11:28; 22:4-7). Everything he touched would become unholy and unclean. One example often used to highlight this truth is the illustration of yeast, which although used in small quantities impacts the whole lump of dough. This further explains the reason why the priest and Levite passed on the other side of the road in the parable of the Good Samaritan

(see Luke 10:30-36). The priests answered Haggai correctly—yes it would be unclean.

Haggai was not the one who was speaking; rather, the Lord was speaking and he was still speaking for God. It was God who was displeased with the attitude of the people who had dishonored Him by their indifference to His house. In verse 14, Haggai drove the message home that they were simply not measuring up to the standards of righteousness and holiness, so everything that they did was unclean. The altar was unclean and so was the site of the ruined Temple—because it had not been properly cleansed. The words "This people" and "this nation" refer to the people previously mentioned in the first sermon. They were the ones who had begun working on the Temple after allowing it to lie in ruins for sixteen years. They were the same ones who brought polluted offerings to the altar. "This people" did not feel it was time to rebuild the house of the Lord. The works of their hands were unclean and the offerings that they brought were unclean and unacceptable. The question is, why?

Why was there a barrier between God and the people? It came about because the people who were offering sacrifices upon the altar were contaminated: "Whatever they offer there [i.e., upon the altar] is defiled." The people assumed that because they were offering sacrifices to God upon the altar (which had been used for many years), this outward action would make them holy and secure the protection and blessing of God for them. They assumed that because they were working on a holy building they would automatically become holy themselves; but they were defiled, said the Lord (see verse 14).

Why were the people unclean? Their lethargic attitude had made them unclean. Their love, their loyalty, and their enthusiasm for God's work had all begun to diminish. They thought that their good works in offering sacrifices upon the altar would make up for their lack of zeal for God's house. They thought their devout actions would make them acceptable in God's eyes. They believed they were pleasing God by offering sacrifices to Him.[1]

Those who come before the Lord in worship must come with clean hands and pure hearts (see Psalm 24:3-4). It matters how one appears before the presence of God. To come with bitterness and anger is to come with a defiled spirit, which renders one's worship futile and defiled.

B. Remember the Cause of the Past Problems (Haggai 2:15-17)

And now, I pray you, consider from this day and upward, from before a stone was laid upon a stone in the temple of the LORD: Since those days were, when one came to an heap of twenty measures, there were but ten: when one came to the pressfat for to draw out fifty vessels out of the press, there were but twenty. I smote you with blasting and with mildew and with hail in all the labours of your hands; yet ye turned not to me, saith the LORD.

These verses pose unique challenges and with some there is difficulty in interpreting them, because they focus the attention of the hearer in three directions at once. Haggai called upon the people to think about a range of things, particularly those times prior to the work beginning. They experienced a series of personal and national setbacks after they began the work and stopped. Verse 15 begins with the word "now" (KJV), which shows a distinct contrast between life before the work began on rebuilding the Temple and life after it

began. Before the work began on rebuilding the Temple, the local economy was in shambles. People were surviving, but their resources were barely able to keep up with their needs and demands. The words *and now* indicated that a new day had dawned. There was desolation and economic destitution caused by the failure of the people to honor God by restoring the destroyed Temple, which had been thoroughly contaminated—going back to the time of the invasion by Babylon (see Haggai 1:6). The preceding examples of personal contamination in verses 11-14 was further developed by reminding the people that their disobedience to the command of God contaminated everything they did and touched. "And now" everything was about to be reversed.

The verse introduced a new thought by calling upon the people to again give very serious reflection and careful thought to all of the things that had gone on over the past few months—that is, the things that had occurred since they began to rebuild the Temple (see Ezra 3:10-13). "From this day onward" ("this day and upward," KJV) looks forward to a time of new and greater prosperity resulting from God's blessings and favor upon the people because of their obedience (see verse 19; compare Deuteronomy 28:1-14).

As long as the people were unwilling to accept responsibility for rebuilding the Temple, their economic fortunes did not improve (verse 16). When they thought they had recovered economically, the net result was the same—instead of finding twenty measures of grain, there were only ten. Instead of there being fifty measures of wine in the vat, there were just twenty. In verse 17, the Lord reminded them that He smote them and everything that they owned, grew, and built. The two most common forms of crop failure in that day were "blight," which was caused by extremely hot winds blowing in off the desert; and mildew, which resulted from the continuing rains of the Mediterranean and the hail that could develop during cold winters. In spite of all the things that were done, their hearts remained stubborn. However, once they laid the foundation and began the work, everything changed.

C. The Lord Promised to Bless His People (Haggai 2:18-19)

Consider now from this day and upward, from the four and twentieth day of the ninth month, even from the day that the foundation of the Lord's temple was laid, consider it. Is the seed yet in the barn? yea, as yet the vine, and the fig tree, and the pomegranate, and the olive tree, hath not brought forth: from this day will I bless you.

Again, Haggai called upon the people to give serious thought to what God's messages meant. The word *consider* is an imperative command that stresses the importance of giving careful and deliberate thought to all of the events of the previous sixteen years. Beginning from the day that work commenced on rebuilding the Temple, things changed in Judah (see Zechariah 8:9-10). Verse 18b could refer to two periods of time—the first being the initial work done during the early days of the return, i.e., 538 BC; or it could refer to the time when work was restarted in 520 BC. What was it that the Lord wanted the people to consider or give serious thought to?

Verse 19 provided the answer. The Judean society was an agricultural economy, so they were very dependent upon the early rains (October–November) and the latter rains (March–April). Rain was always considered to be a sign of the blessings of God upon the land, and the lack of rain was believed to be a sign of disfavor and punishment (see Deuteronomy 11:14; 1 Kings 17:7; Job 29:23; Psalm 84:6 Jeremiah 3:3; 5:24; 14:1-4; James 5:7). Over the previous sixteen years the people had experienced a host of environmental and natural disasters that either ruined the crops and fruit harvests or had been severe enough to produce small yields. By December, all the fields were planted and the time of waiting upon the early rains had begun.

The rhetorical question regarding whether the seed and fruit of the vine had produced crops has been interpreted in several ways. Given the context and the situation of the people, the most likely answer to the question was no. There was no seed in the barn because they had either been consumed or planted. There was no fruit on the vine because the season of harvesting had not arrived. Thus the people were waiting for what they hoped would be a reversal of their fortunes. Instead of delivering another crushing blow, Haggai announced that God was going to bless them. The Hebrew word *barak* can have a variety of meanings, but in this context it denotes the bestowal of divine favor. The Lord was going to bestow upon the people of Judah all of the things necessary to prosper: rain, good weather, and peace in the land. The people would be blessed because they had chosen the path of obedience to God. "From this day forward" (verse 15) could refer to the day they decided to lay the foundation or the day they obeyed. Either case is correct. Everything would work in their favor: the seed would produce a bountiful harvest; and the vine, fig tree, olive tree, and the pomegranate would all yield bountiful blessings upon the people of God.

III. CONCLUDING REFLECTION

One of the central principles that come from this section of the book of Haggai is the matter of holiness and spiritual purity. In our day, people are not as likely to consider whether or not they appear in the Lord's house on Sundays spiritually scarred by the sins of the past week or weekend. Just as the meat could become contaminated by contact with unclean items, people, or places, even so believers can become contaminated by the places and people with whom we become involved. Another principle is the ease with which contamination can be spread. Consider that rumors, lies, and innuendos about others can travel like wildfire and destroy families, relationships, marriages, careers, and reputations. Believers have to always be mindful of the things that we allow to permeate our hearts and minds (see Philippians 4:8-9).

PRAYER

Heavenly Father, may we live in such a way that our lives are always pure and holy. Grant that Your servants will never lose sight of Your glory. Forgive us of our sins. In Jesus' name we pray. Amen.

WORD POWER

Unclean (Hebrew: *tame* [taw–may])—this word covers a wide range of animals and foods which were considered either clean or unclean. According to the Scriptures, a man or woman could become ceremonially unclean. In the book of Leviticus, a man or woman could become unclean through childbirth, menstruation, leprosy, sexual relations, and contact with a corpse (see Leviticus 11–15). It was the responsibility of the priests and Levites to maintain ritual purity and cleanness among themselves and the people.

HOME DAILY BIBLE READINGS
(June 9-15, 2014)

Live Pure Lives
MONDAY, June 9: "A Highway Called the Holy Way" (Isaiah 35)
TUESDAY, June 10: "Established as God's Holy People" (Deuteronomy 28:1-9)
WEDNESDAY, June 11: "You Shall Be Holy" (1 Peter 1:13-21)
THURSDAY, June 12: "You Have Been Born Anew" (1 Peter 1:22–2:3)
FRIDAY, June 13: "You Are God's People" (1 Peter 2:4-10)
SATURDAY, June 14: "You Are the Temple of God" (2 Corinthians 6:14–7:1)
SUNDAY, June 15: "The Hope for God's Blessing" (Haggai 2:10-19)

End Note

---

[1] *Welwyn Commentary Series.* (Welwyn Commentary Series) "Building for God's Glory: Haggai and Zechariah Simply Explained." Wordsearch 10 Edition.

UNIT I: Hope and Confidence Come from God
CHILDREN'S UNIT: Building a Community of Believers
SUMMER QUARTER

LESSON 4
June 22, 2014

HOPE FOR A NEW DAY

FAITH PATHWAY/FAITH JOURNEY TOPIC: **Expect Success**

DEVOTIONAL READING: Psalm 43
PRINT PASSAGE: Haggai 2:20-23; Zechariah 4:5-14
KEY VERSE: Zechariah 4:6

BACKGROUND SCRIPTURE: Nehemiah 7:1-7;
Haggai 2:20-23; Zechariah 4

Haggai 2:20-23; Zechariah 4:5-14—KJV

20 And again the word of the LORD came unto Haggai in the four and twentieth day of the month, saying,

21 Speak to Zerubbabel, governor of Judah, saying, I will shake the heavens and the earth;

22 And I will overthrow the throne of kingdoms, and I will destroy the strength of the kingdoms of the heathen; and I will overthrow the chariots, and those that ride in them; and the horses and their riders shall come down, every one by the sword of his brother.

23 In that day, saith the LORD of hosts, will I take thee, O Zerubbabel, my servant, the son of Shealtiel, saith the LORD, and will make thee as a signet: for I have chosen thee, saith the LORD of hosts.

.....

5 Then the angel that talked with me answered and said unto me, Knowest thou not what these be? And I said, No, my lord.

6 Then he answered and spake unto me, saying, This is the word of the LORD unto Zerubbabel, saying, Not by might, nor by power, but by my spirit, saith the LORD of hosts.

7 Who art thou, O great mountain? before Zerubbabel thou shalt become a plain: and he shall bring forth the headstone thereof with shoutings, crying, Grace, grace unto it.

8 Moreover the word of the LORD came unto me, saying,

9 The hands of Zerubbabel have laid the foundation of this house; his hands shall also finish it; and thou shalt know that the LORD of hosts hath sent me unto you.

10 For who hath despised the day of small things? for they shall rejoice, and shall see the plummet in

Haggai 2:20-23; Zechariah 4:5-14—NIV

20 The word of the LORD came to Haggai a second time on the twenty-fourth day of the month:

21 "Tell Zerubbabel governor of Judah that I will shake the heavens and the earth.

22 I will overturn royal thrones and shatter the power of the foreign kingdoms. I will overthrow chariots and their drivers; horses and their riders will fall, each by the sword of his brother.

23 'On that day,' declares the LORD Almighty, 'I will take you, my servant Zerubbabel son of Shealtiel,' declares the LORD, 'and I will make you like my signet ring, for I have chosen you,' declares the LORD Almighty."

.....

5 He answered, "Do you not know what these are?" "No, my lord," I replied.

6 So he said to me, "This is the word of the LORD to Zerubbabel: 'Not by might nor by power, but by my Spirit,' says the LORD Almighty.

7 What are you, O mighty mountain? Before Zerubbabel you will become level ground. Then he will bring out the capstone to shouts of 'God bless it! God bless it!'"

8 Then the word of the LORD came to me:

9 "The hands of Zerubbabel have laid the foundation of this temple; his hands will also complete it. Then you will know that the LORD Almighty has sent me to you.

10 Who despises the day of small things? Men will rejoice when they see the plumb line in the hand of

the hand of Zerubbabel with those seven; they are the eyes of the LORD, which run to and fro through the whole earth.

11 Then answered I, and said unto him, What are these two olive trees upon the right side of the candlestick and upon the left side thereof?

12 And I answered again, and said unto him, What be these two olive branches which through the two golden pipes empty the golden oil out of themselves?

13 And he answered me and said, Knowest thou not what these be? And I said, No, my lord.

14 Then said he, These are the two anointed ones, that stand by the Lord of the whole earth.

Zerubbabel. (These seven are the eyes of the LORD, which range throughout the earth.)"

11 Then I asked the angel, "What are these two olive trees on the right and the left of the lampstand?"

12 Again I asked him, "What are these two olive branches beside the two gold pipes that pour out golden oil?"

13 He replied, "Do you not know what these are?" "No, my lord," I said.

14 So he said, "These are the two who are anointed to serve the Lord of all the earth."

TOPICAL OUTLINE OF THE LESSON

I. Introduction
  A. Characteristics of Effective Leadership
  B. Biblical Background

II. Exposition and Application of the Scripture
  A. God's Promises to Zerubbabel (Haggai 2:20-23)
  B. Not by Might (Zechariah 4:5-7)
  C. Zechariah's Vision of Success in the Work (Zechariah 4:8-14)

III. Concluding Reflection

LESSON OBJECTIVES

Upon completion of the lesson, the students will be able to do the following:

1. Discover God's promise of eternal reward to the Israelite community because they rebuilt the Temple in obedience to God;
2. Connect the community's restoration of the Temple with God's restoration of the community; and,
3. Express thankfulness to God for the blessings He confers on obedient servants.

POINTS TO BE EMPHASIZED

ADULT/YOUTH
Adult Topic: Expect Success
Youth Topic: The Need for Hope
Adult/Youth Key Verse: Zechariah 4:6
Print Passage: Haggai 2:20-23; Zechariah 4:5-14
—The prophecies in the book of Haggai and the first part of the book of Zechariah are from the same period.

—The book of Haggai suggests that Israel's obedience to God will have positive implications for the entire world.
—Haggai received a seal of guarantee from God that the Temple project would be completed.
—By God's Spirit and power, however, the project would be finished.
—Throughout the process, hope for completion was constantly assured by God's words that came to Zechariah.

CHILDREN
Children Topic: Expecting the Best
Key Verse: Romans 8:24a

Print Passage: Romans 8:18-30
—Today's sufferings are insignificant when compared to the glory that awaits the believer in the future.
—Believers long for the promises of redemption.
—Because of Jesus' resurrection, believers look forward to the rebirth of the entire creation.
—Even when believers do not know what to pray for, the Holy Spirit intercedes and prays for them.
—For those who love God, all things will eventually work out for the good.
—Believers must be reassured that God's purpose is to save them.

I. INTRODUCTION
A. Characteristics of Effective Leadership

Good leaders are hard to find. Good leaders are men and women who can accomplish extraordinary results under difficult and challenging circumstances. All around the world there is a huge demand for good leaders. Every year, *Business Week Magazine* publishes a list of the men and women who they believe are "The Top 25 Managers of the Year." These are men and women who run some of the largest and most profitable corporations in the world. After reading the list, this writer wanted to know if there were any common characteristics that marked these twenty-five top managers.

Four common traits were identified in each of these leaders. First, these leaders were all innovative. They used technology to expand and enhance their businesses to produce double-digit growth. Second, they recognized the need to develop strategic partnerships with other companies around the world. We call this networking. They were willing to work with other organizations to achieve their long-term goals. Third, their perspectives were global. They saw their markets extending beyond their own spheres of operation. They all had a worldwide vision. Fourth, they were willing and able to lead their companies to adapt to changes in the marketplace. They were all willing to restructure and reengineer their businesses to maintain their competitive edge. In other words, they were willing to change to stay out in front.

All of these men and women are highly successful leaders who have been able to achieve great things. There is something to be learned from emulating and imitating meaningful models of leadership. Communities need capable leadership to stay motivated through the completion of a project. Where can Christian communities find this kind of leadership?

God spoke through prophets to affirm that the Temple would be completed under Zerubbabel—not by human might or power, but by the Spirit of the Lord.

B. Biblical Background

Whenever the people of God have needed encouragement and hope, God would raise up a prophet or someone who would speak life into their spirits. During the period of the reconstruction of Jerusalem and the rebuilding of the Temple, the people of God needed such a person. The task of rebuilding the Temple in Jerusalem proved to be one of the most arduous tasks facing the Jews when they returned from exile in Babylon. There was a period of nearly sixteen years when no work was done, because the people had become despondent and discouraged. During one of the most difficult periods in their history, God sent two prophets to encourage the leaders and the people to know that He was with them and to remind them that they would be successful.

They would not need nor have a large army at their disposal. They would be successful because of the presence of the Lord through the Holy Spirit, who would give them the success they desperately longed for.

Zerubbabel the civil leader was heir to the Davidic throne, but this alone was not enough to ensure that he would be successful in leading the rebuilding project. In addition to the prophet Haggai, God pressed into service a man named Zechariah, son of Berekiah, the son of Iddo (see Zechariah 1:1). The name *Zechariah* means "Jehovah is renowned or remembered."

We have very little biographical information about Zechariah, other than what is mentioned in Zechariah 1:1 and Nehemiah 12:16. The prophecy of Zechariah is full of visions and symbolism that can be easily understood when seen in light of the reconstruction project. Both Haggai and Zechariah called the people back to lives of faithfulness and obedience.

II. EXPOSITION AND APPLICATION OF THE SCRIPTURE

A. God's Promises to Zerubbabel (Haggai 2:20-23)

And again the word of the LORD came unto Haggai in the four and twentieth day of the month, saying, Speak to Zerubbabel, governor of Judah, saying, I will shake the heavens and the earth; And I will overthrow the throne of kingdoms, and I will destroy the strength of the kingdoms of the heathen; and I will overthrow the chariots, and those that ride in them; and the horses and their riders shall come down, every one by the sword of his brother. In that day, saith the LORD of hosts, will I take thee, O Zerubbabel, my servant, the son of Shealtiel, saith the LORD, and will make thee as a signet: for I have chosen thee, saith the LORD of hosts.

Haggai preached a final sermon on December 18, 520 BC. He received the Word of the Lord a second time just as he had previously received it (see verse 10). This was a word directed specifically to Zerubbabel, in his role as governor of Judah, and not to the people of Judah. Zerubbabel is not always thought of when we think of the major figures and personalities of the Old Testament era. Yet, he ranks among the giants, because of the courageous leadership he executed during what can be considered as one of the most important periods in the history of Israel. He led in the return from Babylon and the reestablishment of Jewish society and commerce in the land of Judah. This was a daunting task and a lesser man may have folded under the pressures (see Zechariah 4:6-10). We are not told where this event took place or whether it was spoken in the presence of others. It is very likely that there were other people present who heard this word of encouragement and hope. This would have been the final piece of the plan of God to bring Judah back from the brink of destruction. He was going to raise up Zerubbabel to lead in the lineage of David. There are a series of "I will" statements in this message, all intended to increase the courage of Zerubbabel as he faced an uncertain future. What was the message to Zerubbabel?

The Lord said, "I am going to shake the heavens and the earth." This is a repeat of Haggai 2:6, when the exact same words were spoken to the people—yet, this time, they were delivered to the leader. Leaders also need to be reminded of the presence of the Lord when they face mountains of obstacles and challenges. The Lord spoke about something that was going to happen in the future: He was going to shake the world. The impact of what God was going to do would be felt not just on the Earth, but in heaven as well.

Verse 22 is the second of these "I" statements in which the Lord promised to overthrow the thrones, destroy the power of the nations, and utterly destroy their means of waging war and conquest. This depicts a threefold blow to the nations that had exploited the poorer and smaller nations of the Ancient Middle East. The promise was for that time and also for the distant and far-off future. Some interpreters think that this promise had reference to the conflicts revolving around Darius's consolidation of the Persian Empire.

Verse 23 reads, "'On that day,' declares the LORD of hosts, 'I will take you, Zerubbabel, son of Shealtiel, My servant,' declares the LORD, 'and I will make you like a signet *ring,* for I have chosen you,' declares the LORD of hosts." This promise to Zerubbabel was built around a threefold declaration of the Lord's Word. This was not something that Haggai was saying, but after each statement there was the declarative statement that this was the Word of the Lord. "On that day" refers to the immediate context and also the far-off, distant future. So that there would be no mistake about whom the message was intended for, Zerubbabel's father was mentioned.

First, the Lord declared that He had "taken" Zerubbabel. Further, Zerubbabel was called the servant of the Lord, which put him in the same category as Moses and David (see Joshua 1:2; 2 Samuel 3:18). This reference to Zerubbabel as the servant of the Lord has led many interpreters to see this as a messianic prophecy that looks forward to the work of Zerubbabel in his day and also the coming of the true Messiah, Jesus Christ. The Messiah was not only the Anointed One of God; He was also a servant (see Isaiah 42:1; 52:13; 53:11). This statement that Zerubbabel was a servant taken by the Lord was one of possession and ownership. It meant that Zerubbabel would be blessed in his work, protected from his enemies, and guaranteed the divine presence of God. His assignment was specific and critical to the future of the nation of Judah. Zerubbabel was charged with the responsibility of rebuilding the physical house of the Lord God. Jesus Christ came into the world to build a spiritual house and kingdom; both of these servants of God fulfilled some aspect of the Davidic Covenant (see 2 Samuel 7:12-14).

Second, the Lord said that He would make Zerubbabel a signet ring. The word *make* in Hebrew has in it the idea of ordaining, setting aside, establishing, or putting in a new place. Any one of these could refer to Zerubbabel. He did not make himself; the Lord made him or established him in the position of governor of Judah for Himself. What is the significance of a signet ring? This was the seal of the king's authority. It was a ring worn on a finger on the right hand of the king and it was used to stamp documents and/or express his approval (see Esther 8:10; Daniel 6:7).

The third and final promise is expressed in the words, "I have chosen you." The word *chosen* comes from the Hebrew word *bachar* (baw–khar), and it has a wide range of usages, almost all in connection with the choices made by the Lord. In some instances, it refers to the Lord's choosing people (see Deuteronomy 7:6), places (see 2 Chronicles 7:12), and individuals (see 2 Samuel 10:24). Zerubbabel was chosen by the Lord, not because he had earned the right to be used by God, but because God is sovereign and He is free to choose whomever He wants to choose (see Matthew 20:16; John 15:16; 1 Corinthians 1:26-31; Ephesians 1:4; 1 Peter 2:4).

B. Not by Might
(Zechariah 4:5-7)

Then the angel that talked with me answered and said unto me, Knowest thou not what these be? And I said, No, my lord. Then he answered and spake unto me, saying, This is the word of the LORD unto Zerubbabel, saying, Not by might, nor by power, but by my spirit, saith the LORD

of hosts. Who art thou, O great mountain? before Zerubbabel thou shalt become a plain: and he shall bring forth the headstone thereof with shoutings, crying, Grace, grace unto it.

In verses 1-4, Zechariah saw in a vision a gold lamp stand with a bowl at the top and seven lights on it and seven channels to the light. There were two olive trees on either side of the lamp stand. Verse 5 is the answer to a question raised by Zechariah to the angel as to the meaning of this vision. The angel seems to have been surprised that Zechariah did not know what these things meant.

Verse 6 is one of the most familiar and often quoted verses in the entire Bible. The angel gave Zechariah a specific word for Zerubbabel, who was charged with the responsibility of leading in the rebuilding of the Temple in Jerusalem (see Ezra 3:8). The people rebuilding the Temple had encountered stiff opposition and had faced great discouragement and despair (see Ezra 4:4, 24). The work being done was ordered by God and the Temple was for His glory; nothing and no one would be able to stand in its way. Zerubbabel would complete the project—but it would not be with the aid of an army, but by the power of the Holy Spirit (see 2 Chronicles 32:7; Psalm 33:16).

In verse 7, we are faced with the question of who was opposing the work of rebuilding. This is expressed in the personal pronoun "you." Although the person was not mentioned it was more than likely the people of the land who were adamantly opposed to the work from the beginning (see Ezra 4-5). Zerubbabel's opponents are symbolized by the mountains. The mountains that surround Jerusalem have stood as towering citadels since creation (see verse 7; compare with Psalm 125:2). The mountains symbolized might and power, but before the power of God, they were mere molehills that could easily be leveled to the ground. The message was clear that even Zerubbabel's fiercest foe and strongest enemy were nothing by comparison to the power of God. Their enemies would be defeated and the capstone would be put into place. The laying of the capstone was the final word of reassurance that the project would be successful. The completion of the project would be accompanied by shouts of praise, celebration, and acclamation of God's grace and blessings, evidenced by the repetition of the words "God bless it! God bless it!"

C. Zechariah's Vision of Success in the Work (Zechariah 4:8-14)

Moreover the word of the LORD came unto me, saying, The hands of Zerubbabel have laid the foundation of this house; his hands shall also finish it; and thou shalt know that the LORD of hosts hath sent me unto you. For who hath despised the day of small things? for they shall rejoice, and shall see the plummet in the hand of Zerubbabel with those seven; they are the eyes of the LORD, which run to and fro through the whole earth. Then answered I, and said unto him, What are these two olive trees upon the right side of the candlestick and upon the left side thereof? And I answered again, and said unto him, What be these two olive branches which through the two golden pipes empty the golden oil out of themselves? And he answered me and said, Knowest thou not what these be? And I said, No, my lord. Then said he, These are the two anointed ones, that stand by the Lord of the whole earth.

In verse 8, Zechariah announced that the word of the Lord came again. We are not told how it came—more than likely it was in the form of another vision. This time it was a word of affirmation that the Temple would be completed. Zerubbabel had overseen the laying of the foundation of the house of the Lord between 538–537 BC (see Ezra 3:8-11; 5:16).

Not only would he lay the foundation, but the building would be completed. From that day onward there would be no doubt in the minds of people that the Lord had sent Zechariah to encourage Zerubbabel and Joshua for their assignments.

Verse 10 echoes the message of Haggai 2:3-4. When some of the people saw the size of the foundation being laid they felt that it was insignificant in comparison to the Temple built by Solomon (verse 10a). However, Zechariah proclaimed that the people would no longer weep for sadness, but would be filled with joy when they saw the actual work being done on the Temple complex. The plumb line is an instrument made of stone with a long string or thin rope attached. It was used to measure whether or not a wall was straight or vertical. The seven eyes were symbolic of the fullness of God's knowledge. The number "7" means perfection—hence the reference to God having perfect knowledge of every challenge facing the people in the rebuilding of the Temple. God sees all and knows all (see 2 Chronicles 16:9).

Verses 11-14 are a return to the original question of Zechariah to the angel of the Lord that was raised in verse 4, and is an explanation of verses 2-3. There were four elements of the vision that need an explanation: the olive trees, the two branches, the lamp stand, and the two gold pipes. The olive trees were an abundant source of oil, which was used in oil lamps in ancient Israel and throughout the ancient Near East. The two olive branches represented the abundant supply of pure golden oil for the lamp stand used in the Temple to provide light, which was perpetually lit. The gold pipes served as the conduit for filling the lamp stand. What did this mean? It is a reference to verse 6; oil was a symbol of the Holy Spirit and was used to anoint the kings and priests for service. The presence of such an endless supply meant that the power of God's presence would be an inexhaustible source of power for Zerubbabel and Joshua. The two olive trees were Zerubbabel and Joshua, while the lamp stand symbolized the people of God, whose light would never be extinguished by any power on the Earth. These two men were anointed by the Holy Spirit to lead the people of God to accomplish what appeared to be impossible when they first began.

III. CONCLUDING REFLECTION

The messages delivered to Zerubbabel by Haggai and Zechariah have been a source of great help and hope to many pastors and church leaders who have sought to lead building programs. Congregational leaders can face entrenched opposition that is vehemently opposed to progress and change. Yet, this lesson reminds us that our strength is not bound up in how many people we muster to our side, but rests in the knowledge that God is our strength and it is to Him that we must look at all times and in all situations (see Psalm 27:1-6).

PRAYER

Heavenly Father, may we never lose confidence in Your presence nor Your power. Keep us from the dungeons of despair as we seek to do greater works in ministry. In Jesus' name we pray. Amen.

WORD POWER

Shake (Hebrew: *ra-ash*)—denotes a violent upheaval or quaking as that of an earthquake. Here it is not to be understood as a physical event, but more of an eschatological event, that is an event of monumental significance (see Mark 1:14-15; Galatians 4:4).

Take (Hebrew: *laqach* [law–kahl])—This word has in it the idea of marriage or snatching away. Just as a man chooses a wife with great care and consideration, the Lord had specifically chosen Zerubbabel to be the one to lead the people in the rebuilding of the Temple.

HOME DAILY BIBLE READINGS
(June 16-22, 2014)

Hope for a New Day

MONDAY, June 16: "What Hope for the Godless?" (Job 27:8-12)
TUESDAY, June 17: "Hope in God" (Psalm 43)
WEDNESDAY, June 18: "Hope in God's Steadfast Love" (Psalm 33:13-22)
THURSDAY, June 19: "In Hope We Were Saved" (Romans 8:18-25)
FRIDAY, June 20: "Accounting for the Hope in You" (1 Peter 3:13-17)
SATURDAY, June 21: "The Confession of Our Hope" (Hebrews 10:19-24)
SUNDAY, June 22: "I Have Chosen You" (Haggai 2:23; Zechariah 4:1-3, 6-14)

LESSON 5

June 29, 2014

A CALL TO UNITY

FAITH PATHWAY/FAITH JOURNEY TOPIC: Let's All Get Along

DEVOTIONAL READING: **1 Corinthians 12:12-20**
PRINT PASSAGE: **1 Corinthians 1:10-17**

BACKGROUND SCRIPTURE: **1 Corinthians 1:10-17**
KEY VERSE: **1 Corinthians 1:10**

1 Corinthians 1:10-17—KJV

10 Now I beseech you, brethren, by the name of our Lord Jesus Christ, that ye all speak the same thing, and that there be no divisions among you; but that ye be perfectly joined together in the same mind and in the same judgment.

11 For it hath been declared unto me of you, my brethren, by them which are of the house of Chloe, that there are contentions among you.

12 Now this I say, that every one of you saith, I am of Paul; and I of Apollos; and I of Cephas; and I of Christ.

13 Is Christ divided? was Paul crucified for you? or were ye baptized in the name of Paul?

14 I thank God that I baptized none of you, but Crispus and Gaius;

15 Lest any should say that I had baptized in mine own name.

16 And I baptized also the household of Stephanas: besides, I know not whether I baptized any other.

17 For Christ sent me not to baptize, but to preach the gospel: not with wisdom of words, lest the cross of Christ should be made of none effect.

1 Corinthians 1:10-17—NIV

10 I appeal to you, brothers, in the name of our Lord Jesus Christ, that all of you agree with one another so that there may be no divisions among you and that you may be perfectly united in mind and thought.

11 My brothers, some from Chloe's household have informed me that there are quarrels among you.

12 What I mean is this: One of you says, "I follow Paul"; another, "I follow Apollos"; another, "I follow Cephas"; still another, "I follow Christ."

13 Is Christ divided? Was Paul crucified for you? Were you baptized into the name of Paul?

14 I am thankful that I did not baptize any of you except Crispus and Gaius,

15 so no one can say that you were baptized into my name.

16 (Yes, I also baptized the household of Stephanas; beyond that, I don't remember if I baptized anyone else.)

17 For Christ did not send me to baptize, but to preach the gospel—not with words of human wisdom, lest the cross of Christ be emptied of its power.

BIBLE FACT

The term *UNITY* is never used in the sense of uniformity—where everyone looks alike, talks alike and thinks alike. True unity is where believers have the same Jesus, which is to honor God.

UNIFYING LESSON PRINCIPLE

Disagreements in a community may cause division. How can community disagreements be resolved? Paul called the disputing people to find common ground by taking on the mind of Christ.

TOPICAL OUTLINE OF THE LESSON

I. Introduction
A. Communication Is the Key to Community
B. Biblical Background

II. Exposition and Application of the Scripture
A. Paul's Appeal for Unity (1 Corinthians 1:10)
B. Paul's View of the Source and Cause of the Divisions (1 Corinthians 1:11-12)
C. Division over Baptism (1 Corinthians 1:13-17)

III. Concluding Reflection

LESSON OBJECTIVES

Upon completion of the lesson, the students will be able to do the following:

1. Review divisions within the Corinthian faith community;
2. Reflect on the harm caused by divisions within a faith community; and,
3. Examine divisions within the local community and plan ways to achieve unity.

POINTS TO BE EMPHASIZED
ADULT/YOUTH

Adult Topic: Let's All Get Along
Youth Topic: United We Stand
Adult/Youth Key Verse: 1 Corinthians 1:10
Print Passage: 1 Corinthians 1:10-17

—In his appeal, Paul hinted at the liturgical phrase "in the name of our Lord," as used in baptism.
—By calling the conflicting parties "brothers and sisters," Paul softened what was going to be a severe scolding.
—Paul called the Corinthians to remember that they belonged to Christ and not to their baptizers.
—Paul believed that it is baptism that is important, not who does the baptizing.
—The competition among Paul, Peter, and Apollos existed only in the minds of their followers.
—Paul reminded his readers that Christ's message of the Cross remains more important than any who carry the message.

CHILDREN

Children Topic: A United Community
Key Verse: Ephesians 4:6
Print Passage: Ephesians 4:1-6

—Paul encouraged the believers to seek oneness in Christ.
—Paul encouraged the believers to live together, exemplifying humility, gentleness, patience, love, and peace.
—The unity of the church is maintained by the unity of the believers' calling and their doctrine.
—The unity of the church is enabled through the Spirit of God.

I. INTRODUCTION

A. Communication Is the Key to Community

Today, we begin a new unit that looks at the church of Corinth in order to learn how to build and maintain community among believers. What does the word *community* mean within the context of the Christian faith? Community within the Christian faith denotes those who share a common faith and system of belief. It is evidenced through a common worship experience of the risen Christ. Often these early Christian communities were filled with a host of internal problems that were the result of people from varied backgrounds and social standings coming together to form communities of faith. The church in Corinth was the most visible example of a faith community that struggled to overcome internal divisions that plagued communal life.

Nothing grieves the heart of God more than to see His people stuck in quarrels and disagreement. We break the heart of God with our unwillingness to get along. One of Paul's greatest challenges was mending the breach that had developed among the Corinthians. We know from the early chapters that their relational problems were so severe that they became public knowledge. Over the course of thirty-three years in full-time pastoral ministry, this writer has learned a lot about congregational divisions and disagreement—having witnessed conflict erupt in congregations over a host of issues, the majority of which could have been easily settled by open and honest communication. Many of the issues that congregations face take on a life-or-death perspective, and many times it becomes impossible to resolve the simplest issue. Disagreements in a community can cause division. How can community disagreements be resolved? Paul called upon the disputing people to find common ground by taking on the mind of Christ.

B. Biblical Background

The Corinthians were a Greek-speaking congregation, located in the southern tip of ancient Greece. The church was founded and established during Paul's second missionary journey. The account of how the church came to be is found in Acts 18:1-22. According to Acts 18:11, Paul spent eighteen months teaching and preaching in the city of Corinth. He probably spent more time with these believers (at least as far as we know) than with any other church he established. After he left, all hell broke out among the members. The situation was so explosive that Paul wrote several letters trying to address the questions and problems (see 1 Corinthians 5:9).

In verses 10-17, Paul addressed what was a crucial issue within the congregation—division, factions, and cliques. Interpreters have sought to understand the exact nature of the divisions within the congregation. Some have assumed that the problems revolved around the various leaders mentioned—Paul, Apollos, Cephas, and Jesus. It appears that, based upon what we know about Corinthian society, which was riddled by competitive individualism, this spirit of factionalism and ethos identification had spilled into the congregation and infiltrated the relationships of the members of the church. Within that society, wealthy people often wanted to be viewed as social benefactors, who often vied for the loyalty and affection of people in lower social classes. This spirit found its way into the church and people wanted to keep class distinctions based upon gifts and status.

The question was whether or not the people were at odds with Paul or with each other. It appears that they were at odds with each other. Paul knew this because he had been informed by Chloe's people (see verse 11). People were jockeying for power and key positions of leadership and authority within the congregation. Paul wrote with fatherly love and concern, hoping that the Corinthian church members still regarded him as their father in the faith. In the discussion about baptism, it may be that some thought of themselves as having received something special because they were baptized by a particular leader.

II. EXPOSITION AND APPLICATION OF THE SCRIPTURE

A. Paul's Appeal for Unity
(1 Corinthians 1:10)

Now I beseech you, brethren, by the name of our Lord Jesus Christ, that ye all speak the same thing, and that there be no divisions among you; but that ye be perfectly joined together in the same mind and in the same judgment.

The church in Corinth was facing a major internal crisis. Everything that Paul had accomplished during his eighteen months in Corinth was about to be destroyed because of the inability of the congregation to resolve its internal issues. Paul made a personal appeal that they come together to resolve the issues. The word *appeal* (Greek: *parakaleo*) means "to call to one's side for the purpose of encouraging or consoling." Paul wanted the saints in Corinth to understand the magnitude of the situation. As their spiritual father, he appealed to the entire congregation, not only as his children, but moreover as brothers and sisters in Christ (see 2:1; 3:1, 4-6; 6:8; 12:1). Paul wanted the church to end the bickering and bitterness gripping the fellowship. He invoked the only name that should have mattered to them—the Lord Jesus Christ's (see Romans 15:30; 16:17-18; 2 Corinthians 5:20; Ephesians 4:3, 32).

Paul's appeal was threefold: first, that everyone in the congregation agree with one another (see Acts 1:14; 2:42). He did not state the things about which he wanted them to be in agreement. Quite possibly it may have been the need to create a more harmonious climate among themselves. Also, it may have been the very things that he was going to set before them within the body of his letter; second, he appealed to them to end the divisions among them. The term *divisions* (Greek: *schisma*) means "to tear or rent, in some instances it is used to refer to the plowing of a field."[1] In this instance, *schisma* came to denote the deep disagreements over the various leaders within the early Christian community (see John 7:40-43; 10:19-21; 1 Corinthians 11:18); third, Paul appealed to the Corinthians that they perfectly unite in mind and thought (see Philippians

2:1-5). Rather than continue to tear the congregation apart, Paul appealed to them to knit the fellowship back together.

B. Paul's View of the Source and Cause of the Divisions
(1 Corinthians 1:11-12)

For it hath been declared unto me of you, my brethren, by them which are of the house of Chloe, that there are contentions among you. Now this I say, that every one of you saith, I am of Paul; and I of Apollos; and I of Cephas; and I of Christ.

In verse 11, Paul addressed the entire congregation, both men and women. The conflicts had become so pronounced and severe that word had spread throughout the region, and had reached him in Ephesus. He indicated that the source of the information regarding the internal wrangling were people from Chloe's household. Chloe was obviously a very prominent woman in the ancient city of Corinth. She could have been a very wealthy businesswoman or a leading member of the church. We are not sure who she was and any comment beyond this would be speculative. The members of her household could have been slaves, servants, or former slaves who were members of the church in Corinth. Paul had been informed by the members of Chloe's household that there were *quarrels* (Greek: *eris*), meaning "discord" (see 1 Corinthians 6:1; 2 Corinthians 12:20; Philippians 2:14; 2 Timothy 2:23; James 4:1-2).

Verse 12 is Paul's explanation of exactly what he meant. These disputes were not minor between individuals; rather, they were disputes that led to factions being created among the members. They had formed cliques within the congregation around some of the most important Christian leaders of that era. There is no indication that the groups or cliques were formed by the individual Christian leader; rather, they were the result of how the Corinthians idolized men and women of importance and influence. One characteristic of Corinthian society was the infatuation with intellectuals and men and women with larger-than-life social standing and wealth. It was not uncommon, therefore, for the average Corinthian to want to identify with persons whom they believed gave them worth.

The word *follow* means that individuals saw themselves as disciples or students of the names mentioned. It may be that they admired the person for his teaching or preaching, which is certainly similar to what we see in the church today. Apollos, a Jew from Alexandria, Egypt, rose to become one of the most prominent preachers in the first-century Christian church. Outside of the few references to him in the New Testament we know very little about his background or what ultimately happened to him (see Acts 18:24-28; 19:1; 1 Corinthians 3:22; 4:6; 16:12). *Cephas* is the Aramaic name for Peter. There is no record that Peter ever visited Corinth, although it may have been possible during his years of active apostolic ministry. Paul always used the name Cephas when referring to Peter (see 1 Corinthians 3:22; 9:5; 15:5; Galatians 1:18; 2:9, 11). The final group was made up of members of the "Jesus faction." These may have been persons who genuinely wanted to identify with Jesus, or they may have been a group who saw themselves as hyper-spiritual. They may have been a group who dismissed all human teachers and chose to align themselves solely with Jesus Christ. We are not sure what any of these groups believed or taught—neither is it clear if they had a set of beliefs based upon the teachings or preaching of the men they revered.

C. Division over Baptism
(1 Corinthians 1:13-17)

Is Christ divided? was Paul crucified for you? or were ye baptized in the name of Paul? I thank God that I baptized none of you, but Crispus and Gaius; Lest any should say that I had baptized in mine own name. And I baptized also the household of Stephanas: besides, I know not whether I baptized any other. For Christ sent me not to baptize, but to preach the gospel: not with wisdom of words, lest the cross of Christ should be made of none effect.

Verse 13 begins a series of rhetorical questions in which the answer to the question is implied within the question. The questions were phrased in such a way as to confront the Corinthians with the foolishness with which they were carrying on. "Is Christ divided?" The most logical answer is no! "Was Paul crucified for you?" Again, the answer is no! "Or were ye baptized in the name of Paul?" Again, the answer is a resounding no!

Verses 13-17 contain a brief discussion about baptism and how it may have been a source of conflict within the church. The word *Baptism* comes from the Greek word *baptize,* and it means "to dip or submerge in water." It is one of the ritual acts of the Christian faith (see Matthew 28:19; Acts 2:38). The word can be used metaphorically to express the idea of spiritual cleansing or spiritual birth (see Romans 6:3-4; Ephesians 4:5). It is clear from the context of the passage that Paul did not see the baptism of new converts as one of his responsibilities as an apostle. He expressed thanksgiving that he had not been involved in the baptism of any of the people who were at the center of the controversy, except Crispus and Gaius.

Crispus was the ruler of the Jewish synagogue in Corinth and was one of the first and most well-known converts of Paul in that city (see Acts 18:8). Gaius was a common Roman name and identified a man who was converted in Corinth and remained quite loyal to Paul (see Acts 19:29; Romans 16:23). Gaius accompanied Paul on his last journey from Corinth to Jerusalem (see Acts 20:4). The reason why Paul made the statement regarding baptism was so that no one could claim to have been baptized in his name.

In verse 16, Paul mentioned that he had baptized the entire household of Stephanas, which quite possibility refers to his family and his slaves and servants. Beyond the names mentioned, Paul had no recollection of having baptized anyone else. And besides, he had not been sent to baptize, but to preach with power the truth of the Gospel. He reminded them that he was not one for the fanciful rhetoric and catchy sayings that often accompanied much of the preaching of that era.

III. CONCLUDING REFLECTION

All churches have problems. It does not matter about the size, ethnicity, geography, denomination, or any other identifying trait—all churches have problems. We have worked with churches in Nigeria and more recently in Kenya, and we have seen some of the same types of problems there that are experienced here. When we work with pastors and church leaders in Kenya, I say here is a problem that we have—and their response is—"We have that same problem here." Some churches have problems with physical resources, others with people, some with the lack of money, and others have serious leadership issues. Some have internal struggles for power and authority, others have overwhelming concerns with apathy and the lack of member involvement in mission and ministry, others lack visionary leadership, and others lack committed followers; some never grow and soon go out of existence, while others have issues because of their size. The litany of issues that plague all churches can go on and on. I say again, all churches have problems.

The difference between congregations that thrive and grow spiritually has a lot to do with the ability of the leaders to work through problems and resolve them in a manner that is well-pleasing to the plan and purpose of God for that congregation. Some congregational problems go unchecked and unresolved for years, until they eventually eat away at the fabric and heart of the congregation. The Word of God teaches us that God has so fixed the body that every healthy congregation is able to resolve its own unique problems and come to some resolution that empowers the church to grow.

PRAYER

Heavenly Father, grant that by Your Holy Spirit we may learn to live together in harmony and peace. Give Your servants the spirit of humility, so that we deem others more worthy than ourselves. In Jesus' name we pray. Amen.

WORD POWER

Perfectly united (Greek: *katartizo*)—means to "complete" or "mend what has been broken."

HOME DAILY BIBLE READINGS
(June 23-29, 2014)

Let's All Get Along
MONDAY, June 23: "Being of the Same Mind" (Philippians 4:1-7)
TUESDAY, June 24: "Empowered by the Same Spirit" (1 Corinthians 12:4-11)
WEDNESDAY, June 25: "Maintaining the Unity of the Spirit" (Ephesians 4:1-6)
THURSDAY, June 26: "Many Members in One Body" (1 Corinthians 12:12-20)
FRIDAY, June 27: "No Dissension within the Body" (1 Corinthians 12:21-26)
SATURDAY, June 28: "Members of the Body of Christ" (1 Corinthians 12:27-31)
SUNDAY, June 29: "Agreement without Divisions" (1 Corinthians 1:10-17)

End Note

[1]Gordon D. Fee, *The First Epistle to the Corinthians: The New International Commentary on the New Testament* (Grand Rapids: William B. Eerdmans Publishing Co., 1987), 54.

LESSON 6   July 6, 2014

GLORIFY GOD WITH YOUR BODY

Faith Pathway/Faith Journey Topic: Do No Harm

Devotional Reading: Ephesians 4:7-16
Print Passage: 1 Corinthians 6:12-20

Background Scripture: 1 Corinthians 6:12–7:9
Key Verse: 1 Corinthians 6:19

1 Corinthians 6:12-20—KJV

12 All things are lawful unto me, but all things are not expedient: all things are lawful for me, but I will not be brought under the power of any.

13 Meats for the belly, and the belly for meats: but God shall destroy both it and them. Now the body is not for fornication, but for the Lord; and the Lord for the body.

14 And God hath both raised up the Lord, and will also raise up us by his own power.

15 Know ye not that your bodies are the members of Christ? shall I then take the members of Christ, and make them the members of an harlot? God forbid.

16 What? know ye not that he which is joined to an harlot is one body? for two, saith he, shall be one flesh.

17 But he that is joined unto the Lord is one spirit.

18 Flee fornication. Every sin that a man doeth is without the body; but he that committeth fornication sinneth against his own body.

19 What? know ye not that your body is the temple of the Holy Ghost which is in you, which ye have of God, and ye are not your own?

20 For ye are bought with a price: therefore glorify God in your body, and in your spirit, which are God's.

1 Corinthians 6:12-20—NIV

12 "Everything is permissible for me"—but not everything is beneficial. "Everything is permissible for me"—but I will not be mastered by anything.

13 "Food for the stomach and the stomach for food"—but God will destroy them both. The body is not meant for sexual immorality, but for the Lord, and the Lord for the body.

14 By his power God raised the Lord from the dead, and he will raise us also.

15 Do you not know that your bodies are members of Christ himself? Shall I then take the members of Christ and unite them with a prostitute? Never!

16 Do you not know that he who unites himself with a prostitute is one with her in body? For it is said, "The two will become one flesh."

17 But he who unites himself with the Lord is one with him in spirit.

18 Flee from sexual immorality. All other sins a man commits are outside his body, but he who sins sexually sins against his own body.

19 Do you not know that your body is a temple of the Holy Spirit, who is in you, whom you have received from God? You are not your own;

20 you were bought at a price. Therefore honor God with your body.

BIBLE FACT

How do we, as believers, glorify God with our bodies? It is when we recognize that our bodies are the temple of the Holy Spirit; therefore, we are careful about what we allow to come into or go out of our mouths.

TOPICAL OUTLINE OF THE LESSON

I. Introduction
A. No Person Is an Island
B. Biblical Background

II. Exposition and Application of the Scripture
A. A Matter of Perspective (1 Corinthians 6:12)
B. A Matter of Principle (1 Corinthians 6:13-17)
C. A Matter of Privilege (1 Corinthians 6:18-20)

III. Concluding Reflection

LESSON OBJECTIVES

Upon completion of the lesson, the students will be able to do the following:

1. Review the apostle Paul's comparison of the body to a temple;

2. Understand that as members of the community of Christ, their bodies are no longer theirs to abuse, but they must be kept pure; and,

3. Promote clean living within the faith community.

POINTS TO BE EMPHASIZED

ADULT/YOUTH
Adult Topic: Do No Harm
Youth Topic: You Are Not Your Own
Adult/Youth Key Verse: 1 Corinthians 6:19
Print Passage: 1 Corinthians 6:12-20

—*Lawful* means "permissible." *Beneficial* means "to the advantage of the community." (See 6:12.)
—In Corinthian culture, immorality and religious devotion were not seen as mutually exclusive.
—Paul propounded glorifying God as one of a Christian's primary responsibilities.
—Having sexual relations outside of the marriage bond is a perversion of the divinely established marriage union.
—Paul believed that Christians have freedom of choice and that everything is permissible—but not all choices are beneficial.
—Paul reminded the Corinthians that their bodies were "[temples] of the Holy Spirit," places in which God dwells—therefore, they should honor God with their bodies.

CHILDREN
Children Topic: We Must Work Together
Key Verse: Ephesians 4:15
Print Passage: Ephesians 4:7, 11-13, 15-16

—Christ's grace is a gift to all who believe.
—Christ gives various responsibilities and talents to followers.
—All callings and gifts within the body of Christ are given for the benefit of all.
—Believers grow through Christ toward a mature faith.
—As Christians work together in Christ, their faith in God matures.

I. INTRODUCTION

A. No Person Is an Island

Money, sex, and alcohol/drugs have been called the biggest three causes of moral failure in politics and religion. Every year, the Christian church is rocked by revelations of moral failure by some high-profile religious personality. In recent years, there has been a continuous procession of sex scandals that involve senior pastors and priests in both the Protestant and the Roman Catholic churches. Why do these things happen over and over again? Some of the moral failures are the result of what people believe to be their right to freedom of life and the pursuit of personal happiness. Many believe that as long as what they do has no direct impact on the church then what they do is permissible. (For example: the controversy surrounding same-sex marriage and the belief even among some high-profile religious leaders that the Scriptures condone and even endorse the practice.) In many ways the Christian faith is experiencing the infusion of many cultural beliefs and practices into the daily life and theological beliefs of the church.

Personal, moral, and physical purity are beneficial to the community. How does the behavior of one person affect the whole community? Paul said that because Christians are all one within the body of Christ, what harms one will harm other members, and what benefits one will benefit all.

B. Biblical Background

First Corinthians 6:12-20 has been called one of the most difficult passages to swallow in the New Testament. One reason has to do with a clearly defined understanding of the context of the passage and exactly what and to whom Paul was referring when he wrote this letter. It is clear that Paul was addressing some serious issues regarding the moral behavior of members of the church. In this passage, Paul continued to refute the false beliefs and practices held by many Corinthian Christians that they were free to live without restraints. Earlier he had challenged the saints about their willingness to tolerate a man sleeping with or living with his father's wife (see 1 Corinthians 5:1). Furthermore, they continued to practice their desires to litigate every dispute through the legal system and even take each other to court, which was a common social practice in Corinthian society.

Within Corinthian society, it was believed that all things were lawful. "Everything is permissible for me" was most likely a Corinthian maxim that new Christians might have found difficult to give up. It did not matter whether it was meat sacrificed to idols or solicitation of prostitutes—they felt that these things had no impact upon one's spirituality. Were there members in the congregation who consorted with local prostitutes? Were there other cases of sexual immorality that were high-profile incidents like the one mentioned in 5:1? It appears so.

The central theme of the passage focuses on sexual immorality (*porneia*), which is mentioned three times in verses 13 and 18. Having sex outside of marriage was common and condoned in Corinthian society. Paul propounded that glorifying God is one of a Christian's primary responsibilities. Marriage is a sacred union between a husband and wife and the defilement of the marital bed is a perversion in the eyes of God. Paul concluded the passage by reminding the saints in Corinth that their bodies were the temples of the Holy Spirit, and it was their responsibility to guard that sacred place.

II. EXPOSITION AND APPLICATION OF THE SCRIPTURE

A. A Matter of Perspective
(1 Corinthians 6:12)

All things are lawful unto me, but all things are not expedient: all things are lawful for me, but I will not be brought under the power of any.

Paul began this section by highlighting a commonly used Corinthian maxim: "All things are lawful" (*Amplified Bible*). He used this phrase twice in verse 12 to make a point about the flawed perspective from which the Corinthians viewed Christian freedom. Scholars have debated where and how this slogan originated within Corinthian society. Some scholars even believe that Paul may have coined it in his teachings with the Corinthians about Christian liberty (see 1 Corinthians 10:23). Regardless of its origin, there were many within the Corinthian congregation who adopted this slogan as justification for their own sexual activities outside of their marriage.

"Permissible" or "lawful" does not mean that one has the legal right to do what had been previously prohibited. Rather, it indicates freedom from the Law of Moses and the crippling paralysis of traditionalism (see Romans 6:14-15; 1 Corinthians 9:19-21; Galatians 5:1; Colossians 2:21-23). While one may be free to live authentically for Jesus Christ, there is a sense in which freedom is not always beneficial to the larger body of believers (see 1 Corinthians 10:24). One's actions must always be viewed in light of whether it helps or hinders the work of Jesus Christ in the world. In the second part of the verse, Paul made it clear that even though he was free, he would not be bound or enslaved by anything or anyone. The word *mastered* comes from the Greek word *Exousiazo* (ex-oo-see-ad-zo) and literally means "to have full control and mastery over the body or to be brought under the power of anyone." Paul made it clear that believers could not possibly live for Christ and be mastered by their passions and sexual desires.

B. A Matter of Principle
(1 Corinthians 6:13-17)

Meats for the belly, and the belly for meats: but God shall destroy both it and them. Now the body is not for fornication, but for the Lord; and the Lord for the body. And God hath both raised up the Lord, and will also raise up us by his own power. Know ye not that your bodies are the members of Christ? shall I then take the members of Christ, and make them the members of an harlot? God forbid. What? know ye not that he which is joined to an harlot is one body? for two, saith he, shall be one flesh. But he that is joined unto the Lord is one spirit.

In verses 13-17, Paul further refuted the flawed theology of members of the Corinthian church by quoting a second well-known maxim. "Food for the stomach and the stomach for food...." was a common belief that stated that just as food is for the stomach, so the stomach was made for food. It was really not about food, but about the satisfaction of one's personal physical and sexual appetites. Some scholars have questioned whether the maxim included the phrase "but God shall destroy them both"—because it fits and finishes the thought regarding the rationale for being free to engage in any activity that satisfies human cravings. The belief ran something like this: because the stomach and food were physical it did not matter what one did with the body, because one day God would destroy both of them. The thing that mattered most was the preservation of the spirit of a man or woman. One was therefore free to indulge in those things that satisfied the body. These were beliefs and practices that were deeply ingrained within the fabric of ancient Greek culture.

Paul refuted this flawed belief by stating that God did not create the human body for sexual immorality (see Word Power). Rather, the body was made for the Lord and the Lord for the body. Paul was not clear as to exactly what he meant by these statements. It may be that just as God raised Jesus' physical body from the dead, even so one day believers can look forward to the physical resurrection of our bodies (see 1 Corinthians 15:15-58). The physical body must therefore be regarded as sacred and not abused by engaging in illicit sexual activities.

In verse 15, Paul began the first of three rhetorical questions, all beginning with the same formula: "Do you not know" and "Know ye not" (KJV). The implication is either that they were not informed and needed to be informed about matters of sexual immorality, or that they had been taught but continued to allow their cultural beliefs to dictate their conduct. He reminded them that they were members of Christ. When they were born again they were mystically united with Jesus Christ, just as a man is united with his wife in marriage (see Galatians 2:20; Ephesians 5:22-23). Here the reference is not to individuals but to all of them collectively who belonged to Jesus Christ. They were members of His body. Paul raised a follow-up question: "Shall I then take the members of Christ, and make them the members of an harlot?" Was Paul referring to a specific act where a member joined himself with a prostitute, or was he referring to the practice of sacred prostitution, which was common in the pagan temples around Corinth? We cannot be sure, but it seems that Paul was continuing to address the matter of sexual immorality in general. The mention of members indicates that Paul believed that if one member joined himself or herself with a prostitute, then the whole church would be caught up in the act. He answered with an emphatic "No, it cannot be so!"

Verse 16 contains the third rhetorical question, beginning with "Do you not know....?" In this instance, Paul used the Jewish interpretation of marriage to refute the belief that sexual freedom was acceptable even with prostitutes (see Genesis 2:24). When a man and a woman engaged in sexual intercourse the two became one, according to the Law of Moses. Sexual intercourse with a prostitute could not be seen as an innocent personal matter; rather, it created a union that was as deep as that of husband and wife. Paul wanted the church to understand that these actions would have grave spiritual consequences for the church at-large. Rather than unite with prostitutes, Paul called upon the Corinthians to be fully united with the Lord Jesus Christ.

C. A Matter of Privilege
(1 Corinthians 6:18-20)

Flee fornication. Every sin that a man doeth is without the body; but he that committeth fornication sinneth against his own body. What? know ye not that your body is the temple of the Holy Ghost which is in you, which ye have of God, and ye are not your own? For ye are bought with a price: therefore glorify God in your body, and in your spirit, which are God's.

Paul concluded this section with a very strong imperative command: "flee" (Greek: *pheugo* [fyoo-go]), which means to literally "seek safety." Paul exhorted the Corinthians to run away from the very presence of opportunities that presented the temptation to commit sexual immorality (see 2 Timothy 2:22). He stated the reason why they were to flee sexual immorality in the very next line. When a man or woman commits a sexual sin, it is not like any other sin because it involves the very inner being of the people committing the sexual act. The two people are united in ways that were never intended by God. If sexual relations are between a husband and his wife, then the incursion of a third party creates a grave violation of that sacred relationship (see Hebrews 13:4). Because the wife is mystically united with her husband, a violation of that sacred trust means that he has violated himself (see Ephesians 5:28-29). God's will is for the believer to live holy and free from the contamination of sin (see Ephesians 5:3; 1 Thessalonians 4:3).

In verse 19, Paul cited the reason why the believers were to avoid and flee sexual immorality. Their bodies were the temple (*naos*) of the Holy Spirit, who indwells the believer (see John 14:17; Romans 14:7; 1 Peter 2:5). When the Holy Spirit entered the world on Pentecost, He filled the lives of each believer and produced within them the fruit of His presence (see Acts 2:1-4; Galatians 5:22-25). Paul reminded them that this was no ordinary gift, but one received from God. They did not own themselves because they had been purchased with a price. The word *bought* is a translation of the Greek word *agorazo* (ag-or-ad-zo), and it comes from the root word "agora," which refers to the marketplace or the place of commerce and business—a term that they would clearly understand. When Jesus Christ died on the cross, He purchased our salvation and redemption through the shedding of His own blood. Therefore, He owns the church.

III. CONCLUDING REFLECTION

What is sexual immorality? In Western culture, it depends on the person answering the question. There are millions of Americans who see nothing wrong with sexual intercourse outside of marriage. This form of sexual interaction is often depicted in motion pictures and frequently on daytime and primetime television programs. Even within the church there may be people who hold the view that there is nothing wrong or sinful about sexual intercourse outside of marriage, because God created us as sexual beings. The same holds true for prostitution, which is viewed in some places as an acceptable, legal business.

Paul made it clear that sexual intercourse outside of marriage is categorically wrong and sinful. It is destructive of marriage and contaminates the inner sanctuary of the Holy Spirit, which is the body of the believer.

PRAYER

Heavenly Father, teach us to honor You by the way that we live. May we be more attuned to the presence of the Holy Spirit who lives within each of us. Thank You for the precious gift of eternal life through Your Son. In Jesus' name we pray. Amen.

WORD POWER

Sexual Immorality—is a translation of the Greek word *porneia* (por-ni-ah). It refers to illicit sexual intercourse, adultery, fornication, lesbianism, intercourse with animals, and sexual intercourse with a divorced man or woman (see Romans 1:29; compare verses 24-32; Galatians 5:19; Revelation 2:14).

Temple—In the New Testament, there are two Greek words that are translated "temple": *heiron* and *naos*. *Heiron* (hee-er-on) denotes the physical structure of the temple or a sacred place (see John 10:33); the word *naos* is used to designate the most sacred place within the temple precincts—the Holy Place or the Holy of Holies. Paul used the term as a metaphor to denote the sacredness of the believer's physical body as the dwelling place of the Holy Spirit (see 1 Corinthians 3:16-17; Ephesians 2:21). In some instances, he used the term to apply to individuals and on other occasions he used it to refer to the entire church as the body of Christ.

HOME DAILY BIBLE READINGS
(June 30–July 6, 2014)

Glorify God with Your Body

MONDAY, June 30: "Building Up the Body of Christ" (Ephesians 4:7-16)

TUESDAY, July 1: "Building Up the Beloved" (2 Corinthians 12:14-21)

WEDNESDAY, July 2: "Sincerity and Truth in the Body" (1 Corinthians 5:1-8)

THURSDAY, July 3: "Dissociating from Immorality in the Body" (1 Corinthians 5:9-13)

FRIDAY, July 4: "Washed, Sanctified, and Justified" (1 Corinthians 6:1-11)

SATURDAY, July 5: "A Particular Gift from God" (1 Corinthians 7:1-9)

SUNDAY, July 6: "Glorify God in Your Body" (1 Corinthians 6:12-20)

LESSON 7 | July 13, 2014

LOVE BUILDS UP

FAITH PATHWAY/FAITH JOURNEY TOPIC: Love Builds Up

DEVOTIONAL READING: Romans 14:7-12
PRINT PASSAGE: 1 Corinthians 8:1-13

BACKGROUND SCRIPTURE: 1 Corinthians 8
KEY VERSE: 1 Corinthians 8:9

1 Corinthians 8:1-13—KJV

NOW AS touching things offered unto idols, we know that we all have knowledge. Knowledge puffeth up, but charity edifieth.

2 And if any man think that he knoweth any thing, he knoweth nothing yet as he ought to know.

3 But if any man love God, the same is known of him.

4 As concerning therefore the eating of those things that are offered in sacrifice unto idols, we know that an idol is nothing in the world, and that there is none other God but one.

5 For though there be that are called gods, whether in heaven or in earth, (as there be gods many, and lords many,)

6 But to us there is but one God, the Father, of whom are all things, and we in him; and one Lord Jesus Christ, by whom are all things, and we by him.

7 Howbeit there is not in every man that knowledge: for some with conscience of the idol unto this hour eat it as a thing offered unto an idol; and their conscience being weak is defiled.

8 But meat commendeth us not to God: for neither, if we eat, are we the better; neither, if we eat not, are we the worse.

9 But take heed lest by any means this liberty of yours become a stumblingblock to them that are weak.

10 For if any man see thee which hast knowledge sit at meat in the idol's temple, shall not the conscience of him which is weak be emboldened to eat those things which are offered to idols;

11 And through thy knowledge shall the weak brother perish, for whom Christ died?

12 But when ye sin so against the brethren, and wound their weak conscience, ye sin against Christ.

13 Wherefore, if meat make my brother to offend, I will eat no flesh while the world standeth, lest I make my brother to offend.

1 Corinthians 8:1-13—NIV

NOW ABOUT food sacrificed to idols: We know that we all possess knowledge. Knowledge puffs up, but love builds up.

2 The man who thinks he knows something does not yet know as he ought to know.

3 But the man who loves God is known by God.

4 So then, about eating food sacrificed to idols: We know that an idol is nothing at all in the world and that there is no God but one.

5 For even if there are so-called gods, whether in heaven or on earth (as indeed there are many "gods" and many "lords"),

6 yet for us there is but one God, the Father, from whom all things came and for whom we live; and there is but one Lord, Jesus Christ, through whom all things came and through whom we live.

7 But not everyone knows this. Some people are still so accustomed to idols that when they eat such food they think of it as having been sacrificed to an idol, and since their conscience is weak, it is defiled.

8 But food does not bring us near to God; we are no worse if we do not eat, and no better if we do.

9 Be careful, however, that the exercise of your freedom does not become a stumbling block to the weak.

10 For if anyone with a weak conscience sees you who have this knowledge eating in an idol's temple, won't he be emboldened to eat what has been sacrificed to idols?

11 So this weak brother, for whom Christ died, is destroyed by your knowledge.

12 When you sin against your brothers in this way and wound their weak conscience, you sin against Christ.

13 Therefore, if what I eat causes my brother to fall into sin, I will never eat meat again, so that I will not cause him to fall.

TOPICAL OUTLINE OF THE LESSON

I. Introduction

A. The Limits of Personal Freedom

B. Biblical Background

II. Exposition and Application of the Scripture

A. Love versus Knowledge (1 Corinthians 8:1-3)

B. Instructions Regarding Meat Sacrificed to Idols (1 Corinthians 8:4-8)

C. Warnings against Causing Others to Stumble (1 Corinthians 8:9-13)

III. Concluding Reflection

LESSON OBJECTIVES

Upon completion of the lesson, the students will be able to do the following:

1. Explore the positive and negative influences that community members have on one another;

2. Accept that Christians should consider how their behavior might negatively affect others in the community; and,

3. Examine personal behavior for things that might negatively influence others and consider changing the behavior.

POINTS TO BE EMPHASIZED

ADULT/YOUTH

Adult Topic: Love Builds Up

Youth Topic: Building Up the Community

Adult/Youth Key Verse: 1 Corinthians 8:9

Print Passage: 1 Corinthians 8:1-13

—Meat sacrificed to idols in temples was commonly sold in local markets for consumption.

—Some Christians feared that eating idol-sacrificed meat would make them unclean.

—"Stumbling block to the weak" means an impediment or hindrance to their faith.

—The central theme of this passage is unity through building one another up.

—Knowledge sometimes leads to arrogance, which can be a detriment to the unity and harmony of a community of believers.

—The lives of Christians should reflect a careful exercise of their freedom in Christ so they will not be stumbling blocks to others.

CHILDREN

Children Topic: Healthy Eating

Key Verse: 1 Corinthians 8:8

Print Passage: 1 Corinthians 8:1-13

—Eating food that had been sacrificed to idols was an issue for some believers in Corinth.

—Paul felt free to eat anything, but he refrained from some foods for the sake of others.

—All things, including food, have their origin in God.

—Avoid actions that might be obstacles for others as they grow in faith.

I. INTRODUCTION

A. The Limits of Personal Freedom

John was the oldest and longest tenured pastor in the city. He had built a reputation of being a deeply spiritual man whose faith and commitment to the Lord Jesus Christ were greatly admired by other pastors in the city. One of John's long-standing customs was to invite the newest pastor in the city to join him and Emily, his wife, for a get-acquainted dinner. Faith Baptist Church had been without a pastor for more than two years when they called a young seminary graduate named George. Shortly after settling into their new home, John invited George and his wife to join him and Emily for dinner. Shortly after they were seated, the waiter asked if they wanted to order some dinner wine for the occasion. John ordered a very expensive bottle of wine as a way of welcoming the new pastor and his wife to the city. George and his wife were horrified and shocked that John and Emily would order wine in a public setting and then invite them to have a drink with them. Was John wrong, or did the young pastor overreact to the invitation?

In this chapter, Paul wrote to address a serious problem among the Corinthians regarding Christian freedom. There were members of the local church who felt free to eat meat that had been sacrificed idols, and their behavior caused many new believers to stumble. What may be right for some members of a community may not be right for others. How are community members to hold one another accountable? Paul cautioned the faithful to behave in ways that would not cause others to falter in their faith.

B. Biblical Background

The church in Corinth was a congregation filled with strife, division, and cliques. In the previous lesson, we learned how Paul may have come to receive information about the friction going on in the congregation. There were a number of internal problems that had reached a fevered pitch, and unless they were addressed, the church could literally implode. We would probably consider some of the problems to be insignificant; but in that day, they were a major theological and social hurdle. One such issue revolved around whether it was permissible to eat food that had been sacrificed to idols. There were battle lines drawn within the congregation on both sides of the question. One group claimed to possess superior knowledge, which became the source of their freedom and permission to eat food sacrificed to idols. Paul reminded them that real spiritual strength and power does not come from knowledge, but from love. In this passage, we see two very important Jewish precepts: "There are no idols" and "there is no God but one," along with a Christian precept: "one God, one Lord."

Corinth was heavily populated with pagan worshippers and pagan temples. At the center of pagan worship was the sacrifice of animals. The ancient world was filled with superstitions of all sorts. One of the reasons why animals were sacrificed was to purify the food before it was eaten. Many people believed that one of the ways demons entered the body was through food. Therefore, once a portion of it was sacrificed it was then made pure.

The animal sacrificed was usually divided three ways: a portion was burned on the altar, the temple priest received a portion, and finally the person making the sacrifice received what remained. Often the meat that was not used in idol worship services was either eaten at a banquet at the Temple, or was sold on the open market in Corinth. Some Christians feared that eating meat that had been sacrificed to idols would make them unclean and would hinder their faith in Jesus Christ. There were others who believed that it would do no harm at all because they knew that an idol was not God. Paul reminded the church that even though idols did not represent God he would not eat meat if it would cause his brother to stumble.

II. EXPOSITION AND APPLICATION OF THE SCRIPTURE

A. Love versus Knowledge
(1 Corinthians 8:1-3)

NOW AS touching things offered unto idols, we know that we all have knowledge. Knowledge puffeth up, but charity edifieth. And if any man think that he knoweth any thing, he knoweth nothing yet as he ought to know. But if any man love God, the same is known of him.

The Corinthians wrote to Paul and asked that he address a number of questions regarding the social and spiritual life within the church (see 1 Corinthians 7:1). From the reading of this letter, it is clear that there were a group of people in the church who felt that they stood head and shoulders above the others whom they deemed to be the weaker or less experienced among them. In this section of his letter, Paul addressed the issue of meat or food that had been sacrificed to idols. Paul reminded the saints that everyone in the church possessed some degree of knowledge: "We all possess knowledge...." Evidently there were members who felt superior because they knew that an idol was not God, so they were free to enjoy any food, regardless of whether or not it was used in pagan worship.

Paul reminded the Corinthians that they should never see knowledge as the basis for determining how they should live in community with others. He offered three reasons why knowledge was an insufficient basis for making ethical decisions regarding eating food sacrificed to idols. First, he said "knowledge puffs up." The Greek word *phusioo* literally means "to swell." People with knowledge believed that they were stronger or more enlightened than others (see Isaiah 5:21; 47:10). Paul said this was the wrong basis upon which to make ethical decisions regarding food. Love, on the other hand, builds up and edifies the body, which is a theme he would deal with in detail in 13:4 (see Romans 14:19; 15:14).

The second reason is found in verse 2, where Paul stated that the man who thought he knew everything in reality had only limited knowledge (see 1 Corinthians 13:9, 12). It is impossible for any one person to know everything. This is arrogance and pride at its worst. Paul stated that even with our vast storehouse of knowledge there is more to be learned and known.

Verse 3 contains the third reason why

knowledge is inferior to love. It is far better to be known by God than to claim knowledge of God. There are scores of people in local churches who have acquired a great deal of knowledge about God and the Bible, but have never developed a true relationship with God. Hence they know God, but God does not know them. The point that Paul made was akin to Isaiah's: how much can humans truly know about God? (See Isaiah 55:8-9.)

B. Instructions Regarding Meat Sacrificed to Idols (1 Corinthians 8:4-8)

As concerning therefore the eating of those things that are offered in sacrifice unto idols, we know that an idol is nothing in the world, and that there is none other God but one. For though there be that are called gods, whether in heaven or in earth, (as there be gods many, and lords many,) But to us there is but one God, the Father, of whom are all things, and we in him; and one Lord Jesus Christ, by whom are all things, and we by him. Howbeit there is not in every man that knowledge: for some with conscience of the idol unto this hour eat it as a thing offered unto an idol; and their conscience being weak is defiled. But meat commendeth us not to God: for neither, if we eat, are we the better; neither, if we eat not, are we the worse.

In verse 4, Paul returned to the discussion about food that had been sacrificed to idols. He affirmed the position of those in the church who knew that an idol was not God. They all agreed that there was only one God (see Deuteronomy 6:4; Ephesians 4:6; 1 Timothy 2:5). Paul agreed that there were other gods; however, these were not real gods but the works of men's hands (see Psalm 115:4-8; Isaiah 35:19).

We must be careful to avoid the mistake of assuming that Paul affirmed the existence of other gods based upon his statements in verse 5. What Paul affirmed was the existence of the practice of worshipping pagan gods and idols. An idol derives its life from the man or woman who looks to it as a god. Paul reminded the Corinthians that all of life was sustained by the one God, who is both Creator and Sustainer (see Genesis 1:1; Isaiah 40:18-26). While others may claim to be lords, there is but one Lord, Jesus Christ, who is both the source of life and giver of life (see Ephesians 4:4-6). Christians live under the sovereign rule of the Lord Jesus Christ, who is all things to the church (see Ephesians 1:22-23).

In verse 7, Paul agreed that not everyone knew that idols did not really exist. Many of the Christians in the church had come out of pagan religious backgrounds and some of them still affirmed the existence of idol gods. It was inconceivable that an idol could bless anyone, since it did not really exist. Many of the believers had not grown to the point of being free of the shackles of superstitious beliefs and practices associated with pagan worship. Those who were unable to break free were convicted by their conscience, which is the capacity to distinguish between what is morally right and wrong. Paul stated that the tragedy that befell the weaker believer was a defiled conscience and a distorted view of what is morally and spiritually correct and what was corrupted of Christian character. How often does this happen among believers, where the unsuspecting are spiritually demoralized and damaged by those who feel free to do and say whatever they feel free to do and say?

Paul concluded his argument by stating that it is not what goes into a person that weakens him or her spiritually. Eating foods used in pagan sacrifices had no real impact upon one's relationship to Jesus Christ. It did not matter one way or the other whether a person ate food sacrificed to idols or passed on it.

C. Warnings against Causing Others to Stumble (1 Corinthians 8:9-13)

But take heed lest by any means this liberty of yours become a stumblingblock to them that are weak. For if any man see thee which hast knowledge sit at meat in the idol's temple, shall not the conscience of him which is weak be emboldened to eat those things which are offered to idols; And through thy knowledge shall the weak brother perish, for whom Christ died? But when ye sin so against the brethren, and wound their weak conscience, ye sin against Christ. Wherefore, if meat make my brother to offend, I will eat no flesh while the world standeth, lest I make my brother to offend.

In verse 9, the final section of the passage begins with an imperative command: "Be careful." These words were addressed specifically to those who considered themselves to be the stronger and more knowledgeable saints. *Freedom* is translated from the Greek word *exousia*, which means "the power of choice" or the liberty to do as one pleases. The word is sometimes translated to express the idea of power or authority. Paul cautioned them that they did not allow their freedom or right to live free to cause a younger believer to stumble. The term *stumbling block* comes from the word *proskomma*, which metaphorically refers to setting obstacles in the way of others. The knowledge of the stronger saints had become a cause for concern because it created a crisis in the faith of Christians who were not as strong or knowledgeable (see Isaiah 57:14; Matthew 18:6; Romans 14:1, 13, 21; Galatians 5:13; Revelation 2:14).

According to verse 10, anyone with a weak conscience who may believe that eating meat offered to idols is wrong, but who sees a stronger believer eating such meat, could be led to believe that there was nothing wrong with eating such food sacrificed to idols.

Consequently, the weak brother or sister would be defeated and destroyed by the freedom of the believer with knowledge. There is a hint of sarcasm in the words of Paul (verse 11). In verse 12, Paul believed that this kind of reckless use of freedom amounted to sin. He did not say how this came about nor did he attempt to offer an explanation. It may be that to entice someone to participate in an action that he or she believes to be sin is tantamount to being a co-conspirator in the act. If someone believes that an act is sinful, then whether it is sinful or not is not important. In the writings of James, if a person knows to do good and does not do it, to him it is sin (see James 4:17). The same principle is at work in this case. The more grievous consequence is that the act becomes sin against Jesus Christ. Why? Because the stronger person has led a babe in Christ to commit an act that has destroyed him/her spiritually. Some people can never recover from this sort of damage early in their attempts to live for Jesus Christ. Paul concluded that it would be far better for him never to eat meat at all if it was going to be the cause of another believer stumbling and falling over his freedom.

III. CONCLUDING REFLECTION

Congregations can become embroiled in the most senseless conflicts over the most trivial of matters. Many very traditional congregations have strict rules about dress and protocols regarding Communion and who is able to handle the elements of Communion. Is it permissible to touch the Communion table? Are the deacons the only ones with the authority to handle the Communion service items? Are we still saved if we decide to have a glass of wine at dinner? Should churches sponsor dances for young people and members of the congregation who may sense a need to create social events? Because some of these items have long associations with being sinful, it may be unthinkable for many people that a church would sponsor, much less condone, a dance for young people. It is highly unlikely that a very traditional Christian would feel free enough to have a glass of dinner wine with other believers. The point of the passage is not what we are free to do or not do; rather, it is always to live in such a way that our freedom does not become the reason for why another Christian stumbles.

PRAYER

Heavenly Father, may we live in such a way that our freedom never becomes a cause of another believer's moral or spiritual failure. May we live in such a way that Your name is always glorified through us. In Jesus' name we pray. Amen.

WORD POWER

Conscience (Greek: *suneidesis* [soon-i-day-sis])—The word appears thirty-one times in the Scriptures, with all of them being in the New Testament. The word is used in moral theology to draw some distinguishing lines between right and wrong. At its deepest core, the word denotes something akin to our self-awareness of one's personal behavior or decisions. There is no equivalent concept in the Old Testament. The majority of the references to conscience appear in the letters of Paul (see Romans 2:15; 9:1; 13:5; 1 Corinthians 8:10, 12; 10:25, 27, 29; 2 Corinthians 1:12; 4:2; 1 Timothy 1:19).

HOME DAILY BIBLE READINGS
(July 7-13, 2014)

Love Builds Up

MONDAY, July 7: "Regulations for the Interim" (Hebrews 9:1-10)

TUESDAY, July 8: "Human Commands and Teachings" (Colossians 2:16-23)

WEDNESDAY, July 9: "Faith and Knowledge" (2 Peter 1:2-11)

THURSDAY, July 10: "Grow in Grace and Knowledge" (2 Peter 3:14-18)

FRIDAY, July 11: "Honoring and Giving Thanks to God" (Romans 14:1-6)

SATURDAY, July 12: "Accountable to God" (Romans 14:7-12)

SUNDAY, July 13: "Liberty or Stumbling Block?" (1 Corinthians 8)

LESSON 8 — July 20, 2014

OVERCOMING TEMPTATION

FAITH PATHWAY/FAITH JOURNEY TOPIC: **Strength to Meet Temptation**

DEVOTIONAL READING: **Hebrews 3:7-14**
PRINT PASSAGE: **1 Corinthians 10:12-22**

BACKGROUND SCRIPTURE: **1 Corinthians 10:1-22**
KEY VERSE: **1 Corinthians 10:13**

1 Corinthians 10:12-22—KJV

12 Wherefore let him that thinketh he standeth take heed lest he fall.

13 There hath no temptation taken you but such as is common to man: but God is faithful, who will not suffer you to be tempted above that ye are able; but will with the temptation also make a way to escape, that ye may be able to bear it.

14 Wherefore, my dearly beloved, flee from idolatry.

15 I speak as to wise men; judge ye what I say.

16 The cup of blessing which we bless, is it not the communion of the blood of Christ? The bread which we break, is it not the communion of the body of Christ?

17 For we being many are one bread, and one body: for we are all partakers of that one bread.

18 Behold Israel after the flesh: are not they which eat of the sacrifices partakers of the altar?

19 What say I then? that the idol is any thing, or that which is offered in sacrifice to idols is any thing?

20 But I say, that the things which the Gentiles sacrifice, they sacrifice to devils, and not to God: and I would not that ye should have fellowship with devils.

21 Ye cannot drink the cup of the Lord, and the cup of devils: ye cannot be partakers of the Lord's table, and of the table of devils.

22 Do we provoke the Lord to jealousy? are we stronger than he?

1 Corinthians 10:12-22—NIV

12 So, if you think you are standing firm, be careful that you don't fall!

13 No temptation has seized you except what is common to man. And God is faithful; he will not let you be tempted beyond what you can bear. But when you are tempted, he will also provide a way out so that you can stand up under it.

14 Therefore, my dear friends, flee from idolatry.

15 I speak to sensible people; judge for yourselves what I say.

16 Is not the cup of thanksgiving for which we give thanks a participation in the blood of Christ? And is not the bread that we break a participation in the body of Christ?

17 Because there is one loaf, we, who are many, are one body, for we all partake of the one loaf.

18 Consider the people of Israel: Do not those who eat the sacrifices participate in the altar?

19 Do I mean then that a sacrifice offered to an idol is anything, or that an idol is anything?

20 No, but the sacrifices of pagans are offered to demons, not to God, and I do not want you to be participants with demons.

21 You cannot drink the cup of the Lord and the cup of demons too; you cannot have a part in both the Lord's table and the table of demons.

22 Are we trying to arouse the Lord's jealousy? Are we stronger than he?

The pride of individual persons and communities can lead them to act in destructive or harmful ways. How can communities resist the desire to move in harmful directions? Paul reminded the Corinthians that all believers are tempted, but God will not let them be tested beyond their strength—God will provide the way out.

TOPICAL OUTLINE OF THE LESSON

I. Introduction
A. The Powerful Allure of Temptation
B. Biblical Background

II. Exposition and Application of the Scripture
A. Be Careful!
(1 Corinthians 10:12)
B. God Is Faithful
(1 Corinthians 10:13)
C. Flee Idolatry
(1 Corinthians 10:14-22)

III. Concluding Reflection

LESSON OBJECTIVES

Upon completion of the lesson, the students will be able to do the following:

1. Explore Paul's warnings about temptations;
2. Consider what harmful temptations Christians might encounter; and,
3. Make specific decisions to resist specific temptations.

POINTS TO BE EMPHASIZED
ADULT/YOUTH

Adult Topic: Strength to Meet Temptation
Youth Topic: Ignore Warnings, Pay Consequences
Adult/Youth Key Verse: 1 Corinthians 10:13
Print Passage: 1 Corinthians 10:12-22

—Paul's message about God was consistent: God always supplies the needs of those who love Him.

—The references to Communion confirmed that believers are bonded with Jesus Christ.

—Paul appealed to the Corinthian Christians as a community based on their being one body sharing the body of Christ.

—Paul denied that idols have any real being or power. (See verses 19-20.)

—The Corinthian Christians were warned about continuing in idolatry worship.

—Christians have a choice, said Paul, an exit path—and that is to believe that God is faithful and will not let them be tempted beyond their power to flee from idolatry.

CHILDREN

Children Topic: Making Good Choices
Key Verse: 1 Corinthians 10:13b
Print Passage: 1 Corinthians 10:12-15

—Paul knew that the Corinthian believers were tempted in many ways.

—Paul assured the believers that God would not let them be tested beyond their ability to overcome temptation.

—All people are tempted, though not in the same ways.

—Believers are responsible to avoid temptation as much as is possible.

—Through their oneness in Christ, believers can encourage others when they are tempted.

I. INTRODUCTION

A. The Powerful Allure of Temptation

The inability to resist and ward off temptation is one of the most powerful deterrents to our spiritual growth. Satan uses temptation to hinder our growth in grace. He does it with such cunning skill that by the time we realize what has happened, the tragic consequences of our actions have already started to take hold and produce defeat and even death. Adam and Eve plunged the whole world into sin before they realized the gravity of their mistake. Samson was too naive and assumed that he could tamper with God's commandments without any consequences. David stood on his balcony and reveled in the beauty of Bathsheba, while the devil tricked him into committing the most insidious sin of his life. Judas was duped into thinking that thirty pieces of silver were worth selling out His Lord and Master. Temptation is a powerful weapon in the hand of Satan.

Temptation is a force so sinister and powerful that it caused the first spiritual battle that Jesus fought and won (see Matthew 4:1-11). The temptations of Jesus were the first real tests of His resolve and commitment to the Father's redemptive purpose. Believers face many forms and types of temptation. Pride is one of the more subtle forms of temptation which leads to the belief that one can dabble in sinful acts and not be spiritually impacted. The pride of individual persons and communities can lead them to act in destructive or harmful ways. How can communities resist the desire to move in harmful directions? Paul reminded the Corinthians that all believers are tempted but God will not let them be tested beyond their strength—God will provide the way out.

B. Biblical Background

In the previous lesson, the Corinthians were consumed by their own self-delusions and thought that they were above spiritual failure. They believed this primarily because of their possession of a deeper knowledge of the truth. In today's lesson, Paul continued to warn them of the dangers of spiritual pride. In verses 1-11, Paul used the history of the Israelites as the framework for driving home his point in verses 13-22. Although the Israelites all had the same spiritual foundation, yet tens of thousands of them died in the wilderness and never received the promise. The same could have been true of the Corinthians, who believed that eating food sacrificed to idols did no harm to the spiritual well-being of believers. And although Paul concurred with this position, he thought it was necessary to remind the Corinthians that pride can be the downfall of any believer, regardless of how strong he or she believes himself or herself to be.

All Christians face temptation and Paul wanted the church to know that even when temptation comes, God will provide the means of endurance. Paul wanted the church to also know that it was impossible for them to participate in pagan worship, eat food sacrificed to idols, and still feel free to partake of the Lord's Supper. He reminded them that they were one body in Christ, united by His broken body and shed blood.

II. EXPOSITION AND APPLICATION OF THE SCRIPTURE

A. Be Careful!
(1 Corinthians 10:12)

Wherefore let him that thinketh he standeth take heed lest he fall.

Verse 12 forms the conclusion to Paul's discussion of Israel's history that began in verse 1. One of the first things that Paul did was to show a parallel between the failures of the ancient Israelites and that of the Corinthians. In verses 1-11, Paul referred to the wilderness experiences of the Israelites when thousands perished because of their disobedience and idolatry (see Numbers 14:29, 37; 16:41; 17:10; 25:1, 9). Paul wanted the Corinthians to see the past experiences of the Israelites as lessons to be learned and applied. The Corinthians were guilty of believing that they could indulge in their former practices of eating food sacrificed to idols and not be spiritually harmed. Their overconfidence in themselves was a huge mistake and a miscalculation of their strength. The warning was clear: "If you think you are standing firm, be careful." The words "be careful" are expressed in the present imperative tense and indicate the high level of importance attached to the instructions. Paul wanted them to know that it was possible to fall from grace (see Galatians 6:1). Believers make this mistake all the time in thinking that they can dabble in sin and play with the world and not be personally impacted by their carelessness. It is impossible not to be negatively impacted by the practice of sin (see Romans 6).

B. God Is Faithful
(1 Corinthians 10:13)

There hath no temptation taken you but such as is common to man: but God is faithful, who will not suffer you to be tempted above that ye are able; but will with the temptation also make a way to escape, that ye may be able to bear it.

In verse 13, Paul turned his attention from warning to encouraging the Corinthians on how to deal with the temptations associated with the pagan temples. The word *temptation* (*peirasmos*) does not refer to the temptation that leads to sin; rather, it denotes a period of trial or testing for the purpose of proving or validating. The Israelites fell in the wilderness because they were unable to overcome the temptation to trust in themselves and not God.

Paul pointed to two truths that he wanted them to grasp regarding their temptations. First, the Corinthians were not facing anything that others had not already faced before them. However difficult they felt the challenges to be, there were others who had experienced the same struggle. The challenges that they faced regarding the food offered to idols were common to all Christians living in cities with pagan temples, and therefore they should not have seen their situation as unique and different. There are occasions when believers are prone to think that their pain, dilemmas, heartbreak, or disappointments are unique to them. Throughout the history of the Christian faith there is no temptation faced by contemporary believers that has not been previously faced and overcome by saints of past generations.

Second, Paul wanted the Corinthians to realize that God is faithful, which is one of the central affirmations of the Scriptures (see 1 Corinthians 1:9; James 1:12; 2 Peter 2:9; Revelation 3:20). God was not going to allow them to face a challenge or temptation that would jeopardize their ability to overcome. God knew that there was a limit to what they were able to endure and He was fully aware of those limits. He knew their strengths and weaknesses. The one thing God will never do is to desert His people during the moments of their greatest tests and trials.

When they were tempted, God would provide an escape route so that they could endure the trial, even if it was for a brief moment. *Way out* (Greek: *ekbasis* [ek-bas-is]) means "egress." It is the picture of an army that is trapped by the enemy, when all is not lost because there is an escape route through the mountains that keeps them from being defeated. Believers never face temptation, trials, or troubles alone. God will always provide a means by which His people are able to escape or endure the period of testing.

C. Flee Idolatry
(1 Corinthians 10:14-22)

Wherefore, my dearly beloved, flee from idolatry. I speak as to wise men; judge ye what I say. The cup of blessing which we bless, is it not the communion of the blood of Christ? The bread which we break, is it not the communion of the body of Christ? For we being many are one bread, and one body: for we are all partakers of that one bread. Behold Israel after the flesh: are not they which eat of the sacrifices partakers of the altar? What say I then? that the idol is any thing, or that which is offered in sacrifice to idols is any thing? But I say, that the things which the Gentiles sacrifice, they sacrifice to devils, and not to God: and I would not that ye should have fellowship with devils. Ye cannot drink the cup of the Lord, and the cup of devils: ye cannot be partakers of the Lord's table, and of the table of devils. Do we provoke the Lord to jealousy? are we stronger than he?

The instructions regarding the eating of food sacrificed to idols began at 1 Corinthians 8:1. Throughout this lengthy discussion, Paul urged the Corinthian saints to understand that although there was nothing inherently sinful about eating such food, nevertheless they must be aware of the conscience of the weaker brother or sister.

In light of everything that has been stated regarding the practice of eating food sacrificed to idols, Paul strongly urged the Corinthians to "flee from idolatry." The word *Flee* has in it the idea of shunning, or simply flying away or getting as far away from this practice as possible. Paul did not accuse them of practicing idolatry, but the eating of food sacrificed to idols and attendance to the pagan festivals constituted a grave spiritual danger—not just for the individual but for the entire church.

In verse 15, Paul appealed to the intellectual side of the Corinthians. They prided themselves on being filled with wisdom and knowledge, so Paul spoke to that side of them. He wanted the Corinthians to give serious thought to what he had already stated and was about to state. The implication was that after weighing all of the evidence, they would then be in a position to judge for themselves the truthfulness of his arguments. One of the meanings of the word *judge* (Greek: *kino*) is "to separate." In this instance, it implied separating fact from fiction regarding the real harm that resulted from eating food sacrificed to idols.

Beginning at verse 16, Paul made a comparison between the eating of food sacrificed to idols and their participation in the Lord's Supper. Whenever one drinks from the cup, it is his/her full participation in the blood of Christ. Likewise, to break the bread is to fully participate in the body of Christ (see Luke 22:19-20). Participation comes from the Greek word *koinonia*, one of the most important descriptive terms in the New Testament. It indicates "an intimate fellowship or relationship between and among persons" (see Acts 2:42; 1 John 1:3, 7). Believers participate together when they share in the breaking of bread and drinking the cup.

Verse 17 highlights the mystical union of believers with Christ and one another. The one loaf is probably a reference to the single loaf of bread used in the Communion service at that time. The stress in the verse is on the unity of the body (see 1 Corinthians 12:12; Ephesians 4:4-6). Paul wanted the Corinthians to know that there was no such thing as an isolated individual within the body of Christ, no more than there were disconnected body parts (see 1 Corinthians 12:14-27). All were a part of each other and it is symbolized by the one loaf.

Again, in verse 18, Paul appealed to the tradition and practices of the Israelites. Everyone who participated in the sacrifice of the lamb during Passover likewise participated as one body. Everyone who shared in the atonement for sins participated as one body (see Leviticus 16). They were all forgiven and made whole in the eyes of God. Paul continued to make it clear that idols were not living entities, nor did a sacrifice to an idol represent anything significant (verse 19).

According to verse 20, it was clear that sacrificing to an idol was to be viewed with seriousness. This was not an act of worship that could be taken lightly and dismissed as something that had no impact upon a person's life in Christ. When the pagan worshippers offered their sacrifices, they offered them to demons. They were not to have fellowship with demons and eat food that had been sacrificed; to do so represented having fellowship with demons.

In verse 21, Paul drove the point of the message to its fitting conclusion. One could not drink the Lord's cup and then turn around and participate in pagan worship services. One could not sit at the Lord's table and then go and sit at the table of idol worshippers. Engaging in these activities made it clear that one affirmed the practice of sacrificing to idols, and that is certainly not what they meant to do.

Verse 22 refers back to the lessons of verses 1-11, where the ancient Israelites incurred the wrath of God because they would not obey. Paul wanted to know if this was their intention as well. He asked if they were stronger than the Lord.

III. CONCLUDING REFLECTION

One of the questions raised by the text is this: What does it mean to be a role model for other believers? How are those who are strong in the faith to live before believers who are weak and immature? Throughout these lessons, Paul reminded us that the freedom to live in the world must always be tempered by how our actions impact the lives of others. How do we react when we face temptation? What is our response to disappointment? What do we do when we are surrounded by things that produce the lust of the eyes and that produce pride?

The key to overcoming any challenge to

our faith in the Lord Jesus Christ is absolute obedience to the Word of God. The Scriptures are the source of our understanding for all matters of faith and practice. In them we find real-life examples that empower us for service and holy living. Ours is the charge to always ensure that we are following God's blueprint for successful living.

The assurance the believer has is that temptation is common to every human being. What is the implication of this fact? It means that all of humanity has in common a susceptibility to temptation; however, God provides the believer with the necessary avenue of escape. We do not have to submit or succumb to temptation.

PRAYER

Heavenly Father, may we learn the lessons of the Scriptures and be the lights that shine in a world of darkness. Grant that we will know with assurance Your will for our lives. May we learn to love others, not by what we say, but by the examples we set before those who are weak and immature. In the name of Jesus Christ we pray. Amen.

WORD POWER

Temptation (Greek: *peirasmos* [pi–ras–mos])—According to the *Complete Biblical Library*, temptation can mean three different things. First of all, it may mean temptation to sin. This can only come from Satan—never from God. Secondly, people may test God, as Israel did in the wilderness and as the Corinthians were doing. Finally, there is a testing from God that is not enticement to sin but is meant to refine and purify (see Deuteronomy 8:2).

(Complete Biblical Library Commentary—The Complete Biblical Library, Romans–Corinthians.)

HOME DAILY BIBLE READINGS
(July 14-20, 2014)

Overcoming Temptation
MONDAY, July 14: "Turning Aside from God's Commands" (Exodus 32:1-10)
TUESDAY, July 15: "Turning Away from Following God" (Deuteronomy 7:1-6)
WEDNESDAY, July 16: "Putting the Lord to the Test" (Acts 5:1-11)
THURSDAY, July 17: "Search with Heart and Soul" (Deuteronomy 4:25-31)
FRIDAY, July 18: "Holding Firm to the End" (Hebrews 3:7-14)
SATURDAY, July 19: "Examples that Deter from Evil" (1 Corinthians 10:1-8)
SUNDAY, July 20: "God's Faithfulness in Our Testing" (1 Corinthians 10:9-21)

LESSON 9   July 27, 2014

SEEK THE GOOD OF OTHERS

FAITH PATHWAY/FAITH JOURNEY TOPIC: **Build Up Your Neighbor**

DEVOTIONAL READING: **Titus 3:8-14**
PRINT PASSAGE: **1 Corinthians 14:13-26**

BACKGROUND SCRIPTURE: **1 Corinthians 14:13-26**
KEY VERSE: **1 Corinthians 14:26**

1 Corinthians 14:13-26—KJV

13 Wherefore let him that speaketh in an unknown tongue pray that he may interpret.

14 For if I pray in an unknown tongue, my spirit prayeth, but my understanding is unfruitful.

15 What is it then? I will pray with the spirit, and I will pray with the understanding also: I will sing with the spirit, and I will sing with the understanding also.

16 Else when thou shalt bless with the spirit, how shall he that occupieth the room of the unlearned say Amen at thy giving of thanks, seeing he understandeth not what thou sayest?

17 For thou verily givest thanks well, but the other is not edified.

18 I thank my God, I speak with tongues more than ye all:

19 Yet in the church I had rather speak five words with my understanding, that by my voice I might teach others also, than ten thousand words in an unknown tongue.

20 Brethren, be not children in understanding: howbeit in malice be ye children, but in understanding be men.

21 In the law it is written, With men of other tongues and other lips will I speak unto this people; and yet for all that will they not hear me, saith the Lord.

22 Wherefore tongues are for a sign, not to them that believe, but to them that believe not: but prophesying serveth not for them that believe not, but for them which believe.

23 If therefore the whole church be come together into one place, and all speak with tongues, and there come in those that are unlearned, or unbelievers, will they not say that ye are mad?

1 Corinthians 14:13-26—NIV

13 For this reason anyone who speaks in a tongue should pray that he may interpret what he says.

14 For if I pray in a tongue, my spirit prays, but my mind is unfruitful.

15 So what shall I do? I will pray with my spirit, but I will also pray with my mind; I will sing with my spirit, but I will also sing with my mind.

16 If you are praising God with your spirit, how can one who finds himself among those who do not understand say "Amen" to your thanksgiving, since he does not know what you are saying?

17 You may be giving thanks well enough, but the other man is not edified.

18 I thank God that I speak in tongues more than all of you.

19 But in the church I would rather speak five intelligible words to instruct others than ten thousand words in a tongue.

20 Brothers, stop thinking like children. In regard to evil be infants, but in your thinking be adults.

21 In the Law it is written: "Through men of strange tongues and through the lips of foreigners I will speak to this people, but even then they will not listen to me," says the Lord.

22 Tongues, then, are a sign, not for believers but for unbelievers; prophecy, however, is for believers, not for unbelievers.

23 So if the whole church comes together and everyone speaks in tongues, and some who do not understand or some unbelievers come in, will they not say that you are out of your mind?

24 But if an unbeliever or someone who does not understand comes in while everybody is prophesying,

24 But if all prophesy, and there come in one that believeth not, or one unlearned, he is convinced of all, he is judged of all:

25 And thus are the secrets of his heart made manifest; and so falling down on his face he will worship God, and report that God is in you of a truth.

26 How is it then, brethren? when ye come together, every one of you hath a psalm, hath a doctrine, hath a tongue, hath a revelation, hath an interpretation. Let all things be done unto edifying.

he will be convinced by all that he is a sinner and will be judged by all,

25 and the secrets of his heart will be laid bare. So he will fall down and worship God, exclaiming, "God is really among you!"

26 What then shall we say, brothers? When you come together, everyone has a hymn, or a word of instruction, a revelation, a tongue or an interpretation. All of these must be done for the strengthening of the church.

TOPICAL OUTLINE OF THE LESSON

I. Introduction
  A. To Speak or Not to Speak?
  B. Biblical Background

II. Exposition and Application of the Scripture
  A. Praying in Tongues Is Not Beneficial in Worship
     (1 Corinthians 14:13-14)
  B. Speak So that All Understand
     (1 Corinthians 14:15-20)
  C. Tongues Are a Sign for Unbelievers
     (1 Corinthians 14:21-26)

III. Concluding Reflection

LESSON OBJECTIVES

Upon completion of the lesson, the students will be able to do the following:

1. Review what Paul said about the value of speaking in tongues;

2. Understand that an individual person's speaking in a language no one else understands does nothing positive for the community; and,

3. Use good speaking and listening skills with one another.

POINTS TO BE EMPHASIZED
ADULT/YOUTH

Adult Topic: Build Up Your Neighbor
Youth Topic: Make It Plain
Adult/Youth Key Verse: 1 Corinthians 14:26
Print Passage: 1 Corinthians 14:13-26

—Paul did not speak against glossolalia. He participated, but he sought always to edify.

—Prophecy is better for edification than speaking, praying, or blessing in a tongue.

—Paul indicated that speaking in tongues was ecstatic, done without sensibility or using the mind, and required interpretation.

—"Five words" versus "ten thousand words" indicated the huge discrepancy between the value of instruction or prophecy and speaking in tongues.

—As Paul earlier in his letter talked about eating food that was legal but not necessarily wholesome, here he said that speaking in tongues, though a good thing, was not necessarily the most beneficial thing to do.

—Paul addressed the confusion about speaking in tongues and called for words that could be understood.

CHILDREN

Children Topic: Keeping Peace and Order
Key Verse: 1 Corinthians 14:40
Print Passage: 1 Corinthians 14:26-33a, 37-40

—Paul advised the Corinthians regarding their conduct in worship.
—Speaking and listening are vital in worship.
—Some people have particular gifts for speaking and interpreting God's Word.
—Worship should be carried out in an orderly way.
—Worship may include a variety of elements.
—The Holy Spirit gives believers power to recognize and exercise spiritual gifts in worship.

I. INTRODUCTION

A. To Speak or Not to Speak?

Charles Bryant defined the *gift of tongues* as "the extraordinary ability to pray and to praise God with beneficial wordless phrases or utterances not familiar to known languages, and with such a joy-filled intimacy with Christ that faith is strengthened and ministries become effective."[1] Let's break this definition down. First, it is directed to prayer and praise of God. Second, the prayer and praise are uttered in languages that are not part of the world's known languages. Third, this gift is usually experienced during moments of high spiritual ecstasy. Fourth, one of the byproducts of this gift is the building up and strengthening of one's commitment to ministry and mission.

This particular spiritual gift has been at the center of more debate and disagreement than all of the others combined. The concept of speaking in tongues has created a great deal of friction and deep fissures within the Christian community. Communities function best when the members can articulate a shared system of values. How do community members communicate their beliefs to one another? Paul exhorted the Corinthians to speak plainly so that both believers and unbelievers could benefit from the leading of the Spirit.

B. Biblical Background

The Greek word for "tongues" is *Glosselaleo*; the direct translation literally means, "language-speaking." The questions, discussions, debates, and decisions about this subject are legion (many), and I am not sure that there has been or ever will be consensus on exactly what tongues were. What is clear is that Paul believed that there was a kind of language that people spoke in worship that was addressed to God. It had to do with being in an elevated spiritual state. There were obviously several people in the church doing this at the same time. A careful reading of 1 Corinthians 14 reveals that Paul was trying to discourage the speaking of tongues in the context of public worship because of the division it may have been causing among the believers. The practice of speaking in tongues had created a climate of total disorder in worship. Those who had the gift were the "haves" and those did not have the gift were the "have-nots." Paul did not say that the Corinthians needed to abandon the gift; rather, they should practice this gift at home. He was concerned that new people could enter the worship and people would wonder what was going on with all of the speaking in unknown tongues that no one understood. Tongues are unknown because speaking in tongues is not done in a known language.

Paul wanted the Corinthians to be more concerned about edification and prophecy than speaking in tongues.

II. EXPOSITION AND APPLICATION OF THE SCRIPTURE

A. Praying in Tongues Is Not Beneficial in Worship (1 Corinthians 14:13-14)

Wherefore let him that speaketh in an unknown tongue pray that he may interpret. For if I pray in an unknown tongue, my spirit prayeth, but my understanding is unfruitful.

"For this reason" (NIV)—"Wherefore" (KJV) refers back to all that has been previously stated in verses 1-12 regarding the use of (unknown) tongues in worship. Paul was not forbidding speaking in tongues or praying in tongues. Rather, he urged the Corinthians to seek the gift of interpretation (Greek: *diermeneuo* [dee-main-yoo-o]) so that the person praying would understand what was being said. Interpretation is the ability to tell the meaning of what has just been stated. It has in it the idea of being able to explain or expound.

We learn from Paul's statement that the gift of tongues had to do with praying with "my spirit," which is not a reference to praying in the power of the Holy Spirit. He did not indicate what he meant by praying with his spirit.

Verse 14 suggests that one could pray in tongues, which is a form of worship that edifies the person who prays. The problem with praying in tongues stemmed from the fact that the spirit was edified, but the mind was totally barren of any understanding of what was said or done while speaking in tongues. The implication of praying in tongues without understanding is that within public worship no one ultimately understood what had been said. Therefore, if there was no understanding, then no one would be edified.

B. Speak So that All Understand (1 Corinthians 14:15-20)

What is it then? I will pray with the spirit, and I will pray with the understanding also: I will sing with the spirit, and I will sing with the understanding also. Else when thou shalt bless with the spirit, how shall he that occupieth the room of the unlearned say Amen at thy giving of thanks, seeing he understandeth not what thou sayest? For thou verily givest thanks well, but the other is not edified. I thank my God, I speak with tongues more than ye all: Yet in the church I had rather speak five words with my understanding, that by my voice I might teach others also, than ten thousand words in an unknown tongue. Brethren, be not children in understanding: howbeit in malice be ye children, but in understanding be men.

In verse 15, Paul offered instruction to the saints in Corinth by resolving the issue of what to do about speaking in tongues in worship. Paul was open to both practices—that of praying with the spirit or under the influence of the Holy Spirit, and also with his mind. While he could worship God in an intimately powerful way, he would have clear understanding of what was being said. Not only would he pray with the mind and spirit, but he included singing with the mind and spirit as well. The suggestion here is that within the communal worship service, there may have been persons singing in a language that was unintelligible. Singing and music were integral parts of ancient Hebrew worship and were used in the Jewish synagogues (see Psalms 81:1; 95:1; Isaiah 30:29). Music was a vital part of early Christian worship and was often used as a means to edify and encourage the saints, as it does today (see Ephesians 5:19; Colossians 3:16; James 5:13).

Verse 16 presents a hypothetical situation that often occurred in worship. The worship service could be filled with emotional and ecstatic euphoria as men and women were caught up in elevated worship and praise. Someone who comes into the worship and is not familiar with what is going on may find it hard to appreciate what is happening. The person could neither say "Amen" nor join in the celebration. He or she could not even offer words of gratitude or thanksgiving. Why? Because he or she had no idea of what was happening, to say nothing of understanding what was being said.

Paul never made light of the experience of praying in tongues, speaking in tongues, or singing in ecstatic speech. Rather, the focus of the worship is on edification. The other man would not be edified (verse 17). One who spoke in tongues may have enjoyed the experience, but no one else would be blessed. The word *You* is written in such a way that it

denotes a high degree of emphasis. One may mean well in all that one was doing, but who was growing spiritually from this gift? Paul revealed something of his own spiritual life by indicating that he could and did speak in tongues more than anyone in Corinth (verse 18). Since they had never seen him do it, however, more than likely he was driving home the point that speaking in tongues was a gift to be exercised and experienced in the context of one's private residence.

In verse 19, Paul said that in the church he would rather speak five words in plain, easy-to-understand language than to speak ten thousand words that no one understood. He made it clear that instruction was the primary objective of the speaking gifts in worship. What good is spiritual ecstasy without understanding?

This section closes with an appeal to the church as his brothers. In verse 20, he issued an imperative command for them to "stop thinking like children."

C. Tongues Are a Sign for Unbelievers (1 Corinthians 14:21-26)

In the law it is written, With men of other tongues and other lips will I speak unto this people; and yet for all that will they not hear me, saith the Lord. Wherefore tongues are for a sign, not to them that believe, but to them that believe not: but prophesying serveth not for them that believe not, but for them which believe. If therefore the whole church be come together into one place, and all speak with tongues, and there come in those that are unlearned, or unbelievers, will they not say that ye are mad? But if all prophesy, and there come in one that believeth not, or one unlearned, he is convinced of all, he is judged of all: And thus are the secrets of his heart made manifest; and so falling down on his face he will worship God, and report that God is in you of a truth. How is it then, brethren? when ye come together, every one of you hath a psalm, hath a doctrine, hath a tongue,

hath a revelation, hath an interpretation. Let all things be done unto edifying.

Verse 21 is a quote from Isaiah 28:11-12, which was a warning from God that Israel had turned a deaf ear to the Word of God. They had become a nation of disobedient children, and since they would not hear the message of His prophet, God was going to speak to them through the tongues of the Assyrians. Scholars have struggled to make the connection between this Old Testament passage and what Paul was trying to say to the Corinthians. Paul may have been reminding the Corinthians that just as the Jews had refused to hear the Gospel during the life and ministry of Jesus, they were now hearing it in tongues that were foreign to them and their culture.

In verses 22-25, Paul drew a distinction between the benefits of the gift of tongues versus the gift of prophecy. The gift of tongues was a reality in the life of the early Christian church. Paul stated that tongues were a sign for unbelievers (see verse 22). In the next few lines he explained why this was the case. If the entire church was assembled in worship, caught up in the moment of spiritual ecstasy, and were all speaking in tongues, what would people think? Paul was especially concerned about the immature believers and those who were not believers at all. Would they not think that the church was full of people who had gone mad (verse 23)? It would be possible for people to believe that there was something powerfully spiritual taking place in the worship, but without understanding they would miss the point of it all. This would lead to their being pushed further away from Christ—because they could have a problem accepting the fact that God could work in this way.

On the other hand, if the same scenario were repeated and the entire church was prophesying rather than having a negative impact, then the man or woman would be edified and convinced that he or she needed to accept Jesus Christ as his or her personal Lord and Savior. Paul believed that this would bring conviction to the heart of the man or woman who witnessed the service. With such a powerful expression of God's presence taking place, such a person (the man or woman) could only declare that God was clearly among the people.

III. CONCLUDING REFLECTION

Why is there so much confusion over the gift of speaking in tongues? I believe that in the majority of instances, people have misinterpreted the biblical meaning of tongues and imposed a meaning that was never intended by the Holy Spirit. We are reading the biblical text in English and the English language is very limited when it comes to being able to offer clear translations of ancient words. Some words in ancient biblical languages simply do not translate into English. If the translation is not clear, then it stands to reason that the interpretation of a passage will be equally fuzzy and uncertain. This is clearly the case when it comes to understanding the gifts of speaking in tongues and the interpretation of tongues, and many other passages that people simply take out of context or impose some new understanding upon. The problem with speaking in tongues was a situation isolated purely among the Corinthians. We do not know if Christians outside of Corinth had the same issues as the Corinthians when it came to tongues.

The problem with the gift of tongues today centers around the positions that believers take toward the manifestation of the gift within the local church. In many mainline traditional churches, the gift of tongues is seen as having ceased or is not a gift given to believers today. Its presence within the body of the church is frowned upon and even demeaned. In many charismatic and Pentecostal churches, however, the gift of tongues is viewed as evidence of having been baptized by the Holy Spirit. They believe that unless one speaks in unknown tongues, he/she is not saved and certainly is not filled with the Holy Spirit. The New Testament supports neither of these positions.

PRAYER

Heavenly Father, may we forever be grateful for each of the gifts that You have given to us. May we never lose sight of Your presence in our midst and in the world. Grant us the courage to accept those with whom we differ. In Jesus' name we pray. Amen.

WORD POWER

Prophesy (Greek: *propheteuo*)—*Propheteuo* is a speaking gift and it literally means "to speak forth by divine inspiration" (see Acts 11:28). The gift was given to the early Christian church for building up and edifying the body (see 1 Corinthians 14:3-5; Ephesians 4:11-13).
Tongues (Greek: *glossa*)—*Glossa* has a threefold meaning and use in the New Testament. First, it can refer to the physical organ of the tongue. Second, it can refer to a known dialect or language. Third, it is used to identify highly spiritual ecstatic speech. The word used for "tongues" is *glossalia* (see Acts 2:4; 10:46; 19:6; 1 Corinthians 12:10; 14:20-21).

HOME DAILY BIBLE READINGS
(July 21-27, 2014)

Seek the Good of Others
MONDAY, July 21: "Imitate What Is Good" (3 John 2-12)
TUESDAY, July 22: "Doing the Right Thing" (James 4:13-17)
WEDNESDAY, July 23: "Complete in Everything Good" (Hebrews 13:16-21)
THURSDAY, July 24: "Devoted to Good Works" (Titus 3:8-14)
FRIDAY, July 25: "So All Learn and Are Encouraged" (1 Corinthians 14:27-33)
SATURDAY, July 26: "All Done Decently and in Order" (1 Corinthians 14:37-40)
SUNDAY, July 27: "Praying with Spirit and Mind" (1 Corinthians 14:13-26)

End Note

---

[1]Charles V. Bryant, *Rediscovering Our Spiritual Gifts* (Nashville: Upper Room Books, 1991), 124.

LESSON 10   August 3, 2014

CONSOLATION GRANTED THROUGH PRAYER

FAITH PATHWAY/FAITH JOURNEY TOPIC: Does Anyone Care?

DEVOTIONAL READING: Psalm 46
PRINT PASSAGE: 2 Corinthians 1:3-11

BACKGROUND SCRIPTURE: 2 Corinthians 1:3-11
KEY VERSE: 2 Corinthians 1:7

2 Corinthians 1:3-11—KJV

3 Blessed be God, even the Father of our Lord Jesus Christ, the Father of mercies, and the God of all comfort;

4 Who comforteth us in all our tribulation, that we may be able to comfort them which are in any trouble, by the comfort wherewith we ourselves are comforted of God.

5 For as the sufferings of Christ abound in us, so our consolation also aboundeth by Christ.

6 And whether we be afflicted, it is for your consolation and salvation, which is effectual in the enduring of the same sufferings which we also suffer: or whether we be comforted, it is for your consolation and salvation.

7 And our hope of you is stedfast, knowing, that as ye are partakers of the sufferings, so shall ye be also of the consolation.

8 For we would not, brethren, have you ignorant of our trouble which came to us in Asia, that we were pressed out of measure, above strength, insomuch that we despaired even of life:

9 But we had the sentence of death in ourselves, that we should not trust in ourselves, but in God which raiseth the dead:

10 Who delivered us from so great a death, and doth deliver: in whom we trust that he will yet deliver us;

11 Ye also helping together by prayer for us, that for the gift bestowed upon us by the means of many persons thanks may be given by many on our behalf.

2 Corinthians 1:3-11—NIV

3 Praise be to the God and Father of our Lord Jesus Christ, the Father of compassion and the God of all comfort,

4 who comforts us in all our troubles, so that we can comfort those in any trouble with the comfort we ourselves have received from God.

5 For just as the sufferings of Christ flow over into our lives, so also through Christ our comfort overflows.

6 If we are distressed, it is for your comfort and salvation; if we are comforted, it is for your comfort, which produces in you patient endurance of the same sufferings we suffer.

7 And our hope for you is firm, because we know that just as you share in our sufferings, so also you share in our comfort.

8 We do not want you to be uninformed, brothers, about the hardships we suffered in the province of Asia. We were under great pressure, far beyond our ability to endure, so that we despaired even of life.

9 Indeed, in our hearts we felt the sentence of death. But this happened that we might not rely on ourselves but on God, who raises the dead.

10 He has delivered us from such a deadly peril, and he will deliver us. On him we have set our hope that he will continue to deliver us,

11 as you help us by your prayers. Then many will give thanks on our behalf for the gracious favor granted us in answer to the prayers of many.

TOPICAL OUTLINE OF THE LESSON

I. Introduction

A. The Importance of Praying for One Another

B. Biblical Background

II. Exposition and Application of the Scripture

A. Paul's Prayer of Praise to God (2 Corinthians 1:3-4)

B. Paul's Explanation Regarding the Purpose of Suffering (2 Corinthians 1:5-7)

C. Paul's Description of His Suffering (2 Corinthians 1:8-11)

III. Concluding Reflection

LESSON OBJECTIVES

Upon completion of the lesson, the students will be able to do the following:

1. Review what Paul told the Corinthians about affliction and reliance on God for consolation;

2. Increase sensitivity to the whole community's need for God's protection and consolation; and,

3. Find opportunities for the class to offer God's protection and consolation to the community.

POINTS TO BE EMPHASIZED

ADULT/YOUTH

Adult Topic: Does Anyone Care?

Youth Topic: Prayer Works

Adult Key Verse: 2 Corinthians 1:7

Youth Key Verse: 2 Corinthians 1:5

Print Passage: 2 Corinthians 1:3-11

—For Paul, the suffering of the Corinthians was not in vain; it had meaning beyond what they perceived, connecting them to Christ in a real way.

—Paul's belief in the church as the body of Christ is apparent in verses 6 and 7; the Corinthians shared in his suffering and were an integral part of his consolation. (Compare with 1 Corinthians 12:26.)

—The phrase "God of all consolation" (verse 3) goes back to the Hebrew Scriptures (see Psalm 103:13, 17; Isaiah 51:12; 66:13).

—The occasion for Paul's second letter to the Corinthians seems to have been some sort of dispute. The relationship between the apostle and the Corinthian community had deteriorated. Paul defended himself and his mission, attempted to reestablish his apostolic authority, and called on the Corinthians to fulfill their commitments.

—As their hope develops, Christians are able to comfort others through their presence and prayers.

CHILDREN

Children Topic: Caring about Others

Key Verse: 2 Corinthians 1:11

Print Passage: 2 Corinthians 1:3-11

—Paul was grateful for the comfort he received from God through Christ.

—Paul found the knowledge of Christ sufficient in all his suffering.

—Paul longed for the Corinthians to know the same consolation he experienced.

—Paul yearned for the continuing help of the Corinthians through prayer.

—Paul's hope for the Corinthian church was unwavering.

I. INTRODUCTION

A. The Importance of Praying for One Another

There is great value in being part of a Christian community. What would you say are the most prized possessions you have as a Christian? Some might answer that it is their relationship with the Lord Jesus Christ; others might say that it is the opportunity to belong to a fellowship of believers who share a common bond and communal life. Christian congregations are communities of saved individuals who share a common bond in the Lord Jesus Christ. The one important lesson that Jesus wanted His disciples to fully grasp was the need to love one another as He had loved them. It would be this and this alone that would mark them as His disciples (see John 13:34-35).

Whenever the nation or a community has been jolted by a devastating calamity, people seek solace, support, and strength in their houses of worship. The church building represents the visible presence of God in the world. The people of Newtown, Connecticut, gathered at St. Michael's Church to remember their slaughtered children and to join together as a community to pray and to support the grieving families and seek God's face for healing.

In the lesson today, Paul gave testimony of God's consolation in times of hardship and gave thanks for the mutual consolation that comes from praying for one another.

B. Biblical Background

Today, we begin a new unit, which concentrates on Paul's second letter to the Corinthians. The book of 2 Corinthians appears in the New Testament canon as one of two letters written by Paul to a Christian congregation he established on the Greek peninsula. Paul wrote the book of 2 Corinthians while on his third missionary journey, most likely during his stay in Macedonia, sometime in AD 57. The book of 2 Corinthians was Paul's third or maybe even the fourth letter written to address a host of problems within the congregation (see 1 Corinthians 5:9 and 2 Corinthians 2:3-4).

He initially planned to visit the congregation but was forced to change his plans, which set off a firestorm of controversy with some in the church (see 2 Corinthians 1:15-17). Further, the letter was written to refute the presence and teaching of a group of false teachers who had infiltrated the church, wreaking havoc among the members. They made a number of false accusations against Paul—especially in regards to his apostleship—and they raised questions regarding his personal integrity (see 2 Corinthians 1:15-17; 2:1, 4, 17; 7:1-4; 10:1-3). These matters had to be addressed because their continued presence could completely destroy the young congregation. Paul also wrote the letter to remind the Corinthians of their personal commitment to raise an offering for the poor saints in Jerusalem who were suffering from a severe famine (see Acts 11:27-30; 1 Corinthians 16:1-7). Finally, Paul wrote to inform the Corinthians of the suffering that he had faced and endured and to share with them how they must endure suffering just as Jesus Christ had done. Throughout the letter, Paul defended himself and his mission, attempted to reestablish his apostolic authority, and called on the Corinthians to fulfill their commitments.

II. EXPOSITION AND APPLICATION OF THE SCRIPTURE

A. Paul's Prayer of Praise to God
(2 Corinthians 1:3-4)

Blessed be God, even the Father of our Lord Jesus Christ, the Father of mercies, and the God of all comfort; Who comforteth us in all our tribulation, that we may be able to comfort them which are in any trouble, by the comfort wherewith we ourselves are comforted of God.

Paul began the body of his letter by offering praise and adoration to God. The word *praise* (Greek: *eulogetos* [yoo-log-ay-tos]) expresses deep and abounding adoration for God (see Romans 15:5; Ephesians 1:3, 17; 1 Peter 1:3). It can be translated as "blessed" (KJV) or "blessing," and it is used more than four hundred times in the Greek version of the Old Testament, the Septuagint (LXX), to pronounce blessings upon individuals and whole nations (see Genesis 1:28; 49:25; Deuteronomy 11:26-28; Ruth 4:4). Paul gave a theological description of who God is. He would later point out why God is to be praised and lauded. First, God is the Father of our Lord Jesus Christ. Second, He is the Father of compassion, a word synonymous with mercy. God's compassion or mercy is what had sustained Paul during the dark days of his ministry in Asia. The Scriptures point out that God abounds in mercy and compassion (see Nehemiah 9:17; Psalms 62:12; 86:15; Micah 7:18). Third, He is the God of all comfort. Paul made it clear to the Corinthians that there never was and never would be any situation that believers faced, in which the mercy of God would not be available.

One important question is this: Who was Paul referring to in these verses? Did the word *us* refer exclusively to the Corinthians, or did it refer exclusively to his personal situation? The context and the contents of the passage both help us see that Paul was more than likely referring to his personal situation, although the points made were applicable to the Corinthians as well. Remember that Paul had been dealing with a rocky relationship and several thorny issues concerning his integrity and apostolic right to lead the Corinthian church. There were valid reasons why he had not come to visit them, and he began to explain them in the subsequent verses.

In verse 4, Paul turned his attention from talking about who God was to informing the Corinthians of what God does. First, He was their comfort in all times of trouble (see Psalm 27:1-7; 34:6-7; 46:1). The reason why God had given them comfort was for the purpose of their being able to comfort others who were going through similar situations; Paul reminded them that whatever the trial or troubling situation, God had empowered them to meet the challenge. They were to share with others what they had received from God.

In these verses, we learn a valuable lesson about the nature of Christian community, which is to stand with those who find themselves in trouble. Trouble has a way of darkening the doors of everyone, and believers are called not only to pray, but also to be present (see Galatians 6:1; Hebrews 6:10; see especially Matthew 11:28-30).

B. Paul's Explanation Regarding the Purpose of Suffering
(2 Corinthians 1:5-7)

For as the sufferings of Christ abound in us, so our consolation also aboundeth by Christ. And whether we be afflicted, it is for your consolation and salvation, which is effectual in the enduring of the same sufferings which we also suffer: or whether we be comforted, it is for your consolation and salvation. And our hope of you is stedfast, knowing, that as ye are partakers of the sufferings, so shall ye be also of the consolation.

In these verses we note first the distinction between human suffering and the suffering that is the result of one's faith and commitment to Jesus Christ. There is a suffering that is part of the human condition and pilgrimage of life, which is common to all men and women (see John 16:33; 1 Peter 4:15-16). Then there is the suffering that comes because of one's commitment to the Gospel of Jesus Christ. Paul noted that believers can find themselves suffering because of the Gospel of Jesus Christ (see Acts 9:23-25; 14:19-20; 16:20-22; 18:13; 19:26-27; compare with 2 Corinthians 4:7-12; 6:4-10; 11:23-29). "Flow over into" is the translation of a single Greek word, *perisseuo* (per-is-syoo). This word means that suffering can come in abundant quantities such that it floods into

our lives. The words *flow over into* also produce images of a rapidly rising river that overflows its banks until it inundates the plains. Yet, Paul reminded the Corinthians that whatever may have been the challenge, the comfort of God was equal to the task. Just as the suffering could be the result of one's commitment to Jesus Christ, so was the comfort that was able to meet the trial, hardship, or heartache. Believers in every age and generation can take comfort in these words. They stress that although there are periods of deep trial and anxiety, God is able to provide what we need to meet the threat.

"If" (NIV) and "whether" (KJV) in verse 6 is conditional and implies that what follows may or may not have been the case. It is better translated as "whenever," because Paul was telling his listeners that he had been through a great ordeal and he had been severely tested in Asia. The words *we are* are written in the present tense and indicated that at that very moment, he was suffering for Jesus Christ. He did not say what the nature of that suffering was—just that it was beneficial for him and the church in Corinth.

How did his suffering relate to their salvation? It is has already been noted that Paul went through a great deal of suffering, persecution, and near-death experiences during his preaching and missionary work. It would have been easy for him to have withdrawn from Corinth at the first sign of trouble, and opposition to the preaching of the Gospel. He had fresh memories of what had happened in northern Greece at Philippi and Thessalonica. Rather than leave at the first sign of trouble, he stayed, preached, taught, and endured everything that came his way for the sake of the Gospel. He noted in his first letter that when he arrived in Corinth, it was in great fear and trembling (see 1 Corinthians 2:1-5). There is a lesson in Paul's example of courage for everyone who would preach and teach the Gospel of Jesus Christ. Ministry is not all warm and cozy and without tension in congregational settings.

Paul's example of courage, faithfulness, and commitment to the cause of Jesus Christ was beneficial to the Corinthians in two ways. It produced patient endurance, which is a translation of *hupomone* (hoop-om-on-ay)—which means "steadfastness." The word denotes a steadiness that refuses to waver in the midst of a crisis. Paul noted that it was the comforting presence of the Lord Jesus Christ that was producing this quality (*energeo*) in the Corinthians. Although they could not physically see the growth of this quality in themselves, it was being perfected as they learned from Paul how to overcome the trials of life.

Verse 7 concludes this section with Paul announcing that he had no doubts that they would be able to rise to the occasion. Regardless of the pressure or the amount of opposition, Paul knew that by modeling his example, they, too, would be victorious over their suffering.

C. Paul's Description of His Suffering (2 Corinthians 1:8-11)

For we would not, brethren, have you ignorant of our trouble which came to us in Asia, that we were pressed out of measure, above strength, insomuch that we despaired even of life: But we had the sentence of death in ourselves, that we should not trust in ourselves, but in God which raiseth the dead: Who delivered us from so great a death, and doth deliver: in whom we trust that he will yet deliver us; Ye also helping together by prayer for us, that for the gift bestowed upon us by the means of many persons thanks may be given by many on our behalf.

In verse 8, Paul intimated that he was not sure if they personally knew about his troubles and the trials that he faced in Asia (Ephesus). This verse gives us a very good picture of Paul's emotional state as he pondered the prospects of his work in Asia. Throughout the journey through Asia at just about every turn, there was opposition, often accompanied by personal attacks (see Acts 19:23; 1 Corinthians 15:32; 2 Corinthians 4:8). The words "great pressure" (NIV) or "pressed out of measure" (KJV) indicate that pressure was coming in from all sides. Paul said it became so intense that he began to have doubts about whether or not they could survive the situation. We are not sure what the situation was, but all we need do is pick a city and it could very easily have been one of them.

Inwardly they felt that death was a certainty. "The sentence of death" did not necessarily refer to Paul or his companions standing before a criminal tribunal. Rather, it speaks to the gravity of his situation that looked so dire that he may as well have been sentenced to death. There was a reason for the circumstances that he faced: it was so that neither he nor his companions would rely on their own strength, but on the strength and power of God, who raises the dead. Here, the reference was to the resurrection of Jesus Christ. If God can do that, then surely whatever they faced could be overcome by God's power.

Paul wanted it known by the Corinthians that God had delivered them before and there was no doubt that He could do it again (verse 10). Rather than relying on his own strength and intellect, it was better to rely upon God and His faithful care in every circumstance of life. He wanted the church to continue praying for them and giving thanks to God on his behalf. Paul wanted the church to pray that God would keep them and that He would grant them favor and grace to continue to do the work of missions and ministry (verse 11).

III. CONCLUDING REFLECTION

Congregations can be interesting sociological communities that can be filled with relational problems of all kinds. Yet, there is one that is often overlooked and not talked about in the reality of life in a Christian congregation—and that is the support and strength that people gain from other saints in times of trial. In my own congregation, I have watched the members rally to the aid and support of families who were facing difficult periods in their lives. The people of God were not just individuals who were capable of facing and overcoming every challenge they faced alone. Rather, we are people who know that without God, we alone are insufficient for every trial and tribulation we face. Christians believe that God is the one who hears and answers prayer, and without Him, we can do absolutely nothing. This was Paul's message to the Corinthians. While they had had a stormy relationship, nevertheless Paul was still their spiritual father and he loved them with the love of Jesus Christ. There was not anything or anyone who could change that relationship.

PRAYER

Heavenly Father, teach us to rely on You in all things and in all circumstances. Grant that we will never lose hope in Your power to deliver us. In Jesus' name we pray. Amen.

WORD POWER

Comfort (Greek: *parakalein*)—This word is derived from the word *paraklesis,* which literally means "to call near" or summon, especially for the purpose of helping. Jesus used the same word to identify the role of the Holy Spirit as the Paraclete, who comes alongside and aids believers in their trials and work. As believers are comforted by God, they in turn are summoned to come alongside others who may be in distress.

HOME DAILY BIBLE READINGS
(July 28–August 3, 2014)

Consolation Granted through Prayer
MONDAY, July 28: "Our Refuge and Strength" (Psalm 46)
TUESDAY, July 29: "The Shield of Your Help" (Deuteronomy 33:24-29)
WEDNESDAY, July 30: "O Lord, We Rely on You" (2 Chronicles 14:1-12)
THURSDAY, July 31: "Support the Weak" (Acts 20:28-35)
FRIDAY, August 1: "Admonish, Encourage, Help, and Do Good" (1 Thessalonians 5:12-22)
SATURDAY, August 2: "A Cause for Giving Thanks" (Philemon 3-7)
SUNDAY, August 3: "The God Who Consoles Us" (2 Corinthians 1:3-11)

LESSON 11   August 10, 2014

A COMMUNITY FORGIVES

FAITH PATHWAY/FAITH JOURNEY TOPIC: **Restored Relationships**

DEVOTIONAL READING: Luke 17:1-6
PRINT PASSAGE: 2 Corinthians 1:23-24; 2:1-11

BACKGROUND SCRIPTURE: 2 Corinthians 1:23–2:17
KEY VERSE: 2 Corinthians 2:10

2 Corinthians 1:23-24; 2:1-11—KJV

23 Moreover I call God for a record upon my soul, that to spare you I came not as yet unto Corinth.
24 Not for that we have dominion over your faith, but are helpers of your joy: for by faith ye stand.

.....

BUT I determined this with myself, that I would not come again to you in heaviness.
2 For if I make you sorry, who is he then that maketh me glad, but the same which is made sorry by me?
3 And I wrote this same unto you, lest, when I came, I should have sorrow from them of whom I ought to rejoice; having confidence in you all, that my joy is the joy of you all.
4 For out of much affliction and anguish of heart I wrote unto you with many tears; not that ye should be grieved, but that ye might know the love which I have more abundantly unto you.
5 But if any have caused grief, he hath not grieved me, but in part: that I may not overcharge you all.
6 Sufficient to such a man is this punishment, which was inflicted of many.
7 So that contrariwise ye ought rather to forgive him, and comfort him, lest perhaps such a one should be swallowed up with overmuch sorrow.
8 Wherefore I beseech you that ye would confirm your love toward him.
9 For to this end also did I write, that I might know the proof of you, whether ye be obedient in all things.
10 To whom ye forgive any thing, I forgive also: for if I forgave any thing, to whom I forgave it, for your sakes forgave I it in the person of Christ;
11 Lest Satan should get an advantage of us: for we are not ignorant of his devices.

2 Corinthians 1:23-24; 2:1-11—NIV

23 I call God as my witness that it was in order to spare you that I did not return to Corinth.
24 Not that we lord it over your faith, but we work with you for your joy, because it is by faith you stand firm.

.....

SO I made up my mind that I would not make another painful visit to you.
2 For if I grieve you, who is left to make me glad but you whom I have grieved?
3 I wrote as I did so that when I came I should not be distressed by those who ought to make me rejoice. I had confidence in all of you, that you would all share my joy.
4 For I wrote you out of great distress and anguish of heart and with many tears, not to grieve you but to let you know the depth of my love for you.
5 If anyone has caused grief, he has not so much grieved me as he has grieved all of you, to some extent—not to put it too severely.
6 The punishment inflicted on him by the majority is sufficient for him.
7 Now instead, you ought to forgive and comfort him, so that he will not be overwhelmed by excessive sorrow.
8 I urge you, therefore, to reaffirm your love for him.
9 The reason I wrote you was to see if you would stand the test and be obedient in everything.
10 If you forgive anyone, I also forgive him. And what I have forgiven—if there was anything to forgive—I have forgiven in the sight of Christ for your sake,
11 in order that Satan might not outwit us. For we are not unaware of his schemes.

TOPICAL OUTLINE OF THE LESSON

I. Introduction
A. The Seeds for Conflict
B. Biblical Background

II. Exposition and Application of the Scripture
A. Paul's Pastoral Concern (2 Corinthians 1:23-24)
B. Paul's Decision Not to Visit (2 Corinthians 2:1-5)
C. Paul's Plea to Forgive and Restore the Offender (2 Corinthians 2:6-11)

III. Concluding Reflection

LESSON OBJECTIVES

Upon completion of the lesson, the students will be able to do the following:

1. Know what Paul told the Corinthians about the connectedness of all persons in community;
2. Accept the concept that harm or benefit to one in a community is harm or benefit to all; and,
3. Lead the students to forgiveness of any who have harmed another.

POINTS TO BE EMPHASIZED

ADULT/YOUTH

Adult Topic: Restored Relationships

Youth Topic: Forgiveness: A Worthy Venture

Adult/Youth Key Verse: 2 Corinthians 2:10

Print Passage: 2 Corinthians 1:23-24; 2:1-11

—Paul had previously intended to visit the Corinthians on his journey to Macedonia (see 1:16), but later changed his plans (see 1:23; 2:1). This seeming vacillation became a point of contention with the Corinthians, and Paul defended his decision in 1:23–2:4.

—Paul apparently made another visit to Corinth not mentioned in the book of Acts—a visit that did not go well. It resulted in grief or sorrow (see 2:1).

—Second Corinthians 2:5 may give a hint of what took place during Paul's painful visit: an unnamed member of the church grieved not only Paul but also the whole church. This man, probably a key member of the community, publicly challenged Paul and apparently raised considerable opposition to him. (Some scholars consider 2:5 to refer to the discipline discussed in 1 Corinthians 5.)

—Paul feared that the church's discipline of his opponent had gone too far, and urged the Corinthians to forgive and move on by restoring this person to the community.

—Like Jesus, Paul taught that forgiveness has an interpersonal dimension: it heals relationships, restores outcasts, and reconciles those who were estranged.

—Paul apologized to the Corinthians for not visiting them.

—Forgiveness is the way to promote unity and express care for others within the church.

Children Topic: Giving and Receiving Forgiveness

Key Verses: 2 Corinthians 2:5a, 6-7a

Print Passage: 2 Corinthians 2:5-11

—Someone in the Corinthian church caused pain to Paul and the faith community.

—Paul urged the church to forgive the offender.

—Paul promised also to forgive the offender.

—Paul understood forgiveness as being required by faith in Christ and love for Him.

—Believers must comfort the offender so that the person will not be destroyed.

—Failure to forgive is a design of Satan.

I. INTRODUCTION

A. The Seeds for Conflict

Pastor Splimigates had been the senior pastor of the First Church for more than forty-five years. Over the past three years his age and health had started to catch up with him and there were telling signs that his memory and strength were starting to fail. Rather than retire the old pastor, the board of deacons recommended that an assistant pastor be hired to do some of the preaching and counseling. A committee was appointed to recruit and interview candidates for the position. The Reverend Doctor Sue Mae Qualified was selected out of 168 possible candidates for the position. The committee was highly impressed by her leadership skills and preaching and teaching ability. At the church meeting, when the nomination was presented it was hotly debated, because the committee was recommending a woman to become the assistant pastor of First Church. Some members felt that it was against the teachings of the Bible for a woman to hold that position. There were others who saw nothing wrong, either biblically or spiritually, with the nomination.

The nomination caused an uproar among the members of the deacon board and some of the members who voted against the nomination—because the candidate was a woman. At one point the meeting turned into a shouting match, with members calling each other names and some even using profanity when addressing each other. The confusion split the church into two camps, with many of the committee members deciding to leave the church. Families were broken up, long-time friendships were destroyed, and many of the people in the congregation never spoke to each other again.

This is a hypothetical situation that is intended to show that congregational relationships can quickly and easily be destroyed over just about any issue. Congregations can become hotbeds of confusion when persons within the community violate social rules and norms. Many times those persons find it difficult to be accepted again by the larger congregation. Paul reminded the Corinthians that it was important to forgive and restore back to fellowship the man or woman who violated community rules.

B. Biblical Background

Paul had previously planned to visit the Corinthians on his journey to Macedonia (see 2 Corinthians 1:16). At some point he changed his plans and decided not to make that trip (see 1:23; 2:1). The change in plans seemed to some in the church as vacillation on the part of Paul and it was not long before it became a point of contention. Beginning at 1:23–2:4, Paul defended his decision not to come to Corinth.

Apparently, Paul made another visit to Corinth that is not mentioned in the book of Acts. This trip did not go well and resulted in some deep hurt and pain on the part of Paul and the members of the church (see 2 Corinthians 2:1). Paul wrote a "sorrowful letter," attempting to resolve the issues (see 2 Corinthians 2:4). This letter has been at the center of debate by New Testament scholars for years, with no satisfactory conclusion.

Essentially, there are scholars who believe that the books of 1 and 2 Corinthians may be composite letters—that is, they contain the contents of three (maybe four) separate letters. Some scholars consider the book of 1 Corinthians, with its command in 5:5 to hand a member over to Satan, to be the sorrowful letter. Others believe it to be a separate letter that has been lost in time. Still others believe it to be a separate letter that is preserved in 2 Corinthians 10–13. The most likely answer to the problem is that the book of 1 Corinthians is a complete letter, the sorrowful letter has been lost, and the book of 2 Corinthians is a composite letter containing the contents of two letters written by Paul.

II. EXPOSITION AND APPLICATION OF THE SCRIPTURE

A. Paul's Pastoral Concern
(2 Corinthians 1:23-24)

Moreover I call God for a record upon my soul, that to spare you I came not as yet unto Corinth. Not for that we have dominion over your faith, but are helpers of your joy: for by faith ye stand.

In verse 23, Paul returned to a defense related to the change in his travel plans. He called God to be his witness that everything he was about to say was true (see Romans 1:9). The only thing that he had of any real value was his word and his reputation. He stated that the primary reason why he did not return was to spare them. Paul offered no indication as to what he wanted to spare the church from. It may be that he was referring to the trip that went terribly wrong and he wanted to spare them a severe "parental" scolding (see 1 Corinthians 4:19-21; 2 Corinthians 13:2, 10).

Paul did not see himself as an absolute tyrant, ruling and leading the church with an iron fist (see 1 Peter 5:3). This leadership model is foreign to the teachings of Jesus Christ, who taught that those who lead must be willing to first become servants of even the least (see Matthew 23:8; Mark 10:42-45). Rather than attempt to lead by coercion, Paul said that he wanted to work with the church in a way that all of them would have joy. He made it clear that their faith did not rest upon his leadership and his apostolic authority; rather, it was in the finished work of Jesus Christ (see Romans 11:20; 1 Corinthians 2:1-5; 15:1).

B. Paul's Decision Not to Visit
(2 Corinthians 2:1-5)

BUT I determined this with myself, that I would not come

again to you in heaviness. For if I make you sorry, who is he then that maketh me glad, but the same which is made sorry by me? And I wrote this same unto you, lest, when I came, I should have sorrow from them of whom I ought to rejoice; having confidence in you all, that my joy is the joy of you all. For out of much affliction and anguish of heart I wrote unto you with many tears; not that ye should be grieved, but that ye might know the love which I have more abundantly unto you. But if any have caused grief, he hath not grieved me, but in part: that I may not overcharge you all.

Paul indicated in verse 1 that at some point he made up his mind that it would not be profitable for him to return to Corinth for a painful visit. He offered no explanation as to how he arrived at that decision or where he was at the time. There are many New Testament scholars who believe that this statement supports the belief that Paul may have made a visit to Corinth that is not recorded in the book of Acts. He realized that the church was already having a difficult time with what had happened. Rather than bringing each other joy, they had been grieved by Paul's visit and obviously had not gotten over the pain. This reflected a congregational setting that was far different from what Paul experienced in Philippi, a church that he loved and who loved him deeply (see Philippians 1:4, 24-25; 2:2, 17; 4:1). Sometimes leaders make the mistake of believing that they can make demands that the people of God follow their rules and orders without question. There are many hurting people in congregations who have been wounded by leaders and other members.

In verse 3, Paul indicated that he had a reason for writing the way that he did. Scholars differ regarding which letter this may have been (see 2 Corinthians 2:9; 7:8, 12; Background Scriptures). Paul had hoped that the letter would have resolved some of the issues in the congregation and that his rebuke would have restored calm and fellowship. The impact was just the opposite of what he expected. He wanted everything to be resolved so that he would not experience distress and grief from his spiritual children. Paul expressed the belief that the entire church would share his joy and resolve to move forward.

It was his love for the congregation that drove him to write the painful letter (see 1 Corinthians 13:1-7 for Paul's understanding about love). In his first letter, he had taught them of the magnanimous nature of love. True love (agape) is not the kind of love that keeps score or retains its anger forever (see Micah 7:19-20). Paul said that he wrote with tears streaming down his face and a grieving heart. Here, the image is of a brokenhearted parent whose child has just done something so grievous that it literally tears the spirit out of the parent. Whatever the situation was, it had caused Paul a tremendous amount of grief, and he must have vented his frustration and anger in the letter. Sometimes correction can come across as harsh and unusually strong.

Paul displayed the heart of a man more concerned about the people he loved than about himself. In verse 5, he indicated that it was not he himself who had been grieved as much as it was the Corinthians. He was hurt because they were hurt. He qualified his statement by saying that to some extent they had all been grieved. Given what we know about Corinthian culture, some of the people would not have been overly concerned about what had happened. If it was the case of immorality (see 1 Corinthians 5:1), the Corinthians had a different standard of what constituted immorality;

or it involved someone eating food sacrificed to idols and their unwillingness to change; or it may have involved even those who supported the accusers of Paul. The Corinthians had a very different way of reasoning through issues that impacted the church.

C. Paul's Plea to Forgive and Restore the Offender (2 Corinthians 2:6-11)

Sufficient to such a man is this punishment, which was inflicted of many. So that contrariwise ye ought rather to forgive him, and comfort him, lest perhaps such a one should be swallowed up with overmuch sorrow. Wherefore I beseech you that ye would confirm your love toward him. For to this end also did I write, that I might know the proof of you, whether ye be obedient in all things. To whom ye forgive any thing, I forgive also: for if I forgave any thing, to whom I forgave it, for your sakes forgave I it in the person of Christ; Lest Satan should get an advantage of us: for we are not ignorant of his devices.

Verse 6 gives us a window through which to view how the early Christian communities may have handled matters that required the discipline of a member who had violated communal codes or the teaching of Jesus. Evidently, there was a meeting held to hear the evidence and to examine the validity of the charges. They were found to have merit, and Paul indicated that a majority of the church voted to pass judgment upon the offending individual. Scholars have never reached consensus as to who this person was or against whom his offenses were directed. The church responded to the offender with harshness, and may have excluded him from the fellowship. In verse 6, Paul made it clear that whatever punishment had been issued by the church was sufficient.

Instead of continuing to isolate the person, Paul insisted that it was time for healing, forgiveness, and restoration. The reason this was necessary was so that the individual would not be punished further and maybe even pushed away from the church. The word *overwhelmed* means to "drink down," and it presents the image of someone who is swallowed up by problems or circumstances beyond his or her control. While it is certain that there were people who may have believed that the punishment should be harsher, there may well have been others who felt that he had suffered enough (verse 7). The time had come for the person to be forgiven and the church to reaffirm their love for him (verse 8).

Again Paul referred to his painful letter, giving an additional reason why he wrote the letter. It was meant to rebuke them and to restore order, but there was a much larger reason. In verse 9, Paul said the reason for his letter was to test their spirits and faith in Jesus Christ. The test was whether or not the Corinthians would live up to being who they claimed to be in Jesus Christ. A second reason revolved around their willingness to be obedient in every aspect of the teachings of Jesus Christ.

If they were willing to forgive the person, Paul exclaimed that he could do no less. Paul seemed to say that he was not sure that he had anything to forgive the person for. Did he say that whatever may have been the case, he did not count it so severe that he was offended by it? We are not sure, but what we are sure of is that Paul followed the teachings of Jesus and forgave the person and called upon the church to do the same.

There was one final reason why Paul felt it was important to forgive the offender and move on—so that Satan would not outwit the church. What greater ploy than to create a lasting spirit of division and bitterness within the congregation? Paul made it clear that they were shrewd enough to recognize that the inability to forgive and move on was a trick of the enemy.

III. CONCLUDING REFLECTION

Forgiveness is not easy. It is one of the easiest things to say we will do and yet one of the most difficult things to actually do. One of the reasons why we find it hard to forgive is our unwillingness to relive the situation that caused the pain, hear the words that pricked our spirits, or look into the eyes of the one who caused us the pain. Yet, Jesus reminded us that we are to love enough that there are no limits on how often we will forgive those who wrong and offend us (see Mark 11:25-26; Ephesians 4:32). This week, spend some time thinking about all of the persons whom you have wronged or who have hurt you in some way. Then ask God to forgive you or the person and restore the relationship that you once had with that person.

PRAYER

Heavenly Father, teach us how to love and forgive as You have loved and forgiven us. Grant that we may never become the cause of resentment and bitter fights within our local churches. In the name of Jesus Christ we pray. Amen.

WORD POWER

Forgive (Greek: *charizomai* [khar-id-zom-ahee])—literally means to do something pleasant or agreeable. It denotes a spirit of graciousness. In the area of human interpersonal relations it depicts the release of a person from mistakes or failures in the past. The person who forgives another shows that he/she has a heart that is filled with grace.

HOME DAILY BIBLE READINGS
(August 4-10, 2014)

A Community Forgives

MONDAY, August 4: "Sin and Forgiveness" (Acts 13:36-41)

TUESDAY, August 5: "Confession and Forgiveness" (1 John 1:5-10)

WEDNESDAY, August 6: "Repentance and Forgiveness" (Luke 17:1-6)

THURSDAY, August 7: "Redemption and Forgiveness" (Ephesians 1:3-10)

FRIDAY, August 8: "Grace and Justification" (Romans 5:15-21)

SATURDAY, August 9: "Speaking as Persons of Sincerity" (2 Corinthians 2:12-17)

SUNDAY, August 10: "Forgiving and Consoling" (2 Corinthians 1:23–2:11)

LESSON 12

August 17, 2014

TREASURE IN CLAY JARS

FAITH PATHWAY/FAITH JOURNEY TOPIC: Down but Not Out

DEVOTIONAL READING: Jude 17-25
PRINT PASSAGE: 2 Corinthians 4:2-15

BACKGROUND SCRIPTURE: 2 Corinthians 4:2-15
KEY VERSES: 2 Corinthians 4:8-9

2 Corinthians 4:2-15—KJV

2 But have renounced the hidden things of dishonesty, not walking in craftiness, nor handling the word of God deceitfully; but by manifestation of the truth commending ourselves to every man's conscience in the sight of God.

3 But if our gospel be hid, it is hid to them that are lost:

4 In whom the god of this world hath blinded the minds of them which believe not, lest the light of the glorious gospel of Christ, who is the image of God, should shine unto them.

5 For we preach not ourselves, but Christ Jesus the Lord; and ourselves your servants for Jesus' sake.

6 For God, who commanded the light to shine out of darkness, hath shined in our hearts, to give the light of the knowledge of the glory of God in the face of Jesus Christ.

7 But we have this treasure in earthen vessels, that the excellency of the power may be of God, and not of us.

8 We are troubled on every side, yet not distressed; we are perplexed, but not in despair;

9 Persecuted, but not forsaken; cast down, but not destroyed;

10 Always bearing about in the body the dying of the Lord Jesus, that the life also of Jesus might be made manifest in our body.

11 For we which live are alway delivered unto death for Jesus' sake, that the life also of Jesus might be made manifest in our mortal flesh.

12 So then death worketh in us, but life in you.

13 We having the same spirit of faith, according as it is written, I believed, and therefore have I spoken; we also believe, and therefore speak;

2 Corinthians 4:2-15—NIV

2 Rather, we have renounced secret and shameful ways; we do not use deception, nor do we distort the word of God. On the contrary, by setting forth the truth plainly we commend ourselves to every man's conscience in the sight of God.

3 And even if our gospel is veiled, it is veiled to those who are perishing.

4 The god of this age has blinded the minds of unbelievers, so that they cannot see the light of the gospel of the glory of Christ, who is the image of God.

5 For we do not preach ourselves, but Jesus Christ as Lord, and ourselves as your servants for Jesus' sake.

6 For God, who said, "Let light shine out of darkness," made his light shine in our hearts to give us the light of the knowledge of the glory of God in the face of Christ.

7 But we have this treasure in jars of clay to show that this all-surpassing power is from God and not from us.

8 We are hard pressed on every side, but not crushed; perplexed, but not in despair;

9 persecuted, but not abandoned; struck down, but not destroyed.

10 We always carry around in our body the death of Jesus, so that the life of Jesus may also be revealed in our body.

11 For we who are alive are always being given over to death for Jesus' sake, so that his life may be revealed in our mortal body.

12 So then, death is at work in us, but life is at work in you.

13 It is written: "I believed; therefore I have spoken." With that same spirit of faith we also believe and therefore speak,

14 Knowing that he which raised up the Lord Jesus shall raise up us also by Jesus, and shall present us with you.

15 For all things are for your sakes, that the abundant grace might through the thanksgiving of many redound to the glory of God.

14 because we know that the one who raised the Lord Jesus from the dead will also raise us with Jesus and present us with you in his presence.

15 All this is for your benefit, so that the grace that is reaching more and more people may cause thanksgiving to overflow to the glory of God.

TOPICAL OUTLINE OF THE LESSON

I. Introduction
A. The Challenges of Ministry
B. Biblical Background

II. Exposition and Application of the Scripture
A. An Honest Ministry (2 Corinthians 4:2-6)
B. A God-controlled Ministry (2 Corinthians 4:7-12)
C. A Faith-centered Ministry (2 Corinthians 4:13-15)

III. Concluding Reflection

LESSON OBJECTIVES

Upon completion of the lesson, the students will be able to do the following:

1. Know what Paul had to say about proclaiming Jesus Christ as Lord and themselves as slaves for Jesus' sake;

2. Affirm that the power to do good originates in God and not within the community; and,

3. Ask God for power to do the will of God in ministry.

POINTS TO BE EMPHASIZED
ADULT/YOUTH

Adult Topic: Down but Not Out

Youth Topic: Grace Is an Everlasting Treasure

Adult Key Verses: 2 Corinthians 4:8-9

Youth Key Verse: 2 Corinthians 4:7

Print Passage: 2 Corinthians 4:2-15

—Paul described himself as open and sincere, implying that some questioned his character on this point. Paul believed that such people were being unfair: anyone who judged him by moral reasoning (*syneidesis*, "conscience") in the sight of God would find him innocent. (See verse 2.)

—Paul insisted that he and his coworkers did not preach themselves but Jesus Christ (verse 5). This suggests that there were others who did preach themselves; such false teachers were not sincere, but crafty and unreliable in contrast to Paul (verse 2).

—Paul's focus changed in verse 7 from the glory of his ministry to the hardships that such a ministry entails.

—Paul believed that human frailty actually serves to highlight the glory of God's work. Paul developed this theme in considerable detail in subsequent chapters.

—Paul made his defense against those accusers who questioned his lifestyle, preaching, and faith.

—Paul used for his defense the fact that Jesus Christ was the Lord in whom he served, preached, and had faith.

—Clay jars have little value and beauty, but they might contain a special treasure.

—The treasure within believers is the light of the glory of God in the face of Christ.

CHILDREN

Children Topic: Proclaiming Good News
Key Verse: 2 Corinthians 4:5

Print Passage: 2 Corinthians 4:5-12

—Paul reminded the Corinthians of his servant-hood in their midst.

—Paul attributed his message to the power of God in Christ.

—Paul spoke of the Good News as a treasure and of himself and other believers as clay jars.

—Paul had endured much suffering on behalf of the Corinthians.

—As Paul approached his death, life was being restored in the Corinthians.

—Paul encouraged the Corinthians to proclaim Jesus Christ in the face of adversity.

I. INTRODUCTION

A. The Challenges of Ministry

The ministry is a risky vocation. History has shown that the ministry is full of emotional turbulence, financial uncertainty, and social isolation. It is a field of labor that can be filled with heartache and disappointment. Yet, it offers some of the greatest triumphs and moments in life. There are no guarantees of worldly fame or success in the ministry. There are no guarantees of financial security or of becoming wealthy in the ministry. There are no guarantees that people will even receive your message of salvation and redemption in the ministry.

The preacher often finds himself in a love-hate relationship with the world. He is both loved and hated. He is loved by those whom he has helped and blessed. Likewise, he is hated and despised by those whom he has to challenge and confront about their sinfulness. Often the biggest challenge that the preacher faces is within and among those whom he is called to serve, who can at times be his biggest and most vocal critics. This was the case with Paul in Corinth.

B. Biblical Background

Throughout these lessons in the books of Corinthians, we have seen Paul wrestle with the presence of men and women whose motives were less than honorable. In the previous lesson, Paul battled with the presence of internal opposition and misunderstanding relating to his motives. For Paul the call to serve as an apostle was a great honor, yet it was filled with great risks as well (see Romans 1:1; 1 Corinthians 1:1; Galatians 1:11-17; Philippians 3:8-10). Second Corinthians 4 speaks to us from the context of Paul's discussion about the hardships of ministry and the unsurpassed greatness of God's power to sustain His servants. He reminded the Corinthians that in their work for the Lord Jesus Christ, there were times when believers were called to face nothing but trial upon trial and tribulation upon tribulation.

Paul spoke of the conflicts he had faced as he sought to serve God and be obedient and faithful to his calling. He made it clear that there was a distinct difference between the Gospel he preached and the one being preached by others, who preached themselves. There were false teachers in Corinth who were not sincere, but crafty and unreliable in contrast to Paul and his companions. In verses 8-12, Paul taught that regardless of the outward circumstances of life, one's relationship with God never changes.

II. EXPOSITION AND APPLICATION OF THE SCRIPTURE

A. An Honest Ministry
(2 Corinthians 4:2-6)

But have renounced the hidden things of dishonesty, not walking in craftiness, nor handling the word of God deceitfully; but by manifestation of the truth commending ourselves to every man's conscience in the sight of God. But if our gospel be hid, it is hid to them that are lost: In whom the god of this world hath blinded the minds of them which believe not, lest the light of the glorious gospel of Christ, who is the image of God, should shine unto them. For we preach not ourselves, but Christ Jesus the Lord; and ourselves your servants for Jesus' sake. For God, who commanded the light to shine out of darkness, hath shined in our hearts, to give the light of the knowledge of the glory of God in the face of Jesus Christ.

Discouragement and despair are the leading causes of pastoral resignation. Many pastors are so overwhelmed by the constant infighting and petty squabbles that they give up and quit the ministry. This was not the case with Paul, because there was never any doubt in his mind or heart that God had called him for that work (see Galatians 1:11-12, 15-16). Paul had earlier acknowledged that because of the mercy and grace of God, he was committed to the ministry that had been entrusted to him. Rather than cloak his work in secrecy with hidden motives, Paul was adamant that they had not used shameful or secret ways. Neither he nor his companions had been deceptive, which is probably a reference to the accusation that he was collecting the famine relief offering for himself. Paul never preached in such a way that men and women were not able to hear and receive the plain truth of the Gospel (see 1 Corinthians 2:1-5). He called upon the Corinthians to examine their motives and methods. His conscience was clear and he wanted theirs to be clear as well (see verse 2).

In verse 3, Paul made reference to "our gospel," which was not a different message from that preached by the original Twelve (see 1 Corinthians 15:1-4). There was some talk among some of the Corinthians that the preaching of Paul was cloaked in language that was hidden from the average member (see 2 Corinthians 10:2; 2 Peter 3:16). Paul said that "we commend ourselves," which meant to set one with another. The people who were unable to receive the truth of the Gospel were those who were perishing from disobedience and disbelief.

According to verse 4, the reason why they were not able to receive the truth was because they had been blinded by the "god of this age," who is Satan. However, those who had been born again and had been made new creatures in Christ should be able to see the plain truth. Paul made very striking comments about the essence of the Gospel that he preached regarding Jesus Christ. The Gospel was light, and it reflected the glory of Jesus Christ, who is the very image of God (see Colossians 1:15).

In the ancient world, itinerant preachers often traveled from place to place looking for students and a collection. Paul made it clear that his own ministry was not one of self-promotion. They preached Jesus Christ as Lord. There was never any doubt in Paul's mind that Jesus was Lord by virtue of being raised by God from the dead (see Acts 2:36; Romans 10:9; Philippians 2:9-11). Paul identified himself as their servant because of the grace of Jesus Christ.

Verse 6 is not a direct quote from the Old Testament. There are at least two primary interpretations for these words. The first interpretation asserts that this is an allusion to the creation of light in the creation (see Genesis 1:2-4). The second interpretation asserts that this is a reference to Paul's conversion experience on the road to Damascus, where Paul experienced a bright light shining from the heavens (see Acts 9:1-9). Either will fit the context of the verse because those who believe in the atoning death of Jesus Christ upon the cross have come from darkness into the light of God's glory in Jesus Christ.

B. A God-controlled Ministry
(2 Corinthians 4:7-12)

But we have this treasure in earthen vessels, that the excellency of the power may be of God, and not of us. We are troubled on every side, yet not distressed; we are perplexed, but not in despair; Persecuted, but not forsaken; cast down, but not destroyed; Always bearing about in the body the dying of the Lord Jesus, that the life also of Jesus might be made manifest in our body. For we which live are alway delivered unto death for Jesus' sake, that the life also of Jesus might be made manifest in our mortal flesh. So then death worketh in us, but life in you.

Verse 7 begins one of the most encouraging passages in the entire New Testament. Here, Paul spoke about the source of his strength in the midst of the constant turmoil he faced. He compared himself and his companions to inexpensive household pottery that was used for carrying water or holding olive oil. The treasure was a reference to the Gospel and Paul's experience of God's grace and mercy. The reference to "Jars of clay" shows that the unsurpassing power of God is able to preserve the most fragile of vessels for His service. The strength that was in him was not the product of his own creation but was from God, who had called him and filled his life with the Holy Spirit (see Romans 8:34-38).

In verse 8, the metaphor used is of a gladiator who gives his opponent little room for movement, but is unable to drive him into a corner (where there is no escape). Paul was saying that his adversaries pressed him on every side but were never quite able to hem him into a corner. With all of their hostile activities and attempts to stop or slow his preaching and teaching, they never succeeded. He was always given a way out by God (see 2 Corinthians 7:5-7). The key was that God had inspired the spirit of Paul through Titus and the other saints. The Greek word for "perplex," *aporeo*, literally means "to be without resources." It indicates being in a narrow space without room to move. Paul's circumstances often brought him to his wits' end. He was caught up in certain situations, not knowing what to do, where to turn, or who to call on. His was a life of constant pressures. Some of the pressures he experienced came from the churches he established (see 2 Corinthians 11:28). And yet, Paul said that he was not in despair.

In verse 9, Paul noted that he had been *persecuted*, which means "to pursue or chase after." He spoke of being hunted down like an animal by his adversaries.

While we may be persecuted by people, we are never abandoned by God. During his trial before Nero in Rome, Paul reminded Timothy that no one showed up for his defense. Everyone deserted him, but the Lord stood with him (see 2 Timothy 4:16-17). There had been plenty of days when Paul was left alone and abandoned by others, but he was constantly encouraged by the Lord Jesus Christ.

Paul said that he was struck down but not destroyed. He had not been destroyed. Here is the image of a fighter who appears to be on the verge of defeat. His foes knock him down, but he keeps on getting back up (see Psalm 37:24). Here, we see one of the supreme characteristics of the Christian life: though we may fall, we can never be defeated. We may lose a battle, but we will ultimately win the war.

In verses 10-13, Paul made the correlation between his work of ministry and the ministry of Jesus Christ. Jesus was constantly harassed and hounded, and was eventually hunted down, arrested, tried, and crucified. "The death of Jesus" refers to the actual death that Jesus endured. In Jesus, Paul had the perfect model of ministry. All of the troubles he had experienced connected him to Jesus and His persecutions. Just as Jesus was raised to new life, Paul clearly had that same expectation.

"Given over to death" in verse 12 connects the life and ministry of Paul to Jesus, who was given over to Pilate and the Jews. While Paul and his companions were personally giving and sacrificing themselves for the preaching of the Gospel, it was producing life in them (verse 13).

C. A Faith-centered Ministry (2 Corinthians 4:13-15)

We having the same spirit of faith, according as it is written, I believed, and therefore have I spoken; we also believe, and therefore speak; Knowing that he which raised up the Lord Jesus shall raise up us also by Jesus, and shall present us with you. For all things are for your sakes, that the abundant grace might through the thanksgiving of many redound to the glory of God.

Verse 13 is a quote from Psalm 116:10, where the psalmist offered praise and gratitude to God for delivering him from the threat of death. Paul spoke with the same measure and spirit of faith that even though he faced death more than he cared to, he believed that in the end he, too, would be raised from the dead like Jesus. Paul would not allow his persecutors and tormentors to silence his witness of Jesus' death and resurrection. One senses that Paul looked forward to a martyr's death when his work would be vindicated—and he, along with the Corinthians, would be present with the Lord in glory (verse 14).

Why had Paul faced such hardship, trials, and tribulation? It was all for the perfection of the faith of the Corinthians.

III. CONCLUDING REFLECTION

One of the noteworthy characteristics of Christians is not that we do not fall, but that every time we fall, we are able to get up again.

It is not that we are never beaten, but that we are never ultimately defeated. You may lose a battle, but you know that in the end you can never lose the war.[1] We are pressured, perplexed, persecuted, and pummeled, yet we are still more than conquerors through Him who loved us.

No doubt, we have all had times when it seemed as though the world was closing in on us. Society can lock up a person in a ghetto, but it cannot close that person's mind, nor destroy his/her spirit to live. Supervisors may lock a person out of promotions but they cannot kill that person's determination to rise and succeed. Our foreparents were hemmed in on plantations, laboring under the most dehumanizing and morally unjust system known to humankind. Yet that indomitable spirit to be free was never crushed. Many died fleeing to freedom before they would stay and be treated as less than human. Therefore, no matter what situation you may be in now and though things look extremely hopeless, there is always a way out. God will never allow us to be so hemmed in that He does not provide an escape route.

PRAYER

Heavenly Father, give us the spirit of our fore-parents, who refused to be molded by the shackles and chains that enslaved them. Grant that we may have the strength of our Lord Jesus Christ to face and overcome every foe. In Jesus' name we pray. Amen.

WORD POWER

The god of this age (*theos tou ainos toutou*)—In using the word *god,* Paul used language that was common in his day to refer to any and all deities. In following the practice of the ancient rabbinic teachers, Paul made it clear that there was a power that had limited sway over this generation.

HOME DAILY BIBLE READINGS
(August 11-17, 2014)

Treasure in Clay Jars

MONDAY, August 11: "Enduring Troubles and Calamities" (Psalm 71:17-24)
TUESDAY, August 12: "Finding Grace in the Wilderness" (Jeremiah 31:1-6)
WEDNESDAY, August 13: "Sharing Christ's Sufferings and Glory" (1 Peter 4:12-19)
THURSDAY, August 14: "Standing Fast in God's True Grace" (1 Peter 5:8-14)
FRIDAY, August 15: "Walking in Truth and Love" (2 John 1-9)
SATURDAY, August 16: "Waiting for the Lord's Mercy" (Jude 17-25)
SUNDAY, August 17: "Proclaiming Jesus Christ as Lord" (2 Corinthians 4:2-15)

End Note

---

[1]Mattoon's Treasures (Mattoon's Treasures), *Treasures from 2 Corinthians.*

AN APPEAL FOR RECONCILIATION

FAITH PATHWAY/FAITH JOURNEY TOPIC: **Addressing Tensions**

DEVOTIONAL READING: **2 Corinthians 5:16-21**
PRINT PASSAGE: **2 Corinthians 6:1-13; 7:2-4**

BACKGROUND SCRIPTURE: **2 Corinthians 6:1–7:4**
KEY VERSE: **2 Corinthians 7:2**

2 Corinthians 6:1-13; 7:2-4—KJV

WE THEN, as workers together with him, beseech you also that ye receive not the grace of God in vain.
2 (For he saith, I have heard thee in a time accepted, and in the day of salvation have I succoured thee: behold, now is the accepted time; behold, now is the day of salvation.)
3 Giving no offence in any thing, that the ministry be not blamed:
4 But in all things approving ourselves as the ministers of God, in much patience, in afflictions, in necessities, in distresses,
5 In stripes, in imprisonments, in tumults, in labours, in watchings, in fastings;
6 By pureness, by knowledge, by longsuffering, by kindness, by the Holy Ghost, by love unfeigned,
7 By the word of truth, by the power of God, by the armour of righteousness on the right hand and on the left,
8 By honour and dishonour, by evil report and good report: as deceivers, and yet true;
9 As unknown, and yet well known; as dying, and, behold, we live; as chastened, and not killed;
10 As sorrowful, yet alway rejoicing; as poor, yet making many rich; as having nothing, and yet possessing all things.
11 O ye Corinthians, our mouth is open unto you, our heart is enlarged.
12 Ye are not straitened in us, but ye are straitened in your own bowels.
13 Now for a recompence in the same, (I speak as unto my children,) be ye also enlarged.

.....

2 Corinthians 6:1-13; 7:2-4—NIV

AS GOD'S fellow workers we urge you not to receive God's grace in vain.
2 For he says, "In the time of my favor I heard you, and in the day of salvation I helped you." I tell you, now is the time of God's favor, now is the day of salvation.
3 We put no stumbling block in anyone's path, so that our ministry will not be discredited.
4 Rather, as servants of God we commend ourselves in every way: in great endurance; in troubles, hardships and distresses;
5 in beatings, imprisonments and riots; in hard work, sleepless nights and hunger;
6 in purity, understanding, patience and kindness; in the Holy Spirit and in sincere love;
7 in truthful speech and in the power of God; with weapons of righteousness in the right hand and in the left;
8 through glory and dishonor, bad report and good report; genuine, yet regarded as impostors;
9 known, yet regarded as unknown; dying, and yet we live on; beaten, and yet not killed;
10 sorrowful, yet always rejoicing; poor, yet making many rich; having nothing, and yet possessing everything.
11 We have spoken freely to you, Corinthians, and opened wide our hearts to you.
12 We are not withholding our affection from you, but you are withholding yours from us.
13 As a fair exchange—I speak as to my children— open wide your hearts also.

.....

Sometimes the community may ignore the good done by a great leader and may become estranged from the leader. What must be done to end separation of a community from its leaders? Paul reminded the Corinthians of all he had done for the sake of Jesus Christ—and based on that testimony, he asked that they be reconciled to him.

2 Receive us; we have wronged no man, we have corrupted no man, we have defrauded no man.

3 I speak not this to condemn you: for I have said before, that ye are in our hearts to die and live with you.

4 Great is my boldness of speech toward you, great is my glorying of you: I am filled with comfort, I am exceeding joyful in all our tribulation.

2 Make room for us in your hearts. We have wronged no one, we have corrupted no one, we have exploited no one.

3 I do not say this to condemn you; I have said before that you have such a place in our hearts that we would live or die with you.

4 I have great confidence in you; I take great pride in you. I am greatly encouraged; in all our troubles my joy knows no bounds.

TOPICAL OUTLINE OF THE LESSON

I. **Introduction**
   A. Seeds of Discord
   B. Biblical Background

II. **Exposition and Application of the Scripture**
   A. Paul's Appeal for Appreciation (2 Corinthians 6:1-10)
   B. Paul's Appeal for Acceptance (2 Corinthians 6:11-13)
   C. Paul's Appeal for Reconciliation (2 Corinthians 7:2-4)

III. **Concluding Reflection**

LESSON OBJECTIVES

Upon completion of the lesson, the students will be able to do the following:

1. Know that Paul felt estranged from the Corinthians and wanted them to know that he had no bad feelings toward them;

2. Accept that when someone within the community works hard for the benefit of all, disagreements and misunderstandings may yet occur; and,

3. Help to end any misunderstanding and estrangement and restore health to the community.

POINTS TO BE EMPHASIZED
ADULT/YOUTH

Adult Topic: **Addressing Tensions**

Youth Topic: **Walking in Harmony**

Adult Key Verse: **2 Corinthians 7:2**

Youth Key Verse: **2 Corinthians 7:4**

Print Passage: **2 Corinthians 6:1-13; 7:2-4**

—Paul wrote this letter in a time of conflict with the church of Corinth. He said he had planned to visit them recently, but then he decided against it so as to avoid "another painful visit" (2:1).

—In verses 4-10, Paul defended his "credentials" for ministry. These include both the hardships he had endured (verses 4-5) and the virtuous behavior he had displayed (verses 6-7). Paul and his associates had demonstrated these credentials in the context of all of life's contradictions and reversals (verses 8-10).

—Beginning in verse 11, Paul concluded the defense of his ministry that had occupied the bulk of this letter since chapter 2.

—Paul exhorted the Corinthians to "open wide" their hearts (6:13) and "make room" in their hearts (7:2) for him and his associates.

—In 7:3-4, he was effusive in his praise of the Corinthians.

—Paul concluded by assuring the Corinthian church that he had received joy from God's power in the midst of all his troubles.

CHILDREN
Children Topic: Success through Cooperation

Key Verse: 2 Corinthians 6:1

Print Passage: 2 Corinthians 6:1-13

—Paul reminded the Corinthians that God had worked through him for their benefit.

—Paul told the Corinthians that he had endured numerous hardships for them.

—Paul called on the believers to receive God's grace with open hearts.

—As Paul continued to work for Christ, he urged the church people to labor together.

—Paul urged the Corinthians to open their hearts to the Gospel with the same excitement.

I. INTRODUCTION
A. Seeds of Discord

The High-minded Church was an affluent congregation of about 360 members. It had a strong reputation in the community and drew members from many different socioeconomic backgrounds. Their leader, Pastor Hadenough, was highly respected in the church and community. During its annual business meeting, Sister Hazel Jones was nominated to serve as a deaconess. When the nomination was presented by the nominating committee, however, there was some opposition from Sister Socialite. Her opposition centered on the fact that five years ago, Sister Jones had been convicted of welfare fraud and served six months in jail. Since her conversion, Sister Jones had been a faithful and committed disciple of Christ and a strong supporter of the Church's ministry.

Sister Socialite pressed her objection, pointing out that the High-minded Church could not have a woman serving as a deaconess who had been convicted of a felony. Her passionate speech before the congregation persuaded several influential members to go along with her, and the nomination was defeated. Pastor Hadenough tried to reason from the Scriptures that Sister Jones was fully qualified to serve and that God had forgiven her and, therefore, the church must not hold her past over her head. This infuriated many of the affluent members, who turned against the pastor and wanted to force him out of the church. This created the impression among many of the poorer members that the only people welcome to serve in leadership positions were the well-off. The church was thrust into bitter turmoil over the issue.

Sometimes the community may ignore the good done by a great leader and may become estranged from the leader. What must be done to end separation of a community from its leader? Paul reminded the Corinthians of all he had done for the sake of Jesus Christ, and based on that testimony, he asked that they be reconciled to Him.

B. Biblical Background

The Corinthian church was the most difficult congregation to lead. Paul had a love-hate relationship with this congregation. Nowhere else in the New Testament do we see the emotional connections between pastor and people in the ways that we witness them with this congregation. The church was embroiled in several heated exchanges between the people and their founding pastor. Paul wrote this letter at a time of conflict with the church of Corinth. He had previously told them (see 2:1) that he had planned to visit the church, but he changed his plans in order to avoid "another painful visit." Second Corinthians 6:3 lays the groundwork for the very defensive tone Paul would take in chapters 10–13. In verses 4-10, Paul defended his credentials for ministry by reminding the church of the many severe trials, tribulations, and hardships he had personally endured for Christ. He also reminded the church that he had not been dishonest, and spoke of how he had lived a life of complete honesty and integrity.

Beginning at verse 11, Paul concluded his defense of his ministry that included much of the conversation beginning with chapter 2. He appealed to the church for openness and acceptance of himself, since he had not withheld his affection from them. Paul appealed to the church to make room for him and his associates in their hearts (7:3). He reminded them that he had done no wrong to anyone and while they may have been upset with him, it was not his attitude. Paul had confidence in the brothers and sisters in Corinth to such an extent that he was willing to die for them.

II. EXPOSITION AND APPLICATION OF THE SCRIPTURE

A. Paul's Appeal for Appreciation (2 Corinthians 6:1-10)

WE THEN, as workers together with him, beseech you also that ye receive not the grace of God in vain. (For he saith, I have heard thee in a time accepted, and in the day of salvation have I succoured thee: behold, now is the accepted time; behold, now is the day of salvation.) 3 Giving no offence in any thing, that the ministry be not blamed: 4 But in all things approving ourselves as the ministers of God, in much patience, in afflictions, in necessities, in distresses, In stripes, in imprisonments, in tumults, in labours, in watchings, in fastings; By pureness, by knowledge, by longsuffering, by kindness, by the Holy Ghost, by love unfeigned, By the word of truth, by the power of God, by the armour of righteousness on the right hand and on the left, By honour and dishonour, by evil report and good report: as deceivers, and yet true; As unknown, and yet well known; as dying, and, behold, we live; as chastened, and not killed; As sorrowful, yet alway rejoicing; as poor, yet making many rich; as having nothing, and yet possessing all things.

Verse 1 is a continuation and conclusion of Paul's discussion of the ministry of reconciliation brought about through the redemptive work of Jesus Christ (see 5:16-21). In this section of the letter, Paul made two appeals to the Corinthians. In the first appeal, Paul urged (*parakaleo–to call upon*) the Corinthians not to receive God's grace in vain. It appears that there were those in Corinth who raised questions about Paul's authority and calling as an apostle, in addition to challenging him regarding his motives. If they were unwilling to respect him as their spiritual father and see him as God's ambassador, working together with Him, the Gospel preached to them would have been all in vain. Their rejection of him amounted to rejection of his message, so their faith would all be for naught.

Verse 2 is a quote from Isaiah 49:8 and was used parenthetically by Paul to reinforce the urgency of that hour. The verse from the book of Isaiah is set within the context of God's encouragement to the Suffering Servant—so that when He proclaimed the message of salvation, God would help him and give him strength. Paul's use of the verse underscored the urgency of the proclamation of the Gospel of salvation. The time to receive and believe is always "now."

In verse 3, Paul pointed out that no one had stumbled because of his preaching or the ministry entrusted to him. No one would be able to "discredit" (momaomai) their work. The Greek word for "discredit" literally means "to find fault or to lay blame." On the contrary, Paul offered several reasons why they had been honorable servants of God. When Paul's ministry was set beside or alongside that of others, he had proven to be fully capable of enduring some of the most trying and pressing circumstances. Paul was not bragging when he commended his work of ministry. Paul and his companions made it through by enduring the hardships of ministry. Endurance (hupomone) denotes the character of a man or woman who will not quit nor turn from his or her assigned work, regardless of the challenge (verse 4).

Verses 4b and 5 contain a list of nine trials, in groups of three, all of which Paul had faced and was able to overcome because of his willingness to endure. Troubles were those periods of affliction and pressure. Hardships were the times when he was caught between straits. The word distresses has in it the idea of narrow places without much room to move. In the next three trials, Paul recalled being beaten, imprisoned, and in riots (see Acts 13:50; 14:19; 19:29; compare with 2 Corinthians 11:23-27). The final triad of afflictions were the product of his commitment to ministry and preaching the Gospel—long hours of hard work, sleepless nights, and going without food (see 1 Corinthians 4:11; Philippians 4:12).

Verse 6 is a complete change in the tone of Paul's letter. In spite of all that he had been through, it had not affected his spirit.

Paul indicated that his preaching had been saturated with the truth and power of God (see 1 Corinthians 2:5; 4:20). Using a military metaphor, Paul pointed out that he had waged a courageous battle against evil with the weapons of righteousness in both hands (see 2 Corinthians 4:2; 10:4; Ephesians 6:11-18; 1 Thessalonians 5:8).

Verses 8-10 are a series of contrasts in which Paul further explained both the highs and lows of ministry. He had been honored and, yet, dishonored by the same people. There were times when the people bragged about him, and then there were times when his name was connected with scandal. He had been honest, yet he was regarded as an imposter. He was known by them, yet there were times when they acted as though they had no knowledge of him. He had been beaten to the point of death, yet they continued to live on. There had been moments of extreme pain and sorrow, yet he was always rejoicing. Although he would not take any financial support from them and many considered him a poor man, yet he was rich in grace. What looked like nothing to them was in fact everything to him (see Philippians 3:4-13; 4:8-9).

B. Paul's Appeal for Acceptance
(2 Corinthians 6:11-13)

O ye Corinthians, our mouth is open unto you, our heart is enlarged. Ye are not straitened in us, but ye are straitened in your own bowels. Now for a recompence in the same, (I speak as unto my children,) be ye also enlarged.

In this section, Paul poured out his heart to the congregation. They must see that he had withheld nothing from them and that he had labored without fear and compensation to make sure their faith rested upon the power of God. Paul had given them everything that they needed to grow in grace. He had spoken the truth of the Gospel freely and openly and at this point was being very transparent with them. He affectionately referred to them by name: "Corinthians." There was one thing that they had to admit: neither Paul nor his companions had held back their affection from them. These words display a tenderness that bespoke of Paul's overwhelming love for them. As a spiritual father, he appealed to them to remember how he had served them night and day. It was only fair that they, too, would open wide their hearts to him and his companions. Fair exchange indicates an even exchange, and has in it the idea of reciprocity.

C. Paul's Appeal for Reconciliation
(2 Corinthians 7:2-4)

Receive us; we have wronged no man, we have corrupted no man, we have defrauded no man. I speak not this to condemn you: for I have said before, that ye are in our hearts to die and live with you. Great is my boldness of speech toward you, great is my glorying of you: I am filled with comfort, I am exceeding joyful in all our tribulation.

The lesson concludes with Paul making an urgent appeal: "make room"—which is written in the imperative tense. He was not looking for a date on their calendar; rather, he wanted them to find a place in their hearts. He listed three reasons why they needed to follow through on his request. First, they (Paul and his companions) had wronged (*ladikeo*) no one. The word conveys the idea that neither Paul nor his companions had acted in a criminal manner. Second, they had not corrupted (*phtheiro*) the church or any of its members. The word *corrupted* has in it the idea of defiling the faith of another or leading a person astray. Third, they had not exploited (*pleonekteo*) anyone. The word means "to take a larger share or a greater part."

In verse 3, Paul was very careful not to give the Corinthians the wrong impression, which could easily happen. He did not accuse them of any of the three reasons listed above, nor was he trying to condemn them—either individually or collectively. The Corinthians were so dear to them that they (Paul and his companions) would all be willing to die for them. These words express the teaching of Jesus regarding how He wanted His disciples to be known by their love for one another (see John 13:34-35; 15:12-13).

Yet, in spite of how rocky their relationship had been in the past, Paul had not lost confidence in his children. He was extremely confident in them, although he did not say who or what the confidence was directed toward. Quite possibly it was his confidence that they would be able to find room in their hearts for reconciliation and not retaliation.

III. CONCLUDING REFLECTION

Nothing grieves the heart of God more than to see His people stuck in quarrels and disagreements. We break the heart of God with our unwillingness to get along and create congregational settings where peace, harmony, and love abound. One of Paul's greatest challenges was mending the breach that had developed among the Corinthians and between him and them. We know from the early chapters in the first letter that their relational problems were so severe that they became public knowledge (see 1 Corinthians 1:10). Many times congregational conflict can fester for years and even through generations, because leaders and people believe that if they do nothing, say nothing, then things will simply get better and we will all live "happily ever after." Unlike the church in the introduction, Paul has shown us that conflict can be constructively engaged and must be addressed in the spirit of love.

PRAYER

Heavenly Father, help us to see ourselves as You see us. Grant that we may learn to live in harmony and trust each other with our whole hearts. Give our hearts the right spirit and right consciousness when it comes to our relationships with other believers. In Jesus' name we pray. Amen.

WORD POWER

Salvation (*soteria*)—"to save or deliver." In the strictly religious sense, it means to rescue from the penalty of sin and disobedience to God. Within the Old Testament, salvation (or being saved) is used to express deliverance from an actual situation of death or sickness (see Psalm 34:1ff.). Paul used it religiously to express the finished work of Jesus Christ, wherein humans are freed from the penalty of sin, the power of its presence in their lives, and the dominion that it holds (see Romans 6).

HOME DAILY BIBLE READINGS
(August 18-24, 2014)

An Appeal for Reconciliation
MONDAY, August 18: "A Failed Attempt at Reconciliation" (Acts 7:23-28)
TUESDAY, August 19: "Reconciled to God through Christ" (Romans 5:6-11)
WEDNESDAY, August 20: "Making Peace through the Cross" (Colossians 1:15-23)
THURSDAY, August 21: "The Ministry and Message of Reconciliation" (2 Corinthians 5:16-21)
FRIDAY, August 22: "A Harvest of Righteousness" (James 3:13-18)
SATURDAY, August 23: "First Be Reconciled" (Matthew 5:21-26)
SUNDAY, August 24: "Open Wide Your Hearts" (2 Corinthians 6:1-13; 7:2-4)

LESSON 14   August 31, 2014

A COMMUNITY SHARES ITS RESOURCES

FAITH PATHWAY/FAITH JOURNEY TOPIC: Giving to Others

DEVOTIONAL READING: 1 Corinthians 13:1-7
PRINT PASSAGE: 2 Corinthians 8:1-14

BACKGROUND SCRIPTURE: 2 Corinthians 8–9
KEY VERSE: 2 Corinthians 8:7

2 Corinthians 8:1-14—KJV

MOREOVER, BRETHREN, we do you to wit of the grace of God bestowed on the churches of Macedonia;
2 How that in a great trial of affliction the abundance of their joy and their deep poverty abounded unto the riches of their liberality.
3 For to their power, I bear record, yea, and beyond their power they were willing of themselves;
4 Praying us with much intreaty that we would receive the gift, and take upon us the fellowship of the ministering to the saints.
5 And this they did, not as we hoped, but first gave their own selves to the Lord, and unto us by the will of God.
6 Insomuch that we desired Titus, that as he had begun, so he would also finish in you the same grace also.
7 Therefore, as ye abound in every thing, in faith, and utterance, and knowledge, and in all diligence, and in your love to us, see that ye abound in this grace also.
8 I speak not by commandment, but by occasion of the forwardness of others, and to prove the sincerity of your love.
9 For ye know the grace of our Lord Jesus Christ, that, though he was rich, yet for your sakes he became poor, that ye through his poverty might be rich.
10 And herein I give my advice: for this is expedient for you, who have begun before, not only to do, but also to be forward a year ago.
11 Now therefore perform the doing of it; that as there was a readiness to will, so there may be a performance also out of that which ye have.
12 For if there be first a willing mind, it is accepted according to that a man hath, and not according to that he hath not.

2 Corinthians 8:1-14—NIV

AND NOW, brothers, we want you to know about the grace that God has given the Macedonian churches.
2 Out of the most severe trial, their overflowing joy and their extreme poverty welled up in rich generosity.
3 For I testify that they gave as much as they were able, and even beyond their ability. Entirely on their own,
4 they urgently pleaded with us for the privilege of sharing in this service to the saints.
5 And they did not do as we expected, but they gave themselves first to the Lord and then to us in keeping with God's will.
6 So we urged Titus, since he had earlier made a beginning, to bring also to completion this act of grace on your part.
7 But just as you excel in everything—in faith, in speech, in knowledge, in complete earnestness and in your love for us—see that you also excel in this grace of giving.
8 I am not commanding you, but I want to test the sincerity of your love by comparing it with the earnestness of others.
9 For you know the grace of our Lord Jesus Christ, that though he was rich, yet for your sakes he became poor, so that you through his poverty might become rich.
10 And here is my advice about what is best for you in this matter: Last year you were the first not only to give but also to have the desire to do so.
11 Now finish the work, so that your eager willingness to do it may be matched by your completion of it, according to your means.
12 For if the willingness is there, the gift is acceptable according to what one has, not according to what he does not have.

13 For I mean not that other men be eased, and ye burdened:
14 But by an equality, that now at this time your abundance may be a supply for their want, that their abundance also may be a supply for your want: that there may be equality.

13 Our desire is not that others might be relieved while you are hard pressed, but that there might be equality.
14 At the present time your plenty will supply what they need, so that in turn their plenty will supply what you need. Then there will be equality.

TOPICAL OUTLINE OF THE LESSON

I. Introduction
A. The Reality of Poverty
B. Biblical Background

II. Exposition and Application of the Scripture
A. An Example worth Following (2 Corinthians 8:1-6)
B. An Exposition worth Hearing (2 Corinthians 8:7-9)
C. An Expectation worth Matching (2 Corinthians 8:10-12)
D. An Explanation worth Believing (2 Corinthians 8:13-14)

III. Concluding Reflection

LESSON OBJECTIVES

Upon completion of the lesson, the students will be able to do the following:
1. See that Paul attempted to get Christian communities to help one another when there was need;
2. Recognize and accept that several smaller communities may be interrelated in a large community and that the rights and responsibilities pertain to all; and,
3. Lead the class in replicating the grace they have received from God in responding to need in the larger faith community.

POINTS TO BE EMPHASIZED

ADULT/YOUTH
Adult Topic: Giving to Others
Youth Topic: Giving until It Hurts
Adult Key Verse: 2 Corinthians 8:7
Youth Key Verses: 2 Corinthians 8:13-14
Print Passage: 2 Corinthians 8:1-14

—Even though the Macedonian churches had very little, they still gave very much and saw it as a "privilege of sharing" (8:4).
—Paul praised the Corinthians for their passion to give for the Lord's work. This praise may have been Paul's strategy to encourage them to achieve a deeper level of generosity.
—Paul sent Titus and some others to collect an offering from the Corinthians. Titus was glad to go and seems to have had a fondness for the Christians in Corinth. Earlier, Titus had had a successful mission with the Corinthians (see 7:5-7).

—The Corinthians promised to give a generous offering, so Titus was sent to make sure that they gave it and did not make Paul look bad in front of the Macedonians—who had already given sacrificially (see 9:3-5).

—While urging generosity, Paul also assured the Corinthians that God did not expect them to give what they did not have (see 8:12).

—In this passage, Paul appealed to the Corinthians to support a collection of money for the poor in Jerusalem.

—He used the generosity of the Macedonian church, which gave out of limited funds, as an example to follow.

CHILDREN
Children Topic: Helping Others
Key Verse: 2 Corinthians 9:7
Print Passage: 2 Corinthians 8:1-14

—Paul urged the Corinthian Christians to finish the pledge they had made for the Jerusalem church.

—Paul cited the generosity of the churches of Macedonia.

—Paul reminded his readers of the sacrificial gift of Jesus Christ.

—Paul said that any gift given eagerly is acceptable to God.

—Paul advocated a fair balance between the Corinthians' abundance and the need of others.

I. INTRODUCTION
A. The Reality of Poverty

Poverty is probably the number 1 economic problem in the world today. It is estimated by the World Bank and other United Nations agencies that nearly 1.8 billion people live in abject poverty. These are people whose lives are best described as inhumanly deplorable. If you ever see poverty through the eyes of Jesus Christ, it will forever change the way you look at life. This writer and others saw something of this human devastation when we were in California last June. A few of us visited Tijuana, Mexico, and saw firsthand the reasons why so many of the Mexican people want to leave and come across the border to the United States.

If one has ever visited a developing nation, one can see again the real poverty of the world's have-nots. For those of you who have visited Jamaica, Haiti, Bermuda, and some of the other Caribbean Islands, there is another side to the sun and fun that is not always seen—and that is the poverty of many of the people of African descent in that region of the world.

Worldwide poverty must clearly become the most pressing concern of the developed nations of the world. By conservative estimates, nearly 1.5 billion people go to bed hungry each night. Nearly two billion people do not have fresh water to drink. Nearly two billion of the world's people can neither read nor write. The poor that I speak of have no running water in their homes, and they live in makeshift shanties with thatched roofs. They have never had electricity, and most live off of less than $200 per family per year. I say again that poverty is the world's most pressing social and economic problem. Similarly, within the earliest Christian communities, poverty was a critical concern, especially for congregations that were small. The lesson teaches that a small community that possesses much may be part of a larger community that has little and needs the smaller community's assistance. Paul reminded the Corinthians that they were part of a larger faith community and that just as others had been generous to them, they should repay with equal generosity.

B. Biblical Background

This is the final lesson for this quarter. The lesson is part of an extended discussion by Paul to spur the Corinthians to follow the example of the Macedonians in giving to support the famine relief effort for the saints in Jerusalem. In the earlier portions of his letter, Paul had been trying to resolve hurt feelings and broken relationships. Titus had visited the church and brought back news to Paul that encouraged him (see 2 Corinthians 7:5-7, 13). Now it was time to get busy collecting the money that they promised to give.

On the Greek peninsula there were the northern churches of Macedonia, which consisted of the local congregations in Philippi, Berea, Thessalonica, and quite possibly Neapolis. In the south were the churches of Achaia, which consisted of the local congregations in Corinth and Cenchrea. We have no record that other congregations existed in the southern part of Greece. There were considerable differences between the churches in Macedonia and those in Achaia.

At the time that he wrote this letter to the Corinthian Christians, Paul was collecting a love offering for the Christians living in Jerusalem. A severe famine had hit Israel, and saints living there were under severe financial hardship. The Jerusalem church was trying to take care of all of the many different needs of the saints living there. Paul felt led by the Holy Spirit to encourage the churches of Asia, Macedonia, and Achaia to give a special gift to help in the cause of famine relief.

The churches in Macedonia saw this ministry of giving as a privilege given by God to the believer. Ministry was and remains the spiritual birthright of every believer. In Corinth, the churches were beset by internal strife and division. So intense were the conflicts that one wonders if they had a clue about what God was doing in their midst. They were not motivated to do much to help others. Paul had bragged to others about how great these people were, yet he had the greatest difficulty with this group. It was time for the saints to put their money where their mouths were.

II. EXPOSITION AND APPLICATION OF THE SCRIPTURE

A. An Example worth Following
(2 Corinthians 8:1-6)

MOREOVER, BRETHREN, we do you to wit of the grace of God bestowed on the churches of Macedonia; How that in a great trial of affliction the abundance of their joy and their deep poverty abounded unto the riches of their liberality. For to their power, I bear record, yea, and beyond their power they were willing of themselves; Praying us with much intreaty that we would receive the gift, and take upon us the fellowship of the ministering to the saints. And this they did, not as we hoped, but first gave their own selves to the Lord, and unto us by the will of God. Insomuch that we desired Titus, that as he had begun, so he would also finish in you the same grace also.

Up to this point Paul had been working on

his relationship with the Corinthians. Beginning at 8:1 through 9:15, he began an extended discussion about giving and the need for the Corinthians to be just as liberal in giving as they were in everything else.

He began by holding up the churches in Macedonia, a reference most likely to the churches in Philippi, Thessalonica, and Berea. He pointed out that although they were experiencing severe persecution and tribulation, they nonetheless responded to the request with great generosity (see Philippians 1:28-30). It is highly likely that these congregations lived under severe pressure, given the reception and treatment that Paul experienced during his stay in that area.

Verse 2 highlights their situation of severe trial and extreme poverty. Yet, neither of these two conditions interfered with the commitment to be generous toward those in need. Paul called himself as a witness that the saints in Macedonia gave not from the surplus of their earnings or wealth, but gave as much as they were able to give—exceeding their own abilities, given their limited resources. What amazed Paul about the Macedonians was the freedom and spontaneity with which they gave. There was no need for coercion, nor did he have to make demands upon them. They gave entirely on their own.

Verse 4 seems to suggest that Paul looked at their situation and may have tried to persuade them to keep something for themselves. But they would have none of that; rather, they "urgently pleaded" that they be allowed to give up to and beyond the limits of their resources.

Paul shared that they did not give as he had expected, given their enthusiasm for wanting to participate. In the second part of verse 5, Paul stated that which is the absolute prerequisite for being generous toward the work of the ministry. Giving will never precede one's commitment to the Lord Jesus Christ. The Macedonians gave themselves to the Lord first. They became committed disciples and considered the magnanimous grace that had lifted them from sin. And then they gave themselves to their leaders. This was intended to teach two important lessons to the Corinthians: support for the work, and submission to their leaders. Both of these lessons are in keeping with the will of the Lord.

In verse 6, Paul informed the Corinthians that Titus would be the man who would come and collect the offering from them. He urged the church to complete their act of generosity.

B. An Exposition worth Hearing (2 Corinthians 8:7-9)

Therefore, as ye abound in every thing, in faith, and utterance, and knowledge, and in all diligence, and in your love to us, see that ye abound in this grace also. I speak not by commandment, but by occasion of the forwardness of others, and to prove the sincerity of your love. For ye know the grace of our Lord Jesus Christ, that, though he was rich, yet for your sakes he became poor, that ye through his poverty might be rich.

Verse 7 harkens back to the first letter regarding their desire to covet the best spiritual gifts. The Corinthians were always impressed by men and women who spoke with power and who possessed the flashy gifts of faith, speech, tongues, and knowledge. They had been earnest in everything else; at this point, Paul encouraged and exhorted them to excel just as much in the grace of giving.

His words were not to be viewed as a command, but as a gentle nudge in the right direction. He had been bragging to others about their love for him and their generosity. He was willing to set them beside the other congregations and compare their response to that of the Corinthians. It was not for the purpose of competition, but to show that they were equally as generous.

Verse 9 is an important verse in the New Testament, because it lifts up the fact of the incarnation of Jesus Christ. Paul talked about what Jesus gave up in His preexistent, heavenly state. Words are not even sufficient to describe what Jesus left when He came to Earth. Jesus left fellowship with the Father. He left a place of perfect peace. He left a place of perfection. He left a place where there was no pain, no poverty to confront, no heartache to bear, no disparaging disappointments, no crime, no violence, no wars to face, no hate to overcome, no racism, no sexism, no isolationism, no gender gaps, no disagreements, no fights and feuds; there was no sickness, no death, no funerals to attend, no cold weather, no hot weather; there were no storms to face, no burdens to bear, no tears to wipe, no bills to pay, no jobs to try to keep, and no rumors to quell. Jesus left a place where there were no sins to hide, no fears to face, no opposition to fight, no obstacles to overcome, and no problems and pressures to deal with.

When Jesus became a man, He subjected Himself to the worst of humanity's ills. How well the writer of Hebrews 4:15 related this fact in the following: "For we have not a high priest who cannot be touched with the feelings of our infirmities, but was in all points tempted as we are, yet without sin."

Paul reminded the church of what they received when they were saved. Although unspoken, these thoughts are implied within the text, they became rich in love, rich in power, rich in hope, rich in faith, rich in fellowship, rich in healing, rich in praise, rich in worship, and rich in material and spiritual things. Jesus Christ made them richer than they could ever imagine. When He became poor, we became rich.

The whole verse 9 swings on the word *grace*. "For you know the grace of our Lord Jesus Christ." *Grace*, by definition, means "gift." Grace is God's unmerited favor. Grace is God's beneficial goodness bestowed upon undeserving humans like you and me. Grace is God's abundant and abounding love that looks beyond our every fault and sees our needs.

In Ephesians 2:8 and 4:7f, Paul talked about grace. In Ephesians 2:8, he wrote, "For by grace you have been saved through faith; and that not of yourselves, it is the gift of God." But to each one of us grace was given according to the measure of the gift of Christ. Therefore, it says, "When He ascended on high He led captivity captive and He gave gifts to men." Every spiritual gift you have is a gift of grace. Our salvation is a gift of grace. Paul wrote in Romans 3:23-24, "For all have sinned and fall short of the glory of God, being justified as a gift by His grace through the redemption which is in Christ Jesus." In Romans 6:23, the apostle reminded the church, "For the wages of sin is death, but the free gift of God is eternal life in Christ Jesus our Lord." Grace is God's great extension of mercy to sinners.

C. An Expectation worth Matching (2 Corinthians 8:10-12)

And herein I give my advice: for this is expedient for you, who have begun before, not only to do, but also to be forward a year ago. Now therefore perform the doing

of it; that as there was a readiness to will, so there may be a performance also out of that which ye have. For if there be first a willing mind, it is accepted according to that a man hath, and not according to that he hath not.

The Corinthians did not ask Paul for any advice, but he felt it was his obligation and duty to provide it as their spiritual father. He pointed them to what was best for them in this matter of giving. Twelve months prior, they were overflowing with desire to give and to be honest. They were in fact the first to do so. But along the way the relationship between the leader and the people hit a rough place and the desire wilted under the pressure of congregational disharmony.

In verse 11, Paul gently gave an imperative command, "finish the work," or do not drag this out. It was not enough to have the desire and the big talk—the desire and talk had to be matched by work. Christians can at times talk a lot about what they believe they should do to relieve poverty and to engage in foreign missions work—but at the moment of giving, their words are not always matched by their works. It was not a question of what they had or whether or not it would be as much as what others gave. What was important was the willingness to be obedient to what God had called them to do and be. He closed this section by reminding them that they could only give what they had, but possessing little was not a reason not to give anything.

D. An Explanation worth Believing
(2 Corinthians 8:13-14)

For I mean not that other men be eased, and ye burdened: But by an equality, that now at this time your abundance may be a supply for their want, that their abundance also may be a supply for your want: that there may be equality.

Paul addressed, in this closing section, a common myth that many Christians have. If they give away their money to someone else, they in turn will not have enough for themselves. Paul cautioned the Corinthians against believing that they would be left in poverty; rather, they should see their gift for the saints in Jerusalem as reciprocity. Just as they had received the gift of grace and eternal life from Jesus Christ, through the Jews, it was only natural and right that they share their wealth. Quite unlike the church in Jerusalem, there were wealthy Christians in the Corinthian congregation. There would be an equal exchange between the more wealthy Corinthians and the Jews in Jerusalem. Paul seemed to say that the value of what they received through the Gospel far outweighed what they would give up.

III. CONCLUDING REFLECTION

There are basically two kinds of churches when it comes to giving and supporting the causes that are biblically mandated. There are those congregations which are led by men and women who look for reasons not to be generous and who are never challenged to practice giving according to the teachings of Jesus Christ. These are congregations who see tithing as a principle grounded in the Law of Moses; therefore, it is forbidden or unnecessary under grace. Yet, these same congregations give less than 1 percent to causes outside the church, such as feeding the hungry, the poor, and supporting missions around the world.

They are Corinthian in nature. Then there are the churches like those in Macedonia, who recognize that God has given them a great deal, even if it is a little and they therefore are free to give to others without asking for something in return. Which kind of church are you?

Believers are part of a community. This suggests that what affects one part of the community will affect the other part. As believers, it is important that we recognize the interconnectedness of persons in the community. We are our brothers' and sisters' keepers. We are obligated to "look out" for each other. This includes sharing our resources.

PRAYER

Heavenly Father, teach us to love You with our whole hearts and through the sharing of our resources. Grant that Your people will live out their creeds by what we do and say. In Jesus' name we pray. Amen.

WORD POWER

Abundance (*perisseia*)—to overflow. It is the image of a river that is so latent with water that it rushes across its banks and fills the land. Paul used this word to express the unexpectedly generous spirit and contribution of the Macedonians to the famine relief effort.

Afflicting (thlipsis)—means "pressing together," and is a metaphor for oppression and tribulation. The churches of Macedonia were made up of largely poor people. There was no middle class—only the wealthy, the poor, and the poorest. Poverty was one form of affliction in the ancient world.

HOME DAILY BIBLE READINGS
(August 25-31, 2014)

A Community Shares Its Resources
MONDAY, August 25: "Treasure in Heaven" (Mark 10:17-27)

TUESDAY, August 26: "The Measure of Your Gift" (Luke 6:34-38)

WEDNESDAY, August 27: "Giving in Love" (1 Corinthians 13:1-7)

THURSDAY, August 28: "Show Proof of Your Love" (2 Corinthians 8:16-24)

FRIDAY, August 29: "Sowing and Reaping Bountifully" (2 Corinthians 9:1-6)

SATURDAY, August 30: "God Loves a Cheerful Giver" (2 Corinthians 9:7-15)

SUNDAY, August 31: "A Wealth of Generosity" (2 Corinthians 8:1-14)